READER'S CHOICE

Essays and Stories

Canadian Edition

Kim Flachmann
California State University, Bakersfield

Michael Flachmann
California State University, Bakersfield

Alexandra MacLennan
BMO Financial Group Institute for Learning

Prentice
Hall

Toronto

National Library of Canada Cataloguing in Publication Data

Main entry under title:

Reader's choice : essays and stories

Canadian ed.
Includes index.

ISBN 0-13-041874-9

1. College readers. 2. English language—Rhetoric.
I. Flachmann, Kim II. Flachmann, Michael III. MacLennan, Alexandra, 1964–

PE1417.R418 2002   808'.0427   C2002-900949-9

ISBN 0-13-041874-9

Vice President, Editorial Director: Michael J. Young
Acquisitions Editor: Marianne Minaker
Marketing Manager: Christine Cozens
Executive Developmental Editor: Marta Tomins
Production Editor: Avivah Wargon
Copy Editor: Stephanie Fysh
Proofreaders: Patricia Thorvaldson, Ann McInnis
Senior Production Coordinator: Peggy Brown
Page Layout: Jansom
Creative Director: Mary Opper
Cover Design: Sarah Battersby/Michelle Bellemare

Original edition, entitled *The Prose Reader: Essays for Thinking, Reading, and Writing*, Sixth Edition, published by Prentice-Hall, Inc., a division of Pearson Education, Upper Saddle River, NJ. Copyright © 2002 by Prentice-Hall, Inc.

This edition is authorized for sale in Canada only.

3 4 5 6 7 DPC 08 07 06 05

Printed and bound in Canada.

RHETORICAL CONTENTS

   Choyce's essay uses poetic descriptive language to bring alive the vital
   forces at work in a small corner of Nova Scotia.

CHAPTER 2

Narration: *Telling a Story*   68

CHAPTER 3

Example: *Illustrating Ideas* 111

LYNN COADY *Genius or Madness?* 121
Award-winning novelist Lynn Coady offers us some thoughts about socially acceptable behaviour and society's perceptions of those who don't always conform.

SHARON BUTALA *The Myth: The Prairies Are Flat* 125
Prairie writer Butala tackles a common misperception about her region of Canada.

CECIL FOSTER *Why Blacks Get Mad* 130
Using strongly affective examples drawn from his own and his family's lives, Foster speaks forthrightly and personally of the insidious presence of racism in everyday life in Canada.

MARK KINGWELL *Not Available in Stores* 138
Yours for only three easy payments of 39.99 … In this essay, Mark Kingwell, in a column for *Saturday Night*, outlines the appeal and the changing nature of infomercials.

CHAPTER 4

Process Analysis: *Explaining Step by Step* 147

PAUL QUARRINGTON *Home Brew* 157
What golden beverage is a Canadian institution? How do you make this product yourself? The answers to these and other questions are amusingly offered for your enjoyment in Quarrington's essay.

CHAPTER 5

Division/Classification: *Finding Categories*   185

CHAPTER 6

Comparison/Contrast: *Discovering Similarities and*
Differences   217

CHAPTER 9

Argument/Persuasion: *Inciting People to Thought or Action* 351

CHAPTER 10

Documented Essays: *Reading and Writing from*
Sources   393

PART II: Fiction (The Stories)

CHAPTER 11

The Stories   427

PREFACE TO THE INSTRUCTOR

Reader's Choice: Essays and Stories, Canadian Edition, is based on the assumption that lucid writing follows lucid thinking, whereas poor writing is almost inevitably the product of foggy, irrational thought processes. As a result, our primary purpose in this book, as in *Reader's Choice,* Third Canadian Edition, is to help students think more clearly and logically—both in their minds and on paper.

Reading and writing are companion activities that involve students in the creation of thought and meaning—either as readers interpreting a text or as writers constructing one. Clear thinking, then, is the pivotal point that joins together these two efforts. Although studying the rhetorical strategies presented in *Reader's Choice: Essays and Stories* is certainly not the only way to approach writing, it is a productive means of helping students improve their abilities to think, read, and write on progressively more sophisticated levels.

The symbiosis we envision among thinking, reading, and writing is represented in this text by the following hierarchy of cognitive levels:

1. *Literal,* characterized by a basic understanding of words and their meanings;
2. *Interpretive,* consisting of a knowledge of linear connections between ideas and an ability to make valid inferences based on those ideas; and
3. *Critical,* the highest level, distinguished by the systematic investigation of complex ideas and by the analysis of their relationship to the world around us.

FEATURES

The readings in *Reader's Choice: Essays and Stories* will appeal to readers at a variety of levels. *Reader's Choice: Essays and Stories* is organized according to the belief that our mental abilities are generally sequential. In other words, students cannot read or write analytically before they are able to perform well on the literal and interpretive levels. Accordingly, the book progresses from selections that require predominantly literal skills—description, narration, and example—through readings involving more interpretation—process analysis, division/classification, comparison/contrast, and definition—to essays that demand a high degree of analytical thought—cause/effect and argumentation/persuasion. Depending on the calibre of your students and your prescribed curriculum, these rhetorical modes can, of course, be studied in any order.

In addition, the questions at the end of each selection are designed to help students move sequentially from various literal-level responses to interpretation and analysis. These questions deliberately examine both the form and the content of the readings so that your students can cultivate a similar balance in their own writing.

Reader's Choice: Essays and Stories **contains both fiction and non-fiction reading selections.** In addition to essays exemplifying the various rhetorical modes, the book contains ten short stories to broaden the range of genres with which students become familiar and to which they can apply their reading, writing, and thinking skills.

Because students often produce their best writing when they are personally involved in the topics of the pieces they read and in the human drama surrounding those essays, we introduce each selection with biographical information on the author and the original context of the reading. The biographies explain the real experiences from which an essay or a story emerged and help students focus on the purpose, audience, subject of the reading, and perspective on the topic.

The readings in *Reader's Choice: Essays and Stories* represent a broad range of topics. These subjects include national values, discrimination, ethnic identity, TV/media, sports, regional traditions, physical disabilities, mass hysteria, grieving, myths, and human relationships. The readings were selected on the basis of five important criteria: (1) high interest level, (2) effectiveness as models of writing, (3) moderate length, (4) readability, and (5) broad subject variety.

The readings represent writers from across Canada. Together the reading selections portray the universality of human experience as expressed through the viewpoints of men and women, many different ethnic and racial groups, and a variety of ages and social classes.

A website accompanies the book: www.pearsoned.ca/flachmann/ The accompanying website features a glossary of useful terms for students to use in conjunction with this book and includes links to websites relevant to each of the reading selections found in the book

ACKNOWLEDGMENTS

I would like to acknowledge a number of people who helped in the preparation of this edition of *Reader's Choice: Essays and Stories*. I thank David Stover for his encouragement and enthusiasm; and at Pearson Education Canada, for their guidance, patience, and support, Marianne Minaker, Acquisitions Editor; Marta Tomins, Developmental Editor; Avivah Wargon, Production Editor; and Stephanie Fysh, freelance copy editor. For their reviews, which assisted in the development of this book, thank you to Judith Carson, Seneca College; Peter C. Miller, Seneca College; Nancy Line, Durham College; and Rhonda Sandberg, George Brown College.

Finally, at both the Institute for Learning, Bank of Montreal, and Seneca College, I am grateful to my colleagues and friends for their ongoing feedback and advice about *Reader's Choice*.

Alexandra MacLennan

PREFACE TO THE STUDENT

Accurate thinking is the beginning and fountain of writing.

—Horace

THE PURPOSE OF THIS TEXT

Have you ever had trouble expressing your thoughts? If so, you're not alone. Many people have this difficulty—especially when they are asked to write their thoughts down.

The good news is that this "ailment" can be cured. We've learned over the years that the more clearly students think about the world around them, the more easily they can express their ideas through written and spoken language. As a result, this textbook intends to improve your writing by helping you think clearly, logically, and critically about important ideas and issues that exist in our world today. You will learn to reason, read, and write about your environment in increasingly complex ways, moving steadily from a simple, literal understanding of topics to interpretation and analysis. Inspired by well-crafted prose models and guided by carefully worded questions, you can actually raise the level of your thinking skills while improving your reading and writing abilities.

Reader's Choice is organized on the assumption that as a college student you should be able to think, read, and write on three increasingly difficult levels:

1. *Literal, which involves a basic understanding of a selection and the ability to repeat or restate the material;*

2. *Interpretive, which requires you to make associations and draw inferences from information in your reading; and*

3. *Analytical or critical, which invites you to systematically separate, explain, evaluate, and reassemble various important ideas discovered in your reading.*

For example, students with a *literal* grasp of an essay would be able to understand the words on the page, cite details from the selection, and paraphrase certain sections of the essay. Students equipped with *interpretive* skills will see implicit relationships within a selection (such as comparison/contrast or cause/effect), make inferences from information that is supplied, and comprehend the intricacies of figurative language. Finally, students functioning *analytically* will be able to summarize and explain difficult concepts and generate plausible hypotheses from a series of related ideas. In short, this book leads you systematically toward higher levels of thinking and writing.

In order to stimulate your thinking on all levels, this text encourages you to participate in the making of meaning—as both a reader and a writer. As a reader, you have a responsibility to work with the author of each essay and story to help create sense out of the words on the page; as a writer, you must be conscious enough of your audience so that they perceive your intended purpose clearly and precisely through the ideas, opinions, and details that you provide. Because of this unique relationship, we envision reading and writing as companion acts in which writer and reader are partners in the development of meaning.

To demonstrate this vital interrelationship between reader and writer, our text provides you with prose models that are intended to inspire your own thinking and writing. In the introduction to each chapter, we include a student paragraph and a student essay that feature the particular rhetorical strategy under discussion. The essay is highlighted by annotations and by underlining to illustrate how to write that type of essay and to help bridge the gap between student writing and the professional selections in the text. The essays and stories that follow each chapter introduction, selected from a wide variety of contemporary authors, are intended to encourage you to improve your writing through a partnership with some of the best examples of professional prose available today. Just as musicians and athletes richly benefit from studying the techniques of the foremost people in their fields, you will, we hope, grow in spirit and language use from your collaborative work with the writers in this collection.

HOW TO USE THIS TEXT

Reader's Choice contains essays representing the four main purposes of writing:

Description

Narration

Exposition

Persuasion

Our primary focus within this framework is on exposition (which means "explanation"), because you will need to master this type of verbal expression to succeed in both the academic and the professional worlds. Although the essays in this text can be read in any order, we begin with

description

because it is a basic technique that often appears in other forms of discourse. We then move to

narration, or storytelling,

and next to the six traditional expository strategies:

example	*comparison/contrast*
process analysis	*definition*
division/classification	*cause/effect*

The text continues with a chapter on

argument and persuasion,

including a set of opposing viewpoint essays. Chapter 10 discusses and presents

documented research papers,

and the anthology concludes with a selection of short stories.

"Pure" rhetorical types rarely exist, of course, and when they do, the result often seems artificial. Therefore, although each essay in this collection focuses on a single rhetorical mode as its primary strategy, other strategies are always at work in it. These selections concentrate on one primary technique at a time in much the same way a well-arranged photograph highlights a certain visual detail, though many other elements function in the background to make the picture an organic whole.

Each chapter begins with an explanation of a single rhetorical technique. These explanations are divided into six sections that move from the effect of this technique on our daily lives to its integral role in the writing process. The first section catalogs the use of each rhetorical mode in our lives. The second section, "Defining _____" (e.g., "Defining Description"), offers a working definition of the technique and a sample/student paragraph so that we all have the same fundamental understanding of the term. A third section, entitled "Thinking Critically by Using _____," introduces each rhetorical mode as a pattern of thought that helps us organize and more fully understand our experiences. A fourth section, called "Reading and Writing _____ Essays" (e.g., "Reading and Writing Descriptive Essays"), explains the processes of reading and writing an essay in each rhetorical mode, and a fifth section presents an annotated student essay showing this particular rhetorical method "at work." The last part offers some final comments on each rhetorical strategy including a summary review checklist.

Before each reading selection, we have designed some material to focus your attention on a particular writer and topic. This "prereading" segment begins with biographical information about the author and ends with a number of questions to whet your appetite for the selection that follows. The prereading questions forecast not only the material in the essay, but also the questions and writing assignments that follow.

The questions following each reading selection are designed as guides for thinking about the essay. These questions are at the heart of the relationship represented in this book among thinking, reading, and writing. They are divided into four interrelated sections that move you smoothly from a literal understanding of what you have just read, to interpretation, and finally to analysis. The first set of questions, "Understanding Details," focuses on the basic facts and opinions in the selection. The second set of questions, "Analyzing Meaning," asks you to explain certain facts and to evaluate various assumptions of the essay in an effort to understand the entire selection on an analytical level. The third set of questions, "Discovering Rhetorical Strategies," guides your thinking on how the author achieved certain effects through word choice, sentence structure, organization of ideas, and selection of details. This third series of questions often requires you to apply to your reading of an essay material you learned about a particular mode of writing in the chapter introduction. And "Making Connections," the fourth group of questions, asks you to identify and process relationships and connections that you may not have noticed between the essay or story and other selections in the book.

The last section of questions consists of three "Ideas for Discussion/Writing." These topics are preceded by "prewriting" questions to help you generate new ideas. Most of the Discussion/Writing topics specify a purpose (a definite reason for writing the essay) and an audience (an identifiable person or group of people you should address in your essay) so that you can focus your work as precisely as possible. These assignments outline realistic scenes and roles for you to play in those scenes so that, as you write, your relationship to your subject and audience will be clear and precise.

Visit the *Reader's Choice* Web page—**www.pearsoned.ca/ flachmann/**—to find a glossary of useful terms, as well as a collection of Web sites that will give you more information about the readings. This might be information about the author, the original source of the piece of writing, or the topic of the essay you have read.

The word *essay* (which comes from the Old French *essai*, meaning a "try" or an "attempt") is an appropriate label for these writing assignments, because they all ask you to grapple with an idea or problem and then try to give shape to your conclusions in some effective manner. Such "exercises" can be equated with the development of athletic ability in sports: The essay itself demonstrates that you can put together all the various skills you have learned; it proves that you can actually play the sport. After you have studied the different techniques at work in a reading selection, a specific essay assignment lets you practise them all in unison and allows you to discover for yourself even more secrets about the intricate details of effective communication.

INTRODUCTION

■ ■ ■

Thinking, Reading, and Writing

Reading and writing are companion activities that involve students in the creation of thought and meaning—either as readers interpreting a text or as writers constructing one. Clear thinking, then, is the pivotal point that joins these two efforts. Although studying the rhetorical strategies presented in *Reader's Choice* is not the only way to approach writing, it provides a productive means of helping students improve their abilities to think, read, and write on progressively sophisticated levels.

We can improve the way we think, read, and write by exercising our brains on three sequential levels:

1. *The literal level* entails knowing the meanings of words—individually and in relation to one another. In order to comprehend the sentence "You must exercise your brain to reach your full mental potential" on the literal level, for example, someone would have to know the definitions of all the words in the sentence and understand the way those words work together to make meaning.

2. *Interpretation* requires the ability to make associations between details, draw inferences from pieces of information, and reach conclusions about the material. An interpretive understanding of the sample sentence in level 1 might be translated into the following thoughts: "Exercising the brain sounds a bit like exercising the body. I wonder if there's any correlation between the two. If the brain must be exercised, it is probably made up of muscles, much as the body is." None of these particular "thoughts" is made explicit in the sentence, but each is suggested in one way or another.

3. *Thinking, reading, and writing critically*, the most sophisticated form of rational abilities, involves a type of mental activity that is crucial for successful academic work. A critical analysis of our sample sentence might proceed in the following way: "This sentence is talking to me. It actually addresses me with the word *you*. I wonder what *my* mental potential is. Will I be able to reach it? Will I know when I attain it? I certainly want to reach this potential; it will undoubtedly help me succeed scholastically and professionally. The brain is obviously an important tool for helping me achieve my goals in life, so I want to take every opportunity I have to develop and maintain this part of my body." Students who can take an issue or idea apart in this fashion and understand its various components more thoroughly after reassembling them are rewarded intrinsically with a clearer knowledge of life's complexities and the ability to generate creative, useful ideas. They are also rewarded extrinsically with good grades and are more likely to earn responsible jobs with higher pay, because they can apply their understanding of the world effectively to their professional and personal lives.

In this textbook, you will learn to think critically by reading essays and stories written by intelligent, interesting authors and by writing your own essays on a variety of topics.

Thinking Critically

Recent psychological studies have shown that "thinking" and "feeling" are complementary operations. All of us have feelings that are automatic and instinctive. To feel pride after winning first place at a track meet, for example, or to feel anger at a spiteful friend is not behaviour we have to study and master; such emotions come naturally to human beings. Thinking, on the other hand, is much less spontaneous than feeling; research suggests that study and practice are required for sustained mental development.

Thinking critically involves grappling with the ideas, issues, and problems that surround you in your immediate environment and in the world at large. It does not necessarily entail finding fault, which you might naturally associate with the word *critical*, but rather suggests continually questioning and analyzing the world around you. Thinking critically is the highest form of mental activity that human beings engage in. Fortunately, all of us can learn how to think more critically.

Critical thinking means taking apart an issue, idea, or problem; examining its various parts; and reassembling the topic with a fuller understanding of its intricacies. Implied in this explanation is the ability to see the topic from one or more new perspectives. Using your mind in this way will help you find solutions to difficult problems, design creative plans of action, and ultimately live a life consistent with your opinions on important issues that we all must confront on a daily basis.

Our initial goal, then, is to help you think critically when you are required to do so in school, on the job, or in any other area of your life.

Working with the rhetorical modes is an effective way to achieve this goal. With some guidance, each rhetorical pattern can provide you with mental practice to prepare you for writing and critical thinking. Through these various guided thinking exercises, you can systematically strengthen your ability to think analytically.

As you move through the following chapters, we will ask you to isolate each rhetorical mode so that you can concentrate on these thinking patterns one at a time. Each rhetorical pattern we study will suggest slightly different ways of seeing the world, processing information, and solving problems. Looking closely at rhetorical modes or specific patterns of thought helps us discover how our minds work. In the same fashion, becoming more intricately aware of our thought patterns lets us improve our basic thinking skills as well as our reading and writing abilities. Thinking critically helps us discover fresh insights into old ideas, generate new thoughts, and see connections between related issues.

Each chapter introduction provides three exercises specifically designed to help you focus in isolation on a particular pattern of thought. While you are attempting to learn what each pattern feels like in your head, use your imagination to play with these exercises on as many different levels as possible.

When you practise each of the rhetorical patterns of thought, you should be aware of building on your previous thinking skills. As the book progresses, the rhetorical modes become more complex and require a higher degree of concentration and effort. Throughout the book, therefore, you should keep in mind that ultimately you want to let these skills accumulate into a well-developed ability to process the world around you—including reading, writing, seeing, and feeling—on the most advanced analytical level you can master.

Reading Critically

Reading critically begins with developing a natural curiosity about an essay and nurturing that curiosity throughout the reading process. To learn as much as you can from an essay, you should first study any preliminary material you can find, then read the essay to get a general overview of its main ideas, and finally read the selection again to achieve a deeper understanding of its intent. The three phases of the reading process explained below—preparing to read, reading, and rereading—will help you develop this "natural curiosity" so you can approach any reading assignment with an active, inquiring mind.

Preparing to Read

Focusing your attention is an important first stage in both the reading and the writing processes. In fact, learning as much as you can about an essay and its "context" (the circumstances surrounding its development) before you begin reading can help you reach some degree of analysis before writing on the assigned topics. In particular, knowing where an essay was first published, studying the writer's background, and doing some preliminary thinking on the subject of a reading selection will help you understand the writer's ideas and form some valid opinions of your own.

As you approach any essay, you should concentrate on four specific areas that will begin to give you an overview of the material you are about to read. We use an essay by Lewis Thomas to demonstrate these techniques.

1. *Title*. A close look at the title will usually provide important clues about the author's attitude toward the topic, the author's stand on an issue, or the mood of an essay. It can also furnish you with a sense of audience and purpose.

To Err Is Human

From this title, for example, we might infer that the author will discuss errors, human nature, and the extent to which mistakes influence human behaviour. The title is half of a well-known proverbial quotation (Alexander Pope's "To err is human, to forgive, divine"), so we might speculate further that the author has written an essay intended for a well-read audience interested in the relationship between errors and humanity. After reading only four words of the essay—its title—you already have a good deal of information about the subject, its audience, and the author's attitude toward both.

2. *Synopsis.* The Rhetorical Table of Contents in this text contains a synopsis of each essay, very much like the following, so that you can find out more specific details about its contents before you begin reading.

> Physician Lewis Thomas explains how we can profit from our mistakes—especially if we trust human nature. Perhaps someday, he says, we can apply this same principle to the computer and magnify the advantages of these errors.

From this synopsis, we learn that Thomas's essay will be an analysis of human errors and of the way we can benefit from those errors. The synopsis also tells us the computer has the potential to magnify the value of our errors.

3. *Biography.* Learning as much as you can about the author of an essay will generally stimulate your interest in the material and help you achieve a deeper understanding of the issues to be discussed. From the biographies in this book, you can learn, for example, whether a writer is young or old, conservative or liberal, open- or closed-minded. You might also discover if the essay was written at the beginning, middle, or end of the author's career or how well versed the writer is on the topic. Such information will invariably provide a deeper, more thorough understanding of a selection's ideas, audience, and logical structure.

LEWIS THOMAS
1913–1998

Lewis Thomas was a physician who, until his death in 1998, was president emeritus of the Sloan-Kettering Cancer Center and scholar-in-residence at the Cornell University Medical Center in New York City. A graduate of Princeton University and Harvard Medical School, he was formerly head of pathology and dean of the New York University-Bellevue Medical Center and dean of the Yale Medical School. In addition to having written over 200 scientific papers on virology and immunology, he authored many popular scientific essays, some of which have been collected in *Lives of a Cell* (1974), *The Medusa and the Snail* (1979), *Late Night Thoughts on Listening to Mahler's Ninth Symphony* (1983), *Etcetera, Etcetera* (1990), and *The Fragile Species* (1992). The memoirs of his distinguished career have been published in *The Youngest Science: Notes of a Medicine Watcher* (1983). Thomas liked to refer to his essays as "experiments in thought": "Although I usually think I know what I'm going to be writing about, what I'm going to say, most of the time it doesn't happen that way at all. At some point I get misled down a garden path. I get surprised by an idea that I hadn't anticipated getting, which is a little bit like being in a laboratory."

As this information indicates, Thomas was a prominent physician who published widely on scientific topics. We know that he considered his essays "experiments in thought," which makes us expect a relaxed, spontaneous treatment of his subjects. From this biography, we can also infer that he was a leader in the medical world and that, because of the positions he held, he was well respected in his professional life. Last, we can speculate that he had a clear sense of his audience because he was able to present difficult concepts in clear, everyday language.

4. *Preparing to read.* The "Preparing to Read" sections following the biographies are intended to focus your attention and stimulate your curiosity before you begin the essay. They will also get you ready to form your own opinions on the essay and its topic as you read. Keeping a journal to respond to the questions in this section is an excellent idea, because you will then have a record of your thoughts on various topics related to the reading selection that follows.

Discovering where, why, and how an essay was first written will provide you with a context for the material you are about to read: Why did the author write this selection? Where was it first published? Who was the author's original audience? This type of information enables you to understand the circumstances surrounding the development of the selection and to identify any topical or historical references the author makes. All the selections in this textbook were published elsewhere first—in another book, a journal, or a magazine. Some are excerpts from longer works. The author's original audience, therefore, consisted of the readers of that particular publication.

Preparing to Read

The following essay, which originally appeared in the *New England Journal of Medicine* (January 1976), illustrates the clarity and ease with which Thomas explains complex scientific topics. As you prepare to read this essay, take a few moments to think about the role mistakes play in our lives: What are some memorable mistakes you have made in your life? Did you learn anything important from any of these errors? Do you make more or fewer mistakes than other people you know? Do you see any advantages to making mistakes? Any disadvantages?

From the sample "Preparing to Read" material, we learn that Thomas's essay "To Err Is Human" was originally published in the *New England Journal of Medicine*, a prestigious periodical read principally by members of the scientific community. Written early in 1976, the article plays upon its audience's growing fascination with computers and with the limits of artificial intelligence—subjects just as timely today as they were in the mid-1970s.

The questions here prompt you to consider your own ideas, opinions, or experiences in order to help you generate thoughts on the topic of errors in our lives.

Reading

People read essays and stories in books, newspapers, magazines, and journals for a great variety of reasons. One reader may want to be stimulated intellectually, whereas another seeks relaxation; one person reads to keep up with the latest developments in his or her profession, whereas the next wants to learn why a certain event happened or how something can be done; some people read in order to be challenged by new ideas, whereas others find comfort principally in printed material that supports their own moral, social, or political opinions. The selections in this textbook variously fulfill all these expectations. They have been chosen, however, not only for these reasons, but for an additional, broader purpose: Reading them can help make you a better writer.

Every time you read an essay or story in this book, you will also be preparing to write your own essay or story, concentrating on the same rhetorical pattern. For this reason, as you read each selection you should pay careful attention to both its content (subject matter) and its form (language, sentence structure, organization, and development of ideas). You will also see how effectively experienced writers use particular rhetorical modes (or patterns of thought) to organize and communicate their ideas. Each essay in this collection features one dominant pattern that is generally supported by several others.

The questions before and after each piece teach you a way of reading that can help you discover the relationship of a writer's ideas to one another as well as to your own ideas. These questions can also help clarify for you the connection between the writer's topic, his or her style or manner of expression, and your own composing process. The questions are designed to help you understand and generate ideas, discover various choices the writers make in composing their essays, and realize the freedom you have to make related choices in your own writing. Such an approach to the process of reading takes reading and writing out of the realm of mystical creation and places them in the realistic world of the possible; it takes some of the mystery out of reading and writing and makes them manageable tasks at which anyone can become proficient.

The following three general guidelines will help you develop your own system for reading and responding to what you have read:

1. *Read the selection to get an overall sense of it.*

2. *Summarize the reading.*

3. *Read the questions and assignments that follow the selection.*

Guideline 1. *First, read the selection to get an overall sense of it in relation to its title, purpose, audience, author, and publication information.* Write (in the margins, on a separate piece of paper, or in a journal) your initial reactions, comments, and personal associations.

To illustrate, on the following pages is the Thomas essay with a student's comments in the margins, showing how the student reacted to the essay upon reading it for the first time.

Lewis Thomas
(1913–1998)

TO ERR IS HUMAN

Boy is this true!

Everyone must have had at least one personal experience with a computer error by this time. Bank balances are suddenly reported to have jumped from $379 into the millions, appeals for charitable contributions are mailed over and over to people with crazy sounding names at your address, <u>department stores send the wrong bills</u>, utility companies write that they're turning everything off, that sort of thing. If you manage to get in touch with someone and complain, you then get instantaneously typed, guilty letters from the same computer, saying, "Our computer was in error, and an adjustment is being made in your account." 1

Last spring this happened to me.

exactly

These are supposed to be the sheerest, blindest accidents. Mistakes are not believed to be part of the normal behavior of a good machine. If things go wrong, it must be a personal, human error, the result of fingering, tampering, a button getting stuck, someone hitting the wrong key. The computer, at its normal best, is infallible. 2

How can it be?

I wonder whether this can be true. After all, the whole point of computers is that they represent an extension of the human brain, vastly improved upon but nonetheless human, <u>superhuman</u> maybe. A good computer can think clearly and quickly enough to beat you at chess, and some of them have even been programmed to write obscure verse. They can do anything we can do, and more besides. 3

In what way?

Can this be proven?

It is not yet known whether a computer has its own consciousness, and it would be hard to find out about this. When you walk into one of those great halls now built for the huge machines, and stand listening, it is easy to imagine that the faint, distant noises are the sound of thinking, and the turning of the spools gives them the look of wild creatures rolling their eyes in the effort to concentrate, choking with information. <u>But real thinking, and dreaming, are other matters</u>. 4

I expected this essay to be so much more stuffy than it is. I can even understand it.

In what way?

On the other hand, the evidences of something like an unconscious, equivalent to ours, are all around, in every mail. As extensions of the human brain, they have been constructed with the same property of error, spontaneous, uncontrolled, and rich in possibilities. 5

good, clear comparison for the general reader

so true
great image!

<u>Mistakes are at the very base of human thought</u>, embedded there, feeding the structure like <u>root nodules</u>. If we were not provided with the knack of being wrong, we could never get anything useful done. We think our way along by choosing between right 6

I don't understand this

I agree! This is how we learn

and wrong alternatives, and the wrong choices have to be made as frequently as the right ones. We get along in life this way. We are built to make mistakes, coded for error.

We learn, as we say, by "trial and error." Why do we always say that? Why not "trial and rightness" or "trial and triumph"? The old phrase puts it that way because that is, in real life, the way it is done.   7

Another effective comparison for the general reader

A good laboratory, like a good bank or a corporation or government, has to run like a computer. Almost everything is done flawlessly, by the book, and all the numbers add up to the predicted sums. The days go by. And then, if it is a <u>lucky</u> day, and a <u>lucky</u> laboratory, somebody makes a <u>mistake</u>: the wrong buffer, something in one of the blanks, a decimal misplaced in reading counts, the warm room off by a degree and a half, a mouse out of his box, or just a misreading of the day's protocol. Whatever, when the results come in, something is obviously screwed up, and <u>then the action can begin.</u>   8

Isn't this a contradiction?

What?

The misreading is not the important error; <u>it opens the way.</u> The next step is the crucial one. If the investigator can bring himself to say, "But even so, look at that!" then the new finding, whatever it is, is ready for snatching. What is needed, for progress to be made, is <u>the move based on error.</u>   9

aha!

Interesting idea

Could this be related to the human ability to think critically?

Whenever new kinds of thinking are about to be accomplished, or new varieties of music, there has to be an argument beforehand. With two sides debating in the same mind, haranguing, there is an amiable understanding that one is right and the other wrong. Sooner or later the thing is settled, but there can be no action at all if there are not the two sides, and the argument. <u>The hope is in the faculty of wrongness</u>, the tendency toward error. The capacity to leap across mountains of information to land lightly on the wrong side represents the highest of human endowments.   10

I believe Thomas here because of his background.

It may be that this is a uniquely human gift, perhaps even stipulated in our genetic instructions. Other creatures do not seem to have DNA sequences for making mistakes as a routine part of daily living, certainly not for programmed error as a guide for action.   11

Yes, but this is so frustrating

We are at our human finest, <u>dancing with our minds</u>, when there are more choices than two. Sometimes there are ten, even twenty different ways to go, all but one bound to be wrong, and the richness of selection in such situations can lift us onto totally new ground. This process is called exploration and is based on human fallibility. If we had only a single center in our brains, capable of responding only when a correct decision was to be made, instead of the jumble of different, credulous, easily conned clusters of neurones that provide for being flung off into blind alleys, up trees, down dead ends, out into blue sky, along wrong turnings, around bends, we could only stay the way we are today, stuck fast.   12

Nice mental image

This is a great sentence —It has a lot of feeling

I love the phrase "splendid freedom"

<u>The lower animals do not have this splendid freedom.</u> They are limited, most of them, to absolute infallibility. Cats, for all their good side, never make mistakes. <u>I have never seen a maladroit, clumsy, or blundering cat.</u> Dogs are sometimes fallible, occasionally   13

See ¶ 11 Look up "maladroit"

I never thought of mistakes this way

Thomas makes our technology sound really exciting

We need to program computers to make deliberate mistakes so they can help our natural human tendency to learn thru error

Not a contradiction after all.

able to make charming minor mistakes, but they get this way by trying to mimic their masters. <u>Fish are flawless in everything they do</u>. Individual cells in a tissue are mindless machines, perfect in their performance, as absolutely inhuman as bees.

I like this idea

We should have this in mind as we become dependent on more complex computers for the arrangement of our affairs. Give the computers their heads, I say; let them go their way. If we can learn to do this, turning our heads to one side and wincing while the work proceeds, the possibilities for the future of mankind, and computerkind, are limitless. <u>Your average good computer can make calculations in an instant which would take a lifetime of slide rules for any of us</u>. Think of what we could gain from the near infinity of precise, <u>machine-made miscomputation</u> which is now so easily within our grasp. We would begin the solving of some of our hardest problems. How, for instance, should we go about organizing ourselves for social living on a planetary scale, now that we have become, as a plain fact of life, a single community? We can assume, as a working hypothesis, that all the right ways of doing this are unworkable. What we need, then, for moving ahead, is a set of wrong alternatives much longer and more interesting than the short list of mistaken courses that any of us can think up right now. We need, in fact, an infinite list, and when it is printed out we need the computer to turn on itself and select, at random, the next way to go. If it is a big enough mistake, we could find ourselves on a new level, stunned, out in the clear, ready to move again.

14

so true

yes

So mistakes have value!

■ _____ ■

Guideline 2. *After you have read the reading for the first time, summarize its main ideas in some fashion.* The form of this task might be anything, from a drawing of the main ideas as they relate to one another, to a succinct summary. You could draw a graph or map of the topics in the essay; outline the ideas to get an overview of the piece; or summarize the ideas to check your understanding of the main points of the selection. Any of these tasks can be completed from your original notes and underlining.

Guideline 3. *Next, read the questions and assignments following the selection to help focus your thinking for the second reading.* Don't answer the questions at this time; just read them to make sure you are picking up the main ideas from the selection and thinking about relevant connections among those ideas.

Rereading

Following your initial reading, read the piece again, concentrating this time on how the author achieved his or her purpose. The temptation to skip this stage of the reading process is often powerful, but this second reading is crucial to your development as a critical reader in all of your courses as it allows a much deeper understanding of the work under consideration and prepares you to analyze the writer's ideas.

You should also be prepared to look closely at the assumptions the reading is based on: For example, how does the writer move from idea to idea in the piece? What hidden assertions lie behind these ideas? Do you agree or disagree with these assertions? Your assessment of these unspoken assumptions will often play a major role in your critical response to a piece of writing. In the case of Thomas's essay, do you accept the unspoken connection he makes between the workings of the human brain and the computer? What parts of the essay hinge upon your acceptance of this connection? What other assumptions are fundamental to Thomas's reasoning? If you accept his thinking along the way, you are more likely to agree with the general flow of Thomas's essay. If you discover a flaw in his premises or assumptions, your acceptance of his argument will start to break down.

Next, answer the questions that follow the selection. The "Understanding Details" questions will help you understand and remember what you have read on both the literal and the interpretive levels. Some of the questions ask you to restate various important points the author makes (literal); others help you see relationships between the different ideas presented (interpretive).

	Understanding Details
Literal	1. According to Thomas, in what ways are computers and humans similar? In what ways are they different?
Lit./Interp	2. In what ways do we learn by "trial and error"? Why is this a useful way to learn?

Interpretive   3. What does Thomas mean by the statement, "If we were not provided with the knack of being wrong, we could never get anything useful done" (paragraph 6)?

Interpretive   4. According to Thomas, in what important way do humans and "lower" animals differ? What does this comparison have to do with Thomas's main line of reasoning?

The "Analyzing Meaning" questions require you to analyze and evaluate some of the writer's ideas in order to form valid opinions of your own. These questions demand a higher level of thought than the previous set and help you prepare more specifically for the discussion/writing assignments that follow the questions.

Analyzing Meaning

Analytical   1. What is Thomas's main point in this essay? How do the references to computers help him make this point?

Analytical   2. Why does Thomas perceive human error as such a positive quality? What does "exploration" have to do with this quality (paragraph 12)?

Analytical   3. What could we gain from "the near infinity of precise, machine-made miscomputation" (paragraph 14)? In what ways would our civilization advance?

The "Discovering Rhetorical Strategies" questions ask you to look closely at what strategies the writer uses to develop his or her thesis, and how those strategies work. The questions address features of the writer's composing process, such as word choice, use of detail, transitions, statement of purpose, organization of ideas, sentence structure, and paragraph development. The intent of these questions is to raise various elements of the composing process to the conscious level so you can use them in creating your own essays.

Discovering Rhetorical Strategies

1. Thomas begins his essay with a list of experiences most of us have had at one time or another. Do you find this an effective beginning? Why or why not?

2. Which main points in his essay does Thomas develop in most detail? Why do you think he chooses to develop these points so thoroughly?

3. Explain the simile Thomas uses in paragraph 6: "Mistakes are at the very base of human thought, embedded there, feeding the structure like root nodules." Is this comparison between "mistakes" and "root nodules" useful in this context? Why or why not? Find another simile or metaphor in this essay, and explain how it works.

A final set of questions, "Making Connections," asks you to consider the selection you have just read in reference to other pieces in the book. Your instructor will assign these questions according to the selections you have read. The questions may have you compare the writers' treatment of an idea, the authors' style of writing, the difference in their opinions, or the similarities between their views of the world. Such questions will help you see connections in your own life—not only in your reading and your immediate environment, but also in the larger world around you. These questions, in particular, encourage you to move from specific references in the selections to a broader range of issues and circumstances that affect your daily life. (See box, opposite.)

Because checklists can provide a helpful method of reviewing important information, we offer here a series of questions that represent the three stages of reading just discussed. All these guidelines can be generalized into a checklist for reading any academic assignment in any discipline. (See "Reading Inventory.")

Making Connections

1. Cecil Foster ("Why Blacks Get Mad") refers both directly and indirectly to learning from mistakes. Would Lewis Thomas agree with his approach to this topic? In what ways do these authors think alike about the benefits of making errors? In what ways do they differ on the topic? Explain your answer.

2. Lewis Thomas and Tony Leighton ("The New Nature") both discuss the usefulness of computers. In what ways do their ideas complement each other? In what ways do they differ?

3. Thomas says, "The lower animals . . . are limited, most of them, to absolute infallibity." Compare this perspective with that of Stanley Coren in "Dogs and Monsters." Do you think Coren would agree that "[o]ther creatures do not seem to have DNA sequences for making mistakes as a routine part of daily living, certainly not for programmed error as a guide for action"? Explain why or why not.

Reading Inventory

Preparing to Read

Title

1. What can I infer from the title of the essay about the author's attitude toward the subject or the general tone of the essay?
2. Who do I think is the author's audience? What is the principal purpose of the essay?

Synopsis

1. What is the general subject of the essay?
2. What is the author's approach to the subject?

Biography

1. What do I know about the author's age, political stance, and general beliefs?

2. How qualified is the author to write on this subject?

3. When did the author write the essay? Under what conditions? In what context?

4. Where was the essay first published?

Content

1. What would I like to learn about this topic?

2. What are some of my opinions on this subject?

Reading

1. What are my initial reactions, comments, and personal associations in reference to the ideas in this essay?

2. What are the essay's main ideas?

3. Did I read the questions and assignments following the essay?

Rereading

1. How does the author achieve his or her purpose in this essay?

2. What assumptions underlie the author's reasoning?

3. Do I have a clear literal understanding of this essay? What words do I need to look up in a dictionary?

4. Do I have a solid interpretive understanding of this essay? Do I understand the relationship among ideas? What conclusions can I draw from this essay?

5. Do I have an accurate analytical understanding of this essay? Which ideas can I take apart, examine, and put back together again? What is my evaluation of this material?

6. Do I understand the rhetorical strategies the writer uses and the way they work? Can I explain the effects of these strategies?

Writing Critically

The last stage of responding to the reading selections in this text offers you various "Ideas for Discussion/Writing" that will allow you to demonstrate the different skills you have learned in each chapter. You will be most successful if you envision each writing experience as an organic process that follows a natural cycle of prewriting, writing, and rewriting.

Preparing to Write

The prewriting phase involves exploring a subject, generating ideas, selecting and narrowing a topic, analyzing an audience, and developing a purpose. Preceding the writing assignments are "Preparing to Write" questions you should respond to before trying to structure your thoughts into a coherent essay. These questions will assist you in generating new thoughts on the topics and may even stimulate new approaches to old ideas. Keeping a journal to respond to these questions is an excellent technique, because you will then have a record of your opinions on various topics related to the writing assignments that follow.

Preparing to Write

Write freely about an important mistake you have made: How did the mistake make you feel? What (if anything) did you learn from this mistake? What did you fail to learn that you should have learned? Did this mistake have any positive impact on your life? What were its negative consequences? How crucial are mistakes in our lives?

Responses to these questions can be prompted by a number of different "invention" techniques and carried out by you individually, with another student, in small groups, or as a class project. Invention strategies can help you generate responses to these questions and discover related ideas through the various stages of writing your papers. Because you will undoubtedly vary your approach to different assignments, you should be familiar with the following choices available to you:

Brainstorming. The basis of brainstorming is free association. Ideally, you should get a group of students together and bounce ideas, words, and thoughts off one another until they begin to cluster around related topics. If you don't have a group of students handy, brainstorm by yourself or with a friend. In a group of students or with a friend, the exchange of thoughts usually starts orally, but should transfer to paper when your ideas begin to fall into related categories. When you brainstorm by yourself, however, you should write down everything that comes to mind. The act of recording your ideas in this case becomes a catalyst for other thoughts. Then, keep writing down words and phrases that occur to you until they begin to fall into logical subdivisions, or until you stop generating new ideas.

Freewriting. Freewriting means writing to discover what you want to say. Set a time limit of about ten minutes, and just write by free association. Write about what you are seeing, feeling, touching, thinking; write about having nothing to say; recopy the sentence you just wrote—anything. Just keep writing on paper, on a typewriter, or on a computer. After you have generated some material, locate an idea that is central to your writing assignment, put it at the top of another page, and start freewriting again, letting your thoughts take shape around this central idea. This second type of preparation is called *focused freewriting,* and is especially valuable when you already have a specific topic.

Journal Entries. Journal entries are much like freewriting, except you have some sense of an audience—probably either your instructor or yourself. In a journal, anything goes. You can respond to the "Preparing to Write" questions, jot down thoughts, paste up articles that spark your interest, write sections of dialogue, draft letters (the kind you never send), record dreams, or make lists.

Direct Questions. This technique involves asking a series of questions useful in any writing situation to generate ideas, arrange thoughts, or revise prose. One example of this strategy is to use the inquiries journalists rely on to check the coverage in their articles:

Who:	*Who played the game?*
	Who won the game?
What:	*What kind of game was it?*
	What happened in the game?
Why:	*Why was the game played?*
Where:	*Where was the game played?*
When:	*When was the game played?*
How:	*How was the game played?*

If you ask yourself extended questions of this sort on a specific topic, you will begin to produce thoughts and details that will undoubtedly be useful to you in the writing assignments that follow.

Clustering. Clustering is a method of drawing or mapping your ideas as fast as they come into your mind. Put a word, phrase, or sentence in a circle in the centre of a blank page. Then, put every new idea that comes to you in another circle and show its relationship to a previous thought by drawing a line to the circle containing the previous idea. You will probably reach a natural stopping point for this exercise in two to three minutes.

Although you can generate ideas in a number of different ways, the main principle behind the "Preparing to Write" questions in this text is to encourage you to do what is called *expressive writing* before you tackle any writing assignment. This is writing based on your feelings, thoughts, experiences, observations, and opinions. From this reservoir, you can then choose the ideas you want to develop into an essay and begin writing about them one at a time.

As you use various prewriting techniques to generate responses to the "Preparing to Write" questions, you should know that these responses can be expressed using lists, outlines, random notes, sentences and paragraphs, charts, graphs, or pictures—whatever keeps the thoughts flowing smoothly and productively. One of our students used a combination of brainstorming and clustering to generate the following thoughts in response to the prewriting exercise following the Thomas essay:

Brainstorming

Mistakes:
- *happen when I'm in a hurry*
- *make me feel stupid*
- *love*
- *Bob*
- *learned a lot about people*
- *people aren't what they seem*
- *getting back on track*
- *parents*
- *corrections*

- *relationships*
- *trip back East*
- *pride*
- *going in circles*
- *learning from mistakes*
  - *I am a better person*
  - *my values are clear*
- *mistakes help us change*
  - *painful*
  - *helpful*
  - *valuable*

Clustering

From the free-flowing thoughts you generate, you next need to decide what to write about and how to limit your subject to a manageable length. Our student writer chose topic 2 from the "Choosing a Topic" list after the essay (see page 23). Her initial responses to the prewriting questions helped her decide to write on "A Time I Got Lost." She then generated more focused ideas and opinions in the form of a journal entry. It is printed here just as she wrote it, errors and all.

Journal Entry

The craziest mistake I think I ever made was on a trip I took recently——I was heading to the east coast from British Columbia and reached Fredericton. I was so excited because I was going to get to see the Atlantic Ocean for the first time in my life and Fredericton was one of my last towns before I reached the sea. In Fredericton I was going to have to change from a northeast direction to due east.

When I got there the highway was under construction. I took the detour, but got all skrewed up till I realized that I had gone the wrong direction. By this time I was lost somewhere in downtown Fredericton and didn't know which way was east. I stoped and asked a guy at a gas station and he explained how to get back on the east–bound highway. The way was through the middle of town. By the time I got to where I was supposed to turn right I could only turn left. So I started left and then realized I couldn't turn back the other way! I made a couple of other stops after that, and one jerk told me I "just couldn't get there from here." Eventually I found a truck driver heading toward the same eastbound highway, and he told me to follow him. An hour and forty minutes after reaching Fredericton's city limits I finally managed to leave going east. I felt as if I had spent an entire month there!

The thing I learned from this was just how egocentric I am. I would not have made this error if I had not been so damn cocky about my sense of direction. My mistake was made worse because I got flustered and didn't listen to the directions clearly. I find that the reason I most often make a mistake is because I don't listen carefully to instructions. This has been a problem all my life.

After I got over feeling really dum I decided this kind of thing was not going to happen again. It was too much a waste of time and gas, so I was going to be more careful of road signs and directions.

This all turned out to be a positive experience though. I learned that there are lots of friendly, helpful people. It was kind of reassuring to know that other folks would help you if you just asked.

I feel this and other mistakes are crucial not only to my life but to personal growth in general. It is the making of mistakes that helps people learn where they are *misdirecting their energies. I think mistakes can help all of us learn to be more careful about some part of our lives. This is why mistakes are crucial. Otherwise, we would continue in the same old rut and never improve.*

This entry served as the foundation upon which the student built her essay. Her next step was to consider *audience* and *purpose* (which are usually specified in the writing assignments in this text). The first of these features identifies the person or group of people you will address in your essay. The second is a declaration of your principal reason for writing the essay, which usually takes the form of a thesis statement (the statement of purpose or the controlling idea of an essay). Together these pieces of information consciously or subconsciously help you make the most of the decisions you are faced with as you write: what words to choose, what sentence structures to use, what order to present ideas in, which topics to develop, and which to summarize. The more you know about your audience (age, educational background, likes, dislikes, biases, political persuasion, and social status) and your purpose (to inform, persuade, and/or entertain), the easier the writing task will be. In the rough draft and final draft of the essay in the section that follows, the student knew she was writing to a senior English class at her old high school in order to convince them that mistakes can be positive factors in their lives. This clear sense of audience and purpose helped her realize she should use fairly advanced vocabulary, call upon a variety of sentence structures, and organize her ideas chronologically to make her point most effectively to her intended audience.

At this stage of the writing process, some people benefit from assembling their ideas in the form of an outline. Others use an outline as a check on their logic and organization after the first draft has been written. Whether your outlines are informal (a simple list) or highly structured, they can help you visualize the logical relationship of your ideas to each other. We recommend using your outline throughout the prewriting and writing stages to ensure that your work will be carefully and tightly organized. Your outline, however, should be adjusted to your draft as it develops.

Writing

The writing stage asks you to draft an essay based upon the prewriting material you have assembled. Because you have already made the important preliminary decisions regarding your topic, your audience, and your purpose, the task of actually writing the essay should follow naturally. (Notice we did not say this task should necessarily be easy—just natural.) At this stage, you should look upon your essay as a way of solving a problem or answering a question: The problem/question is posed in your writing assignment, and the solution/answer is your essay. The three "Choosing a Topic" assignments that follow the prewriting questions in the text require you to consider issues related to the essay you just read. Although they typically ask you to focus on one rhetorical pattern, they draw on many rhetorical strategies (as do all writing assignments in the text) and require you to support your statements with concrete examples. These assignments refer to the Lewis Thomas essay and emphasize the use of example, his dominant rhetorical strategy.

Choosing a Topic

1. You have decided to write an editorial for your local news-paper concerning the impact of computers on our lives. Cite specific experiences you have had with computers to help make your main point.

2. You have been invited back to your high school to make a speech to a senior English class about how people can learn from their mistakes. Write your speech in the form of an essay explaining what you learned from a crucial mistake you have made. Use examples to show these students that mistakes can be positive factors in their lives.

3. In an essay for your writing class, explain one specific human quality. Use Thomas's essay as a model. Cite examples to support your explanation.

The following essay is our student's first-draft response to topic 2. After writing her journal entry, the student drafted a tentative thesis statement: "I know there are positive attitudes that can come from making a mistake because I recently had an opportunity to learn some valuable lessons in this way." This statement helped the student further develop and organize her ideas as she focused finally on one well-chosen example to illustrate her thesis. At this point, the thesis is simply the controlling idea around which the other topics take shape; it is often revised several times before the final draft.

First Draft: A Time I Got Lost

Parents and teachers frequently pressure us to avoid committing errors. Meanwhile, our friends laugh at us when we make mistakes. With all these different messages, it is hard for us to think of mistakes as positive events. But if any of you take the time to think about what you have learned from mistakes, I bet you will realize all the good things that have come from these events. I know there are positive attitudes that can come from making a mistake because I recently had an opportunity to learn some valuable lessons in this way.

While travelling back east this last summer, I made the mistake of turning west on an interprovincial detour in order to reach the Atlantic Ocean. The adventure took me into the heart of Fredericton, where I got totally lost. I had to get directions several times until two hours later I was going in the right direction. As I was driving out of town, I realized that although I had made a dumb mistake, I had learned a great deal. Overall, the detour was actually a positive experience.

The first thing I remember thinking after I had gotten my wits together was that I had definitely learned something from making the mistake. I had the opportunity to see a new city, filled with new people— 3000 kilometres from my own hometown, but very much like it. I also became aware that the beach is not always toward the west, as it is in British Columbia. The entire experience was like getting a geography lesson firsthand.

As this pleasant feeling began to grow, I came to another realization. I was aware of how important other people can be in making a mistake into a positive experience. My first reaction was "Oh no, someone is going to know I made a mistake!" But the amazing part about this mistake was how supportive everyone was. The townspeople had been entirely willing to help someone they did not know. This mistake helped me to learn that people tend to be nicer than I had imagined.

The final lesson I learned from getting lost in Fredericton was how to be more cautious about my actions so as not to repeat the same mistake. It was this internalization of all the information I gleaned from making the mistake that I see as the most positive part of the experience. I realized that in order to avoid such situations in the future I would have to be less egocentric in my decisions and more willing to listen to directions from other people. I needed to learn that my set way of doing things was not always the best way. If I had not made the mistake, I would not have been aware of my other options.

By making this mistake I learned that there is a more comprehensive manner of looking at the world. In the future, if we could all stop after making a mistake and ask ourselves, "What can I learn from this?" we would be less critical of ourselves and have a great many more positive experiences. If I were not able to make mistakes, I would probably not be able to expand my knowledge of my environment, my understanding of people, and my choice of various actions.

Rewriting

The rewriting stage includes revising, editing, and proofreading. The first of these activities, *revising*, actually takes place during the entire writing process as you change words, recast sentences, and move whole paragraphs from one place to another. Making these linguistic and organizational choices means you will also be constantly adjusting your content to your purpose (what you want to accomplish) and your audience (the readers) in much the same way you alter your speech to communicate more effectively in response to the gestures, eye movements, or facial expressions of your listener. Revising is literally the act of "reseeing" your essay, looking at it through your readers' eyes to determine whether or not it achieves its purpose. As you revise, you should consider matters of both content and form. In *content*, do you have an interesting, thought-provoking title for your essay? Do you think your thesis statement will be clear to your audience? Does your introduction capture the readers' attention? Is your treatment of your topic consistent throughout the essay? Do you support your assertions with specific examples? Does your conclusion sum up your main points? In *form*, is your essay organized effectively? Do you use a variety of rhetorical strategies? Are your sentence structure and vocabulary varied and interesting?

Editing entails correcting mistakes in your writing so that your final draft conforms to the conventions of standard written English. Correct punctuation, spelling, and mechanics will help you make your points and will encourage your readers to move smoothly through your essay from topic to topic. At this stage, you should be concerned about such matters as whether your sentences are complete, whether your punctuation is correct and effective, whether you have followed conventional rules for using mechanics, and whether the words in your essay are spelled correctly.

Proofreading involves reading over your entire essay, slowly and carefully, to make certain you have not allowed any errors to slip into your draft. (Most writing instructors don't look upon errors as kindly as Thomas does.) In general, good writers try to let some time elapse between writing the final draft and proofreading it (at least a few hours, perhaps a day or so). Otherwise, they find themselves proofreading their thoughts rather than their words. Some writers even profit from proofreading their papers backward—a technique that allows them to focus on individual words and phrases rather than on entire sentences.

Because many writers work well with checklists, we present here a set of guidelines that will help you review the entire writing process.

Writing Inventory

Preparing to Write

1. Have I explored the prewriting questions through brainstorming, freewriting, journal entries, direct questions, or clustering?
2. Do I understand my topic or assignment?
3. Have I narrowed my topic adequately?
4. Do I have a specific audience for my essay? Do I know their likes and dislikes? Their educational level? Their knowledge about the topic?
5. Do I have a clear and precise purpose for my essay?

Writing

1. Can I express my topic as a problem or question?
2. Is my essay a solution or an answer to that problem or question?

Rewriting

Revising the Content

1. Does my essay have a clear, interesting title?

2. Will my statement of purpose (or thesis) be clear to my audience?

3. Will the introduction make my audience want to read the rest of my essay?

4. Do I pursue my topic consistently throughout the essay?

5. Have I included enough details to prove my main points?

6. Does my conclusion sum up my central points?

7. Will I accomplish my purpose with this audience?

Revising the Form

1. Have I organized my ideas as effectively as possible for this audience?

2. Do I use appropriate rhetorical strategies to support my main point?

3. Is my sentence structure varied and interesting?

4. Is my vocabulary appropriate for my topic, my purpose, and my audience?

5. Do I present my essay as effectively as possible, including useful graphic design techniques on the computer, where appropriate?

Editing and Proofreading

1. Have I written complete sentences throughout my essay?

2. Have I used punctuation correctly and effectively (check especially the use of commas, colons, and semicolons)?

3. Have I followed conventional rules for mechanics (capitalization, underlining or italics, abbreviations, and numbers)?

4. Are all the words in my essay spelled correctly? (Use a dictionary when in doubt.)

Following is the student's revised draft of her essay on making mistakes in life. The final draft of this typical student's essay represents the entire writing process at work. We have made notes in the margin to highlight various effective elements in her essay, and we have underlined substantial changes in words and phrases from earlier drafts.

Mistakes and Maturity

Catchy title; good change from first draft

Rapport with audience and point of view established

Parents and teachers frequently <u>harp</u> on us to <u>correct</u> our errors. Meanwhile, our friends laugh at us when we make mistakes. With all these <u>negative</u> messages, most of us have a hard time believing that problems can be positive experiences. But if we take the time to think about what we have learned from various <u>blunders</u>, we will realize all the good that has come from these events. <u>I know making mistakes can have positive results because I recently learned several valuable lessons from one unforgettable experience.</u>

Clear, stimulating introduction for high school seniors

Good brief summary of complex experience (see notes from Preparing to Write)

While <u>I was</u> travelling to the east coast last summer, I made the mistake of turning west on an interprovincial detour <u>in an attempt</u> to reach the Atlantic Ocean. This adventure took me into the <u>centre</u> of Fredericton, where I <u>became</u> totally lost, bewildered, and angry at myself. I had to <u>ask for</u> directions several times until two hours later, when I <u>finally found the correct highway toward the ocean.</u> As I was driving out of town, I realized that although I had made a "dumb" mistake, I had actually learned a great deal. Overall, <u>my adventure had been quite positive.</u>

Background information

Good details

The first <u>insight</u> I remember having after my wits returned was that I had definitely learned more about Canadian geography from making this mistake. <u>I had become intimately acquainted with a town 4827 kilometres from home that greatly resembled my own city, and I had become aware that the beach is not always toward the west, as it is in British Columbia. I had also met some pleasant strangers. Looking at my confusion as a learning experience encouraged me to have positive feelings about the mistake.</u>

First topic (Topics are in chronological order)

Adequate number of examples

Nice close to this paragraph

<u>As I relaxed and let</u> this happy feeling grow, I came to another realization. I <u>became</u> aware of how important other people can be in <u>turning</u> a mistake into a positive event. Although my first reaction had been "Oh, no! Someone is going to know <u>I'm lost</u>," I was amazed by how supportive other people were <u>during my panic and embarrassment. From an old man swinging on his front porch to an elementary school boy crossing the street with his bright blue backpack, I found</u> that the townspeople of Fredericton were entirely willing to help someone they did not <u>even</u> know. <u>I realized that people in general</u> are nicer than <u>I had previously thought.</u>

Second topic

Clear explanation with details

Good summary statement

The final lesson I learned from <u>making this mistake</u> was how to be more cautious about <u>my future decisions</u>. <u>This insight was, in fact,</u> the most positive part of the entire experience. <u>What</u> I realized I must do to <u>prevent</u> similar <u>errors</u> in the future was to relax, <u>not be so bullheaded</u> in my decisions, and be more willing to listen to directions from other people. <u>I might never have had these positive realizations if I had not made this mistake.</u>

Third topic

Specific details

Clear transition statement

        Thus, by <u>driving in circles for two hours, I developed</u> a more com-prehensive way of looking at the world. If I were unable to make mis-takes, I probably would not have had this chance to <u>learn</u> about my environment, <u>improve my impressions of strangers,</u> and <u>reconsider the egocentric way in which I act in certain situations.</u> Perhaps there's <u>a lesson here for all of us.</u> Instead of <u>criticizing ourselves unduly,</u> if each one of us could <u>pause</u> after we make an error and ask, "<u>How</u> can I <u>profit</u> from this?" <u>we would realize that mistakes can often be turned into positive events that will help us become more confident and mature.</u>

Concluding statement applicable to all readers

Good summary of three topics without being repetitive

Nicely focused concluding remark

As these various drafts of the student paper indicate, the essay assignments in this book encourage you to transfer to your own writing your understanding of how form and content work together. If you use the short-answer questions after each reading selection as a guide, the writing assignments will help you learn how to give shape to your own ideas and to gain control of your readers' thoughts and feelings. In essence, they will help you recognize the power you have through language over your life and your environment.

Conclusion

As you approach the essays and stories in this text, remember that both reading and writing function most efficiently as processes of discovery. Through them, you educate and expand your own mind and the minds of your readers. They can provide a powerful means of discovering new information or clarifying what you already know. Reading and writing lead to understanding. And just as you can discover how to read through writing, so too can you become more aware of the details of the writing process through reading. We hope your time spent with this book is both pleasant and profitable as you refine your ability to discover and express effectively the good ideas within yourself.

CHAPTER 1

DESCRIPTION

∎ ∎ ∎

Exploring Through the Senses

All of us use description in our daily lives. We might, for example, try to convey the horrors of a recent history exam to our parents, or help a friend visualize someone we met on vacation, or describe an automobile accident for a police report. Whatever our specific purpose, description is fundamental to the act of communication: We give and receive descriptions constantly, and our lives are continually affected by this simple yet important rhetorical technique.

Defining Description

Description may be defined as the act of capturing people, places, events, objects, and feelings in words so that a reader (or listener) can visualize and respond to them. Unlike narration, which traditionally presents events in a clear time sequence, description essentially suspends its objects in time, making them exempt from such limits of chronology. Narration tells a story, while pure description contains no action or time. Description is one of our primary forms of self-expression; it paints a verbal picture that helps the reader understand or share a sensory experience through the process of "showing" rather than "telling." *Telling* your friends, for example, that "the campgrounds were filled with friendly, happy activities" is not as engaging as *showing* them by saying, "The campgrounds were alive with the smell of spicy baked beans, the sound of high-pitched laughter, and the sight of happy families sharing the warmth of a fire." Showing your readers helps them understand your experience through as many senses as possible.

Descriptions range between extremes: (1) totally objective reports (with no trace of opinions or feelings), such as we might find in a dictionary or an encyclopedia, and (2) very subjective accounts, which focus almost exclusively on personal impressions. The same horse, for instance, might be described by one writer as "a large, solid-hoofed herbivorous mammal having a long mane and a tail" (objective) and by another as "a magnificent and spirited beast flaring its nostrils in search of adventure" (subjective). Most descriptive writing, however, falls somewhere between these two extremes: "a large, four-legged beast in search of adventure."

Objective description is principally characterized by its impartial, precise, and emotionless tone. Found most prominently in technical and scientific writing, such accounts might include a description of equipment to be used in a chemistry experiment, the results of a market survey for a particular consumer product, or a medical appraisal of a heart patient's physical symptoms. In situations like these, accurate, unbiased, and easily understandable accounts are of the utmost importance.

Subjective description, in contrast, is intentionally created to produce a particular response in the reader or listener. Focusing on feelings rather than on raw data, it tries to activate as many senses as possible, thereby leading the audience to a specific conclusion or state of mind. Examples of subjective descriptions are a parent's disapproving comments about one of your friends, a professor's glowing analysis of your most recent "A" paper, or a basketball coach's critique of the team's losing effort in last night's big game.

In most situations, the degree of subjectivity or objectivity in a descriptive passage depends to a large extent upon the writer's purpose and intended audience. In the case of the heart patient mentioned above, the person's physician might present the case in a formal, scientific way to a group of medical colleagues; in a personal, sympathetic way to the invalid's spouse; and in financial terms to a number of potential contributors in order to solicit funds for heart disease research.

The following paragraph describes one student's fond memories of visiting "the farm." As you read it, notice the writer's use of subjective description to communicate to her readers the multitude of contradictory feelings she connects with this rural retreat.

The shrill scream of the alarm shatters a dream. This is the last day of my visit to the place I call "the farm," an old ramshackle house in the country owned by one of my aunts. I want to go out once more in the peace of the early morning, walk in the crisp and chilly hour, and breathe the sweet air. My body feels jarred as my feet hit the hard-packed clay dirt. I tune out my stiff muscles and cold arms and legs and instead focus on two herons playing hopscotch on the canal bank: Every few yards I walk toward them, they fly one over the other an almost equal distance away from me. A killdeer with its piercing crystalline cry dips its body as it flies low over the water, the tip of its wing leaving a ring to reverberate outward. The damp earth has a strong, rich, musky scent. To the east, dust rises, and for the first time I hear the clanking and straining of a tractor as it harrows smooth the soil before planting. A crop duster rises close by just as it cuts off its release of spray, the acrid taste of chemical filtering down through the air. As the birds chatter and peck at the fields, I reluctantly return to my life in the city.

Thinking Critically by Using Description

Each rhetorical mode in this book gives us new insight into the process of thinking by providing different options for arranging our thoughts and our experiences. The more we know about these options, the more conscious we become of how our minds operate and the better chance we have to improve and refine our thinking skills. (For a more thorough definition of the term *rhetorical mode*, see the Web site **www.pearsoned.ca/flachmann/**)

As you examine description as a way of thinking, consider it in isolation for a moment—away from the other rhetorical modes. Think of it as a muscle you can isolate and strengthen on its own in a weight-training program before you ask it to perform together with other muscles. By isolating description, you will learn more readily what it entails and how it functions as a critical thinking tool. In the process, you will also strengthen your knowledge of how to recognize and use description more effectively in your reading, in your writing, and in your daily life.

Just as you exercise to strengthen muscles, so too will you benefit from doing exercises to improve your skill in using descriptive techniques. As you have learned, description depends to a great extent on the keenness of your senses. So as you prepare to read and write descriptive essays, do the following tasks so that you can first learn what the process of description feels like in your own head. Really use your imagination to play with these exercises on as many different levels as possible. Also write when you are asked to do so. The combination of thinking and writing is often especially useful when we practise our thinking skills.

1. Make a list of five descriptive words you would use to trigger each of the following senses: taste, sight, hearing, touch, and smell.

2. Find a picture of a person, an animal, a bouquet of flowers, a sunset, or some other still-life portrait. List words you would use to describe this picture to a classmate. Then, list a few similes and metaphors that actually describe this still life. How would your description differ if you were seeing the subject in real life rather than in a picture?

3. Choose an unusual object and brainstorm about its physical characteristics. Then, brainstorm about the emotions this object evokes. Why is this object so unusual or special? Compare your two brainstorming results and draw some conclusions about their differences.

Reading and Writing Descriptive Essays

All good descriptions share four fundamental qualities: (1) an accurate sense of audience (who the readers are) and purpose (why the essay was written), (2) a clear vision of the object being described, (3) a careful selection of details that help communicate the author's vision, and (4) a consistent point of view or perspective from which a writer composes. The dominant impression or main effect the writer wishes to leave with a specific audience dictates virtually all of the verbal choices in a descriptive essay. Although description is featured in this chapter, you should also pay close attention to how other rhetorical strategies (such as example, division/classification, and cause/effect) can best support the dominant impression.

How to Read a Descriptive Essay

Preparing to Read. As you approach the reading selections in this chapter, you should focus first on the author's title and try to make some initial assumptions about the essay that follows: Does Ray Guy reveal his attitude toward his subject in the title "When

Jannies Visited"? Can you guess what the general mood of "What a Certain Visionary Once Said" will be? Then, scan the essay to discover its audience and purpose: What do you think Lesley Choyce's purpose is in "Thin Edge of the Wedge"? Who is Dave Bidini addressing in "Kris King Looks Terrible"? You should also read the synopsis of each essay in the Rhetorical Table of Contents (on pages iii–xi); these brief summaries will provide you with helpful information at this point in the reading process.

Next, learn as much as you can about the author and the conditions under which the essay was composed, information that is provided in the biographical statement before each essay. For a descriptive essay, the conditions under which the author wrote the essay, coupled with his or her purpose, can be very revealing: Can you determine when Ray Guy's piece was written? Does it describe the narrator's life now or in the past? What do Dave Bidini's interests tell you about his motivations for writing "Kris King Looks Terrible"? What concerns might have led Lesley Choyce to have written "Thin Edge of the Wedge"? What does Tomson Highway's background suggest about his perspective in "What a Certain Visionary Once Said"? Learning where the essay was first published will also give you valuable information about its audience.

Last, before you begin to read, try to do some brainstorming on the essay's title. In this chapter, respond to the Preparing to Read questions before each essay, which ask you to begin thinking and writing about the topic under consideration. Then, pose your own questions: What image do you have of "the north" (Highway)? Do you know what jannies are (Guy)? What have your preconceptions been about hockey arenas (Bidini)? What might you want to learn about the life of an island (Choyce)?

Reading. As you read each essay for the first time, jot down your initial reactions to it, and try to make connections and see relationships among the author's biography; the essay's title, purpose, and audience; and the synopsis. In this way, you will create a context or framework for your reading. See if you can figure out, for example, what Highway might be saying about people's attitudes toward the land in his essay, "What a Certain Visionary Once Said," or why Ray Guy wrote an essay about mummering in "When Jannies Visited." Try to discover what the relationship is between purpose, audience, and publication information in Lesley Choyce's essay.

Also determine at this point if the author's treatment of his or her subject is predominantly objective (generally free of emotion) or subjective (heavily charged with emotion). Or perhaps the essay falls somewhere between these two extremes.

In addition, make sure you have a general sense of the dominant impression each author is trying to convey. Such an initial approach to reading these descriptive selections will give you a foundation upon which to analyze the material during your second, more in-depth reading.

Finally, at the end of your first reading, take a look at the questions after each essay to make certain you can answer them. This material will guide your rereading.

Rereading. As you reread these descriptive essays, you should be discovering exactly what each essay's dominant impression is and how the author created it. Notice each author's careful selection of details and the way in which these details come together to leave you with this impression. Also try to determine how certain details add to and detract from that dominant impression and how the writer's point of view affects it: How does Tomson Highway create a sense of respect for the environment in "What a Certain Visionary Once Said"? How does Dave Bidini help us to share the experience of visiting SkyRink?

Try to find during this reading other rhetorical modes that support the description. Although the essays in this chapter describe various persons, places, or objects, all of the authors call upon other rhetorical strategies (especially example and comparison/contrast) to communicate their descriptions. How do these various rhetorical strategies work together in each essay to create a coherent whole?

Finally, answering the questions after each essay will check your understanding of the author's main points and help you think critically about the essay in preparing for the discussion/writing assignments that follow.

For an inventory of the reading process, you may want to review the checklists on pages 15–16 of the Introduction.

How to Write a Descriptive Essay

Preparing to Write. Before you choose a writing assignment, use the prewriting questions that follow each essay to help you discover your own ideas and opinions about the general topic of the essay. Next, choose an assignment or read the one assigned to you. Then, just as you do when you read an essay, you should determine the audience and purpose for your description (if these are not specified for you in the assignment). To whom are you writing? And why? Will an impartial, objective report be appropriate, or should you present a more emotional, subjective account to accomplish your task? In assessing your audience, you need to determine what they do and do not know about your topic. This information will help you make decisions about what you are going to say and how you will say it. Your purpose will be defined by what you intend your audience to know, think, or believe after they have read your descriptive essay. Do you want them to make up their own minds about hockey arenas or cultural traditions, for example, based on an objective presentation of data, or do you hope to sway their opinions through a more subjective display of information? Or perhaps you will decide to blend the two techniques, combining facts and opinions, in order to achieve the impression of personal certainty based on objective evidence. What dominant impression do you want to leave with your audience? As you might suspect, decisions regarding audience and purpose are as important to writing descriptions as they are to reading descriptions, and will shape your descriptive essay from start to finish.

The second quality of good description concerns the object of your analysis and the clarity with which you present it to the reader. Whenever possible, you should thoroughly investigate the person, place, moment, or feeling you wish to describe, paying particular attention to its effect upon each of your five senses. What can you see, smell, hear, taste, and touch as you examine it? If you want to describe your house, for example, begin by asking yourself a series of pertinent questions: How big is the house? What colour is it? How many exterior doors does the house have? How many interior doors? Are any of the rooms wallpapered? If so, what are the colour and texture of that wallpaper? How many different shades of paint cover the walls? Which rooms have constant noises (from clocks and other mechanical devices)? Are the kitchen appliances hot or cold to the touch? What is the quietest room in the house? The noisiest? What smells do you notice in the laundry? In the kitchen? In the basement? Most important, do any of these sensory questions trigger particular childhood memories? Although you will probably not use all of these details in your descriptive essay, the process of generating and answering such detailed questions will help reacquaint you with the object of your description as it also assists you in designing and focusing your paper. To help you generate some of these ideas, you may want to review the prewriting techniques introduced on pages 17–22.

Writing. As you write, you must select the details of your description with great care and precision so that you leave your reader with a specific impression. If, for instance, you want your audience to feel the warmth and comfort of your home, you might concentrate on describing the plush carpets, the big upholstered chairs, the inviting scent of hot apple cider, and the crackling fire. If, on the other hand, you want to gain your audience's sympathy, you might prefer to focus on the sparse austerity of your home environment: the bare walls, the quietness, the lack of colour and decoration, the dim lighting, and the frigid temperature. You also want to make sure you omit unrelated ideas, like a conversation between your parents you accidentally overheard. Your careful choice of details will help control your audience's reaction.

To make your impression even more vivid, you might use figurative language to fill out your descriptions. Using words "figuratively" means using them imaginatively rather than literally. The two most popular forms of figurative language are *simile* and *metaphor*. A *simile* is a comparison between two dissimilar objects or ideas introduced by *like* or *as*: Choyce describes "two dents in the ground as if some giant had punched down into a massive surface of dough." A *metaphor* is an implied comparison between two dissimilar objects or ideas that is not introduced by *like* or *as*: At age eight, Ray Guy's life is a collection of "pieces of the great jigsaw ..." Besides enlivening your writing, figurative language helps your readers understand objects, feelings, and ideas that are complex or obscure by comparing them with things that are more familiar.

The last important quality of an effective descriptive essay is point of view, your physical perspective on your subject. Because the organization of your essay depends on your point of view, you need to choose a specific angle from which to approach your description. If you verbally jump around your home, referring first to a picture on the wall in your bedroom, next to the microwave in the kitchen, and then to the quilt on your bed, no reasonable audience will be able to follow your description. Nor will they want to. If, however, you move from room to room in some logical, sequential way, always focusing on the details you want your readers to know, you will be helping your audience form a clear, memorable impression of your home. Your vision will become their vision. In other words, your point of view plays a part in determining the organization of your description. Working spatially, you could move from side to side (from one wall to another in the rooms we have discussed), from top to bottom (from ceiling to floor), or from far to near (from the farthest to the closest point in a room), or you might progress from large to small objects, from uninteresting to interesting, or from funny to serious. Whatever plan you choose should help you accomplish your purpose with your particular audience.

Rewriting. As you reread each of your descriptive essays, play the role of your audience and try to determine what dominant impression you receive by the end of your reading.

1. Do you communicate the dominant impression you want to convey?
2. Do you have a clear point of view on your subject?
3. How does the essay make you feel?
4. What does it make you think about?
5. Which senses does it stimulate?
6. Do you use similes or metaphors when appropriate?
7. Could you, for example, add more detailed information, reorganize some of the essay, or omit irrelevant material?

For additional suggestions on the writing process, you may want to consult the checklists on pages 26–27 of the Introduction.

Student Essay: Description at Work

In the following essay, a student relives some of her childhood memories through a subjective description of her grandmother's house. As you read it, pay particular attention to the different types of sensual details the student writer chooses in order to communicate to readers her dominant impression of her grandmother's home. Notice also her use of carefully chosen details to "show" rather than "tell" us about her childhood reminiscences, especially her comparisons, which make the memory as vivid for the reader as it is for the writer.

Grandma's House

Writer's point of view or perspective

<u>My most vivid childhood memories</u> are set in my Grandma Goodlink's house, a curious blend of familiar and mysterious treasures. Grandma lived at the end of a dead-end street, in the same house she had lived in since the first day of her marriage. That was half a century and thirteen children ago. A set of crumbly steps made of concrete mixed with gravel led up to her front door. I remember a big gap between the house and the steps, <u>as if someone had not pushed them up close enough to the house.</u> Anyone who looked into the gap <u>could see old toys and books</u> that had fallen into the crack behind the steps and had remained there, forever irretrievable.

Dominant impression

Comparison (simile)

Sight

Only a hook-type lock on the front door protected Grandma's many beautiful antiques. Her living room was set up <u>like a church or schoolroom</u>, with an <u>old purple velvet couch</u> against the far wall and two chairs immediately in front of the couch facing the same direction. <u>One-half of the couch was always buried in old clothes, magazines, and newspapers, and a lone shoe sat atop the pile, a finishing touch to some bizarre modern sculpture</u>. To one side was an aged and <u>tuneless</u> upright piano with <u>yellowed keys</u>. The ivory overlay was missing so that <u>the wood underneath showed through</u>, and many of the keys made only a <u>muffled and frustrating thump</u>, no matter how hard I pressed them. On the wall facing the piano was the room's only window, draped with <u>yellowed lace curtains</u>. Grandma always left that window open. I remember sitting near it, <u>smelling the rain</u> while the curtains <u>tickled my face.</u>

Comparison (simile)

Sight

Comparison (metaphor)

Sound

Sight

Sight

Sound

Sight

Smell

Touch

For no apparent reason, <u>an old curtain</u> hung in the door between the kitchen and the living room. In the kitchen, a large Formica-topped table always held at least a half-dozen varieties of <u>homemade jelly, as well as a loaf of bread, gooseberry pies, or cherry pies with the pits left in, boxes of cereal,</u> and anything else not requiring refrigeration, <u>as if the table served as a small, portable pantry.</u> Grandma's kitchen always <u>smelled of toast</u>, and I often wondered—and still do—if she lived entirely on toast. <u>A hole had eaten through the kitchen floor</u>, not just the warped yellow linoleum, but all the way through the floor itself. My sisters and I never wanted to take a bath at Grandma's house, because we discovered that anyone who lay on the floor on his stomach and put one eye to the hole <u>could see the bathtub</u>, which was kept in the <u>musty</u> basement because the upstairs bathroom was too small.

Sight

Taste

Comparison (simile)

Smell

Sight

Sight

Smell

The back bedroom was near the kitchen and adjacent to the basement stairs. I once heard one of my aunts call that room a firetrap, and indeed it was. The room was <u>wallpapered with the old</u> Sight <u>newspapers</u> Grandma liked to collect, and the bed was stacked

Sight high with <u>my mother's and aunts' old clothes</u>. There was no space between the furniture in that room, only a narrow path against one wall leading to the bed. A sideboard was shoved against the opposite wall; a sewing table was pushed up against the sideboard; a short chest of drawers lay against the sewing table; and so on. But no one could identify these pieces of forgotten furniture ⎬Sight without digging through the sewing patterns, half-made dresses, dishes, and books. Any outsider would just think this was a part of the room where the floor had been raised to about waist-level, so thoroughly was the mass of furniture hidden.

Comparison   Stepping off Grandma's sloping back porch was <u>like stepping</u>
(simile) <u>into an enchanted forest</u>. The grass and weeds were hip-level,
Comparison with a tiny dirt path leading to nowhere, <u>as if it had lost its way in</u>
(simile) <u>the jungle</u>. A <u>fancy white fence</u>, courtesy of the neighbors, bordered Sight the yard in back and vainly attempted to hold in the <u>gooseberries,</u>
Sight <u>raspberries, and blackberries</u> that grew wildly along the side of
Sight Grandma's yard. <u>Huge crabapple, cherry, and walnut trees</u> shaded the house and hid the sky. I used to stand under them and look up, pretending to be deep in a magic forest. The ground was <u>cool and</u> Touch <u>damp</u> under my bare feet, even in the middle of the day, and my head would fill with the <u>sweet fragrance of mixed spring flowers</u> Smell
Sound <u>and the throaty cooing of doves</u> I could never find but could always hear. But, before long, the wind would shift, and the <u>musty</u>
Smell <u>aroma of petroleum</u> from a nearby refinery would jerk me back to reality.

Grandma's house is indeed a place for memories. Just as her decaying concrete steps store the treasures of many lost child-
Dominant hoods, <u>her house still stands, guarding the memories of generations</u>
impression
rephrased <u>of children and grandchildren.</u>

Some Final Thoughts on Description

Because description is one of the most basic forms of verbal communication, you will find descriptive passages in most of the reading selections throughout this textbook. Description provides us with the means to capture our audience's attention and clarify certain points in all of our writing. The examples chosen for the following section, however, are predominantly descriptive—the main purpose in each being to involve the readers' senses as vividly as possible. As you read through each of these essays, try to determine its intended audience and purpose, the object of the description, the extent to which details are included or excluded, and the author's point of view. Equipped with these four areas of reference, you can become an increasingly sophisticated reader and writer of descriptive prose.

Description in Review

Reading Descriptive Essays

Preparing to Read

1. What assumptions can you make from the essay's title?
2. Can you guess what the general mood of the essay is?
3. What is the essay's purpose and audience?
4. What does the synopsis in the Table of Contents tell you about the essay?
5. What can you learn from the author's biography?
6. Can you guess what the author's point of view toward the subject is?
7. What are your responses to the Preparing to Read questions?

Reading

1. Is the essay predominantly objective or subjective?
2. What dominant impression is the author trying to convey?
3. Did you preview the questions that follow the essay?

Rereading

1. How does the author create the essay's dominant impression?
2. What other rhetorical modes does the author use to support the essay's purpose?
3. What are your responses to the questions after the essay?

Writing Descriptive Essays

Preparing to Write

1. What are your responses to the Preparing to Write questions?

2. What is your purpose? Will you be primarily objective or subjective?

3. Who is your audience?

4. What is the dominant impression you want to convey?

5. Do you know the object of your description well?

Writing

1. Do the details you are choosing support your dominant impression?

2. Do you use words literally and figuratively?

3. What is your point of view toward your subject?

4. Do you *show* rather than *tell* your dominant impression?

Rewriting

1. Do you communicate the dominant impression you want to convey?

2. Do you have a clear point of view on your subject?

3. How does the essay make you feel?

4. What does it make you think about?

5. Which senses does it stimulate?

6. Do you use similes or metaphors when appropriate?

7. Are you *showing* rather than *telling* your description?

Lesley Choyce

THIN EDGE OF THE WEDGE

Lesley Choyce is a Renaissance man with a multitude of jobs: Choyce teaches English at University of Dalhousie, he hosts a television show called *Choyce Words,* he runs a literary publishing house called Pottersfield Press, he is a musician with a band called The Surf Poets, but he is best known as a writer. After having his first book published by Fiddlehead Press in 1980, he has written more than 40 books representing a range of genres including poetry, young adult fiction, and science fiction and appealing to a variety of audiences. In addition, Choyce is an accomplished surfer as evidenced by his winning of the Men's Open Canadian National Surfing Championship in 1995.

Choyce was born in New Jersey in 1951 and immigrated to Nova Scotia in 1979. His stories are often set around Lawrencetown where he now lives, and tell the stories of people, most often young adults, who share his passions.

Preparing to Read

Environmentalists tell us that we are not separate from nature, that we are part of a greater biological pattern. Our lives affect and are affected by the total health and energy of the world around us. Lesley Choyce's essay "Thin Edge of the Wedge," first published in the spring of 1997 in *Canadian Geographic*, describes the dynamic life of an island in Nova Scotia. Interspersed between geological descriptions of the changes being wrought on this small piece of land is the portrayal of the human experience of this territory. The vivid passages show Choyce's intense fascination with his subject. As you read "Thin Edge of the Wedge," think about an island, a park, a beach, or some natural environment you know well. How has time changed this place? Does it have a rhythm, a life of its own? What patterns in your place's life belong to the cycles of nature, and what changes have people made?

■_____■

Wedge Island is barely discernible on a road map of Nova   1
Scotia because there are no roads leading there. Although it is not truly an island, its tether to the eastern shore is so tenuous that it remains remote and seemingly adrift. Eroded by the forces of the North Atlantic, it is a mere fragment of what was once a formidable headland. Within a lifetime, it will most likely be reduced to a rubble of stone, an insignificant reef at high tide. But for now, the Wedge exists, a reminder that nothing is permanent on this shore. Geologists define it as a "drowned coast" because the sea is gradually engulfing it. It has been for a long time.

Something like a dinosaur's bony spine of boulders leads a   2
wary hiker from the salt-bleached fish shacks on the mainland to the Wedge. If it's a fine July day—blue sky, big and bold above— the hiker might slide his hand along the silky beards of sea oats as he leaves solid land, then dance from rock to rock. Low tide is the best bet to make it there in one piece. Still, waves will spank the rocks from both sides, slap cold saltwater on his shoes and spit clean, frothy Atlantic into his face.

Wedge Island is a defeated drumlin, a dagger-shaped 3
remnant of land stretching a good kilometre out to sea. Smashed
lobster traps, shreds of polypropylene rope as well as bones of
birds and beasts litter the rocks near the shore. Thirty metres up
the red dirt cliff sits a parliament of herring gulls peering down
at a rare visitor with some suspicion. If the visitor scurries up
the side of crumbling dirt, the gulls will complain loudly at his
intrusion, then take to the sky and let him pass.

At the top is a grassy peninsula a mere 60 centimetres wide 4
where both sides have been sculpted away by rains and pounding
seas. It's a place of vertigo and lost history. The land widens as
it extends seaward onto this near-island of bull thistles, raspberry
bushes and grass that seems cropped short as a putting green.

Farther out, at the very tip of the island, bare ribs of bedrock 5
protrude into the sea. This is the same rock you'd find if you
could make one giant leap from here across the Atlantic and step
ashore on the edge of the Sahara. It is the very rock that was
once part of the super-continent that drifted north to crash into
this coast, then drag itself away to form Africa.

This island is a forgotten domain on the edge of the continent. 6
It is easy to imagine that no man has ever been here before. But on
the way back to the mainland, the truth reveals itself on the western
shore. Not three metres from the edge of a cliff eight storeys high
is a circle of lichen-covered rocks in the grass. A man-made well.
The water is deep and long-legged insects skim along its obsidian
surface. The well is full, nearly to the brim—it seems impossible
given its elevation on this narrow wedge of land.

Nearby are two dents in the ground, as if some giant had 7
punched down into a massive surface of dough. Those two dents
were once the foundations of a farmhouse and barn. Nearby
fields sprouted cabbage and turnips. A family lived on vegetables
from the stony soil, cod and mackerel from the sea. There were
no roads, no cars, nothing but boats for commerce with Halifax.
A way of life long gone.

The rains and seas will continue to conspire to undo the 8
ribbon of land left between the well's fresh water and the sky.
The well's stone walls will collapse. The drumlin's cliff will be
pried by ice, and pocked by pelting rain. The sea will slip out
stones from beneath the hill, the turf up above will tumble, and
eventually the water of the farmer's well will gush out of the
heart of the headland and race down to meet the sea.

UNDERSTANDING DETAILS

1. What does Choyce predict will happen to Wedge Island? When?
2. How do geologists define Wedge Island? Why?
3. What is Wedge Island? What evidence is there of human habitation of the island?

ANALYZING MEANING

1. How does Choyce feel about his subject? How do you know this?
2. What is Choyce's thesis, and how does the description of the disappearance of Wedge Island develop his thesis?
3. What is the "truth [that] reveals itself on the western shore" in paragraph 6?

DISCOVERING RHETORICAL STRATEGIES

1. Choyce's essay contains several relatively unusual verbs that make his description particularly vivid. Find five examples of such verbs and explain why they are effective choices.
2. There are several striking similes and metaphors in Choyce's descriptive passages. The waves "spank the rocks," "slap cold saltwater on his shoes and spit clean, frothy Atlantic into his face" (paragraph 2) and the grass "seems cropped short as a putting green" (paragraph 4). What does Choyce's use of these figures of speech show the reader about the author's view of his subject? How does it contrast with Choyce's use of scientific details?
3. Choyce frequently uses alliteration in "Thin Edge of the Wedge." Identify five examples of alliteration and explain how this figure of speech enhances Choyce's description.

MAKING CONNECTIONS

1. Like Tomson Highway ("What a Certain Visionary Once Said") Lesley Choyce is describing an environment he knows well. Compare and contrast the attitudes of these two writers to their subjects.
2. Lesley Choyce employs sentence fragments and several short, simple sentences in this essay. How is his style similar to, or different from that of Joe Fiorito ("Breakfast in Bed")?

IDEAS FOR DISCUSSION/WRITING

Preparing to Write

Write freely about a place in the natural environment that you have known for some time. Why is it special to you? How long have you been familiar with this place? How often do its natural features change, and what causes these changes? What details stand out most clearly in your mind, and why? Do you see echoes of, or similarities to, your experience of life's patterns in any aspects of your special place?

Choosing a Topic

1. Basing your essay on specific sense details, describe your special place to a friend who has never been there. Decide on the main reason why your place is so meaningful to you, and try to communicate this dominant impression of your place as clearly as possible.
2. Are cities or towns as alive as a beach or a forest? Why? Using a logical order for arranging your arguments, describe exactly to someone whose point of view is not known which aspects of city or natural life make either or both living entities.
3. Using your imagination, travel backward in time to view and describe your special place as it might have been 500 years ago. What would be different from the way it looks today? Write an essay that describes the differences and similarities in the two visions. Compare what your imagination's eye sees to what you see today, and decide on your point of view in the comparison.

Tomson Highway

■□■

WHAT A CERTAIN VISIONARY ONCE SAID

In the following essay, Tomson Highway (1951–) presents a loving and vibrant description of the region of Canada where he comes from. The eleventh of twelve children, Highway was born and raised on the Brochet Reserve in northern Manitoba where his first language was Cree. Highway didn't begin learning English until he was six years old when he was sent away to a Catholic boarding school. He graduated from the University of Western Ontario with a B.A. in music and English, and began writing at about age 30. Now a resident of Toronto, Highway is the founder and was the first director of the Native Earth Performing Arts Theatre, and has received wide acclaim for the plays that he has written and produced including the Dora Mavor Moore Award, the Toronto Arts Award (1990), and the Chalmers Canadian Play Award in 1986 for *The Rez Sisters* and again in 1990 for *Dry Lips Oughta Move to Kapuskasing*.

In an article in the *Toronto Sun*, John Coulbourn described Highway's "gentle, quiet humour, his great but unassuming pride, his passion and the dignity and strength of his spirit ..." These qualities are undoubtedly among those that contributed to Highway being made a Member of the Order of Canada in 1994 and being chosen by *Maclean's* magazine as one of the 100 most important Canadians in history.

In 1997 Highway published his first novel, *Kiss of the Fur Queen*, a largely autobiographical story about two Cree brothers. *Rose*, a full-length musical sequel to *The Rez Sisters* and *Dry Lips*, was first produced in 2000. Most recently Highway has published *Caribou Song*, the first in a series of three illustrated books for children.

This essay first appeared as an insert in *The Bank of Montreal Annual Report (1992)*.

Preparing to Read

The following essay is a vivid description of a part of the country Tomson Highway respects and admires. Before reading, think about the Canadian North. In your mind, travel north from the 49th parallel. How does the weather change as you progress? What do you notice about the landscape and the terrain? What happens to the population? What observations do you make about the vegetation? What about the wildlife? Are there any assumptions that you make about the seasons? Does your mode of transportation change as you travel north? What colours stand out to you? Are there any distinctive smells? What sounds do you hear? What sounds do you not hear?

■_____■

As you travel north from Winnipeg, the flatness of the prairie 1 begins to give way. And the northern forests begin to take over, forests of spruce and pine and poplar and birch. The northern rivers and northern rapids, the waterfalls, the eskers, the northern lakes—thousands of them—with their innumerable islands encircled by golden-sand beaches and flat limestone surfaces that slide gracefully into water. As you travel farther north, the trees themselves begin to diminish in height and size. And get smaller, until, finally, you reach the barren lands. It is from these reaches that herds of caribou in the thousands come thundering down each winter. It is here that you find trout and pickerel and pike and whitefish in profusion. If you're here in August, your eyes will be glutted with a sudden explosion of colour seldom seen in any southern Canadian landscape: fields of wild raspberries, cloud-berries, blueberries, cranberries, stands of wild flowers you never believed such remote northern terrain was capable of nurturing. And the water is still so clean you can dip your hand over the side of your canoe and you can drink it. In winter, you can eat the snow, without fear. In both winter and summer, you can breathe, this is your land, your home.

Here, you can begin to remember that you are a human   2
being. And if you take the time to listen—really listen—you can begin to hear the earth breathe. And whisper things simple men, who never suspected they were mad, can hear. Madmen who speak Cree, for one, can in fact understand the language this land speaks, in certain circles. Which would make madmen who speak Cree a privileged lot.

Then you seat yourself down on a carpet of reindeer moss   3
and you watch the movements of the sky, filled with stars and galaxies of stars by night, streaked by endlessly shifting cloud formations by day. You watch the movements of the lake which, within one hour, can change from a surface of glass to one of waves so massive in their fury they can—and have—killed many a man. And you begin to understand that men and women can, within maybe not one hour but one day, change from a mood of reflective serenity and self-control to one of depression and despair so deep they can—and have—killed many a man.

You begin to understand that this earth we live on—once   4
thought insensate, inanimate, dead by scientists, theologians and such—has an emotional, psychological and spiritual life every bit as complex as that of the most complex, sensitive and intelligent of individuals.

And it's ours. Or is it?   5

A certain ancient aboriginal visionary of this country once   6
said: "We have not inherited this land, we have merely borrowed it from our children."

If that's the case, what a loan!   7

Eh?   8

UNDERSTANDING DETAILS

1. For Highway, what is the essential appeal of the North?
2. In contrast to the view of traditional scientists and theologians, how does Highway characterize the earth? In your own words, characterize Highway's attitude towards the earth.
3. How many senses does Highway invoke in this description? Give one example of each from this essay.

ANALYZING MEANING

1. What is Highway's purpose in writing this description? Who is he writing it for?
2. In paragraph 2, Highway refers to madmen. Who are these madmen and why does Highway label them this way? Does he really believe that they are mad?
3. Explain Highway's conclusion. Why does he end on a questioning note?

DISCOVERING RHETORICAL STRATEGIES

1. Is this description objective or subjective? Explain. How might a land surveyor's description of this area differ from Highway's?
2. How many times does the writer use the words "north" or "northern" in this essay? What effect does this have on the reader? How would more specific place names change the impression?
3. Does "What a Certain Visionary Once Said" contain the four fundamental qualities of descriptive essays that are outlined at the beginning of this chapter? Support your answer with specific details.

MAKING CONNECTIONS

1. Neil Bissoondath ("Pieces of Sky") describes sitting by a blazing fire at night under a sky filled with stars (paragraphs 11–12). Does this experience have the same effect on Bissoondath that it has on Highway? Explain why or why not.
2. In "Teeth," Brian Lewis writes about the attitude of white men toward Ottochie, a native Canadian. How does this attitude compare to Highway's comments about perceptions of people who can "understand the language the land speaks"?
3. Tomson Highway refers several times to the place he has journeyed to as "home." What does he value in his home? How do these things compare to the things that Allen Abel values in his "A Home at the End of the Journey"?

IDEAS FOR DISCUSSION/WRITING

Preparing to Write

Write freely about weather. How would you describe the climate of Canada generally? How would you describe the region where you live? What accommodations have you made in your life for the weather you experience? What kind of weather do you most enjoy? How does the weather influence your mood? Why is the weather such a common topic of conversation?

Choosing a Topic

1. In an essay for newcomers to your region of the country, describe your favourite season. Focus on the natural physical aspects of that season, as well as the effects they have on you and your community.
2. Three recent television programs are set in northern towns: *Northern Exposure* (in America), and *The Rez* and *North of 60* (in Canada). If you have seen any of these shows, write an essay in which you discuss how their depiction of the northern communities has either confirmed or changed your impressions.
3. Highway obviously feels very strongly about the place he describes. Write a short essay in which you describe a place that you very strongly dislike. Provide enough detail so that your audience will be sure to avoid this spot.

Dave Bidini

KRIS KING LOOKS TERRIBLE

According to *Quill and Quire*, in his first book, *On a Cold Road: Tales of Adventure in Canadian Rock*, "Bidini manages to layer and link themes and variations on our country's musical community, history, and players— famous and obscure—with equal measures of intricate (but unobtrusive) craft and gut-honest openness, creating a book rich and ripe with voices that bear repeated listening." *On a Cold Road* is Bidini's memoir of the adventures of the Rheostatics, for which he is the rhythm guitarist, and the tales of many other Canadian musicians. The same qualities of humour, honesty, and strong, vivid portraits come through when Bidini turns his focus to the world of hockey in *Tropic of Hockey*, his tales of his search for hockey in unlikely places. Bidini (1962–), a Toronto-based musician and writer, has also been a regular columnist for the *Toronto Star* and a book reviewer for the *Globe and Mail*, as well as a regular contributor to the radio program *Definitely Not the Opera*. He is also a contributor to *The Original Six: True Stories from Hockey's Classic Era*, a collection edited by Paul Quarrington.

Preparing to Read

In 1999, Dave Bidini, along with his wife, Janet, set out for China as the first destination in Bidini's quest to find hockey in unlikely places. The selection here comes from Bidini's second book, *Tropic of Hockey*, the resulting collection of tales. With what countries do you associate hockey? Within those countries, where is hockey played? What is characteristic of an outdoor hockey rink? What are hockey arenas typically like? What are some places that you would consider it unlikely to find hockey?

A fter a full day's rest, we headed into town to find SkyRink, the home of the tournament. 1

The thought crossed my mind that SkyRink might not be anything close to what its name suggested. I almost expected to be disappointed since, these days, arena names make little sense. For instance, not only does the National Car Rental Center, home of the Florida Panthers, promise little in the way of aesthetics, you can't even rent a car there. Same with the horseless Saddledome in Calgary. And despite the nation's affection for the old Maple Leaf Gardens, there's probably more foliage growing on the Hoover Dam. These erroneous names aren't reserved only for the pro ranks, either. In Toronto, new hockey complexes are being called Ice Gardens, Ice Land, and Ice Palace, names better suited to the American south, where the word "ice" is required so that people don't show up in shorts clutching frozen cappuccinos. But in Canada, what does one expect to find in an arena? Beach volleyball? The Antiques Roadshow? A name like Ice Land is proof of how insidious the American lexicon is in Canada's game. I prefer rinks to be named after dead people— Ted Reeve, Jimmy Simpson, Max Bell. The names suggest a persona, a link to the past, the warmth of someone's den. 2

Judging by the nature of other arenas with *Sky* in their name, SkyRink did not hold much promise. SkyDome, the home of the 3

Toronto Blue Jays, is fine if you enjoy the perils of sitting in a place where slabs of concrete have been known to come crashing down. In Edmonton, the Skyreach Centre is now the home of the Edmonton Oilers. The building used to be called Northlands Coliseum—a name that evokes hoarfrost and mulled wine and poplar trees—but the name was changed to Skyreach—which evokes nothing—when the local telephone company tossed a few million at the club, aping a trend that has besmirched more than a few stadia. The acquisition of naming rights is one of the scourges of modern sport. Candlestick Park in San Francisco was renamed 3Com Park after a software company, Jack Murphy Stadium in San Diego became QUALCOMM Stadium (software again), and Joe Robbie Stadium in Miami became Pro Player Stadium (you guessed it: men's underwear). Perhaps the most extreme example is the STAPLES Center, the home of the LA Kings. Until I heard the name, I hadn't realized how much hockey reminded me of the fast-paced world of office supplies.

The road out of the Bay was trimmed with long-armed trees 4 cupping orange and pink blossoms like altar boys holding candles. The flowers hung in bunches over the road and whipped against the flank of the bus, which rushed along the winding road gripping the edge of the cliff. The bus tilted and tipped as it fought corners and, with each turn, small vistas of the city were revealed: knots of blue and white high-rises; the shimmering green track of the Happy Valley raceway; a whitewashed mansion with guard dogs and gold gates; a regatta of iron ships floating in the bay; the stone shelves of an old terraced graveyard rising over the city; and, at the bottom of a street of Victorian homes, a procession of checker-skirted schoolgirls.

We drove under one overpass, then another, and suddenly 5 the city was very loud. The first few moments entering a strange city are always stage-directed by your senses. They're so inflamed by the newness of the environment that you find yourself thinking things like, "My God! That exhaust smells so wonderful and strange!" or "That garbage over there is just so darned colourful!" even as the locals are making choking sounds. While abroad, the senses refuse to be burdened by the mundane. They're wearing sombreros and drinking umbrella drinks and carrying on.

The bus let us off on Cheung Sha Wan Road in Kowloon 6 market, renowned throughout the world as the hub of the pirated electronics underground. The market rattled at full pelt. Stereo salesmen had dragged their tallest sound systems to the edge of the sidewalk and were blasting Canto-Pop at ear-splitting volumes. There was junk everywhere. An electronics boneyard littered the sidewalk with hacked-apart eight-tracks and CB radios—not to mention the obligatory box of used LPs with the same unloved Seals and Crofts albums you'd find at home—laid out on old newspapers and blankets. Fruit vendors came at me bearing weird-looking apples. In narrow alleyways, goat carcasses and pig heads and groupers the size of cricket bats hung under vinyl canopies. A corner apothecary offered boxes of Leung Chi See Dog Pills, Ping On Ointment, Essence of Deer, and Atomic Enema in its window; next door a young man sat, legs crossed behind a row of typewriters with flowers stemmed through their print bars; wholesale clothing depots flooded three city blocks—Fancy Fashion, Funny Fashion, Top and Top Fashion, Bukky Fashion and, of course, Fukky Fashion; shops tented in the middle of the street and lit by bare bulbs were festooned with cables, speaker wires, baskets of fuses, watches, and belt buckles; and a small pastry shop sold crates of sea prune, liquorice prune, and dried sour-cream prune, which young girls pressed into their mouths by the handful. The high clucking pitch of restaurant crowds filled the air.

I was in Parkdale no longer.   7

We stood in front of Dragon Centre mall, a huge building 8 that loomed arms-crossed over the market. The entrance was filled with a circus of laughing children being scooped up by an escalator. We rode with them, upwards into the building behind a floor-to-ceiling glass façade. The ride was spectacular. We stared out at Kowloon across acres of high-rises pressed shoulder to shoulder, their sides thistled with television antennae. Laundry waved in a parade of coloured flags. Beyond that: smokestacks, the sea, the red horizon.

We floated higher.   9

Finally, on the eighth floor of the mall, I heard hockey—the 10 honking of the score-clock, the bang of the puck against the boards, the referee's whistle, skates chopping snow. I smelled the chemicals of the ice and the Zamboni diesel, and then I saw it: a rink small enough to fit in your palm, a sprite's pond, a place for Tom Thumb, Gabby Boudreau. To best describe it I have to use a word not often associated with the greatest sporting stadia of our time: cute.

It was a play rink.   11

It was one-fifth the size of an NHL oval—18 metres by 42   12
metres, to be exact. Perhaps a homesick architect from Trois-
Rivières had been left with a narrow concrete channel and
decided to fill it with ice. It was maybe the width of three bowling
lanes. I suspected that bigger puddles had been left by the
monsoon. Every element of SkyRink was odd. Since it was eight
storeys up inside a glass tower, you could look out and forecast
the weather from the way the clouds rolled in off the South China
Sea. There was a mezzanine with an arcade—pinball machines,
toy cars, and robotic clowns—that cantilevered over the rink and
filled the air with the sound of bells and horns and children
crying out to each other. Between the mezzanine and the rink
was a yellow roller coaster that was close enough to the ice that
you could reach up with a hockey stick and tap it. It was a flame-
tongued, turquoise dragon that hurtled over the ice at high
speeds, a frightful spectacle for even the most steel-nerved
goaltender. It seemed that SkyRink had been designed with the
idea of marrying amusement-park folly to hockey, and while
hockey has experimented with this theme before—San Jose's
shark blimp and Anaheim's daredevil duck come to mind, as do
the barrel jumping and dogsled races that were part of
intermissions in the 1920s—at least those novelties were kept at
a safe distance from the action. But at SkyRink, there was no
barrier or railing to prevent someone in the arcade from pelting
the players with eggs or worse, and it did nothing to allay my
fears of being killed by a large metal lizard.

At both ends of the ice, loose white netting was strung up   13
behind the goals. It reminded me of the mesh in those old Soviet
rinks, which Team Canada used to complain about. The SkyRink
netting served two purposes: to catch pucks and to act as a curtain
for the dressing area, which lay just behind the end boards. It
did neither job well. It whipped pucks back to the ice, and, like
Cheryl Tiegs' macramé tank top, if you looked closely enough,
you could see everything. Behind the netting, players freely
changed in and out of their clothes. The scene was like something
out of a rogue health club: fellows in towels strode to and from
the bathrooms, the odd player revealing his bare ass and hairy
stomach (or bare, hairy ass). This abundance of flesh did little
to ease my fear of being naked before strangers, and while not
every player flashed skin—some used a series of towels like
semaphore flags to guard their parts—many treated the area like

a Roman bath. Exhibitionists would dig SkyRink. I thought of that brazen Canadian couple who were caught love-making in the windows of the SkyDome Hotel. Here, you could press ham before eight million people.

SkyRink had a Zamboni. It was old and dented and looked as   14
if it had stood in the way of a Matthew Barnaby shitfit. It had South China Ice Hockey League written in Chinese and English on the side and was driven by a young Chinese man in yellow sweats who was far too slender to bring any credibility to his job.

SkyRink had other credibility problems. Frankly, it didn't   15
smell bad enough. Let's face it: hockey stinks. It's a bloated, heavy odour that you can poke with your finger. The first time I set foot in a rink after years away from the game, I rushed a hockey sock to my face to guard myself from the stench. Of course, after a few weeks in my equipment bag, the sock was well stewed and I was forced to wrap something else around my mouth. When I ran out of socks, I had to embrace the game's feral miasma.

But SkyRink smelled like jasmine (I should have been   16
grateful, I know). The source of this fragrance was Kathy K's Pro Shop, which was stocked with a surprising complement of top-of-the-line hockey gear. Unlike many skate-sharpening depots— which tend to smell of plugged plumbing and are operated by large, unshaven men—Kathy K's carried the scent of blossoms, and if that wasn't strange enough, Kathy thanked you for your business and offered a bowl of candies by the cash register, allowing you to take to the ice chewing a gumball and spitting rainbow trails of purple, blue, and red.

There was also the food problem. And again, it wasn't so   17
much a problem as, well, a treat. There was no snack bar at SkyRink, unless you counted the Jack in the Box, which I only ever saw used by ex-pats teary-eyed for the taste of grease. Instead, there was a food court opposite the rink, where women with faces carved by time spooned sea snails the size of silver dollars and braised aubergine and double-cooked pork onto plastic plates, the aroma of garlic and soya and sesame oil scenting the air. There were kiosks selling blackened grouper, lemon chicken, bean curd seared in garlic and peppers, sushi, and hot soup with prawns—not your typical hockey cuisine.

The crowd at SkyRink was also its own. It was mostly seniors   18
who had wandered over from the food court (proving that, no matter where you go in the world, you'll find the same people

hanging out in malls). It was a rare treat to skate along the boards and exchange glances with a group of old men who could have been extras in *The Last Emperor*. After a few days, I discovered that they appreciated pratfalls and gaffes rather than athletic grace and beauty. If someone scored an end-to-end goal, they'd get little reaction, but if they tripped over the net or were slew-footed or got slashed in the eye, the old men would laugh and pantomime their fall. The less able you were on your skates the more you were liked by the gallery; before the tournament ended, there was a real chance that I'd be a star.

UNDERSTANDING DETAILS

1. To Bidini, "these days arena names make little sense." Why? How does Bidini believe they should be named? Explain his rationale.
2. What is it about SkyRink that leads Bidini to call it "cute"?
3. Who comes to SkyRink? Why, typically, do they come there?

ANALYZING MEANING

1. Does Bidini like SkyRink? Why or why not?
2. Bidini claims that SkyRink has "credibility problems" (paragraph 15). What are the credibility problems? What does Bidini mean by this term?
3. Paragraph 7 is a single sentence: "I was in Parkdale no longer." Explain what Bidini means by this sentence.

DISCOVERING RHETORICAL STRATEGIES

1. Bidini's writing includes details that appeal to each of the five senses. Find at least one example of each and then decide which you find most effective.
2. In addition to description, Bidini is using the rhetorical technique of comparison and contrast in this piece of writing. What is he comparing and contrasting? Why? What effect does this have on his intended audience?
3. Bidini fills his writing with specific examples, such as the names of fashion stores, the list of products available at the apothecary, and the names of different sports facilities. Explain the effect of these specific examples on Bidini's description.

MAKING CONNECTIONS

1. Dave Bidini and Charlotte Gray ("The Temple of Hygiene") both write about travelling to an Asian destination. How are their experiences similar? How do they differ?
2. Hockey is the subject of Bidini's essay as well as that of Michael McKinley ("Opera Night in Canada"). How do the two authors feel about the topic of hockey? How is the attitude of each conveyed?
3. Bidini and Paul Quarrington ("Home Brew") have collaborated on a book about hockey entitled *The Original Six*. What aspects of their writing styles are similar? Are there stylistic points on which you think they might have disagreed?

IDEAS FOR DISCUSSION/WRITING

Preparing to Write

Brainstorm or make a list of the trips you've taken in your life. What places stand out particularly vividly in your mind? What details make those places especially memorable? Are there any places that have disappointed you? If so, how did reality compare to your expectations? How do you choose what places you will visit? Are you more likely to revisit familiar places or to select new destinations? How much research do you do before travelling somewhere? How do you know what to expect when you visit a new place?

Choosing a Topic

1. Recall a time when you faced a significant new experience. Write a narrative essay in which you recreate the events and your feelings about them for your audience.
2. Choose a destination, real or imagined, and write a promotional article for your student newspaper about it. What might make readers want to visit your location, and why? How can you best make your location interesting to your audience?
3. Imagine that a new stadium is being built where you live. Write a 500-word essay explaining what it should be named and why.

Ray Guy

■ □ ■

WHEN JANNIES VISITED

Ray Guy's memories of childhood in the small town of Arnold's Cove, Placentia Bay, Newfoundland, give his essays and newspaper columns amusingly authentic and deftly apt details of a life most Canadians only occasionally consider. Born in 1939, Guy attended Memorial University in St. John's and Ryerson Polytechnical Institute in Toronto, and is an award-winning freelance journalist who lives today in St. John's, Newfoundland. He is also the author of a play, and in the great Newfoundland "story-spinning" tradition, of a collection of radio monologues. A glance at the titles of some of his published works confirms his decided preference for a humorous tone: *You May Know Them As Sea Urchins Ma'am* (1975), *Outhouses of the East* (1978), *This Dear and Fine Country* (1985), and a collection of essays, *Ray Guy's Best* (1987). His skill as a comic writer won him the Stephen Leacock Medal in 1977, and his continuing loyalty to the voice and story of his native province resulted in the Newfoundland Arts Council Award in 1985 and an honourary doctoral degree from Memorial University in 2001.

Preparing to Read

This essay first appeared in *Canadian Geographic* magazine in November/December 1993. Here Ray Guy evokes images associated with Christmas in his childhood home. Particularly strong is the image of the "dreadful" masked jannies that would come to each home and dance and wreak havoc before moving on. As Guy explains, their power resided primarily in their anonymity. What other festivities or events are characterized by masks or disguises? What effects does anonymity have on people's behaviour? What is the difference between a costume and a disguise? In what situations do people assume each? What famous characters can you think of who wore masks or disguises to hide their true identity?

■—————————————————————————————————■

Jannies didn't spoil Christmas for me but they surely put a crimp 1
in it. I was terrified of them. Even when I was old enough to be
one myself there was still something dreadful about jannies.

On Boxing Day after supper at about eight there would come 2
a heavy rapping at the door. Nobody else ever knocked, they

just stamped snow off their boots on the porch in winter or cleared their throats in the summer. Nobody ever knocked except strangers ... and jannies!

Christmas 1947 stands out more than any before or since, 3 perhaps because I was eight that year. When you get to be eight a good many things clang into focus, the pieces of the great jigsaw seem to have grown larger, you can count past 10 without taking off your socks. So I knew, by then, that jannies, or mummers, were really only people.

Still, there was that gut-flopping dread. Someone went out 4 onto the dark porch and opened the door and you heard the King Jannie speak in a harsh, gabbling rasp of words made while sucking the breath in: "Any jannies in tonight?"

"Yes. OK. But ..." There'd be a feeble attempt to set 5 conditions. Not too much noise, granny wasn't well. Not too rowdy, the youngsters were scared. But nothing short of a deathbed constrained them.

Out of the dark and the frosty air they blundered and 6 bumped and bundled, into the heat of the kitchen and the soft light of the kerosene lamp, roistering, hulking, tripping, stomping, lurching. They were big and bloated and mostly mute.

They had grotesque humps on their backs or obscenely 7 protruding bellies, sometimes both at once. Their faces were mummified with scraps of old lace curtains or masked blank with cardboard that had torn-out holes for eyes. They stank, they reeked.

A raw sheepskin hung over this one's deformed back, cow's 8 horns attached to a piece of bloody skull were lashed to that one's head. Another wore a jouncing girdle of fox pelts, two or three were in oilskins turned inside out, putrid with bilge water and week-old fish.

They danced a lumpish dance, shuddering the floorboards, 9 trembling the teapot atop the stove, flaring the lamp in its wall bracket, led in their floundering by a mouth organ crudely played by one of their number through its soggy mouth cloth.

The only game to it was to guess who they were. If a jannie 10 was guessed he had to unmask on the spot, which drained the dread away and destroyed the whole mob of them. But although there were fewer than 200 people in the whole village of Arnold's Cove, Newfoundland, jannies' identities were seldom guessed.

They carried staves or hook-tipped gaffs, and if you tugged 11 at their disguises they hit, not with raps or taps, but with bruising, bone-deadening clouts. Even your father, gamely smiling, gave off a fear of them.

They might lunge and seize anyone and drag them into their   12 ogreish dance, prodding and fumbling them in a most improper way. Or they might spitefully smash a bowl or upset a water bucket. At some unseen signal they all moved to leave, were offered a shot of rum or a tumbler of water, and blundered and reeled off into the night.

Two or three other gangs of jannies might show up before   13 the night was over, or on any night of the twelve days of Christmas, between December 26 and Old Christmas Day on January 6.

There seemed little reason to tolerate this mummering except   14 that it was the "done thing" and had been since time out of mind. Later, when I was old enough to join in the jannying, I glimpsed a dark attraction—the power of being that capricious Unknown, and feared.

Compared to jannies, most else about Christmas then was   15 bright and beautiful. For instance, snotty var. It was the very essence of the season and still is the most powerful trigger of memory.

At school in the first week of Advent, the teacher began   16 shoring up our spiritual foundations. We were catechized after morning prayer with questions like: "What is the first thing that must come to our minds when we think of Christmas?"

She asked again, this time ending the word "Christmas" with   17 a definite hiss. "Please, Miss," said one of the Bigger Boys, Leonard, I'd guess, "Snotty var, Miss." She twisted both his ears until they stayed red for an hour.

He'd been guilty of insolence, blasphemy and lapsing into   18 the local dialect, his mother tongue. Teachers strove to knock all three out of you, especially the latter. There was a whole dictionary full of punishable words, and on top of that a tireless knuckle-rapping campaign against wrong pronunciation of right words.

In 30 years, had he lived that long, Leonard might have said   19 that the first thing that came to his mind when he thought of Christmas was the pungent tang of balsam fir sap. Not snotty var. By then he might have learned the new language in which emmets were ants, dumbledores were bees, piss-a-beds were dandelions and a merrybegot was an illegitimate child.

But schooling then was like that. Now that I was eight I knew   20 that the green light said "go" and how to spell "squirrel" although there was neither one nor the other within a hundred miles. I could draw a soldier of the Roman legions and we sent coded notes to each other in the Phoenician alphabet. But it was long after I'd finished 17 years of schooling that I learned that John Guy, merchant adventurer out of Bristol, had met the Beothuks on a beach just over the hill. In 1612.

Or that my mother's people lived across the harbour at a   21
place known as "Burdle," but which was once a French plantation called Bordeaux.

My hometown of Arnold's Cove (nobody named "Arnold"   22
lived there) lies on the eastern shore of Placentia Bay, Newfoundland's largest bay, a great triangle 80 miles long and 60 miles across at its southern base. Its three main landmarks are Cape St. Mary's, Chapeau Rouge, and, at its northern point, Pipers Hole. Arnold's Cove is about 10 miles south of Pipers Hole.

The village was on a low, treeless peninsula a couple of miles   23
long and a quarter mile wide, and the wind roared across it from every direction. It was like a monstrous raft at sea. But at its western end the peninsula rose up to become the High Head with cliffs that dropped straight down 250 feet to the ocean.

One day in June when I was eight the Bigger Girls came to   24
borrow me. While you were still in short pants the Bigger Girls seemed to like minding you. After that you were allowed to hang around in places where the men worked.

They were taking me, they said, to pick crowberries behind   25
the old graveyard, but we went much farther than that. We went along the goat path through the bogs and by the low cliffs to the Otter Rub, where the Americans had watched for submarines. Beyond that, we went on and on ...

Then, scrambling up through the scrubby spruce and the dusty   26
rockslides, we came out at the top of the High Head. Here was my sudden enlightenment of a lifetime. Down in the village, the line of sight of an eight-year-old extended from the cat in the shade of the dooryard rhubarb to a glimpse of blue hills an improbable distance away. But now I could see where I was in the world.

There were the islands of the bay, Long Island, Red Island,   27
Iona, Merasheen. On them were villages like Jean de Gaunt and Peaches Cove, Harbour Buffett and Tacks Beach, Rose au Rue and Haystack. The islets of Bread and Cheese, the next cove north from us, called Come By Chance. And Bay Bulls Arm across the narrow Isthmus of Avalon in Trinity Bay, where John Guy first met "ye savages of ye clime."

I could see now where the fishing boats went after they   28
thumped away around the point in the early morning to the
fishing grounds, as well known to them as the fertile patches of
a farmer's field: The Jerseyman, called "Jasmin," Burdle Banks,
Goose Island Ground, The Pancake, the Big Neverfail and the
Little Neverfail.

That was all full and plenty, but then one of the Bigger Girls   29
said: "There's only one salt water in the world, you know, and it
goes on and on and on. To China and to where the King lives. To
where the cowboys is in the States, even!" I wanted to run
headlong down from the High Head to the beach away below
and throw so big a rock in the water as would make waves that
might go to China. To where the palm trees were. I reserved
doubts about the cowboys.

This great enlightenment from the top of the High Head all   30
went to make me especially remember 1947 and the Christmas of it.

Christmas then seemed like a test or a statement of readiness;   31
all was as ready as could or would be to face the winter to come. In
the weeks before Christmas the stacked firewood on the back porch
rose toward the ceiling, enough to last those 12 work-free days of
the season. Most of it was dry, had seasoned for a few years, but
some was raw green fir, oozing sap and covered with turpentine
blisters, and used to damp the kitchen stove when a winter's gale
drew the fire like a blacksmith's forge and the stovepipe glowed
dangerously hot. Potatoes gathered in mid-October were heaped in
earthen root cellars, and by the end of November all the animals for
killing had been killed and their carcasses hung at the back of fish
sheds built on stilts over the water.

Each family had a dozen or more sheep; nearly everyone   32
had a pony to plow the potato fields in May and to haul firewood
throughout the winter. There were hens, ducks and occasionally
geese. And there was a pig or two to rend the still fall air on its
fatal day.

You knew it was pig day when the advisory went around   33
for women and children to stay indoors. A monstrous cauldron
used for tanning nets was lugged up from the beach, set over a
fire by the pig pen and set steaming. Soon, the loud and
prolonged squeals of the pig arose. I was eight and convinced
they were boiling it to death. Granny reassured me: "That's only
the way pigs are, 'tis a pig's nature to make a great fuss over
every sort of little thing."

The Bigger Boys claimed the pig's bladder, which was 34 inflated and covered in sail canvas and used in great formless games of football, played during Christmas before the heavy snows of January set in.

A few people kept cows so there might be a calf or two for 35 slaughter, and the larder was further stocked with game: moose, caribou, rabbits, ducks and ptarmigan. In December there was a secure feeling of sufficiency and just a tinge of trepidation about "the long and hungry month of March." The basic, rock-bottom ration against a shortfall in that lean time at the end of the winter was the setting aside of one barrel of potatoes and one barrel of salted herring for each family member.

A Newfoundland fishing village at that time had a subsistence 36 economy in which broody hens, spavined ponies and haystacks had as important a part as salt cod, dories and a following sea. Which is probably why a Quebec farm journal, *The Family Herald and Weekly Star*, was the journal of choice all over the island.

A mini-ritual sometime in mid-December was "The Opening 37 of The Gaps." Gaps in the maze of fences that enclosed potato fields, hay meadows and cabbage patches were opened up to create a new road cutting through them all—the winter road, the slide path.

As soon as the ice on the ponds was thick enough, a caravan 38 of ponies in jingling harness set out in the morning for the firewood places beyond the railway tracks—stands of spruce and fir that were hereditary and had names like Whiffen's Droke, The Level Brook, The Place Where Poor Bill Lost The Pocketknife or The Pond Where Uncle Steve Caught The Otter.

They filed back in the early winter dusk, slides loaded with 39 firewood for the insatiable kitchen stoves, a boat knee (the rib of a boat) or a stem of larchwood on top that might have been noticed 10 or 15 years before for its unusual shape, a brace or two of partridge or rabbits swinging from the slide, harness bells jingling, steam wafting from the pot-bellied ponies, sparks from the runners where the winter road was bare.

Sometimes at Christmas a dozen or more men were missing. 40 The herring fishery was the last of the year. The boats went out 10 miles or more to a reach between islands in the bay where the shoals of herring appeared. They stayed away for a fortnight … and hoped for "light nights" (nights when the moon shone clear and bright) at Christmas.

If the nights were moonless or stormy, the herring couldn't see   41
the nets, the catch was abundant, and even Christmas was no
excuse to leave such bounty and come home. But if it chanced
that there were light nights, the boats came back for a day or two.

That Christmas of 1947 when I was eight there was a full   42
moon, but dark and heavy clouds night after night. On December
23 the sky cleared and the moon and stars glared down. As the
church bell rang near midnight on Christmas Eve, the boats were
heard coming far off, and they rounded the point into the cove,
their masts hung with lanterns and green boughs. As they came
they made a trail of stars on the black glass of the water.

Not only had the herring men brought themselves back in   43
good time, they'd met a moonshiner among the islands who was
freshly back from St. Peter's—as they called the French island
of Saint-Pierre. So there was tobacco and a better-quality spirit to
enliven that Christmas.

What other rum there was for Christmas, Easter, weddings   44
and wakes, was called swish. Fisherman were entitled to the thick-
staved puncheons that brought undiluted rum from the West
Indies. These were sawed in two and used as tubs for salting fish.

But if three or four gallons of water were poured into these   45
empty casks and let stand for a week and the casks rolled back
and forth to swish it around, it was the Wedding in Cana all over
again. The staves gave up their essence and you had three or
four gallons of the best Demerara rum.

So then it was Christmas. The church decorated all up and   46
down the lamp posts with balsam fir and tissue-paper roses.
Socials, dances, soup suppers, "meat teas," concerts in the school
every other night. Card games and singing and stories and
midnight "scoffs" in the houses and … jannies.

That year I got an orange, a fifty-cent piece, an American   47
chocolate bar, a prayer book and a new pair of mitts in my
stocking, but the big thing was my father had made me a slide out
of a salt pork barrel and it went like billy-be-damned down the
hill in our meadow along the icy winter road.

Since there were 12 days of yuletide—and all the baking   48
done as well as the firewood laid in—there seemed to be no
frantic festive pace, just that assured and designated time in the
darkest part of the year when people came to your house every
night or you went to theirs.

It was an obvious portion of the year. Between pig-killing 49
time and Candlemas Day, February 2, when the lamps were not
lit until after supper. Then to the middle of February when the
bleating of new lambs was added to the evening's sounds and on
to early March, when the hammering to repair the boats on the
beaches began.

Thirty-five years later I was living in a St. John's suburb with 50
cable TV and a microwave oven. One evening in early January two
station wagons stopped out front. A mob of mummers debouched.

By now, jannies, like much else, had gone full circle and 51
beyond, from being a base embarrassment, a low practice from
the past, to being folkloric and historic and a piece of precious
heritage. The two-faced Roman god, Janus, had been brought
into the picture, an actual script of the mummer's play had been
reconstituted, there were elaborate costumes and the university
crowd delighted in floating a revival.

They banged on the door. They said, "Any jannies in 52
tonight?"

"No," I said. I was a big boy, now. 53

UNDERSTANDING DETAILS

1. What are jannies and at what time of year do they typically appear?
2. Why do people tolerate the mummers?
3. What is snotty var? Why is one of the boys punished for saying
   that this was the first thing that came to his mind when he
   thought about Christmas?

ANALYZING MEANING

1. In paragraph 3, Guy says, "When you get to be eight a good
   many things clang into focus ..." and later he speaks of the great
   enlightenment he experienced the year he was eight. What is
   it that "clangs into focus" for Guy in 1947?
2. What is the role of the jannies in the community that Guy is evok-
   ing in the reader's mind's eye? How does their role change by
   the time Guy opens his door to them in St. John's 35 years later?
3. Characterize the community in which Guy grew up. What things
   dominate the lives of the inhabitants of Arnold's Cove? What
   influences seem particularly strong in the lives of these people?

DISCOVERING RHETORICAL STRATEGIES

1. Guy's essay is a series of snapshots of a time and place from his experience. What unifies the incidents and images that he describes?
2. Guy uses many specific place names in his description of his childhood in Arnold's Cove. Why does he choose to include these specific details? What do these names add to Guy's description?
3. Reread the description of the jannies that Guy recalls from his childhood (paragraphs 6–12) and keep track of all of the verbs used to describe their actions. What is the effect of Guy's word choices here? What language might the jannies themselves use to describe their antics?

MAKING CONNECTIONS

1. While Ray Guy writes about jannying, Kim Pittaway's "Dead Wrong" describes another kind of ritual. Compare and contrast Pittaway's and Guy's attitudes toward these rituals.
2. How do you think Stephen King ("Why We Crave Horror Movies") would explain the appeal of jannying? What role does it play in Guy's society?
3. Ray Guy gives us a vivid description of childhood in a part of Atlantic Canada. How does this compare to Wayson Choy's ("I'm a Banana and Proud of It") childhood in Vancouver? How does it compare to your own memories of childhood?

IDEAS FOR DISCUSSION/WRITING

Preparing to Write

Write freely about an experience that you found frightening or intimidating when you were young. What made it unsettling? How did you respond? Did others share your feelings? Did your reaction to it change as you grew up?

Choosing a Topic

1. Choose a particular event or activity to which your reaction has changed over time. Describe your experience of that event so that your initial feelings about it are apparent to your audience both through the details that you include and the language choices you make.

2. Write an essay describing the three most memorable people you have met in your life. Why did you choose these particular people? Do they have qualities in common? Where and how did you meet each one? Remember to link the sections of your essay and to choose a logical order for presentation of your characters.

3. The dialect of Arnold's Cove is one of the elements in Guy's description that makes it vivid. Choose a familiar scene that involves interaction between people and write a script for this scene in which you pay particular attention to making the dialogue realistic. Your scene might be a family meal, a child asking permission to use the car, explaining why you got home late, or the half-time or intermission conversation at a sporting event you are attending with your friends.

CHAPTER 2

NARRATION

■ ■ ■

Telling a Story

A good story is a powerful method of getting someone's attention. The excitement that accompanies a suspenseful ghost story, a lively anecdote, or a vivid joke easily attests to this effect. In fact, narration is one of the earliest verbal skills we all learn as children, providing us with a convenient, logical, and easily understood means of sharing our thoughts with other people. Storytelling is powerful because it offers us a way of dramatizing our ideas so that others can identify with them.

Defining Narration

Narration involves telling a story that is often based on personal experience. Stories can be oral or written, real or imaginary, short or long. A good story, however, always has a point or purpose. It can be the dominant mode (as in a novel or short story), supported by other rhetorical strategies, or it can serve the purpose of another rhetorical mode (as in a persuasive essay, a historical survey, or a scientific report).

In its subordinate role, narration can provide examples or explain ideas. If asked why you are attending college or university, for instance, you might turn to narration to make your answer clear, beginning with a story about your family's hardships in the past. The purpose of telling such a story would be to help your listeners appreciate your need for higher education by encouraging them to understand and identify with your family history.

Unlike description, which generally portrays people, places, and objects in *space*, narration asks the reader to follow a series of actions through a particular *time* sequence. Description often complements the movement of narration, though. People must be depicted, for instance, along with their relationships to one another, before their actions can have any real meaning for us; similarly, places must be described so that we can picture the setting and understand the activities in a specific scene. The organization of the action and the time spent on each episode in a story should be based principally on a writer's analysis of the interests and needs of his or her audience.

To be most effective, narration should prolong the exciting parts of a story and shorten the routine facts that simply move the reader from one episode to another. If you were robbed on your way to work, for example, a good narrative describing the incident would concentrate on the traumatic event itself rather than on such mundane and boring details as what you had for breakfast and what clothes you had put on prior to the attack. Finally, just like description, narration *shows* rather than *tells* its purpose to the audience. The factual statement "I was robbed this morning" could be made much more vivid and dramatic through the addition of some simple narration: "As I was walking to work at 7:30 a.m., a huge and angry-looking man ran up to me, thrust a gun into the middle of my stomach, and took my money, my new wristwatch, all my credit cards, and my pants— leaving me penniless and embarrassed."

The following paragraph written by a student recounts a recent parachuting experience. As you read this narrative, notice especially the writer's use of vivid detail to *show* rather than *tell* her message to the readers.

> I have always needed occasional "fixes" of excitement in my life, so when I realized one spring day that I was more than ordinarily bored, I made up my mind to take more than ordinary steps to relieve that boredom. I decided to go parachuting. The next thing I knew, I was stuffed into a claustrophobically small plane with five other terrified people, rolling down a bumpy, rural runway, droning my way to 3500 feet and an exhilarating experience. Once over the jump area, I waited my turn, stepped onto the strut, held my breath, and then kicked off into the cold, rushing air as my heart pounded heavily. All I could think was, "I hope this damn parachute opens!" The sensation of falling backward through space was unfamiliar and disconcerting till my chute opened with a loud "pop," momentarily pulling me upward toward the distant sky. After several minutes of

floating downward, I landed rudely on the hard ground. Life, I remembered happily, could be awfully exciting. And a month later, when my tailbone had stopped throbbing, I still felt that way.

Thinking Critically by Using Narration

Rhetorical modes offer us different ways of perceiving reality. Narration is an especially useful tool for sequencing or putting details and information in some kind of logical order, usually chronological. Working with narration helps us see clear sequences separate from all other mental functions.

Practising exercises in narrative techniques can help you see clear patterns in topics you are writing about. Although narration is usually used in conjunction with other rhetorical modes, we are going to isolate it here so that you can appreciate its specific mechanics separately from other mental activities. If you feel the process of narration in your head, you are more likely to understand exactly what it entails and thus to use it more effectively in reading other essays and in organizing and writing your own essays.

For the best results, we will once again single out narration and do some warm-up exercises to make your sequencing perceptions as accurate and successful as possible. In this way, you will actually learn to feel how your mind works in this particular mode and then be more aware of the thinking strategies available to you in your own reading and writing. As you become more conscious of the mechanics of the individual rhetorical modes, you will naturally become more adept at combining them to accomplish the specific purpose and the related effect you want to create.

The following exercises, which require a combination of thinking and writing skills, will help you practise this particular strategy in isolation. Just as in a physical workout, we will warm up your mental capabilities one by one as if they were muscles that can be developed individually before being used together in harmony.

1. Make a chronological list of the different activities you did yesterday, from waking in the morning to sleeping at night. Randomly pick two events from your day, and treat them as the highlights of your day. Now, write freely for five minutes, explaining the story of your day and emphasizing the importance of these two highlights.

2. Recall an important event that happened to you between the ages of five and ten. Brainstorm about how this event made you feel at the time it happened. Then, brainstorm about how this event makes you feel now. What changes have you discovered in your view of this event?

3. Create a myth or story that illustrates a belief or idea that you think is important. You might begin with a moral that you believe in and then compose a story that "teaches" or demonstrates that moral.

Reading and Writing Narrative Essays

To read a narrative essay most effectively, you should spend your time concentrating on the writer's main story line and use of details. To create an effective story, you have some important decisions to make before you write and certain variables to control as you actually draft your narrative.

During the prewriting stage, you need to generate ideas and choose a point of view through which your story will be presented. Then, as you write, the preliminary decisions you have made regarding the selection and arrangement of your details (especially important in a narrative) will allow your story to flow more easily. Carefully controlled organization, along with appropriate timing and pacing, can influence your audience's reactions in very powerful ways.

How to Read a Narrative Essay

Preparing to Read. As you prepare to read the narratives in this chapter, try to guess what each title tells you about that essay's topic and about the author's attitude toward that topic: Can you tell, for example, what Evelyn Lau's attitude toward her subject is from her title in "I Sing the Song of My Condo" or how Abel feels about Canadian citizenship in "A Home at the End of the Journey"? Also, scan the essay and read its synopsis in the Rhetorical Table of Contents to help you anticipate as much as you can about the author's purpose and audience.

The more you learn from the biography about the author and the circumstances surrounding the composition of a particular essay, the better prepared you will be to read the essay. For a narrative essay, the writer's point of view or perspective toward the story and its characters is especially significant. From the biographies, can you determine something about Brian Lewis's view of the treatment of the Inuit in "Teeth" or Alison Wearing's reason for writing her essay, "Last Snowstorm"? What do you learn about Steven Heighton's views about war in "Elegy in Stone"? Last, before you begin to read, answer the Preparing to Read questions and then try to generate some of your own inquiries on the general subject of the essay: What do you want to know about health and living conditions among Native Canadians in the Arctic (Lewis)? What are your thoughts about Canadian citizenship (Abel)? What do you think about the value of owning a home (Lau)?

Reading. As you read a narrative essay for the first time, simply follow the story line and try to get a general sense of the narrative and of the author's general purpose. Is Lewis's purpose to make us feel sympathetic or annoyed about the responses of the bureaucrats to the needs of the Inuit people? Is Steven Heighton trying to encourage us to visit the monument at Vimy Ridge or is he simply trying to show us more about the nature of Canada? Record your initial reactions to each essay as they occur to you.

Based on the biographical information preceding the essay and on the essay's tone, purpose, and audience, try to create a context for the narrative as you read. How do such details help you understand your reading material more thoroughly? A first reading of this sort, along with a survey of the questions that follow the essay, will help prepare you for a critical understanding of the material when you read it for the second time.

Rereading. As you reread these narrative essays, notice the author's selection and arrangement of details. Why does Abel organize his essay one way and Lewis another? What effect does their organization create? Also pay attention to the timing and the pacing of the story line. What do the detailed descriptions of her son's outfit add to Wearing's narrative? What does the quick pace of Abel's "A Home at the End of the Journey" communicate?

In addition, consider at this point what other rhetorical strategies the authors use to support their narratives. Which writers use examples to supplement their stories? Which use definitions? Which use comparisons? Why do they use these strategies?

Finally, when you answer the questions after each essay, you can check your understanding of the material on different levels before you tackle the discussion/writing topics that follow. For a general checklist of reading guidelines, please see pages 15–16 of the Introduction.

How to Write a Narrative Essay

Preparing to Write. First, you should answer the prewriting questions to help you generate thoughts on the subject at hand. Next, as in all writing, you should explore your subject matter and discover as many specific details as possible. (See pages 17–22 of the Introduction for a discussion of prewriting techniques.) Some writers rely on the familiar journalistic checklist of Who, What, When, Where, Why, and How to make sure they cover all aspects of their narrative. If you were using the story of a basketball game at your college or university to demonstrate the team spirit of your school, for example, you might want to consider telling your readers *who* played in the game and/or *who* attended; *what* happened before, during, and after the game; *when* and *where* it took place; *why* it was being played (or *why* these particular teams were playing each other or *why* the game was especially important); and *how* the winning basket was shot. Freewriting, or a combination of freewriting and the journalistic questions, is another effective way of getting ideas and story details on paper for use in a first draft.

Once you have generated these ideas, you should always let your purpose and audience ultimately guide your selection of details, but the process of gathering such journalistic information gives you some material from which to choose. You will also need to decide whether to include dialogue in your narrative. Again, the difference here is between *showing* and *telling*: Will your audience benefit from reading what was actually said, word for word, during a discussion, or will a brief description of the conversation be sufficiently effective? In fact, all the choices you make at this stage of the composing process will give you material with which to create emphasis, suspense, conflict, and interest in your subject.

Next, you must decide upon the point of view that will most readily help you achieve your purpose with your specific audience. Point of view includes the (1) person, (2) vantage point, and (3) attitude of your narrator. *Person* refers to who will tell the story: an uninvolved observer, a character in the narrative, or an omniscient (all-knowing) narrator. This initial decision will guide your thoughts on *vantage point*, which is the frame of reference of the narrator: close to the action, far from the action, looking back on the past, or reporting on the present. Finally, your narrator will naturally have an *attitude*, or *personal feeling*, about the subject: accepting, hostile, sarcastic, indifferent, angry, pleased, or any of a number of similar emotions. Once you adopt a certain perspective in a story, you must follow it for the duration of the narrative. This consistency will bring focus and coherence to the story.

Writing. After you have explored your topic and adopted a particular point of view, you need to write a thesis statement and to select and arrange the details of your story coherently so that the narrative has a clear beginning, middle, and end. The most natural way to organize the events of a narrative, of course, is chronologically. In your story about the school basketball game, you would probably narrate the relevant details in the order in which they occurred (i.e., sequentially, from the beginning of the game to its conclusion). More experienced writers may elect to use flashbacks: An athlete might recall a significant event that happened during the game, or a coach might recollect the contest's turning point. Your most important consideration is that the elements of a story follow some sort of time sequence, aided by the use of clear and logical transitions (e.g., "then," "next," "at this point," "suddenly") that help the reader move smoothly from one event to the next.

Rewriting. As you reread the narrative you have written, pretend you are a reader and make sure you have told the story from the most effective point of view, considering both your purpose and your audience:

1. Is your purpose (or thesis) clearly stated?
2. Who is your audience?
3. To what extent does this narrator help you achieve your purpose?

Further, as you reread, make certain you can follow the events of the story as they are related:

1. Does one event lead naturally to the next?
2. Are all the events relevant to your purpose?
3. Do you show rather than tell your message?

For more advice on writing and editing, see pages 26–27.

Student Essay: Narration at Work

The following essay characterizes the writer's mother by telling a story about an unusual family vacation. As you read it, notice that the student writer states her purpose clearly and succinctly in the first paragraph. She then becomes an integral part of her story as she carefully selects examples and details that help convey her thesis.

A Vacation With My Mother

First-person narrator <u>I had an interesting childhood</u>—not because of where <u>I</u> grew up General subject and not because I ever did anything particularly adventuresome or thrilling. In fact, I don't think my life seemed especially interesting to me at the time. But now, telling friends about my supposedly ordinary childhood, I notice an array of responses ranging Specific subject from astonishment to hilarity. <u>The source of their surprise and amusement is my mother</u>—gracious, charming, sweet, and totally out of synchronization with the rest of the world. <u>One strange</u> Thesis statement <u>family trip we took when I was eleven captures the essence of her zaniness.</u>

My two sets of grandparents lived in Calgary and Regina, respectively, and my parents decided we would spend a few weeks Narrator's attitude driving to those cities and seeing all the sights along the relaxed and rambling way. <u>My eight-year-old brother, David, and I had</u> <u>some serious reservations</u>. If Dad had ever had Mom drive him to school, we reasoned, he'd never even consider letting her help drive us anywhere out of town, let alone out of Vancouver. If we weren't paying attention, we were as likely to end up at her office or the golf course as we were to arrive at school. Sometimes she'd Examples drop us off at a friend's house to play and then forget where she'd left us. The notion of going on a long trip with her was really unnerving.

Transition <u>How can I explain my mother to a stranger?</u> Have you ever watched reruns of the old *I Love Lucy* with Lucille Ball? I did as a child, and I thought Lucy Ricardo was normal. I lived with somebody a lot like her. Now, Mom wasn't a redhead (not usually, anyway), and Dad wasn't a Cuban nightclub owner, but <u>at home</u> Narrator's vantage point <u>we had the same situation of a loving but bemused husband trying to deal with the off-the-wall logic and enthusiasm of a frequently exasperating wife. We all adored her, but we had to admit it: Mom was a flaky, absent-minded, genuine eccentric.</u>

Transition   <u>As the first day of our trip approached</u>, David and I reluctantly said good-bye to all of our friends. Who knew if we'd ever see any of them again? Finally, the moment of our departure arrived, and we loaded suitcases, books, games, some camping gear, and a tent into the car and bravely drove off. We bravely drove off again two hours later after we'd returned home to get the purse and traveller's cheques that Mom had forgotten.

Careful selection of details

Use of dialogue   David and I were always a little nervous when using gas station bathrooms if Mom was driving while Dad napped: "You stand outside the door and play lookout while I go, and I'll stand outside the door and play lookout while you go." I had terrible visions: "Honey, where are the kids?" "What?! Oh, gosh . . . I thought they were being awfully quiet. Uh . . . Lethbridge?" We were never actually abandoned in a strange city, but we weren't about to take any chances.

Examples

Transition   <u>On the fourth or fifth night of the trip</u>, we had trouble finding a motel with a vacancy. After driving futilely for an hour, Mom suddenly had a great idea: Why didn't we find a house with a likely-looking back yard and ask if we could pitch our tent there? To her, the scheme was eminently reasonable. Vowing quietly to each other to hide in the back seat if she did it, David and I groaned in anticipated mortification. To our profound relief, Dad vetoed the idea. Mom never could understand our objections. If a strange family showed up on her front doorstep, Mom would have been delighted. She thinks everyone in the world is as nice as she is. We finally found a vacancy in the next town. David and I were thrilled—the place featured bungalows in the shape of tepees.

Passage of time

Example

Transition   <u>The Native motif must have reminded my parents that we had not yet used the brand-new tent, Coleman stove, portable mattress, and other camping gear we had brought.</u> We headed to a national park the next day and found a campsite by a lake. It took hours to figure out how to get the tent up: It was one of those deluxe models with mosquito-net windows, canvas floors, and enough room for three large families to sleep in. It was after dark before we finally got it erected, and the night had turned quite cold. We fixed a hurried campfire dinner (chicken burned on the outside and raw in the middle) and prepared to go to sleep. That was when we realized that Mom had forgotten to bring along some important pieces of equipment—our sleeping bags. The four of us huddled together on our thin mattresses under the carpet from the station-wagon floor. That ended our camping days. Give me a stucco tepee any time.

Chronological order

Careful selection of details

We drove through three provinces and saw lots of interesting sights along the way: a working mine, a logging camp, caves, mountains, waterfalls, even a haunted house. David and I were excited and amazed at all the wonders we found, and Mom was just as enthralled as we were. Her constant pleasure and sense of the world as a beautiful, magical place was infectious. I never realized until I grew up how really childlike—in the best sense of the word—my mother actually is. She is innocent, optimistic, and always ready to be entertained. *Examples (spatial order)*

Transition <u>Looking back on that long-past family</u> vacation, <u>I now realize that my childhood was more special because I grew up with a mother who wasn't afraid to try anything and who taught me to look at the world as a series of marvellous opportunities to be explored.</u> What did it matter that she thought England was bordered by Germany? We were never going to try to drive there. So what if she was always leaving her car keys in the refrigerator or some other equally inexplicable place? <u>In the end, we always got where we were going—and we generally had a grand time along the way.</u> *Narrator's attitude*

Examples

Concluding remark

Some Final Thoughts on Narration

Just as with other modes of writing, all decisions regarding narration should be made with a specific purpose and an intended audience constantly in mind. As you will see, each narrative in this section is directed at a clearly defined audience. Notice, as you read, how each writer manipulates the various features of narration so that the readers are simultaneously caught up in the plot and deeply moved to feel, act, think, and believe the writer's personal opinions.

Narration in Review

Reading Narrative Essays

Preparing to Read

1. What assumptions can you make from the essay's title?
2. Can you guess what the author's mood is?
3. What is the essay's purpose and audience?
4. What does the synopsis in the Rhetorical Table of Contents tell you about the essay?

5. What can you learn from the author's biography?

6. Can you guess what the author's point of view toward the subject is?

7. What are your responses to the Preparing to Read questions?

Reading

1. What is the essay's general story line?

2. What is the author's purpose?

3. Did you preview the questions that follow the essay?

Rereading

1. What details did the author choose and how are they arranged?

2. How does the author control the pace of the story?

3. What other rhetorical modes does the author use to support the essay's purpose?

4. What are your responses to the questions after the essay?

Writing Narrative Essays

Preparing to Write

1. What are your responses to the Preparing to Write questions?

2. What is your purpose?

3. Who is your audience?

4. What is your narrator's point of view—including person, vantage point, and attitude toward the subject?

Writing

1. What is your thesis?

2. What details will best support this thesis?

3. How can you arrange these details most effectively?

4. Do you *show* rather than *tell* your story?

5. Does your narrative essay follow a time sequence?

Rewriting

1. Is your purpose (or thesis) clearly stated?

2. Who is your audience?

3. To what extent does your narrator help you achieve your purpose?

4. Does one event lead naturally to the next?

5. Are all the events relevant to your purpose?

6. Do you *show* rather than *tell* your message?

Allen Abel

A HOME AT THE END OF THE JOURNEY

Born in Brooklyn, New York in 1950, Allen Abel grew up to be a sports writer in his early years as a newspaper journalist. Now a resident of Toronto, he is a writer and broadcaster of wide-ranging interests and talents. After receiving a Bachelor of Science degree in 1971 from Rensselaer Polytechnic in New York State, Abel's focus of activities took an abrupt turn into a career as a sports journalist, where he won a number of journalism awards. He moved to Toronto in the late 1970s, and became a well-known sports columnist for the *Globe and Mail* from 1977 until 1983. Abel has also worked as a sports commentator for CFRB and wrote a documentary about the Canadian women's Olympic hockey team going to the Nagano Olympics. Abel's *Globe* columns always revealed an intelligent and ironic style, and often some more "serious" interests, which may have resulted in an extraordinary career shift for the author: The *Globe* made him their Peking correspondent in 1983 and in 1986 he became a reporter and producer of CBC-TV's *The Journal* for eight years. His career as a political observer has also led him into the production of documentary films of international interest, including *The Price of Freedom* (about East Germany) and *The Fires of Kuwait*. Allen Abel is the author of several books, including *But I Loved It Plenty Well* (1983), *Scaring Myself to Death: Adventures of a Foreign Correspondent* (1992), *Flatbush Odyssey: A Journey to the Heart of Brooklyn* (1995), and *Abel's Outback: Explorations and Misadventures on Six Continents, 1990–2000* (2001) and he has also served as a columnist for the *National Post*.

Preparing to Read

"A Home at the End of the Journey" first appeared in *Maclean's* magazine in January of 1995. In this narrative essay Abel relates the experience of becoming a Canadian citizen, and particularly the citizenship ceremony in which he participated. Before you read about Abel's experience, think about the concept of citizenship. What does it mean to be a citizen of a country? What rights and responsibilities accompany citizenship? How do these obligations and opportunities vary from one country to another? What difference is there between being a citizen of a country by birth and being a citizen of that country through choice? What do people need to do to become citizens of Canada?

■──────────────────────────────────────■

On an early winter evening in the bottomlands of Toronto's   1
untamed River Don, 70 would-be Canadians file into a blinding bright conference room and take their seats in the alphabetical order of their mutually incomprehensible names. Outside, a first frosting has rendered this quadrant of the city even more picturesque than usual. The coatracks are crammed like Tokyo commuters; overshoes slump limply on the floor.

The 70 are to take the Oath of Citizenship, pledging allegiance   2
to the woman in England—and her lovelorn son and *his* son and so forth forever—who still embodies the vast, infant Canadian state. In front of the oath-takers, a speaker's podium has been set up, and there is a small desk on which are piled the certifying documents, emblazoned with Lion and Unicorn, that each new citizen will receive. I'm a little nervous, my throat a bit dry. I am one of the 70.

Now the clerk of the court comes out, a tall, energetic woman   3
in billowing robes, dashing around like a refugee claimant from the cast of *Sister Act 2*. The ceremony will begin soon, she announces. When the oath has been sworn, she instructs, we new Canadians are to proceed from our seats in a seamless serpentine to shake the hand of the presiding judge and then, doing a single axel in front of the podium, we are to return immediately to our assigned chairs. All of this is to be accomplished swiftly, to leave more time for speeches.

Photography is permitted, the clerk says, but not during the   4
swearing of the oath itself. This act, it seems, is as sacred as the fox dance of the British Columbia Musqueam, and snapshots would defile the affair. But Beta cameramen from local television stations are here, and they will roll right over the taboo, and no one will complain or try to halt them.

It is International Human Rights Week, so the ceremony is to   5
include more ceremony than usual. Decorated dignitaries from various ethnic communities of Metro Toronto have been invited to witness the swearing-in and then—it is a lovely touch—they

are to reaffirm their own loyalty to Crown and Canada by taking the oath themselves. A red-coat Mountie stands at crisp attention, and officers of the Canadian Jewish Congress warmly greet each immigrant family. It is they who are hosting this group naturalization, here at their modern headquarters in this snowbound suburban vale.

I study my fellow foreigners as they arrive, and I try to guess 6 which ones are war orphans and day laborers and entrepreneurs, and which ones are gangsters and welfare cheats. Tonight's new Canadians, we are informed, have come from 27 countries, borne by the strange and sweeping currents of life to reunite, for this brief instant, in the saying of 43 words. Then, we will scatter into the infinite city, to meet again in fear or fellowship only at bus shelters, and some other less Toronto-centric place. But around me now, as the presiding judge arrives and the crowded room falls to a hush, I see the faces I have faced as a foreign correspondent in the refugee camps of Kurdistan, the back alleys of Havana, the cages of Hong Kong that hold escaped Vietnamese. It is a swirling sensation—that I have been sent from this city to their worlds and now their worlds have joined with mine.

(An hour earlier, I had thought: this is the night I finally leave 7 Brooklyn, my home town, behind me. But then, my wife and I had jumped into a taxi to make the ceremony on time and it had been outfitted with a bullet-proof partition between driver and passenger, an emblem of the new urban Canada. No one spoke; I stared glumly at the snow. Brooklyn had followed me north.)

The presiding judge greets us. An immigrant herself from 8 some European duchy, I cannot locate her accent—Latvia? Luxembourg?—she has performed this procedure manifold times but her voice still swells with proud anticipation. We are gaining a new country, she tells us. The gifts of this land will be limited only by the capacity of our hearts.

We stand at the clerk's command and begin the affirmation, 9 some of us mumbling, some nearly shouting, others utterly lost in the antiquated Anglophile creed ("I will be faithful and bear true allegiance..."). The cameras are on us. We will observe the laws of Canada, we utter. We will fulfil our duties. We will remain standing and do it all over again, says the presiding judge—in French.

The slow parade to the podium begins. I clasp the judge's 10 hand, receive my Commemoration of Canadian Citizenship.

Now, the Canadians who have been citizens for longer than six minutes are invited to restate their vows. In the peanut gallery to my right, I see my Canadian wife with her right hand raised, serenely chanting along. But I am already contemplating the fruits of my neonate heritage: seats on royal commissions; diplomatic postings to warm, benign republics; poets' allowances; jury duty. Shaking me from this reverie, *O Canada* begins, sung by two young stars of *Miss Saigon*.

The ceremony is over. We take our coats and re-enter the   11
intemperate night. Shivering, our teeth playing marimba melodies, we give up on the bus after a couple of minutes and hail another cab. I slide in, expecting more anticrime plastic, more mistrust, more silence.

Instead there is a slim, blushing Arab in the driver's seat and   12
a giggling Chinese woman right beside him. They both are in their 20s, lost in laughter. Turning east on Sheppard, skating sideways on the pond, the pilot turns around to shake my hand and to introduce his companion.

"Don't be afraid," the driver says. "This is my girlfriend."   13

"Congratulations!" I tell him. I'm thinking: Maybe this place   14
can work.

UNDERSTANDING DETAILS

1. Abel is relating an event in which there are many participants. What is his relationship to the participants of this citizenship ceremony?
2. What does Abel mean when he says "Brooklyn had followed me north"?
3. Explain the significance of the ceremony that Abel is depicting in this essay. How might the importance of this ceremony vary for the range of participants that Abel describes?

ANALYZING MEANING

1. What is Abel's thesis in this essay? What specific examples does he include that develop this central idea?
2. How many different nationalities or cultures does Abel refer to in "A Home at the End of the Journey"? Why does he include such a variety of references?
3. Characterize Abel's tone in this essay. What does the tone convey about the author's attitude toward his subject?

DISCOVERING RHETORICAL STRATEGIES

1. Abel uses many stylistic devices to make his writing interesting and effective. Find examples of similes, metaphors, personification, and alliteration in this essay.
2. How is Abel's past experience as a foreign correspondent and a sports writer reflected in the details and images he chooses to include in this essay?
3. How does Abel give his narrative a sense of completion? How does the conclusion of his essay link back to the introduction?

MAKING CONNECTIONS

1. The citizenship ceremony described in "A Home at the End of the Journey" has made Abel a Canadian. How does Abel's view of what is a Canadian compare to the view of Bissoondath ("Pieces of Sky")?
2. Steven Heighton ("Elegy in Stone") conveys a sense of pride in Canada for the understatement, quiet dignity, and reluctance to glorify war that he finds reflected in the park at Vimy Ridge. How do you think Allen Abel would react to this little piece of Canada in France?

IDEAS FOR DISCUSSION/WRITING

Preparing to Write

Before you begin writing, think of a ceremony in which you have participated that stands out in your mind. It might have been a graduation or a wedding or a coming-of-age ceremony such as a Bar or Bat Mitzvah, or it might have been a citizenship ceremony such as Abel's. What do you remember about the event? Who attended? What rituals were involved? How did you feel about the ceremony beforehand? Did you feel differently during the event? After it was over, what emotions do you recall experiencing? Did your participation in that ceremony give you any particular understanding about the world or the people in it?

Choosing a Topic

1. Abel uses his narrative to make a point about the multicultural nature of Canada. Choose a particular incident or event in which you have participated or that you have witnessed that illustrates your view about this aspect of Canada. Write a narrative essay

in which you recreate that incident or event and link it clearly to your view about multiculturalism in Canada.

2. Choose an incident or event from your life that has given you particular insight into human nature. Relate the event in a narrative essay with a clear thesis.

3. Ceremonies often change to adapt to a progressive world. Write a narrative essay in which you describe one ceremony you have attended or participated in that in some way did not follow tradition or convention. Use your essay to show how our world is changing. Make it clear through your choice of details and language whether you consider this change positive or negative.

Steven Heighton

ELEGY IN STONE

"If being a poet is possessing a heightened sense of perception, then in his latest collection of essays, *The Admen Move on Lhasa: Writing and Culture in a Virtual World*, Steven Heighton is every inch a poet. Here he is sometimes chatty, even wistful; at other times, wholly serious, even lamenting; and at others still, lyrical, poetic. But whatever voice he assumes, he is sure to hold your attention."

So opens L. Brent Robillard's review in the *Backwater Review* of Heighton's collection of essays from which the selection here is taken. *The Admen Move on Lhasa* (1997) follows the publication of three collections of poetry: *Stalin's Carnival* (1989), *Foreign Ghosts* (1989), and *The Ecstasy of Skeptics* (1994); and two books of fiction: *Flight Paths of the Emperor* (1992) and *On earth as it is* (1995). Steven Heighton has consistently been recognized for his writing with awards including The Canadian Authors Association Air Canada Award for most promising young writer in 1989, The Gerald Lampert Memorial Award (1990), and a National Magazine Awards gold medal for fiction in 1992. In addition, Heighton's *Flight Paths of the Emperor* was a Trillium Book Award finalist in 1993 and *On earth as it is* was nominated for the Governor General's Award for poetry in 1995. In 2000, Heighton's novel *The Shadow Boxer* was published.

Steven Heighton was born in Toronto in 1961 and grew up there and in Red Lake in Northern Ontario. After graduating from Queen's

University with a B.A. and an M.A. in English, he spent time teaching in Japan and then returned to Kingston where he became editor of *Quarry* magazine. He has also lived in Alberta and British Columbia, and now lives and works as a writer, with his family, in Kingston, Ontario.

Preparing to Read

"Elegy in Stone" is taken from a collection of essays entitled *The Admen Move on Lhasa* (1996). In this essay Steven Heighton relates his visit to the national park and monument at Vimy Ridge in France. Before reading Heighton's essay, think about war and the attitudes toward war. What images are evoked by the terms honour, valour, and bravery? How have attitudes toward war changed with new technologies that change the way wars are fought? How has increased understanding about the psychological effects of war on survivors (e.g., post-traumatic stress syndrome) changed our attitudes about war?

■ _____ ■

Vimy Ridge, April 1992

The park's entrance—a border crossing, really—was modest 1
enough: a small sign you could easily miss if you were driving past. But we were on foot. And though it turned out to be a much longer walk than we'd expected, it was a good place to walk, the fields along the road billowing with mustard, wheat, and poppies, the oaks and maples fragrant with new growth. We could be in Canada, I thought—then remembered that, for official purposes, we were.

The wind as we neared the ridge grew chilly, the sky grey.   2

Before long the road passed through a forest of natural 3
growth and entered an old plantation of white pines, thick and towering, a spacious colonnade receding in the gloom. Fences appeared along the road, then signs warning us not to walk among the trees where sheep foraged above grassed-in trenches, shell holes, unexploded mines. In the blue-green, stained-glass light of the forest, the near-silence was eerie, solemn, as in the cathedral at Arras.

Finally we heard voices, saw a file of parked cars ahead 4
through the trees and came out at the main exhibit site of the park, some distance below the monument that crowns Vimy Ridge. Here, in 1917, from a line of trenches now preserved in concrete and filled daily with French tourists, the Canadian troops had launched their attack. Preserved likewise is the first obstacle

they had met: the front-line German trench, barely a grenade's throw away. This whites-of-their-eyes proximity surprised us and made stories of verbal fraternization between the lines—of back and forth banter in broken English and German—all the more plausible, and poignant.

A few years after the end of the First World War the 5 government of France gave Canada a sizeable chunk of the cratered, barren terrain around Vimy Ridge, where 20,000 Canadians fell before the ridge was finally taken on 12 April 1917. Today many Canadian visitors to France pass the memorial park en route to Arras or Lille without realizing the site is officially a small piece of Canada. Though "plot" might be a better word, for although the trenches where Canadian and Allied soldiers lived and died during their siege have healed over, the fields are scarred with cemeteries and the woodlots filled with unmarked graves.

We'd arrived the night before in nearby Arras, finding a 6 hotel and visiting the town's medieval cathedral. The hotel manager had elaborately regretted that we hadn't come two weeks earlier, on Easter Monday, when French President François Mitterand and Prime Minister Brian Mulroney and a handful of Vimy veterans had arrived for the seventy-fifth anniversary of the ridge's fall. I told the manager that I'd read about the ceremony back home, but felt the park was probably best experienced without the crowds and fanfare of an official visit. I could have said more but didn't trust my French enough to try explaining how disturbed I'd been by photographs of those heads of state and their aides beaming glibly among the hunched veterans, whose nation-building sacrifice was clearly far from the politicians' minds.

Nation-building sacrifice sounds far too much like the kind of 7 pious, pushy rhetoric I've learned to mistrust and fear, yet for years the bloody achievement of the Canadians on Vimy Ridge did stand, like the ridge itself, as a landmark, a high point around which the idea of a distinct Canadian identity could form.

"*C'est magnifique*," the manager told us when we explained 8 we wanted to go. "*Magnifique.*"

At the park's main exhibit site we went into a small, 9 undistinguished brick building to see about a tour of the tunnel system under the trenches. The young guides, in Parks Canada uniforms, explained that we'd just missed the tour and unfortunately would have to wait for the next. But as we turned and went outside to confer, they must have noticed the small Canadian flag sewn onto my backpack, because one of them came out after us and beckoned us toward the tunnels. "You should have told us you're Canadian," he said with a soft Manitoba-French accent. "We don't get all that many."

The low-ceilinged, labyrinthine "subways"—where men ate 10 and slept before the attack and couriers ran with their messages and sappers set charges under the German lines—have been carefully restored, but more or less unembellished. The impression, as above in the trenches, was sobering. I was relieved that this sad, clammy underworld had not been brightened up into some gaudy monument to Our Glorious Past; I was relieved that it still looked, and felt, like a tomb. It reminded me of the tunnels of the besieged Huguenots under the cathedral in Arras.

It was good to get back up into the daylight. We agreed to 11 meet Mario and the other guides for a beer that night in town.

We followed the road up the last part of the ridge to the 12 monument, wind blowing over the bare fields in a steady barrage. Seventy-five years before, the Canadians had advanced at dawn through driving sleet and snow, and now, nearing the exposed crown of the ridge, we could see how weather of that intensity must be quite common. The monument stands atop Hill 145, the Canadians' final objective and the highest point for miles around—but on the morning of the attack it must have been invisible through the snow and the timed barrage behind which the men were advancing.

Before the hilltop and the monument came in sight I'd felt 13 uneasy, recalling the many monuments I had seen that stylized or made over the true face of war so as to safeguard an ideology, to comply with aesthetic conventions, or to make life easier for the recruiters of future wars. But as we neared the monument—two enormous white limestone pillars that meet at the base to form a kind of elongated U—I was impressed. And, as before, relieved. I'd first become anxious when the hotel keeper had told us to expect something "magnifique," but now I saw that in a sense he was right, for here was something magnificent in its simplicity, its solemnity, its understatement. And brilliant in its implication, because the pillars did not quite form a triumphant V, as you might expect, but a shape uncannily resembling the sights mounted on machine guns of the First World War—the kind that claimed tens of thousands of Canadian lives in the war and several thousand on the morning of the attack.

I don't believe such resemblances can be assigned to chance. 14 An artist's hand is always guided in large part by the subconscious. I don't know whether the architect of the Vimy monument was ever asked about his intentions, conscious or subconscious, but in a sense they're no longer the point; unlike so many other old monuments, Walter Seymour Allward's is strikingly modern because of the way it surpasses, or second-guesses, all conventional intent.

We drew closer. Our feeling that this monolith was more a 15 cenotaph, a vast elegy in stone instead of petrified hot air, grew stronger. And with it a feeling of pride. But a kind of pride very different, I think, from the tribal, intolerant swagger so many monuments have been built to inspire. A shy pride in our country's awkwardness at blowing its own horn—because sooner or later every country that does blow its own horn, with flamboyance, starts looking for somebody else to outblow. A pride in our reluctance—our seeming inability—to canonize brave, scared, betrayed adolescents as bearded heroes of mythic dimension, larger than life. Unreal.

And the monument is a cenotaph: we find its base inscribed 16 with the names of the 11,285 Canadians whose final resting place is unknown. Blown to pieces. Lost in the mud, or buried anonymously in the graveyards below the ridge. The parade of names marches on and on, a kind of elegy whose heartbreaking syllables are English- and French-Canadian, Ojibway, Ukrainian, Dutch, German, Italian, Japanese ...

Many are the names of our own distant relations. 17

The figures carved on and around the monument, though 18 dated in style, are not blowing trumpets or beating breasts or drums. They seem instead to grieve. We round the monument and the Douai Plain fans out below us: another figure, much larger, cloaked, stands apart at the edge of the monument overlooking the plain. Behind her a sparely worded inscription, in English and French, tells of the ridge's fall.

The figure, we will learn later that night, is Canada, 19 "mourning her lost sons."

Tonight in Arras we'll learn other things as well from the 20 Canadian guides we meet for a beer. That the whole park is planted with shrubs and trees from Canada. That 11,285 pines were planted after the war for every lost man whose name appears on the monument. That the prime minister's Easter visit was indeed a grand and lavish affair—everything the monument itself is not—but that the old soldiers on display carried themselves with dignity and a quiet, inconspicuous pride. And it's that feeling we end up coming back to towards the end of the night when the drinks have made us a bit more open and, I suppose, sentimental. Because we learn that these young expatriates have all felt just as we have about the austerity of the Vimy monument—and, by implication, the Canadian tendency to downplay the "heroism" of our achievements, to refuse to idealize, poeticize, and thus censor an obscene, man-made reality.

Or am I wrong to offer Canada these drunken toasts on a 21 virtue that's largely a matter of historical and political necessity? Perhaps what I'm trying to say is that Canadians are lucky to have been spared, so far, that sense of collective power combined with intense tribal identity that makes every imperial nation so arrogant, competitive, and brutal. And as our friends guide us back to our hotel, I wonder if Canadians will ever stop berating themselves for not believing—as too many other nations have believed, and keep on believing—that they're better than others, that they're the chosen, the elect, the Greatest Nation on Earth, with God on their side.

"Make sure to let people back home know about the 22 memorial," Mario calls out as we enter our hotel. And I reflect that a visit to the monument and the many battlefields around it might help convince some Canadians that there are worse things than uncertainty and understatement.

And if the monument doesn't convince them, or the 23 battlefields, then surely the graveyards will. In the park or within walking distance lie thirty cemeteries where the remains of over 7,000 Canadians are buried. They are peaceful places, conscientiously tended. Flowers bloom over every grave. Many are poppies. The paint on the crosses is fresh, a dazzling white in the April sun. Here, no doubt, many of the boys whose names appear on the monument are actually buried, beneath long files of anonymous crosses, or stones ranked like chairs in a vast, deserted cathedral. Another endless parade, this time of the nameless—though here and there we do find stones inscribed with a name, an age. David Mahon, 1901–1917. IN MEMORY OF OUR DEAR AND ONLY CHILD.

We recite the words aloud, but this time the feeling they   24
inspire has little to do with pride. The huge limestone gunsight
looms above us on the ridge as we enter yet another aisle, and
read, yet again:

A SOLDIER OF THE GREAT WAR
A Canadian Regiment
Known Unto God

UNDERSTANDING DETAILS

1. What is the significance of Vimy Ridge? Explain why there is a park situated here.
2. What does the monument Heighton finds in the park look like? Draw a picture of the monument incorporating as many details as possible. When was it built? By whom?
3. What is the role of Mario in Heighton's essay?

ANALYZING MEANING

1. According to Heighton, what aspects of Canada do the monument and park at Vimy Ridge reflect? Does Heighton see these aspects as positive or negative?
2. Why is Heighton glad he missed the Prime Minister's visit?
3. Describe Heighton's reaction to all that he finds at Vimy Ridge. Why is he "relieved that this sad, clammy underworld had not been brightened up into some gaudy monument to Our Glorious Past; I was relieved that it still looked, and felt, like a tomb" (paragraph 10)?

DISCOVERING RHETORICAL STRATEGIES

1. What is the dominant tone of Heighton's essay? How does this tone suit the purpose of the essay?
2. Heighton incorporates many figures of speech into this essay. Find examples of alliteration, metaphor, simile, and personification. What is the effect of each of these on Heighton's essay?
3. While narration is the primary rhetorical strategy used in Heighton's essay, he also writes very descriptively. Find examples in "Elegy in Stone" of particularly vivid descriptive images or passages. How do these enhance Heighton's narration?

MAKING CONNECTIONS

1. Heighton's essay is largely about war and the ways that citizens of different countries view war. Barbara Ehrenreich ("The Ecstasy of War") summarizes different theories about the way wars are waged. What do you think Heighton's "theory of war" would be?
2. Both Steven Heighton and Neil Bissoondath ("Pieces of Sky") are writing about the national character of Canada and Canadians. Whose view do you agree with more strongly? Why?
3. In his description of visiting Vimy Ridge, Heighton mentions several symbolic elements (the monument, the crosses, the trees and shrubs) but the only flag seems to be the one sewn on his backpack. What do you think military historian Gwynne Dyer ("Flagging Attention") would think about the apparent absence of flags?

IDEAS FOR DISCUSSION/WRITING

Preparing to Write

Write freely about monuments constructed to remember people or events. What purpose do monuments serve? Who builds them? Who maintains them? What kinds of monuments are public? Which are personal? What monuments are you familiar with? What kinds of emotions do they evoke?

Choosing a Topic

1. Write an essay in which you describe a place that is a good representation of Canada's identity or reflection of values. Link the aspects of the place clearly with the qualities you believe they represent.
2. Write a narrative essay about a visit you have made to some site of historical significance. Why did you go there? What was your predominant impression of this place?
3. Monuments are sometimes built in recognition of people who have been killed in some tragic way. Choose a situation such as a specific natural disaster and then outline, in a descriptive essay, what kind of monument you would design to recognize and remember this person or people.

Evelyn Lau

I Sing the Song of My Condo

In *Reference West: A Monthly Review of Books for BC Readers*, poet Robin Skelton said that each of Lau's books merits "attention for its artistry, its vision, and its pure intelligence." An online profile by Anders Blichfeldt identifies "the soul-mark of Evelyn Lau's writing: poignancy and a sense of deep emotional disorientation, at once subtle and nightmarish." Lau (1972–) has typically focused her artistry, her vision, and her poignant portrayals of characters and situations on the dark fringes of society but she says, "I have always wanted to move from the 'margin' to the 'centre' in my writing; I want to train my powers of observation and imagery on more 'normal' lives than I have previously been able to chronicle." Perhaps the essay included here is one such attempt to shift to the "centre."

The hard, gritty details of Evelyn Lau's life first became familiar to many with the success of her book, *Runaway: Diary of a Street Kid*, published in 1989. This autobiographical work that was, five years later, made into a television movie, chronicles Lau's experiences as a 14-year-old runaway who became a prostitute and a junkie on the way to becoming a writer. She has also published three books of poetry, including *Oedipal Dreams* (1992)—which made her the youngest nominee ever for the Governor General's Award for poetry—two books of short stories entitled *Fresh Girls and Other Stories* (1983) and *Choose Me* (1999), and a novel, *Other Women* (1985). Lau's most recent book is *Inside Out: Reflections on a Life So Far*, a collection of personal essays.

Preparing to Read

This article from *The Globe and Mail* in June of 1995 appeared in a column entitled "Middle-Class Dreams." From Lau's previous work she might not seem an obvious choice as a writer for this column, but here Lau relates an experience familiar to many middle-class Canadians: that of purchasing her first home. It may be fitting that this piece comes from a writer who first made her mark writing about running away from home.

Here Lau explains why she decided to take this step, pulls us through the range of emotions that she experienced, and introduces us to the variety of people who decorated the path to eventual home ownership. The rough and marginal characters of much of Lau's work are replaced here by the Vancouver real estate agents and young married couples with new babies whose lives cross hers in her search for a place in the carefree "world of mortgage brochures."

Before reading about Lau's experience, think about buying a home and the dream of home ownership that dominates many lives. What role do real estate agents play in the search for a home? How does a real estate agent differ from a salesperson selling you any other product or service? What image do you have of real estate agents? If you have ever purchased a home, what about the process stands out in your mind?

L ate in the spring of last year, my fancy turned to thoughts of 1 real estate and I joined the growing ranks of Canadians in their 20s who were looking for their first homes.

I had been a renter since I was 16 and I never wanted to deal 2 with a landlord again. Instead, I wanted to know what it was like to worry if I spilled wine on my carpet, to agonize over the exact placement of a picture before pounding a nail in my wall, to open a closet door or rest my forehead against a kitchen cabinet and think, "I own this."

I went to the bank with a bundle of tax returns under my 3 arm to prequalify for a first mortgage. After a long meeting during which the bank manager and I peered morosely at a computer screen and juggled numbers for savings, RRSPs and a writer's erratic income into a yearly figure, I walked out with a brochure titled Information for First Home-buyers in my hand.

The people depicted in the brochures were not like anyone I 4 knew. The women were blond, with sunny smiles, and their husbands looked both chiselled and paternal. They were engaged in chummy family activities, like washing the dog or puttering in the garden, with the help of their model children. A white picket fence stood in soft focus in the background.

I knew then I wanted to live in the world of the mortgage 5 brochures, which never showed these middle-class people lying awake among twisted sheets in their new master bedrooms or throwing up into their ceramic sinks from panic at hefty mortgages and rising interest rates. I wanted to sing the love song of the middle class. I wanted this to be the song of myself— a litany of mortgage payments and car payments, the weeping and gnashing at tax time, maximum RRSP payments and mutual funds, credit cards and credit's twin, debt.

Laura Cavanagh, the real-estate agent I acquired through a 6 friend's connections, was an outgoing woman with tanned skin, long hair and hips so slim it seemed impossible she had two teenaged children. The male realtors we met in front of apartment buildings always held her hand for a beat too long and fastened their eyes upon hers with much intent and private meaning.

Together we toured a depressing number of 500-square-foot 7 one-bedrooms listed by young married couples who had just had their first baby. Their apartments smelled of sour milk and spoiled food, and in the bedrooms a crib took up whatever space the double bed did not already occupy. The vendor's agent would gamely point out that new carpets weren't that expensive, really, and if I enlisted the help of friends I could easily strip away the velvet-textured and dung-coloured wallpaper. He would flick on all the light switches and then exclaim, "And look at how bright this unit is!"

I became increasingly dejected at what my savings could 8 afford in Vancouver, when I knew the same amount could buy a house, with acreage attached, in Saskatoon. Laura, however, remained true to her business card's slogan—"The realtor with a positive attitude"—and came to my apartment several times a week to show me yet another suite.

Over the months I grew fond of her. She was different from 9 some of the other agents we encountered, who drove gold Mercedes and who staggered about in high heels and silk scarves, arrived late for appointments and then whipped us through the apartment while their pagers and cell phones incessantly beeped and rang. Laura held my hand when I made my first offer—and my second, third and fourth, all unsuccessfully—and comforted me after I had spent another sleepless night over interest-rate calculations.

As summer passed into fall, I discovered that acquiring a 10 real-estate agent was like acquiring a stray kitten or a runaway child—it was a lifetime commitment. She reminded me of little Gertrude in John Cheever's *The Country Husband*, with her uncanny knack of showing up in places I did not expect. I would open my front door on a Saturday morning to pick up the paper and there she would be, showered and perfumed, standing in the hallway and proffering the latest figures on a suite in which I had expressed a moment's interest. See, here's its sales history, its current assessment. Would I like to see it in 15 minutes? She would be wearing such a brave smile that I could only admire her and never find it in my heart to turn her away.

Meanwhile, my friends, who were older and therefore 11 wealthier, were actually buying places. I went to a friend's house-warming party with a smile of congratulations on my face and envy in my heart. My former foster parent bought a penthouse with 12-foot ceilings in a new building; another friend purchased an actual house with the help of his well-off parents. I went to a cocktail party at his parents' home, where a hundred guests fit neatly into the kitchen. I was surrounded by half a dozen empty bedrooms, Jacuzzis and soaker tubs and murderous chandeliers in the marble foyer. Resentment blazed in me.

Now when I walked the streets of Vancouver, I glared up at   12
the high windows of the condominiums and felt the owners were not as special as me, nor as deserving. When I gave poetry readings, I looked out at the audience and wondered how many of them owned their own homes. It came to me that I had rarely wanted anything this much before.

One afternoon Laura took me to the opening of a converted   13
building where she said the suites were priced below market value. Balloons were tied to the gates and hedges, and dozens of would-be buyers stood about the grounds, gazing up at the suites with their brochures shielding their eyes.

The display suite was bustling with activity—realtors wearing   14
suits and flustered smiles, the women with green eye-shadow and trailing a scent of White Shoulders. They paced back and forth with their clients, pulling out calculators to demonstrate price per square foot and the amount of monthly payments. Even as I sat there, someone called out that suite 312 had just been sold and 105 down the hall, and they were expecting an offer on 210.

The cell phones rang and rang and the anxiety of the buyers   15
became a frenzy of panic. It was a fever that sparked smiles on the faces of the realtors. Offers were recklessly written, and a slim-waisted woman in a floral dress who represented the financing company stepped forward to give or withhold her approval.

I was tempted by the display suite, which was small but fully   16
renovated, boasting a marble fireplace and slate tiles. Loden wallpaper in the bathroom was printed with female Greek statues clutching scraps of fabric to their breasts. I realized that the suite was a good bargain, but as I sat on the rented leather couch I found I could not pull out my chequebook and write an offer, not without at least a night's reflection.

"In all good conscience, I can say you aren't going to lose   17
money on this one," Laura said, but I was immobilized with terror. An hour later she drove me home. I spent the evening drinking heavily and calculating my finances.

The suite was priced within my range, and by the light of   18
morning I had decided I would make my move. I went back to
the suite where I had sat on the couch and looked around my
new home—this was where I would put my desk, my bed. I
approached the sales agent—a beefy, blond man with a distracted
air and an incessantly warbling pager—and said I would buy
the display suite.

"Oh. That was sold yesterday," the man said, already turning   19
away.

I surprised myself with my own reaction—it was grief. I very   20
nearly heard the crack of my heart breaking. This was not the
relief I felt when one of my previous offers had fallen through;
this was my *home* being taken away.

I stumbled out in a daze and walked the three kilometres   21
home, wiping away tears with the back of my hand the whole
way. It seemed my song would be a different one after all, it
would be the song of Rainer Maria Rilke's *Autumn Day*:
"Whoever has no house now will never have one." It was all
very well for Rilke—he had owned houses. He had written his
famous elegies while staying in Princess Marie von Thurn und
Taxis-Hohenlohe's castle. I wished bankruptcy, illness and death
upon whoever had bought my suite.

What surprised me for weeks afterward was how entirely   22
alike this feeling of bereftness was to losing the person you love.
Somehow the real, intelligent, sensible desire to buy a first home
and stop paying rent had mutated over the months into an
obsession that was like a woman's obsession for a man who had
deserted her, whom she could love only at a distance.

When I slept I was tortured by dreams in which I walked   23
through beautiful apartments that were within my price range,
then just as I pulled out my chequebook I would wake up. Several
times I dreamed I bought an apartment with three balcony doors
but no balconies, and I knew that one day I would open the
doors, step out and fall to my death. In another, I had just moved
into a new condominium and discovered that with the removal
of the previous owner's furniture and pictures, I could see that the
walls were pocked with holes the size of my fist.

Over the course of a year, my realtor and I saw 50 suites. I sat   24
on 50 strangers' sofas, looked into their cupboards, sniffed inside
their refrigerators, inspected their drapes and light switches. I
checked the drains in their balconies and flushed their toilets. I

looked for my own books on their bookshelves and was dismayed by the rows of American bestsellers or educational texts I found there. I peered into their closets and discovered if the owners were people who shopped in vintage stores or Sears or Holt Renfrew.

Once I saw the apartment of a little old lady whose obsession 25 was turtles—troops of ceramic, glass and jade turtles filed across every available counter and desktop. She owned an aquarium of turtles, posters of turtles, a bedspread with a turtle stitched on it.

After 12 months of searching, I no longer believed I would 26 purchase anything soon. I had visions of my realtor and me setting out at the turn of the millennium to look at our 300th suite.

When at last I found the right place, it happened so suddenly 27 that the frustrations of the year vanished overnight. I went to an open house on Sunday and on the Monday Laura presented my offer. It was accepted that afternoon. She stopped by to give me the news and when she came down the hallway her eyes were shining.

"You have a home now," she said. 28

The rest of the week flashed by in a blur of telephone calls 29 and meetings with the bank manager. I signed contracts, read by-laws and city council meeting minutes and certified deposit cheques. It was so stressful that I felt disconnected from reality. I vacillated between happiness, numb panic and a great, swelling pride. I had never been in debt for anything before, had never even owned a car or a computer, and now here I was committing myself to a $100,000 mortgage for 650 square feet. I had made a decision that was going to affect the rest of my life.

I take possession of the suite at the end of June, just days 30 before my 24th birthday. I may never sleep again. But at last I'm a homeowner.

UNDERSTANDING DETAILS

1. Why has Lau decided to purchase a home at this stage in her life?
2. Describe Lau's feelings about the process of purchasing her first home. How does Lau react to the prospect of this commitment?
3. Describe Laura Cavanagh. How is she different from the other real estate agents?

ANALYZING MEANING

1. How does Lau characterize the real estate sales people she meets as she searches for her home? Why does she give us these details about them?
2. What does Lau believe that home ownership will bring to her life? In your opinion, is she being realistic?
3. What are the effects on Lau of this experience of purchasing a home? Contrast Lau's reactions to discovering that the display suite was already sold, and her actual purchase.

DISCOVERING RHETORICAL STRATEGIES

1. Explain the title of Lau's essay. Where in her essay is the idea of a song repeated?
2. Identify the details that Lau has chosen that particularly effectively *show* you her experience rather than *tell* about it?
3. Where does Lau use figurative language to help convey her experience vividly to her readers?

MAKING CONNECTIONS

1. Evelyn Lau and Steven Heighton ("Elegy in Stone") are both poets as well as prose writers. What aspects of their essays reflect their poetic interests?
2. In "I Sing the Song of My Condo," Lau references two other writers; in "Opera Night in Canada," Michael McKinley mentions three different operas; in "The Myth: The Prairies Are Flat," Sharon Butala evokes W.O. Mitchell's novel *Who Has Seen the Wind*. What function do these cultural references play in their respective essays?

IDEAS FOR DISCUSSION/WRITING

Preparing to Write

Write freely about the biggest purchase you have ever made. Like Lau, this might have been a home, or it might have been a car, a computer, a college or university education, a stereo, or a special outfit. What motivated you to make this purchase? How did you feel at the time? Did you save money beforehand or did you buy on credit and pay off the debt later? Would you make the same choices about your purchase if you had it to do over again?

Choosing a Topic

1. Lau tells us that in 1994 she "joined the growing ranks of Canadians in their 20s who were looking for their first homes." Write an article for your college/university or community newspaper in which you explain to young Canadians the advantages of owning a home over renting. What motivations to purchase can you supply that will outweigh the hesitation that most people feel about making such a large financial commitment?

2. Before becoming a homeowner, Lau describes the extreme disappointment she felt when the display suite she decided to purchase was no longer available. Write an essay in which you describe a major disappointment that you have experienced at some time in your life. What anticipation led up to this disappointment? What went wrong? How did you deal with the letdown when your hopes or expectations were not fulfilled?

3. Is home ownership a realistic dream for most young Canadians? Write an essay in which you argue either that Lau's experience is one within the reach of others like herself, or that it is an unreachable dream for most of her peers.

Brian Lewis

TEETH

Originally from Wales, Brian Lewis came to Canada for a year of peace and quiet, and stayed. After working as a high school teacher in Wales, Lewis began teaching in British Columbia and then moved to Baffin Island in 1963 to teach English as a second language.

In 1968 Lewis published an arctic reading series in Inuktitut, the Inuit language, and in 1970 he completed his M.A. thesis at the University of Toronto on teaching English to Canadian "Eskimos." More recently Lewis served two terms as a member of the Legislative Assembly of the Northwest Territories. Lewis writes as a hobby to keep himself amused and occupied. Other articles by Lewis about life in the north have appeared in *Up Here*, where this piece was found.

Preparing to Read

"Teeth" appeared first in *Up Here* magazine in 1990. Brian Lewis relates a story from just after World War II about an aged Inuit hunter's experiences with Canadian bureaucracy. Ottochie, the main character, had a straightforward solution to the problem of losing his teeth. His homemade dentures became the focus of fascination to representatives of medicine, religion, law enforcement, business, and the army. Ottochie's reactions to his new city-made dentures puzzled his audience of officials as well. As you read Lewis's account of the incident and its resolution, consider your own reactions to governments and other dispensers of "rules and regulations." How often are the authorities' judgments "a good fit"? How much or how little do most Canadians know about Northern Aboriginal People? How many assumptions do we make based on ignorance of our own country and its varied peoples? How often are native people seen as "museum artifacts" or media stereotypes?

In Norman Wells this past winter, Ipellie Kilabuk, the MLA from   1
Pangnirtung, complained to the Legislative Assembly of the Northwest Territories about the declining quality of dentures supplied through the Northern Health Service.

Joe Arlooktoo, MLA from Lake Harbour, agreed with him.   2

It seems dentists nowadays no longer provide their patients   3
with heavy-duty false teeth, which Inuit need to masticate large quantities of meat. Even moderate chewing pressure makes today's dentures crack.

The two experienced legislators from Nunavut wondered   4
whether young dentists assume Northern diets now consist exclusively of Kraft dinner.

A story that dates from the early years of dental practice on   5
Baffin Island suggests diet has too often been ignored in the design of Northern dentures.

During the Second World War, the sea often threw pieces of   6
metal flotsam onto the Arctic shore. One summer an old hunter named Ottochie, who was sadly lacking in teeth, found a promising piece of aluminum on a beach in Foxe Strait. With infinite care, he carved himself a set of dentures from the metal.

This was at a time when all ships had been pressed into war   7
duty and Northern supply and service had been reduced to a trickle. But after the war the Government of Canada resumed its Arctic patrol, checking into the health and living conditions of the Inuit. When the *Nascopie* arrived at Cape Dorset fresh from its

triumphs on the Murmansk run, there was a young dentist aboard. He set directly to work.

One of the cabins in the *Nascopie* had been fixed up as a 8 dentist's office. Passengers, including an Anglican missionary, a Bay clerk, a Mountie and a retired colonel were sitting around the edge of the cabin like villagers watching a road repair gang at work.

The dentist whirled Ottochie around in the antique dentist's 9 chair, holding the gleaming jaws ajar for everyone to see.

"Beautiful set," exclaimed the missionary, who had never 10 been heard to utter a discouraging word.

"Must have taken a long wee while to make," added the Bay 11 clerk, in his cautious, ever-calculating manner.

Through an interpreter, the dentist explained how he would 12 make Ottochie a proper set of dentures. But he really had to have those home-made ones.

Reluctantly, Ottochie parted with his teeth and grimaced at 13 the thought of gumming it through a long Arctic winter.

The young dentist promised he'd return with some real 14 dentures the following August. Ottochie said he'd be waiting.

To the watching passengers, it was a wonderful thing to see 15 the State once more assuming its proper responsibilities.

"Here," declared the ever-practical Mountie, handing 16 Ottochie a black-handled pen knife. "You're going to have to cut your walrus real small."

Ottochie shook hands with everyone in the cabin and left. 17

A year later, almost to the day, the *Nascopie* anchored off 18 Kingait. Ottochie kayaked over to the ship, anxious to get his teeth. He was the first patient into the dentist's chair. Again there was a fringe of inquisitive passengers in the cabin, though none of them knew the history of Ottochie's teeth: they just hung around like gossips in a corner store, waiting to hear something sensational.

When the young dentist revealed with a flourish the finest 19 dentures money could buy, the passengers sensed they were witnessing something special. They ooh'd and aah'd at the blushing pink gums and the dainty porcelain sheen of the teeth.

Ottochie also sensed the occasion as the dentist stood over 20 him holding the dentures like an Archbishop holding a coronet waiting to crown him king. The fringe of passengers moved strategically closer.

"There," said the dentist, inserting the dentures. "How does   21
that feel?"

"Qannohitppa?" the missionary asked Ottochie.   22

"Taikoa piuniqsaulausingmamatik," responded Ottochie,   23
clearly distraught.

"What did he say?" asked the dentist querulously, fearing   24
the worst.

"The ones he used to have were better."   25

"Oh," said the dentist, devastated. He motioned Ottochie to   26
open his mouth and smile into a small hand-held mirror.

Ottochie obliged, but it was a glum smile. He gave a mutter   27
only the missionary could understand.

"He wants his old teeth back," said the missionary. "Where   28
are they?"

"In the Smithsonian," gulped the dentist. "In the United   29
States. For the world to see."

There was a brief exchange between Ottochie and the   30
missionary.

"What was that about?" asked the dentist, his anxiety turning   31
to suspicion.

"Ottochie can't imagine why people would go all the way   32
to the United States just to see a set of false teeth on a shelf. He
says teeth should be in a mouth."

The dentist shrugged.   33

Ottochie carefully extracted the dentures from his mouth   34
and returned them to the young dentist. The gesture held
profound sadness. He moved among the passengers, shaking
hands. Then he began wandering around the cabin, examining
windows and cupboards.

"He's reluctant to leave," observed the dentist.   35

"I do believe he's looking for another piece of metal," said the   36
missionary. "Something malleable."

UNDERSTANDING DETAILS

1. What was Ottochie's response to the type and quality of dentures supplied to him? Why would the dentist find it necessary
   to replace the hunter's handmade set?
2. Why is it necessary for the Northern Health Service to supply
   a different type of false teeth to inhabitants of the Arctic?

3. How do people's differing reactions to Ottochie's aluminum teeth compare to the hunter's responses to the professionally made dentures?

ANALYZING MEANING

1. Why is the young dentist so determined to take away Ottochie's aluminum dentures? Does his estimated replacement date of "the following August" seem reasonable?
2. What does Ottochie's opinion about the proper place for a set of false teeth tell you about the Inuit approach to life?
3. What does Ottochie's ritual gesture of handshaking at the end of the two meetings suggest about both the meetings and about the hunter's innate sense of behaviour?

DISCOVERING RHETORICAL STRATEGIES

1. What is the writer's purpose in relating a story he did not experience personally? Why do you think that he begins with more contemporary statements from Native Canadian politicians?
2. Which descriptive details best illustrate the author's sympathies? How are Ottochie's reactions described? How are those of the observers described?
3. Lewis tells Ottochie's story in a two-part anecdote divided by a year's passage of real time. Which aspects of the two parts of the story are similar, or parallel, and which differ? Why? What device links the beginning and end of the essay?

MAKING CONNECTIONS

1. Brian Lewis opens his essay with an anecdote about the needs of Inuit people being ignored by the Northern Health Service. How is this similar to the story Judy Rebick ("The Culture of Overwork") tells about the woman who is overworked?
2. Cecil Foster ("Why Blacks Get Mad") writes about preconceived notions affecting people's behaviour and attitudes. How do the preconceived ideas of the young dentist affect the way he treats Ottochie? What would Foster say about the treatment of Ottochie in this essay?
3. Charlotte Gray ("The Temple of Hygiene") and Brian Lewis both incorporate languages other than English into their essays

although it is unlikely that the majority of their readers will understand Inuktitut or Japanese. What is the purpose of this technique? Do you find it effective? Why or why not?

IDEAS FOR DISCUSSION/WRITING

Preparing to Write

How have government legislation or bureaucratic rules made your life more difficult, or easier, and why? Have you ever felt that a judgment or rule that originated in the government or some other policy-setting body made no sense to a situation in your own life? Did you believe that such rules may have been created without any consultation of those most directly concerned? Whose welfare seems to be at stake in the situations where you find such regulations to be impediments?

Choosing a Topic

1. For your student newspaper, write a narrative article describing a mix-up or misunderstanding in your own life that involved dealing with authority figures and rules. Describe and evaluate your reaction to the results of your dilemma as they affected your life.
2. Write a narrative essay in the form of a letter to your Member of Parliament that explains why you feel that government-sponsored health care is a good or a bad thing. Use examples taken from your or your family's lives to show why you feel as you do.
3. Write a letter to an imagined penpal in a different part of Canada, in which you explain aspects of your everyday life which you believe that the reader would find different or re-markable. Why have you chosen such incidents or behaviour? How would they differ from things "normal" to an inhabitant of another region?

Alison Wearing

■ □ ■

LAST SNOWSTORM

Alison Wearing (1968–) is the winner of the National Magazine Awards Gold Medal for Travel Writing, the recipient of the Western Magazine Award for Travel Writing, and a runner-up for the Journey Prize for fiction. This reflects her writing ability in both fictional and non-fictional genres. Wearing, who lives near Peterborough, Ontario, is probably most widely known for her book *Honeymoon in Purdah*, her story of travelling for a year through Iran. In addition to this book, however, Wearing has had travel stories published in a range of national newspapers and journals and her work has been broadcast on CBC Radio.

Preparing to Read

Before reading Wearing's poignant narrative about a visit she makes to Montreal, think about growing old. When does someone become old? What distinguishes an old person from a middle-aged person? Why do people often resist growing old? How do they resist aging?

The airport limo arrives. My eight-month-old baby is bundled 1 up in a fleecy suit with ears that make him look like a little bear. I don't normally go in for this kind of cutesy stuff, but the outfit was a gift and, despite myself, I quite like it. In addition to Noah, I am carrying only one small backpack containing three essential items: my wallet, the airline tickets, a diaper. All other bags are in the car, which J (Noah's father) is driving to the same destination to which Noah and I are about to fly. The reasons for these travel arrangements are too tedious to get into right now. Main thing is: the bags are in the car. J leaves about twenty minutes before I do and jokes that he'll probably get to Montreal first.

Then the limo arrives. As I was saying. 2

Now, I'm not sure who coined the phrase "airport limo," 3 but whoever it was didn't live in Toronto. What we climb into is just a regular old, beat-up cab that happens to go to the airport, this one with such a foul smell that I begin to wonder if the cabbie has a wet dog riding up front with him. I even lean forward and peek down at the floor—don't see anything. We get to the airport. I hoist Noah onto my hip (where he spends most of his life), fling my ultralight pack onto my shoulder, and go to check in. Then I look around quizzically, because that cabbie's wet dog seems to have followed us into the airport. Or ... no.

I lift Noah's butt up to my nose. Head for the nearest 4 washroom. I realize I'm in trouble the moment I sit him on the counter between the sinks. The mess has soaked right through his cute little bear suit.

Wads and wads of paper towel later, I have most of it off his 5 body, though he has so many little rolls and creases in his thighs that it's difficult to be sure. Also, since my left hand is busy keeping him from sliding into the sink or onto the floor, and my right hand is trying to work the water and reach for more paper towels, I'm incapable of doing a thorough job. The worst part is the little jumpsuit, which has the stuff oozing out of the back, the front, the legs, even—inexplicably—up near the neck. I can't wet it, as it's freezing outside and this is the only thing the sweet babe has to wear. I decide just to wipe it out with dry paper towel and live with the results. Somewhere in the middle of this exercise a woman comes out of one of the stalls and says, as she is washing her hands, "You should always travel with an extra set of little clothes." Then, with emphasis, "... for *Exactly This Reason.*"

Only because I am otherwise occupied do I refrain from 6 saying, "I'm So Glad you're not my mother."

With the reeking outfit back on again, and a layer of paper 7 towels between us, I hoist a smiling Noah onto my hip and we catch our plane. We land in Montreal just after six. Noah and I have dinner plans for seven. We take a cab first to the hotel, in the distant hope that J will have arrived before us and will be able to provide for a change of wardrobe. No such luck. I do a bit more cursory wiping of the shitsuit and hail another cab. Step out in front of that exquisite house and ring the bell.

"Hi Alison, come in, come in."   8

He has aged so much in a single year. He now radiates the 9 lightness that comes with age, when the eyes have stopped focusing on dailiness and detail; when, even as they are looking at you, they are looking into distance. There is a sadness in this light, but also a serenity. He knows I notice. Looks apologetic. Or slightly embarrassed.

I take this moment to introduce Noah, who shows off his   10
two bottom teeth and clings to me, giggling. "I'm going to have
to ask you to hold him while I take off my coat," I start, "but be
careful because he's had a bit of an accident." I hand the little
poo-bear over and watch how easily he is taken into this old
man's arms. "Don't worry about accidents," he says, "they're
part of life." We move to the kitchen and sit on stools at the
counter. Noah cranes his head to see who is holding him, then
reaches up and sticks his finger in the man's nose.

We laugh together, all of us.   11

He moves so slowly, it is painful to watch. A minute to cross   12
the kitchen. Several frustrating, fruitless minutes to open a
package: the frozen dinners we're eating tonight. He is full of
apologies. Hopes I don't mind. "It's not caviar," he says, putting
the plastic trays in the microwave, "but they're not bad."

We pick at each other's lasagna and Chinese food—both   13
think the other's tastes better—and talk of Mexican villages, the
startling irrelevance of book reviews, canoe routes in Temagami,
babies, the reason his hands are shaking.

"I should probably tell you, I have Parkinson's ... You don't   14
die from it, but it makes you look like an old man, even if you
don't feel like one."

He takes another trembling bite.   15

"I don't care what you look like, you're not an old man to me."   16

He stops, puts his fork down, we look into each other's sad   17
eyes, and smile.

Noah paws at my shirt.   18

"If you don't mind," I say, "I'm just going to nurse him right   19
here."

"I don't mind, as long as you don't mind if I watch."   20

"Not at all," I laugh and cradle Noah in my lap. When I look   21
up, across the table, the old man is staring so tenderly, as though
he were witnessing a miracle. Eyes full of tears.

After dinner, we move into the living room—the room with   22
thirty-foot ceilings and an emptiness that is impossible to fill.
There is a portrait of his youngest son resting against the wall,
waiting to be hung. My eyes are drawn to it, again and again. It
is haunting, the way the young man's spirit swims in these slicks
of coloured oils. We don't say a word about it, or him, though we
stand at the window and watch the snowstorm together, and it
amounts to the same thing.

When it is time to leave, Noah cries while I put my coat on.   23

"He wants his mother," the man says, shifting the baby   24
around in his arms. "He's got good taste."

We wait for the taxi by the front door and talk about the   25
Schubert Lieder I once sang at the (out of tune) piano here. Words
that, when sung, rise to the heavens:

Ruhn in Frieden, alle Seelen	Rest in peace, all souls
Die vollbracht ein banges Quälen,	Who have had done with anxious torment,
Die vollendet süssen Traum,	Who have had done with sweet dreams,
Lebenssatt, geboren kaum,	Who, sated with life and hardly born,
Aus der Welt hinüberschieden	Have departed from this world:
All Seelen ruhn in Frieden.	All souls, rest in peace.

Smiles. A touch of hands. A long, deep hug. We say nothing of   26
"next time" or "soon." We say nothing.

Outside, a few steps from the road, Noah folded up   27
under my coat, I turn to wave. I stand, instead, in the
falling snow, and watch his door, gently, close.

UNDERSTANDING DETAILS

1. Where is Wearing travelling and how? Why does she question
   the term "airport limo"?
2. What is the source of the "wet dog" smell in the cab?
3. Describe Wearing's reaction to the man she goes to visit.

ANALYZING MEANING

1. Who is the old man Wearing visits in Montreal? Why has she
   gone to visit him?
2. Reread the final paragraph of the essay. Instead of waving, why
   does Wearing "stand, instead, in the falling snow and watch
   his door, gently, close"?
3. Much of the communication between Wearing and the old man
   is non-verbal. What unspoken messages are being conveyed?
   How are those messages transmitted?

DISCOVERING RHETORICAL STRATEGIES

1. Although she is writing a narrative piece, Wearing incorporates many descriptive details into her story. Find at least four examples of particularly vivid descriptive phrases that help Wearing's narrative come to life.
2. How would you describe the pacing of Wearing's narrative? How has she achieved this effect?
3. Narrative is made effective through the careful selection of detail. Why has Wearing incorporated the detail about the music she sang in the past?

MAKING CONNECTIONS

1. Much of the communication in Wearing's narrative is non-verbal. What role does non-verbal communication play in stories such as that of Steven Heighton's visit to Vimy Ridge ("Elegy in Stone")?
2. Wearing is best known as a travel writer. Dave Bidini ("Kris King Looks Terrible") writes about his travels to Hong Kong and Charlotte Gray ("The Temple of Hygiene") writes about her trip to Japan. Are there similarities in the writing style of these three authors as they relate the stories of their visits to their respective destinations?

IDEAS FOR DISCUSSION/WRITING

Preparing to Write

Write freely about non-verbal communication. How do people communicate without using words? What techniques do people have for conveying ideas without using words? Why do people often use looks or touch to communicate emotions rather than voicing those feelings? What percentage of a message is typically communicated through non-verbal rather than verbal means?

Choosing a Topic

1. Write an essay in which you convey the potential confusion created by non-verbal communication by relating a specific personal story of a misunderstanding. Make sure that you select and organize your details effectively to serve your purpose clearly.

2. Recall a time when you faced a significant new experience. Write a narrative essay in which you recreate the events and your feelings about them for your audience. Be sure to show your audience the events and feelings rather than telling about them.

3. Write a narrative essay in which you relate an interaction between two people in which no words were exchanged. Show your readers clearly what message or messages were conveyed and how.

CHAPTER 3

EXAMPLE

■ ■ ■

Illustrating Ideas

Citing an example to help make a point is one of the most instinctive techniques we use in communication. If, for instance, you state that being an internationally ranked tennis player requires constant practice, a friend might challenge that assertion and ask what you mean by "constant practice." When you respond "about three hours a day," your friend might ask for more specific proof. At this stage in the discussion, you could offer the following illustrations to support your statement: When not on tour, Martina Hingis practises three hours per day; Pete Sampras, four hours; and Michael Chang, two hours. Your friend's doubt will have been answered through your use of examples.

Defining Examples

Well-chosen examples and illustrations are an essay's building blocks. They are drawn from your experience, your observations, and your reading. They help you *show* rather than *tell* what you mean, usually by supplying concrete details (references to what we can see, smell, taste, hear, or touch) to support abstract ideas (such as faith, hope, understanding, and love), by providing specifics ("I like chocolate") to explain generalizations ("I like sweets"), and by giving definite references ("Turn left at the second stoplight") to clarify vague statements ("Turn in a few blocks"). Though illustrations take many forms, writers often find themselves indebted to description or narration (or some combination of the two) in order to supply enough relevant examples to achieve their rhetorical intent.

As you might suspect, examples are important ingredients in producing exciting, vivid prose. Just as crucial is the fact that carefully chosen examples often encourage your readers to feel one way or another about an issue being discussed. If you tell your parents, for instance, that living in a college residence is not conducive to academic success, they may doubt your word, perhaps thinking that you are simply attempting to coerce money out of them for an apartment. You can help dispel this notion, however, by giving them specific examples of the chaotic nature of residence life: the party down the hall that broke up at 2 a.m. when you had a chemistry exam that same morning at 8 o'clock; the stereo next door that seems to be stuck on its highest decibel level at all hours of the day and night; and the new "friend" you recently acquired who thinks you are the best listener in the world—especially when everyone else has the good sense to be asleep. After such a detailed and well-documented explanation, your parents could hardly deny the strain of this difficult environment on your studies. Examples can be very persuasive.

The following paragraphs, written by a student, use examples to explain how he reacts to boredom in his life. As you read this excerpt, notice how the writer shows rather than tells the readers how he copes with boredom by providing exciting details that are concrete, specific, and definite:

> We all deal with boredom in our own ways. Unfortunately, most of us have to deal with it far too often. Some people actually seek boredom. Being bored means that they are not required to do anything; being boring means that no one wants anything from them. In short, these people equate boredom with peace and relaxation. But for the rest of us, boredom is not peaceful. It produces anxiety.
>
> Most people deal with boredom by trying to distract themselves from boring circumstances. Myself, I'm a reader. At the breakfast table over a boring bowl of cereal, I read the cereal box, the milk carton, the wrapper on the bread. (Have you ever noticed how many of those ingredients are unpronounceable?) Waiting in a doctor's office, I will gladly read weekly news magazines of three years ago, a book for five-year-olds, advertisements for drugs, and even the physician's odd-looking diplomas on the walls. Have you ever been so bored you were reduced to reading through all the business cards in your wallet? Searching for names similar to yours in the phone book? Browsing through the *National Enquirer* while waiting in the grocery line? At any rate, that's my recipe for beating boredom. What's yours?

Example   113

Thinking Critically by Using Examples

Working with examples gives you yet another powerful way of processing your immediate environment and the larger world around you. It involves a manner of thinking that is completely different from description and narration. Using examples to think critically means seeing a definite order in a series of specific, concrete illustrations that are related in some way that may or may not be immediately obvious to your readers.

Isolating this rhetorical mode involves playing with related details in such a way that they create various patterns that relay different messages to the reader. Often, the simple act of arranging examples helps both the reader and the writer make sense of an experience or idea. In fact, ordering examples and illustrations in a certain way may give one distinct impression, while ordering them in another way may send a completely different message. Each pattern creates a different meaning and, as a result, an entirely new effect.

With examples, more than with description and narration, patterns need to be discovered in the context of the topic, the writer's purpose, and the writer's ultimate message. Writers and readers of example essays must make a shift from chronological to logical thinking. A writer discussing variations in faces, for example, would be working with assorted memories of people, incidents, and age differences. All of these details will eventually take shape in some sort of statement about faces, but these observations would probably not follow a strictly chronological sequence.

The exercises here will help you experience the mental differences among these rhetorical modes and will also prepare you to make sense of details and examples through careful arrangement and rearrangement of them in your essay. These exercises will continue to give you more information about your mind's abilities and range.

1. For each sentence below, provide two to three examples that would illustrate the generalization:
   a. I really liked (disliked) some of the movies released this year.
   b. Many career opportunities await a college graduate.
   c. Some companies make large sums of money by selling products with the names of professional sports teams on them.
2. Give an example (as specific as possible) of each item listed here: car, pizza, song, musician, event, friend, emotion, vacation, plant.

3. Jot down five examples of a single problem on campus that bothers you. First, arrange these examples in an order that would convince the president of your school that making some changes in this area would create a more positive learning environment. Second, organize your five examples in such a way that they would convince your parents that the learning environment at your current school cannot be salvaged and you should immediately transfer to another school.

Reading and Writing Essays That Use Examples

A common criticism of college- and university-level writers is that they often base their essays on unsupported generalizations, such as "All sports cars are unreliable." The guidelines discussed in this introduction will help you avoid this problem and use examples effectively to support your ideas.

As you read the essays in this chapter, take time to notice the degree of specificity the writers use to make various points. To a certain extent, the more examples you use in your essays, the clearer your ideas will be and the more your readers will understand and be interested in what you are saying.

Notice also that these writers know when to stop—when "more" becomes too much and boredom sets in for the reader. Most students err by using too few examples, however, so we suggest that, when in doubt about whether or not to include another illustration, you should go ahead and add it.

How to Read an Essay That Uses Examples

Preparing to Read. Before you begin reading the essays in this chapter, take some time to think about each author's title: What can you infer about Lynn Coady's attitude toward her subject from her title "Genius or Madness?"? What do you think Cecil Foster's view is of blacks in Canadian society? In addition, try to discover the writer's audience and purpose at this point in the reading process. Scanning the essay and surveying its synopsis in the Rhetorical Table of Contents will provide you with useful information for this task.

Also important as you prepare to read is information about the author and about how a particular essay was written. Most of this material is furnished for you in the biography preceding each essay. From it, you might learn why Lynn Coady is qualified to write about "anti-social behaviour" or why Sharon Butala wrote "The Myth: The Prairies Are Flat."

Example   115

Finally, before you begin to read, take time to answer the Preparing to Read questions and to make some associations with the general subject of the essay: What do you want to know about infomercials (Mark Kingwell)? What are some of your opinions on racism in Canada (Cecil Foster)?

Reading. As you first read these essays, record any thoughts that come to mind. Make associations freely with the content of each essay, its purpose, its audience, and the facts about its publication. For example, try to determine why Cecil Foster writes about black discontent in Canadian society or why Lynn Coady titles her essay "Genius or Madness?". At this point, you will probably be able to make some pretty accurate guesses about the audience each author is addressing. Creating a context for your reading—including the writer's qualifications; the essay's tone, purpose, and audience; and the publication information—is an important first step toward being able to analyze your reading material in any mode.

Finally, after you have read an essay in this section once, preview the questions after the selection before you read it again. Let these questions focus your attention for your second reading.

Rereading. As you read the essays in this chapter for a second time, focus on the examples each writer uses to make his or her point: How relevant are these examples to the thesis and purpose of each essay? How many examples do the writers use? Do they vary the length of these examples to achieve different goals? Do the authors use examples their readers can easily identify with and understand? How are these examples organized in each case? Does this arrangement support each writer's purpose? For example, how relevant are Lynn Coady's examples of famous people's behaviour to her central idea? How many examples does Kingwell use to make each point? Does Cecil Foster vary the length of each of his examples to accomplish different purposes? How does Sharon Butala organize her examples? Does this arrangement help her accomplish her purpose? In what way? Does Cecil Foster use examples that blacks, as well as people of other races, can identify with? How effective are his examples? How effective are Butala's examples?

As you read, consider also how other rhetorical modes help each writer accomplish his or her purpose. What are these modes? How do they work along with examples to help create a coherent essay?

Last, answering the questions after each essay will help you check your grasp of its main points and will lead you from the literal to the analytical level in preparation for the discussion/writing assignments that follow.

For a thorough summary of reading tasks, you might want to consult the checklists on pages 15–16 of the Introduction.

How to Write an Essay That Uses Examples

Preparing to Write. Before you can use examples in an essay, you must first think of some. One good way to generate ideas is to use some of the prewriting techniques explained in the Introduction (pages 17–22) as you respond to the Preparing to Write questions that appear before the writing assignments for each essay. You should then consider these thoughts in conjunction with the purpose and the audience specified in your chosen writing assignments. Out of these questions should come a number of good examples for your essay.

Writing. In an example essay, a thesis statement or controlling idea will help you begin to organize your paper. (See page 22 for more information on thesis statements.) Examples become the primary method of organizing an essay when they guide the readers from point to point in reference to the writer's thesis statement. The examples you use should always be relevant to the thesis and purpose of your essay. If, for instance, the person talking about tennis players cited the practice schedules of only unknown players, her friend certainly would not be convinced of the truth of her statement about how hard internationally ranked athletes work at their game. To develop a topic principally with examples, you can use one extended example or several shorter examples, depending on the nature and purpose of your assertion. If you are attempting to prove that Canadians are more health conscious now than they were 20 years ago, citing a few examples from your own neighbourhood will not provide enough evidence to be convincing. If, however, you are simply commenting on a neighbourhood health trend, you can legitimately refer to these local cases. Furthermore, always try to find examples with which your audience can identify so that they can follow your line of reasoning. If you want your parents to help finance an apartment, citing instances from the lives of current rock stars will probably not prove your point, because your parents may not sympathize with these particular role models.

Example 117

The examples you choose must also be arranged as effectively as possible to encourage audience interest and identification. If you are using examples to explain the imaginative quality of Canada's Wonderland, for instance, the most logical approach would probably be to organize your essay by degrees (i.e., from least to most imaginative or most to least original). But if your essay uses examples to help readers visualize your bedroom, a spatial arrangement of the details (moving from one item to the next) might be easiest for your readers to follow. If the subject is a series of important events, like graduation weekend, the illustrations might most effectively be organized chronologically. As you will learn from reading the selections that follow, the careful organization of examples leads quite easily to unity and coherence in your essays. *Unity* is a sense of wholeness and interrelatedness that writers achieve by making sure all their sentences are related to the essay's main idea; *coherence* refers to logical development in an essay, with special attention to how well ideas grow out of one another as the essay develops. Unity and coherence produce good writing—and that, of course, helps foster confidence and accomplishment in school and in your professional life.

Rewriting. As you reread your example essays, look closely at the choice and arrangement of details in relation to your purpose and audience:

1. Have you included enough examples to develop each of your topics adequately?
2. Are the examples you have chosen relevant to your thesis?
3. Have you selected examples that your readers can easily understand?
4. Have you arranged these examples in a logical manner that your audience can follow?

For more detailed information on writing, see the checklists on pages 26–27 of the Introduction.

Student Essay: Examples at Work

In the following essay, a student uses examples to explain and analyze her parents' behaviour as they prepare for and enjoy their grandchildren during the Christmas holidays. As you read it, study the various examples the student writer uses to convince us that her parents truly undergo a transformation each winter.

Mom and Dad's Holiday Disappearing Act

General topic Often during the winter holidays, people find surprises: Children discover the secret contents of brightly wrapped packages that Details to capture holiday spirit have teased them for weeks; cooks are astonished by the wealth of smells and memories their busy kitchens can bring about; workaholics stumble upon the true joy of a few days' rest. My surprise over the past few winters has been the personality transformation my parents go through around mid-December as they change from Dad and Mom into Poppa and Granny. Yes, they become grandparents and are completely different from the people I know the other eleven and a half months of the year.

Background information

Thesis statement

The first sign of my parents' metamorphosis is the delight they take in visiting toy and children's clothing stores. These two people, who usually despise anything having to do with shopping malls, become crazed consumers. While they tell me to budget my money and shop wisely, they are buying every doll, dump truck, and velvet outfit in sight. And this is only the beginning of the holidays!

First point

Examples relevant to thesis

Transition When my brother's children arrive, Poppa and Granny come into full form. First they throw out all ideas about a balanced diet for the grandkids. While we were raised in a house where everyone had to take two bites of broccoli, beets, or liver (foods that appeared quite often on our table despite constant groaning), the grandchildren never have to eat anything that does not appeal to them. Granny carries marshmallows in her pockets to bribe the littlest ones into following her around the house, while Poppa offers "surprises" of candy and cake to them all day long. Boxes of chocolate-covered cherries disappear while the bran muffins get hard and stale. The kids love all the sweets, and when the sugar revs up their energy levels, Granny and Poppa can always decide to leave and do a bit more shopping or go to bed while my brother and sister-in-law try to deal with their supercharged, hyperactive kids.

Second point

Humorous examples (organized from most to least healthy)

Transition Once the grandchildren have arrived, Granny and Poppa also seem to forget all of the responsibility lectures I so often hear in my daily life. If little Tommy throws a fit at a friend's house, he is "overwhelmed by the number of adults"; if Mickey screams at his sister during dinner, he is "developing his own personality"; if Nancy breaks Granny's vanity mirror (after being told twice to put it down), she is "just a curious child." But, if I track mud into the house while helping to unload groceries, I become "careless";

Third point

Examples in the form of comparisons

Example 119

if I scold one of the grandkids for tearing pages out of my calculus book, I am "impatient." If a grandchild talks back to her mother, Granny and Poppa chuckle at her spirit. If I mumble one word about all of this doting, Mom and Dad reappear to have a talk with me about petty jealousies.

Transition to conclusion

When my nieces and nephews first started appearing at our home for the holidays a few years ago, I probably was jealous, and I complained a lot. But now I spend more time simply sitting back and watching Mom and Dad change into what we call the "Incredible Huggers." They enjoy their time with these grandchildren so much that I easily forgive them their Granny and Poppa faults.

Writer's attitude

I believe their personality change is due to the lack of responsibility they feel for the grandkids: In their role as grandparents, they don't have to worry about sugar causing cavities or temporary failures of self-discipline turning into lifetime faults. Those problems are up to my brother and sister-in-law. All Granny and Poppa have to do is enjoy and love their grandchildren. They have all the fun of being parents without any of the attendant obligations. And you know what? I think they've earned the right to make this transformation—at least once a year.

Writer's analysis of situation

Concluding remark

Specific reference to introduction

Some Final Thoughts on Examples

Although examples are often used to supplement and support other methods of development—such as cause/effect, comparison/contrast, and process analysis—the essays in this section are focused principally on examples. A main idea is expressed in the introduction of each, and the rest of the essay provides examples to bolster that contention. As you read these essays, pay close attention to each author's choice and arrangement of examples; then, try to determine which organizational techniques are most persuasive for each specific audience.

Example in Review

Reading Example Essays

Preparing to Read

1. What assumptions can you make from the essay's title?
2. Can you guess what the general mood of the essay is?

3. What is the essay's purpose and audience?

4. What does the synopsis in the Rhetorical Table of Contents tell you about the essay?

5. What can you learn from the author's biography?

6. Can you guess what the author's point of view toward the subject is?

7. What are your responses to the Preparing to Read questions?

Reading

1. What general message is the author trying to convey?

2. Did you preview the questions that follow the essay?

Rereading

1. What examples help the author communicate the essay's general message?

2. How are these examples organized?

3. What other rhetorical modes does the author use to support the essay's purpose?

4. What are your responses to the questions after the essay?

Writing Example Essays

Preparing to Write

1. What are your responses to the Preparing to Write questions?

2. What is your purpose?

3. Who is your audience?

4. What is the message you want to convey?

Writing

1. What is your thesis or controlling idea?

2. Do the examples you are choosing support this thesis?

3. Are these examples arranged as effectively as possible?

4. What is your point of view toward your subject?

5. How do you achieve unity and coherence in your example essay?

Rewriting

1. Have you included enough examples to develop each of your topics adequately?

2. Are the examples you have chosen relevant to your thesis?

3. Have you arranged these examples in a logical manner that your audience can follow?

Lynn Coady

GENIUS OR MADNESS?

In 1998 Lynn Coady (1970–) received national recognition for her first novel, *Strange Heaven*, with a nomination for the Governor General's Award for fiction and the Canadian Authors Association's Air Canada award for the most promising writer under 30.

Lynn Coady comes from Cape Breton, Nova Scotia, but, after receiving a B.A. from Carleton University in Ottawa and living in New Brunswick, she moved to British Columbia to study creative writing at the University of British Columbia. Now living in Vancouver, Coady has been publishing short stories since 1992 and is also a playwright. Her play, *Monster*, was a finalist in Theatre BC's 1996 National Playwriting Competition. A collection of Coady's stories entitled *Play the Monster Blind*, published in 2000, continues to portray contemporary life in Cape Breton and earn Coady accolades. Coady's second novel, *Saints of Big Harbour*, "a study in what makes a person a loser in his own ideas and in the ideas of the world...," will be published in 2002.

Preparing to Read

This essay originally appeared in the *Globe and Mail* as part of an advertisement for Chapters bookstore. This ad was part of a series of essays by notable Canadian writers, musicians, and thinkers. In "Genius or Madness?" Lynn Coady writes about the fine line between unconventional behaviour that is admired and that which is viewed negatively. Before reading Coady's essay, think about people who are considered geniuses. In what ways are they exceptional? In what way do their lives differ from those of everyone else? Who decides that an individual is a genius? At what point in a person's life is the designation of genius typically applied?

■───■

In my hometown, perhaps small towns in general, it's easy to   1
be crazy. As an adolescent, I didn't talk much and liked to read
books in my room. That was all it took. Other people were crazy
for different reasons. There were a couple of other kids who stayed
in their rooms and played guitar (or oboe, or drums ...). Someone
else was a vegetarian and an environmentalist—this in a town
whose lifeblood consisted of the pulp of razed forests. Then there
was the elementary school art teacher who wore high-heels,
chunky jewelry, and low-cut tops. He also had a big, fluffy white
mat he liked to lounge on during class, making us kids fidget
uncomfortably on the minuscule carpet-samples he provided for us.

In the glare of small-town scrutiny, any deviation from the   2
norm stands out wildly. The art teacher, because he was an adult,
and well-established in the community, was treated with a faux-
friendly indulgence that in any modern city would instantly be
recognized for the covert bigotry it was. In our town it passed
for tolerance. Weirdo adolescents, however, were less kindly
indulged—the assumption always being that teenagers exist in a
developmental limbo with no solid values or proclivities of their
own, and can, therefore, with firm guidance, easily be molded
into well-adjusted citizens.

As it turned out, the conformity expected in my hometown   3
actually served as a handy preview of what was to come—the
larger-scale conformity that defines the urban adult. Like many
a small-town girl, I lived in the hope of getting out and going
where not talking much and reading books was even a marginally
acceptable pastime and I wouldn't be considered crazy anymore.
Off I went to the big city. All I've learned in the ten year interim
since is that reading books is *okay*, in moderation, but not wanting
to talk remains a no-no. Small-town hicks and urban sophisticates
alike can't help but take it personally. People harangue me for
never answering my phone, for example. But I don't like
answering my phone. "But it's *anti-social*," they warn, ominously.

This is the crux of crazy, apparently. *Anti-social behavior* is   4
our euphemism for everything from the dabblings of people like
the Unabomber, to that hairy street-wanderer who talks and
titters to himself as he makes ready to pee on the sidewalk, to

Emily Dickinson, in near-obscurity, penning some of the most shattering verse ever written. If you believe what people tell you, it's all the same, and it's all bad. There was probably much concern and consternation over Emily's doings at the time, existing in a cocoon of grief and isolation, only rousing herself to scribble her terse, morbid observations of the world. Anti-social? Definitely. Crazy? According to some, yes. There's one important thing to keep in mind, however. She was also ground-breaking.

Society is not so much afraid of full-blown chemically-imbalanced madness as it is of non-conformity. To not conform to societal norms is to insult the painstaking codes of conduct enshrined by our ancestors so that we could live in civilization. The dilemma has always been that a civilization can never move forward until some nut-job flouts one or two of its standards, with the ultimate aim of toppling them. This scares the bejeezus out of people, particularly those who may have spent their lives upholding such precarious tenets. Thus when Socrates starts advising the youth of Athens to question everything around them, the citizens get a bit squirrelly. When Hamlet expresses his rampant disgust at the world and humanity, Elizabethans pop a collective garter. When the young Holden Caulfield denounces his clean-cut compatriots as phonies and whores, post-war America recoils.   5

You would think by now that we would see the need for this kind of crazy, after centuries of conformity and blind obedience leading us over cliffs. Yet even today, we dare not step out of line. Try not answering your phone for an afternoon.   6

UNDERSTANDING DETAILS

1. Describe the kind of town where Coady grew up.
2. In her essay Coady cites several examples of people who might have been considered crazy. Who are these people? Why has she chosen these particular examples?
3. Why does Coady not answer her phone? What conclusion does this lead people to draw about her?

ANALYZING MEANING

1. Why are people afraid of nonconformity? Compare and contrast the reaction of adults and adolescents to nonconformist behaviour.

2. In paragraph 2 Coady contrasts covert bigotry and tolerance. Explain the difference between the two.
3. This essay appeared as an advertisement in the *Globe and Mail* for Chapters bookstore. Why would a bookstore pay for a full-page ad of this type in a national newspaper? Why do you think this topic was chosen for this audience? Explain where you think Coady would position herself on the spectrum of conformity/nonconformity.

DISCOVERING RHETORICAL STRATEGIES

1. Where in this essay do you find Coady's purpose most clearly stated? How does the organization of the major examples in this essay demonstrate the author's thesis statement?
2. Coady makes some careful language choices in this essay. Explain the effectiveness of her introduction of the elementary school teacher (paragraph 1). Why has Coady alternated between fairly sophisticated vocabulary (e.g., "To not conform to societal norms is to insult the painstaking codes of conduct enshrined by our ancestors so that we could live in civilization." paragraph 5) and very informal word choices (e.g., "nut-job," "bejeezus," "squir-relly," and "pop a collective garter" in paragraph 5)?
3. Although the author's dominant rhetorical method is the use of example, what other strategies has Coady used to organize her information? Give examples of these strategies.

MAKING CONNECTIONS

1. Stephen King ("Why We Crave Horror Movies"), like Lynn Coady, explores the division between the emotions that society accepts and fosters and those that are viewed as unacceptable or indicative of insanity. How do the views of these two writers compare? How would King characterize Coady's anti-social behaviour?
2. Lynn Coady was the 1998 recipient of the Canadian Authors Association's Air Canada award for the most promising writer under 30. This award was won in previous years by Steven Heighton ("Elegy in Stone") and Evelyn Lau ("I Sing the Song of My Condo"). Choose one of these essays and identify any similarities between their writing and Coady's that may have made the Canadian Authors Association choose them as recipients of this award.

IDEAS FOR DISCUSSION/WRITING

Preparing to Write

Write freely about a particular person who is or was considered a genius. What is his or her special area of expertise? What makes this person so remarkable? What do you most admire about this person? Is this person a nonconformist in any way? Is this behaviour considered an asset or a liability?

Choosing a Topic

1. Write an essay about one area of life in which nonconformity is applauded. Is this always the case or are there specific conditions that make this nonconformity positive?
2. Choose a particular award and nominate your candidate. You might focus on an award in your school or community; an industry award such as the Juno Awards for Canadian music or the Academy Awards for movies; or an international organization award such as the Nobel Prize for Literature, Peace, or Science. Select the individual who you believe is the most deserving recipient and write your nomination piece, giving the selection committee plenty of specific examples that set your candidate apart from the other contenders and demonstrate why he or she is the obvious choice.
3. Are all geniuses or heroes a little eccentric? What makes anyone unique or special? Are we all a little odd? Are our odd qualities or apparent weaknesses sometimes assets? Using examples drawn from your own experience, write a character portrait of someone who seems unique to you.

Sharon Butala

THE MYTH: THE PRAIRIES ARE FLAT

Sharon Butala's name is familiar to many Canadians, as it has appeared on both the fiction and non-fiction best-seller lists during her writing career. Butala (1940–) is an award-winning author who writes, as in this selection, about life on and around the Saskatchewan ranch where she has lived for over two decades.

After teaching at the University of Saskatchewan, Butala began her career as a writer when she was 38 years old. Since then she has published novels, short stories, plays, magazine and newspaper essays and articles, and works of non-fiction, including *Perfection of the Morning* (1994), which was nominated for the Governor General's award for non-fiction, and *Wild Stone Heart.*

Preparing to Read

In this essay, first published in *En Route*, Air Canada's inflight magazine, Sharon Butala presents an effective argument against a common perception about the region of the country in which she resides. Before you read "The Myth: The Prairies Are Flat," think about the Prairies. What provinces fall within the Prairies? What image do you have of the Prairies? Where does that image come from? Have you seen the Prairies? If so, how would you describe the terrain? Geographically, is it consistent or varied? Is the prairie landscape appealing? Why or why not?

■_____■

Yesterday I relaxed as I set the car on cruise and leaned back to   1
enjoy the scenery along the 145-kilometre stretch between Rosetown and Swift Current, my favourite part of the trip from Saskatoon to my home in southwest Saskatchewan. I like the way the land rolls, rising and falling and rising again, spreading out around me for miles until it meets the far-off horizon.

There is a pleasant scarcity of people as I travel between   2
small, half-deserted villages through an expansive landscape uncluttered by forests, rushing streams, waterfalls or mountains. There's no denying that wide-openness takes getting used to, as the first settlers often reported to their less adventurous relatives back in Europe. But contrary to popular belief, that soul-stirring spaciousness is far from being a boring stretch of flatness.

In school I learned that the word *prairie* refers to a plain—a   3
flat area—while *Prairies* is an abbreviation for the Prairie provinces, Alberta, Saskatchewan and Manitoba, which are flat. I was baffled by this because I was born and spent my earliest years among the trees, lakes and rivers in the immense northern bush country of east-central Saskatchewan, none of which is flat. And, like most everyone, I learned at school that Alberta is defined by its Rocky Mountains. I was 20 before I saw the Regina Plains, a glacial lake bed that is as flat as flat ever gets. My

understandably astonished reaction was, "Oh, so this is what the teachers meant when they said the Prairies are flat."

When I met a rancher from Saskatchewan's south-west, who 4 I later married, I'd never been south of the Trans-Canada Highway other than around Regina. Since the Trans-Canada runs through the flattest land in western Canada, I remember asking my husband-to-be a little nervously before my first visit to his ranch, "Is it flat?"

Not at all. I was amazed to discover a vast, wide-open 5 country of grassy, high, rolling hills. On unbearably hot Sundays in July, we would go with most of our neighbours up to the Cypress Hills to revel in the coolness of the 1,400-metre altitude. "Didn't you know," my husband asked in surprise, "that the Cypress Hills is the highest point in Canada between the Rockies and Labrador?"

On other occasions, we went to the Great Sand Hills, an area 6 of sand dunes covering 3,400 square kilometres. But you won't find these either, unless you leave the Trans-Canada Highway. No wonder many Canadians believe that the vast area from Ontario to the Rockies, from the 49th parallel to the Arctic, is as flat as a billiard table.

Both my parents were raised on Prairie farms and since 7 agricultural equipment couldn't negotiate steep hills or fill in and level low, boggy areas back then, they spent their first 20 years on flat land. This included the horrendous Dust Bowl of the 1930s when the rest of the country was inundated with images of massive dust clouds sweeping across expanses of the flattest land where farms once flourished. And because these places were the worst afflicted, they got all the press. The fact is that forests grow over half of Manitoba and Alberta and a third of Saskatchewan, and lakes cover one-fifth of Manitoba.

Literature is also to blame. W.O. Mitchell's *Who Has Seen the* 8 *Wind*, published in 1947 and one of Canada's great novels, remains the most widely read book to come out of Saskatchewan. And it's set—guess where—on the Regina Plains. That story continues to perpetuate the myth of flatness for thousands who've never seen the Prairies.

Since the Dust Bowl era and the publication of *Who Has Seen* 9 *the Wind,* there have been countless more books about the Prairies, with full-colour cover photos of the flattest land possible and a sky that fills three-quarters of the page—as if the Prairie provinces offer no other landscapes. No graphic artist would think of putting Nistowiak Falls on the cover of a book called *Saskatchewan*, nor a picture of Lake Winnipeg to identify Manitoba.

Yesterday, as I sped across the wide landscape toward the distant, mirage-ridden horizon, watching the clouds through my windshield as they shifted and changed and sent shadows chasing each other across the sweep of hills and fields, I felt fully free. And I pitied all those "flat and boring" philosophers who fail to see, whether level as a tabletop or not, the exquisite and singular beauty of the Prairies.   10

UNDERSTANDING DETAILS

1. What is the difference between "prairie" and "the Prairies"? Why is Butala confused about the definition of "the Prairies"?
2. What or who has perpetrated the myth that the Prairies are flat?
3. According to Butala, what is the truth about the Prairies?

ANALYZING MEANING

1. Butala uses the term "soul-stirring spaciousness" to describe the terrain in her region of the country. What does she mean by this phrase?
2. What is Butala's purpose in writing this essay? Given the original source of publication, who do you think is her intended audience?
3. Why do myths get created and perpetuated? What role do they play in helping people deal with the world in which they live?

DISCOVERING RHETORICAL STRATEGIES

1. Butala has used multiple examples to make her point about the myth that the Prairies are flat. How has she selected these examples? Which do you find most effective? Why?
2. The language Butala uses is particularly descriptive and incorporates metaphors and similes. Identify at least four examples of figures of speech in Butala's essay.
3. Consider Butala's perspective on this subject. What biographical details give her argument credibility?

MAKING CONNECTIONS

1. Butala writes with a passion about the land where she lives. How does her attitude toward her subject compare to that of Lesley Choyce ("Thin Edge of the Wedge") or Tomson Highway ("What a Certain Visionary Once Said")?

2. Malcolm Gladwell ("Is the Belgian Coca-Cola Hysteria the Real Thing?") explains one way in which ideas become contagious and spread, even though they may have no basis in fact. In what way is the mass hysteria that Gladwell describes similar to the way in which the myth of the flat Prairies has been spread?

3. Sharon Butala writes to counter a myth about a landscape. In what ways is her purpose similar to that of Drew Hayden Taylor ("Pretty Like a White Boy") or Cecil Foster ("Why Blacks Get Mad")?

IDEAS FOR DISCUSSION/WRITING

Preparing to Write

What is a myth? Write freely about myths and the role that they play in a community or society. How are myths created? What is the appeal of myth? What sustains myths? How are myths debunked? Can myths do harm if they are misrepresenting something? How are contemporary myths different from traditional myths? What do they have in common?

Choosing a Topic

1. Think of a popular myth about the area of the country where you live. Write an essay for the readers of *En Route* magazine in which you debunk that myth, supporting your point with specific illustrative examples.

2. Create a myth about a place with which you are familiar. Select specific examples to support your claim and to make it credible.

3. Urban myths and legends are frequently transmitted over the Internet. Write an essay in which you explain the reason for the prevalence of urban myths and legends in an online environment. Use specific examples to illustrate your points.

Cecil Foster

■ □ ■

WHY BLACKS GET MAD

Cecil Foster (1954–) is a journalist and novelist who lives in Toronto with his wife and two sons. Foster immigrated to Canada in 1979 from Barbados. He has worked in a variety of journalistic positions both in Barbados and in Canada. The former editor of *Contrast,* a Toronto black community newspaper, Foster has also worked as a senior editor at *The Financial Post,* the host of a talk show on CFRB radio, special advisor to Ontario's Progressive Conservative minister of culture, and a teacher of journalism at Ryerson University and Humber College. Foster's first novel, *No Man in the House,* was published in 1991 and was written for his children to help them understand one aspect of the experience of immigration. It was followed in 1995 by *Sleep on Beloved,* the award-winning *A Place Called Heaven* (1996), *Slammin' Tar* (1998), a memoir entitled *Island Wings* (1998), and most recently, *Dry Bone Memories* (2001). Foster can also be heard occasionally on CBC Radio.

Preparing to Read

In this article from *Chatelaine* magazine, Foster examines the problem of racism in Canada. Before reading Foster's views, think about racism. What is racism? What distinguishes racism from other forms of discrimination? Have you ever been subjected to racism? Do you consider yourself racist? What examples of racism have you observed in Canada? What causes racism? How can racism be overcome or eliminated?

■ ━━━━━━━━━━━━━━━━━━━━━━━━━━━━━━━━━━━━━━━ ■

I felt totally helpless the night of May 4, as I sat in front of my television set watching Toronto's Yonge Street reduced to skirmishes between the police and angry, alienated young people—many of them black.

Only a few nights earlier, my wife, Glenys, and I had been glued to the set while youths across the United States torched sections of Los Angeles, Atlanta and New York. The Rodney King verdict, which exonerated L.A.'s finest in a monstrous beating of a black man, had triggered the worst outbreak of violence since the Watts riots of 1965.

Now, it was Toronto's turn, and those of us in the black   3
community who had predicted such an eruption for years could
only agonize about what we were witnessing. Glenys and I
thought about our two sons, Munyonzwe, 10, and Michello, 9,
sleeping upstairs. Would they feel compelled to take to the streets
in another six or seven years?

This clash between black and white was particularly poignant   4
for middle-class blacks like Glenys and me. In our late 30s, with
a fairly comfortable home and jobs—I am a senior editor at *The
Financial Post* and a novelist, Glenys owns a Pizza Pizza franchise
in Toronto—we may be said to have achieved many of the
dreams we brought with us from Barbados in the '70s. But when
the rampage started, we understood its roots as no white viewer
could, because we too know the bitterness and frustration blacks
experience every day in white society.

We didn't expect it to be this way. When I was growing up   5
in Barbados, I believed that, if I got myself an education, I would
achieve success as a writer. Later on, I believed that, if I
immigrated to Canada and did well, I would find acceptance in
a multicultural society.

As it turned out, I did work hard, did achieve success, but   6
acceptance is another matter. The worst thing about racism in
Canada is that it is not open but subtle. I can't remember anybody
ever calling me nigger and yet I feel the pain of racism in the way
people talk to me, handle me or just simply assume I am up to
no good. It's what blacks call white stereotypical expectations.

I first encountered this stereotyping when I visited Canada in   7
1976, the year of the Montreal Olympics. I was still living in the
West Indies and preparing to study mass communications at the
Jamaican campus of the University of the West Indies on a
scholarship later that year. I had saved every penny for almost
two years to get to Montreal, see the Olympics and spend three
weeks with my girlfriend, Glenys, also from Barbados.

I arrived at Mirabel airport with all my papers in order but,   8
while white passengers were processed quickly, I was held back
for questioning. Would I be looking for a job? Would I take a
job—even part-time—if offered?

I had been warned to expect this by Barbadians who had   9
visited Canada earlier. The immigration officer, they told me,
would automatically assume I planned to be an illegal immigrant.

Three years later, in 1979, aged 24, I did immigrate—legally—   10
and joined Glenys, whom I had known since high school. She

had taken the gamble in 1975 of coming to Montreal to study secretarial science at the then Sir George Williams University. We were planning to marry and we chose Toronto as our future home, lured by the promise of economic improvement and of raising our kids in an environment that would allow them to develop to the best of their ability.

Finding a job was a problem at first. I remember being at a   11
Friday night dominoes session at a friend's house when the question of a job came up. I said my only skill was reporting. "Reporting!" a friend echoed. "Look at that television and tell me what you see." There was a Stanley Cup game on the screen. "That is Canada there. All white. If you see a black face, it must be a Buffalo station."

I was living in my brother Errol's apartment at this time. To   12
cover my living expenses, I became a bad telephone salesman for Grolier at night, hawking encyclopedias, and by day editing *Contrast*, the now-defunct black newspaper. I also started university courses at York, eventually completing two B.A. degrees in administrative studies and economics.

One day, as I was walking to a West Indian store to buy some   13
week-old Barbadian newspapers, a young white policeman pulled up on a motorcycle. An interrogation began: Who was I? Did I have any identification? Was I a legal immigrant in the country? I was frightened. My voice broke when I answered. No, I didn't have any I.D. I had neglected my brother's advice— never go out without a passport. And I became very conscious of the gun on this policeman's hip. In Barbados, policemen don't carry guns.

Finally, he said I could go; he was on the lookout for someone   14
just like me. My friends laughed at this when I told them. "He didn't mistake you. He just wanted to stop you."

During those early days, I left applications and résumés at   15
every Toronto media house. My hopes rose when I learned there was an opening at The Canadian Press news agency. Believing my experience at Reuters and the Caribbean News Agency would be an asset, I asked for the editor concerned. The man said he would be delighted to chat with me. He told me his desk was right across from the elevator, so he would see me when I got off. I should bring my clippings.

The conversation sounded so promising, but when I got off   16
the elevator, the man at the nearest desk checked his watch and frowned. I waited. Eventually, he said, "Are you Mr. Foster?" He

apologized for promising me an interview. He should have known it was going to be a busy day and he wouldn't have time for a longish chat. In any case, the opening he had in mind was filled, but he'd keep me in mind. He never looked at my clippings.

But I did get a job in late 1979 at *The Toronto Star*. I now had   17
a regular paycheque, but this did not save me from stereotyping. One day, I went to interview the head of a volunteer group for some charity. She had told me to come to the back of her affluent home in North Toronto, as she was having renovations made to the front. As I walked around piles of gravel and sand, I heard a woman shout angrily from the doorway, "So now you decide to show up? Do you know how long I've been waiting for you?"

"Didn't we agree on 10 o'clock?"   18

"Who are you?"   19

"The reporter from *The Star*."   20

"Oh, my God," she said. In spite of my jacket and briefcase,   21
one glance had been enough for her to classify me as a construction worker. It was not the only time someone has assumed that a reporter with an anglicized name at a major newspaper must be white. This is one reason we gave our sons African first names.

In 1980, Glenys and I were married and went to live in the St.   22
James Town apartment complex in downtown Toronto. It was our first home together. I was working steadily and attending college at night, she was working as a secretarial clerk in a freight-forwarding company. Life was looking better, and we started to plan for our own family. The next year, Glenys became pregnant with our first son.

But however positive we felt about our new life, the racist   23
undercurrent remained. By this time, I was working for *The Globe and Mail*'s *Report on Business*. I was assigned to interview the executive director of some business association. As I waited in his outer office, I could see the executive through the glass. He was on the phone, and his assistant put a note on his desk, informing him of my arrival. The man got off the phone, took up some papers, looked at his watch and did some more work. Then, he made more phone calls. One of them, I learned later, was to my office, asking why I had not arrived. Finally, I asked the assistant to find out when he would see me.

The executive came out, very apologetic. He had not read   24
the note, he said, had assumed I was someone seeing his assistant. Now, it was too late for the interview.

Blacks put up with such incidents in the name of our   25
paycheques, but they frustrate and anger us.

In 1983, our second son, Michello, was born, and over the   26
next several years, Glenys and I worked hard to build the kind of
life we'd dreamed about in Barbados. As well as working as a
reporter by day and studying by night, I started writing fiction,
as a means of escape. *No Man in the House,* my first novel, was
published in Canada in 1991 and was well received. This fall, it
is being released in the U.S.

In 1989, we were able to take out a mortgage on a small house   27
in the suburbs. At about that time, Glenys realized a dream she
had had from the time when she used to help her brother with his
grocery store in Barbados. She had always wanted to run her
own business and, when the chance came to buy into a Pizza
Pizza franchise, she took the plunge.

She enjoys the work, but stereotyping is routine. White   28
customers often bypass her to speak to white employees. Once,
two yuppies saw her sweeping up and offered her a job cleaning
their homes.

"I don't try to explain anymore," Glenys says. "Being black   29
and a woman, they just don't expect me to be the owner."

Because Glenys and I are adults, we can laugh about these   30
incidents, but they are not funny when they affect our kids. Four
years ago, our son Michello, then 5, faced his first racist incident.

We knew something was up when he ran home from school   31
and burrowed under his brother's bedcover. A classmate had
not invited him to her birthday party. Her parents didn't like
blacks, she told him. My son believed that, if he slept in his
brother's bed under his cover, he would become like him—fairer-
skinned—and get the invitation.

We were devastated. What could we tell him? That it   32
wouldn't happen again? We knew it would. But why should a kid
so young be robbed of his innocence?

He's older now, and racist taunts in the schoolyard are   33
common. He tries to give as good as he gets, but "How many
times can I call them 'vanilla'?" he asks us. "They have so many
names for me: 'brown cow,' 'peanut butter,' 'chocolate cookie.'"

We encourage him to be tolerant but as peer pressure grows,   34
he may try his own solutions. In fact, at about the time of the
Yonge Street incidents, the principal sent home a note saying
my son had hit someone in the mouth.

Anger, like racism, starts young. And it builds up, fueled by   35
successive slights. "You go into work on Monday morning and

you hear everybody in the office talking about the party, the picnic over the weekend or the invitations to the cottage, and you say to yourself, why wasn't I invited?" says my friend Lloyd, a midmanagement worker at a trust company. It should surprise no one when rage erupts, as it did recently in Toronto, Montreal and Halifax. Blacks have felt for too long that they are not invited to the party.

The riots last May told us just how desperate young blacks 36 feel about their prospects. But if the violence jolted the whites, there was also a shock in store for middle-class blacks. We discovered that these youths believe that middle-class blacks are as big a problem as white supremacists.

Pioneer blacks who have become doctors, chartered 37 accountants, journalists, bank managers, even elected politicians are perceived not as role models but as sellouts, Uncle Toms, house niggers, Oreos (black outside, white within). We are accused of failing to confront racism, of swallowing our anger and being too careful not to rock the boat.

Blacks have a term for this: white burnout. It comes when 38 you give up trying to fight the system. Austin Clarke, an outstanding novelist, also from Barbados, who used to speak out vehemently, now says, "I had two daughters at The Bishop Strachan School [an expensive private school]. I found it easier to pay the fees working inside the system than outside."

There is also the fear that, if we do fight the system, we 39 endanger our jobs.

As middle-class blacks watch violence erupt, a kind of 40 paralysis sets in. We know we must support the kids on the streets and help them build a secure future—but we also know that because of the deep resentment they feel toward us we aren't any damn use at this point.

So, whites who expect "role model" blacks to act as 41 intermediaries between them and militant youths should look elsewhere. Role model blacks are too busy patching things up with their fellow blacks.

As Austin Clarke told me the day after the riots, "I remember, 42 back in the '60s, saying the next generation of blacks is not going to stand for this shit. The next generation has now grown up."

And what the new generation sees is discouraging. Look at 43 Toronto blacks: our unemployment rate is high, and 87 percent make less than $25,000 annually. Single parent homes are three times more common among black families, and 25 percent of these families rely on government for all income.

The result is hopelessness, and the result of that has now   44
become clear to everyone: I haven't met any black community
leader who doesn't anticipate more violence. If our kids'
frustrated rage is to be replaced by a new sense of hope, we will
need to reform the place where most of their problems have their
roots—the educational system. At present, 60 percent of black
youths in Toronto do not finish high school. But kids must remain
in school if they are to get the tools to prepare themselves for
better jobs and escape the poverty cycle. A college degree will
go a long way toward instilling confidence in young people,
even when facing the most bigoted employer. An educated kid
knows about antidiscrimination laws and regulations and will
use them to battle overt racism. More than that, he or she will
have choices in employment.

Meanwhile, governments must act fast to open up institutions   45
to blacks. This means continuing to put pressure on government
agencies such as the police and the judicial system who deal
daily with blacks. Professions such as law and medicine must
reexamine their entry criteria to rid them of racial biases.

But perhaps the best thing the wider society can do is simply   46
to let blacks feel that we belong, that there's a place for us in the
schools, in politics, the arts and, most importantly, in the work
force. Simply put, that we are Canadians and equal. Society has
brought pressure to bear on smoking, drunk driving and sexism
in the workplace. Now, it must make people equally
uncomfortable about stereotyping blacks.

At the same time, there is a lot of work to be done by the black   47
community. Not only must we create the peer pressure to make our
kids want to stay in school, but more adults must be willing to
sacrifice time, effort and even money to guide them. We have to
teach them how to live in a racist society and, hard as it is, we
cannot afford to appear to be losing hope. We must encourage
youths to dream, to believe they can bring about changes.

And it must be done fast. Already, too many blacks believe   48
they will always be on the outside looking in. Too many blacks
feel betrayed by Canadian schools, churches, human-rights
commissions, law courts and police. And too many blacks already
believe this society isn't worth maintaining and are willing to
try to destroy it.

The prospects are that bleak.   49

UNDERSTANDING DETAILS

1. In what aspects of his life has Foster experienced racism?
2. Why did Foster and his wife, Glenys, give their sons African names?
3. What does Foster believe governments should do to overcome racism? What about professions? Wider society? The black community?

ANALYZING MEANING

1. Why did Foster immigrate to Canada? Have his expectations been fulfilled? Explain.
2. "Anger, like racism, starts young" (paragraph 35). Explain this statement with specific examples you have experienced or observed.
3. Define the following terms and give specific examples to help differentiate between them: discrimination, racism, stereotyping.

DISCOVERING RHETORICAL STRATEGIES

1. How has Foster organized his examples? Is this pattern effective? Why or why not?
2. Describe the tone that Foster creates in this article. How does he establish this tone? Is this tone appropriate for his intended audience?
3. Foster's examples come from his own experience. What effect does this have on the readers?

MAKING CONNECTIONS

1. Allen Abel finishes his essay ("A Home at the End of the Journey") with the comment, "I'm thinking: Maybe this place can work." How do you think Foster would respond to Abel's story of his citizenship ceremony and his concluding comment about Canada?
2. Drew Hayden Taylor ("Pretty Like a White Boy") and Cecil Foster both write about the difficulties of being judged on their appearance and "not looking the part" but their essays have very different tones. While Taylor uses humour, Foster is very serious. Which approach do you find more effective? Explain why.

3. Foster uses personal experience to make his point about discrimination. Compare and contrast this strategy to that chosen by Judy Rebick in "The Culture of Overwork."

IDEAS FOR DISCUSSION/WRITING

Preparing to Write

Write freely about expectations. What expectations do you have for your life? What things do you hope to achieve? What goals have you set? To what degree are your expectations shaped by others in your family, your peer group, or your community? How is your behaviour influenced by the expectations of those around you?

Choosing a Topic

1. "Overall, Canada is a good country in which to live." Write an essay in which you support this statement with plenty of specific examples.
2. Foster discusses the problem of feeling caught in the middle that many middle-class blacks face in Canada. Write an essay in which you describe an experience of feeling "caught in the middle." Use specific, detailed examples to convey your position clearly.
3. Write an essay for a college- or university-educated audience in which you claim that your school or your community is either more racist or less racist than it used to be. Specific examples will help you to build a convincing argument.

Mark Kingwell

NOT AVAILABLE IN STORES

In a column in the *Toronto Star*, Jim Coyne adamantly declares that he hates Kingwell and calls Kingwell "the purple loosestrife of pop-cult pundits." It is hardly a flattering description, but Coyne's point is that Kingwell seems to be everywhere, and that has created some resentment.

Douglas Bell, however, goes further in examining the reasons for Kingwell's huge appeal. Kingwell views his nonacademic writing as serious but accessible and Michael Ignatieff points out that Kingwell is "... interesting because he seems to know things about popular culture while also knowing something about Aristotle [and] ... he has a sense of humour." For a variety of reasons Kingwell is being called on from all sides for comments, reactions, ideas, and commentary on topics ranging from the nature of happiness to the appeal of Melrose Place, from Princess Diana's death to the millennium.

Kingwell was born in Toronto in 1963 and grew up primarily in Winnipeg, southwestern Ontario, and Prince Edward Island. He graduated from the University of Toronto with a B.A., went to the University of Edinburgh for a Master's degree in literature and philosophy, and then earned a Ph.D. in philosophy at Yale. Since his graduation from Yale, Kingwell has taught at Yale, York University, and the University of Toronto, where he was made Assistant Professor of Philosophy in 1993. Kingwell's academic writing has been published in several journals including the *Journal of Philosophy*, the *Journal of Speculative Philosophy*, *International Philosophical Quarterly*, *Ethics*, and the *Yale Journal of Law and the Humanities*. In addition he has been television columnist for *Saturday Night*, the ideas columnist for the *University of Toronto Magazine*, and a contributing editor to *Descant*, *Shift*, and *Gravitas*. His writing can also be found in a variety of other periodicals including *Adbusters*, the *Globe and Mail*, the *Toronto Star*, the *National Post*, *Queen's Quarterly*, and *Harper's*. Kingwell has also published books: *A Civil Tongue: Justice, Dialogue, and the Politics of Pluralism* (1995), *Dreams of Millennium: Report from a Culture on the Brink* (1996), *Better Living: In Pursuit of Happiness from Plato to Prozac* (1998), *Marginalia: A Cultural Reader* (1999), and *The World We Want: Virtue, Vice, and the Good Citizen* (2000). Kingwell also speaks frequently on television and radio on cultural and political issues.

Preparing to Read

"Not Available in Stores" is an essay that first appeared as a column in *Saturday Night* magazine in 1998. Kingwell, as a well-known popular culture commentator, here discusses the appeal and success of infomercials as well as the trends that are changing the genre of infomercials. Before reading Kingwell's essay, think about television advertising. Do you sit and watch television commercials or do you use them as a chance to get a snack or check what is on on other channels? What is your favourite television commercial? Your least favourite? Do you ever make a point of watching infomercials?

It begins like one of those cosy Women's Television Network 1 chat shows, complete with bad lighting, fuzzy lenses, and warm looks. The host is an attractive, soft-spoken woman of a certain age. She purrs at the camera. She and her guests are here to tell you about what she chucklingly calls "Hollywood's breast-kept secret." Yes, it's true: Accents, the Plasticine bust enhancers favoured by movie stars and models alike, are now available to you, the lowly viewer. No surgery. No hideous contraptions. You don't even have to leave home to get them.

And what a difference they make! Soon a line-up of gorgeous 2 but slightly flat-chested women are being transformed before your eyes into jiggly supermodels or "Baywatch" lifeguards. These flesh-coloured slabs of silicone gel that "fit into any underwire bra" and "within minutes warm to your natural body temperature" can actually be used in the swimming pool! At the end of the half-hour, the ever-smiling host and her guests admit that *they are all wearing Accents themselves*! Well, shut my mouth.

"Accents" is only the most outrageous of the current crop 3 of television infomercials: those over-the-top attempts to hawk make-up, cleaning products, and ab-flexers under the guise of a genial talk show ("Kathie Lee Talks") or breathless science programme ("Amazing Discoveries!"). Turn on your television late at night or on a weekend afternoon—even, these days, at midmorning—and the good-natured hosts, a has-been actress (Ali McGraw) or never-was celeb (Ed McMahon), are touting cosmetics or miracle car wax as if they are doing us a public service. Information + commercial = infomercial. Line up the word, and the phenomenon, next to those long advertising features in newspapers and magazines, often slyly imitating the publication's actual typeface and design, known as "advertorials."

Patently absurd, maybe, but if emerging trends continue, 4 infomercials will not remain what they have been so far: a marginal and benign, if irritating, television presence. With the loosening of CRTC regulations, the explosion of cable channels, and the crude economics that can make them more lucrative than regular programming for network affiliates, infomercials are showing up in more and more places on the TV schedule, elbowing aside such popular quality fare as Sunday-afternoon sports, syndicated comedies, and old movies. They are also getting more and more sophisticated, as big-name companies with mainstream products—Ford Motor Co., Procter & Gamble, Apple Canada—enter the infomercial market.

And if, as enthusiasts in the business press insist, this is the 5 future of TV advertising, then that is very bad news indeed for television and its viewers. But not because there is anything inherently wrong with infomercials, at least not as they have existed until now. The delicate pact between ads and shows that makes television possible has always been able to withstand the amateurish, ad-becomes-show genre they represent. But when infomercials are everywhere, and especially when they go high market, that pact is in danger of being overturned, and the thin line between entertainment and pitch may be erased for good.

Blame Ron Popeil. Blame him a lot, and at length. Blame him   6 until his smiling, trout-like face is imprinted on your mind as the fount of all evil. Because Popeil is the one who started the sort of television hard sell that reaches its tacky terminus in today's infomercials. Founder of Ronco, restless inventor of the Popeil Pocket Fisherman, the Patti-Stacker, and other cheesy "labour-saving" devices too numerous to mention, Popeil is the guy who all but invented television shopping. In the 1970s he discovered that people got very excited, and very willing to spend, at the thought that you need never leave your couch to have the entire Ronco or K-Tel product line delivered to your home. His favourite author was the guy who came up with *Call this toll-free number now*.

Popeil has recently come out from behind the camera to   7 appear in his own convection-oven and pasta-machine infomercials. Looking like an also-ran from a professional tanning competition, he slops flour and water into slowly spinning machines that disgorge brightly coloured goo for thirty minutes. Your own fresh pasta every night! Operators are standing by!

It isn't hard to decipher what makes these and other low-   8 end infomercials so successful. Potential buyers are never made to feel bad, even as their baser desires are being pandered to. For example, we are told at least four times that Accents "are shipped confidentially" and arrive at your door in (get this) "a beautiful designer chest that will look great on your vanity." The Accents people even muster expert opinion, the *sine qua non* of the TV hard sell. In this case, it's a panel of Hollywood make-up artists and photographers. "I tried everything," says one. "Foam pads, wires, push-up bras, duct tape. Nothing works like Accents." (Duct tape?)

The same forms of reassurance are visible on all the successful   9 infomercials now airing, from The Stimulator to the Ab-Roller Plus. The Stimulator—a small syringe-like device that is supposed to kill pain by means of mild electric shock, a sort of mini stun gun—also produces what has to be the funniest infomercial moment of all time. Evel Knievel, the all-but-forgotten daredevil of the 1970s, shares, over footage of his famous Caesars Palace motorcycle crash, his belief in the pain-relieving properties of The Stimulator. "If it hepped me," Knievel twangs, "it can hep you." Now that's expert opinion.

This is so silly that it is easy to imagine a kind of self-parody   10 operating, of the sort in the hilarious "Money Show" spots on CBC's "This Hour Has 22 Minutes": "Gus, I want to pay less in taxes, but I'm not sure how." "Marsha, it couldn't be easier; stop filing your returns!" But that would misread the intentions of the makers—and the attitudes of the audience, whose response to infomercials has been wholehearted. Canadians spent $100-million on infomercial products in 1995, up thirty-four per cent from 1994. One Ontario company, Iona Appliances Inc., quadrupled annual sales of its "dual-cyclonic" vacuum cleaner when it started marketing via infomercial.

In fact, the point of infomercials has so far been their lack of   11 sophistication. The niche is still dominated by the charmingly inept likes of Quality Special Products, the Canadian company responsible for such thoroughly trailer-park items as the Sweepa ("The last broom you'll ever have to buy!") and the Sophist-O-Twist hair accessory ("French braids made easy!").

Most current efforts eschew the cleverness and quality visible   12 on more traditional commercial spots in favour of the low-ball aesthetic of public-access cable. Instead of competing with shows for our attention—and therefore being pushed to find better writing, multimillion-dollar budgets, and gilt-edged directorial talent—infomercials become the shows. Yet they do so in ways so obviously half-hearted that nobody, not even the quintessential couch-potato viewer, could actually be fooled. The talk-show cover story is really nothing more than a tacit agreement between marketer and viewer that they're going to spend half an hour in each other's company, working over a deal.

And this is what many critics miss: most infomercials, as   13 they now appear, aren't really trying to dupe the viewer. They are instead the bottom-feeding equivalent of the irony observable in many regular commercials. Bargain-basement infomercials offer a simpler form of customer complicity than the crafty self-mockery and self-reference that appeals to young, kitsch-hungry viewers. Infomercials are a pure game of "let's pretend," taken straight from the carnival midway.

That's why the entry of high-end marketers into the field is   14 so alarming. Big-money companies are not content to maintain the artless façade that now surrounds infomercials. They break the carny-style spell of cheap infomercials, where we know what we see is fake, but we go along anyway, and offer instead the high production quality, narrative structure, and decent acting of actual shows.

A recent Apple Canada effort, for example, which aired last   15
year in Toronto, Calgary, and Vancouver, is set up as a saccharine half-hour sitcom about a white-bread family deciding to buy a home computer ("The Marinettis Bring Home a Computer"). It is reminiscent of "Leave It To Beaver" or "The Wonder Years," complete with Mom, Pop, Gramps, the family dog, and an annoying pre-teen narrator named TJ. Gramps buys the computer, then bets grumpy Pop that the family will use it enough to justify the expense. Soon TJ is bringing up his slumping math grades, Mom is designing greeting cards for profit, and Gramps is e-mailing fellow opera buffs. It's nauseating, but effective. Heather Hutchison, marketing communications manager for Apple Canada, explains the company's decision to enter the infomercial universe this way: "Having produced something of higher quality," she says, "there's a recognition at—I hesitate to use the word 'subconscious,' but at a lower level—that it says something about the quality of the product. The Canadian market responds well to this kind of softer sell."

We all know that television, as it now operates, is primarily   16
a vehicle for the delivery of advertising. That is, we know that if it weren't for ads, nobody would get to spend a million dollars on a single episode of an hour-long drama or employ some of the best dramatic writers and directors now working. True, this symbiosis is uneasy at best, with good shows all but free-riding on the masses of dreck that keep the advertisers happily reaching their targets. That's fine—or at least not apocalyptic. We can accept that advertising is the price we have to pay (every seven minutes) for good television.

But slick infomercials, unlike their cheapo forbears, threaten to   17
destroy this shaky covenant. Only a moron could mistake a low-end infomercial for a real show. (And only a condescending jerk could think that all people who buy Sweepas and Abdomenizers are, in fact, morons.) Up-market infomercials have a much greater potential to muddy the waters between advertising and programming. It may be that, without the cheesy aesthetics and side-show barker style, these new infomercials won't find an audience. But it's more likely that big companies with big budgets

and top advertising talent will be able to suck even non-morons into these narrative ads that masquerade as entertainment. The new corporate offerings, in other words, may actually do what Ron Popeil couldn't: strip TV of extraneous effects like quality programming so that it finally reveals its essential nature—selling things, selling things, and selling things.

    When that's true, maybe it's time to turn the damn thing off   18 for good.

UNDERSTANDING DETAILS

1. What recent trend in infomercials does Kingwell identify? Why is this happening? How does Kingwell feel about this trend?
2. Who is Ron Popeil? Why is he significant in the world of infomercials?
3. What makes traditional low-end infomercials successful?

ANALYZING MEANING

1. How does Kingwell feel about the change that is happening in the world of infomercials?
2. What is Kingwell's thesis? How is it revealed in the examples that he relates in his essay?
3. Characterize Kingwell's attitude toward traditional infomercials? How does this compare to his attitude toward the "new, slick" infomercials?

DISCOVERING RHETORICAL STRATEGIES

1. The use of examples to illustrate his point characterizes Kingwell's essay. How many examples of infomercials does Kingwell include? Which example do you find the most effective?
2. In paragraph 9, Kingwell illustrates his point about the use of "expert opinion" with a quotation from Evel Knievel. Why does Kingwell deliberately misspell words in this quotation? How does this reinforce his point about traditional infomercials?
3. Kingwell's essay finishes with a very short final paragraph. Explain how this serves as an effective conclusion to "Not Available in Stores."

MAKING CONNECTIONS

1. Jennifer Cowan ("TV Me Alone") writes about the pervasiveness of television in our society. How do you think that Cowan would respond to Kingwell's points about infomercials and the essential nature of television?
2. Mark Kingwell's sense of humour is apparent in "Not Available in Stores" although he is making some serious points. Compare Kingwell's use of humour to that of Drew Hayden Taylor ("Pretty Like a White Boy"), Dave Bidini ("Kris King Looks Terrible"), or David Suzuki ("The Right Stuff").
3. Kingwell outlines the evolution of infomercials into something quite threatening. Tony Leighton ("The New Nature") talks about the technological evolution of image manipulation and the effect that this evolution is having on our society. Evan Solomon ("The Babar Factor") discusses the changes in children's entertainment from traditional storybooks to contemporary video games. Outline the development of one other thing that has progressed from being relatively benign to threatening.

IDEAS FOR DISCUSSION/WRITING

Preparing to Write

Brainstorm or make a list of the products you've seen advertised in infomercials. What are the first words and thoughts and images that come to mind about each? Are there connections between any of these patterns of words? Why do people watch infomercials? What sustains a whole channel of infomercials (the Home Shopping Network)? Have you ever purchased anything after watching an infomercial for it? If so, what convinced you to purchase it? Were you satisfied with your purchase? Why or why not?

Choosing a Topic

1. Advertisements pervade all aspects of our lives, sometimes blatantly and other times more subtly. As advertisers continue to look for new and innovative ways to promote their products, advertisements appear in more and more unusual places including the doors of washroom stalls, computer screen savers, on people's bodies in the form of temporary tattoos, on stickers on produce in the supermarket, and in strategic product placement in movies. Write an essay in which you argue for or against three of the more unusual places you have seen ads.

2. Write a script for an infomercial for a product or a service of your choice. Decide whether you are going to follow a traditional infomercial approach or employ the more recent stylistic trends. Make sure you include specific details to make your product/service appealing.

3. Things do not always turn out to be as they initially appear. Products and services may be presented appealingly in advertisements but don't always fulfill our expectations. Write a letter to the company from which you purchased a product or service that didn't turn out to be as it originally appeared. Remember to be specific about your dissatisfaction and the course of action you expect from the vendor.

CHAPTER 4

PROCESS ANALYSIS

■ ■ ■

Explaining Step by Step

Human nature is characterized by the perpetual desire to understand and analyze the process of living well. The best-seller list is always crowded with books on how to know yourself better, how to be assertive, how to become famous, how to avoid a natural disaster, or how to be rich and happy—all explained in three easy lessons. Open almost any popular magazine, and you will find numerous articles on how to lose weight, how elections are run in this country, how to dress for success, how political rallies evolved, how to gain power, or how to hit a successful topspin backhand. People naturally gravitate toward material that tells them how something is done, how something happened, or how something works, especially if they think the information will help them improve their lives in a significant way.

Defining Process Analysis

A *process* is a procedure that follows a series of steps or stages; *analysis* involves taking a subject apart and explaining its components in order to better understand the whole. Process analysis, then, explains an action, a mechanism, or an event from beginning to end. It concentrates on either a mental or a physical operation: how to solve a chemistry problem, how to tune up your car, how the Canadian Senate is formed, how the Internet works. In fact, the explanation of the writing process, beginning on page 16 of this book, is a good case in point: It divides writing into three interrelated verbal activities and explains how they work—separately and together.

A process analysis can take one of two main forms: (1) It can give directions, thereby explaining how to do something (directive), or (2) it can give information about how something happened (informative). The first type of analysis gives directions for a task the reader may wish to attempt in the future. Examples include how to make jelly, how to lose weight, how to drive to Saskatoon, how to assemble stereo equipment, how to make money, how to use a microscope, how to knit, how to resuscitate a dying relationship, how to win friends, how to discipline your child, and how to backpack.

The second type of analysis furnishes information about what actually occurred in specific situations. Examples include how Hiroshima was bombed, how certain rock stars live, how the tax system works, how *Titanic* was filmed, how Mario Lemieux earned a place in the Hockey Hall of Fame, how gold was first discovered in the Yukon, how computers work, how a kibbutz functions, and how the Gulf War began. These subjects and others like them respond to a certain fascination we all have with mastering some processes and understanding the intricate details of others. They all provide us with opportunities to raise our own standard of living, either by helping us directly apply certain processes to our own lives, or by increasing our understanding of how our complex twentieth-century world functions.

The following student paragraph analyzes the process of constructing a garden compost pit. Written primarily for people who might wish to make such a pit, this piece is directive rather than informative. Notice in particular the amount of detail the student calls upon to explain each stage of the process and the clear transitions she uses to guide us through her analysis.

> No garden is complete without a functioning compost pit. Here's a simple, inexpensive way to make your garbage work for you! To begin with, make a pen out of hog wire or chicken wire, four feet long by eight feet wide by four feet high, splitting it down the middle with another piece of wire so that you end up with a structure that looks like a capital "E" on its side. This is a compost duplex. In the first pen, place a layer of soda ash, just sprinkled on the surface of the dirt. Then, pile an inch or so of leaves, grass clippings, or sawdust on top of the soda ash. You're now ready for the exciting part. Start throwing in all the organic refuse from your kitchen (no meat, bones, or grease, please). After the food is a foot or so deep, throw in a shovelful of steer manure, and cover the entire mess with a thin layer of

dirt. Then water it down. Continue this layering process until the pile is three to three-and-a-half feet high. Allow the pile to sit until it decomposes (from one month in warm climates to six months in colder weather). Next, take your pitchfork and start slinging the contents of pen one into pen two (which will land in reverse order, of course, with the top on the bottom and the bottom on the top). This ensures that everything will decompose evenly. Water this down and begin making a new pile in pen one. That's all there is to it! You now have a ready supply of fertilizer for your garden.

Thinking Critically by Using Process Analysis

Process analysis embodies clear, careful, step-by-step thinking that takes one of three different forms: chronological, simultaneous, or cyclical. The first follows a time sequence from "first this" to "then that." The second forces you to deal with activities or events that happen or happened at the same time, such as people quietly studying or just getting home from work when the major 1994 earthquake hit Los Angeles. And the third requires you to process information that is continuous, like the rising and setting of the sun. No other thinking pattern will force you to slow down as much as process analysis, because the process you are explaining probably won't make any sense if you leave out even the slightest detail.

Good process analysis can truly help your reader see an event in a totally new light. An observer looks at a product already assembled or at a completed event and has no way of knowing without the help of a good process analysis how it got to this final stage. Such an analysis gives the writer or speaker as well as the observer a completely new way of "seeing" the subject in question. Separating process analysis from the other rhetorical modes lets you practise this method of thinking so that you will have a better understanding of the various mental procedures going on in your head. Exercising this possibility in isolation will help you feel its range and its intricacies so that you can become more adept at using it, fully developed, in combination with other modes of thought.

1. List as many examples of each type of process (chronological, simultaneous, and cyclical) that you can think of. Share your list with the class.
2. Write out the process of tying a shoe step by step. Have another person follow your steps exactly to test how well you have analyzed this process.

3. Write a paragraph telling how *not* to do something. Practise your use of humour as a technique for creating interest in the essay by emphasizing the "wrong" way, for example, to wash a car or feed a dog.

Reading and Writing Process Analysis Essays

Your approach to a process analysis essay should be fairly straightforward. As a reader, you should be sure you understand the author's statement of purpose and then try to visualize each step as you go along. As a writer, you need to adapt the mechanics of the way you normally write to the demands of a process analysis paper, beginning with an interesting topic and a number of clearly explained ideas or stages. As usual, the intended audience determines the choice of words and the degree of detail.

How to Read a Process Analysis Essay

Preparing to Read. Preparing to read a process analysis essay is as uncomplicated as the essay itself. The title of Paul Quarrington's essay in this chapter, "Home Brew," tells us exactly what we're going to learn about. Maureen Littlejohn's phrase "You are a contract painkiller, code name ASA" describes clearly what her article will teach us about. Scanning each selection to assess the author's audience will give you an even better idea of what to expect in these essays, while the synopsis of each in the Rhetorical Table of Contents will help focus your attention on its subject.

Also important as you prepare to read these essays are the qualifications of each author to write on this subject: Has he or she performed the task, worked with the mechanism, or seen the event? Is the writer's experience firsthand? When Paul Quarrington tells us about making beer at home, is he actually writing from personal experience? Has Maureen Littlejohn actually experienced the effect of ASA on pain or fever? What is Stanley Coren's experience with dogs? How does he know about the genetic engineering of dogs? The biography preceding each essay will help you uncover this information and find out other publication details that will encourage you to focus on the material you are about to read.

Finally, before you begin reading, answer the prereading questions, and then do some brainstorming on the subject of the essay: What do you want to know about mass hysteria (Gladwell)? How much do any of us really know about how ASA works, and why might we want to know more?

Reading. When you read the essays in this chapter for the first time, record your initial reactions to them. Consider the preliminary information you have been studying in order to create a context for each author's composition: Why did Maureen Littlejohn write "You Are a Contract Painkiller"? What circumstances prompted Coren's "Dogs and Monsters"? Who do you think is Fiorito's target audience in "Breakfast in Bed"?

Also determine at this point whether the essay you are reading is *directive* (explaining how to do something) or *informative* (giving information about how something happened). This fundamental understanding of the author's intentions, along with a reading of the questions following the essay, will prepare you to approach the contents of each selection critically when you read it a second time.

Rereading. As you reread these process analysis essays, look for an overview of the process at the beginning of the essay so you know where each writer is headed. The body of each essay, then, is generally a discussion of the stages of the process.

This central portion of the essay is often organized *chronologically* (as in Quarrington's essay), with clear transitions so that readers can easily follow the writer's train of thought. Other methods of organization are *cyclical* (such as the process of genetic engineering described by Coren), describing a process that has no clear beginning or end, and *simultaneous* (such as the effects of ASA outlined in Littlejohn's essay), in which many activities occur at the same time with a clear beginning and end. Most of these essays discuss the process as a whole at some point. During this second reading, you will also benefit from discovering what rhetorical modes each writer uses to support his or her process analysis and why these rhetorical modes work effectively. Do the historic examples that Littlejohn uses add to our understanding of the process she is explaining? What do Paul Quarrington's step-by-step instructions, complete with scientific data and cause-and-effect explanations of results, add to his essay on beer-making? How do all the rhetorical modes in each essay help create a coherent whole? After reading each essay for a second time, answer the questions that follow the selection to see if you are understanding your reading material

on the literal, interpretive, and analytical levels before you take
on the discussion/writing assignments.

For an overview of the entire reading process, you might
consult the checklists on pages 15–16 of the Introduction.

How to Write a Process Analysis Essay

Prewriting. As you begin a process analysis assignment, you
first need to become as familiar as you can with the action, mechanism, or event you are going to describe. If possible, try to go
through the process yourself at least once or twice. If you can't actually carry out the procedure, going through the process mentally and taking notes is a good alternative. Then, try to read
something about the process. After all this preparation (and careful consideration of your audience and purpose), you should be
ready to brainstorm, freewrite, cluster, or use your favourite
prewriting technique (see pages 17–22 of the Introduction) in response to the prewriting questions before you start composing
your paper.

Writing. The essay should begin with an overview of the
process or event to be analyzed. This initial section should introduce the subject, divide it into a number of recognizable steps,
and describe the result once the process is complete. Your thesis
in a process essay is usually a purpose statement that clearly and
briefly explains your approach to the procedure you will discuss: "Building model airplanes can be divided into four basic
steps" or "The American courts follow three stages in prosecut-
ing a criminal case."

Next, the directive or informative essay should proceed
logically through the various stages of the process, from
beginning to end. The parts of a process usually fall nicely into
chronological order, supported by such transitions as "at first,"
"in the beginning," "next," "then," "after that," and "finally."
Some processes, however, are either simultaneous, forcing the
writer to choose a more complex logical order for the essay (such
as classification), or cyclical, requiring the writer to choose a
starting point and then explain the cycle stage by stage. Playing
the guitar, for example, involves two separate and simultaneous
components that must work together: holding the strings against
the frets with the fingers of one hand and strumming with the
other hand. In analyzing this procedure, you would probably

want to describe both parts of the process and then explain how the hands work together to produce music. An example of a cyclical process would be the changing of the seasons. To explain this concept to a reader, you would need to pick a starting point, such as spring, and describe the entire cycle, stage by stage, from that point onward.

In a process paper, you need to be especially sensitive to your intended audience, or it will not be able to follow your explanation. The amount of information, the number of examples and illustrations, and the terms to be defined all depend on the prior knowledge and background of your readers. A writer explaining to a group of amateur cooks how to prepare a soufflé would take an entirely different approach to the subject than he or she would if the audience were a group of bona fide chefs hoping to land jobs in elegant French restaurants. The professional chefs would need more sophisticated and precise explanations than their recreational counterparts, who would probably find such an approach tedious and complicated because of the extraneous details.

The last section of a process analysis paper should consider the process as a whole. If, for example, the writer is giving directions on how to build a model airplane, the essay might end with a good description or drawing of the plane. The informative essay on our legal system might offer a summary of the stages of judging and sentencing a criminal. And the essay on cooking a soufflé might finish with a photograph of the mouth-watering dish.

Rewriting. In order to revise a process analysis essay, first make sure your main purpose is apparent throughout your paper:

1. Have you written a directive or an informative essay?
2. Is your purpose statement clear?

Next, you need to determine if your paper is aimed at the proper audience:

1. Have you given your readers an overview of the process you are going to discuss?
2. Do you go through the process you are explaining step by step?
3. At the end of the essay, do you help your readers see the process as a complete entity?

The checklists on pages 26–27 will give you further guidelines for writing, revising, and proofreading.

Student Essay: Process Analysis at Work

The student essay that follows analyzes the process of using a "home permanent" kit. Notice that, once the student gives an overview of the process, she discusses the steps one at a time, being careful to follow a logical order (in this case, chronological) and to use clear transitions. Then, see how the end of the essay shows the process as a whole.

Follow the Simple Directions

Although fickle hairstylists in Paris and Hollywood decide what is currently "in," many romanticists disregard fashion and yearn for a mane of delicate tendrils. Sharing this urge but resenting the cost, I opted for a "home perm" kit. Any literate person with normal dexterity could follow illustrated directions, I reasoned, and the eight easy steps would energize my limp locks in less than two hours. "Before" and "after" photos of flawless models showed the metamorphosis one might achieve. Confidently, I assembled towels, rollers, hair clips, waving lotion, neutralizer, end papers, and a plastic cap. While shampooing, I chortled about my ingenuity and economy.

After towel-drying my hair, I applied the gooey, acidic waving lotion thoroughly. Then I wrapped an end paper around a parted section and rolled the first curl ("securely but not too tightly"). Despite the reassuring click of the fastened rollers, as I sectioned each new curl the previous one developed its own volition and slowly unrolled itself. Resolutely, I reapplied waving lotion and rewound—and rewound—each curl. Since my hair was already saturated, I regarded the next direction skeptically: "Apply waving lotion to each curl." Faithfully, however, I complied with the instructions. Ignoring the fragile state of the fastened rollers, I then feigned assurance and enclosed my entire head in a plastic cap. In forty minutes, chemical magic would occur.

Restless with anticipation, I puttered about the house; while absorbed in small chores, I felt the first few drops of lotion escape from the plastic tent. Stuffing wads of cotton around the cap's edges did not help, and the small drops soon became rivulets that left red streaks on my neck and face and splattered on the floor. (Had I overdone the waving lotion?) Ammonia fumes so permeated each room that I was soon asked to leave. Retreating to the bathroom, I opened the window and dreamed of frivolous new hairstyles.

Marginal annotations:
Purpose statement for informative process analysis

Overview

First step (chronological order)

Second step

Third step

Transition

Fourth step

Transition

Fifth step

Transition   <u>Finally, the waving time had elapsed; neutralizing was next</u>. I removed my plastic cap, carefully heeding the caution: "Do not   Sixth step disturb curlers as you rinse waving lotion from hair." With their usual impudence, however, all the curlers soon bobbed in the sink; undaunted, I continued. "This next step is critical," warned the instructions. Thinking half-hearted curls were better than no curls

Transition at all, I poured the entire bottle of neutralizer on my hair. <u>After a drippy ten-minute wait, I read the next step: "Carefully remove</u>

Seventh step <u>rollers." As this advice was superfluous, I moved anxiously to the</u> Transition <u>finale: "Rinse all solution from your hair, and enjoy your curls."</u> Eighth step

    Lifting my head from the sink and expecting visions of

Final Aphrodite, I saw instead Medusa's image in the mirror. Limp
product question-mark spirals fell over my eyes, and each "curl" ended in an explosion of steel-wool frizz. Reflecting on my ineptitude, I knew why the direction page was illustrated only with drawings. After washing a large load of ammonia-scented towels, I took two aspirin and called my hairdresser. <u>Some repair services are cheap</u> Concluding
<u>at any price.</u>   remark

Some Final Thoughts on Process Analysis

In this chapter, a single process dictates the development and organization of each of the essays. Both directional and informational methods are represented here. Notice in particular the clear purpose statements that set the focus of the essays in each case, as well as the other rhetorical modes (such as narration, comparison/contrast, and definition) that are used to help support the writers' explanations.

Process Analysis in Review

Reading Process Analysis Essays

Preparing to Read

1. What assumptions can you make from the essay's title?
2. Can you guess what the general mood of the essay is?
3. What is the essay's purpose and audience?
4. What does the synopsis in the Rhetorical Table of Contents tell you about the essay?
5. What can you learn from the author's biography?

6. Can you guess what the author's point of view toward the subject is?

7. What are your responses to the Preparing to Read questions?

Reading

1. Is the essay *directive* (explaining how to do something) or *informative* (giving information about how something happened)?

2. What general message is the author trying to convey?

3. Did you preview the questions that follow the essay?

Rereading

1. Does the author furnish an overview of the process?

2. How is the essay organized—*chronologically, cyclically,* or *simultaneously*?

3. What other rhetorical modes does the author use to support the essay's purpose?

4. What are your responses to the questions after the essay?

Writing Process Analysis Essays

Preparing to Write

1. What are your responses to the Preparing to Write questions?

2. What is your purpose?

3. Who is your audience?

4. Are you as familiar as possible with the action, mechanism, or event you are going to explain?

Writing

1. Do you provide an overview of the process at the beginning of the essay?

2. Does your first paragraph introduce your subject, divide it into recognizable steps, describe the result once the process is complete, and include a purpose statement?

3. Is your process analysis essay either *directive* or *informative*?

4. Do you proceed logically through the various steps of the process?

5. Are the essay's details organized *chronologically, simultaneously,* or *cyclically*?

6. What is your audience's background?

7. Does your essay end considering the process as a whole?

Rewriting

1. Have you written a *directive* or an *informative* essay?

2. Is your purpose statement clear?

3. Have you given your readers an overview of the process you are going to discuss?

4. Do you go through the process you are explaining step by step?

5. At the end of the essay, do you help your readers see the process as a complete entity?

Paul Quarrington

HOME BREW

Fly fisherman, beermeister, rock musician, and acclaimed young Canadian novelist: meet Paul Quarrington (1953–). Quarrington, whose brother and fellow brewer is a musician with the Toronto Symphony, grew up in suburban Toronto. Following a brief stint in academia at the University of Toronto this prolific and lively writer-to-be published his first novel, *The Service* (1978), at twenty-five. If beer is one of Quarrington's consuming interests, as he suggests, then rock music—beer's inevitable companion—has been another amusing sideline in his career. He has played bass and co-produced LPs performed with yet another Quarrington brother as part of the group Joe Hall and the Continental Drift, during the heyday of Toronto's Queen Street night culture. Quarrington's interest in rock gave him the subject of another of his best-selling novels, *Whale Music* (1989), which concerns itself with a fictionalized version of the reclusive Brian Wilson of the Beach Boys. This novel won Quarrington the Governor General's Award for fiction in 1990. His ability to make stories out of his interests produced three novels about sports: *Home Game* (1983), *King Leary* (1987), and

Hometown Heroes (1988), a collection of stories edited by Quarrington entitled *Original Six: True Stories from Hockey's Classic Era* (1996), and a work
of nonfiction, *Fishing With My Old Guy* (1995). In addition, Quarrington
has written screenplays for popular television shows *Due South, Once a
Thief,* and *Power Play.* Quarrington lives in Toronto and his latest books include *The Boy on the Back of the Turtle* (1997), a nonfiction book about travelling through the Galapagos Islands with his seven-year-old daughter and
his seventy-three-year-old father, and *The Spirit Cabinet* (1999).

Preparing to Read

Paul Quarrington's lively tribute to "Home Brew," which first appeared
in *Harrowsmith* magazine in the spring of 1992, presents this writer's
adventures with the pleasures and problems of making Canada's favourite
beverage at home. The contents of the ubiquitous brown and green bottles have been brewed by humans since the beginning of civilization. But
does this mean that making beer is an easy process? As you prepare to try
"Home Brew," think of what might motivate you to try to make "home-
made anything": Would it be your fondness for that product? Would it be
the chance to save money? Would it be the challenge of trying to better a
commercial product? Or would you be driven by curiosity about the
process of making something yourself? Could you then teach someone else
to follow your procedure successfully?

■───────────────────────────────────────■

The first thing I must explain is that my brother helped me with   1
this project. We share certain traits my brother and I, and chief
among them is a fondness, nay an *over*-fondness for beer. We have
even developed a Trivial Pursuit-type game featuring questions
about beer. Indeed, every question can be answered by bellowing, "Beer!" My brother and I take a foolish delight in ordering
drinks in the same fashion, screaming out "Beer!" at helpful bar-
tenders and waiters, deviating from this only to the extent of making it "More beer!" as the evening progresses.

At any rate, when asked by this fine journal if I would look   2
into the making of beer—home brewing—my brother stepped
into the breach (I could not stop him), and his presence shall
make itself known. For example, at one point during the
procedure, I took to ruminating aloud. "Making beer," I mused,
"is as natural as childbirth."

"True," agreed my brother, "but the child could be a   3
homicidal maniac."

By which my brother made oblique reference to the truly   4
vile bogswill that people had forced upon us in days long gone
by, bottles filled half with a dull, cloudy liquid, half with some

other-worldly sludge. It used to be that no words filled me with as much dread as "homemade beer." But I have learned much— the aforementioned bogswill was likely the doing of "the wild yeasties"—and, while learning, have tasted many exceptional beers. My brother and I are very pleased with our own batch and have spent several lovely evenings in his living room, occasionally glancing up at each other and bellowing, "Beer!"

But let us get down to basics; let us make sure we all know 5 exactly what is going on here. Beer is a beverage that is fermented from cereals and malt and flavoured with hops. From this simple statement, all else shall follow, so it is good to fix it in your mind, to repeat it inwardly a couple of times. (Or, put as a question in our game: What beverage is fermented from cereals and malt and flavoured with hops? Answer: Beer!)

The first significance arising from the statement is that beer 6 is made with cereals rather than with fruit as is, say, wine. The process of fermentation occurs when a molecule of sugar splits, creating two molecules of carbon dioxide (CO_2) and two molecules of ethyl alcohol (C_2H_5OH). Starch, such as that found in those cereals, cannot be converted into alcohol. This would be extremely bad news for us beer lovers, except for a vegetable enzyme called amylase. You see, starch is, chemically speaking, a long chain of molecules ($C_6H_{10}O_5$, et cetera, et cetera). Amylase breaks up the chain, pairs the molecules and adds a water molecule, thus creating $C_{12}H_{22}O_{11}$, which is a maltose sugar molecule that can thence undergo fermentation, praise the Lord. It is this process that is carried out at malting houses, which is why we begin our beermaking with a large can of malt extract (usually hopped malt extract) rather than with a bucketful of barley.

I will abandon the pseudoscientific tone now. It is bound to 7 go down in flames right around the time I try to throw in the scientific name for the yeast used to make lager beers, *Saccharomycescarlsbergensis*. That yeast, you see, was named for the place where it was discovered, and do not be embarrassed if you, too, failed to realize that there are all sorts of different yeasts with all sorts of fancy names—not to mention those unruly thugs and hooligans, the wild yeasties. Yeast is what does the actual work of fermentation. It is a plant organism, a living thing; and when it dies, it sinks to the bottom and forms sludge.

Malt and yeast are all you truly need to make beer, and 8 humankind has been making it for something like 8,000 years. (Q: What has humankind been making for 8,000 years? A: Beer!)

Hops did not appear on the European scene until the 12th century, and even at that time, there was resistance in the form of laws forbidding their use. Hops are the flowers of the female hop vine (an aggressive spreader, it has earned the lovely nomenclature *Humulus lupulus* and is also known as the "wolf of the willows"), and their resins and oils impart flavour of a slightly bitter nature to the beer.

There are many different kinds of hops; they all have different names (Cluster, Fuggles, Tetenang), and they come in either pellet or leaf form. It really is quite mind-boggling. That is why it is important to have a firm grip on the basics. (Q: Combine malt, hops, yeast and water, and in time, you will have what? A: Beer!) This is no more mysterious than, say, the baking of bread. Not coincidentally, the Old English *breowan* gives us both "brew" and "bread." 9

The first step in making beer at home is to leave it—your home, that is—and hie down to a specialty shop. We chose a Wine-Art/Brewers-Art store (in Toronto) because it happened to be closest, but Wine-Art/Brewers-Art stores also have a reputation for helpfulness, and many of the home brewers I spoke with steered me in that direction. And indeed, we were greeted by a friendly sort, Martin Jordan (manager), who spent a long time explaining things. The process detailed below is, in fact, Martin's Improved Method. 10

You need to acquire some basic equipment: a primary fermenter, a secondary fermenter and a siphoning hose. This should run you somewhere between $30 and $40. Allow me a moment to deal with the financial advantages of home brewing. Clearly, home brew is a lot less expensive than buying beer at the beer store. This seems to me, however, to be one of the least noble reasons for undertaking the endeavour. You will encounter people who brew because it is cheap, and they usually give themselves away by saying something like, "And the beer is just as good as the stuff you buy." 11

These people are missing the point, I think. The great thing about home brewing is that you can make some really wonderful beers, you can alter recipes to suit your individual taste and if it ends up being economical, that is a fact to be savoured rather than gloated over. Besides, it may not be all that economical: although the three items listed above are all you really need, they are not all you will end up carting out of the store. 12

You will want a hydrometer to measure specific gravity (I will 13
explain in a moment). You will want a vapour lock, and you will
want a plastic J-tube which is crooked at the bottom so that you
don't have to stand there holding the siphoning hose. You will
want a hose clamp for when you are bottling, which reminds me—
you need some bottles. And caps. And a capper. And you will
want some potassium metabisulphite crystals to cleanse and
disinfect all that stuff.

The primary fermenter is typically a large plastic pail— 14
preferably a food-grade pail, but nothing used for oils or vinegars—
with a tight-fitting lid. The secondary fermenter is typically a large
glass bottle (such as might contain a genie). These are called, for
reasons that have not been explained to my satisfaction, carboys.
They come in two sizes, 19 and 23 litres. Those are the two
quantities you make beer in, 19 and 23 litres. We are going to be
making 23 litres.

Now that you have your basic equipment, you need to 15
purchase the ingredients for the wort. The wort is the combination
of malt, grains and hops whence flows your batch of beer. My
brother and I chose to make an English-style bitter and purchased
a can of hopped malt extract with the word BITTER printed on it.
You could purchase Brown Ale, American Light, Stout, Pale Ale, et
cetera. Each can contains 1.5 kilograms of hopped malt extract,
yeast and instructions, and costs around $15. One could make a
batch of beer just by using the stuff in the can (actually, you need
some corn sugar), but Martin Jordan suggested that we also
purchase some roasted barley and bittering hops. This we did,
because he said the resulting beer would taste like Smithwick's, a
statement that had my brother and me leaping about the store like
puppies.

So now you are all loaded up, and it cost approximately $75, of 16
which perhaps $55 was a one-time investment. Therefore, for about
$20, you are going to get 23 litres of beer. (I find it hard not to get
excited.)

The first step takes place in the kitchen, where you cook up 17
the wort in a huge pot. To begin, you bring four to six litres of
water to a boil. You add the bittering hops. The hops look like
rabbit pellets, which is a bit off-putting. Martin Jordan suggested
that in the course of cooking the wort, you occasionally take a single
hop and fling it with a certain élan into the mixture. I think this is
sage advice. I doubt that a single hop affects the flavour much, but
it does help the novice brewmaster to relax.

At any rate, you let the hops boil for 15 to 20 minutes, at which   18
point you add the sugar. Let that boil for another five minutes,
then add the crushed malt grains. (Take a pinch and eat them;
you'll be surprised how good they taste.) Let that simmer for five
minutes, then add the malt extract, which you will discover is a
thick, glutinous syrup with the consistency of molasses. Return
the mixture to a low simmer.

While the wort is cooking (and whenever you are not flinging   19
hop pellets into it) is a good time to clean and disinfect your primary
fermenter—or, in my case, a good time to discover that your brother
has an obsessive-compulsive personality disorder. I counsel
thoroughness rather than monomania. For instance, if, having
disinfected your primary fermenter, you then pick it up to move it
closer to the stove, it is not necessary—although my brother found
it so—to redisinfect where the offending fingers were placed. It is
a good idea to mark the 23-litre level on the inside of the container.

Now put some cold water in that primary fermenter. (A tip   20
from Mr. Jordan: You might draw the water the day before and let
it sit overnight, which helps get rid of the chlorine taste.) You now
strain the wort into it. You stir and then add more water until you
reach the 23-litre mark. You pitch the yeast, which is less strenuous
than it sounds, adding it when the mixture is between 70 and 80
degrees F. (Warning: If it is too hot, you will kill the yeast.)

Now, ahem, allow me to get a little scholarly here. The   21
specific gravity of water is 1.000. Liquids containing sugar have
a higher specific gravity because they are denser. Alcohol is
lighter than water. Therefore, during fermentation, the specific
gravity of your brew will drop as more and more of the sugar
is converted into alcohol. Some of the malt will not convert (which
is what gives beer its taste), so although the final specific gravity
will approach 1.000 again, it will never truly arrive.

A rule of thumb is that when the specific gravity stops   22
dropping, fermentation is complete. Got it? For this reason, we
now take our hydrometer, which looks like a futuristic fishing
float, and place it in our beer-to-be. It might read, say, 1.046. The
higher the figure, the more potential alcohol, and some recipes
will even say, "At this point, your starting s.g. should be 1.048,"
in which case you would add more malt and/or sugar until that
level is attained.

All right now. Fermentation splits a molecule of sugar into   23
ethanol and carbon dioxide. The latter is gas, gas that is exuded
with a series of very satisfying mulching galoomps. So we need

to let the gas escape. But if we leave the container uncovered, guess what's going to get into it? The wild yeasties! For even though many yeasts are civilized and gentrified, there are unruly yeasts floating about in the air, little gangs of them just looking to mess up somebody's beer. To get into it and produce *off flavours*. That is Martin Jordan's way of saying the wild yeasties will make, you know, bogswill. You therefore cover your primary fermenter very securely, having purchased a lid for that purpose. You will notice that the lid has a largish hole dead centre, which seems foolish until you see that your fermentation lock's rubber stopper will plug it admirably. The fermentation lock is a twisted piece of tubing, half-filled with water, which will let out the CO_2, and vent the last gasps of expiring yeast without admitting the dreaded hordes.

You then move down to the basement, especially if you are 24 attempting to make a lager. Lager, derived from the German for "storage," cannot be properly made when the weather is too warm, so if you are doing this in the summer, you had best make an ale. Ale is fermented at higher temperatures, which causes most of the yeast to rise to the top. Ale is thus a top-fermenting brew, lager a bottom-fermenting brew. And there, at last, we know the difference between the two.

You can relax now for approximately five days. It should be 25 easy to determine whether fermentation is taking place (bubbles in the vapour lock), although our brew appeared strangely inactive. Martin Jordan suggested that the gas was probably escaping from somewhere else, perhaps from around the lid rather than through the vapour lock, and by taking a series of readings with the carefully sterilized hydrometer, we were able to determine that all was as it should be.

On day five, you siphon into the secondary fermenter. Your 26 primary fermenter will have developed a sludgy bottom layer made up of yeast corpses, and although the siphoning tube has a crook at the bottom, hopefully raising it above it all, great care should be taken not to transfer the sludge. By the way, you realize I am assuming that all of this stuff has been cleansed and sterilized. Any slip-up on the sanitation front could result in *off flavours*, so never let down your guard. (While we were making our beer, a number of bad batches were reported to Martin Jordan at his store, as if the wild germs and yeasties had gone on a citywide rampage. Beware.)

On day 15, you add the "finings," commonly isinglass, which 27
is made from the scrapings of sturgeons' swim bladders. This
makes your beer less cloudy. Don't ask how, just do it.

On day 20, you bottle. Beer's effervescence is created from 28
extra fermentation at the end of the process, so you now add a
little more corn sugar or finishing malt. You could add about
half a teaspoon of sugar per bottle, although the sensible thing to
do is add 1-1/4 cups to the 23-litre carboy. Siphon off some beer,
dissolve the sugar in it, then reintroduce it to the brew. Don't
start stirring in your carboy, lest you disturb the sludge.

My brother and I bottled in plastic litre bottles with screw-on 29
plastic caps, which I realize is cheating, but I thought it worked
wonderfully. A potential downside is that you need to drink a
litre whenever you want a beer, but my brother and I conceived
of this as *no big problem.* You might choose to bottle the standard
341-millilitre size, which you would then cap in the traditional
manner. My big tip here is to purchase a clamp for the end of
your siphoning tube, a simple device that stops the flow
momentarily as you move from bottle to bottle.

If you are still in the basement at this point, it might be an idea 30
to move your lot upstairs where it is warmer to sort of kick-start this
last bit of fermentation. Five days later, you should return your
beer to a cool place, and five days after that, you could drink one.
Which is to say, it is the earliest you should drink one, but time
will only improve your beer. Many claim it is best in three months.

Perhaps the diciest aspect of home brew comes with the 31
actual drinking. That final bit of fermentation produced bubbles,
a little more alcohol and some dead yeast cells, which are now
lying on the bottom of the bottle. When pouring the beer, it is
best to hold the bottle in front of a light so that you can view the
sludge's advent toward the neck. The trick is to avoid dead yeast
without leaving behind half a bottle of beer. And once you have
poured the beer, rinse out the bottle immediately, because as the
remaining liquid evaporates, the sludge will adhere to the inside
and render it useless as a beer receptacle.

So there you have it. The procedure is simple, virtually idiot- 32
proof—nothing can stop those yeasts from splitting up sugar
molecules—and also educational.

Q: What beverage contains pelletized wolf of the willows and 33
sturgeon swim bladder scrapings?

A: You got it. 34

UNDERSTANDING DETAILS

1. What are the constituent parts of the recipe for beer? What role does each play in making the finished beverage?
2. What living ingredient plays a vital role in the fermentation of beer? How does it work? Why might it sometimes produce "vile bogswill," or a brewed offspring which is "a homicidal maniac"?
3. Describe the preparation of wort. What must be added to wort to produce beer? What is the function of each added ingredient?

ANALYZING MEANING

1. Has Quarrington convinced you that making your own beer is "simple" and "virtually idiot-proof"? Which of his instructions seems the easiest to follow, and which the most difficult? Why?
2. With which characteristics of the author do you identify? Where do you find evidence of such in the essay? Do these aspects of his personality make him more or less credible as someone writing a real set of instructions?
3. Quarrington's essay contains several sidetrips into what he calls "the pseudoscientific tone," passages that explain the chemical aspects of beer production. Are these passages clear and understandable to you? Explain why or why not.

DISCOVERING RHETORICAL STRATEGIES

1. Although "Home Brew" is very clearly both a directive and descriptive piece of process writing, other rhetorical strategies are used. Giving details from the essay to support your answer, explain which other rhetorical forms you discover.
2. Humour in writing often deflates the importance of the speaker, or discounts the seriousness of what is said. Is this true of Paul Quarrington's use of humour? What comic concept does he use as a unifying thematic link throughout the essay?
3. In spite of the writer and his brother being portrayed to some degree as "Garth and Wayne," there are clear evidences of Quarrington's fondness for using new and delightful words. Where do you find examples of interesting word use? How do these shifts in diction affect you as a reader? What do they add to your perception of the writer? How do they affect the overall tone of the essay?

MAKING CONNECTIONS

1. Paul Quarrington, like Joe Fiorito ("Breakfast in Bed") is basing his essay on a recipe. Explain how each of these authors makes a recipe interesting and entertaining to read.
2. Quarrington, like Drew Hayden Taylor ("Pretty Like a White Boy") and Susan Swan ("Nine Ways of Looking at a Critic"), is noted for the humour that characterizes his writing. How do each of these writers achieve a humorous tone in their respective essays?
3. In this essay, Quarrington incorporates stories of his family members. Compare the effect of this personalization to Ray Guy's ("When Jannies Visited") use of family anecdotes in his essay.

IDEAS FOR DISCUSSION/WRITING

Preparing to Write

Write freely about one of your more memorable experiments with trying to make something on your own for the first time. What were you trying to make? Why? Had you been given any prior instructions? Were you trying your "recipe" alone, or with someone else? What were the results of your first "do it yourself" attempt? Were they humorous at the time? Were the results a success, or even usable? What happens when you try to show someone else how to do something you do well?

Choosing a Topic

1. Your school newspaper has just asked you to write the first column in a "Student Cooking" series. Write an article based on the process format in which you tell readers who have cooking skills similar to yours how to make a dish you've learned to cook. Include such information as why this dish is suitable to student cooking abilities, available equipment and facilities, how many it will serve, and what it would cost.
2. Using your own experience with a hobby or with making something which others might buy from a store, write a process essay that persuades the reader to try this "do it yourself" project. Explain your reasons for finding the activity and the end-product valuable and enjoyable as you give detailed instructions for making the same thing.

3. Beer, cola, wine, mineral water, coffee: We all have favourite beverages. Explain in a process essay why your favourite drink holds such appeal to you. What do you know about this beverage that will interest your readers? Choose a tone and clear points of detailing that will be most interesting to your audience.

Malcolm Gladwell

IS THE BELGIAN COCA-COLA HYSTERIA THE REAL THING?

Since growing up in Elmira, Ontario, Malcolm Gladwell (1963–) has experienced impressive success in his writing career. After holding the positions of reporter and northeastern bureau chief of the *Washington Post*, Gladwell moved to writing a popular column in *The New Yorker* magazine and a book called *The Tipping Point* in which he examines the idea of social epidemics and the ways in which change happens in a society.

Gladwell was born in England and lived there, as well as in the United States and Jamaica, before his family settled in rural Ontario in 1969. In 1984, he graduated from the University of Toronto with a history degree and got an internship at the *American Spectator* in Indiana. Less than a year later, he landed a job as a reporter at the *Washington Post* and, over time, moved from writing on topics with a business focus to those with a more general science bent. After complementing his work at the *Post* with freelance assignments for *The New Yorker*, Gladwell eventually won a contract as a staff writer with *The New Yorker* in 1996. Gladwell continues to write for *The New Yorker* and to do public speaking engagements based on *The Tipping Point*.

Preparing to Read

In the summer of 1999, Malcolm Gladwell wrote the following essay that appeared in *The New Yorker*. "Is the Belgian Coca-Cola Hysteria the Real Thing?" relates the story of an apparent food poisoning outbreak in Belgium and then speculates as to the real cause of the affliction that struck about 100 children. Before reading Gladwell's essay, think about food safety. What responsibility do food manufacturers have for food safety? How should a company respond to complaints that their products have caused illness? What role should government legislation play in up-holding standards of food safety?

_____

The wave of illness among Belgian children last month had the 1
look and feel—in the beginning, at least—of an utterly typi-cal food poisoning outbreak. First, forty-two children in the Belgian town of Bornem became mysteriously ill after drinking Coca-Cola and had to be hospitalized. Two days later, eight more school chil-dren fell sick in Bruges, followed by thirteen in Harelbeke the next day and forty-two in Lochristi three days after that—and on and on in a widening spiral that, in the end, sent more than one hun-dred children to the hospital complaining of nausea, dizziness, and headaches, and forced Coca-Cola into the biggest product re-call in its hundred-and-thirteen-year history. Upon investigation, an apparent culprit was found. In the Coca-Cola plant in Antwerp, contaminated carbon dioxide had been used to carbonate a batch of the soda's famous syrup. With analysts predicting that the scare would make a dent in Coca-Cola's quarterly earnings, the soft-drink giant apologized to the Belgian people, and the world re-ceived a sobering reminder of the fragility of food safety.

The case isn't as simple as it seems, though. A scientific study 2
ordered by Coca-Cola found that the contaminants in the carbon dioxide were sulfur compounds left over from the production process. In the tainted bottles of Coke, these residues were present at between five and seventeen parts per billion. These sulfides can cause illness, however, only at levels about a thousand times greater than that. At seventeen parts per billion, they simply leave a bad smell—like rotten eggs—which means that Belgium should have experienced nothing more than a minor epidemic of nose-wrinkling. More puzzling is the fact that, in four of the five schools where the bad Coke allegedly struck, half of the kids who got sick hadn't drunk any Coke that day. Whatever went on Belgium, in other words, probably wasn't Coca-Cola poisoning. So what was it? Maybe nothing at all.

"You know, when this business started I bet two of my 3
friends a bottle of champagne each that I knew the cause," Simon Wessely, a psychiatrist who teaches at the King's College School of Medicine in London, said.

"It's quite simple. It's just mass hysteria. These things usually 4
are."

Wessely has been collecting reports of this kind of hysteria for 5
about ten years and now has hundreds of examples, dating back
as far as 1787, when millworkers in Lancashire suddenly took
ill after they became persuaded that they were being poisoned by
tainted cotton. According to Wessely, almost all cases fit a pattern.
Someone sees a neighbor fall ill and becomes convinced that he
is being contaminated by some unseen evil—in the past it was
demons and spirits; nowadays it tends to be toxins and gases—
and his fear makes him anxious. His anxiety makes him dizzy
and nauseous. He begins to hyperventilate. He collapses. Other
people hear the same allegation, see the "victim" faint, and they
begin to get anxious themselves. They feel nauseous. They
hyperventilate. They collapse, and before you know it everyone
in the room is hyperventilating and collapsing. These symptoms,
Wessely stresses, are perfectly genuine. It's just that they are
manifestations of a threat that is wholly imagined. "This kind
of thing is extremely common," he says, "and it's almost normal.
It doesn't mean that you are mentally ill or crazy."

Mass hysteria comes in several forms. Mass motor hysteria, 6
for example, involves specific physical movements: shaking,
tremors, and convulsions. According to the sociologist Robert
Bartholomew, motor hysteria often occurs in environments of
strict emotional repression; it was common in medieval nunneries
and in nineteenth-century European schools, and it is seen today
in some Islamic cultures. What happened in Belgium, he says,
is a fairly typical example of a more standard form of contagious
anxiety, possibly heightened by the recent Belgian scare over
dioxin-contaminated animal feed. The students' alarm over the
rotten-egg odor of their Cokes, for example, is straight out of the
hysteria textbooks. "The vast majority of these events are
triggered by some abnormal but benign smell," Wessely said.
"Something strange, like a weird odor coming from the air
conditioning."

The fact that the outbreaks occurred in schools is also typical 7
of hysteria cases. "The classic ones always involve schoolchildren,"
Wessely continued. "There is a famous British case involving
hundreds of schoolgirls who collapsed during a 1980
Nottinghamshire jazz festival. They blamed it on a local farmer
spraying pesticides." Bartholomew has just published a paper
on a hundred and fifteen documented hysteria cases in schools
over the past three hundred years. As anyone who has ever been
to a rock concert knows, large numbers of adolescents in confined

spaces seem to be particularly susceptible to mass hysteria. Those intent on pointing the finger at Coca-Cola in this sorry business ought to remember that. "We let the people of Belgium down," Douglas Ivester, the company's chairman, said in the midst of the crisis. Or perhaps it was the other way around.

UNDERSTANDING DETAILS

1. What were the symptoms experienced by the Belgian children in Gladwell's essay? What caused these symptoms?
2. List the steps in the process of mass hysteria setting in.
3. What causes mass hysteria?

ANALYZING MEANING

1. How did Coca-Cola respond to the apparent poisoning of the people in Belgium? Was this response appropriate? Why or why not?
2. What is Gladwell's purpose in this essay? What is the main topic of Gladwell's essay?
3. Who is particularly susceptible to mass hysteria? Why?

DISCOVERING RHETORICAL STRATEGIES

1. A significant portion of Gladwell's essay is spent describing a series of events in Belgium. Explain why he spends so much time detailing these events.
2. Gladwell has quoted and cited other people in his essay. Why has he done this? What effect does this have?
3. What is Gladwell's purpose in this essay? Does he achieve this purpose?

MAKING CONNECTIONS

1. Gladwell is fascinated with the popularity of different social phenomena and the reasons people behave the way they do. Imagine a conversation between Gladwell and Mark Kingwell ("Not Available in Stores"). What do these two writers have in common? What topics of conversation do you imagine might engage them?

2. Lynn Coady ("Genius or Madness?") and Judy Rebick ("The Culture of Overwork") both cite examples of people's behaviour being modelled on that of those around them. Are these examples of the mass hysteria that Gladwell outlines? Why or why not?
3. Like Gladwell, David Foot ("Boomers Dance to a New Beat") is interested in factors that influence the behaviour of groups of people. How do you think Foot would explain Gladwell's point about cases of mass hysteria typically involving schoolchildren?

IDEAS FOR DISCUSSION/WRITING

Preparing to Write

Write freely about contagious behaviour. What types of behaviour are "contagious"? What kinds of things do we do because we observe others around us doing them? Can yawning or blushing be caused by suggestion? If we observe others around us yawning, is it possible to keep ourselves from yawning as well?

Choosing a Topic

1. In a process essay directed to your classmates, explain how you believe a company should react in a case where their product seems to be contaminated. Decide on your tone and purpose before you begin.
2. Write an essay for a local newspaper or magazine in which you outline the process for ensuring that the foods you consume at home are safe.
3. Gladwell explains how mass hysteria takes hold and what factors create it. Write a narrative essay in which you relate a story illustrating the power of the "mob mentality." How did the actions of individuals get dictated by the group of which they were a part? Were the consequences of this behavioural influence positive or negative?

Stanley Coren

■ □ ■

DOGS AND MONSTERS

You can see Stanley Coren as a guest on numerous television shows as well as in the role of host on his weekly television show "Good Dog"; you can hear him on radio programs such as *Dan Rather*, *Ideas*, *Quirks and Quarks*, *Basic Black*, and *The Osgood Report*; and you can read his work in articles published in *USA Today*, the *Globe and Mail*, the *New York Times*, the *Chicago Tribune*, *Time*, *People*, *Maclean's*, *Cosmopolitan*, and *Entertainment Weekly*. Coren has also published several books about dogs, including *How to Speak Dog*, *Why We Love the Dogs We Do*, *The Intelligence of Dogs*, and *Sleep Thieves*. He has published a multitude of academic and scientific writings related to his research into various areas of psychology and his current role as a professor and director of the Human Neuropsychology and Perception Laboratory at the University of British Columbia. If you wanted to meet Coren, you could register for a psychology class he teaches at UBC, you could take a course with the Vancouver Dog Obedience Training Club, or you could attend one of the many fundraising events for the SPCA in which he participates.

Coren was born in Philadelphia in 1942 and educated at the University of Pennsylvania (undergraduate) and Stanford University (doctorate). This prolific writer and researcher now lives in Vancouver with his wife, two dogs, and a cat.

Preparing to Read

One recent cellular phone ad campaign highlights the similarities in appearance between people and the dogs they choose as pets. Do you have a dog? If so, what kind of dog do you have? What characteristics made you choose that type of dog? Generally, do you think dogs are good pets? Why or why not? How has the role of pets changed over the last century? In this essay, originally published in *Saturday Night* magazine in May 2000, Stanley Coren outlines the process of bio-engineering dogs to adapt to the current technologies and needs of their human owners.

Today's headlines routinely raise fears about genetic engineer- 1
ing. The biggest concern is that "tampering with creation" to fashion new strains of plants and animals may result in the devastation of the world by upsetting the natural balance among

species. Even Prince Charles has joined the debate, claiming that genetic engineering "takes us into areas that should be left to God. We should not be meddling with the building blocks of life in this way." But the genetic manipulation of species is far from new. In fact, it began at least 14,000 years ago, when human beings created the first deliberately engineered organism—the dog.

The bioengineered canine was not created in a high-level 2 biocontainment lab; rather, its beginnings were accidental. Wolves and jackals (the domestic dog's predecessors) were attracted to human camps because primitive humans left bones, bits of skin, and other scraps of leftover food scattered near their dwellings. The wolves and jackals learned that by loitering around the settlement they could grab an occasional bite to eat without the exertion involved in hunting. These primitive dogs were initially tolerated by humans because they functioned as de facto garbage-disposal units.

The dogs near the campsite provided another key benefit: 3 security. They barked whenever wild beasts or strangers approached, removing the need for human guards to be posted at night, and thus affording the villagers more rest and increased safety. The bark was critical—the most effective guard dogs, obviously, were those with loud, persistent barks. And so a selective breeding program was begun: those dogs that barked loudly were kept and bred with other loud barkers, while those that did not bark were simply killed or chased off. In fact, one of the major distinctions between wild canines and domestic dogs today is that domestic dogs bark, while wild dogs seldom do. The persistent racket that irritates so many people is actually a human innovation.

It wasn't until the end of the fifteenth century, though, that 4 the dog as a genetic creation became truly unique—almost more an invention than a species. At this point people began cross-breeding dogs, not just to cater to their changing needs, but to suit advancing technology. Typically, humans had tailored machines to suit organisms. With dogs, they began modifying an organism to fit a machine. The machine was the gun, and the organism was the gun dog.

The earliest gun dogs were the pointers, which appeared in 5 Europe in the 1500s. The hunting weapon of choice at the time was the muzzle-loading musket, a primitive device that was notoriously laborious to use. On sighting his quarry, a hunter had to take out his powder horn, dump gunpowder down the barrel, followed by a lead ball wrapped with oiled paper or cloth, and tamp down the shot and powder with a tamping rod; then he had to fire the gun. The process took a minimum of thirty seconds, all in the service of a weapon with an effective range of twenty-five to fifty yards. To accommodate musket technology, the pointer was designed to be slow, silent, and patient. The pointer's job was to find a bird, then to hold its position while pointing at the bird's location for the agonizingly long time it took the hunter to load and shoot his weapon. If a lucky shot actually killed a bird the pointer was expected to go out and bring the game back as well. But the retrieval was window-dressing; the pointer's genetic value lay in its ability to stretch time out, to live in a slow-motion world.

As weapons technology improved, guns became easier to 6 load, with better range and accuracy. To match this new equipment, dog breeders in the late 1700s created a new kind of dog—the setter. Setters moved much more quickly than pointers, and indicated their proximity to the prey not by the stillness of their point but by the beat of their tails. The faster a setter wagged its tail, the closer it was to the game.

As more land was cultivated and cities and towns sprang up, 7 hunters were forced to turn to wilderness areas, particularly wetlands, where they hid behind blinds and waited for their quarry to come to them. These circumstances placed a premium on a dog that was not simply quiet, as the pointer had been, but that possessed an almost preternatural obedience and patience. Thus, the retriever became the bioengineered star of the next century. Retrievers were bred to wait—to do nothing: not to point, not to flush, not to run, not to bark—and retrieve. They were bred to be less, not more, which, given the physiognomy of the species, may have been the more remarkable biotechnological feat.

Canada is responsible for the newest and most intriguing 8 genetic invention in the retriever group: the Nova Scotia duck tolling retriever, a handsome, auburn-hued dog that stands about twenty inches high and weighs about forty-five pounds. The need for the toller arose when duck hunters found that they could better attract their quarry by having wooden "lures," or decoys, carved to look like ducks, floating in the nearby water. Ducks are also attracted to unusual movement and activities. This is where the toller comes in. Tolling simply means that the dog runs back and forth on the shore, spinning and making noise, or swims erratically near the shore to attract the birds. Curious ducks fly near to see what all the activity is about, and come within range of the hunter's gun. Tollers will do this for hours if needed. Of course, once the bird is shot the dog is then expected to swim out and bring it back to its lazy master.

Like any piece of technology—the 78 rpm record player, or 9
the pedal-driven sewing machine—a bioengineered dog can become outmoded and obsolete. One of the most common breeds of the eighteenth and nineteenth centuries, the Spanish pointer, was so popular in its day that it can be seen in scores of early paintings of hunts. These dogs were perfect for the era of the muzzle-loading musket—slow, quiet, and the most meticulous of the pointers. Today the breed is effectively extinct. Spanish pointers were simply too slow for impatient modern hunters, with their new, superior equipment—both guns and dogs.

Walk into homes today, and what you'll find are dogs 10
engineered for a wholly different piece of technology: the TV remote control. Perhaps our faith in biogenetic engineering would be improved if we recognized that for those of us who don't hunt, some dogs have also been designed specifically to be our companions—to fit the couch-potato mentality of our current, leisure-addicted era. It is a wonder to me that starting with the DNA of a wolf, we have spent 14,000 years of biotechnology and genetic manipulation in the creation of the little white beast who is right now gently snoring with his head resting against my foot.

UNDERSTANDING DETAILS

1. What is Coren's thesis? Where in the essay is it stated?
2. Outline the significant stages of development in the process of breeding dogs. What key characteristics identify each stage?
3. What has motivated humans to genetically engineer dogs over the last 14,000 years? What is the relationship between dogs and various forms of technology?

ANALYZING MEANING

1. Explain the title "Dogs and Monsters." Is it effective? Why or why not?
2. In the first paragraph of Coren's essay, he refers to the fear about genetic modification found in current headlines. How does Coren's discussion of the bio-engineering of dogs relate to foods that are now the focus of the genetic modification controversy?

3. What is Coren's purpose in writing this essay? What gives him credibility in his discussion of genetic modification and bio-engineering?

DISCOVERING RHETORICAL STRATEGIES

1. What strategies has Coren used to unify the introduction and conclusion of his essay?
2. In addition to chronologically outlining the history of the bio-engineering of dogs, Coren uses other rhetorical strategies in his essay. What other methods of organization has he employed?
3. Which of the three forms of process analysis does Coren's essay follow? Explain your answer.

MAKING CONNECTIONS

1. In what ways are the views of Tony Leighton ("The New Nature") and Stanley Coren complementary in regard to human manipulation of processes such as photography and animal breeding?
2. Coren explains that dogs have been bred over time to adapt to the current technology available to people. Imagine that Coren is in conversation with Evan Solomon ("The Babar Factor") about adaptation to technology. In what ways have our forms of entertainment adapted over time to suit the technology available? Do you think Coren and Solomon would agree on the beneficial value of this type of adaptation?
3. Stanley Coren adds interest to his essay with the personal detail about his own dog in his conclusion. Compare this strategy to that of Gwynne Dyer ("Flagging Attention") or Judy Rebick ("The Culture of Overwork").

IDEAS FOR WRITING/DISCUSSION

Preparing to Write

Coren opens his essay by pointing to recent fears about genetic modification. Write freely about genetic modification and the implications it has for our society. In what areas of our life are you aware of genetic modification happening? Do you see it as a good thing or a bad thing? Why does genetic modification frighten people? What are the benefits of genetic modification?

Should the government prohibit the production of genetically modified organisms?

Choosing a Topic

1. Write an essay in which you argue for or against companies being allowed to bio-engineer foods. Make sure you support your position with specific examples.
2. Humans are constantly inventing new tools to help them adapt to a changing environment. Think of one particular technological advance of the last 20 years, and outline how and why that change happened.
3. Write an essay for the humane society newsletter in which you outline the process for adopting a pet. Be sure to explain clearly how people should select the pets they wish to adopt.

Maureen Littlejohn

YOU ARE A CONTRACT PAINKILLER

For a writer, "it is important to listen and never assume" as well as to "ask a lot of questions," according to Maureen Littlejohn, a journalist who has specialized in pop culture for about 15 years. Littlejohn began her journalistic career working on *Campus Digest* (now *Campus Canada*) after graduating with an honours B.A. (General Arts) from the University of Toronto and completing the magazine journalism program at Ryerson Polytechnic Institute, and then moved on to roles including Entertainment/ Lifestyles features writer at the *Winnipeg Free Press* and editor of the annual Juno Souvenir Program. While at U of T, Littlejohn, who always wanted to go into the field of communications, worked at the *Varsity* campus newspaper as a writer and typesetter. Later, Littlejohn further developed her writing skills through participating in the Banff Publishing Workshop. Littlejohn also worked as an on-air music critic for Global TV for three years and edited *Network* magazine for six years.

Articles Littlejohn has written have appeared in a variety of publications including the *Financial Post* magazine, *Flare* magazine, the Canadian Airlines in-flight magazine, *The Music Scene, CARAS News, Canadian Musician, Network,* and *Equinox,* where the piece included here was first published.

Preparing to Read

ASA, or aspirin, is a medication that is readily available and familiar to most of us. In this essay, Maureen Littlejohn outlines the process by which ASA works to relieve our pain and the process through which ASA was developed. Before reading this essay, think about familiar medications. What do you typically keep stocked in your medicine cabinet at home? Do you ever use aspirin? When? Why? What other nonprescription medications do you use? Do you favour medications available from pharmacies or more natural remedies? Why?

■_____■

You are a contract painkiller, code name ASA, also known to 1
your clients as aspirin. Pain is your gain—Canadians swallow almost one billion of your agents each year. You have achieved renown by destroying headaches but you are equally effective in countering sprains, burns, or blows. You stop swelling and reduce fever and research suggests you may even help prevent heart attack and stroke.

On your latest mission, your client has just had a fight with 2
her boss, and her head is pounding. Involuntary muscle contractions on her scalp and at the back of her neck, triggered by the argument, are now causing swelling and throbbing. In reaction, her body has produced an enzyme called prostaglandin, which is sensitizing the nerve endings in her scalp, especially around her temples and sending a message of pain to her brain.

Taken with a modest stream of water or ginger ale, your 3
chalky, round self begins the mission by moving through the host's esophagus, into the stomach, then the upper small intestine, where you are dissolved and passed into the bloodstream. There, you slop into a molecular chain of events and disable the enzyme that converts the acid in cell membranes into prostaglandins. The nerve endings are now desensitized, that pain message to the brain is stopped, and your host is smiling again.

You reduce fever in a similar way. If your host were suffering 4
from the flu, her white blood cells would be fighting the virus by producing prostaglandins that, in turn, cause the body's temperature to rise. You head off the prostaglandins and bring the fever down.

You are not the only pain relieving agent at work. Ibuprofen 5
and other aspirinlike drugs known as nonsteroidal anti-inflammatory drugs (NSAIDs) do much the same thing. You all share possible side effects—in 2 to 6 percent of your clients, you

cause stomach irritation and possibly bleeding and, in extreme cases, kidney failure. Prostaglandins help maintain the integrity of the stomach lining, and in their absence, the acidic NSAIDs give the host a queasy feeling.

As a tonic for hire, you have been around for a century, but 6 your family tree goes back much further. In ancient Greece, Hippocrates noted that chewing on willow leaves reduced fever. In the 1800s, two Italian chemists confirmed that willow bark contains one of your main ingredients, the antipyretic (fever-reducing) salicin. A Swiss pharmacist then found that meadowsweet, a shrub in the spirea family, has even more of the magic substance than willow bark. And while experimenting with salicin, a German chemist created salicylic acid (the SA of ASA). He called it *Spirsäure* after spirea, hence the "spirin" part of your name. The "a" was added for "acetyl," the substances—including a salt—that made the SA easier on the stomach. In 1893, Felix Hoffmann at the Bayer AG Chemical Works in Germany purified and stabilized you, and that's when you first claimed celebrity status as one of the world's most popular, inexpensive pain relievers. Today you are synthesized from coal tar or petroleum instead of plants.

Beyond garden-variety aches and pains, you are prescribed 7 as a remedy for arthritis because of your genius for blocking prostaglandins that trigger the pain and swelling of joints. Your most recent prostaglandin-fighting potential is to prevent heart attack and stroke. There is even talk that you may help ward off cancer and senility. Mission impossible? We'll see.

UNDERSTANDING DETAILS

1. What is ASA made from? What does ASA stand for?
2. When was ASA invented? By whom?
3. Explain how ASA works to relieve pain and reduce fever.

ANALYZING MEANING

1. Why has ASA become so popular over time? What do you anticipate its status will be in the future?
2. Describe Littlejohn's attitude toward her subject. What specific examples contribute to this impression?
3. Explain why ASA is now synthesized from coal tar or petroleum. Why have we moved beyond simply ingesting willow leaves and meadowsweet?

DISCOVERING RHETORICAL STRATEGIES

1. Littlejohn uses the second person to detail the history and the effect of ASA. What is the effect of casting the reader in the role of an ASA tablet? Why has she chosen this strategy? How effective is her choice to address the inanimate subject of her essay directly?
2. In this essay Littlejohn uses an extended metaphor. To what does she compare ASA? List five examples where she makes this connection.
3. Is this essay a directive or a descriptive process analysis? Why is this an appropriate strategy for this topic?

MAKING CONNECTIONS

1. Littlejohn uses an extended metaphor in this essay to make her subject more interesting and easier to understand. Explain how her use of metaphor compares to that of Lesley Choyce ("Thin Edge of the Wedge") or Dave Bidini ("Kris King Looks Terrible").
2. "You Are a Contract Painkiller" addresses the reader directly as "you" and, in fact, casts the reader as the subject of the essay. How is this approach similar to that of Joe Fiorito's "Breakfast in Bed"? How is the role of the reader different in these two essays?
3. Maureen Littlejohn is presenting scientific information in this essay and incorporating terminology that may initially be unfamiliar to her readers. What strategies has she used to make this subject accessible and interesting to her audience? How does her approach compare to that of Tony Leighton ("The New Nature")?

IDEAS FOR DISCUSSION/WRITING

Preparing to Write

Write freely about common pain medications with which you are familiar. What do you do if you burn yourself on an iron? How do you remedy a headache? What do you do for bee stings? What is the best way to relieve sunburn pain? How do you treat a sprain? How did you learn about these treatments? How do you gauge their effectiveness?

Choosing a Topic

1. Think of a practice that was once commonly accepted for treating some ailment. It might be the use of mustard plasters or cod liver oil to cure or prevent colds, electric shock therapy to treat psychological problems, amputation to prevent the spread of infection, or lobotomies to cure psychological disorders. In a short essay, explain how and why this practice fell out of favour.
2. There are many things that we may find disagreeable but that we do because we recognize the benefits that they offer. This might include getting our teeth cleaned at the dentist's, exercising, or cleaning the bathroom. Describe one such process, focusing on its positive aspects.
3. Taking medication is one response to relieving pain but many people are resistant to taking medications such as ASA. Write an essay in which you present some alternative responses to treating a headache or other "garden-variety aches and pains."

Joe Fiorito

BREAKFAST IN BED

Originally from Thunder Bay, Ontario, Joe Fiorito (1948–) began his writing career in Montreal, Quebec, where he worked as a columnist for the *Montreal Gazette* and *Hour* magazine. Fiorito now lives in Toronto where he contributes regular columns to Air Canada's *EnRoute* magazine and the *National Post*. He has worked for CBC Radio, where he produced *The Food Show*, and he is also a published poet. His book *Comfort Me with Apples* (1994) is a collection of essays that originally were published as a weekly column in *Hour* magazine. While Fiorito has no formal journalism training, in 1996 he won a national newspaper award for his *Gazette* columns. A collection of these profiles, or "people pieces," has now been published in a book entitled *Tango on the Main*. Most recently, Fiorito has written a memoir, *The Closer We Are to Dying* (1999), about his family.

Preparing to Read

While "Breakfast in Bed" is taken from *Comfort Me with Apples*, it originally appeared in *Hour* magazine in 1993. In this short essay, Fiorito gives the reader a recipe and a reason for making popovers. Before you begin to

read, think about the importance of smell in your life. What is the difference between a smell and a scent? What about an odour? What smells
do you find appealing? What smells are repulsive or annoying? Do you
have a favourite perfume or cologne? What is it? How would you describe its scent?

■_____■

The Inuit greet face to face, but they don't rub noses, exactly,   1
and you shouldn't call it kissing. It is a form of greeting every
bit as intimate as a kiss, but it goes deeper than that; it's a way for
friends to take in each other's smell. It's how friends fill the empty
places caused by absence.

Smell is fundamental to happiness. I know a man who travels   2
with a piece of his wife's clothing sealed in a plastic bag. When
the separation is too much to bear, he opens the bag and breathes.

Traces of this signature mark our sheets and pillows; this is   3
what makes crawling into bed on a cold night such a comfort.

Smell is one of the many nameless things you miss when   4
love goes wrong. That smell will linger, it will haunt you and
exhaust you long after your lover has gone.

Think I'm exaggerating? Wake early one Sunday and smell   5
the person sleeping next to you. Do it. Lean over. The side of the
neck will do, just below the ear. Take a deep breath. The
knowledge of this scent is lodged in the deepest part of your
brain. Breathe deeply, if only to remind yourself of why you are
where you are, doing what you're doing.

Now go to the kitchen. Throw two eggs into a bowl with a   6
cup of milk and a cup of flour. Add a quarter teaspoon of salt
and a tablespoon of melted butter. Mix until smooth, but don't
overdo it.

Pour the batter into buttered muffin tins, filling the cups no   7
more than half full. Put the tins in a cold oven. Turn on the heat
to 450°F. After fifteen minutes, turn the oven down to 350°F.
Wait fifteen minutes more.

This recipe comes from the *Fannie Farmer Baking Book* by   8
Marion Cunningham. It's an important book, with clear recipes
and much new thinking. For example, prior to Marion, popovers
were always started in a hot oven. This is a small thing, but one
which changed my life.

While you're changing yours, make some coffee and squeeze   9
a couple of oranges. Do what you want with a pear or a pineapple.
Get a tray ready to take back to bed.

Now open the oven. It will make you smile. They don't call 10
these things popovers for nothing. They look like little domes,
golden brown and slightly crisp on the outside. The texture inside
is as soft as your partner's neck. The smell is just as warm and
every bit as earthy.

Take them out of the muffin tins and put them in a basket. 11
They'll steam as you break them open. Eat them with a little
butter and the best jam or honey in the cupboard. A soft
camembert isn't out of place if you have it.

Breakfast together is the second- or third-most intimate thing 12
you can share. If someone new is sleeping over and you want
to make an impression, make these. If you're worried about what
to talk about while you're eating, remember what Oscar Wilde
said. Only dull people are brilliant at breakfast.

If you haven't got a partner, make popovers anyway. It's 13
easy enough to cut this recipe in half. It's good practice. It's its
own reward. The butter melts into the jam and the sun pours
onto your breakfast bed. And you have another way to fill the
emptiness caused by absence.

UNDERSTANDING DETAILS

1. How does Fiorito suggest that one can fill the emptiness that
   results from loneliness?
2. What process is Fiorito explaining in this essay?
3. What are popovers? How did they get their name?

ANALYZING MEANING

1. Explain the relationship between smell and memory.
2. What does Fiorito mean when he says that smell is fundamental to happiness?
3. Explain why, in Fiorito's estimation, breakfast together is such
   an intimate experience.

DISCOVERING RHETORICAL STRATEGIES

1. In this essay, Fiorito is giving the readers a recipe. How does it
   differ from the way a popover recipe might be written in *The Joy
   of Cooking* or any other cookbook?
2. How does Fiorito link the beginning and the end of his essay?
   Does he have an effective introduction and conclusion?
3. Describe Fiorito's tone in this essay. Use specific examples to
   show how his style (use of language) creates this tone.

MAKING CONNECTIONS

1. Joe Fiorito's writing is distinguished by a conversational tone and an informal style. Compare his style to that of Laura Robinson ("Starving for the Gold") or Tony Leighton ("The New Nature"). Whose style do you find more effective? Why?

2. Fiorito takes a subject that seems relatively simple and potentially boring and creates interest through the incorporation of specific detail. Explain how this approach makes his topic interesting and entertaining. How does this compare to the approach of Sharon Butala ("The Myth: The Prairies Are Flat") or Dave Bidini ("Kris King Looks Terrible")?

IDEAS FOR DISCUSSION/WRITING

Preparing to Write

Write freely about your favourite food. What do you know about its national origins or about the history of its preparation? Where and when do you eat this food? Do you associate it with any particular events or people in your life? Could you write a recipe for this food yourself? What ingredients does it contain? Is your favourite food healthy and nutritious, junk food, or a bit of both?

Choosing a Topic

1. Write an essay in which you include a recipe for one of your favourite foods that is fairly simple to prepare. Instead of writing it in "cookbook instruction style," present the information in a narrative like Fiorito did, in which you also provide a context and some subjective information about this dish. Make sure that you provide enough detail that your reader will be able to follow your recipe.

2. In "Breakfast in Bed" Fiorito says that breakfast together is one of the most intimate experiences you can share. Think of some particular ritual that you share with others that involves food. This might be preparing or eating a family meal, preserving fruit or vegetables, making wine or beer, or going out for a drink after work. How often does this ritual happen? Who participates? Where does this ritual fall on the intimacy scale? Write an essay in which you describe this event in a descriptive process analysis.

3. In "Breakfast in Bed" Fiorito cites Oscar Wilde as saying, "Only dull people are brilliant at breakfast." Write an essay in which you explain to your audience how to appear brilliant at any meal you choose.

CHAPTER 5

DIVISION/CLASSIFICATION

■ ■ ■

Finding Categories

Both division and classification play important roles in our everyday lives: Bureau drawers separate one type of clothing from another; kitchen cabinets organize food, dishes, and utensils into proper groups; grocery stores shelve similar items together so shoppers can easily locate what they want to buy; school notebooks with tabs help students divide up their academic lives; newspapers classify local and national events in order to organize a great deal of daily information for the general public; and our own personal classification systems assist us in separating what we like from what we don't so that we can have access to our favourite foods, our favourite cars, our favourite entertainment, our favourite people. The two processes of division and classification are so natural to us, in fact, that we sometimes aren't even aware we are using them.

Defining Division/Classification

Division and classification are actually mirror images of each other. Division is the basic feature of process analysis, which we studied in the last chapter: It moves from a general concept to subdivisions of that concept or from a single category to multiple subcategories. Classification works in the opposite direction, moving from specifics to a group with common traits or from multiple subgroups to a single, larger, and more inclusive category. These techniques work together in many ways: A college, for example, is *divided* into departments (single to multiple), whereas courses are *classified* by department (multiple to single); the medical field is *divided* into specialties, whereas doctors are *classified* by a single specialty; a cookbook is *divided* into chapters, whereas recipes are *classified* according to type; and athletics is *divided* into specific sports, whereas athletes are *classified* by the sport in which they participate. Division is the separation of an idea or an item into its basic parts, such as a home into rooms, a course into assignments, or a job into various duties or responsibilities; classification is the organization of items with similar features into a group or groups, such as ordering furniture to decorate a dining room, dropping all carbohydrates from your diet, or preferring to date only tall, sun-tanned swimmers.

Classification is an organizational system for presenting a large amount of material to a reader or listener. This process helps us make sense of the complex world we live in by letting us work with smaller, more understandable units of that world. Classification must be governed by some clear, logical purpose (such as focusing on all lower-division course requirements), which will then dictate the system of categories to be used. The plan of organization that results should be as flexible as possible, and it should illustrate the specific relationship to each other of items in a group and of the groups themselves to one another.

As you already know, many different ways of classifying the same elements are possible. If you consider the examples at the outset of this chapter, you will realize that bureau drawers vary from house to house and even from person to person; that no one's kitchen is set up exactly the same way as someone else's; and that grocery stores have similar but not identical systems of food classification. (Think, for instance, of the many different schemes for organizing dairy products, meats, diet foods, etc.) In addition, your friends probably use a method different from yours to organize their school notebooks; different newspapers vary their presentation of the news; and two professors will probably teach the same course material in divergent ways. We all have distinct and uniquely logical methods of classifying the elements in our own lives.

The following student paragraph about friends illustrates both division and classification. As you read it, notice how the student writer moves back and forth smoothly from general to specific and from multiple to single:

> The word "friend" can refer to many different types of relation-
> ships. Close friends are "friends" at their very best: people for whom
> we feel respect, esteem, and, quite possibly, even love. We regard

these people and their well-being with kindness, interest, and goodwill; we trust them and will go out of our way to help them. Needless to say, we could all use at least one close friend. Next come "casual friends," people with whom we share a particular interest or activity. The investment of a great amount of time and energy in developing this type of friendship is usually not required, though casual friends often become close friends with the passage of time. The last division of "friend" is most general and is composed of all those individuals whose acquaintance we have made and who feel no hostility toward us. When one is counting friends, this group should certainly be included, since such friendships often develop into "casual" or "close" relationships. Knowing people in all three groups is necessary, however, because all types of friends undoubtedly help us live healthier, happier lives.

Thinking Critically by Using Division/ Classification

The thinking strategies of division and classification are the flip sides of each other: Your textbook is *divided* into chapters (one item divided into many), but chapters are *classified* (grouped) into sections or units. Your brain performs these mental acrobatics constantly, but to be as proficient at this method of thinking as possible, you need to be aware of the cognitive activities you go through. Focusing on these two companion patterns of thought will develop your skill in dealing with these complex schemes as it simultaneously increases your overall mental capabilities.

You might think of division/classification as a driving pattern that goes forward and then doubles back on itself in reverse. Division is a movement from a single concept to multiple categories, while classification involves gathering multiple concepts into a single group. Dividing and/or classifying helps us make sense of our subject by using categories to highlight similarities and differences. In the case of division, you are trying to find what differences break the items into separate groups, while, with classification, you let the similarities among the items help you put the material into meaningful categories. Processing your material in this way helps your readers see your particular subject in a new way and often brings renewed insights to both reader and writer.

Experimenting with division and classification is important to your growth as a critical thinker. It will help you process complex information so you can understand more fully your options for dealing with material in all subject areas. Practising division and classification separately from other rhetorical modes makes you concentrate on improving this particular pattern of thinking before adding it to your expanding arsenal of critical thinking skills.

1. Study the table of contents of a magazine that interests you. Into what sections is the magazine divided? What distinguishing features does each section have? Now study the various advertisements in the same magazine. What different categories would you use to classify these ads? List the ads in each category.
2. Make a chart classifying the English instructors at your school. Explain your classification system to the class.
3. List six to eight major concerns you have about Canadian society. Which of these are most important? Which are least important? Now classify these concerns into two or three distinct categories.

Reading and Writing Division/Classification Essays

Writers of division/classification essays must first decide if they are going to break down a topic into many separate parts or group together similar items into one coherent category; a writer's purpose will, of course, guide him or her in this decision. Readers must likewise recognize and understand which of these two parallel operations an author is using to structure an essay. Another important identifying feature of division/classification essays is an explanation (explicit or implicit) of the significance of a particular system of organization.

How to Read a Division/Classification Essay

Preparing to read. As you approach the selections in this chapter, you should study all the material that precedes each essay so you can prepare yourself for your reading. First of all, what hints does the title give you about what you are going to read? To what extent does Amy Willard Cross reveal in her title her attitude toward the pace of life? Who do you think Susan Swan's audience is in "Nine Ways of Looking at a Critic"? Does David Foot's title give us any indication about his point of view in "Boomers Dance to a New Beat"? Then, see what you can learn from scanning each essay and reading its synopsis in the Rhetorical Table of Contents.

Also important as you prepare to read the essays in this chapter is your knowledge about each author and the conditions under which each essay was written: What does the biographical material tell you about Gwynne Dyer's "Flagging Attention"? Knowing where these essays were first published will give you even more information about each author's purpose and audience.

Finally, before you begin to read, answer the Preparing to Read questions, and then, think freely for a few minutes about the general topic: What do you want to know about the different types of book critics discussed by Susan Swan in "Nine Ways of Looking at a Critic." What are some of your own stories about living in a time-conscious society (Cross)?

Reading. As you read each essay for the first time, write down your initial reactions to the topic itself, to the preliminary material, to the mood the writer sets, or to a specific incident in the essay. Make associations between the essay and your own experiences.

In addition, create a context for each essay by drawing on the preliminary material you just read about the essay: What is David Foot telling us about the baby boom generation and why is this of interest? What is Swan saying about the role of the critic in the creative process? According to Dyer, why are the designs of our flags significant?

Also, in this first reading, notice whether the writers divided (split up) or classified (gathered together) their material to make their point. Finally, read the questions after each essay, and let them guide your second reading of the selection.

Rereading. When you read these division/classification essays a second time, notice how the authors carefully match their dominant rhetorical approach (in this case, division or classification) to their purpose in a clear thesis. What, for example, is Swan's dominant rhetorical approach to her subject? How does this approach further her purpose? What other rhetorical strategies support her thesis? Then, see how these writers logically present their division or classification systems to their readers, defining new categories as their essays progress. Finally, notice how each writer either implicitly or explicitly explains the significance or value of his or her division/classification system.

How does Gwynne Dyer explain his system of organization? And how does Cross give her organizing principle significance? Now, answer the questions after each essay to check your understanding and to help you analyze your reading in preparation for the discussion/writing topics that follow.

For a more complete survey of reading guidelines, you may want to consult the checklist on pages 15–16 of the Introduction.

How to Write a Division/Classification Essay

Preparing to Write. You should approach a division/classification essay in the same way you have begun all your other writing assignments—with some kind of prewriting activity that will help you generate ideas, such as the Preparing to Write questions featured in this chapter. The prewriting techniques outlined in the Introduction on pages 17–22 can help you approach these questions imaginatively. Before you even consider the selection and arrangement of details, you need to explore your subject, choose a topic, and decide on a specific purpose and audience. The best way to explore your subject is to think about it, read about it, and then write about it. Look at it from all possible angles, and see what patterns and relationships emerge. To choose a specific topic, you might begin by listing any groups, patterns, or combinations you discover within your subject matter. Your purpose should take shape as you form your thesis, and your audience is probably dictated by the assignment. Making these decisions before you write will make the rest of your task much easier.

Writing. As you begin to write, certain guidelines will help you structure your ideas for a division/classification essay:

1. First, declare an overall purpose for your classification.
2. Then, divide the item or concept you are dealing with into categories.
3. Arrange these categories into a logical sequence.
4. Define each category, explaining the difference between one category and another and showing that difference through specific examples.
5. Explain the significance of your classification system. (Why is it worth reading? What will your audience learn from it?)

All discussion in such an essay should reinforce the purpose stated at the beginning of the theme. Other rhetorical modes—

such as narration, example, and comparison/contrast—will naturally be used to supplement your classification.

To make your classification as workable as possible, take special care that your categories do not overlap and that all topics fall into their proper places. If, for example, you were classifying all the jobs performed by students in your writing class, the categories of (1) indoor work and (2) outdoor work would probably be inadequate. Most delivery jobs, for example, fall into both categories. At a pizza parlour, a florist, or a gift shop, a delivery person's time would be split between indoor and outdoor work. So you would need to design a different classification system to avoid this problem. The categories of (1) indoor work, (2) outdoor work, and (3) a combination of indoor and outdoor work would be much more useful for this task. Making sure your categories don't overlap will help make your classification essays more readable and more accurate.

Rewriting. As you rewrite your division/classification essays, consider carefully the probable reactions of your readers to the form and content of your paper:

1. Does your thesis communicate your purpose clearly?
2. Have you divided your topic into separate and understandable categories?
3. Are these categories arranged logically?
4. Are the distinctions between your categories as clear as possible?
5. Do you explain the significance of your particular classification system?

More guidelines for writing and rewriting are available on pages 26–27 of the Introduction.

Student Essay: Division/Classification at Work

The following student essay divides skiers into interesting categories based on their physical abilities. As you read it, notice how the student writer weaves the significance of his study into his opening statement of purpose. Also, pay particular attention to his logical method of organization and clear explanation of categories as he moves with ease from multiple to single and back to multiple again throughout the essay.

People on the Slopes

<u>When I first learned to ski</u>, I was amazed by the shapes who   Subject
whizzed by me and slipped down trails marked only by a black diamond signifying "most difficult," while others careened awkwardly down the "bunny slopes." <u>These skiers, I discovered, could</u>
<u>be divided into distinct categories—for my own entertainment</u>   Overall
<u>and for the purpose of finding appropriate skiing partners</u>.   purpose

Thesis statement appears to the left of the underlined thesis lines.

First are the <u>poetic skiers</u>. They glide down the mountainside   First category
silently with what seems like no effort at all. They float from side
to side on the intermediate slopes, their knees bent perfectly above   Definition
parallel skis, while their sharp skills allow them to bypass slower   Supporting details
skiers with safely executed turns at remarkable speeds.

The <u>crazy skiers</u> also get down the mountain quickly, but with   Second category
a lot more noise attending their descent. At every hill, they yell a
loud "Yahoo!" and slam their skis into the snow. These go-for-   Definition
broke athletes always whiz by faster than everyone else, and they   Supporting details (with humour)
especially seem to love the crowded runs where they can slide
over the backs of other people's skis. I often find crazy skiers in
mangled messes at the bottoms of steep hills, where they are yelling
loudly, but not the famous "Yahoo!"

<u>After being overwhelmed by the crazy skiers</u>, I am always glad   Transition
to find other skiers like myself: the <u>average ones</u>. We are polite   Third category
on the slopes, concentrate on improving our technique with every
run, and ski the beginner slopes only at the beginning of the day   Definition
to warm up. We go over the moguls (small hills) much more cau-   Supporting details (comparative)
tiously than the crazy or poetic skiers, but we still seek adventure
with a slight jump or two each day. We remain a silent majority on
the mountain.

<u>Below us in talent, but much more evident on the mountain-</u>   Fourth category
<u>side</u>, are what I call <u>the eternal beginners</u>. These skiers stick to the   Transition
same beginner slope almost every run of every day during their va-   Definition
cation. Should they venture onto an intermediate slope, they
quickly assume the snowplow position (a pigeon-toed stance) and
never leave it. Eternal beginners weave from one side of the run to   Supporting details
the other and hardly ever fall, because they proceed so slowly;
however, they do yell quite a bit at the crazies who like to run
over the backs of their skis.

<u>Having always enjoyed people-watching, I have fun each time</u>   Transition
<u>I am on the slopes observing the myriad of skiers around me. I</u>   Significance of classification system
<u>use these observations to pick out possible ski partners for my-</u>
<u>self and others</u>. Since my mother is an eternal beginner, she has
more fun skiing with someone who shares her interests than with

my dad, who is a poetic skier with solitude on his mind. After taking care of Mom, I am free to find a partner I'll enjoy. My sister, the crazy skier of the family, just heads for the rowdiest group

Concluding remarks she can find! <u>As the years go by and my talents grow, I am trusting my perceptions of skier types to help me find the right partner for life on and off the slopes. No doubt watching my fellow skiers will always remain an enjoyable pastime.</u>

Some Final Thoughts on Division/ Classification

The essays collected in this chapter use division and/or classification as their primary organizing principle. All of these essays show both techniques at work to varying degrees. As you read these essays, you might also want to be aware of the other rhetorical modes that support these division/classification essays, such as description and definition. Finally, pay particular attention to how these authors bring significance to their systems of classification and, as a result, to their essays themselves.

Division/Classification in Review

Reading Division/Classification Essays

Preparing to Read

1. What assumptions can you make from the essay's title?
2. Can you guess what the general mood of the essay is?
3. What is the essay's purpose and audience?
4. What does the synopsis in the Rhetorical Table of Contents tell you about the essay?
5. What can you learn from the author's biography?
6. Can you guess what the author's point of view toward the subject is?
7. What are your responses to the Preparing to Read questions?

Reading

1. What do you think the "context" of the essay is?
2. Did the author use division or classification most often?
3. Did you preview the questions that follow the essay?

Rereading

1. How does division or classification help the author accomplish his/her purpose?

2. What other rhetorical strategies does the author use to support the essay's purpose?

3. How does the writer explain the significance of his/her division/classification system?

4. What are your responses to the questions after the essay?

Writing Division/Classification Essays

Preparing to Write

1. What are your responses to the Preparing to Write questions?

2. What is your purpose?

3. Who is your audience?

Writing

1. Do you declare an overall purpose for your essay?

2. Do you divide the item or concept you are dealing with into categories?

3. Do you arrange these categories into a logical sequence?

4. Do you define each category, explaining the difference between one category and another and demonstrating that difference through examples?

5. Do you explain the significance of your division/classification system?

6. Are the categories in your essay distinct from one another so they don't overlap?

7. What rhetorical strategies support your essay?

Rewriting

1. Does your thesis communicate your purpose clearly?

2. Have you divided your topic into separate and understandable categories?

3. Are these categories arranged logically?

4. Do you explain the significance of your particular classification system?

David Foot

■□■

BOOMERS DANCE TO A NEW BEAT

David Foot is a professor of Economics at the University of Toronto who has become very well known for his work concerning the role of demographics in determining societal and economic trends. Foot's book, *Boom, Bust and Echo: How to Profit from the Coming Demographic Shift*, co-written with Daniel Stoffman, quickly became a best-seller and has made Foot a popular speaker and authority on future Canadian trends.

Prior to the 1996 publication of *Boom, Bust and Echo,* Foot had published two other books: *Canada's Population Outlook: Demographic Futures and Economic Challenges* (1982) and, with Blossom T. Wigdor, *The Over Forty Society* (1988). Foot's other publications are listed on his Web site (**www.footwork.com**).

David Foot was born in England in 1944, grew up in Australia where he completed an undergraduate degree, and then continued his education at Harvard University where he earned a doctorate in economics. While his writing has attracted much attention for Dr. Foot, he has also been recognized for his teaching ability. He is a two-time recipient of the University of Toronto undergraduate teaching award. As well, in 1992, he received a 3M Award for Teaching Excellence from the Society for Teaching and Learning in Higher Education, which recognizes outstanding Canadian university educators.

Preparing to Read

Before you read this essay, think about different generations. To what generation do you belong? What generation are your parents a part of? What defines a generation? What is a "generation gap"? Which generation has had the most significant impact on our society? Why?

Cocooning is dead, the trend-spotters have proclaimed. 1

In the eighties, North Americans hunkered down in their 2 house-fortresses with remote control to avoid an increasingly unsafe world. Now, this cocooning trend, first labelled by guru Faith Popcorn, is in reverse.

Canadians and Americans are watching less TV and going 3 out more to movies, museums, the performing arts and restaurants. Crime rates have stopped rising and, in many jurisdictions, they are falling.

All forms of home entertainment are either stagnant or 4 declining in popularity. The Internet does not seem to be catching on as home entertainment or as a shopping vehicle. There has been a resurrection of city streets and a renewed concern for communities. According to a recent *Globe and Mail* article, we are rejecting the "bland fruits of wired isolation."

But is all this so surprising? A careful understanding of 5 demographic trends provides a logical and easily understood explanation. For managers and marketers, it also serves as a foundation for anticipating new trends.

In a person's teens and 20s, "action" is important. The 6 downtown core of major cities provide this action. Being "grounded" by a tough parent is real punishment; moving out, usually into a city apartment, is a common goal.

Growing up into the late 20s and early 30s often means 7 partnering and family formation. For many parents, the city core doesn't seem like a great place to raise kids, so they buy houses in the suburbs. This means a mortgage and other loans to purchase furniture, appliances and the minivan.

So it was with the baby boomer generation, which has 8 dominated, if not determined, postwar economic and social trends in North America. The 10 million boomers in Canada, born between 1947 and 1966, comprise the biggest generation in the history of this country. Watching them can provide an understanding of these trends.

The first boomer became a teen-ager in 1960. So the sixties 9 and seventies were dominated by boomers moving through their teen-age years into their 20s. They rushed into cities, stimulating massive urbanization. They rented apartments, driving down vacancies and increasing rents. They went to movies and rock concerts and they ate lots of cheap food.

In 1977, a significant event went almost unnoticed—the first 10 boomer reached the dreaded age of 30. The early boomers started buying homes in the suburbs. By the mid-eighties, the new trend became an avalanche. Suburbanization took off.

Debt levels soared and the "echo generation" was spawned. 11 Minivan sales took off. Young children and lots of debt put a damper on going out. Technology and TV in particular, including video rentals, became the main entertainment media. Cocooning was established.

So Faith Popcorn was right, but it was not because of new 12 societal values. The biggest generation in history was leaving its action years behind and moving into its family ones. Not surprisingly, family values emerged as a new social trend. Rental housing, movie theatres and take-out restaurants experienced much slower growth and, in some cases, decline.

Spending growth was focused on family and home. Pet-food 13 sales were still brisk but convenience-store sales sagged. Boomers started paying off their loans and mortgages, leaving no cash for luxuries or savings.

With kids to raise and careers to manage, the boomers in 14 their 30s and 40s were running "99 Lives"—another Popcorn trend. They were trying to be good parents to their kids and good children to their aging parents. They were working overtime and competing for promotion to ever-fewer mid-management positions. Woe betide any organization that wasted their time. The "vigilante consumer" had arrived in full force.

But last year, another watershed was reached—the first 15 boomers turned 50. This is mid-life crisis time. The kids are beginning to leave home and those sprained ligaments are taking longer to heal.

Running shoes have become walking shoes, and the treadmill 16 purchased to replace visits to the fitness centre now induces guilt. Resting has become a pleasurable activity, especially at the cottage. Anyone ignorant of the power of demographics might think values are changing again.

With lower interest rates and evaporating loans, there is 17 more discretionary income, making it possible to afford a luxury or a sports-utility vehicle, a restaurant meal, and a show.

The teen-age or twentysomething kids don't need babysitting 18 any more, so going out is possible again. But the show is less likely to be a movie or a rock concert unless, of course, the Rolling Stones are back in town. Increasingly, the lavish musical, the symphony and maybe the opera hold more attraction.

So boomers are emerging from their cocoons. Surprise! They 19 are watching less TV—home entertainment is dropping in popularity—they are shopping in their neighbourhoods and they are not using the Internet. Their beloved pets are aging and the vet is becoming as familiar as the doctor.

Their parents are also getting old and mortality has come 20 closer to home. Aging has entered a deeply psychological, almost spiritual phase. Boomers are snapping up books on the topic, provided the print is large.

But the seven million "echo" kids are also having an impact.   21
Movie attendance is rising, mainly because of the increased
numbers of teen-agers. Similarly, the growth in confectionary,
pop and some fast-food sales has little to do with boomers trying
to relive youth. Their echo kids born in the eighties are delivering
these trends.

The marketplace of the future is becoming more complex.   22
While the leading boomers are killing cocooning, their kids are
reigniting the trends of the sixties. Rock stars have a bright future,
as does new technology. Of course, it should not be surprising to
see a reversal of the downward trend in crime rates as the echo
generation enters its prime crime-prone ages.

But will this drive the boomers back to cocoons? Hardly.   23
They are finding time to volunteer, to give to charity and to
support their communities. They are increasingly worried about
pensions, investing in the market and thinking about moving
out of the urban rat race. These are the trends of the future.

The boomer generation is predictably shifting into the next   24
phase of life: They are beginning to move from parenthood to
grandparenthood.

Managing this new trend is both a personal and a societal   25
challenge, with all the associated opportunities and tribulations.
Demographic analysis can provide us with a window to
understand these changes, to disentangle them and to predict
them. What more could the successful manager ask for?

UNDERSTANDING DETAILS

1. List the stages of life that Foot identifies including the defining
   events and interests.
2. Who are the two groups currently impacting trends? Explain
   why.
3. Who exactly are the baby boomers and why have they had such
   a big impact on major trends in our society?

ANALYZING MEANING

1. Why is demographic analysis important?
2. What trends are likely to emerge in the next decade as a result
   of demographics, given the influences that Foot outlines?

3. "Anyone ignorant of the power of demographics might think values are changing again" (paragraph 16). Explain this quotation from Foot's essay. What is the distinction between changing values and the power of demographics?

DISCOVERING RHETORICAL STRATEGIES

1. How does Foot organize his categories in this essay? Why does he place these categories in this particular order?
2. Describe the author's intended audience. What makes you think he is directing his comments to this group?
3. What other rhetorical modes does Foot use in this essay besides division and classification? How do these other modes support the author's division/classification system?

MAKING CONNECTIONS

1. David Foot outlines how the baby boomer generation has influenced economic and societal trends in postwar North America. How might Foot explain the phenomena of television in public places (Cowan, "TV Me Alone") and the increasing homogeneity/suburbanization of places like Sudbury (Ferguson, "The Sudbury Syndrome")?
2. Amy Willard Cross ("Life in the Stopwatch Lane") is part of the boomer generation. At what stage in the boomers' lives was her essay originally published? How do you think that demographics may have contributed to the categories of time Cross has identified in her essay? If she were writing this essay today how might it be different?
3. Mark Kingwell ("Not Available in Stores") has written about infomercials and the changes that they have undergone. Based on demographics, what would you predict for the future of infomercials? For television generally?

IDEAS FOR DISCUSSION/WRITING

Preparing to Write

Write freely about your thoughts on your generation. What things define your generation? What music? What attitudes and ideas? What leisure activities? What clothing? What values identify someone of your generation? Do you like the image of your generation? Why or why not? What would you like to change about your generation?

Choosing a Topic

1. As a young entrepreneur you want to start a small business in the next decade. Explain what kind of business you believe would be successful, based on the demographic trends that are outlined in Foot's essay.
2. You are a manager of a mid-size company and you want to hire and retain the best employees. Describe what kind of working environment you will aim to establish to appeal to the workforce of the early 2000s. Where will your employees be located? What kinds of benefits will you offer them? What hours will your employees be expected to work?
3. Imagine you are contributing to the second edition of *Reader's Choice: Essays and Stories* in 2005. Find one new essay that you think should be included. Write a letter to the editor of this text in which you justify your choice based on its merits including its appeal to your audience.

Amy Willard Cross

■ ☐ ■

LIFE IN THE STOPWATCH LANE

Amy Willard Cross is a writer who manages to divide her time between the stopwatch pace of the city and the more relaxed tempo of her other home "in the woods." *The Summer House: A Tradition of Leisure* (1992) is Cross's first book. In it, she examines the North American practice of escaping to the more leisurely life of a cottage or summer house. Born in Washington, D.C. in 1960, Cross currently lives in Canada. Her articles can be found in *City and Country Home*, the *Globe and Mail*, and *Cottage Life*, and she is currently Health Editor at *Chatelaine*.

Preparing to Read

This article first appeared in the *Globe and Mail*'s "Facts and Arguments" column in 1990. In "Life in the Stopwatch Lane," Amy Willard Cross examines the trend toward dividing time into progressively smaller units and labelling different types of time. Before reading this essay, think about the concept of time and how it has changed. How is time viewed differently in different cultures? What value do you place on your time? How do you measure time and what labels do you use to identify different divisions of time?

■──■

If time is money, the rates have skyrocketed and you probably 1
can't afford it. North Americans are suffering a dramatic time shortage since demand greatly exceeds supply. In fact, a recent survey revealed that people lost about 10 hours of leisure per week between 1973 and 1987. Maybe you were too busy to notice.

Losing that leisure leaves a piddling 16.6 hours to do 2
whatever you want, free of work, dish-washing or car-pooling. In television time, that equals a season of 13 *thirtysomething* episodes, plus 3 1/2 reruns. Hardly enough time to write an autobiography or carry on an affair.

How has replacing free time with more billable hours affected 3
society? It has created a new demographic group: the Busy Class—who usurped the Leisure Class. Easy to recognize, members of the Busy Class constantly cry to anyone listening, "I'm *soooooo* busy." So busy they can't call their mother or find change for a panhandler. Masters of doing two things at once, they eke the most out of time. They dictate while driving, talk while calculating, entertain guests while nursing, watch the news while pumping iron. Even business melts into socializing—people earn their daily bread while they break it.

In fact, the Busies must make lots of bread to maintain 4
themselves in the standard of busy-ness to which they've become accustomed. To do that, they need special, expensive stuff. Stuff like call waiting, which lets them talk to two people at once. Stuff like two-faced watches, so they can do business in two time zones at once. Neither frenzied executives nor hurried housewives dare leave the house without their "book"—leather-bound appointment calendars thick as bestsellers. Forget hi-fi's or racing cars, the new talismans of overachievers also work: coffee-makers that brew by alarm; remote-controlled ignitions; or car faxes. Yet, despite all these time-efficient devices, few people have time to spare.

That scarcity has changed how we measure time. Now it's 5
being scientifically dissected into smaller and smaller pieces. Thanks to digital clocks, we know when it's 5:30 (and calculate we'll be home in three hours, eight minutes). These days lawyers

can reason in 1/10th of an hour increments; they bill every six minutes. This to-the-minute precision proves time's escalating value.

Time was, before the advent of car phones and digital clocks, 6 we scheduled two kinds of time: time off and work hours. Not any more. Just as the Inuit label the infinite varieties of snow, the Busy Class has identified myriad subtleties of free time and named them. Here are some textbook examples of the new faces of time:

Quality time. For those working against the clock, the quality 7 of time spent with loved ones supposedly compensates for quantity. This handy concept absolves guilt as quickly as rosary counting. So careerist couples dine à deux once a fortnight. Parents bond by reading kids a story after nanny fed and bathed them. When pressed for time, nobody wastes it by fighting about bad breath or unmade beds. People who spend quality time with each other view their relationships through rose-coloured glasses. And knowing they've created perfect personal lives lets the Busy Class work even harder—guilt-free.

Travel time. With an allowance of 16.6 hours of fun, the Busy 8 Class watches time expenditures carefully. Just like businesses do while making bids, normal people calculate travel time for leisure activities. If two tram rides away, a friendly squash game loses out. One time-efficient woman even formulated a mathematical theorem: fun per mile quotient. Before accepting any social invitation, she adds up travel costs, figures out the time spent laughing, drinking and eating. If the latter exceeds the former, she accepts. It doesn't matter who asks.

Downtime. Borrowed from the world of heavy equipment 9 and sleek computers, downtime is a professional-sounding word meaning the damn thing broke, wait around until it's fixed. Translated into real life, downtime counts as neither work nor play, but a maddening no-man's land where nothing happens! Like lining up for the ski-lift, or commuting without a car phone, or waiting a while for the mechanic's diagnosis. Beware: people who keep track of their downtime probably indulge in less than 16 hours of leisure.

Family time. In addition to 60-hour weeks, aerobics and dinner 10 parties, some people make time for their children. When asked to brunch, a young couple will reply, "We're sorry but that's our family time." A variant of quality time, it's Sunday afternoon between lunch and the Disney Hour when nannies frequent Filipino restaurants. In an effort to entertain their children without exposure to sex and violence, the family attends craft fairs, animated matinees or tree-tapping demonstrations. There, they converge with masses of family units spending time alone with the kids. After a noisy, sticky afternoon, parents gladly punch the clock come Monday.

Quiet time. Overwhelmed by their schedules, some people 11 try to recapture the magic of childhood when they watched clouds for hours on end. Sophisticated grown-ups have rediscovered the quiet time of kindergarten days. They unplug the phone (not the answering machine), clutch a book and try not to think about work. But without teachers to enforce it, quiet doesn't last. The clock ticks too loudly. As a computer fanatic said, after being entertained at 16 megahertz, sitting still to watch a sunset pales by comparison.

As it continues to increase in value, time will surely divide 12 into even smaller units. And people will share only the tiniest amounts with each other. Hey, brother, can you spare a minute? Got a second? A nanosecond?

UNDERSTANDING DETAILS

1. Summarize the various categories into which Cross divides time. How many categories does she believe used to exist?
2. Why do busy people divide time into so many different categories?
3. What technological innovations does Cross mention that have allowed us to "maximize our efficient use of time"?

ANALYZING MEANING

1. What is Cross's purpose in this essay? To what extent does she achieve this purpose?
2. What is responsible for our measuring time in smaller and smaller units? What implications does this have for the way that we live?
3. Why has increased efficiency resulted in less leisure time?

DISCOVERING RHETORICAL STRATEGIES

1. While Cross's main division is that of time, she also divides people into groups. On what basis has she divided each of these subjects?

2. How would you describe the tone that Cross adopts in this essay? How does she feel about the "Busy Class" and the categories of time they have created? How do you know this?

3. Humour and unexpected phrasing are used effectively in describing the people that are featured in this essay and the different categories of time. Which details are particularly effective in conveying Cross's point of view?

MAKING CONNECTIONS

1. Amy Willard Cross identifies several types of time in her essay. Imagine a conversation between Cross and Tomson Highway ("What a Certain Visionary Once Said"). Do you think these two writers would view time the same way? Explain why or why not.

2. David Foot ("Boomers Dance to a New Beat") discusses the role of demographics in societal trends. How is Cross's division of time a reflection of the generation to which she belongs?

3. Amy Willard Cross identifies each of the categories in her essay with a clear heading. How does this compare to the strategies used by Susan Swan ("Nine Ways of Looking at a Critic") and Gwynne Dyer ("Flagging Attention")? Why has each author chosen his or her respective approach?

IDEAS FOR DISCUSSION/WRITING

Preparing to Write

Write freely about the effects of technology. What technological developments have made us more efficient? What expectations have changed as a result of changing technology? What positive effects do you see from things such as computers, cellular telephones, and fax machines? What negative consequences have these pieces of equipment had on our lives?

Choosing a Topic

1. In a short essay outline the ways in which some technological development has changed your life. Before you start writing, make sure that you choose a purpose and a particular point of view.

2. The way time is viewed varies greatly across cultures. Write an essay, to be distributed at an international conference on ed-

ucation, which gives teachers from a variety of different countries an idea of how a typical North American student spends her/his time. Use a clear system of division to convey your message effectively.

3. Write an essay in which you classify the various people you know, in categories. First, decide on a principle for classification, and then use specific detail to explain where individuals are placed.

Gwynne Dyer

FLAGGING ATTENTION

Gwynne Dyer is described on the CBC *Ideas* Web site as "one of Canada's media renaissance men, an outstanding journalist, broadcaster, producer, author, and filmmaker." Dyer was born in St. John's, Newfoundland in 1943, and has earned degrees from Memorial University of Newfoundland (B.A., History), Rice University in Houston (M.A., Military History), and King's College, University of London (Ph.D., Military and Middle Eastern History). That education, along with his experience serving in the Royal Canadian Naval Reserve, the U.S. Naval Reserve, and the British Royal Naval Reserve and reporting on the Gulf War, has prepared Dyer well for the writing, producing, directing, and hosting of a multitude of radio productions, films, and television series, mainly dealing with topics related to war, defence, militarism, international conflict, and human politics. Dyer also writes a twice-weekly syndicated column on international affairs that appears in about 150 papers in around 30 countries.

Preparing to Read

The following essay, taken from *EnRoute* (Air Canada's in-flight magazine), discusses the range of flags that exist and the qualities that allow us to categorize them. As you prepare to read this article, think about flags. What do flags represent? Who designs flags? What rules of conduct govern people's behaviour in relation to flags? What does it mean to burn a flag? Where are flags typically displayed? At what times of year or at what events are flags typically highly visible?

If you want to see my favourite flag in the whole world—more   1
bizarre than the Nepalese flag, which looks like two scraps of
red bikini fluttering in the wind; more literal-minded even than
Cyprus's flag, which consists of an orange map of Cyprus on a
white background—you don't have to go that far. Just go to
Vancouver.

I spent some time in the Navy during the late Jurassic, and   2
reservists I knew from Vancouver would actually boast about
it. It was the flag of Her Majesty's Canadian Ship Discovery
(which is actually a building, or "stone frigate"). How will you
know which one that is? Easy. It's a neat little circle nestled in
the crotch of a large letter "Y." Or to put it another way: It is a
"disc over" a "Y."

Visual puns are to ordinary puns as Ebola fever is to measles.   3
A long time ago (back when I had pimples) I used to collect visual
puns, but after HMCS Discovery I just gave up. You can search
the front and back pages of any dictionary you like, and no flag
in the world even begins to approach it for sheer awfulness.
Though they do try.

All this stuff about flags came up after my six-year-old, Kate,   4
saw *Mulan* and wanted to know what the Chinese flag looked
like. So out with the trusty dictionary, and there it was in all its
minimalist splendour: a plain red flag with some stars in the corner.

She seemed a bit disappointed by China's flag, so to cheer   5
her up I started making fun of some of the more lurid flags that
jostled alongside it on the page. Brazil's, for example, has the
slogan of a dead political movement—*Ordem e Progresso* (Order
and Progress)—written on a white band stretched like an equator
across a blue globe with the southern night sky superimposed
on it, and the whole mess being contained within a yellow
diamond on a green background. Kate was riveted.

While there were about 50 flags at the back of the dictionary   6
when I was a kid, there are now close to 200, and the style has
changed.

Boring old horizontal or vertical stripes are out. Diagonal   7
slashes, nested triangles and heraldic animals are in, and any
flag with less than five colours just isn't in the running. I get
around a lot, but I haven't seen even half of them in real life—
except maybe outside the United Nations building in New York,
where the flagpoles are now crowded so closely together that
you can't make anything out.

What struck both me and my daughter was that there are   8
obviously three quite different kinds of flags. There are the
traditional ones, with a few dignified stripes and maybe some
stars or a crest. There are the designer ones, ranging from ad-
agency flash to play-school messy. And there are the ones that are
just trying too hard, like Mozambique's flag: crossed black hoe
and AK-47 superimposed on an open white book, all on a yellow
star, which is, in turn, on a red triangle, with broad green, thin
white, broad black, thin white and broad yellow stripes off to
the right. (Yes, I know it's all symbolic, but even so ...)

Canada's flag falls into the designer category. Three vertical   9
stripes, red-white-red, still look quite traditional, and if you were
feeling bold you might even get away with having a discreet
little shield or badge on the middle stripe—in fact, more than
half the flags of Latin America follow exactly that pattern—but
the maple leaf is just too big and in-your-face to qualify as
traditional. This is a flag halfway to being a logo. Well, good.
The whole idea of a new Canadian flag, back in the '60s, was to
re-brand the country, and it has worked a treat: Everybody now
understands that we're not British, we're Canadian. Québec went
through a similar exercise 15 years before, adopting the old pre-
revolutionary French flag in colour-reverse, with an equally
satisfactory rise in the recognition factor.

If it works, don't knock it. But what you notice, looking across   10
the pages and pages of flags, is that (a) most of the good ideas
were taken some time ago; (b) the smaller the country, the more
elaborate the flag; and (c) there are fashions in flags, as in
everything else. The new South African flag, for example, looks
like a collision between Jamaica's and Vanuatu's. After 200 other
countries have dipped into the pot, there aren't any elegant
designs left. While Japan (pop. 125 million) has made do with a
plain red circle on a white background for over 1,000 years,
latecomer Grenada (pop. 101,000) wound up with a multi-
coloured extravaganza involving stars, circles, triangles,
rectangles and what appears to be a leaf shape.

As for fashion, it's not just Muslim countries putting crescent   11
moons on their flags, or half the countries of Africa going in for
stars. For some reason, it has become de rigueur among small
island states—Trinidad and Tobago, St. Kitts-Nevis, the Marshall
Islands, the Solomon Islands—to put bold diagonal slashes on
their flags.

But no matter how gaudy or silly the flag, somewhere a   12
bunch of school kids or army conscripts is being taught to love it,
pledge allegiance to it, maybe even kill or die for it. Now, I
understand the need for a sense of unity and community, and I
realize that people need symbols. In my time, I have served in
various people's navies and saluted their flags without feeling
abused or humiliated. It's just part of the package. Once, in the
Canadian Navy, I was the guy out in front with the sword and
shiny boots when we did the Sunset Ceremony, and even felt a
surge of emotion myself at the climax of the ceremony.

We are all tribesmen under the skin, and there's no point in   13
beating ourselves up about it. But we don't have to fall for it
either; we are not *only* tribesmen. I'll pledge allegiance to any
flag you like if it will keep me out of jail. But frankly, I'd rather
pledge allegiance to a bedspread.

UNDERSTANDING DETAILS

1. What are the three categories of flags that Dyer identifies? What
   characterizes each of these categories? Into which category does
   the Canadian flag fall? Why?
2. In paragraph 3, Dyer discussed visual puns. What is a visual
   pun? How does Dyer feel about them?
3. What is the purpose of a national flag? What need or needs
   does it fulfill?

ANALYZING MEANING

1. Dyer ends his essay by saying, "We are all tribesmen under the
   skin ... [but] we are not *only* tribesmen. I'll pledge allegiance to
   any flag you like if it will keep me out of jail. But frankly, I'd
   rather pledge allegiance to a bedspread." Explain what Dyer
   means in this conclusion.
2. In paragraph 6, Dyer comments on the increase in the number
   of flags and the change in their style. Why is there such an increase in the number of flags, and what accounts for the stylistic changes in flag design?
3. Dyer has an M.A. and a Ph.D. in military history. In addition, the
   focus of his writing, films, and broadcasting has been militarism
   and war in many different nations. Why is it the curiosity of his
   six-year-old daughter that alerts him to the variety of flags and
   their significance?

DISCOVERING RHETORICAL STRATEGIES

1. How would you describe the tone that Dyer adopts in this essay? How has Dyer created this tone?
2. Throughout his essay, Dyer makes several interesting word choices and uses several figures of speech. Identify at least four examples of this type of language usage and explain the effect they have on Dyer's essay.
3. Dyer makes a few references to belonging to the navy. What role do these references play in his essay?

MAKING CONNECTIONS

1. Neil Bissoondath ("Pieces of Sky") writes about symbols that represent the values of Canada. How are the values Bissoondath evokes reflected in the flags that Dyer describes?
2. How does Dyer's attitude toward patriotism compare to that of Allen Abel in "A Home at the End of the Journey" or of Steven Heighton in "Elegy in Stone"?

IDEAS FOR DISCUSSION/WRITING

Preparing to Write

Write freely about patriotism. In what ways do people demonstrate their patriotism? Why do people feel such strong loyalty to their countries? In what ways is patriotism created? How is it maintained? What types of behaviour are considered particularly patriotic? What is the opposite of being patriotic?

Choosing a Topic

1. Write an essay in which you classify specific examples of behaviour into those that are distinctly patriotic and those that are counter to patriotism. Be clear about your attitude toward each category of behaviour.
2. Assume that you are responsible for another "rebranding of Canada." Describe the flag that you would design and its significance. What new aspects of Canada are you hoping to convey with this flag?
3. National anthems are another symbol of a country intended to inspire patriotism and reflect the values of a nation. In the same way that Dyer has categorized flags, categorize a range of national anthems with which you are familiar.

Susan Swan

■ □ ■

NINE WAYS OF LOOKING AT A CRITIC

"Swan has a gift for the provocative ..." says Joe Hooper of *Mirabella*, and in the essay that appears here, Swan does not shy away from provoking her audience.

Born in Midland, Ontario in 1945, Swan was a student at Havergal College in Toronto in the early 1960s and received a B.A. from McGill University in 1967. In the 1970s Swan became involved in theatre, both writing and performing. She is now a novelist, a journalist, a script writer, a faculty member for the Humber School for Writers' correspondence program, and a professor of Humanities at York University in Toronto.

Susan Swan's novels include *The Biggest Modern Woman in the World* (1983), the story of a giantess who exhibited with P.T. Barnum; *The Last of the Golden Girls* (1989); and *The Wives of Bath* (1993), about a murder in a girls' boarding school. Swan's most recent book is *Stupid Boys Are Good to Relax With* (1998) and she is currently working on a novel called *What Casanova Told Me*. While Swan has received a very positive response to her work, as evidenced by her nominations for Canada's Governor General's Award, the UK Guardian Award, and Ontario's Trillium Award, she has also created controversy as sexuality figures prominently in all of Swan's novels. Suanne Kelman, in a 1994 story about "Can Lit's bad girls" from *Chatelaine* magazine, summarizes Swan's attitude as follows: "Swan writes the way she thinks: raised to be a pillar of society, she's still trying to free herself—and her readers—from what she sees as a phony concept of female virtue."

Preparing to Read

In this humorous essay, which originally appeared in the *Globe and Mail*, Susan Swan divides book reviewers into nine different categories. Before you begin reading, think about the job of a reviewer whether that person is reviewing books, movies, restaurants, concerts, or any other work or performance. Who is the audience the reviewer is targeting? What is the goal of a reviewer? Are there reviewers whose opinions you particularly value? Are there reviewers with whom you disagree? What makes a good reviewer? How do you think reviewers are perceived by those whose work they review?

As a writer, I naturally have some idealistic notions about book 1 reviewing. For instance, I admire Alexander Pope's list of necessary qualities for a critic—integrity, modesty, tact, courage and an awareness of the critic's own limitations. I also like Matthew Arnold's claim that a critic should possess an eager, open mind and the ability to rise above a sect or clique.

But a reviewer with these qualities is not a person most 2 authors get to meet very often, no matter how much we might long for an intelligent review. The more books I write and the more reviews I receive (whether good, bad or indifferent), the more I see how elusive this ideal reviewer is. What I notice instead are the clearly recognizable types of unsatisfactory reviewers no author can avoid meeting in the pages of our newspapers and magazines. I'm not talking so much about academic journals, although you can probably spot my reviewing types there too.

The following is a list of eight types of less-than-ideal 3 reviewers I've met in my 20 years of writing fiction and 30 years of reviewing.

Number one are The Masturbators, a common category. 4 These are the reviewers who feel they could have written a better book on the subject, given half the chance. In their eyes, the author got it all wrong, and the only value in the book is that it reminds the reviewers that they have superb and untested writing skills which, for one reason or another, they haven't got around to putting into practice.

Sometimes, the direction these reviewers suggest the book 5 take are strange and hilarious. For instance, G.K. Chesterton was fond of quoting the reviewer who liked Charles Dickens's novel *Martin Chuzzlewit*, but complained that it shed no light on the marital customs of Norway.

Number two are The Spankers. Canada, which has an 6 abundance of good writers, also teems with Spankers, who are out to administer discipline over anything from ill-conceived plot-lines to misplaced commas. If Spankers are male, they often display a macho zest—"a real man calls crap crap." If they are female, Spankers can indulge in a scolding, martyred tone—as in, "I have better things to do, but for the good of literature I will dirty my hands in pronouncing this book not worth the reader's time."

Once in a while, in my writerly paranoia, I think the Canadian 7 style *is* to punish and admonish. After all, Canadians tend to look suspiciously at anyone who upholds what is good. Like our pioneers, who distrusted emotions and the body—viz. French-Canadian Jansenism and English-Canadian Calvinism—we prefer the canny so-and-so who won't be fooled by what is bad.

But Spankers can be found anywhere, particularly if the book 8 tries to tackle sexuality. "D.H. Lawrence has a diseased mind. He is obsessed with sex ... we have no doubt that he will be ostracized by all except the most degenerate coteries in the literary world," an English reviewer once wrote in *John Bull*.

The third category, closely aligned with Spankers, is The 9 Young (and Old) Turk. This group sees the review solely as an opportunity to demonstrate its literary superiority and above-average intelligence. (Not only was I once one of these—dismissing older, established writers in a few sentences—I have been the victim of Young Turks, too. This may be my karma for assuming earlier that my limited life experience and barely developed writing skills were the very qualities that allowed me to see the tinny emptiness of the older writer's celebrity.)

It's probably a good thing Turks can sometimes leave us with 10 memorable witticisms that may be remembered long after the book they reviewed. Who can forget Oscar Wilde's riposte that it took a heart of stone to read of the death of Little Nell without laughing?

The fourth category is Gushers: They skip over discussion of 11 the book; they just want to communicate the enjoyment of reading it. The best example of Gushers can be found in the book ads of publications like *The New York Times Book Review*, where phrases lifted from reviews proclaim: "major"; "ground-breaking"; "compulsively readable"; "new genius that will change the face of literature"; "the first truly great novel since Tolstoy," and so on. Americans excel at the use of superlatives, trotting out for different authors the same laudatory manifestos of praise week after week. Few writers will object to this habit, for obvious reasons.

The fifth category is The Diviners, a sympathetic but 12 misguided lot. Diviners claim to know the author's reasons for writing the book. They may even deliver an up-to-the-minute and totally fabricated psychological analysis of the author as an incest victim or recovering alcoholic as evidence for their position. (Authors are wise to hold their tongues when confronted with these well-wisher divinations.)

Sixth are The Puritans, who don't like a book if they think its 13 characters have bad morals. They have trouble separating the author from the people in the story.

Seventh come The Grumps, who may like the book but 14
begrudge its author too much praise. Grumps are fond of making
congratulatory noises and then lingering for much of their review
over typos and small mistakes as if they were major boo-boos
that undermined the book's credibility. Most authors I know
would feel grateful (although embarrassed) if the reviewer
pointed out a major mistake. But to be taken to task for tiny errors
by reviewers who say they love the book is the sort of thing that
can make a writer want to take up brick-laying.

My eighth and final category—to date—is that of The Flat- 15
Earthers. These reviewers believe all fiction should be true-to-
life, relying, like non-fiction, on fact. Flat-Earthers tend to say
things like, "This would never happen so it's no good." In this
category, a film like *Thelma and Louise* would be a failure because
how often have you heard of two women driving their car over
a cliff into the Grand Canyon?

Flat-Earthers also have an astonishing ability to know what 16
life is really like. I don't mean the reviewer who is upset by a
writer sloppily sticking wrong details into a piece of fictional
realism, like putting palm trees on Baffin Island. The Flat-Earther
has more hubris than that; a book must support his or her
definition of what it's like to be alive, as he or she knows it. The
idea that fiction can present a reality altogether different from
the life the reviewer knows is unheard of to a Flat-Earther.

All right. I've told you about the types of reviewers writers 17
often meet. But if a writer like me could construct the ideal critic
the way I make up a character, what qualities would I give this
creature? First of all, most writers I know want professional
standards. Curiously enough, many reviewers aren't know-
ledgeable about literature. Nor are they experienced enough with
reviewing to know what they're doing. Would you let your child
take English lessons from somebody newly arrived from a non-
English-speaking country? Canada now has an abundance of
good writers, but the quality of our reviewers hasn't kept up
with the quality of our books. Much of the blame for this belongs
to the media, which has eliminated space for book reviews and
is still paying reviewers roughly what it did when I started
reviewing back in the late 1960s.

No other profession I know could get away with such sub- 18
standard pay. A good reviewer needs credentials and a living
wage, otherwise getting your book reviewed is like having your
teeth pulled in the Wild West. Instead of a trained dentist, you

face the equivalent of a drunken cowboy with pliers, who has the confidence to think he can do a good job. The idea that he might leave a hole in your head for the rest of your life doesn't occur.

As Pope said, a writer appreciates a reviewer who is brave   19
enough to declare a bias. Why review Jane Austen if you are a Jack Kerouac fan who hates 19th-century British writers, unless you are going to admit up front that Austen isn't your cup of tea? (Book columnists are an exception because readers get to know their taste and can put their judgments in perspective.)

"Says who?," I often think reading reviewers with no   20
particular credentials to engage the book's subject, or who lack the courage to admit that a certain style isn't their specialty.

By contrast, good reviews will represent the book (without   21
lapsing into long-winded plot summaries) so the reader gets a sense of what the book is like whether the reviewer likes it or not. And the best reviews offer an informed reading that will provide an interesting or revealing point of view from which the book can be perceived. In other words, a well-written review gives us not only the reviewer's personal reaction, it adds to our knowledge of the book.

Pure opinion is a cheat; it belongs to talk radio stations, not   22
reviews. In some ways, personal reaction is the most uninteresting thing a reviewer has to offer.

UNDERSTANDING DETAILS

1. List the types of critics Swan identifies. Explain the apparent contradiction between the title, which prepares you for nine groupings, and the sentence in paragraph 3 that introduces eight types of critics.
2. According to Swan, what is the difference between a good review and a bad review?
3. Into which category of reviewer does Swan put herself? Does she believe she still belongs in this category? Why or why not?

ANALYZING MEANING

1. Explain why Swan has chosen the name "The Flat-Earthers" for the category of reviewers who "believe all fiction should be true-to-life"? Is this an effective name for this group?

2. In this essay, Swan refers to a variety of people ranging from Alexander Pope to Jack Kerouac. Who are the people she mentions and why has she made reference to them in this essay?
3. Explain which of the eight types of "less-than-desirable" reviewers you think would be the worst in the opinion of most writers. Which would be the best? Why?

DISCOVERING RHETORICAL STRATEGIES

1. Why do you think that Susan Swan has written this essay? What is her purpose? Where is this made clear?
2. Who is the intended audience of this essay? Explain why you have identified this group of people.
3. Explain the effectiveness of Swan's introduction and conclusion. How has she linked the beginning and end of her essay?

MAKING CONNECTIONS

1. In this essay Swan identifies one category as being particularly Canadian and another as being typically American. How do these qualities compare to the contrasts between Canadians and Americans that are pointed out by Allen Abel ("A Home at the End of the Journey")?
2. In "The Babar Factor," Evan Solomon reviews video games by comparing them to Babar books. In Swan's terms, what category does Solomon fit into as a reviewer?
3. In "Genius or Madness?" Lynn Coady considers the opinions of others and the way that people are classified. Imagine a discussion between Coady and Swan about the role of the critic in the life of a writer. Do you think they would see the critic's role the same way? Why or why not?

IDEAS FOR WRITING/DISCUSSION

Preparing to Write

Write freely about a book you have read. What was the book about? Did you like it? What was good about it? What didn't you like? Was there anything about it that confused you? Would you read other books by the same author? What would you say to the author if you met him or her? How would you rate the book overall? Would you recommend it to others?

Choosing a Topic

1. In this essay Swan divides book reviewers into different categories. Write an essay in which you divide movie reviewers into a series of appropriate categories.

2. Using the Internet or periodical indexes, find a review of one of Swan's books. Read the review and then decide in which of Swan's categories the reviewer best fits. Explain why the reviewer fits the category you have chosen.

3. Stores classify their merchandise into various categories to help shoppers locate the things they are looking for. Think of a type of store where things are often difficult to find and propose a new system of classification that you think would be more effective. You might choose a music store, a grocery store, a hardware store, a department store, or some other type of store with which you are familiar.

CHAPTER 6

COMPARISON/CONTRAST

■ ■ ■

Discovering Similarities and Differences

Making comparisons is such a natural and necessary part of our everyday lives that we often do so without conscious effort. When we were children, we compared our toys with those of our friends, we contrasted our height and physical development to other children's, and we constantly evaluated our happiness in comparison with that evidenced by our parents and childhood companions. As we grew older, we habitually compared our dates, teachers, parents, friends, cars, and physical attributes. In college or university, we learn about anthropology by writing essays on the similarities and differences between two African tribes, about political science by contrasting the Liberal and Reform platforms, about business by comparing annual production rates, and about literature by comparing Atwood with Munro or Shakespeare with Marlowe. Comparing and contrasting various elements in our lives helps us make decisions, such as which course to take or which house to buy, and it justifies preferences that we already hold, such as liking one city more than another or loving one person more than the next. In these ways and in many others, the skillful use of comparison and contrast is clearly essential to our social and professional lives.

Defining Comparison/Contrast

Comparison and contrast allow us to understand one subject by putting it next to another. Comparing involves discovering likenesses or similarities, whereas contrasting is based on finding differences. Like division and classification, comparison and contrast are generally considered part of the same process, because we usually have no reason for comparing unless some contrast is also involved. Each technique implies the existence of the other. For this reason, the word *compare* is often used to mean both techniques.

Comparison and contrast are most profitably applied to two items that have something in common, such as cats and dogs or cars and motorcycles. A discussion of cats and motorcycles, for example, would probably not be very rewarding or stimulating, because they do not have much in common. If more than two items are compared in an essay, they are still most profitably discussed in pairs: for instance, motorcycles and cars, cars and bicycles, or bicycles and motorcycles.

An analogy is an extended, sustained comparison. Often used to explain unfamiliar, abstract, or complicated thoughts, this rhetorical technique adds energy and vividness to a wide variety of college-level writing. The process of analogy differs slightly from comparison/contrast in three important ways: Comparison/contrast begins with subjects from the same class and places equal weight on both of them. In addition, it addresses both the similarities and the differences of these subjects. Analogy, conversely, seldom explores subjects from the same class, and focuses principally on one familiar subject in an attempt to explain another, more complex one. Furthermore, it deals only with similarities, not with contrasts. A comparison/contrast essay, for example, might study two veterans' ways of coping with the trauma of the Gulf War by pointing out the differences in their methods as well as the similarities. An analogy essay might use the familiar notion of a fireworks display to reveal the chilling horror of the lonely hours after dark during this war: "Nights in the Persian Gulf were similar to a loud, unending fireworks display. We had no idea when the next blast was coming, how loud it would be, or how close. We cringed in terror after dark, hoping the next surprise would not be our own death." In this example, rather than simply hearing about an event, we participate in it through this highly refined form of comparison.

The following student paragraph compares and contrasts married and single life. As you read it, notice how the author compares similar social states and, in the process, justifies her current lifestyle:

> Recently I saw a bumper sticker that read, "It used to be wine, women, and song, and now it's beer, the old lady, and TV." Much truth may be found in this comparison of single and married lifestyles.

When my husband and I used to date, for example, we'd go out for dinner and drinks and then maybe see a play or concert. Our discussions were intelligent, often ranging over global politics, science, literature, and other lofty topics. He would open doors for me, buy me flowers, and make sure I was comfortable and happy. Now, three years later, after marriage and a child, the baby bottle has replaced the wine bottle, the smell of diapers wipes out the scent of roses, and our nights on the town are infrequent, cherished events. But that's ok. A little bit of the excitement and mystery may be gone, but these intangible qualities have given way to a sturdy, dependable trust in each other and a quiet confidence about our future together.

Thinking Critically by Using Comparison/Contrast

Comparison and contrast are basic to a number of different thought processes. We compare and contrast quite naturally on a daily basis, but all of us would benefit greatly from being more aware of these companion strategies in our own writing. They help us not only in perceiving our environment but also in understanding and organizing large amounts of information.

The basic skill of finding similarities and differences will enhance your ability to create accurate descriptions, to cite appropriate examples, to present a full process analysis, and, of course, to classify and label subjects. It is a pattern of thought that is essential to more complex thinking strategies, so perfecting the ability to use it is an important step in your efforts to improve your critical thinking.

Once again, we are going to practise this strategy in isolation to get a strong sense of its mechanics before we combine it with other rhetorical modes. Isolating this mode will make your reading and writing even stronger than they are now, because the individual parts of the thinking process will be more vigorous and effective, thus making your academic performance more powerful than ever.

1. Find magazine ads that use comparison/contrast to make a point or sell a product. What is the basis of each comparison? How effective or ineffective is each comparison?
2. Compare or contrast the experience of spending time with a special person to another type of experience (e.g., a roller-coaster ride, sleeping, or a trip across Canada). Be as specific as possible in your comparison.

3. Have you ever been to the same place twice? Think for a moment about how the first and second visits to this place differed. How were they similar? What were the primary reasons for the similarities and differences in your perceptions of these visits?

Reading and Writing Comparison/Contrast Essays

Many established guidelines regulate the development of a comparison/contrast essay and should be taken into account from both the reading and the writing perspectives. All good comparative studies serve a specific purpose. They attempt either to examine their subjects separately or to demonstrate the superiority of one over the other. In evaluating two different types of cars, for example, a writer might point out the amazing gas mileage of one model and the smooth handling qualities of the other, or the superiority of one car's gas consumption over that of the other. Whatever the intent, comparison/contrast essays need to be clear and logical and to have a precise purpose.

How to Read a Comparison/Contrast Essay

Preparing to Read. As you begin reading this chapter, pull together as much preliminary material as possible for each essay so you can focus your attention and have the benefit of prior knowledge before you start to read. In particular, you are trying to discover what is being compared or contrasted and why. What does Will Ferguson's title ("The Sudbury Syndrome") suggest to you? From the title of his essay, can you tell what Michael McKinley is comparing in "Opera Night in Canada"? From glancing at the essay itself and reading the synopsis in the Rhetorical Table of Contents, what does Gloria Steinem's essay try to accomplish?

Also, before you begin to read these essays, try to discover information about the author and about the conditions under which each essay was written. Why is Ferguson qualified to write about various Canadian cities? Does he reveal his background in his essay? What is Charlotte Gray's job? To what extent do you expect this to colour her comparison of Japanese and Canadian cultures?

Finally, just before you begin to read, answer the Preparing to Read questions, and then make some free associations with the general topic of each essay. For example, what are some of the similarities and differences between hockey and opera (Michael McKinley)? What is your general view on women's bodybuilding (Gloria Steinem)?

Reading. As you read each comparison/contrast essay for the first time, be sure to record your own feelings and opinions. Some of the issues presented in this chapter are highly controversial. You will often have strong reactions to them, which you should try to write down as soon as possible.

In addition, you may want to comment on the relationship between the preliminary essay material, the author's stance in the essay, and the content of the essay itself. For example, what motivated Solomon to write "The Babar Factor"? Who was his primary audience? What is Ferguson's tone in "The Sudbury Syndrome," and how does it further his purpose? Answers to questions such as these will provide you with a context for your first reading of these essays and will assist you in preparing to analyze the essays in more depth on your second reading.

At this point in the chapter, you should make certain you understand each author's thesis and then take a close look at his or her principal method of organization: Is the essay arranged (1) point by point, (2) subject by subject, (3) as a combination of these two, or (4) as separate discussions of similarities and differences between two subjects? (See the chart on page 224 for an illustration of these options.) Last, preview the questions that follow the essay before you read it again.

Rereading. When you read these essays a second time, you should look at the comparison or contrast much more closely than you have up to now. First, look in detail at the writer's method of organization (see the chart on page 224). How effective is it in advancing the writer's thesis?

Next, you should consider whether each essay is fully developed and balanced: Does McKinley compare similar items? Does Solomon discuss the same qualities for his subjects? Does Gray deal with all aspects of the comparison between Japanese and Canadian people? Is Steinem's treatment of her two subjects well balanced? And does Ferguson give his audience enough specific details to clarify the extent of his comparison? Do all the writers in this chapter use well-chosen transitions so you can move smoothly from one point to the next? Also, what other rhetorical modes support each comparison/contrast in this chapter? Finally, answering the questions after each selection will let you evaluate your understanding of the essay and help you analyze its contents in preparation for the discussion/writing topics that follow.

For a more thorough inventory of the reading process, you should turn to pages 15–16 in the Introduction.

How to Write a Comparison/Contrast Essay

Preparing to Write. As you consider various topics for a comparison/contrast essay, you should answer the Preparing to Write questions that precede the assignments and then use the prewriting techniques explained in the Introduction to generate even more ideas on these topics.

As you focus your attention on a particular topic, keep the following suggestions in mind:

1. Always compare/contrast items in the same category (e.g., compare two professors, but not a professor and a swimming pool).
2. Have a specific purpose or reason for writing your essay.
3. Discuss the same qualities of each subject (if you evaluate the teaching techniques of one professor, do so for the other professor as well).
4. Use as many pertinent details as possible to expand your comparison/contrast and to accomplish your stated purpose.
5. Deal with all aspects of the comparison that are relevant to the purpose.
6. Balance the treatment of the different subjects of your comparison (i.e., don't spend more time on one than on another).
7. Determine your audience's background and knowledge so that you will know how much of your comparison should be explained in detail and how much can be skimmed over.

Next, in preparation for a comparison/contrast project, you might list all the elements of both subjects that you want to compare. This list can then help you give your essay structure as well as substance. At this stage in the writing process, the task may seem similar to pure description, but a discussion of two subjects in relation to one another rapidly changes the assignment from description to comparison.

Writing. The introduction of your comparison/contrast essay should (1) clearly identify your subjects, (2) explain the basis of your comparison/contrast, and (3) state your purpose and the overall limits of your particular study. Identifying your subject is, of course, a necessary and important task in any essay. Similarly, justifying the elements you will be comparing and contrasting creates reader interest and gives your audience some specifics to look for in the essay. Finally, your statement of purpose or thesis (for example, to prove that one professor is superior to another) should include the boundaries of your discussion. You cannot cover all the reasons for your preference in one short essay, so you must limit your consideration to three or four basic categories (perhaps teaching techniques, the clarity of the assignments given, classroom attitude, and grading standards). The introduction is the place to make all these limits known.

You can organize the body of your paper in one of four ways: (1) a point-by-point, or alternating, comparison; (2) a subject-by-subject, or divided, comparison; (3) a combination of these two methods; or (4) a division between the similarities and differences. (See the chart on page 224.)

The point-by-point comparison evaluates both subjects in terms of each category. If the issue, for example, is which of two cars to buy, you might discuss both models' gasoline consumption first; then, their horsepower; next, their ease in handling; and, finally, their standard equipment. Following the second method of organization, subject by subject, you would discuss the gasoline consumption, horsepower, ease in handling, and standard equipment of car A first and then follow the same format for car B. The third option would allow you to introduce, say, the interior design of each car point by point (or car by car) and then to explain the mechanical features of the automobiles (kilometres per litre, horsepower, gear ratio, and braking system) subject by subject. To use the last method of organization, you might discuss the similarities between the two models first and the differences second (or vice versa). If the cars you are comparing have similar kilometres-per-litre (km/L) ratings but completely different horsepower, steering systems, and optional equipment, you could discuss the gasoline consumption first and then emphasize the differences by mentioning them later in the essay. If, instead, you are trying to emphasize the fact that the km/L ratings of these models remain consistent despite their differences, then reverse the order of your essay.

Methods of Organization

Point by Point

km/L, car A
km/L, car B

horsepower, car A
horsepower, car B

handling, car A
handling, car B

equipment, car A
equipment, car B

Subject by Subject

km/L, car A
horsepower, car A
handling, car A
equipment, car A

km/L, car B
horsepower, car B
handling, car B
equipment, car B

Combination

Interior, car A
Interior, car B

———

km/L, car A
horsepower, car A

km/L, car B
horsepower, car B

Similarities/Differences

similarities:
  km/L, cars A & B

differences:
  horsepower, cars A & B
  handling, cars A & B
  equipment, cars A & B

When confronted with the task of choosing a method of organization for a comparison/contrast essay, you need to find the pattern that best suits your purpose. If you want single items to stand out in a discussion, for instance, the best choice will be the point-by-point system; it is especially appropriate for long essays, but has a tendency to turn into an exercise in making lists if you don't pay careful attention to your transitions. If, however, the subjects themselves (rather than the itemized points) are the most interesting feature of your essay, you should use the subject-by-subject comparison; this system is particularly good for short essays in which the readers can retain what was said about one subject while they read about a second subject. Through this second system of organization, each subject becomes a unified whole, an approach to an essay that is generally effective unless the theme becomes awkwardly divided into two separate parts. You must also remember, if you choose this second method of organization, that the second (or last) subject is in the most emphatic position because that is what your readers will have seen most recently. The final two options for organizing a comparison/contrast essay give you some built-in flexibility so that you can create emphasis and attempt to manipulate reader opinion simply by the structure of your essay.

Using logical transitions in your comparison/contrast essays will establish clear relationships between the items in your comparisons and will also move your readers smoothly from one topic to the next. If you wish to indicate comparisons, use such words as *like, as, also, in like manner, similarly,* and *in addition;* to signal contrasts, try *but, in contrast to, unlike, whereas,* and *on the one hand/on the other hand.*

The conclusion of a comparison/contrast essay summarizes the main points and states the deductions drawn from those points. As you choose your method of organization, remember not to get locked into a formulaic approach to your subjects, which will adversely affect the readability of your essay. To avoid making your reader feel like a spectator at a verbal table tennis match, be straightforward, honest, and patient as you discover and recount the details of your comparison.

Rewriting. When you review the draft of your comparison/contrast essay, you need once again to make sure that you communicate your purpose as effectively as possible to your intended audience. Two guidelines previously mentioned should help you accomplish this goal:

1. Do you identify your subjects clearly?
2. Does your thesis clearly state the purpose and overall limits of your particular study?

You will also need to pay close attention to the development of your essay:

1. Are you attempting to compare/contrast items from the same general category?
2. Do you discuss the same qualities of each subject?
3. Do you balance the treatment of the different subjects of your essay?
4. Did you organize your topic as effectively as possible?
5. Does your conclusion contain a summary and analysis of your main points?

For further information on writing and revising your comparison/contrast essays, consult the checklists on pages 26-27 of the Introduction.

Student Essay: Comparison/Contrast at Work

The following student essay compares the advantages and disadvantages of macaroni and cheese versus tacos in the life of a harried first-year college or university student. As you read it, notice that the writer states his intention in the first paragraph and then expands his discussion with appropriate details to produce a balanced essay. Also, try to determine what effect he creates by using two methods of organization: first subject by subject, then point by point.

Student Chef

To this day, I will not eat either macaroni and cheese or tacos. *Topics*
No, it's not because of any allergy; it's because during my first *Basis of comparison* year at college, I prepared one or the other of these scrumptious dishes more times than I care to remember. <u>However, my choice</u> *Thesis statement: Purpose and limits of comparison* <u>of which culinary delight to cook on any given night was not as</u> <u>simple a decision as one might imagine.</u>

Macaroni and cheese has numerous advantages for the student *Paragraph on Subject A: Macaroni and cheese* chef. <u>First of all, it is inexpensive.</u> No matter how poor one may be, *Point 1 (Price)* there's probably enough change under the couch cushion to buy a box at the market. All that starch for only 89¢. What a bargain! <u>Second, it can be prepared in just one pan.</u> This is especially im- *Point 2 (Preparation)* portant given the meagre resources of the average student resi- *Point 3 (Odour)* dence kitchen. <u>Third, and perhaps most important, macaroni and</u> <u>cheese is odourless.</u> By odourless, I mean that no one else can smell it. It is a well-known fact that students hate to cook and that they love nothing better than to wander dejectedly around the kitchen with big, sad eyes after someone else has been cooking. But with macaroni and cheese, no enticing aromas are going to find their way into the nose of any would-be mooch.

Tacos, <u>on the other hand</u>, are a different matter altogether. For *Paragraph on Subject B: Tacos* *Transition* the student cook, <u>the most significant difference is obviously the</u> *Point 1 (Price)* <u>price</u>. To enjoy tacos for dinner, the adventurous student gourmet must purchase no fewer than five ingredients from the market: corn tortillas, beef, lettuce, tomatoes, and cheese. Needless to say, *Point 2 (Preparation)* this is a major expenditure. <u>Second, the chef must adroitly shuffle</u> <u>these ingredients back and forth among his very limited supply of</u> <u>pans and bowls. And finally, tacos smell great.</u> That wouldn't be *Point 3 (Odour)* a problem if the tacos didn't also smell great to about twenty of the cook's newest—if not closest—friends, who appear with those same pathetic, starving eyes mentioned earlier. When this happens, the cook will be lucky to get more than two of his own creations.

Subject B
Paragraph on Point 4: Taste
Tacos, then, wouldn't stand much of a chance if they didn't **Transition** outdo <u>macaroni and cheese</u> in one area: taste. Taste is almost— **Subject A** but not quite—an optional requirement in the opinion of a frugal student hash-slinger. Taste is just important enough so that tacos are occasionally prepared, despite their disadvantages.

Transition
Paragraph on Point 5: Colour
But <u>tacos</u> have other advantages besides their taste. With their **Subject B** enticing, colourful ingredients, they even look good. The only thing that can be said about the colour of <u>macaroni and cheese</u> is **Subject A** that it's a colour not found in nature.

Transition
Paragraph on Point 6: Time
On the other hand, <u>macaroni and cheese</u> is quick. It can be pre- **Subject A** pared in about ten minutes, while <u>tacos</u> take more than twice as **Subject B** long. And there are occasions—such as final exam week—when time is a scarce and precious resource.

Transition
Analysis
As you can see, quite a bit of thinking went into my choice of **Summary** food in my younger years. These two dishes essentially got me through my first year and indirectly taught me how to make im- portant decisions (like what to eat). <u>But I still feel a certain revul-</u> **Concluding** <u>sion when I hear their names today.</u> **statement**

Some Final Thoughts on Comparison/Contrast

The essays in this section demonstrate various methods of organization as well as a number of distinct stylistic approaches to writing a comparison/contrast essay. As you read these selections, pay particular attention to the clear, well-focused introductions; the different logical methods of organization; and the smooth transitions between sentences and paragraphs.

Comparison/Contrast in Review

Reading Comparison/Contrast Essays

Preparing to Read

1. What assumptions can you make from the essay's title?
2. Can you guess what the general mood of the essay is?
3. What is the essay's purpose and audience?
4. What does the synopsis in the Rhetorical Table of Contents tell you about the essay?

5. What can you learn from the author's biography?

6. Can you guess what the author's point of view toward the subject is?

7. What are your responses to the Preparing to Read questions?

Reading

1. What is the author's thesis?

2. How is the essay organized: Point by point? Subject by subject? As a combination of the two? As separate discussions of similarities and differences between two subjects?

3. Did you preview the questions that follow the essay?

Rereading

1. Is the writer's method of organization effective for advancing the essay's thesis?

2. Is the essay fully developed?

3. What other rhetorical strategies does the author use to support the essay's purpose?

4. What are your responses to the questions after the essay?

Writing Comparison/Contrast Essays

Preparing to Write

1. What are your responses to the Preparing to Write questions?

2. What is your purpose?

3. Are you comparing/contrasting items in the same category (e.g., two professors, but not a professor and a swimming pool)?

4. Do you have a specific purpose or reason for writing your essay?

5. Are you going to discuss the same qualities of each subject?

6. Have you generated as many pertinent details as possible to expand your comparison/contrast and to accomplish your stated purpose?

Writing

1. Does your introduction (1) clearly identify your subjects, (2) explain the basis of your comparison/contrast, and (3) state your purpose and the overall limits of your particular study?

2. Does your thesis include the boundaries of your discussion?

3. Have you limited your discussion to three or four basic categories?

4. Is your paper organized in one of the following ways: point by point, subject by subject, as a combination of the two, or as separate discussions of similarities and differences between two subjects?

5. Does your conclusion summarize your main points and state the deductions you made from those points?

Rewriting

1. Do you identify your subjects clearly?

2. Does your thesis clearly state the purpose and overall limits of your particular study?

3. Are you attempting to compare/contrast items from the same general category?

4. Do you discuss the same qualities of each subject?

5. Do you balance the treatment of the different subjects of your essay?

6. Have you organized your topic as effectively as possible?

7. Does your conclusion contain a summary and analysis of your main points?

Charlotte Gray

THE TEMPLE OF HYGIENE

Charlotte Gray (1948–) has been a regular contributor to three magazines: *Chatelaine* (a parenting column), *Saturday Night* (where her focus is national politics and for which she was the Ottawa editor), and the *Canadian Medical Association Journal* (in which she examines a wide scope of health-care-related issues). This range is testament to Gray's ability as a writer and her capacity to enable her reader to relate to many different experiences. Originally from Sheffield, UK, Gray earned her B.A. from Oxford University in 1969, and went on to work as the assistant editor and then the editor of *Psychology Today* (UK). She is, in addition, the author of Governor General's Award nominee *Mrs. King: The Life & Times of Isabel Mackenzie King* (1997) (for which she won the Canadian Authors Association Birks Family Foundation Award for a biographical work about a Canadian by a Canadian) and *Sisters in the Wilderness: The Lives of Susanna Moodie and Catharine Parr Traill* (1999). The mother of three children, Gray lives and works in Ottawa and appears periodically on radio and television speaking on political issues. She is currently working on a biography of the Mohawk poet, E. Pauline Johnson.

Preparing to Read

This essay first appeared in *Saturday Night* magazine in 1989, and was subsequently included in *The Saturday Night Traveller,* a collection of travel writing pieces. In this essay Charlotte Gray discusses a trip she took to Japan, with particular attention to her visit to a traditional Japanese bathhouse. Before reading, think about trips that you have taken and the elements of those experiences that stand out in your memory. Are the geographic details or the recollections of the people more vivid in your mind?

■_____■

Some years ago, I bought a nineteenth-century Japanese print of   1
a fight in a bathhouse. The snarling intensity of the naked, dishevelled women always intrigues me—it's so at odds with the impassive neatness of the ranks of workers, schoolchildren, or commuters featured in the standard documentaries about the Japanese "economic miracle." So when I arrived in Japan on a Japanese government programme for foreign journalists, I ranked a *sento* above a teahouse on the "preferred excursions" list I was told to prepare. I made my request to Mr. Kondo, head of the foreign ministry's international press division, who processed foreigners along the conveyor belt of Constructive Japanese Experience. He listened, stony-faced. Organized tours around factories, yes. Voyeurism in the temples of hygiene—well, even an official guest and her accompanying spouse would have to organize that for themselves.

I persisted. The hospitality service of the foreign ministry   2
had provided George and me with an escort: pretty, thirty-year-old Kaoru. Beneath Kaoru's demure smile and dutiful attention to my every whim, there bubbled a nonconformist streak. She always drank coffee instead of green tea. She refused to wear a kimono at her cousin's wedding, even though the most Westernized women in her family stuck to the national dress for

the rites of passage. Most seriously, she had already rejected three suitors selected by her parents because they were too traditional, and would not have permitted her to continue working after marriage. Now, Kaoru giggled, she was "Christmas cake"—Japanese shorthand for women beyond their twenty-fifth birthday, as unwanted as Christmas cake beyond December 25.

"Kaoru, please could you take us to a *sento*?" I asked. Her smile   3 froze for a second, then she replied, "Do you mean a swimming pool?" The limits of Japanese nonconformity began to show. I insisted that I wanted to visit an authentic bathhouse—not a swimming pool, or a gussied-up version in which Westerners outnumbered residents. We sparred for five minutes, then Kaoru got out her little notebook. The previous time the notebook had appeared was when I had asked to visit the gate of Tokyo's Imperial Palace so I could see the crowds of tiny, bent old women keeping a death watch on the occupant of the Chrysanthemum Throne. Kaoru had found that expedition a little tacky: foreign television cameras outnumbered well-wishers during most of my visit. Nevertheless, she had written down the request and taken me.

The bathhouse opportunity finally arose in Kyoto. The ancient   4 capital of Japan is now a badly planned, crowded city. Buddhist temples, Zen gardens, and ancient palaces are pools of serenity amongst bleak modern buildings. We were staying in a *ryokan*—a Japanese inn where smiling women in kimonos served us an elaborate meal at the traditional knee-level table in our own room. "Maybe tonight we'll visit a *sento*?" Kaoru suggested out of the blue. I uncurled from a cartilage-cracking kneel with enthusiasm. Kaoru summoned a cab, which ferried us through the "night area" of Kyoto—an exuberant bustle of bars, nightclubs, and restaurants.

Through the cab windows we saw the same kinds of street   5 scenes that had fascinated us in Tokyo. Clutches of neatly groomed men, wearing navy suits and carrying briefcases, strolled along, often propping up one of their number who was swaying like a stage lush. These "sararimen" (salary-men) had been male-bonding over beer or Scotches before lurching home to their wives. I had spent an afternoon with a sarariman's wife in a Tokyo suburb. Mrs. Hama's life had horrified me: she was trapped at home with only a microwave, electric bread maker, electric rice steamer, and koto (long harplike instrument) for company. Her days appeared to be spent ferrying her twelve-year-old daughter and sixteen-year-old son between schools and cramming classes. Once a week, she joined a group of other housewives for a gym class. She never knew when her husband would come home.

Mrs. Hama obviously found my life equally horrifying— 6 though the merest shadows of shock flitted across her permanent smile. Why did I need to work if my husband was a government *sarariman*? What was I doing leaving my three little boys with someone who was looking after them only for money? Wasn't I worried that, in a country like Canada, they might marry somebody from a different background—even a different race? As Kaoru escorted me home after the visit, her self-control dissolved. "I thought she would choke you when you ate a grape *whole*, without removing the skin," she giggled, overcome by the hilarious culture clash between two forty-year-old mothers. "And then, when you told her that your seven-year-old rarely has homework ..."

The cab finally dropped Kaoru, George, and me at the end of 7 an unlit lane. Towels in hand, we walked past the back doors of noodle shops and brightly lit windows with metal grilles in front of them. The bathhouse looked like a shabby municipal office. People scurried in and out, some wearing baggy pyjamas. A lick of hot, damp air curled round the door as we entered—George to the right and Kaoru and I to the left. We walked straight into a large, tiled locker room, with the inevitable row of neatly paired shoes by the entrance. A curtain separated the men's and women's changing rooms. A watchful attendant in a navy apron was seated at a raised counter which straddled the changing rooms. We paid her our 240 yen (about two dollars) each and went over to a bank of lockers.

Through a glass wall directly in front of us, I could see naked 8 figures moving in clouds of steam. Around me, six women were silently getting dressed or undressed, another was drying her hair at a long horizontal mirror. A naked septuagenarian in a brown leather armchair grunted with concentration—the chair appeared to be some kind of La-Z-Boy back-massager and she was rhythmically squirming against a set of rollers behind her. On a high shelf stood a row of twenty-five plastic bowls, neatly tied up in pink, blue, or purple gauze scarves. These contained the washing equipment of the regulars. The whole place looked entirely functional—a human laundrette rather than a health spa.

On the way over, Kaoru admitted that she had visited a 9 bathhouse only once before; her family had always had their own bathroom. Once, communal bathhouses had been the centre

of community life. In feudal Japan, there was a clear bathhouse
pecking order: the samurai families used the bathhouses in the
mornings, when the water was cleanest; the merchants in
the afternoon; the peasants, workers, and household servants
in the evening after they had toiled in fields and kitchens. As
recently as ten years ago, more households had colour televisions
than had bathtubs. But a twentyfold increase in GNP since the
war has allowed the Mrs. Hamas of this world to have baths as
well as bread makers (and, inevitably, reinforced their isolation).
Only the poor continue to rely on bathhouses. Most of the women
around Kaoru and me in the changing room seemed to be
students or grannies.

It was hard to take the scene in, however, because bathing   10
meant business. Kaoru didn't waste a second as she stripped
and scuttled towards the door into the inner sanctum—the
bathhouse proper. I was so busy keeping up that I forgot to pick
up my *oke*, or water scoop, on my way through. A lady who had
appeared oblivious to my presence caught my arm as I opened
the big door and handed me one. If this had been a fancy Tokyo
bathhouse, now geared to tourists and joggers, it would have
been a beautifully turned little pail made of cypress wood, bound
with copper hoops. What I was handed, however, was a
utilitarian blue plastic bowl.

There were four separate baths in the bathhouse: a large   11
Jacuzzi that could accommodate about eight people; a whirlpool
in which six people could sit; a smaller tub filled with freezing
cold water; and another tub filled with hot water that I didn't
immediately see anything special about. Each bath was sunk into
the floor, close to the wall, and covered in white tile. At two-foot
intervals along the wall between the baths, and along a low wall
down the middle of the room, were taps about eighteen inches off
the ground.

Over each tap was a mirror with an advertising slogan pasted   12
across it, for soft drinks including Coca-Cola and one
unfortunately named Sweat, for different kinds of soap, and for
electrical equipment. I could recognize the brand names, which
were in the Roman alphabet (*romaji*), though the other words
were all indecipherable to me. A few were in *kanji*, the elaborate
Chinese pictographs that the Japanese adopted between the
fourth and the ninth centuries; most were in *hiragana*, the much
simpler, abbreviated system of forty-eight phonetic symbols that
the Japanese evolved from the ninth century onwards. (Japanese

schoolchildren are expected to master all three scripts by the age of eight—a feat that makes the challenge of bilingualism look Mickey Mouse.) Painted on the tile of the end wall was a large landscape, filled with the familiar clichés of a Hokusai print: a lavender Mount Fuji hovered in the distance; black-jacketed peasants in coolie hats toiled on the left; foam-tipped waves curled over on the right.

Kaoru bustled over to a tap, squatted in front of it, and hid   13 her self-consciousness in the ferocity of her ablutions. Occasionally she gave me a slightly conspiratorial smile, as I followed her example. We soaped all over, then scrubbed with the long cotton cloths we had brought with us, then poured bowls of hot water over ourselves. We repeated the ritual three times. The seven other women in the bathhouse appeared completely indifferent to us as we soaped, even though I was as inconspicuous as a yellow Labrador in a cluster of Siamese cats. After a while, I noticed suspicious glances reflected in the mirrors, so I rubbed with ostentatious fervour. Kaoru had warned me that Japanese people don't trust Westerners in their bathhouses: they find our predilection for wallowing in our own dirty water disgusting.

One woman sat in the Jacuzzi, her eyes closed, her knees   14 bunched up, her chin resting on her fist. Two other women squatted by the central row of taps, holding an animated conversation while one energetically scrubbed the other's back pink with a bristle brush. Another washed her hair with furious energy, creating bowlfuls of lather which she sluiced off and down the drain that circled the room. One crouched figure stared intently at her face in a mirror. She appeared to be stroking her forehead and cheeks: after a few minutes I realized that she was methodically shaving every inch of her face, except for her carefully outlined eyebrows.

All the bodies around me were virtually hairless (except for   15 pubic hair). They were also far firmer than the bodies that surround me on Canadian beaches every summer. Not a ripple of cellulite ruffled the surface of thighs or buttocks—not even on a couple of thickset, middle-aged women. Western women would die for such marble-smooth agelessness. Yet nearly every body in a fashion magazine or face on a store mannequin was Occidental. "Why don't I ever see Japanese women in commercials?" I asked Kaoru. "Because your people are more beautiful than us," she replied firmly.

After taking the top layer of my skin off with merciless 16 scrubbing, I did the rounds of the baths. My gasp of shock when I moved from the heat of the Jacuzzi to the icy cold bath triggered smiles from fellow bathers. I was quite startled: by now I'd become accustomed to the studied indifference to foreigners that the Japanese exhibit (partly through respect for privacy, partly through fear of "getting involved" and actually having to take responsibility for a stranger). The impenetrability of the language, combined with Japanese *enryo* (usually translated as reserve or restraint), often made me feel I was knocking against a locked and soundproofed glass door. But for a moment, the door opened. The Rodin thinker in the Jacuzzi opened her eyes and asked Kaoru where I was from. When Kaoru replied "Canada," a few more faces turned towards me. One of the two back scrubbers nodded vigorously. "Ben Johnson," she sang out, and assumed an expression of condolence. There was a muted chorus of sympathetic "Aaahs," then everyone returned to her own bath business.

The real shock came in the fourth, "mystery" bath. It was 17 rectangular in shape, and had yellow panels with pinholes in them on the two long sides. I slid in at one end, and cautiously stuck my foot into the hot water between the two panels. An electric shock immediately zapped my calf. The current seemed to vary: sometimes it just tingled, other times, especially when I stood between the panels, it was torture. It was the perfect therapy for muscles aching from all the unaccustomed kneeling in teahouses, private homes, and the *ryokan*.

We'd arranged to meet George outside at ten o'clock. I rose 18 from the electric-shock bath, where I'd given my neck a last zap, and carelessly draped myself in the nice fluffy towel I'd brought from the *ryokan*, as though I'd just finished swimming. Another breach of bathhouse etiquette—the patrons didn't go in for big fluffy towels. They patted themselves dry with the thin white cloth, then draped that in front of themselves as their only concession to modesty when they left the bathhouse area.

Back in the changing room I watched with covert fascination 19 as one woman dressed in three layers of underwear, including thermal long johns, before donning the regulation dark skirt and polyester blouse that is the universal attire of middle-aged women. No wonder domestic energy consumption in Japan is one-quarter the level in Canada. Underwear is their primary heating source.

George emerged a few minutes after us. His side of the   20
bathhouse had been more crowded and sociable. Bull-shaped
men had roared at each other across the waters, while a couple
of crones moved around, cleaning the place. But the bathing
had been equally purposeful and thorough. He had not
exchanged a word with his fellow bathers, and they had
studiously ignored him. Even in the steamy intimacy of the *sento*,
we had been firmly kept at arm's length. Only a mention of our
Olympic steroid-user, who had committed the unforgivable sin
(in Japanese eyes) of disgracing his family and his nation, had
broken through the *enryo*.

UNDERSTANDING DETAILS

1. What are some of the specific areas in which Gray points out differences between Japan and Canada? Which traditions, customs, and institutions, and which other aspects of life does Gray
   mention? How do these differences affect people in the essay?
2. How is Kaoru's nonconformity as a young Japanese woman illustrated? Give specific examples.
3. Gray uses several Japanese words or expressions in this essay.
   Explain the following terms that appear in "The Temple of
   Hygiene": Christmas cake, *sento*, *ryokan*, *sararimen*, *enryo*. What
   effect does Gray hope to achieve by using Japanese words such
   as *sento* and *enryo* rather than English translations of these terms?

ANALYZING MEANING

1. Why is Kaoru reluctant to take her guests to the bathhouse?
   How does she demonstrate this reluctance? What does Kaoru's
   reluctance about taking her guests to the bathhouse indicate
   about Japanese attitudes toward this institution?
2. How would you summarize Gray's view of the Japanese people and Japanese life? Which of Gray's examples best demonstrate her perception of the Japanese people and Japanese life?
   Does she only point out differences or are there also similarities?
3. The use of the word *temple* in the title suggests ritual. What ritual patterns do you see in the actions of the people in the bathhouse? What does this attitude toward a bath suggest to you
   about Japanese life?

DISCOVERING RHETORICAL STRATEGIES

1. What is the point of view of the narrator of this essay? In what context has Gray made this trip to Japan? How does this influence her experience and her perspective? What is the purpose of Gray's trip?
2. In this essay, Gray compares and contrasts aspects of Japanese life and Canadian life. What specific details or examples does she use to make the differences vivid and memorable? Which specific paragraphs of detailed description give you the clearest pictures of Gray's reactions to her unique Japanese experience? Why?
3. Gray has used a simile to highlight the difference between herself and the other women in the bathhouse in paragraph 13. Explain what makes this metaphor effective. Identify other similes, metaphors, or analogies that Gray has used in this comparison and contrast.
4. The structure of Gray's essay follows the progress of a miniature journey, with Kaoru as the guide. Using specific examples, trace the progress of the trip or journey in the essay, and identify the primary method of organization Gray has used. Why do you think Gray might have selected this pattern?

MAKING CONNECTIONS

1. Charlotte Gray and Allen Abel ("A Home at the End of the Journey") both consider what it means to be Canadian by contrasting Canadians and Canadian experience with people and experiences from other countries. In your view, what does it mean to be Canadian? How are Canadians and how is Canada different from at least one other specific country?
2. Charlotte Gray introduces some Japanese vocabulary into her essay just as Brian Lewis ("Teeth") incorporates some Inuktitut phrases into his. Explain why these authors have added bits in languages that the majority of their readers are unlikely to know? What effect does this create for their readers?
3. "Kris King Looks Terrible" (Dave Bidini) and "The Temple of Hygiene" (Charlotte Gray) both relate experiences of Canadians travelling to parts of Asia. How are Bidini and Gray's observations consistent? Where do they differ? How does each of their situations affect their experience of this foreign place?

IDEAS FOR DISCUSSION/WRITING

Preparing to Write

Write freely about Japan. What associations do you have with this country? What images come to mind when you think about Japan? How have these impressions been developed? What different sources have contributed to your overall view of Japan and of Japanese people? Which of your impressions are objective and which are subjective? What Japanese products are you familiar with? What Japanese personalities or public figures can you name?

Choosing a Topic

1. As people travel more frequently and more easily, aspects of different cultures and countries blend. Which aspects of the Japanese society that Gray describes do you see as desirable to introduce into Canada? Are there any aspects that you would not want to see merged into Canadian society? Are there any examples of Japanese influence already in Canada that you have observed?

2. *It's a Small World* travel magazine has asked you to write an essay about a trip you have taken or another place you have lived. In your essay compare another city, province, or country to the one you live in now. Focus on specific elements so you can provide substantial detail.

3. Gray questions Kaoru about the lack of Japanese women in advertisements and is firmly told that "Your people are more beautiful than us." What gives Kaoru this impression? How are general standards of beauty established? Maintained?

Will Ferguson

▪ ☐ ▪

THE SUDBURY SYNDROME

Originally from Fort Vermilion in northern Alberta, Will Ferguson (1964–) has lived and worked in a wide variety of places both in Canada and abroad, including five years in Japan. These experiences provide the basis for the books he has written and the commentary he occasionally provides on CBC radio. Ferguson's *I Was a Teenage Katima-Victim* (1998) is a memoir of the period he spent participating in the national Katimavik volunteer program that brought together young people from across the country to work on various projects in different communities. *Hokkaido Highway Blues: Hitchhiking Japan* (1998) and *The Hitchhiker's Guide to Japan* (1998) are both products of Ferguson's 1996 hitchhiking trip over the length of Japan. The book from which the selection here was taken is *Why I Hate Canadians* (1997), a humorous analysis of what Canada is and the meaning of being Canadian. A graduate of York University with a B.F.A. in film studies, Ferguson now lives with his wife and son in Calgary, Alberta. His recent works include *Bastards and Boneheads* (1998), *Canadian History for Dummies* (2000), and *How to Be a Canadian (Even If You Already Are One)*, co-written with his brother.

Preparing to Read

In this essay, Ferguson introduces Sudbury as one of Canada's "scars" rather than one of its "smiles." Before you read Ferguson's essay, think about a specific place that you would characterize as a "scar" instead of a "smile." Why is it a scar? What specific details illustrate its ugliness or lack of appeal? Does it have any redeeming qualities? Does it seem to be improving or getting worse?

■━━━━━━━━━━━━━━━━━━━━━━━━━━━━━━━━━━━■

So far we have been discussing Canada largely in the abstract. 1 Let's now take a closer look at some of the places and spaces we occupy. Canada on the street corner of a specific town or city is far different from the Canada of the imagination. With that in mind, I give you the city of Sudbury. And remember as you read this that (A) I love Sudbury, and (B) our scars define us every bit as much as our smiles, and our *collective* scars define us even further. Plastic surgery is *not* the answer.

England may have the White Cliffs of Dover, but Canada has 2 the Black Cliffs of Sudbury. And unlike the cliffs of Dover, which are really more of an *off*-white, the cliffs of Sudbury are black. Even better, they are man-made.

You see the cliffs as you drive into town, Sudbury's slag-pile 3 glaciers, the scorched tailings of the city's infamous nickel mines. Rail-cars roll up to the edge, then pause, tilt and pour out the molten slag, casting an orange echo against the sky, like the castle defences of a medieval siege. The slag cools into a crust, then blackens, and is in turn covered.

No animal can live off its own waste. This is a basic rule of 4 biology, and yet Sudbury, a city of 90,000 in the scrub-backed

land of the Canadian Shield, seems to defy this. Folk singer
Murray McLaughlin called it a "hard-rock town." Others have
been less charitable. But if Sudbury has a bad reputation, it came
by it honestly. It may be ugly, but it was a damn sight uglier and
nastier just a few years ago. (*Suggested town motto:* You think it
stinks now, you should have seen it before!)

Sudbury started in 1883 as a muddy, backwoods rail town at   5
the junction of two main lines. With the discovery of the world's
richest nickel deposits came an economic boom. Two companies
blasted their way to the top of the slag pile and stayed there:
Falconbridge Mines and the almighty American-based
International Nickel Company, now known simply as INCO.

INCO ruled Sudbury for almost eighty years. As final courts   6
of appeal, there was God, Ottawa and INCO, but not necessarily
in that order. As late as 1964, the mayor of Sudbury was
cheerfully informing newcomers to the city: "INCO calls the
shots around here, and don't ever forget it."

> Oh the girls are out to bingo,
> and the boys are gettin' stink-o,
> And we'll think no more of INCO
> on a Sudbury Saturday night.

So sang Stompin' Tom Connors, and the words ring true of   7
a company town that ate its own. The pollution was horrific.
Every dollar earned was wrestled from the earth, carved, blasted,
crushed, melted down and skimmed off. For miles around the
vegetation was dead, the land was barren and sullied. Lung
cancer, acid rain, lakes turned to vinegar, bedrock torched bare:
Sudbury had it all. It was—and still is—a hard-drinking, blue-
collar place, with a rowdy mix of French and English. An
archetypal mining town, a sorrowful and sickly place.

And yet never were a people so proud of their town. The   8
good citizens of Sudbury will defend their rocky home amid the
smokestacks with the same fierce stubbornness that a parent
defends a particularly ugly child. It's a town with a chip on its
shoulder, and so it should. If you were the brunt of innumerable
jokes, if in high school you were always voted most likely to die
of industrial disease, you too would get pissed off at writers like
me who come into town, shake their heads and declare it a
"sorrowful and sickly place."

Later, INCO built Superstack, the tallest chimney in the   9
world, to throw the emissions out higher and over a larger area.

This massive, spewing smokestack is a symbol of Sudbury as much as the Giant Nickel on the road into town. (In his travel book *Last Train to Toronto*, Terry Pindell recalls meeting Miss Nude Canada, the amply endowed Kathy Stack, in her home town of Sudbury. Her stage name was XTC, but everyone around town called her Superstack, though I believe this nickname may not have been in reference to the INCO chimney.)

10 The glory of nude dancing aside, Sudbury went into free-fall sometime around 1980 and just kept tumbling. A series of bitter strikes and layoffs was followed hard by recession and terminal unemployment and the apocalyptic INCO strike. The picket lines, the cutbacks, the false minibooms that came and went like death spasms, all weighed heavy on the City That Nickel Built.

11 The story of Sudbury doesn't end there, though by all logic it should; it was a one-industry town and its time had run out. But then, like a minor miracle, the clouds broke and the Sudbury Renaissance began. A streak of civic pride, as deep as any nickel core, saved them. (That and millions of dollars in federal and corporate aid.) The strategy was simply, the mantra short: diversify or die.

12 And what do you think they decided to base their recovery on? You'll never guess. Never. They decided to make Sudbury a centre for *tourism*. That's right, tourism. "I don't know, honey, this year it's either Paris or Sudbury, I just can't decide." The crazy thing is, it worked. Tourism is now a major, multimillion-dollar industry in Sudbury and one of the cornerstones of the city's recovery plan.

13 INCO donated $5 million towards the construction of Science North, a tourist-orientated interactive centre. It was the biggest single corporate donation to a community project in Canadian history—something which INCO never tires of pointing out.

14 Science North is "science beyond the classroom." The buildings are designed in the shape of snowflakes, *stainless steel* snowflakes, that are connected via bedrock tunnels. And how do they entice you to come to the complex? With the promise that you will *"Pet a tarantula! Hold a porcupine! and lie on a bed of nails!"* Tarantulas? Bed of nails? Just how does this tour end? Do they poke you in the eye with a stick and set your hair on fire? In fact, Science North is a lot of fun. And yes, as I discovered, you *can* pet a porcupine. His name is Ralf, he likes to have his belly rubbed, and no, his quills don't come off. Unless he's angry. So you should try to stay on his good side.

Sudbury has reinvented itself, and with tourism now   15
booming, people are actually ending up in Sudbury *on purpose!*
The city's concentrated tree-planting and beautification project
finally paid off when *Chatelaine* magazine—that purveyor of
good taste—ranked Sudbury as one of the ten best Canadian
cities to live in. *Crowds cheer! Balloons fly! Parades parade!*

Now then, let's not go overboard. Sudbury, no matter how   16
many trees you plant is still, well, Sudbury. Many of the newly
built and much ballyhooed residential complexes were really just
the generic Canadian Suburb transplanted whole into what was
once, and still is, a rough northern town. All the trees by the side
of the road are not going to hide the rock and refineries. (*Suggested
Motto:* As far as industrial wastelands go, we're not that bad!)

It's true, the United Nations Environment Committee has   17
applauded Sudbury's urban renewal efforts. (*Crowds cheer,
balloons fly*, etc. etc.) Do you remember back in grade school,
when the teacher used to give special silver stars to that slow
kid who tried really, really hard but was still a bit thick? They
called the award Most Improved. Well, Sudbury is that student,
and she wears her star proudly.

From the top of the hill, beside the giant stainless steel nickel,   18
she proclaims, like Scarlett O'Hara in *Gone with the Wind*, "As
God as my witness, I will never be ugly again!"

And on the other side, across the hill, the slag cars rumble   19
and roll, pouring the fire that slides down like lava and cools
into blackness on the edge of town.

Tucked in within Sudbury's Copper Cliff townsite is a place   20
called Little Italy. Built by migrant workers to resemble the
mountain villages of their native land, it is a small enclave of
narrow random streets and oddly angled houses. From Little
Italy to the Giant Nickel, from the Black Cliffs to the Superstack
itself, Sudbury has stories to tell. Love her or hate her, there is no
place quite like her. Sudbury *is* ugly. It is a city with a past, a
city covered with scars, but it is also a city with that elusive
quality we call *character*, and character is not something you can
buy. But it is something you can lose.

Every time you pass through Sudbury, you will notice the   21
encroaching sameness of suburbia. It is happening across Canada.
I call it the Sudbury Syndrome: the desire to eradicate the scars
and birthmarks of a place and import instead the shiny surfaces
and retail clones of a common urban/suburban culture. It is

nothing short of the Blanding of Canada. Local character and diversity is slowly being watered down, and our cities and towns are fast becoming as interchangeable as shopping malls.

The town of Sudbury, with its gritty working-class roots and 22 nickel-plated pride, epitomizes this. A campaign has been under way since the early 1990s to change Sudbury's image, to make it more like every other town, to make it as innocuous as possible. To make it as nice as everybody else.

Let me take you now to Saint John, New Brunswick, or, as I like 23 to call it, Sudbury-by-the-sea. Living as I do in the fey little town of St. Andrews, I have come to rely on Saint John (population: 79,000) as my pipeline to consumer goods, import foods, cinemas, and adult sex shoppes (*sic*).

St. Andrews, with a population less than 1,300, has a mind- 24 boggling variety all its own, a riffraff collection of greying hippies, faded back-to-the-landers, imported salmon researchers, restless college kids, price-gouging landlords, wealthy elders and assorted craftspeople. The town has also, wisely and with more than a little smugness, decided to resist the drift towards mass commercialization. The town stewards have kept fast-food chains and discount department stores at bay and the result is an expensive but largely unspoiled town. Quaint. Historic. Narcoleptic.

The city of Saint John, an hour and a half down the road, is 25 a world away from St. Andrews, and the two coexist like a dowager aunt and a tattooed dock-worker: uneasily.

Let's be frank. Saint John is a functionally illiterate city. 26 Trying to find a decent used bookstore in Saint John is like trying to find a decent restaurant in Regina. Much like Sudbury, Saint John is a blue-collar, gaseous, foul-smelling, knocked-about town. And just as Sudbury has been cursed and blessed—but to my mind, mostly cursed—by the presence of INCO, so has Saint John suffered at the hands of its own capitalist overlords: the Clan Irving.

To me, the Irvings have always seemed to be old-school 27 caricatures: cigar-smoking, round-bellied, union-busting capitalists of nineteenth-century America. Except it isn't the nineteenth century any more (a fact which no one has had the nerve to tell the Irvings) and Saint John remains a city in thrall.

Have you ever started packing to move, and you start out 28 by boxing and labelling everything and then arranging them carefully by content and size, but by the time you are done you are throwing things into boxes and shoving them wherever the hell they can fit? Well, it's the same with Saint John. There may have been a plan way back when, but the city is now a stack of random boxes jumbled along the bedrock, wedged in among highway overpasses and Irving shipyards. With its one-way streets and sadistic bypasses, Saint John is an unforgiving city; take a wrong turn and it's *Hello Moncton!*

And yet, for all that—because of that—I love Saint John. It's 29 a great place. The Old City is filled with surprises and the people are as raw and real as they come. Whether you're eating the meatloaf sandwich and spicy fries at Reggie's Diner or waiting for the Reversing (yawn) Falls to do their stench-side trick, it is hard not to feel a begrudging admiration for Saint John. Like Sudbury, it has a character all its own. Which makes it all the more depressing that it was in Saint John that I experienced my worst case of Urban Amnesia ever.

Fredericton, meanwhile, is a government town. Inhabited largely 30 by bureaucrats, poets and students, Fredericton can't quite make up its mind if it wants to be eccentric or snooty and has settled on a kind of eccentric snootiness that puzzles as much as it captivates. Like most Canadian cities, Fredericton (population: 45,000) is inflicted with a perimeter rim of shopping malls and fast-food emporiums. Like Saint John, Fredericton is about an hour and a half from St. Andrews.

Where Saint John is pure grit, Fredericton is pampered and 31 refined. Where Saint John is masculine, Fredericton is feminine. Where Saint John is dark, Fredericton is light. It's yin, it's yang. It's the fiddle vs. the violin. It's diner coffee vs. cappuccino. Saint John is unforgiving, Fredericton is welcoming.

The two cities are as different as any two could be, and yet, 32 during a grey winter outing as I wandered down a hermetically sealed shopping mall corridor, I suddenly lost all sense of place. I couldn't remember if I was in Saint John or Fredericton. Everything was completely familiar—and yet I had absolutely no idea where I was. It must be the way a victim of amnesia feels.

Which city was I in? Fredericton? Saint John? There was 33 nothing to distinguish it either way. Shopping malls, like suburbs, have no character. They are, by their very nature, generic.

It turned out I was in Saint John, which I discovered only 34 after I stopped someone and asked. (And boy, did I get a funny look.) It was a heart-sinking moment to realize just how standardized modern Canadian culture has become. It is cheerful and clean and comfortable. And soulless.

What this country needs is more Sudburys and fewer 35 shopping malls.

UNDERSTANDING DETAILS

1. How has Sudbury changed between the 1980s and the late 1990s when Ferguson's essay was written? Give specific examples that show the progression.
2. How are Saint John and Fredericton similar? In what ways do they differ?
3. What force has been primarily responsible for the establishment and development of Sudbury?

ANALYZING MEANING

1. In this essay Ferguson introduces a trend he labels "the Blanding of Canada." Explain exactly what "the Blanding of Canada" is. What is Ferguson's attitude toward this trend?
2. How does Ferguson feel about his hometown of St. Andrews, New Brunswick? Is his attitude consistent with the characteristics he uses to introduce St. Andrews? Explain the apparent contradiction in Ferguson's approach.
3. Ferguson concludes his essay with a call for more Sudburys and fewer shopping malls. Explain why Ferguson sees this as the ideal.

DISCOVERING RHETORICAL STRATEGIES

1. Which of the four patterns of organization has Ferguson chosen in this essay?
2. Reading reviews of *Why I Hate Canadians*, in which this essay first appeared, shows that Ferguson offends many readers with his views about Canada and Canadians. The tone that Ferguson uses and his tendency to exaggerate to make a point may exacerbate this reaction. Explain why Ferguson hasn't adopted a more diplomatic, even tone in conveying the ideas he has about his subject matter.
3. Ferguson uses many metaphors and similes to make his writing interesting and vivid. Find four examples of Ferguson's use of these figures of speech. Which do you find the most effective? Why?

MAKING CONNECTIONS

1. Ferguson concludes his essay by saying that "[w]hat this country needs is more Sudburys and fewer shopping malls." Imagine that Ferguson is having a conversation about Canada with Neil Bissoondath ("Pieces of Sky"), Sharon Butala ("The Myth: The Prairies Are Flat"), and Tomson Highway ("What a Certain Visionary Once Said"). Who in this group do you think would agree with Ferguson? Who would disagree? Who would you most closely agree with?

2. In "Kris King Looks Terrible," Dave Bidini writes about a section of Hong Kong. How does Bidini's depiction of Hong Kong compare to Ferguson's depiction of St. Andrews? Would Bidini describe Hong Kong as a "scar" or a "smile" on the face of China?

3. Ferguson uses an informal and humorous tone in this essay. Identify the specific techniques he employs to achieve this tone. How do those techniques compare to the strategies used by Drew Hayden Taylor ("Pretty Like a White Boy")?

IDEAS FOR DISCUSSION/WRITING

Preparing to Write

In "The Sudbury Syndrome" Ferguson writes about the value of character in a place. Write freely about a place you know that has character. What makes this place unique? Is it generally viewed positively or negatively? Why? Are the elements of character valued? How has this place changed over time? Has that enhanced its character or diminished it?

Choosing a Topic

1. Think about a city or town you know well. Compare and contrast what that place is like today with what it was like when you first knew it. Using specific examples, show how it has changed. In your view, has the change been an improvement or a deterioration?

2. Ferguson laments the uniformity and consistency of shopping malls and the lack of unique character that they possess. Using specific examples with which you are familiar, write an essay in which you either advance Ferguson's view or counter it with a defence of shopping malls.

3. Choose two people who work in the same field and compare and contrast their approaches to the job. You might consider two teachers, two newscasters, two DJs, two store clerks, two servers in a restaurant, or two politicians.

Gloria Steinem

THE POLITICS OF MUSCLE

Once described as a writer with "unpretentious clarity and forceful expression," Gloria Steinem is one of the foremost organizers and champions of the modern women's movement. She was born in Toledo, Ohio in 1934, earned a B.A. at Smith College, and pursued graduate work in political science at the universities of Delhi and Calcutta in India before returning to America to begin a freelance career in journalism. One of her earliest and best-known articles, "I Was a Playboy Bunny," was a witty exposé of the entire Playboy operation written in 1963 after she had worked undercover for two weeks in the New York City Playboy Club. In 1968 she and Clay Felker founded *New York* magazine; then, in 1972, they started *Ms.* magazine. Steinem's subsequent publications have included *Outrageous Acts and Everyday Rebellions* (1983), *Marilyn: Norma Jean* (1986), *Bedside Book of Self-Esteem* (1989), and *Moving Beyond Words* (1994). She has also written several television scripts and is a frequent contributor to such periodicals as *Esquire, Vogue, Cosmopolitan, Seventeen,* and *Life.* An articulate and passionate spokesperson for feminist causes, Steinem has been honoured nine times by the *World Almanac* as one of the 25 most influential women in America.

Preparing to Read

Taken from the author's newest book, *Moving Beyond Words,* "The Politics of Muscle" is actually an introduction to a longer essay entitled "The Strongest Woman in the World," which celebrates the virtues of women's bodybuilding champion Bev Francis. In this introductory essay, Steinem examines the sexual politics of women's weight lifting and the extent to which a "new beauty standard" has begun to evolve because of pioneers in the sport like Francis. As you prepare to read this essay, examine for a few minutes your own thoughts about the associations people make with weakness and strength in both men and women: Which sex do you think of as stronger? In our society, what does strength have to do with accomplishment? With failure? Do these associations vary for men and women? What does weakness suggest in North American culture? Do these suggestions vary for men and women? What are the positive values North Americans associate with muscles and strength? With helplessness and weakness? What are the negative values North Americans associate with muscles and strength? With helplessness and weakness? From your experience, what connections have you made between physical strength and gender roles?

■───■

I come from a generation who didn't do sports. Being a cheer- 1
leader or a drum majorette was as far as our imaginations or
role models could take us. Oh yes, there was also being a strutter—one of a group of girls (and we were girls then) who marched and danced and turned cartwheels in front of the high school band at football games. Did you know that big football universities actually gave strutting scholarships? That shouldn't sound any more bizarre than football scholarships, yet somehow it does. Gender politics strikes again.

But even winning one of those rare positions, the stuff that 2
dreams were made of, was more about body display than about the considerable skill they required. You could forget about trying out for them if you didn't have the right face and figure, and my high school was full of girls who had learned to do back flips and twirl flaming batons, all to no avail. Winning wasn't about being the best in an objective competition or achieving a personal best, or even about becoming healthy or fit. It was about *being chosen.*

That's one of many reasons why I and other women of my 3
generation grew up believing—as many girls still do—that the most important thing about a female body is not what it does but how it looks. The power lies not within us but in the gaze of the observer. In retrospect, I feel sorry for the protofeminist gym teachers who tried so hard to interest us in half-court basketball and other team sports thought suitable for girls in my high school, while we worried about the hairdo we'd slept on rollers all night to achieve. Gym was just a stupid requirement you tried to get out of, with ugly gym suits whose very freedom felt odd on bodies accustomed to being constricted for viewing. My blue-collar neighborhood didn't help much either, for it convinced me that sports like tennis or golf were as remote as the country clubs where they were played—mostly by men

anyway. That left tap dancing and ballet as my only exercise, and though my dancing school farmed us out to supermarket openings and local nightclubs, where we danced our hearts out in homemade costumes, those events were about display too, about smiling and pleasing and, even during the rigors of ballet, about looking ethereal and hiding any muscles or strength.

My sports avoidance continued into college, where I went 4 through shock about class and wrongly assumed athletics were only for well-to-do prep school girls like those who brought their own lacrosse sticks and riding horses to school. With no sports training to carry over from childhood—and no place to become childlike, as we must when we belatedly learn basic skills—I clung to my familiar limits. Even at the casual softball games where *Ms.* played the staffs of other magazines, I confined myself to cheering. As the *Ms.* No Stars, we prided ourselves on keeping the same lineup, win or lose, and otherwise disobeying the rules of the jockocracy, so I contented myself with upsetting the men on the opposing team by cheering for their female team members. It's amazing how upset those accustomed to conventional divisions can become when others refuse to be divided by them.

In my case, an interest in the politics of strength had come not 5 from my own experience but from observing the mysterious changes in many women around me. Several of my unathletic friends had deserted me by joining gyms, becoming joggers, or discovering the pleasure of learning to yell and kick in self-defense class. Others who had young daughters described the unexpected thrill of seeing them learn to throw a ball or run with a freedom that hadn't been part of our lives in conscious memory. On campuses, I listened to formerly anorexic young women who said their obsession with dieting had diminished when they discovered strength as a third alternative to the usual fat-versus-thin dichotomy. Suddenly, a skinny, androgynous, "boyish" body was no longer the only way to escape the soft, female, "victim" bodies they associated with their mothers' fates. Added together, these examples of before-and-after strength changes were so dramatic that the only male analogues I could find were Vietnam amputees whose confidence was bolstered when they entered marathons in wheelchairs or on artificial legs, or paralyzed accident survivors whose sense of themselves was changed when they learned to play wheelchair basketball. Compared to their handicapped female counterparts, however, even those men seemed to be less transformed. Within each category, women had been less encouraged to develop whatever muscle and skills we had.

Since my old habits of ignoring my body and living inside my 6
head weren't that easy to break, it was difficult to change my nonathletic ways. Instead, I continued to learn secondhand from watching my friends, from reading about female strength in other cultures, and from asking questions wherever I traveled.

Though cultural differences were many, there were political 7
similarities in the way women's bodies were treated that went as deep as patriarchy itself. Whether achieved through law and social policy, as in this and other industrialized countries, or by way of tribal practice and religious ritual, as in older cultures, an individual woman's body was far more subject to other people's rules than was that of her male counterpart. Women always seemed to be owned to some degree as the means of reproduction. And as possessions, women's bodies then became symbols of men's status, with a value that was often determined by what was rare. Thus, rich cultures valued thin women, and poor cultures valued fat women. Yet all patriarchal cultures valued weakness in women. How else could male dominance survive? In my own country, for example, women who "belong" to rich white men are often thinner (as in "You can never be too rich or too thin") than those who "belong" to poor men of color; yet those very different groups of males tend to come together in their belief that women are supposed to be weaker than men; that muscles and strength aren't "feminine."

If I had any doubts about the psychological importance of 8
cultural emphasis on male/female strength difference, listening to arguments about equality put them to rest. Sooner or later, even the most intellectual discussion came down to men's supposedly superior strength as a justification for inequality, whether the person arguing regretted or celebrated it. What no one seemed to explore, however, was the inadequacy of physical strength as a way of explaining oppression in other cases. Men of European origin hadn't ruled in South Africa because they were stronger than African men, and blacks hadn't been kept in slavery or bad jobs in the United States because whites had more muscles. On the contrary, males of the "wrong" class or color were often confined to laboring positions precisely because of their supposedly greater strength, just as the lower pay females received was often rationalized by their supposedly lesser

strength. Oppression has no logic—just a self-fulfilling prophecy, justified by a self-perpetuating system.

The more I learned, the more I realized that belief in great 9 strength differences between women and men was itself part of the gender mind-game. In fact, we can't really know what those differences might be, because they are so enshrined, perpetuated, and exaggerated by culture. They seem to be greatest during the childbearing years (when men as a group have more speed and upper-body strength, and women have better balance, endurance, and flexibility) but only marginal during early childhood and old age (when females and males seem to have about the same degree of physical strength). Even during those middle years, the range of difference *among* men and *among* women is far greater than the generalized difference *between* males and females as groups. In multiracial societies like ours, where males of some races are smaller than females of others, judgments based on sex make even less sense. Yet we go right on assuming and praising female weakness and male strength.

But there is a problem about keeping women weak, even in a 10 patriarchy. Women are workers, as well as the means of reproduction. Lower-class women are especially likely to do hard physical labor. So the problem becomes: How to make sure female strength is used for work but not for rebellion? The answer is: Make women ashamed of it. Though hard work requires lower-class women to be stronger than their upper-class sisters, for example, those strong women are made to envy and imitate the weakness of women who "belong" to, and are the means of reproduction for, upper-class men—and so must be kept even *more* physically restricted if the lines of race and inheritance are to be kept "pure." That's why restrictive dress, from the chadors, or full-body veils, of the Middle East to metal ankle and neck rings in Africa, from nineteenth-century hoop skirts in Europe to corsets and high heels here, started among upper-class women and then sifted downward as poor women were encouraged to envy or imitate them. So did such bodily restrictions as bound feet in China, or clitoridectomies and infibulations in much of the Middle East and Africa, both of which practices began with women whose bodies were the means of reproduction for the powerful, and gradually became generalized symbols of femininity. In this country, the self-starvation known as anorexia nervosa is mostly a white, upper-middle class, young-female phenomenon, but all women are encouraged to envy a white and impossibly thin ideal.

Sexual politics are also reflected through differing emphases   11
on the reproductive parts of women's bodies. Whenever a
patriarchy wants females to populate a new territory or replenish
an old one, big breasts and hips become admirable. Think of the
bosomy ideal of this country's frontier days, or the *zaftig*, Marilyn
Monroe–type figure that became popular after the population
losses of World War II. As soon as increased population wasn't
desirable or necessary, hips and breasts were deemphasized.
Think of the Twiggy look that arrived in the 1960s.

But whether bosomy or flat, *zaftig* or thin, the female ideal   12
remains weak, and it stays that way unless women ourselves
organize to change it. Suffragists shed the unhealthy corsets that
produced such a tiny-waisted, big-breasted look that fainting
and smelling salts became routine. Instead, they brought in
bloomers and bicycling. Feminists of today are struggling against
social pressures that exalt siliconed breasts but otherwise stick-
thin silhouettes. Introducing health and fitness has already led to
a fashion industry effort to reintroduce weakness with the waif
look, but at least it's being protested. The point is: Only when
women rebel against patriarchal standards does female muscle
become more accepted.

For these very political reasons, I've gradually come to believe   13
that society's acceptance of muscular women may be one of the
most intimate, visceral measures of change. Yes, we need progress
everywhere, but an increase in our physical strength could have
more impact on the everyday lives of most women than the
occasional role model in the boardroom or in the White House.

UNDERSTANDING DETAILS

1. According to Steinem, what is "gender politics" (paragraph 1)?
2. In what ways does Steinem equate "winning" with "being chosen" (paragraph 2)? Why is this an important premise for her
   essay?
3. What does Steinem mean when she says, "Oppression has no
   logic" (paragraph 8)? Explain your answer in detail.
4. In what ways does "power" lie with the observer rather than
   within the female?

ANALYZING MEANING

1. Why does Steinem call the female body a "victim" body (paragraph 5)? What did girls' mothers have to do with this association?
2. Do you agree with the author that a woman's body is "far more subject to other people's rules than [is] that of her male counterpart" (paragraph 7)? Explain your answer giving examples from your own experience.
3. What is Steinem implying about the political overtones connected with female weakness and male strength? According to Steinem, why are these judgments so ingrained in North American social and cultural mores?
4. What are Steinem's reasons for saying that "Society's acceptance of muscular women may be one of the most intimate visceral measures of change" (paragraph 13)? Do you agree with this statement or not? Explain your reaction in detail.

DISCOVERING RHETORICAL STRATEGIES

1. Who do you think is Steinem's intended audience for this essay? On what evidence do you base your answer?
2. In your opinion, what is Steinem's primary purpose in this essay? Explain your answer in detail.
3. How appropriate is the title of this essay? What would be some possible alternate titles?
4. What rhetorical modes support the author's comparison/contrast? Give examples of each.

MAKING CONNECTIONS

1. To what extent would Laura Robinson ("Starving for the Gold") agree with Gloria Steinem's assertion that "the most important thing about a female body is not what it does but how it looks" (paragraph 3)? Do you agree or disagree with this assertion? Give at least three reasons for your opinion.
2. If Steinem is correct that American women have not traditionally found power in their muscles, where have they found it? If you were able to ask Naheed Mustafa ("My Body Is My Own Business") or Michele Lemon ("Understanding Does Not Always Lead to Tolerance") this same question, what do you think their answers would be? With whom would you agree most? Explain your answer.

3. Steinem's essay explores women in a realm that is traditionally male-dominated. How does her presentation of the experience of women in bodybuilding compare to Judy Rebick's position about women in a world that is traditionally male-dominated? What elements make a difference in these experiences?

IDEAS FOR DISCUSSION/WRITING

Preparing to Write

Write freely about the definition and role of strength and weakness in North American society: What does strength generally mean in our society? What does weakness mean? What association do you have with both modes of behaviour? Where do these associations come from? What are the political implications of these associations? The social implications? In what ways are strength and weakness basic to the value system in North American culture?

Choosing a Topic

1. Compare two different approaches to the process of succeeding in a specific job or activity. Develop your own guidelines for making the comparison; then write an essay for your fellow students about the similarities and differences you have observed between these two different approaches. Be sure to decide on a purpose and a point of view before you begin to write.
2. Interview your mother and father about their views on physical strength in their separate family backgrounds. If you have grandparents or step-parents, interview them as well. Then compare and contrast these various influences in your life. Which of them are alike? Which are different? How have you personally dealt with these similarities and differences? Be sure to decide on a purpose and a point of view before you begin to write.
3. In her essay, Steinem argues that "an increase in our [women's] physical strength could have more impact on the everyday lives of most women than the occasional role model in the boardroom or in the White House" (paragraph 13). Do you agree with the author? Write an essay to be published in your local newspaper explaining your views on this issue.

Michael McKinley

■□■

OPERA NIGHT IN CANADA

Michael McKinley is a screenwriter, journalist, and author of three books about hockey. *Hockey Hall of Fame Legends*, *Putting a Roof on Winter*, and *Etched in Ice* are all sports history books that reflect McKinley's love of this traditional Canadian game. In addition, McKinley, who graduated from the University of British Columbia and Oxford University, wrote and produced *Sacred Ballot*, a documentary on papal elections for CBC's *Witness*. In his role as a journalist, McKinley has written for many publications, including the *Chicago Sun-Times*, the *New York Daily News*, the *Daily Mail* (London), the *Guardian* (London), the *Los Angeles Times*, the *New York Observer*, *Saturday Night*, and *Sports Illustrated*. McKinley, who lives in Vancouver, is the program director for The Cambridge Tradition, an international academic program.

Preparing to Read

"Opera Night in Canada" first appeared in *Saturday Night* magazine with the subtitle "hockey and opera are more similar than you think, which is bad news for hockey." In this essay Michael McKinley shows the commonalities between these two apparently disparate forms of entertainment. What are your thoughts about hockey? Do you play hockey? Do you like to watch hockey? Do you attend hockey games? Do you like opera? Have you ever attended an opera? To what types of people do these forms of entertainment typically appeal? Why do you think McKinley sees the similarities between hockey and opera as bad news for hockey?

■───────────────────────────────────■

In late August, a new opera by composer Leslie Uyeda and 1
librettist Tom Cone debuted at Festival Vancouver, an international showcase for music. Of course, the premiere of an opera at a music festival is hardly newsworthy, but the subject matter of this opera was: *Game Misconduct* is an opera about hockey.

The ninety-minute opera takes place in the seventh game of 2
a playoff series between a Canadian team and their American rivals, and follows eight characters over three periods, plus overtime, as they watch the action from the bleachers. Each character represents a theme: there's Larry, a hot-dog and

popcorn vendor, who will lose his job of twenty years when the arena is torn down; Rita, a fan whom Larry loves; Rene, the father of the Canadian team's goalie; Blossom, who loves hockey for the fighting; Snake and Sylvia, for whom hockey fills the gaps in their relationship; Hugo, an obnoxious fan from Anaheim; and Trish, a hockey virgin at her first game.

For those of us who love both hockey and opera, the idea of these two art forms being united after all this time is as shocking as Pinkerton returning to marry Madame Butterfly or the Leafs being united with the Stanley Cup. Hockey and opera would seem to exist on opposite ends of the cultural spectrum; a closer look, however, reveals that they have a lot in common. Hockey has three periods; most operas have three acts. Hockey has six positions—a centre, two wingers, two defencemen, and the goalie—while opera has six major "positions"—soprano, mezzo, contralto, tenor, baritone, and bass. Opera's favourite themes are love and death, and hockey echoes these themes, giving us something to love (the game) in the season of death (winter).   3

Perhaps the most interesting parallel, though, is that both opera and hockey were, in the early stages of their development, hugely popular, and populist, forms of entertainment. Venice saw the world's first public opera house open in 1637, and by 1670, the city had twenty of them. Opera houses had also sprouted up in Rome, Florence, Genoa, Bologna, and Modena. In fact, all across Europe, "real people" were piling in to see tragedy and comedy set to a few good tunes, even if they couldn't understand the Italian, an oversight that Mozart addressed in 1791 when he wrote *The Magic Flute* in his native language of German—a move that brought even more common folk into the stalls.   4

A century later, opera enjoyed a similar flowering on this side of the Atlantic. Places as far-flung as Dawson City built ice rinks in the service of hockey—but an opera house was just as important to a Canadian small town. Indeed, the country's towns and cities did not consider themselves civilized until they had an opera house to call their own, and both urban Brahmin and rugged frontiersman would think nothing of going to the opera one night and a hockey game the next. When the Kenora Thistles won the Stanley Cup in 1907, the team from the smallest town ever to win the trophy (population 10,000) could only hold their civic reception in a place as hallowed as the ice rink: the Kenora Opera House. The champion Thistles sat in the opera boxes, their faces reflecting the "barricade of silverware"—including   5 the Cup—that lined the stage as the ecstatic townspeople serenaded their heroes with speeches and song. The occasion itself was operatic.

Nearly a quarter of a century later, Conn Smythe was 6 inventing the Maple Leafs as "Canada's Team" (or English Canada's Team) and looking to raise them a temple at Carlton and Church Streets. He wanted to build a place that could not only house the Stanley Cup champions to come, but where people could also dress as though they were going to the opera. On November 12, 1931, 13,000 people—many of them in evening dress, as if at *Siegfried* (or later, under Harold Ballard, at *I Pagliacci*)—turned out for the Gardens opening. As speeches droned on at centre ice, impatient shouts of "Play hockey!" roared down from the rafters, where sat many of the men who had built the place, eager to see if the one-dollar MLG common shares they had taken were going to be worth anything.

The image of proles in the cheap seats shouting "Get on with 7 it" recalls the vocal passion of early opera audiences, but it also highlights the downward trajectory of opera in the twentieth century. Movies, radio, and eventually television rendered a night at the opera a largely upper-class pursuit; the importance of opera to the common folk was confined to that parodic phrase beloved of sports announcers: "It ain't over until the fat lady sings." Opera drifted from its populist roots, becoming rarefied, culturally adrift, and, arguably, irrelevant, at least to the public at large.

Opera's current cultural relevance—or lack of same—is one 8 of the reasons that *Game Misconduct*'s composer chose to tackle hockey as a theme. "'Contemporary' has become a frightening word to a lot of people," Uyeda says. "I don't understand why people don't want to see themselves reflected [in opera]. And that is exactly the reason that I went for this theme of hockey, because it has something to do with me, and with this great country."

Ironically, just as people no longer see themselves reflected 9 in opera, it may not be long before they no longer see themselves reflected in hockey. Just as opera has its corporate-sponsorship drives, the NHL now fights for the corporate patron with its mega-arenas bearing corporate logos and perks like wine cellars and humidors and, at the Staples Center in Los Angeles, fireplaces in the corporate boxes. In fact, top tickets for a Maple Leafs game cost a whopping $325 each, or almost three times what you'd pay to sit in the front row at a Canadian Opera Company performance.

When the swank Air Canada Centre opened in Toronto, Leafs   10
coach Pat Quinn saw the future of hockey—and it was not good.
Asked if he feared losing the blue-collar fan, Quinn said, "We've
already lost the blue-collar fan. I'm worried about the white-
collar fan." It's something that *Game Misconduct* worries about
too. Opera, once central, lost touch with the common fan. In the
ultimate irony of the hockey-opera relationship, the fat lady may
be singing for the national game as well.

UNDERSTANDING DETAILS

1. The differences between opera and hockey are obvious; McKinley
   focuses on similarities. List the similarities he identifies.
2. Why did Uyeda choose to create an opera about hockey?
3. Why has the popularity of opera diminished over time? What
   effects have these forces had on hockey?

ANALYZING MEANING

1. Why has McKinley chosen to compare opera and hockey? What
   is his purpose in this essay?
2. Explain the "parodic phrase beloved of sports announcers: 'It
   ain't over until the fat lady sings.'" What does McKinley mean
   by his reference to this phrase in the final sentence of his essay?
3. Is McKinley's outlook for the future of hockey optimistic or
   pessimistic? Explain.

DISCOVERING RHETORICAL STRATEGIES

1. Which of the four main methods of organizing a comparison
   and contrast essay has McKinley used? Why do you think he has
   made this choice?
2. In addition to comparison and contrast, what rhetorical strategies has McKinley employed in his essay? Where do you see
   evidence of these strategies?
3. How does McKinley give his essay cohesiveness? What details
   link the conclusion back to the beginning of the essay?

MAKING CONNECTIONS

1. Michael McKinley and Dave Bidini ("Kris King Looks Terrible")
   both write about hockey. If they were to attend a hockey game
   together, on what aspects of the experience do you think they
   would agree? Where might their views differ?

2. David Foot ("Boomers Dance to a New Beat") attributes various social trends to changing demographics. How do changing demographics contribute to the changing nature of the experience of attending a hockey game?
3. Imagine that McKinley and Evan Solomon ("The Babar Factor") are having a discussion about popular entertainment. What does hockey have in common with the stories about Babar the elephant? What about opera in comparison to Babar?

IDEAS FOR DISCUSSION/WRITING

Preparing to Write

Michael McKinley writes about the popular and populist beginnings of both opera and hockey, but he suggests that both have become "rarefied" or inaccessible to the public at large. Write freely about entertainment events and their appeal. What type of events have the broadest public appeal? Where do they take place? What type of events do you like to attend? To what do you attribute their appeal? What type of audience do those events tend to attract? Is there a cost associated with those events? Are there types of entertainment events that you avoid? If so, why? How do you learn about events that are happening in your community? Are there types of events you have attended in the past but that have now become inaccessible?

Choosing a topic

1. Write an essay for a group of your classmates in which you propose attending an event or participating in an activity that won't have immediate appeal. To convince them to participate, show the similarities between this type of event or activity and another that you know they enjoy.
2. Write an essay in which you compare and contrast two events that you have attended. Make sure you point out both similarities and differences, and clarify for your audience which one you preferred.
3. Hockey is often considered the national sport of Canada (although that title is officially shared with lacrosse). Compare and contrast the role of hockey in Canada to the role of baseball in the United States, football in Brazil or Italy, cricket in the West Indies, tae kwon do in Korea, or sumo wrestling in Japan. Have the roles of these respective sports changed over time? If so, in what way?

Evan Solomon

■□□■

THE BABAR FACTOR

A graduate of McGill University with degrees in English literature and religious studies, Evan Solomon (1968–) is the cofounder and executive editor of *Shift* magazine, a freelance journalist, and a fiction writer. For four years he was the host of a weekly show on Newsworld called *Futureworld* and he is now the host of Newsworld's *Hot Type*. He has also worked as a reporter for the *South China Morning Post* and is a regular contributor to CBC's *The National*, as a guest host and a contributor of cultural essays. Solomon's success is evidenced, in part, by the fact that he has received three Gemini nominations for *Futureworld*. His first novel, *Crossing the Distance*, the story of two brothers, was published in 1999.

Preparing to Read

"The Babar Factor" first appeared in *Shift* magazine in the spring of 1994. In this essay Evan Solomon looks at the distinctions between the stories of childhood and the enormously popular video games that have made a fairly recent appearance. In preparing to read this essay think about the stories that you remember from your own childhood. Do you remember reading books or having them read to you? Were stories told to you by the adults in your life? Are there characters from traditional stories that you can recall? Do you remember any specific stories that you particularly liked? What role did stories and books play in your childhood?

■——————————————————————————————————■

People come from all over the world to Celesteville-on-the-Sea. It has 1
the most beautiful beach in the land of the elephants.

And so begins another adventure with Jean de Brunhoff's 2
noble elephant-king Babar. Remember him? He was a great hero.
So were Curious George, Madeline, Mike Mulligan and his steam
shovel Mary Anne. This is a memorial to them. This is a memorial
to popular stories without interactive characters.

Super Mario sets foot in the door . . . 3

Accompanied by a catchy digital melody, these lines begin 4
another adventure in the ongoing saga of that noble video game

plumber Mario. Do you know him? Apparently, he's a great hero. So is Sonic the Hedge Hog and Dino Man. This is a memorial to them. This a memorial to popular video game characters who have yet to be forgotten.

Listen: 5

Two very interesting documents were recently made public. 6 One is called the Nintendo Co. 1993 *Annual Report* and the other is the year-end numbers for Sega Canada. Both are filled with extraordinary figures like this:

1. Over 75% of the 9.9 million households in Canada own video games.
2. The video game market is worth $400 million in Canada and $6 billion worldwide.
3. Nintendo has sold more than 100 million Mario video games worldwide.

Dazzling figures. So dazzling that they induce me to throw 7 away my Luddite bias and embark on a quest to understand why video games are popular.

Because my background is filled with books rather than video 8 games, I decide to measure the quality of the games by the Babar factor. Is a game more interesting than a story about Babar? Are the graphics more compelling than Jean de Brunhoff's famous watercolours? Is there more action, are the characters better developed? In short, what would I rather do, play with a game or read a Babar?

I begin by playing those games which boil CRTC chief Keith 9 Spicer's lobster. First there's Night Trap, an adventure where vampire-like gentlemen in black costumes stalk women and suck out their blood. Called a "live action game" because it contains video images complete with incredibly bad acting, this beauty is now available from 3DO. Translation: The company 3DO uses better graphics than the much touted 16-bit machines from Sega and so the women's blood is more visible.

Cheers from the vidiots, jeers from the worry-warts. 10 Summary: an altogether dreary game with less graphic violence than the Ren and Stimpy show (stay with me now as I connect with these cultural touchstones). Definitely less interesting than a Babar story—even those which focus too much on Babar's pesky nephew Arthur—but only slightly more sexist.

Then there's the controversial Mortal Kombat, details of   11
which I will spare you, but needless to say, it revolves around
a tournament where players fight to the death. With a multicultural cast of sadistic characters, this action-packed thriller is
clearly fluent in the vernacular of fun.

Home versions of the game don't allow players to see   12
essentials like blood spurting from a decapitated corpse, and
that has some customers crying foul. But what these customers
don't realize is that every home unit of the Sega system is, in
fact, secretly encoded with a way to unleash Mortal Kombat's
gory potential. Here is that secret code. Move your joy stick in the
following sequence: Down, Up, Left, Left, press button A, then
Right, and finally Down. Now, I'm no expert in mnemonics, but
there is an easy way to remember the code. The first letters spell
the word DULLARD. Go check. Is this a profound semiotic irony
or merely hacker humour that I don't get? I decide to rate Mortal
Kombat highly. While not as strong on narrative as Brunhoff's
work, the game is far more compelling. Just think, if only Celeste
had ripped out Babar's tusks in a bloody domestic dispute. What
a read! And those would have been watercolours worth saving.

But enough of the violent games. What of Mario and Sonic,   13
the real driving forces behind the video game explosion? Getting
to know them is slightly more difficult. First Mario. Resides in
Brooklyn. Plumber. First appeared as "Jumpman" in the 1981
version of Donkey Kong. Nimble of foot. On a mission to save one
of his three lovers. Last year Mario slipped the surly bonds of
the video game world and became a movie star. Played by the
irrepressible Bob Hoskins, Mario emerges as a bumbling fool
with a good heart. Bob did such a fine job effacing any nuance in
Mario's character that children went wild and a sequel went into
production.

And then Sonic, Sega's champion character. Sonic: video   14
game star, Saturday morning cartoon hero, leader of an
interactive video empire worth an estimated 3.5 billion dollars.
And the recent Q-score independent research ratings in the States
concluded that Sonic is more recognizable than Mickey Mouse.
Hmm, makes you look twice at this hedgehog.

And if you do look twice, here is what you will find. Not   15
only are Mario and Sonic childishly underdeveloped characters,
they do not even function within a narrative framework. But
because of a sophisticated marketing campaign, the lines between

story and game have become blurred. And so we mistake these exercises in hand-eye coordination for valuable narratives.

The campaign to blur these lines begins in promotional 16 literature. "Fun is an international language," a Nintendo report says, and then continues, "and Mario helps kids experience fun." Loaded words like "language" and "experience" are used to enrich the basic idea of fun, while positive characteristics such as bravery and loyalty are grafted onto one-dimensional game characters. By dressing up chase-games in the garb of story, marketing possibilities are exponentially greater. After all, it's easier to sell a person than a pixel.

And so, Mario the game piece becomes Mario the lovable 17 hero, and Sonic the blue graphic becomes Sonic the precocious child. Now they can be sold as role models. It's interactive literature, the press releases say, and the kids relate to it, don't you see? I, for one, don't see. Because despite the cartoons, the movies, and the proliferation of games, no real narrative structure exists at all. And everyone in the industry knows it.

"Mario is goofy and awkward, but he works hard and thus 18 can do superhuman things like flying and leaping over buildings," says Nintendo marketing vice president Peter Main, desperate to give Mario some depth. Notice how Main is not compelled to justify Mario's actions in a coherent way. Rather, the *non sequitur*—"he works hard therefore he can fly"—suffices. It suffices because the games move too fast for anyone to notice.

But contrast this shallow imaginative universe to that of 19 Babar. Babar, whose mother is tragically gunned down in front of him. Babar, who unites the elephants after the old king dies from poison. Babar who builds a city, fights enemies and teaches his children valuable, hard-learned lessons.

Because video games have no story, they are unable to create 20 or sustain dramatic tension. The excitement generated by overcoming obstacles is not dramatic because players can always replay the game if they fail. Nothing of value is ever won or lost. In Babar, on the other hand, there is always the potential for tragedy. Each story is compelling because we rely on the eminently mortal Babar to save the situation. But in video games, the "Play Again" factor is the prevailing eschatology, dulling the pleasures derived from emotional uncertainty.

Ultimately, this debases our understanding of the heroic. 21 Mario and Sonic are no more than Pavlovian dogs, conditioned to either pursue or retreat. Nothing they do requires risk or choice. The fact that Pavlov's bell has been substituted by a quarter and the dog biscuit by a princess should not fool us. Mario and Sonic are neither heroes nor role models, they are cute exercise tools that amuse, distract and ultimately bore.

As video games continue to grow in popularity, our 22 imaginative universe continues to shrink. While classic forms of entertainment like Babar demand a willing suspension of disbelief, video games only demand a willing suspension—that is to say, the choice to believe or disbelieve is irrelevant because there is nothing to believe or disbelieve in. With no context, there is no way to explore the heights and depths of human experience, which, after all, is the fundamental task of stories. In the end, all there is left to do is unplug the mind, plug in the game and play.

I don't like to wax nostalgic for books. I keep up with 23 developments in CD-ROMs. Heck, I just recently got myself an e-mail address. But when it comes to Mario and Sonic, I have simple advice: turn back from these wicked ways and read your holy Babar.

UNDERSTANDING DETAILS

1. What is Solomon comparing and contrasting (a) specifically and (b) generally?
2. Who is Babar? Who are Super Mario and Sonic?
3. Why does Solomon choose to measure the appeal of video games against a story about Babar?

ANALYZING MEANING

1. What is the essential difference between video games and stories?
2. Explain the popularity of video games such as Mortal Kombat and Super Mario.
3. Explain Solomon's conclusion. What do books have to offer that video games do not?

DISCOVERING RHETORICAL STRATEGIES

1. Describe Solomon's tone in this essay. Point out specific examples that create this tone.

2. In addition to comparison and contrast, what rhetorical modes has Solomon used in "The Babar Factor"?
3. Explain what strategies Solomon uses to make his introduction particularly effective.

MAKING CONNECTIONS

1. Evan Solomon and Will Ferguson ("The Sudbury Syndrome") are contemporaries who are both writing about change. In both cases they conclude that the original is preferable to the newer, although many people see the newer form (video games or shopping malls) as more desirable. Why do these writers advocate for resisting the change and returning to what has gone before? Do you agree with their positions?
2. In addition to being writers, Solomon, Coren ("Dogs and Monsters"), and Rebick ("The Culture of Overwork") are all television hosts. Is there anything in their writing that reflects their TV style?
3. Much of Solomon's essay considers the impact of new technology. Imagine a conversation between Evan Solomon and Tony Leighton ("The New Nature") about the significance of the impact of new technology on our society. How do the views of these two men compare? Do you believe they would essentially agree or disagree? How does your view fit into the conversation?

IDEAS FOR DISCUSSION/WRITING

Preparing to Write

In this essay Solomon cites statistics that demonstrate the overwhelming popularity of video games. Write freely about the role that video games play in our lives. Who plays video games? When and where are they played? What is their appeal? What accounts for their success? Do you think that their popularity will last?

Choosing a Topic

1. Choose two forms of entertainment and write an essay in which you compare and contrast them. Use your examination of their similarities and differences to determine which is the better option.

2. Choose a character from a story that you think resembles you or someone you know in appearance and/or character. You might choose a childhood story or one that you have read as an adult. Write an essay in which you describe the similarities between your two subjects.
3. Your student council is going to purchase a new video game for the student lounge at your school. Write an essay in which you compare and contrast two of the available games in order to make a recommendation about which one they should purchase.

Definitions vary from short, dictionary-length summaries to longer, "extended" accounts that determine the form of an entire essay. Words or ideas that require expanded definitions are usually abstract, complex, or unavoidably controversial; they generally bear many related meanings or many shades of meaning. Definitions can be *objective* (technically precise and generally dry) or *subjective* (coloured with personal opinion), and they can be used to instruct or entertain, or to accomplish a combination of these two fundamental rhetorical goals.

In the following excerpt, a student defines "childhood" by putting it into perspective with other important stages of life. Though mostly entertaining, the paragraph is also instructive as the student objectively captures the essence of this phase of human development:

> Childhood is a stage of growth somewhere between infancy and adolescence. Just as each developmental period in our lives brings new changes and concerns, childhood serves as the threshold to puberty—the time we learn to discriminate between good and bad, right and wrong, love and lust. Childhood is neither a time of irresponsible infancy nor responsible adulthood. Rather, it is marked by duties that we don't really want, challenges that excite us, feelings that puzzle and frighten us, and limitless opportunities that help us explore the world around us. Childhood is a time when we solidify our personalities in spite of pressures to be someone else.

Thinking Critically by Using Definition

Definitions are building blocks in communication that help us make certain we are functioning from the same understanding of terms and ideas. They give us a foundation to work from in both reading and writing. Definitions force us to think about meanings and word associations that make other thinking strategies stronger and easier to work with.

The process of thinking through our definitions forces us to come to some understanding about a particular term or concept we are mentally wrestling with. Articulating that definition helps us move to other modes of thought and higher levels of understanding. Practising definitions in isolation to get a feel for them is much like separating the skill of peddling from the process of riding a bike. The better you get at peddling, the more natural the rest of the cycling process becomes. The following

CHAPTER 7

DEFINITION

■ ■ ■

Limiting the Frame of Reference

Definitions help us function smoothly in a complex world. All effective communication, in fact, is continuously dependent on our unique human ability to understand and employ accurate definitions of a wide range of words, phrases, and abstract ideas. If we did not work from a set of shared definitions, we would not be able to carry on coherent conversations, write comprehensible letters, or respond to even the simplest radio and television programs. Definitions help us understand basic concrete terms (such as automobiles, laser beams, and the gross national product), discuss various events in our lives (such as snow skiing, legal proceedings, and a New Year's celebration), and grasp difficult abstract ideas (such as the concepts of democracy, ambition, and resentment). The ability to comprehend definitions and use them effectively helps us keep our oral and written level of communication accurate and accessible to a wide variety of people.

Defining Definition

Definition is the process of explaining a word, object, or idea in such a way that the reader (or listener) knows as precisely as possible what we mean. A good definition sets up intellectual boundaries by focusing on the special qualities of a word or phrase that set it apart from other similar words or phrases. Clear definitions always give the writer and the reader a mutual starting point on the sometimes bumpy road to successful communication.

exercises ask you to practise definitions in a number of different ways. Being more conscious of what definition entails will make it more useful to you in both your reading and your writing.

1. Define one of the concrete words and one of the abstract words listed here in one or two sentences. What were some of the differences between the process you went through to explain the concrete word and the abstract word? What can you conclude from this brief exercise about the differences in defining abstract and concrete words? Concrete: *cattle, book, ranch, water, gum.* Abstract: *freedom, progress, equality, fairness, boredom.*

2. Define the word "grammar." Consult a dictionary, several handbooks, and maybe even some friends to get their views on the subject. Then, write a humorous definition of grammar that consolidates all these views into a single definition.

3. In what ways can you "define" yourself? What qualities or characteristics are crucial to an understanding of you as a person?

Reading and Writing Definition Essays

Extended definitions, which usually range from two or three paragraphs to an entire essay, seldom follow a set pattern of development or organization. Instead, as you will see from the examples in this chapter, they draw on a number of different techniques to help explain a word, object, term, concept, or phenomenon.

How to Read a Definition Essay

Preparing to Read. As you begin to read each of the definition essays in this chapter, take some time to consider the author's title and the synopsis of the essay in the Rhetorical Table of Contents: What is Michael Clugston's attitude toward lightning in "Twice Struck"? What do you sense is the general mood of Neil Bissoondath's "Pieces of Sky"?

Equally important as you prepare to read is scanning an essay and finding information from its preliminary material about the author and the circumstances surrounding the composition of the essay. What do you think is Wayson Choy's purpose in his definition of "banana"? And what can you learn about Drew Hayden Taylor and his qualifications for writing "Pretty Like a White Boy"?

Last, as you prepare to read these essays, answer the prereading questions before each essay, and then, spend a few minutes thinking freely about the general subject of the essay at hand: What role does your appearance play in your life (Taylor)? What information do you need about being a "banana" (North American of Chinese ancestry) (Choy)? What values do you consider distinctively Canadian (Bissoondath)?

Reading. As you read a definition essay, as with all essays, be sure to record your initial reactions to your reading material. What are some of your thoughts or associations in relation to each essay?

As you get more involved in the essay, reconsider the preliminary material so you can create a context within which to analyze what the writer is saying: Who do you think is Taylor's primary audience? Do you think his essay will effectively reach that group of people? In what ways is Wayson Choy qualified to write about being a "banana"?

Also, determine at this point whether the author's treatment of his or her subject is predominantly objective or subjective. Then, make sure you understand the main points of the essay on the literal, interpretive, and analytical levels by reading the questions that follow.

Rereading. When you read these definition essays for a second time, check to see how each writer actually sets forth his or her definition: Does the writer put each item in a specific category with clear boundaries? Do you understand how the item being defined is different from other items in the same category? Did the author name the various components of the item, explain its etymology (linguistic origin and history), discuss what it is not, or perform a combination of these tasks?

To evaluate the effectiveness of a definition essay, you need to reconsider the essay's primary purpose and audience. If Taylor is trying to get the general reader to understand the experience of not "looking the part," how effective is he in doing so? In like manner, is Clugston successful in explaining the nature of lightning and humans' understanding of it? Especially applicable is the question of what other rhetorical strategies help the author communicate this purpose. Through what other modes does Bissoondath define what it is to be Canadian?

For an inventory of the reading process, you can review the guidelines on pages 15–16 of the Introduction.

How to Write a Definition Essay

Preparing to Write. As with other essays, you should begin the task of writing a definition essay by answering the prewriting questions featured in this text and then by exploring your subject and generating other ideas. (See the explanation of various prewriting techniques on pages 17–19 of the Introduction.) Be sure you know what you are going to define and how you will approach your definition. You should then focus on a specific audience and purpose as you approach the writing assignment.

Writing. The next step toward developing a definition essay is usually to describe the general category to which the word belongs and then to contrast the word with all other words in that group. To define *exposition*, for example, you might say that it is a type of writing. Then, to differentiate it from other types of writing, you could go on to say that its main purpose is to "expose," or present information, as opposed to rhetorical modes such as description and narration, which describe and tell stories. In addition, you might want to cite some expository methods, such as example, process analysis, division/classification, and comparison/contrast.

Yet another way to begin a definition essay is to provide a term's etymology. Tracing a word's origin often illuminates its current meaning and usage as well. *Exposition*, for example, comes from the Latin *exponere*, meaning "to put forth, set forth, display, declare, or publish" (*ex* = out; *ponere* = to put or place). This information can generally be found in any good dictionary or in a good encyclopedia.

Another approach to defining a term is to explain what it does *not* mean. For example, *exposition* is not creative writing. By limiting the readers' frame of reference in these various ways, you are helping to establish a working definition for the term under consideration.

Finally, rhetorical methods that we have already studied, such as description, narration, example, process analysis, division/classification, and comparison/contrast, are particularly useful to writers in expanding their definitions. To clarify the term *exposition*, you might **describe** the details of an expository theme, **narrate** a story about the wide use of the term in today's classroom, or **give examples** of assignments that would produce good expository writing. In other situations, you could **analyze** various writing assignments and discuss the **process** of producing an expository essay, **classify** exposition apart from creative writing and then **divide** it into categories similar to the headings of this book, or **compare** and **contrast** it with creative writing. Writers also use definition quite often to support other rhetorical modes.

Rewriting. Reviewing and revising a definition essay is a relatively straightforward task:

1. Have you chosen an effective beginning for your paper?
2. Did you create a reasonable context for your definition?
3. Have you used appropriate rhetorical strategies to develop your ideas?
4. Have you achieved your overall purpose as effectively as possible?

Other guidelines to direct your writing and revising appear on pages 26–27 of the Introduction.

Student Essay: Definition at Work

In the following essay, a student defines "the perfect yuppie." Notice how the writer puts this term in a category and then explains the limits of that category and the uniqueness of this term within the category. To further inform her audience of the features of "yuppiedom," the student calls on the word's etymology, its dictionary definition, an itemization of the term's basic characteristics, a number of examples that explain those characteristics, and, finally, a general discussion of causes and effects that regulate a yuppie's behaviour.

The Perfect Yuppie

Etymology/ dictionary definition Many people already know that the letters YUP stand for "young urban professional." *Young* in this context is understood to mean thirtyish; *urban* often means suburban; and *professional* means most *Subject* definitely college-educated. Double the *P* and add an *I* and an *E* at the end, and you get *yuppie*—that 1980s bourgeois, the marketers' darling, and the 1960s' inheritance. But let's not generalize. Not *Limitations set* every thirty-year-old suburban college graduate qualifies as a yuppie. Nor is every yuppie in his or her thirties. True yuppiness involves much more than the words that make up the acronym. *Writer's credibility* Being the little sister of a couple of yups, I am in an especially good position to define the perfect yuppie. I watched two develop.

The essence of yuppiness is generally new money. In the yuppie's defence, I will admit that most yuppies have worked hard

General category of word being defined

Why the dictionary definition is inadequate

General characteristic

Cause/
Effect — for their money and social status. Moreover, the baby boom of which they are a part has caused a glut of job seekers in their age bracket, forcing them to be competitive if they want all the nice things retailers have designed for them. But with new money comes

General characteristic — an interesting combination of wealth, naiveté, and pretentiousness.

Specific example — For example, most yuppies worthy of the title have long ago traded in their fringed suede jackets for fancy fur coats. Although they were animal rights activists in the 1960s, they will not notice the irony of this change. In fact, they may be shameless enough to parade in their fur coats—fashion-show style—for friends and family. Because of their "innocence," yuppies generally will not see the vulgarity of their actions. — Cause/effect; Specific example

General characteristic — Because they are often quite wealthy, yuppies tend to have a lot of "things." They are simply overwhelmed by the responsibility of spending all that money. For example, one yup I know has fourteen pairs of sunglasses and seven watches. She, her husband, and their three children own at least twenty collections of everything from comic books to Civil War memorabilia. Most yuppies have so much money that I often wonder why the word "yuppie" does not have a dollar sign in it somewhere. — Specific example; Specific example

General characteristic — Perhaps in an effort to rid themselves of this financial burden, all good yuppies go to Europe as soon as possible. Not Germany or France or Portugal, mind you, but Europe. They do not know what they are doing there and thus generally spend much more money than they need to—but, after all, no yuppie ever claimed to be frugal. Most important, they bring home slides of Europe and show them to everyone they know. A really good yuppie will forget and show you his or her slides more than once. Incidentally, when everyone has seen the slides of Europe twice, the yuppie's next stop is Australia. — Cause/effect; Cause/effect

General characteristic — A favourite pastime of yuppies is having wine-tasting parties for their yuppie friends. At these parties, they must make a great to-do about tasting the wine, cupping their faces over the glass with their palms (as if they were having a facial), and even sniffing the cork, for goodness sake. I once knew a yuppie who did not understand that a bottle of wine could not be rejected simply because he found he "did not like that kind." Another enjoyed making a show of having his wife choose and taste the wine occasionally, which they both thought was adorable. — Specific example; Specific example; Specific example

What it is not — Some yuppie wanna-be's drive red or black BMWs, but don't let them fool you. A genuine, hard-core yuppie will usually own a gold or silver Volvo station wagon. In this yuppie-mobile, the — General characteristic

Specific examples yuppie wife will chauffeur her young yuppettes to and from <u>their modelling classes, track meets, ballet, the manicurist, and boy scouts, for the young yuppie is generally</u> as competitive and socially active as his or her parents. On the same topic, one particularly annoying trait of yuppie parents is bragging about their yuppettes. You will know yuppies by the fact that they <u>have the</u> *General character-istic* <u>smartest, most talented children in the world</u>. They <u>will show you</u> <u>their kids' report cards, making sure you notice any improve-</u> *Specific example* <u>ments from last quarter</u>.

Division/ classification   Perhaps I have been harsh in my portrayal of the perfect yuppie, and, certainly, I will be accused by some of stereotyping. But consider this: I never classify people as yuppies who do not so classify themselves. <u>The ultimate criterion for being yuppies is</u> *General char-acteristic and concluding statement* <u>that they will always proudly label themselves as such.</u>

Some Final Thoughts on Definition

The following selections feature extended definitions whose main purpose is to explain a specific term or idea to their readers. Each essay in its own way helps the audience identify with various parts of its definitions, and each successfully communicates the unique qualities of the term or idea in question. Notice what approaches to definition each writer takes and how these approaches limit the readers' frame of reference in the process of effective communication.

Definition in Review

Reading Definition Essays

Preparing to Read

1. What assumptions can you make from the essay's title?
2. Can you guess what the general mood of the essay is?
3. What is the essay's purpose and audience?
4. What does the synopsis in the Rhetorical Table of Contents tell you about the essay?
5. What can you learn from the author's biography?
6. Can you guess what the author's point of view toward the subject is?
7. What are your responses to the Preparing to Read questions?

Reading

1. Have you recorded your reactions to the essay?
2. Is the author's treatment of the subject predominantly subjective or objective?
3. Did you preview the questions that follow the essay?

Rereading

1. How does the author lay out the definition?
2. What is the essay's main purpose and audience?
3. What other rhetorical strategies does the author use to support the essay's purpose?
4. What are your responses to the questions after the essay?

Writing Definition Essays

Preparing to Write

1. What are your responses to the Preparing to Write questions?
2. Do you know what you are going to define and how you will approach your topic?
3. Who is your audience?

Writing

1. Does the beginning of your essay suit your purpose?
2. Do you use effective strategies to define your word or concept?
3. What rhetorical strategies do you use to expand your definition essay?

Rewriting

1. Have you chosen an effective beginning for your paper?
2. Did you create a reasonable context for your definition?
3. Have you used appropriate rhetorical strategies to develop your ideas?
4. Have you achieved your overall purpose as well as possible?

Drew Hayden Taylor

PRETTY LIKE A WHITE BOY:
THE ADVENTURES OF A
BLUE-EYED OJIBWAY

Living in Toronto but originally from the Curve Lake Reserve near Peterborough, Ontario, Drew Hayden Taylor (1962–) is quoted in a profile from the *Montreal Gazette* as follows: "I hate the technical part of writing … I hate it with a passion." And yet he had achieved enviable success by his early thirties—as a writer.

Since graduating from the broadcasting program at Seneca College, Taylor has worked as a radio reporter, a sound recordist for a film company, a trainee producer with the CBC, a promoter at the Canadian Native Arts Foundation, and a freelance writer. In addition to articles and stories that have appeared in *Maclean's*, the *Globe and Mail*, *This* magazine, *Anishinabek News*, *Cinema Canada*, and *Windspeaker*, Taylor has written episodes for *The Beachcombers* and *Street Legal*. He is also an award-winning playwright who has served as the writer-in-residence for the Native Earth Performing Arts Theatre. His published works include several plays (*Toronto at Dreamer's Rock, Someday, Only Drunks and Children Tell the Truth,* and *The Baby Blues)*, a collection of essays (*Funny, You Don't Look Like One: Observations from a Blue-Eyed Ojibway*), and a book of short stories (*Fearless Warriors*). Taylor's most recent works include *The Boy in the Treehouse/Girl Who Loved Her Horses* (2000), *alterNatives* (2000), and *The Buz'Gem Blues*, the third play in Drew Hayden Taylor's *Blues Quartet* (2002).

Taylor brings a strong sense of humour to his work, which centres primarily around native issues. One of his aspirations is described in a quotation from a profile in *Windspeaker*: "With Native People writing their own stories, Canadians and people in other countries may get a more accurate view of (our people)," says Taylor. "It may help abolish the popular concept that Indians are all the same …" The essay "Pretty Like a White Boy: The Adventures of a Blue-Eyed Ojibway" conveys Taylor's frustrating experiences of not "looking the part."

Preparing to Read

In this essay, Drew Hayden Taylor presents examples from his own life that illustrate the problems that occur as we categorize and define people by their heritage and appearance. Taylor's definition of a new term that accurately defines who he is provides a concluding summary to his discussion of stereotypes and the difficulties of not fitting neatly into the already existing categories. As you prepare to read, consider the terms "Indians," "Native people," and "white man." What associations do you have with each of these? Are they positive labels or negative ones? How do you distinguish people from these groups? What does an Indian look like? In what way does a white person differ in appearance? What does the title of this essay tell you about the author's attitude toward his topic?

In this big, huge world, with all its billions and billions of people, it's safe to say that everybody will eventually come across personalities and individuals that will touch them in some peculiar yet poignant way. Individuals that in some way represent and help define who you are. I'm no different, mine was Kermit the Frog. Not just because Natives have a long tradition of savouring Frogs' legs, but because of his music. If you all may remember, Kermit is quite famous for his rendition of 'It's Not Easy Being Green.' I can relate. If I could sing, my song would be 'It's Not Easy Having Blue Eyes in a Brown Eyed Village.' 1

Yes, I'm afraid it's true. The author happens to be a card-carrying Indian. Once you get past the aforementioned eyes, the fair skin, the light brown hair, and noticeable lack of cheekbones, there lies the heart and spirit of an Ojibway storyteller. Honest Injun, or as the more politically correct term may be, honest aboriginal. 2

You see, I'm the product of a white father I never knew, and an Ojibway woman who evidently couldn't run fast enough. As a kid I knew I looked a bit different. But, then again, all kids are paranoid when it comes to their peers. I had a fairly happy childhood, frolicking through the bullrushes. But there were certain things that, even then, made me notice my unusual appearance. Whenever we played cowboys and Indians, guess who had to be the bad guy, the cowboy. 3

It wasn't until I left the Reserve for the big bad city, that I became more aware of the role people expected me to play, and the fact that physically I didn't fit in. Everybody seemed to have this preconceived idea of how every Indian looked and acted. One guy, on my first day of college, asked me what kind of horse I preferred. I didn't have the heart to tell him 'hobby.' 4

I've often tried to be philosophical about the whole thing. I have both white and red blood in me, I guess that makes me pink. I am a 'Pink' man. Try to imagine this, I'm walking around on any typical Reserve in Canada, my head held high, proudly 5 announcing to everyone 'I am a Pink Man.' It's a good thing I ran track in school.

My pinkness is constantly being pointed out to me over and over and over again. 'You don't look Indian?' 'You're not Indian, are you?' 'Really?!?' I got questions like that from both white and Native people, for a while I debated having my status card tattooed on my forehead.   6

And like most insecure people and specially a blue-eyed Native writer, I went through a particularly severe identity crisis at one point. In fact, I admit it, one depressing spring evening, I dyed my hair black. Pitch black.   7

The reason for such a dramatic act, you may ask? Show Business. You see, for the last eight years or so, I've worked in various capacities in the performing arts, and as a result I'd always get calls to be an extra or even try out for an important role in some Native oriented movie. This anonymous voice would phone, having been given my number, and ask if I would be interested in trying out for a movie. Being a naturally ambitious, curious, and greedy young man, I would always readily agree, stardom flashing in my eyes and hunger pains from my wallet.   8

A few days later I would show up for the audition, and that was always an experience. What kind of experience you may ask? Picture this, the picture calls for the casting of seventeenth-century Mohawk warriors living in a traditional longhouse. The casting director calls the name 'Drew Hayden Taylor' and I enter.   9

The casting director, the producer, and the film's director look up from the table and see my face, blue eyes flashing in anticipation. I once was described as a slightly chubby beachboy. But even beachboys have tans. Anyway, there would be a quick flush of confusion, a recheck of the papers, and a hesitant 'Mr. Taylor?' Then they would ask if I was at the right audition. It was always the same. By the way, I never got any of the parts I tried for, except for a few anonymous crowd shots. Politics tells me it's because of the way I look, reality tells me it's probably because I can't act. I'm not sure which is better.   10

It's not just film people either. Recently I've become quite involved in Theatre, Native theatre to be exact. And one cold October day I was happily attending the Toronto leg of a province-wide tour of my first play, *Toronto at Dreamer's Rock*. The place was sold out, the audience very receptive and the performance was wonderful. Ironically one of the actors was also half white.   11

The director later told me he had been talking with the actor's 12
father, an older non-Native type chap. Evidently he had asked a
few questions about me, and how I did my research. This made
the director curious and he asked about his interest. He replied
'He's got an amazing grasp of the Native situation for a white
person.'

Not all these incidents are work related either. One time a 13
friend and I were coming out of a rather upscale bar (we were out
Yuppie watching) and managed to catch a cab. We thanked the
cab driver for being so comfortably close on such a cold night, he
shrugged and nonchalantly talked about knowing what bars to
drive around. 'If you're not careful, all you'll get is drunk
Indians.' I hiccuped.

Another time this cab driver droned on and on about the 14
government. He started out by criticizing Mulroney, and
eventually to his handling of the Oka crisis. This perked up my
ears, until he said 'If it were me, I'd have tear-gassed the place by
the second day. No more problem.' He got a dime tip. A few
incidents like this and I'm convinced I'd make a great undercover
agent for one of the Native political organizations.

But then again, even Native people have been known to look 15
at me with a fair amount of suspicion. Many years ago when I
was a young man, I was working on a documentary on Native
culture up in the wilds of Northern Ontario. We were at an
isolated cabin filming a trapper woman and her kids. This one
particular nine-year-old girl seemed to take a shine to me. She
followed me around for two days both annoying me and
endearing herself to me. But she absolutely refused to believe
that I was Indian. The whole film crew tried to tell her but to no
avail. She was certain I was white.

Then one day as I was loading up the car with film 16
equipment, she asked me if I wanted some tea. Being in a hurry
I declined the tea. She immediately smiled with victory crying out
'See, you're not Indian, all Indians drink tea!'

Frustrated and a little hurt I whipped out my Status card 17
and thrust it at her. Now there I was, standing in a Northern
Ontario winter, showing my Status card to a nine-year-old non-
status Indian girl who had no idea what one was. Looking back,
this may not have been one of my brighter moves.

But I must admit, it was a Native woman that boiled 18
everything down in one simple sentence. You may know that
woman, Marianne Jones from 'The Beachcombers' television

series. We were working on a film together out west and we got
to gossiping. Eventually we got around to talking about our
respective villages. Hers on the Queen Charlotte Islands, or Haida
Gwaii as the Haida call them, and mine in central Ontario.

Eventually childhood on the Reserve was being discussed   19
and I made a comment about the way I look. She studied me for
a moment, smiled, and said 'Do you know what the old women
in my village would call you?' Hesitant but curious, I shook my
head. 'They'd say you were pretty like a white boy.' To this day
I'm still not sure if I like that.

Now some may argue that I am simply a Métis with a Status   20
card. I disagree, I failed French in grade 11. And the Métis as
everyone knows have their own separate and honourable culture,
particularly in western Canada. And of course I am well aware
that I am not the only person with my physical characteristics.

I remember once looking at a video tape of a drum group,   21
shot on a Reserve up near Manitoulin Island. I noticed one of
the drummers seemed quite fairhaired, almost blond. I mentioned
this to my girlfriend of the time and she shrugged saying 'Well,
that's to be expected. The highway runs right through the
Reserve.'

Perhaps I'm being too critical. There's a lot to be said for   22
both cultures. For example, on the left hand, you have the Native
respect for Elders. They understand the concept of wisdom and
insight coming with age.

On the white hand, there's Italian food. I mean I really love   23
my mother and family but seriously, does anything really beat
good Veal Scallopini? Most of my aboriginal friends share my
fondness for this particular brand of food. Wasn't there a warrior
at Oka named Lasagna? I found it ironic, though curiously logical,
that Columbus was Italian. A connection I wonder?

Also Native people have this wonderful respect and love for   24
the land. They believe they are part of it, a mere chain in the
cycle of existence. Now as many of you know, this conflicts with
the accepted Judeo-Christian i.e. western view of land
management. I even believe somewhere in the first chapters of the
Bible it says something about God giving man dominion over
Nature. Check it out, Genesis 4:?, 'Thou shalt clear cut.' So I grew
up understanding that everything around me is important and
alive. My Native heritage gave me that.

And again, on the white hand, there's breast implants. Darn   25
clever them white people. That's something Indians would never

have invented, seriously. We're not ambitious enough. We just take what the Creator decides to give us, but no, not the white man. Just imagine it, some serious looking white man, and let's face it people, we know it was a man who invented them, don't we? So just imagine some serious looking white doctor sitting around in his laboratory muttering to himself, 'Big tits, big tits, hmmm, how do I make big tits?' If it was an Indian, it would be 'Big tits, big tits, white women sure got big tits' and leave it at that.

So where does that leave me on the big philosophical 26 scoreboard? What exactly are my choices again? Indians—respect for Elders, love of the land. White people—food and big tits. In order to live in both cultures I guess I'd have to find an Indian woman with big tits who lives with her grandmother in a cabin out in the woods and can make Fettucini Alfredo on a wood stove.

Now let me make this clear, I'm not writing this for sympathy, 27 or out of anger, or even some need for self-glorification. I am just setting the facts straight. For as you read this, a new Nation is born. This is a declaration of independence, my declaration of independence.

I've spent too many years explaining who and what I am 28 repeatedly, so as of this moment, I officially secede from both races. I plan to start my own separate nation. Because I am half Ojibway and half Caucasian, we will be called the Occasions. And I of course, since I'm founding the new nation, will be a Special Occasion.

UNDERSTANDING DETAILS

1. Does Drew Hayden Taylor affiliate himself more closely with Native or white culture? Give specific examples to support your answer.
2. What advantages does Taylor associate with being Native? What advantages does Taylor link with being white?
3. According to Taylor, why would he make a great undercover agent for a Native political organization?

ANALYZING MEANING

1. What is the author's purpose in this essay? Does he take an objective or a subjective approach in defining his subject?
2. Explain why Drew Hayden Taylor does not consider himself to be Métis.

3. Why do you think that Taylor did not get the parts in the films for which he auditioned?

DISCOVERING RHETORICAL STRATEGIES

1. What tone is established in this essay? How does Taylor create this tone? Is it effective?
2. What rhetorical strategies is Taylor employing in this essay in addition to definition? Give specific examples to support your answer.
3. Why does Taylor settle on the term "Special Occasion" rather than "Pink Man" as a way to define himself? What definition strategy has resulted in his final title?

MAKING CONNECTIONS

1. Drew Hayden Taylor credits Tomson Highway ("What a Certain Visionary Once Said") with "helping him to get his feet wet" in native theatre. What similarities are there between Taylor's essay and Highway's?
2. Imagine Cecil Foster ("Why Blacks Get Mad") and Drew Hayden Taylor having a conversation about their experiences of being judged based on their appearance. In what respects are their experiences similar? How do they differ? Do the two respond to appearance-based judgment in the same way? Give specific examples to support your answer.
3. Drew Hayden Taylor has chosen humour as a vehicle for making a difficult subject more palatable to his readers. Compare this strategy to that of Laura Robinson ("Starving for the Gold"). Explain which you think is the more effective approach.

IDEAS FOR DISCUSSION/WRITING

Preparing to Write

Write freely about your ethnic background, race, or heritage. How would you define yourself? Do existing categories work for you or do you feel the need to create a new category to capture who you are? What physical characteristics define you as part of the group you have identified? What personality characteristics affiliate you with this group? How would you categorize children of mixed heritage?

Choosing a Topic

1. Think of a term to define yourself in a way that reflects various aspects of your heritage/background. Others may belong to this group, but focus on the aspects that make you unique from other, already existing categories. Write an essay for a general interest magazine in which you define your term using examples from your own life to make your definition clear.
2. Often our expectations are not borne out by reality. Write an essay for college or university students in which you define a particular job or profession based on your knowledge of someone in that position.
3. In paragraph 1, Taylor refers to "individuals that in some way represent and help define who you are." Describe one such individual in your life and explain how he or she has contributed to making you who you are.

Wayson Choy

I'M A BANANA AND PROUD OF IT

Now a teacher of English at Toronto's Humber College and a faculty member at the Humber School for Writers, Wayson Choy (1939–) was born and raised in British Columbia, where he was the first Chinese Canadian to enroll in the University of British Columbia's creative writing program. Since that time, Choy has won the 1996 Trillium Award and the 1996 Vancouver City Book Award for his first novel, *The Jade Peony*, which is about Vancouver's Chinatown during the Depression and World War II. Choy followed *The Jade Peony* with the critically acclaimed *Paper Shadows: A Chinatown Childhood*, a memoir about his own experiences growing up in Vancouver's Chinatown and the discovery of hidden truths about his childhood. Choy describes his childhood as being "like a Chinese box that opens in a variety of different ways, revealing different levels, each sliding compartment a secret"; in *Paper Shadows*, he explores the challenges of growing up with his Chinese heritage often in conflict with the influences of the North American culture in which he was living.

Choy is currently working on a new novel, a sequel to *The Jade Peony* called *The Ten Thousand Things*.

Preparing to Read

In this essay, which first appeared in the *Globe and Mail*'s Facts and Arguments column, Wayson Choy proudly defines himself as a "banana," an affectionate nickname for integrated North American children of Chinese parents. Before reading this essay think about nicknames and the role that they play in our lives. Who assigns nicknames? Who uses them? What makes some nicknames stick and others fade? Are nicknames positive or negative? Do you have a nickname? Do you like it? Does it appropriately reflect who you are?

■_____■

Because both my parents came from China, I took Chinese. But I cannot read or write Chinese and barely speak it. I love my North American citizenship. I don't mind being called a "banana," yellow on the outside and white inside. I'm proud I'm a banana.

After all, in Canada and the United States, native Indians are "apples" (red outside, white inside); blacks are "Oreo cookies" (black and white); and Chinese are "bananas." These metaphors assume, both rightly and wrongly, that the culture here has been primarily anglo-white. Cultural history made me a banana.

History: My father and mother arrived separately to the B.C. coast in the early part of the century. They came as unwanted "aliens." Better to be an alien here than to be dead of starvation in China. But after the Chinese Exclusion laws were passed in North America (late 1800s, early 1900s), no Chinese immigrants were granted citizenship in either Canada or the United States.

Like those Old China village men from *Toi San* who, in the 1850s, laid down cliff-edge train tracks through the Rockies and the Sierras, or like those first women who came as mail-order wives or concubines and who as bond-slaves were turned into cheaper labourers or even prostitutes—like many of those men and women, my father and mother survived ugly, unjust times. In 1917, two hours after he got off the boat from Hong Kong, my father was called "chink" and told to go back to China. "Chink" is a hateful racist term, stereotyping the shape of Asian eyes: "a chink in the armour," an undesirable slit. For the Elders, the past was humiliating. Eventually, the Second World War changed hostile attitudes toward the Chinese.

During the war, Chinese men volunteered and lost their lives as members of the American and Canadian military. When hostilities ended, many more were proudly in uniform waiting to go overseas. Record Chinatown dollars were raised to buy War Bonds. After 1945, challenged by such money and ultimate sacrifices, the Exclusion laws in both Canada and the United States were revoked. Chinatown residents claimed their citizenship and sent for their families.

By 1949, after the Communists took over China, those of us 6 who arrived here as young children, or were born here, stayed. No longer "aliens," we became legal citizens of North America. Many of us also became "bananas."

Historically, "banana" is not a racist term. Although it clums- 7 ily stereotypes many of the children and grandchildren of the Old Chinatowns, the term actually follows the old Chinese tendency to assign endearing nicknames to replace formal names, semicomic names to keep one humble. Thus, "banana" describes the generations who assimilated so well into North American life.

In fact, our families encouraged members of my generation 8 in the 1950s and sixties to "get ahead," to get an English educa- tion, to get a job with good pay and prestige. "Don't work like me," Chinatown parents said. "Work in an office!" The *lao wah- kiu* (the Chinatown old-timers) also warned, "Never forget—you still be Chinese!"

None of us ever forgot. The mirror never lied. 9

Many Chinatown teen-agers felt we didn't quite belong in 10 any one world. We looked Chinese, but thought and behaved North American. Impatient Chinatown parents wanted the best of both worlds for us, but they bluntly labelled their children and grandchildren "*juk-sing*" or even "*mo no.*" Not that we were totally "shallow bamboo butt-ends" or entirely "no brain," but we had less and less understanding of Old China traditions, and less and less interest in their village histories. Father used to say we lacked Taoist ritual, Taoist manners. We were, he said, "*mo li.*"

This was true. Chinatown's younger brains, like everyone 11 else's of whatever race, were being colonized by "white bread" U.S. family television programs. We began to feel Chinese home life was inferior. We co-operated with English-language magazines that showed us how to act and what to buy. Seductive Hollywood movies made some of us secretly weep that we did not have movie- star faces. American music made Chinese music sound like noise.

By the 1970s and eighties, many of us had consciously or 12 unconsciously distanced ourselves from our Chinatown histories. We became bananas.

Finally, for me, in my 40s or 50s, with the death first of my   13
mother, then my father, I realized I did not belong anywhere
unless I could understand the past. I needed to find the
foundation of my Chinese-ness. I needed roots.

I spent my college holidays researching the past. I read   14
Chinatown oral histories, located documents, searched out early
articles. Those early citizens came back to life for me. Their long
toil and blood sacrifices, the proud record of their patient, legal
challenges, gave us all our present rights as citizens. Canadian
and American Chinatowns set aside their family tongue
differences and encouraged each other to fight injustice. There
were no borders. "After all," they affirmed, "*Daaih ga tohng yahn*
… We are all Chinese!"

In my book, *The Jade Peony*, I tried to recreate this past, to   15
explore the beginnings of the conflicts trapped within myself, the
struggle between being Chinese and being North American. I
discovered a truth: these "between world" struggles are universal.

In every human being, there is "the Other"—something that   16
makes each of us feel how different we are to everyone else, even
to family members. Yet, ironically, we are all the same, wanting
the same security and happiness. I know this now.

I think the early Chinese pioneers actually started "going   17
bananas" from the moment they first settled upon the West Coast.
They had no choice. They adapted. They initiated assimilation. If
they had not, they and their family would have starved to death.
I might even suggest that all surviving Chinatown citizens
eventually became bananas. Only some, of course, were more
ripe than others.

That's why I'm proudly a banana: I accept the paradox of   18
being both Chinese and not Chinese.

Now at last, whenever I look in the mirror or hear ghost   19
voices shouting, "You still Chinese!", I smile.

I know another truth: In immigrant North America, we are all   20
Chinese.

UNDERSTANDING DETAILS

1. What does the term "banana" mean? How is this different from
   "apple" and "Oreo cookie"?
2. Describe the experience of Choy's parents coming to Canada.
3. What motivated Choy to research the past? What type of
   research did he do? Did he find what he was looking for?

ANALYZING MEANING

1. Choy differentiates between racist terms and nicknames. What is the difference between them? Can a term be both a racist term and a nickname? Can it move from being one to the other?
2. In the '50s and '60s, why did Chinatown parents encourage their children to assimilate?
3. Explain Choy's discovery of the "… truth [that] these 'between world' struggles are universal" (paragraph 15).

DISCOVERING RHETORICAL STRATEGIES

1. Choy centres his essay around the use of the term "banana." How does he extend this metaphor in his essay?
2. What is Choy's thesis? Where is it found?
3. Who is Choy's intended audience?

MAKING CONNECTIONS

1. Choy defines the term "banana" as an affectionate nickname which he groups with the metaphors "apple" and "Oreo cookie." Imagine Choy is having a conversation with Cecil Foster ("Why Blacks Get Mad") about the use of these terms. On what points would the two agree? Are there areas where they would disagree?
2. Choy's essay is one of self-definition. In what ways is "I'm a Banana and Proud of It" similar to Drew Hayden Taylor's "Pretty Like a White Boy"? What differences do you find in the strategies these two writers use to define themselves?
3. In "I'm a Banana and Proud of It," Wayson Choy talks about the importance of understanding the past. Steven Heighton ("Elegy in Stone") also recognizes value in understanding the past. Why is an understanding of our history important to our sense of belonging in the present? How does the larger context enrich our lives in the present?

IDEAS FOR DISCUSSION/WRITING

Preparing to Write

Wayson Choy talks in this essay about what the Chinatown parents wanted for their children. Write freely about parental aspirations or dreams for their children. What dreams did your parents have for you as you were growing up? Were these messages conveyed explicitly or implicitly? Did you share these aspirations? What hopes would you have for your children if you were a parent?

Choosing a Topic

1. Think of a nickname you have now or have had in the past, and write an essay in which you explain how this nickname defines you.
2. Wayson Choy, in writing *The Jade Peony* as an exploration of his roots, discovered the combination in every human being of "the Other" and the desire for the same security and happiness. Using your own personal history, write a narrative essay showing this combination of elements in a person or people you know.
3. In this essay, Wayson Choy introduces a food metaphor that defines many North Americans. Write an essay in which you use an animal metaphor to describe the various members of your family. Make sure you keep your metaphor consistent.

Michael Clugston

TWICE STRUCK

A Canadian journalist, Michael Clugston has had articles published in a variety of magazines, including *Equinox*, from which this essay was taken; *Reader's Digest*; the *Globe and Mail*'s *Destinations*; and *Canadian Geographic*, where he was an editor until 1996. After spending most of the last five years as a news editor in Japan, where he grew up, Clugston is now living in Aylmer, Quebec.

Preparing to Read

In *Equinox*, where "Twice Struck" originally appeared in 1991, Clugston's essay is accompanied by a picture of a spectacular bolt of lightning. Before you begin reading, think about lightning and thunderstorms. How do you feel about thunderstorms? Have you ever been frightened by a crack of thunder or a flash of lightning? What kind of emotions do thunder and lightning typically evoke in people? In animals? What associations do you have with thunder and lightning in movies you have seen or stories you have read? What gives Clugston's subject its lasting appeal and interest?

■——■

Tennyson called it a "flying game." Benjamin Franklin termed 1 it a "sudden and terrible mischief." In Roman mythology, the god Jupiter used spiky thunderbolts as letters to the editor when he chose to show displeasure with the poor mortals below.

By whatever name, lightning is a spectacular natural event. 2 Captured in photographs, its grandeur and beauty are safely petrified in static portraits of primal energy. In reality, at 24,000 to 28,000 degrees C, it is four times hotter than the surface of the sun. It can vaporize steel, plough up fields, shatter giant trees and scatter livid incendiary sparks over vast forests. Each day, it kills 20 people.

Its horror is the haphazard nature of its violence, a random 3 Russian-roulette threat beyond control. If you are caught out in the open during a thunderstorm, it can look like oncoming headlights of celestial chaos. Lightning can terrify you, charm you with its beauty, fry you, or, prosaically enough, bring on asthma, drowsiness and other discomforting side effects from the ionized air it creates.

Ask a scientist what lightning is, and he or she will most 4 likely remind you of the electric kiss you get indoors on a dry winter day when you walk across a carpet and then touch an electric switch or another person. That nasty little jolt is the micro version of the heaven-sent tracery that can look as delicate as needlepoint while travelling between 100,000 and 300,000 kilometres per second.

But the scientist will also tell you that there is still a 5 considerable mystery to lightning. "In some areas, we really don't know what's happening up there," says Andrew Podgorski, a senior research officer at the National Research Council of Canada in Ottawa and head of the Electromagnetic Interference/ Electromagnetic Compatibility Programme. "It's very difficult to predict where the lightning is being initiated and how the lightning channels are defined. Nor do we know how the lightning bolt itself can grow so quickly to the huge channel that we perceive."

What is known, though, is fascinating enough. If nature 6 abhors a vacuum, electricity abhors imbalance. Like water, which seeks its own level, electricity tries to even out the imbalance on charges between two neighbouring bodies by leaping the gap with a bright spark. However, when we see that spark in the form of lightning, what we see is not what we think we see.

The colossal structures we know as thunderheads are giant   7
electrical generators. They occur when weather conditions create rapid updrafts of warm, moist air that travel high in the atmosphere. Furious updrafts and downfalls of water and ice particles create regions of positive and negative charge. Lightning can travel between the opposite charges within the clouds or between the cloud and ground. The negative base of a thunderhead creates a positive charge in the ground immediately below and sets the scene for the gaudy short circuits overhead.

Majestic bolts such as those pictured here were probably   8
preceded by a weak electrical spark that descended from the negatively charged clouds to the positively charged earth. The weak spark is called the "stepped leader," named for its rootlike branchings. Near the earth, the spindly leader intersects with a shorter leader rising from the ground to meet it. This creates a conductive pathway of ionized air—a bridge of ions from heaven to earth. The stage is then set for the real business to begin.

A few millionths of a second later, a bright channel of light   9
and heat—a lightning bolt—leaps back up the bridge, but the human eye is not fast enough to distinguish the leader from the bolt. If lightning appears to be branched downward, it is because the upward-moving charge flows through all the ionized side routes established by the leader. It is the return stroke that causes most of the thunder we hear.

Last year, Podgorski conducted lightning experiments inside   10
the top of Toronto's CN Tower during a thunderstorm. "I thought about Ben Franklin while I was up there," he says. "But the tip is protected by metal, so I didn't even realize lightning was striking the tower while I was inside."

Franklin, the Philadelphian Renaissance man, flew his famous   11
kite in 1752 to prove that clouds were electrified, an experiment which led him to the invention of lightning rods. By 1782, the only building in Philadelphia that did not sport one of Franklin's rods was the French Embassy. One official died when it was struck by lightning that year.

Ever since Franklin's experiment and well into the 1800s,   12
lightning, and protection against it, has caught the public imagination. For a few years, people could be seen carrying

lightning-rod umbrellas, which lofted a sharp metal rod on top and trailed ground wires behind them.

While we may think of such a device as a silly momentary 13 fad, it was a big step forward in understanding from the Middle Ages in Europe. Then people believed that ringing church bells in thunderstorms kept the lightning from striking nearby buildings. In this way, the call of duty sent hundreds of bell ringers on sudden ascensions to heaven before the curious custom belatedly became unpopular. The words *fulgura frango* ("I break the lightning") can still be found on some medieval bells.

We still cannot "break" lightning, but we can study it. 14 Experiments have shown that lightning saturates the air with positive ions—atoms that have lost one or more electrons. The heat of lightning produces ions by searing electrons away from the atoms in its path. For some people, these can bring on a host of unpleasant effects. "Weather-sensitive people have reported insomnia, irritability, tension, chills, sweats, dizziness and loss of balance, migraines and other types of headaches, visual disturbances, nausea and vomiting," writes bacteriologist Julius Fast in his book of reactions.

But whatever the folklore or science of the day, our 15 perception of lightning remains rooted in the universal reactions of wonder and respect.

UNDERSTANDING DETAILS

1. In your own words, define lightning.
2. List the various effects that lightning can have.
3. Explain the words "fulgura frango" that can be found on some medieval church bells.

ANALYZING MEANING

1. In "Twice Struck," Clugston cites scientific knowledge about lightning as well as folklore on this subject. What is the relationship between these two realms of understanding our world?
2. Explain why Clugston says that wonder and respect are universal reactions to lightning.
3. In the Middle Ages people rang church bells to ward off lightning; in the 1800s they carried lightning rod umbrellas. What do people in the 1990s do to protect themselves against the "flying flames"? Are these practices based on science or folklore?

DISCOVERING RHETORICAL STRATEGIES

1. Is Clugston's definition objective or subjective? Explain your answer.
2. In his essay, Clugston cites Benjamin Franklin, Andrew Podgorski, Julius Fast, and Alfred Lord Tennyson. Who is each of these people and why is each mentioned in "Twice Struck"?
3. Reread paragraph 3 of "Twice Struck." Identify all the examples of figurative language that you can find in this paragraph. What effect do these uses of language have on you as a reader?

MAKING CONNECTIONS

1. Michael Clugston cites other people in his essay as do Judy Rebick ("The Culture of Overwork") and Malcolm Gladwell ("Is the Belgian Coca-Cola Hysteria the Real Thing?"). Explain why these authors have incorporated quotations from others into each of their essays.
2. In "Twice Struck" Clugston describes a particular natural phenomenon and our reactions to it. How do the responses to lightning that Clugston details compare to the reactions to other natural processes such as that described by Lesley Choyce ("Thin Edge of the Wedge")?
3. Michael Clugston says that wonder and respect are universal reactions to lightning. How do you think Tomson Highway ("What a Certain Visionary Once Said") would respond to this assertion? Explain your answer.

IDEAS FOR DISCUSSION/WRITING

Preparing to Write

Write freely about the weather. In what ways does the weather affect your life? How are our lives generally governed by weather? What is the most severe storm you have ever experienced? How did you react to it? Why do we consider weather predictions important? What need sustains whole television stations devoted to weather?

Choosing a Topic

1. While science has come a long way in explaining lightning, there are still some things we don't know. Traditionally, myths

and legends have been invented to explain events that we don't entirely understand. Write a myth to explain a particular weather phenomenon.

2. Write an essay in which you explain how the weather that you experience in your region of the country has contributed to defining you as a person.

3. Weather is often said to influence people's behaviour in fairly significant ways. This might be an ongoing condition like Seasonal Affective Disorder (SAD) or it might be a more specific behaviour related to a dramatic change in temperature or humidity or a phase of the moon. Write an essay in which you explore the connection between people's behaviour and the weather.

Neil Bissoondath

PIECES OF SKY

Neil Bissoondath (1955–) is the Trinidadian-born Canadian author of three novels and two collections of short stories. Known internationally for his fiction, Bissoondath has probably become best known in Canada for his contentious views on multiculturalism as put forth in his first non-fiction book, *Selling Illusions: The Cult of Multiculturalism in Canada.* "Pieces of Sky," which appeared in the *Globe and Mail*'s "National Values" column in May 1995, is drawn from *If You Love This Country: 15 Voices for a Unified Canada,* an anthology of essays by Canadians concerned about the possible outcome of the then-approaching October 1995 referendum and published by Penguin Books Canada Limited.

Preparing to Read

In this selection, Bissoondath discusses the values that he sees as uniquely Canadian and why values are important. Before reading Bissoondath's essay, think about Canadian values. What makes Canadians distinctive as a people? What distinguishes Canadians from Americans? From people of other nationalities? How is the Canadian culture a unique one? Which values are national and which are regional?

*W*e are what the geography of the country has made us ... That is   1
why we are, in a sense, nearer to English Canadians than to
Frenchmen. After a month in Paris, which I loved with all my heart, I just
the same got very lonesome for our trees, and the sight of the Laurentides
and the horizon of Quebec. I felt lonesome for the Canadian sky so vast and
so grandiose. In Paris, you have pieces of sky.

> —Rodger Lemelin, Quebec novelist,
> from a letter written in English, 1950.

It has become popular in recent years for many, in both public   2
and private life, to insist that there are no such things as Canadian
values and, by extension, a Canadian culture. This is a peculiar
notion in a country that has existed as a political entity for almost
130 years and as a historical one for even longer. It is a way of
saying that Canada and Canadians have no reality.

But the nation, fractious and uneasy as it frequently is, does   3
exist, and so do its values. They may not always be readily
identifiable, they may not always be easily defined, but their
effect can be sniffed in the very air that surrounds us. Canada
may physically resemble the United States in many ways, but
when I cross the border I know immediately that I am in a foreign
land. The psychic electricity is different, alien. It tells me that I am
no longer at home.

Principles, values and beliefs—words used by Pierre Elliott   4
Trudeau in a statement of affirmative values attached to the
Charter of Rights and Freedoms—are the playthings of moral
philosophers, the rallying cries of religious fundamentalists, the
linguistic torches of politicians seeking a tone of higher order.
They have also become concepts of battle plans in a Canada
profoundly shaped by the ideas of Mr. Trudeau.

They say there was a time when you could tell the Canadian   5
easily; he was the one who would stuff empty candy wrappers
and gnawed apple cores into his pockets until he came to a
garbage can. Then he'd stand there as if in holy communion,
muttering phrases that ended with "... eh?" and making offerings
at the altar of civic pride.

We have always defined our pride differently. But this   6
particular trait was set on the path to a slow death by the advent
some years ago of the word "biodegradable." Silently assuring
ourselves that nature would take care of it, Canadians began
acquiring new abilities; surreptitious flicks of the wrist and—

"Nice lookin' clouds up there, eh?"—eyes that wandered resolutely away from the flight paths of balled paper or empty cigarette packs. Today, the Canadian litters with the best of them. Specificity, it must be said, may be dwindling.

And yet, they say, the Canadian continues to reveal himself 7 most readily in other ways, with an overheated politeness. For instance: Tread accidentally on a Canadian's foot, and he falls all over himself apologizing to you. Many view this as a silly trait. I do not. In some parts of the world, you'd be lucky to get away with just a scowl. In others, you'd be lucky to get away with your life. The Canadian's urge to apologize for having got his shoe under yours strikes me as endearing and eminently civilized.

We cannot trust stereotype, of course. The best it can offer is 8 general direction. But this part is, I hope, true. For it suggests the principles, values and beliefs that define the character of a people. So just what, at this time in our history, are Canadians' values?

This is a question often posed by those who would deny 9 their existence. Instead, the very asking of the question tends to be an attempt to belittle the notion itself, as if the identification of a value as Canadian is somehow meant to deny it to others. But of course this is not so.

I suspect we glimpsed one such value in the thousands of 10 get-well messages Bloc Québécois Leader Lucien Bouchard received from Canadians outside Quebec during his life-threatening illness: To abhor the man's political dream is not necessarily to abhor the man. Values such as this—the recognition that the human being is worth more than political principle— lend texture to a society. Such an attitude is not exclusive to Canada, but I would suggest that its being shared by others does not make it less Canadian.

A blazing campfire late at night, beneath a sky luminous 11 with more stars than the mind could comfortably conjure: nature's way, you think, of dwarfing the human imagination, not into insignificance but into a proper perspective of its place in the larger world. Like the prairie sky, perhaps, or the reach of the Rockies, which have a way of dampening arrogance, of imposing a vital modesty.

Way up there, in a sky so large it defies the mind to go 12 beyond cliché, a single tiny light cuts a rapid course through the glittering darkness, the satellite's path somehow deepening the silence that is already as profound, as all-encompassing, as that of the world before time. You feel yourself alone despite the companionship of neighbouring campfires lit by people— anglophone, francophone—who offer little more than a smile, a nod, a wave: No more is required, no more expected. The communality of purpose is sufficient. The experience we are sharing goes beyond words or invitations or the usual requirements of social convention.

It was the writer Margaret Visser who pointed out to me that   13
camping—this safest of engagements with the natural world—can justly be viewed as a Canadian ritual. And ritual, let us remember, is the physical representation of values. To sit there, then, between campfire and tent, in the utter safety of a national park, is to feel the self part of a larger, miraculous whole. It is to immerse yourself, however fleetingly, in the power of a social value rarely seen as such: to understand the modesty for which Canadians are justly known.

It was Prime Minister John Diefenbaker who, in protest   14
against apartheid at the 1961 Commonwealth Conference, arranged the expulsion of South Africa from the organization. And it was Prime Minister Brian Mulroney, who many years later at another Commonwealth Conference, earned the enmity of British Prime Minister Margaret Thatcher by leading the battle for the imposition of severe trade sanctions against the government in Pretoria.

The battle against racism by Canadians may be imperfect—   15
here at home, for instance, discomfort can be found in attitudes toward blacks and Asians, and in conditions on numerous Native reserves—but it has been many decades since the principle of racial segregation has found any public favour in this country. Individuals continue to struggle with their own racism, trying to bridge the chasm between the heart—which has been taught racial distrust—and the mind, which has recognized the evil of it.

And yet ...   16

Even as apartheid slides steadily into the history books, even   17
as South Africa under the leadership of Nelson Mandela struggles to achieve a society free of racial segregation, we here in Canada are seeing it take root—in the name of equality. In Ontario, demands are made for the public funding of segregated schools. In British Columbia, a Chinese parents' association is set up. The Writers' Union of Canada funds a racially segregated conference, and governments across the country implement hiring policies based partly on race.

A queer thing is happening, then, to this value so long 18
cherished. It is not so much slipping away as metamorphosing
into an ugly version of itself, acquiring the justification that the
founders of apartheid once used for that abhorrent system: that,
somehow, separate could also mean equal.

The difference between innocence and naiveté is not always 19
clear, yet the former can be seen as a positive trait—as in the
innocence of children—while the second is reviled as being a
small step away from stupidity. Innocence implies having a
trusting nature, while naiveté implies simplemindedness.

And so I opt for the word "innocence" to describe what seems 20
to constitute an enduring and laudable Canadian quality. Indeed, so
ingrained is it that I would go so far as to call it a Canadian value.

Consider, for instance, the public outrage that met the 21
broadcast of videotapes from the Canadian Airborne Regiment.
What those tapes offered were the antics of brutes who happened
to be Canadian. To anyone who has seen Gwynne Dyer's superb
documentary series, *War*, the behaviour on our television screens
was distressing but hardly surprising.

We found it distressing because this is not how we see 22
ourselves. We believe in our own clean-cut, good-guy image.
And even if we know that the military does not aim to create
Boy Scouts, even if we know that the ultimate goal of military
training is to produce efficient killers, we still want them to reflect
our image of ourselves: We want our killers clean-cut, polite and
well-behaved.

It was suggested to me at the time that the outrage merely 23
revealed the profound naiveté of the Canadian public. On
reflection, I agreed, but suggested the word "innocence" instead.
I did not see this as condemnation. Instead, I thought it a
becoming innocence, heartening proof of how seriously we take
our notions of goodness. I saw it as a confirmation of idealism.

Five or six years ago, my companion and I were on vacation 24
in France. Wandering around Nice one morning, we spotted on
a deserted street two 500-franc notes (about $250 in all), one lying
on the sidewalk, the other under a parked car. With visions of
some frantic pensioner in our heads, we entered a nearby bank in
the hopes that a customer may have reported their loss.

We were met with utter incredulity. As we stood there, the 25
bills held uneasily in our hands, they asked where we were from,
and on being told, mumbled, "*Ahh, les gentils Canadiens ...*" in a
way that you knew stories would be told of the innocent

Canadians, that we would be objects of mirth. And yet, for once, condescension did not rankle. After all, in the larger scheme of things it was not a bad image to leave behind.

We took our leave, feeling a little silly, a little guilty—and, as   26
far as I was concerned, glad to be innocent Canadians in a world that saw naiveté in simple honesty.

Innocence, naiveté: Call it what you will. But to give up on it   27
is to surrender our essential idealism. We seem at times to be in danger of doing just that. The signs are there: in those, for instance, who would break Quebec away from Canada as well as in those who, through weariness or short-sightedness, would allow Quebec to break away; in a willingness to sacrifice the unfortunate of our society in the name of fiscal responsibility; and in marvelling at the multiplicity of languages on European cereal boxes while raging at the other official language printed on our own.

Principles, values and beliefs are big words easily tossed   28
around. Politicians and philosophers believe they give them weight, but they rarely ever do; they merely make evident the weight with which they have already been invested by the public. And it is our little actions that give them weight, lend them meaning; that give us as a people, anglophone and francophone, a specific personality that is not always easily perceived but that is there nonetheless, shaping us and being shaped by us in an act of mutual and ongoing creation.

Canada has always been an act of faith—and acts of faith   29
depend on idealism. To give up on our innocence is to give up on our idealism, is to give up on ourselves. It is to stigmatize our eyes, so that what we see is not the whole sky but just pieces of it.

UNDERSTANDING DETAILS

1. In the stereotype cited by Bissoondath, what traits would identify a Canadian in the past? Are these still characteristic be-
   haviours today?
2. Explain the difference between innocence and naiveté. Which
   does Bissoondath see as a Canadian quality?
3. What, at this time in our history, are Canadian values, according to Bissoondath? Do you agree with him? Are there other
   values that you would add to the list that are definitively
   Canadian?

ANALYZING MEANING

1. Bissoondath's view of employment equity and multicultural-ism programs has been the subject of much debate. How does he regard such programs? Why?
2. Explain the importance of principles, values, and beliefs in defining a nation.
3. Bissoondath says that the writer Margaret Visser pointed out to him that camping is a Canadian ritual. Why has camping become so important to Canadians? What values are reflected in this pastime?

DISCOVERING RHETORICAL STRATEGIES

1. Is Bissoondath's definition primarily an objective or a subjective one? Explain your conclusion.
2. Bissoondath refers to several politicians in the course of this essay. Why does he mention all of these people? How do these references help Bissoondath accomplish his purpose?
3. In this essay Bissoondath uses a variety of rhetorical modes to help him define distinctive Canadian values. Explain what other rhetorical modes Bissoondath has employed in "Pieces of Sky."

MAKING CONNECTIONS

1. Imagine a conversation among Allen Abel ("A Home at the End of the Journey"), Will Ferguson ("The Sudbury Syndrome"), and Neil Bissoondath about characteristic Canadian values. On which points would these three writers agree? On which would they disagree? With whom do you identify most closely on this subject?
2. Cecil Foster ("Why Blacks Get Mad") and Neil Bissoondath both write about racism in Canada. Compare and contrast their views on this topic.
3. Wayson Choy ("I'm a Banana and Proud of It") identifies himself as a "banana," the child of Chinese parents, who has assimilated well into North American life. How would Bissoondath react to this characterization and to this metaphor representing one who is "yellow on the outside and white inside"?

IDEAS FOR DISCUSSION/WRITING

Preparing to Write

Bissoondath says that rituals are the physical representation of values. What rituals are important in your life? How were those rituals established? How are they maintained? Who else partakes in the rituals of your life? What underlying values are represented by those rituals? List the five most important values in your life, or principles that guide you in your life. Where did those values come from? Have they changed over time?

Choosing a Topic

1. Write an essay for a newspaper or magazine outside Canada in which you define what a Canadian is. Make sure that you provide specific examples to make your definition clear to your readers.
2. Choose a group to which you belong and write a definition of that group, based on the common values, beliefs, or rituals that unite its members and distinguish them from other similar groups. The group might be your family; a sports club or team to which you belong; members of the congregation of your synagogue/church/temple/mosque, etc.; a group of volunteers for some cause, event, or organization; a gang; or a group of students with whom you particularly identify.
3. Canadians have an easier time travelling internationally than people with passports from many other countries. Write an essay explaining why travelling Canadians generally get a warm reception from most other countries.

CHAPTER 8

CAUSE/EFFECT

■ ■ ■

Tracing Reasons and Results

Wanting to know why things happen is one of our earliest, most basic instincts: Why can't I go out, Mommy? Why are you laughing? Why won't the dog stop barking? Why can't I swim faster than my big brother? These questions, and many more like them, reflect the innately inquisitive nature that dwells within each of us. Closely related to this desire to understand *why* is our interest in *what* will happen in the future as a result of some particular action: What will I feel like tomorrow if I stay up late tonight? How will I perform in the track meet Saturday if I practise all week? What will be the result if I mix together these two potent chemicals? What will happen if I turn in my next English assignment two days early?

A daily awareness of this intimate relationship between causes and effects allows us to begin to understand the complex and interrelated series of events that make up our lives and the lives of others. For example, trying to understand the various causes of the conflict in the Middle East teaches us about international relations; knowing our biological reactions to certain foods helps us make decisions about what to eat; understanding the interrelated reasons for the outbreak of World War II offers us insight into historical trends and human nature; knowing the effects of sunshine on various parts of our bodies helps us make decisions about how much ultraviolet exposure we can tolerate and what suntan lotion to use; and understanding the causes of Canada's most recent recession will help us respond appropriately to the next economic crisis we encounter. More than anything else, tracing causes and effects teaches us how to think clearly and react intelligently to our multifaceted environment.

In college or university, you will often be asked to use this natural interest in causes and effects to analyze particular situations and to discern general principles. For example, you might be asked some of the following questions on essay exams in different courses:

Anthropology: Why did the Mayan culture disintegrate?

Psychology: Why do humans respond to fear in different ways?

Biology: How do lab rats react to caffeine?

History: What were the positive effects of building the Trans-Canada Highway?

Business: Why did so many computer manufacturing companies go bankrupt in the early 1980s?

Your ability to answer such questions will depend in large part on your skill at writing a cause/effect essay.

Defining Cause/Effect

Cause/effect analysis requires the ability to look for connections between different elements and to analyze the reasons for those connections. As the name implies, this rhetorical mode has two separate components: cause and effect. A particular essay might concentrate on cause (Why do you live on campus?), on effect (What are the resulting advantages and disadvantages of living on campus?), or on some combination of the two. In working with causes, we are searching for any circumstances from the past that may have caused a single event; in looking for effects, we seek occurrences that took place after a particular event and resulted from that event. Like process analysis, cause/effect makes use of our intellectual ability to analyze. Process analysis addresses *how* something happens, whereas causal analysis discusses *why* it happened and *what* the result was. A process analysis paper, for example, might explain how to advertise more effectively to increase sales, whereas a cause/effect study would discover that three specific elements contributed to an increase in sales: effective advertising, personal service, and selective discounts. The study of causes and effects, therefore, provides many different and helpful ways for humans to make sense of and clarify their views of the world.

Looking for causes and effects requires an advanced form of thinking. It is more complex than most rhetorical strategies we have studied because it can exist on a number of different and progressively more difficult levels. The most accurate and effective causal analysis accrues from digging for the real or ultimate causes or effects, as opposed to those that are merely superficial or immediate. Actress Angela Lansbury would have been out of work on an episode of the television show *Murder, She Wrote*, for example, if her character had stopped her investigation at the immediate cause of death (slipping in the bathtub) rather than searching diligently for the real cause (an overdose of cocaine administered by an angry companion, which resulted in the slip in the tub). Similarly, voters would be easy to manipulate if they considered only the immediate effects of a tax increase (a slightly higher tax bill) rather than the ultimate benefits that would result (the many years of improved education that our children would receive because of the specialized programs created by such an increase). Only the discovery of the actual reasons for an event or an idea will lead to the logical and accurate analysis of causes and effects important to a basic understanding of various aspects of our lives.

Faulty reasoning assigns causes to a sequence of actions without adequate justification. One such logical fallacy is called *post hoc, ergo propter hoc* (after this, therefore because of this): The fact that someone lost a job after walking under a ladder does not mean that the two events are causally related; by the same token, if we get up every morning at 5:30 a.m., just before the sun rises, we cannot therefore conclude that the sun rises *because* we get up (no matter how self-centred we are!). Faulty reasoning also occurs when we oversimplify a particular situation. Most events are connected to a multitude of causes and effects. Sometimes one effect has many causes: A student may fail a history exam because she's been working two part-time jobs, she was sick, she didn't study hard enough, and she found the instructor very boring. One cause may also have many effects. If a house burns down, the people who lived in it will be out of a home. If we look at such a tragic scene more closely, however, we may also note that the fire traumatized a child who lived there, helped the family learn what good friends they had, encouraged the family to double their future fire insurance, and provided the happy stimulus that they needed to make a long-dreamed-of move to another city. One event has thus resulted in many interrelated effects. Building an argument on insecure foundations or oversimplifying the causes or effects connected with an event will seriously hinder the construction of a rational essay. No matter what the nature of the cause/effect analysis, it must always be based on clear observation, accurate facts, and rigorous logic.

In the following paragraph, a student writer analyzes some of the causes and effects connected with the controversial issue of euthanasia. Notice how he makes connections and then analyzes those connections as he consistently explores the immediate and ultimate effects of being able to stretch life beyond its normal limits through new medical technology:

> Along with the many recent startling advances in medical technology have come a number of complex moral, ethical, and spiritual questions that beg to be answered. We now have the ability to prolong the life of the human body for a very long time. But what rights do patients and their families have to curtail cruel and unusual medical treatment that stretches life beyond its normal limits? This dilemma has produced a ripple effect in society. Is the extension of life an unquestionable goal in itself, regardless of the quality of that life? Modern scientific technology has forced doctors to reevaluate the exact meaning and purpose of their profession. For example, many medical schools and undergraduate university programs now routinely offer classes on medical ethics—an esoteric and infrequently taught subject only a few years ago. Doctors and scholars alike are realizing that medical personnel alone cannot be expected to decide on the exact parameters of life. In like manner, the judicial process must now evaluate the legal complexities of mercy killings and the rights of patients to die with dignity and without unnecessary medical intervention. The insurance business, too, wrestles with the catastrophic effects of new technology on the costs of today's hospital care. In short, medical progress entails more than microscopes, chemicals, and high-tech instruments. If we are to develop as a thoughtful, just, and merciful society, we must consider not only the physical well-being of our nation's patients, but their emotional, spiritual, and financial status as well.

Thinking Critically by Using Cause/Effect

Thinking about causes and effects is one of the most advanced mental activities that we perform. It involves complex operations that we must think through carefully, making sure all connections are reasonable and accurate. Unlike other rhetorical patterns, cause/effect thinking requires us to see specific relationships between two or more items. To practise this strategy, we need to look for items or events that are causally related—that is, one that has caused the other. Then, we can focus on either the causes (the initial stimulus), the effects (the results), or a combination of the two.

Searching out causes and effects requires a great deal of digging that is not necessary for most of the other modes. Cause/effect necessitates the ultimate in investigative work. The mental exertion associated with this thinking strategy is sometimes exhausting, but it is always worth going through when you discover relationships that you never saw before or you uncover links in your reasoning that were previously unknown or obscure to you.

If you've ever had the secret desire to be a private eye or an investigator of any sort, practising cause/effect reasoning can be lots of fun. It forces you to see relationships among multiple items and then to make sense of those connections. Completing exercises in this skill will help you perfect the logistics of cause/effect thinking before you mix and match it with several other thinking strategies.

1. Choose a major problem you see in our society, and list what you think are the main causes of this problem on one side of a piece of paper and the effects on the other side. Compare the two lists to see how they differ. Then, compare and contrast your lists with those written by other students.

2. What "caused" you to become a student? What influences led you to this choice at this point in your life? How has being a student affected your life? List several overall effects.

3. List the effects of one of the following: getting a speeding ticket, winning an Olympic medal, graduating from college or university, or watching TV until the early hours of the morning.

Reading and Writing Cause/Effect Essays

Causal analysis is usually employed for one of three main purposes: (1) to prove a specific point (such as the necessity of stricter gun control), in which case the writer generally deals totally with facts and with conclusions drawn from those facts; (2) to argue against a widely accepted belief (for example, the assertion that cocaine is addictive), in which case the writer relies principally on facts, with perhaps some pertinent opinions; or

(3) to speculate on a theory (for instance, why the crime rate is higher in most major cities than it is in rural areas), in which case the writer probably presents hypotheses and opinions along with facts. This section will explore these purposes in cause/effect essays from the standpoint of both reading and writing.

How to Read a Cause/Effect Essay

Preparing to Read. As you set out to read the essays in this chapter, begin by focusing your attention on the title and the synopsis of the essay you are about to read and by scanning the essay itself: What do you think Stephen King is going to talk about in "Why We Crave Horror Movies"? What does the synopsis in the Rhetorical Table of Contents tell you about Laura Robinson's "Starving for the Gold"?

Also, at this stage in the reading process, you should try to learn as much as you can about the author of the essay and the reasons he or she wrote it. Ask yourself questions like the following: What is King's intention in "Why We Crave Horror Movies"? Who is Kim Pittaway's intended audience in "Dead Wrong"? And what is Trina McQueen's point of view in "Why We Crave Hot Stuff"?

Finally, before you begin to read, answer the prereading questions for each essay and then consider the proposed essay topic from a variety of perspectives: For example, concerning Pittaway's topic, have you ever attended a celebrity funeral or watched one on TV? Do you read tabloid news stories? Have you participated in competitive sports? Was it a positive or negative experience? What do you want to know about digital manipulation of photographs from Tony Leighton?

Reading. As you read each essay in this chapter for the first time, record your spontaneous reactions to it, drawing as often as possible on the preliminary material you already know: What do you think of horror movies (King)? Why did Pittaway choose the title she did? What is McQueen suggesting about "hot stuff" stories? Whenever you can, try to create a context for your reading: What is the tone of Robinson's discussion about young female athletes? How does this tone help her communicate with her audience? What do you think Robinson's purpose is in her essay on athletes and eating disorders? How clearly does she get this purpose across to you?

Also, during this reading, note the essay's thesis and check to see if the writer thoroughly explores all possibilities before settling on the primary causes and/or effects of a particular situation; in addition, determine whether the writer clearly states the assertions that naturally evolve from a discussion of the topic. Finally, read the questions following each essay to get a sense of the main issues and strategies in the selection.

Rereading. When you reread these essays, you should focus mainly on the writer's craft. Notice how the authors narrow and focus their material, how they make clear and logical connections between ideas in their essays, how they support their conclusions with concrete examples, how they use other rhetorical modes to accomplish their cause/effect analysis, and how they employ logical transitions to move us smoothly from one point to another. Most important, however, ask yourself if the writer actually discusses the real causes and/or effects of a particular circumstance: What does King say are the primary reasons people crave horror movies? What does McQueen consider the main cause of the appeal of "hot stuff" stories? How does the ability to manipulate photographs with ease change the way we view the world, according to Leighton? What are the primary causes and effects of eating disorders?

For a thorough outline of the reading process, consult the checklist on pages 15–16 of the Introduction.

How to Write a Cause/Effect Essay

Preparing to Write. Beginning a cause/effect essay requires—as does any other essay—exploring and limiting your subject, specifying a purpose, and identifying an audience. The Preparing to Write questions before the essay assignments, coupled with the prewriting techniques outlined in the Introduction, encourage you to consider specific issues related to your reading. The assignments themselves will then help you limit your topic and determine a particular purpose and audience for your message. For cause/effect essays, determining a purpose is even more important than usual, because your readers can get hopelessly lost unless your analysis is clearly focused.

Writing. For all its conceptual complexity, a cause/effect essay can be organized quite simply. The introduction generally presents the subject(s) and states the purpose of the analysis in a clear thesis. The body of the paper then explores all relevant causes and/or effects, typically progressing either from least to most influential or from most to least influential. Finally, the concluding section summarizes the various cause-and-effect relationships established in the body of the paper and clearly states the conclusions that can be drawn from those relationships.

The following additional guidelines should assist you in producing an effective cause/effect essay in all academic disciplines:

1. Narrow and focus your material as much as possible.
2. Consider all possibilities before assigning real or ultimate causes or effects.
3. Show connections between ideas by using transitions and key words—such as *because, reasons, results, effects,* and *consequences*—to guide your readers smoothly through your essay.
4. Support all inferences with concrete evidence.
5. Be as objective as possible in your analysis so that you don't distort logic with personal biases.
6. Understand your audience's opinions and convictions, so that you know what to emphasize in your essay.
7. Qualify your assertions to avoid overstatement and oversimplification.

These suggestions apply to both cause/effect essay assignments and exam questions.

Rewriting. As you revise your cause/effect essays, ask yourself the following important questions:

1. Is your thesis stated clearly at the outset of your paper?
2. Does it include your subject and your purpose?
3. Do you accomplish your purpose as effectively as possible for your particular audience?
4. Do you use logical reasoning throughout the essay?
5. Do you carefully explore all relevant causes and/or effects, searching for the real (as opposed to the immediate) reasons in each case?
6. Do you state clearly the conclusions that can be drawn from your paper?

More specific guidelines for writing and revising your essays appear on pages 26–27 of the Introduction.

Student Essay: Cause/Effect at Work

In the following essay, the student writer analyzes the effects of contemporary TV soap operas on young people: Notice that she states her subject and purpose at the beginning of the essay and then presents a combination of facts and opinions in her exploration of the topic. Notice also that, in her analysis, the writer is careful to draw clear connections between her perceptions of the issue and various objective details in an attempt to trace the effects of this medium in our society today. At the end of her essay, look at her summary of the logical relationships she establishes in the body of the essay and her statements about the conclusions she draws from these relationships.

Distortions of Reality

Background Television's contributions to society, positive and negative, have been debated continually since this piece of technology invaded the average Canadian household in the 1950s. Television has brought an unlimited influx of new information, ideas, and cultures into our homes. However, based on my observations of my thirteen-year-old cousin, Katie, and her friends, I think we need to take a closer look at the effects of soap operas on adolescents today. The distortions of reality portrayed on these programs are frighten- Thesis ingly misleading and, in my opinion, can be very confusing to statement young people.

Transition   During the early 1990s, the lifestyle of the typical soap opera "family" has been radically transformed from comfortable pretentiousness to blatant and unrealistic decadence. The characters neither live nor dress like the majority of their viewers, who are generally middle-class Canadians. These television families live First in large, majestic homes that are flawlessly decorated. The actors distortion of reality Concrete are often adorned in beautiful designer clothing, fur coats, and examples expensive jewellery, and this opulent lifestyle is sustained by people with no visible means of income. Very few of the characters seem to "work" for a living. When they do, upward mobility—without the benefit of the proper education or suitable training—and a well-planned marriage come quickly.

Transition   From this constant barrage of conspicuous consumption, my cousin and her friends seem to have a distorted view of everyday First effect economic realities. I see Katie and her group becoming obsessed with the appearance of their clothes and possessions. I frequently

Concrete examples

hear them berate their parents' jobs and modest homes. With noticeable arrogance, these young adolescents seem to view their parents' lives as "failures" when compared to the effortless, luxurious lifestyles portrayed in the soaps.

Transition

One of the most alluring features of this genre is its masterful use of deception. Conflicts between characters in soap operas are based on secrecy and misinformation. Failure to tell the truth and to per-

Concrete examples

form honourable deeds further complicates the entangled lives and love affairs of the participants. But when the truth finally comes out and all mistakes and misdeeds become public, the culprits and offenders hardly ever suffer for their actions. In fact, they appear to leave the scene of the crime guilt-free.

Second distortion of reality

Transition

Regrettably, Katie and her friends consistently express alarming

Concrete examples

indifference to this lack of moral integrity. In their daily viewing, they shrug off underhanded scenes of scheming and conniving, and they marvel at how the characters manipulate each other into positions of powerlessness or grapple in distasteful love scenes. I can only conclude that continued exposure to this amoral behaviour is eroding the fundamental values of truth and fidelity in these kids.

Second effect

Transition

Also in the soaps, the powers-that-be conveniently disregard any sense of responsibility for wrongdoing. Characters serve jail

Concrete examples

terms quickly and in relative comfort. Drug or alcohol abuse does not mar anyone's physical appearance or behaviour, and poverty is virtually nonexistent. Usually, the wrongdoer's position, wealth, and prestige are quickly restored—with little pain and suffering.

Third distortion of reality

Adolescents are clearly learning that people can act without regard for the harmful effects of their actions on themselves and others when they see this type of behaviour go unpunished. Again, I notice the result of this delusion in my cousin. Recently, when a businessman in our community was convicted of embezzling large sums of money from his clients, Katie was outraged because he

Third effect

Concrete examples

was sentenced to five years in prison, unlike her daytime TV "heartthrob," who had been given a suspended sentence for a similar crime. With righteous indignation, Katie claimed that the victims, many of whom had lost their entire savings, should have realized that any business investment involves risk and the threat of loss. Logic and common sense evaded Katie's reasoning as she insisted on comparing television justice with real-life scruples.

The writers and producers of soap operas argue that the shows are designed to entertain viewers and are not meant to be reflections of reality. Theoretically, this may be true, but I can actually see how these soap operas are affecting my cousin and her crowd. Although my personal observations are limited, I cannot believe they are unique or unusual. <u>Too many young people think that they can amass wealth and material possessions without an edu-</u> Ultimate effect <u>cation, hard work, or careful financial planning; that material goods are the sole measure of a person's success in life; and that honesty and integrity are not necessarily admirable qualities.</u>

Proposed solution   <u>Soap operas should demonstrate a realistic lifestyle and a re-</u><u>sponsible sense of behaviour.</u> The many hours adolescents spend in front of the television can obviously influence their view of the world. As a society, we cannot afford the consequences resulting from the distortions of reality portrayed every day in these shows.

Some Final Thoughts on Cause/Effect

The essays in this chapter deal with both causes and effects in a variety of ways. As you read each essay, try to discover its primary purpose and the ultimate causes and/or effects of the issue under discussion. Note also the clear causal relationships that each author sets forth on solid foundations supported by logical reasoning. Although the subjects of these essays vary dramatically, each essay exhibits the basic elements of effective causal analysis.

Cause/Effect in Review

Reading Cause/Effect Essays

Preparing to Read

1. What assumptions can you make from the essay's title?
2. Can you guess what the general mood of the essay is?
3. What is the essay's purpose and audience?
4. What does the synopsis in the Rhetorical Table of Contents tell you about the essay?
5. What can you learn from the author's biography?
6. Can you guess what the author's point of view toward the subject is?
7. What are your responses to the Preparing to Read questions?

Reading

1. What is the author's thesis?
2. What are the primary causes and/or effects in the essay?
3. Did you preview the questions that follow the essay?

Rereading

1. How does the writer narrow and focus the essay?
2. Does the writer make clear and logical connections between the ideas in the essay?
3. What concrete examples support the author's conclusions?
4. Does the writer discuss the real causes and effects?
5. What are your responses to the questions after the essay?

Writing Cause/Effect Essays

Preparing to Write

1. What are your responses to the Preparing to Write questions?
2. What is your purpose?
3. Who is your audience?

Writing

1. Do you narrow and focus your material as much as possible?
2. Do you consider all possibilities before assigning real or ultimate causes or effects?
3. Do you show connections between ideas by using transitions and key words?
4. Do you support all inferences with concrete evidence?
5. Are you as objective as possible in your analysis so that you don't distort logic with personal biases?
6. Do you understand your audience's opinions and convictions, so that you know what to emphasize in your essay?
7. Do you qualify your assertions to avoid overstatement and oversimplification?

Rewriting

1. Is your thesis stated clearly at the outset of your paper?
2. Does it include your subject and your purpose?

3. Do you accomplish your purpose as effectively as possible for your particular audience?

4. Do you use logical reasoning throughout the essay?

5. Do you carefully explore all relevant causes and/or effects, searching for the real (as opposed to the immediate) reasons in each case?

6. Do you state clearly the conclusions that can be drawn from your paper?

Stephen King

WHY WE CRAVE HORROR MOVIES

"People's appetites for terror seem insatiable," Stephen King once remarked, an insight which may help justify his phenomenal success as a writer of horror fiction since the mid-1970s. After early jobs as a janitor, a laundry worker, and a high school English teacher in Portland, Maine, King turned to writing full time following the spectacular sales of his first novel, *Carrie* (1974), which focuses on a shy, socially ostracized young girl who takes revenge on her cruel classmates through newly developed telekinetic powers. King's subsequent books have included *The Shining* (1976), *Firestarter* (1980), *Cujo* (1981), *Pet Sematary* (1983), *Misery* (1987), *The Stand* (1990), *The Waste Lands* (1992), *Dolores Claiborne* (1993), *Rose Madder* (1995), *Desperation* (1996), *Bag of Bones* (1998), and *Dreamcatcher* (2001). Asked to explain why readers and moviegoers are so attracted to his tales of horror, King told a *Chicago Tribune* interviewer that most people's lives "are full of fears—that their marriage isn't working, that they aren't going to make it on the job, that society is crumbling all around them. But we're really not supposed to talk about things like that, and so they don't have any outlets for all those scary feelings. But the horror writer can give them a place to put their fears, and it's ok to be afraid then, because nothing is real, and you can blow it all away when it's over." A cheerful though somewhat superstitious person, King, who now lives in Bangor, Maine, admits to doing most of his best writing during the morning hours. "You think I want to write this stuff at night?" he once asked a reviewer.

Preparing to Read

As you prepare to read this article, consider your thoughts on Canada's emotional condition: How emotionally healthy are Canadians? Were they more emotionally healthy twenty years ago? A century ago? What makes a society emotionally healthy? Emotionally unhealthy? How can a society maintain good health? What is the relationship between emotional health and a civilized society?

■_____■

I think that we're all mentally ill; those of us outside the asylums   1
only hide it a little better—and maybe not all that much better, after all. We've all known people who talk to themselves, people who sometimes squinch their faces into horrible grimaces when they believe no one is watching, people who have some hysterical fear—of snakes, the dark, the tight place, the long drop … and, of course, those final worms and grubs that are waiting so patiently underground.

When we pay our four or five bucks and seat ourselves at   2
tenth-row center in a theater showing a horror movie, we are daring the nightmare.

Why? Some of the reasons are simple and obvious. To show   3
that we can, that we are not afraid, that we can ride this roller coaster. Which is not to say that a really good horror movie may not surprise a scream out of us at some point, the way we may scream when the roller coaster twists through a complete 360 or plows through a lake at the bottom of the drop. And horror movies, like roller coasters, have always been the special province of the young; by the time one turns 40 or 50, one's appetite for double twists or 360-degree loops may be considerably depleted.

We also go to reestablish our feelings of essential normality;   4
the horror movie is innately conservative, even reactionary. Freda Jackson as the horrible melting woman in *Die, Monster, Die!* confirms for us that no matter how far we may be removed from the beauty of a Robert Redford or a Diana Ross, we are still light-years from true ugliness.

And we go to have fun.   5

Ah, but this is where the ground starts to slope away, isn't it?   6
Because this is a very peculiar sort of fun, indeed. The fun comes from seeing others menaced—sometimes killed. One critic has suggested that if pro football has become the voyeur's version of combat, then the horror film has become the modern version of the public lynching.

It is true that the mythic, "fairy-tale" horror film intends to take away the shades of gray .... It urges us to put away our more civilized and adult penchant for analysis and to become children again, seeing things in pure blacks and whites. It may be that horror movies provide psychic relief on this level because this invitation to lapse into simplicity, irrationality, and even outright madness is extended so rarely. We are told we may allow our emotions a free rein ... or no rein at all.

If we are all insane, then sanity becomes a matter of degree. If your insanity leads you to carve up women, like Jack the Ripper or the Cleveland Torso Murderer, we clap you away in the funny farm (but neither of those two amateur-night surgeons was ever caught, heh-heh-heh); if, on the other hand, your insanity leads you only to talk to yourself when you're under stress or to pick your nose on your morning bus, then you are left alone to go about your business ... though it is doubtful that you will ever be invited to the best parties.

The potential lyncher is in almost all of us (excluding saints, past and present; but then, most saints have been crazy in their own ways), and every now and then, he has to be let loose to scream and roll around in the grass. Our emotions and our fears form their own body, and we recognize that it demands its own exercise to maintain proper muscle tone. Certain of these emotional muscles are accepted—even exalted—in civilized society; they are, of course, the emotions that tend to maintain the status quo of civilization itself. Love, friendship, loyalty, kindness—these are all the emotions that we applaud, emotions that have been immortalized in the couplets of Hallmark cards and in the verses (I don't dare call it poetry) of Leonard Nimoy.

When we exhibit these emotions, society showers us with positive reinforcement; we learn this even before we get out of diapers. When, as children, we hug our rotten little puke of a sister and give her a kiss, all the aunts and uncles smile and twit and cry, "Isn't he the sweetest little thing?" Such coveted treats as chocolate-covered graham crackers often follow. But if we deliberately slam the rotten little puke of a sister's fingers in the door, sanctions follow—angry remonstrance from parents, aunts and uncles; instead of a chocolate-covered graham cracker, a spanking.

But anticivilization emotions don't go away, and they demand periodic exercise. We have such "sick" jokes as, "What's the difference between a truckload of bowling balls and a truckload of dead babies?" (You can't unload a truckload of bowling balls with a pitchfork ... a joke, by the way, that I heard originally from a ten-year-old.) Such a joke may surprise a laugh or a grin out of us even as we recoil, a possibility that confirms the thesis: If we share a brotherhood of man, then we also share an insanity of man. None of which is intended as a defense of either the sick joke or insanity but merely as an explanation of why the best horror films, like the best fairy tales, manage to be reactionary, anarchistic, and revolutionary all at the same time.

The mythic horror movie, like the sick joke, has a dirty job to   12
do. It deliberately appeals to all that is worst in us. It is morbidity unchained, our most base instincts let free, our nastiest fantasies realized ... and it all happens, fittingly enough, in the dark. For those reasons, good liberals often shy away from horror films. For myself, I like to see the most aggressive of them—*Dawn of the Dead*, for instance—as lifting a trap door in the civilized forebrain and throwing a basket of raw meat to the hungry alligators swimming around in that subterranean river beneath.

Why bother? Because it keeps them from getting out, man. It   13
keeps them down there and me up here. It was Lennon and McCartney who said that all you need is love, and I would agree with that.

As long as you keep the gators fed.   14

UNDERSTANDING DETAILS

1. Why, in King's opinion, do civilized people enjoy horror movies?
2. According to King, in what ways are horror movies like roller coasters?
3. According to King, how are horror films like public lynchings?
4. What is the difference between "emotions that tend to maintain the status quo of civilization" (paragraph 9) and "anticivilization emotions" (paragraph 11)?

ANALYZING MEANING

1. How can horror movies "reestablish our feelings of essential normality" (paragraph 4)?
2. What is "reactionary, anarchistic, and revolutionary" (paragraph 11) about fairy tales? About horror films?
3. Why does the author think we need to exercise our anticivilization emotions? What are some other ways we might confront these emotions?

4. Explain the last line of King's essay: "As long as you keep the gators fed" (paragraph 14).

DISCOVERING RHETORICAL STRATEGIES

1. What is the cause/effect relationship King notes in society between horror movies and sanity?
2. Why does King begin his essay with such a dramatic statement as "I think that we're all mentally ill" (paragraph 1)?
3. Who do you think is the author's intended audience for this essay? Describe them in detail. How did you come to this conclusion?
4. What different rhetorical strategies does King use to support his cause/effect analysis? Give examples of each.

MAKING CONNECTIONS

1. Apply Stephen King's definition of the appeal of horror to such experiences as attending a celebrity funeral (Pittaway). In what way does participating in the ritual of death compare to watching a horror movie? What are the principal differences between watching a horror movie and living through a real-life celebrity death?
2. The effect of a horror movie can be contagious, like the hysterical behaviour described by Malcolm Gladwell ("Is the Belgian Coca-Cola Hysteria the Real Thing?"). In what way might a horror movie trigger mass hysteria?
3. Compare King's comments about "fear" with similar insights into fear by other authors such as Laura Robinson ("Starving for the Gold"), Lynn Coady ("Genius or Madness?"), and Ray Guy ("When Jannies Visited"). How would each of these writers define the term differently? With which author's definition would you most likely agree? Explain your answer.

IDEAS FOR DISCUSSION/WRITING

Preparing to Write

Write freely about how most people maintain a healthy emotional attitude: How would you define emotional well-being? When are people most emotionally healthy? Most emotionally unhealthy? What do your friends and relatives do to maintain a healthy emotional life? What do you do to maintain emotional health? What is the connection between our individual emotional health and the extent to which our society is civilized?

Choosing a Topic

1. Think of a release other than horror films for our most violent emotions. Is it an acceptable release? Write an essay for the general public explaining the relationship between this particular release and our "civilized" society.
2. If you accept King's analysis of horror movies, what role in society do you think other types of movies play (e.g., love stories, science fiction, and comedies)? Choose one type, and explain its role to your composition class.
3. Your psychology instructor has asked you to explain your opinions on the degree of sanity or insanity in Canada at present. In what ways are we sane? In what ways are we insane? Write an essay for your psychology instructor explaining in detail your observations along these lines.

Trina McQueen

WHY WE CRAVE HOT STUFF

Trina McQueen is now the Executive Vice President of the CTV Network after working at the CBC for 25 years in positions ranging from on-air reporter and program host to director of news and current affairs, and then serving as the President of the Discovery Channel. McQueen also serves as the chair of the Action Group on Violence in Television and sits on the boards of the Banff Television Foundation, the World Wildlife Fund, and the Canadian Journalism Foundation. In 1999 McQueen was recognized for her contribution to Canadian broadcasting with the A.D. Dunton Alumni Award from her alma mater, Carleton University. The essay that appears here was published in the *Globe and Mail* and is an adaptation of a piece that appears in a collection of essays entitled *Journalism in the New Millennium*, published to commemorate the opening of the University of British Columbia's Sing Tao School of Journalism. According to McQueen, "The ability to write well, to rivet people's attention, is absolutely the most essential skill anyone can have ..."

Preparing to Read

In this essay, Trina McQueen considers the role of journalism in our lives
and presents an argument for the appeal of "tabloid" news stories. Before
you begin reading, consider the appeal of stories about people such as
Bill Clinton, O.J. Simpson, Princess Diana, Pamela Anderson, and Gillian
Guess. Why are we fascinated by the lives of people who are "beset with
extremely interesting personal demons"? What kinds of items in the news
catch your attention? What kinds of items do you ignore?

■_____■

Journalism about ethics reminds me of those "thin book" jokes. 1
There isn't much of it. Even when an event seems to have a
moral centre, journalists will report around, over, under and
through the moral issue.

One case in point: the controversy over providing financial 2
aid to people who had contracted hepatitis C from tainted blood.
The controversy was hugely reported. The facts of the matter
were well documented. There was extensive background analysis
of surrounding issues. What got very little ink and air time were
the principles that a society might use in deciding whether
compensation was justified. Much was made of the tears
streaming down the face of a dissident Liberal who voted with
the government. But how had she come to her original decision
that compensation was a moral duty? And how had she balanced
those principles against the principles used in deciding her
political duty? In mainstream journalism, the moral issues were
mostly edited out or weren't even there to be edited.

But before we consider what's left out, let's consider what 3
is lately there: Princess Diana, Bill Clinton, Margaret Trudeau,
O.J. Simpson, Mr. and Mrs. Matthew Barrett, Pamela Anderson.
Beautiful, rich and sensational, their characters are redolent of
power and sexuality, and all are beset by extremely interesting
personal demons.

Many academics and journalists wonder why there is so 4
much in newspapers, magazines and television about these folks
and so little about Chiapas and hydroelectric restructuring. They
argue about it at conferences; they write books and columns and
theses. It's called the "tabloidization of news." Some of this
tabloidization is wild rumour and some of it is outright lies. It is
acknowledged that this is deplorable. It is also agreed that some
tabloid journalism is true but there is too much of it.

Today, tabloid journalism may have reached terminal 5
velocity. The next U.S. president, for example, cannot reasonably
be expected to provide the wealth of embarrassingly riveting
intimate material that the current one does. Yet we can predict
that attempts will be made and that the coverage of them will
be exuberant.

What distresses some media thinkers about tabloid news is 6
that it fits uncomfortably into the usually accepted noble purposes
of news. The word "noble" is not being used sarcastically here.
The practice of journalism has, in most democracies, special
protections and rights because it is one of the people's defences
against tyranny and injustice. Tabloid stories—let's call them
hot-stuff stories—are not likely to inspire the people to rise
against their oppressors.

So hot stuff is not part of the core competencies of journalism: 7
politics and business. It has no advice for us on our democratic
responsibilities and duties. It may tell us something of the
character of powerful people, but it is silent on the systems and
processes that rule us. It deep-backgrounds not nor does it spin.

Nor is hot stuff related to another accepted use of journalism: 8
to determine whether we are safe. Stories about war, crime,
disasters and the environment are all said to answer these
important questions. Is my family safe? Is my community safe?
Is my world safe? But few of us can learn much that we did not
know about safety from Diana's death. We had already decided
whether to do up our seat belts and ask our chauffeurs to slow
down in Paris tunnels.

Hot stuff is not "news you can use," as are stories about 9
health, consumerism, hobbies and education. And I would argue
that hot stuff is not truly human interest, as are features about
feisty centenarians and champion pumpkin carvers. The
characters in hot stuff are truly characters; the demonic killers, the
fabulous babes, the hot commander-in-chief and the angelic
princess. They are dramatis personae.

Hot stuff certainly fills one of the chief purposes of 10
journalism, which is to sell copies and increase ratings. The
Columbia Journalism Review, in an issue devoted to what it calls
"money lust," opines that "more so than at any other moment
in journalism's history, the news product that lands on
newsstands, doorsteps and television screens is hurt by a
heightened, unseemly lust at many companies for ever greater
profits." The periodical warns that today's "diminished and

deracinated journalism ... could lead to a fatal erosion of the ancient bond between journalists and the public."

Certainly if profits are the question, hot stuff is one terrific 11 answer. In the past five years, hot stuff has produced all the ecstatic revenue moments of the news business. From the first shot of the white Bronco on the freeway, O.J. drove CNN ratings, revenue and stock prices. *Time* and *Newsweek* covers on Diana—two each in a row—produced the biggest newsstand sales in the magazines' histories. CBC Newsworld drew huge audiences even at midnight the night Diana died. The numbers for her funeral service were as much as 60 times higher than normal.

The Diana phenomenon was the breathtaking culmination 12 of a change in news choices that had begun years before. The *Times* of London probably shows that change most dramatically. *The Economist* has noted that in a newspaper historically celebrated for its international news (Stanley finds Livingstone, the Charge of the Light Brigade), the *Times'* front page recently had only one foreign piece: it was about Leonardo DiCaprio's new girlfriend.

Rupert Murdoch—he of Fox TV and sensational tabloids— 13 had a heretical vision. Like many other heretical visions, it has become commonplace. The Project for Excellence in Journalism analyzed stories on television, newsmagazines and front pages and concluded that stories of celebrity, gossip and scandal took up 43 per cent of the total space—three times more than 20 years ago. It all seems to have worked out nicely. Profits at most newspaper chains are showing healthy gains, and television news departments have become profit centres.

None of these choices and changes would have been made if 14 the public had not responded. Hot stuff sells. Right now I'm reading every word of *The Globe and Mail*'s comprehensive and straight-faced coverage of the trial of a dominatrix in Richmond Hill, Ont.

There are many theories about why scandal and gossip are so 15 popular.

Margaret Thatcher said "there is no such thing as society: 16 only individuals and their families." In her time, politicians, associations and even nation states began to be seen as ineffective and even irrelevant (incorrectly seen so, in my view). Philosopher Mark Kingwell in his book *Better Living* says this is an age in which "the individual is granted an unprecedented moral, political and epistemological influence." So it is hardly surprising that the intensely personal becomes an important subject of journalism.

A simpler theory is that ordinary people are rather stupid,   17
moving their lips as they read the latest about Brad Pitt. Although
there is a definite bozo factor in the population, it is my
experience that most people want to expand their experience.
Working at the Discovery Channel, where a hot-stuff story is the
uncovering of a new dinosaur skeleton, I'm constantly humbled
by the knowledge and the intelligence of our public. But
Discovery Channel's ratings hit their lowest the week of Aug.
31, 1997. Our viewers had the same fascination for the Diana
story as everyone else.

And it was a Story. That is the attraction of hot stuff. Most of it   18
has the pure and elemental force of story. There is a narrative; there
are characters. Storytelling is simply the most powerful form of
human communication. We are wired to absorb and comprehend
the world through constructing, telling and hearing stories.

But journalism is more than storytelling. It is about witnessing   19
faithfully and intelligently, it is about recording carefully, it is
about hard questioning and intense listening, and it is about
skepticism and empathy. But when all of that is done, there is
still a story to tell. And in most traditional journalism, from daily
news to documentaries, this is the element most forgotten.

There are dangers to journalistic storytelling: Sometimes the   20
facts won't fit a neat narrative; bits have to be crammed in or
left out. But the story rules, and unless journalists are willing to
study the craft of storytelling so they can apply it to subjects that
are difficult and foreign but relevant, they will fight a losing
battle against the natural story. And why should the Devil have
all the good tunes?

It is important to consider also that hot-stuff journalism   21
brings the storyteller and audience directly together. Political,
business or labour reporters all want and need the respect of
those about whom they write. The result is often a kind of insider
writing that puts the onus on the viewer or reader to fight his
or her way into the inner sanctum where the reporter and subject
live. In much of hot-stuff reporting, that's not so. No journalist
really cared what Monica Lewinsky or Louise Woodward thought
about their press. The reporters were free to think only about
the viewers and their needs.

Hot stuff, however, has another appeal: the moral questions   22
it raises. When I was a young journalist, idealistic, arrogant and
hopeful, I thought my profession might change the world—

expose injustice, inspire citizenship, provoke thought, preserve democracy, increase decency.

I have read a survey of people who described the uses they   23 made of journalism. They found news to be very important in their lives, but they did not say they used it to help them fulfill the duties of citizenship or to decide their economic courses of action or to galvanize themselves into political action. They used the news as something to talk about. How trivial, I thought, raging. They see the world as small talk.

I now think that using the news as something to talk about is   24 terribly important. I think it may even be the way of linking information to personal decisions, what U.S. cultural critic Neil Postman might call adding wisdom to data.

And I suspect that one of the appeals of hot-stuff journalism   25 is that it gives people a simple and effective opportunity to explore and discuss morals and ethics, to test their own standards and principles, to answer Socrates' question, "What is the life that is worth living?"

We make many more ethical decisions than we do political   26 ones. We will be called on to vote perhaps once a year. But every day we face moral decisions, big and small: Should I give money to a squeegee kid? Should I walk back four blocks to return the extra $10 the cashier gave me? Is that man lying on the street drunk or sick? And there are horrific dilemmas: My unborn child is deformed; my dying father begs me to help him go sooner. Or how do we deal with a nasty neighbour, a daughter-in-law of a different religion, a drug-addicted friend? What does it mean to be a good parent, spouse, child or employee? Perhaps when we gather in the lunchroom to discuss O.J. or Paul Bernardo or Paula Jones or Alan Eagleson or Diana, we are really discussing our moral options and ourselves.

There is a paradox here: People clearly seek out and desire   27 information about morality; and they are just as clearly rejecting more of the traditional sources of that information.

But mainstream journalism is curiously absent from this   28 arena. It offers "news you can use" on almost every subject: RRSPs, removing stains, starting a neighbourhood action group, writing a résumé, taking vitamins. It educates us endlessly on politics, personal finance and health. But on ethics and spirituality, the great presses and the great networks can offer only whispers. There are a few religion columns and essays.

Business ethics receive some attention, and journalistic ethics are covered. CBC Newsworld, in fact, will begin airing a new program titled *The Moral Divide* in the new year. It is probably the first of its kind. Perhaps it is the first of a trend.

It makes me squeamish to try to "sell" journalism about ethics, 29 but I think it is possible to find utility as well as virtue in the subject.

The more we consider the importance—the value and the 30 wonderful stories of moral and ethical decisions—the more curious the lack of their presence in journalism is. The Greeks had a word for those unacquainted with ethics: *idiot*.

UNDERSTANDING DETAILS

1. Explain the term "tabloidization of news" (paragraph 4).
2. What are the noble purposes of journalism identified by McQueen? What element does she say is forgotten (paragraph 19)? How has her view of the profession of journalism shifted over time?
3. In McQueen's opinion, what is the attraction of "hot stuff" stories?

ANALYZING MEANING

1. McQueen repeatedly uses the example of Princess Diana in her essay. Why is this example particularly significant?
2. Describe McQueen's attitude toward journalistic storytelling. Do you agree with her position?
3. To what extent do you think news stories shape behaviour and public opinion on socially relevant issues? According to McQueen, why is journalism about ethics so rare (paragraph 28)?

DISCOVERING RHETORICAL STRATEGIES

1. In this essay McQueen uses many examples to illustrate the points she is making. Why has she employed so many examples in her essay? Which examples are the most effective?
2. Characterize the tone McQueen uses in this essay. Why has she made this choice? How is the tone appropriate for the subject matter and the audience she is addressing?
3. Explain McQueen's conclusion to this essay. What comment is she making about the importance of ethics in our lives?

MAKING CONNECTIONS

1. McQueen's title has obvious similarities to the title of Stephen King's essay ("Why We Crave Horror Movies"). What do the topics they have chosen to write about have in common?

2. McQueen attributes some of the attraction of "hot stuff" to the appeal of story. How would Michael McKinley ("Opera Night in Canada") respond to McQueen's position? What about Evan Solomon ("The Babar Factor")?

3. Imagine a conversation between Trina McQueen and David Foot ("Boomers Dance to a New Beat"). How do you think Foot would account for the appeal and the growing prevalence of "hot stuff" stories? On what points do you think McQueen and Foot would agree? Where might they disagree? Whose view is closer to your own?

IDEAS FOR DISCUSSION/WRITING

Preparing to Write

Write freely about a major news topic that has captured your attention over the last year. How much detail do you have about this topic? What about it attracted your attention? What retained your interest? What made it a "news-worthy" event? Did your friends or family members share your interest in this story? Why or why not?

Choosing a Topic

1. Editors and producers of news stories constantly have decisions to make about what kinds of stories to pursue and report on as well as what angle should be taken on a story. Write an essay for your school newspaper in which you discuss the role you believe that journalism should play in our society.

2. McQueen suggests that using the news as something to talk about may be a way of exploring personal morals and ethics. Choose a well-known news story such as that of Monica Lewinsky, Alan Eagleson, or Gary Condit and Chandra Levy, and write an essay in which you discuss how you support the behaviour of one of the participants in the story, or argue that he or she should have behaved differently.

3. One of the questions McQueen poses in her essay is "What does it mean to be a good parent, spouse, child, or employee?"

Choose one of these roles and write an essay in which you answer this question. Include specific details and examples to
support your argument.

Laura Robinson

STARVING FOR THE GOLD

A former member of Canada's national cycling and nordic skiing teams,
Laura Robinson (1958–) is known for her articles on sports and recre-
ation, and particularly women athletes. Her commentaries have appeared
in the *Toronto Star*, the *Globe and Mail*, *Canadian Living*, *Toronto Life*, *Saturday
Night*, *NOW Magazine*, and *Up Here*. She has also published *She Shoots,
She Scores: Canadian Perspectives on Women in Sport* (1997) and *Crossing the
Line: Sexual Assault in Canada's National Sport* (1998), a book that details the
abuse in the world of minor league hockey; she is currently working on
Clearing Hurdles: The Business and Politics of Women in Sport. Robinson no
longer participates in sports competitively. Instead, she enjoys recreational ski racing, cycling, and running. In this article Robinson portrays
a frightening picture of the way young female athletes are treated by their
male coaches.

Preparing to Read

As you prepare to read think about competitive sports and athletes. What
does it take for someone to become a top athlete? How does pursuing
this level of achievement influence the lives of those athletes? What is
the appeal of competitive sports, both to the participants as well as to the
observers? What benefits does one enjoy as a top athlete? What disadvantages or drawbacks might there be? In international competitions,
such as the Olympic Games, why are some countries consistently winners in particular sports? Think specifically of sports such as gymnastics
and figure skating, where many young women compete. As either a participant or a spectator, what role do you see coaches playing in competitive sports?

Imagine for a moment you are an Olympic athlete. If you pictured   1
a male athlete, try again. Actually, you are a woman, engaged in
rigorous year-round training. Now, imagine that your body-fat
percentage is less than half the average for a reasonably active
woman your age. As a result, your menstrual cycle has stopped;
you no longer have a period. You are a textbook case of anorexia
nervosa, obsessed with weight and body shape. Perhaps you are
bulimic, and resort to compulsive binge eating, followed by violent
purging—vomiting, fasting or the taking of laxatives and diuret-
ics. If you are a junior athlete, in your early teens, you are effectively delaying the onset of puberty and stunting normal growth.

A rational observer would conclude that you are seriously ill.   2
A rational observer would not suspect that you had been driven
to these life-threatening disorders by your coach.

According to five women, former members of Canada's   3
national sports teams, their coaches' insistence on excessive
thinness threatened their physical health. The athletes' identities
have been disguised for reasons that will presently be made clear.

The first woman, while still a junior, was told by her coach   4
that she should "think about" losing weight. "I was 5-foot-5 and
weighed 135, but he said, 'Look, all the top women, all the senior
women are thin.' So I thought, 'Maybe I am a little chubby.' I
started to train for the Calgary Olympics. By late 1987, I weighed
less than 110. I was constantly hungry, but I told myself, 'This
is a good feeling.' I lost another five pounds the week before our
qualifying competition, but I felt extremely weak and didn't
make the team." Her standing began to suffer, and two years
later she retired from active competition.

Says another woman, "Looking back, I can see how stupid it   5
was. The coaches were saying, 'Hey, we've got the thinnest team
around, the girls are looking great.' We didn't have great results,
but that didn't seem to matter. I was just a teenager, and a coach's
attitude means everything when you're young. Now, I'm angry.
They screwed up my mind, and I'll never be able to look at food
again the way I did before."

A third athlete, now attending university, wrote in a study of   6
athletic amenorrhea (cessation of the menstrual period): "Pressure
was always felt to be lean, and considerable emphasis was placed
on being beneath 12 per-cent body fat. It seemed that the primary
goal was to maintain a low body-fat composition. Often, it was
felt this was more important than actual performance."

This pressure was applied in unmistakable ways. One coach   7
held contests to see who could leave the most food uneaten on her
plate at training camp. Yet another athlete experienced anxiety
attacks over the caliper tests and pool dunking (total submersion
in order to accurately gauge a subject's body fat). "After the tests,
we'd compare results," she says. "Our coach would announce
at dinner who had the lowest fat percentage, and the roller-
coaster eating would start all over again."

One's first reaction to these charges is a measure of disbelief.   8
We hesitate to think that coaches would do such things—but not
so long ago, our athletes were supplied with anabolic steroids
because it was "necessary" in order to win, because "everyone
else did it." A conspiracy of silence surrounded these activities.
Ben Johnson's and Angella Issajenko's physiques were obviously
artificial: the changes in their bodies couldn't be attributed to
natural causes. Every athlete, every sports journalist and sports
official had ample cause for suspicion. No one spoke up.

Next, one might ask: Where are the women coaches, who   9
presumably wouldn't participate in this nonsense? An answer
is suggested by the dismissal in February of Ken Porter, Athletics
Canada's former director of track and field technical programs.
Mr. Porter claimed that he was fired in part because he wished to
promote black and women coaches, and deplored the relegation
of women to "a ghetto-type position as team chaperone."

Third, why hasn't coaching malfeasance come to light? Well,   10
it has. The Dubin Report, commissioned after Ben Johnson tested
positive for anabolic steroids at the 1988 Seoul Olympics,
concluded that coaches must assume responsibility for the "health,
welfare, moral education and preparation for life of the athlete."
Since then, another report, prepared for the federal Minister of
Fitness and Amateur Sport, found that athletes feel they are
coerced into "harmful practices . . . and believe their concerns on
the subject of personal harm are ignored." A third report,
undertaken on behalf of the same ministry, is due within the next
month. It is said to address the issue of physical and sexual abuse.

The reports stack up, the problems are studied to death, and   11
the bad-apple coaches are seldom weeded out.

According to Marion Lay, manager of the Women's Program   12
at Sport Canada (the funding agent for our national teams),
"Coaches who manipulate through food and body image are
robbing women of their self-esteem and self-respect. But what
safe place is there for an athlete who feels abused?"

The women who confided in me asked for anonymity 13
because some of them intend to work within the system; but
even those who maintain only a casual interest fear that if they
speak out they will be perceived as "traitors" to sport. Ms. Lay's
reaction says it all: "Of course, they can't reveal their identities.
There's no mechanism to protect them."

Why this particular form of abuse? Helen Lenskyj, a sports 14
sociologist at the Ontario Institute for Studies in Education, cites the
emergence during the 1970s of a prepubescent body type—the
very young, very thin gymnast, minus hips and breasts, whose
appearance continues to influence judges when it comes to
awarding points for artistic merit in the so-called esthetic sports. As
a result, coaches everywhere decided that their athletes should
look like Soviet gymnast Olga Korbut. In fact, leanness is a factor in
both esthetic and endurance sports—to a point. Athletes shouldn't
carry extra pounds. The trouble is that not everyone is prepubescent
and can't possibly look that way, no matter what she does.

Another factor, according to Marion Lay, is simply resistance 15
to change. The last two decades have seen a dramatic increase
in the number of female competitors. Ms. Lay feels that often
coaches haven't come to terms with this fact: "There's an attitude
of, 'Yes, we'll let you in, but you have to play the game our way,
look the way we want you to look.' Women have to give things
up in order to enter sports." In other words, the predominant
view (because men control sports) is that sports are male. If a
woman is going to take part, she'd better resemble a man. If she's
got womanly hips, she can't really be an athlete, because real
athletes aren't women—and so on, all round the vicious circle.

Little wonder that even so cautious an organization as the 16
Coaching Association of Canada (CAC) raises the shocking notion
that nearly one-third of all women athletes have some sort of
eating disorder. This figure, culled from unspecified studies,
appears in the National Coaching Certification Program's Level
III Course—mandatory at a national-team level. The course
describes the symptoms of anorexia and bulimia, and provides
checklists for their detection, but assumes that the person
studying the materials isn't the source of the difficulty. According
to Tom Kinsman, the CAC's executive director, "These are
problems that weren't talked about before, so we didn't write
about them. I hope a new awareness will go a long way in helping
people raise the issues with dignity and security. But I can tell you
the process won't be nice, clean and clear-cut."

Apparently not. In fact, these issues were under discussion   17
when I began competing over 20 years ago. One of the problems
has always been, as Mr. Kinsman admits, if a coach acts
improperly, it's up to the sport's governing body, not the CAC,
to discipline him—an unlikely scenario if athletes are too
intimidated to lodge complaints, and "believe their concerns are
ignored" when and if they do so.

It is important not to trivialize the issue here. Demeaning   18
comments and sexist behaviour aren't confined to the world of
sports. Yes, it's crude and counterproductive to criticize an athlete
in front of her peers. If a coach's first reaction to every woman
who passes by is "What a lardass," the message sinks in. These
things are wounding, but women everywhere face similar
indignities daily. Nor do I suggest that every coach is like Charlie
Francis, Ben Johnson's steroid supplier.

A skeptic would argue that plenty of non-athletic teenagers   19
are anorectic, that countless women punish their bodies for
doubtful ends (silicone implants and face-lifts spring to mind),
that a certain number of women athletes would succumb to eating
disorders even with the most supportive and caring coach. As
well, an athlete places such extraordinary demands on her body
that it's hard to pinpoint cause and effect.

All this may be so. But it can't be denied that Canada's most   20
senior coaches are exacerbating—if not creating—a problem of
terrible magnitude.

With devastating results. First, long-term amenorrheics are   21
susceptible to a loss in bone density or osteoporosis (abnormally
porous or weakened bones). If these conditions persist, one in
three such athletes will suffer a fracture. A 1985 study found that
even athletes with irregular (as opposed to nonexistent) periods
were nearly four times more prone to stress fractures than those
whose periods were uninterrupted.

Next, and more serious, is the fact that athletes engage in   22
regular aerobic activity, which reduces low-density lipoprotein-
cholestrol. So far, so good—LDL-C is a contributing factor in
coronary ailments. But because an amenorrheic woman's estrogen
secretions are low, this positive effect is reversed. Up go the LDL-
C levels; up goes the risk of heart disease.

Lastly, it's been predicted that almost 15 per cent of anorectics   23
and bulimics will die over the course of 30 years as a direct result
of their disorders. There hasn't been a verifiable instance yet
among Canadian athletes—but these are early days.

So the question remains. Why would a coach encourage such 24
dangerous behaviour? Anorectic athletes are too unhealthy to
do well over the long haul; you can't compete at the international
level if you're starving yourself. Many athletes eventually break
down and disappear from view. Unless they're household names,
no one notices. They're interchangeable, there are plenty more
where they came from.

One answer has been suggested by Ms. Lenskyj, the OISE 25
sports psychologist: it's imitative crime. In addition to underage
gymnasts like Olga Korbut, a fair number of older European athletes
are much too thin. I could name an entire cycling team whose
members are plainly anorectic. They're fast on the road, but they're
burning out even faster. Watch for them at the Barcelona Olympics,
because they won't be competing in a couple of years.

But Marion Lay's comments earlier about forced make-overs 26
may be closer to the mark. Notes Karin Jasper, a Toronto
psychotherapist, "The athletic look is lean with narrow hips, and
we have learned that women dislike the size of their hips,
stomachs and thighs, those areas most connected with
pregnancy." Constant harping on these areas—the first ones to
catch a male coach's eye—is enough to stir up instant insecurity.
"The ideal male athlete has narrow hips, but that's not normal for
women," says Ms. Lenskyj. "Dieting can't change skeletal
structure. Only a few girls have bodies that correspond to a male's
in terms of leanness. If coaches use weight and fat percentages as
a tool to manipulate athletes, it is a form of sexual abuse."

The inescapable conclusion is that the coach, unused to 27
women in sport, wants them to look like boys. Or, failing that, like
little girls. This syndrome assumes even more ominous overtones
when you consider the inordinate number of women athletes
and coaches who wind up as romantic items. I remember a
Canadian national team where every member was living with
or married to her coach or technical adviser. One hesitates to
speculate on these unions. According to Karin Jasper, an
unfortunate side-effect of self-starvation is often a loss of sexual
drive. The coach gets less than he bargained for in that
department. The other possibility is that his fondest wish has
come true—he has found someone who's lost all outward signs
of womanhood—no breasts, no hips, no period. It makes you
wonder whether he might not be happier coaching little boys.

The real imperative here is obviously control over someone 28
less powerful, someone malleable and eager to please. Given

that girls begin their athletic careers very young, they don't get a chance to develop into well-rounded human beings in any sense. I personally believe that many male coaches don't like, and are ill-equipped to deal with, grown women. There's no other explanation for the ceaseless humiliation and ridicule— the construction of a closed system where trauma becomes a tool to produce great-looking girls, the thinnest team around.

Is change possible in the world of organized sports? Let's give coaches the benefit of the doubt. Maybe they think that all these things will actually help us bring home lots of medals. Remember the outcry when Canada's skaters "failed" to win Gold and had to "settle for" Bronze. Third-best in the world translated as "not good enough." (The logical extension of this sort of thinking is that, whatever an athlete's body is like, it's never right. It's too fat, too thin, too this or too that.) 29

When our athletes, being human, made mistakes, they were savagely criticized by the media. As a result, every athlete, man or woman, becomes a performance machine. Karin Jasper is not surprised: "We talk to girls and women about overcoming perfectionism, about not basing their evaluation of themselves on all-or-nothing standards. But athletes are taught to see themselves this way. Either they win, or they don't. When their entire value is based on performance, they won't be viewed as a whole person, they're one-dimensional." 30

Under these conditions, even an influx of women coaches would do little good. Until the system asks what's best for a given person, not an athlete, it's stuck in the all-or-nothing groove. For male coaches to change, they'd have to re-examine their priorities, their own sexuality, their entire basis for coaching. That's not going to happen. 31

The real tragedy is that sports can feel so good, so refreshing and exciting and freeing. I entered organized sports when I was 14. I was lucky. I had people who made sure I got to the races on time, but also gave me plenty of books to read. Still, I couldn't help but be affected to some degree. I was obsessed with exercise; I overtrained. That was my response to the pressure, and it wasn't healthy. Even now, I tend to avoid scales. I have to think twice if someone asks me if I consider myself thin. I escaped the worst of it, but my attitudes remain. 32

One of the women whose own sad story I recounted earlier has started to coach girls between the ages of 12 and 16. "They ask 33 me if they're overweight," she says, "and I tell them, 'If you think you can work with your weight, then you're fine. This is the body God has given you, so enjoy it.'" That's encouraging, as far as it goes—although the fact that 12-year-old athletes anguish about their weight is food for thought. But, because of her experiences, this woman is incapable of saying, "This is the body God has given me, so I'll enjoy it." That has been taken from her and nothing can compensate her for such a loss.

UNDERSTANDING DETAILS

1. Why, in Robinson's opinion, are male coaches starving their female athletes?
2. Why don't the athletes challenge the coaches about their food consumption?
3. According to Robinson, what is necessary for this unhealthy pattern to be broken?

ANALYZING MEANING

1. What does the title tell you about the tone of this article?
2. Do you agree that the use of weight and fat percentages as a tool to manipulate athletes is a form of sexual abuse (paragraph 26)? Why or why not?
3. In her discussion of this problem, Robinson identifies a chain of reaction. She considers both the causes and effects of the coaches' behaviour, as well as the causes and effects of the athletes' behaviour. Rank these four categories according to the amount of attention Robinson gives to each. Which ranks the highest? Why has Robinson chosen this focus?

DISCOVERING RHETORICAL STRATEGIES

1. What is Robinson's main purpose in this essay? Has she achieved her goal? Explain.
2. Describe Robinson's intended audience.
3. At what points in this essay does Robinson analyze the causes of this problem? When does she study the effects? Is a pattern apparent?

MAKING CONNECTIONS

1. Imagine a conversation between Gloria Steinem ("The Politics of Muscle") and Laura Robinson about the role of sport in women's lives. On what points do you think they would agree? Where might they disagree? Whose view would you most closely agree with?
2. Laura Robinson and Naheed Mustafa ("My Body Is My Own Business") both discuss body image in their essays. Compare and contrast the views of these two writers.
3. In this essay Laura Robinson discusses her own experience but she also includes many quotations from others and cites many experts in the field of sports psychology, coaching, and psychotherapy. How does this approach compare to that used by Cecil Foster ("Why Blacks Get Mad") and Judy Rebick ("The Culture of Overwork")?

IDEAS FOR DISCUSSION/WRITING

Preparing to Write

Write freely about participation in sports. Do you participate in any sports? If so, what sports? Do individual sports or team sports hold more appeal? Would you rather be involved in sports recreationally or competitively? What sports do you like to watch? Do sports play a role in your school life now? Should participation in sports be mandatory in elementary school? In secondary school? Why or why not?

Choosing a Topic

1. In an article for a fashion magazine, promote participation in sports for the beneficial effects that it can have. Provide specific examples to generate a convincing argument.
2. Body image is a major concern, particularly for young women. Why do females, especially, work so hard to achieve a certain prescribed image? What effects does this obsession with appearance have? Write an essay for teenagers that points out the problems of striving to be something that does not come naturally.
3. Think of a situation in which your behaviour was influenced either positively or negatively by the expectations of another individual, such as a parent, friend, teacher, or other relative. Write an essay for that person in which you outline and explain the effects of those expectations.

Kim Pittaway

∎ ☐ ∎

DEAD WRONG

As a freelance writer and regular contributor to *Chatelaine* magazine, Kim Pittaway (1964–) tackles a broad range of subjects of concern, particularly to Canadian women. In addition, Pittaway sits on the editorial board of *This* magazine and the board of directors of the National Magazine Awards foundation.

Preparing to Read

The following essay, taken from *Chatelaine* magazine, takes a clear position on our society's attitudes about grieving and reactions to death. As you prepare to read this article, think for a few minutes about funeral customs in our society: Have you attended a funeral service recently? Which rituals seemed particularly vivid to you? Who else attended the funeral? What relationship did the people there have to the deceased? How do people typically react to the death of a family member or close friend? What provisions are made at your school or workplace to deal with the death of a friend or relative? How do you react to the death of celebrities who you don't know personally?

∎————————————————————∎

The pundits can't condemn them loudly enough: the celebrity- 1
death rituals of the 1990s, with their flowery shrines and on-camera weeping by complete strangers. It's distasteful, they say. A symptom of our obsession with media-manufactured personalities, when even the kid next door can end up in *People* magazine if she's unlucky enough to be caught in the crossfire of the latest school shooting. A sign of the times, when we feel closer to JFK Jr. or Princess Di or a murdered child than to the people in our own homes.

The naysayers heap scorn on those who line up to leave 2
flowers, bad poetry and children's drawings in remembrance and they mutter about the empty lives of those who have time to indulge in all this artificial grief. They, of course, are too busy being interviewed about the "problem" on yet another current affairs program to have time for such nonsense.

And they're dead wrong.   3

I'll admit that I once agreed with the cynics on the issue of   4
public grieving. I'm not proud to admit it now, but I once took a
side trip to Graceland for the sole purpose of laughing at the
kitschiness of it all and snickered at the visitors crying and leaving
letters at Elvis's grave. (Though Graceland was pretty kitschy,
what with the Jungle Room and its shag-carpeted floors and
ceilings. And, really, when someone says the King is buried in the
backyard, I think "dog" not "rock 'n' roll legend." But there he
was, with his mom, baby brother and Colonel Parker.)

But time and, perhaps more important, personal experiences   5
with grief have made me change my mind. We live in a society
where publicly mourning our personal losses is discouraged.
Your best friend dies? Use a vacation day for the funeral; no,
actually, use half a vacation day—and be back to work after
lunch. Lose your mom or a child? Check your company policy or
collective agreement and you'll likely find you get three days
off. Then move on—and try not to depress your friends and
coworkers with the details. Miscarry? Well, that one doesn't
count at all. After all, you can try again soon.

Still feeling the pain of your loss months later? Get the   6
mourning-after pill: Prozac should take the edge off that grief.
You'll be back on your feet—and back to work—in no time. And
if you must cry, do it quietly in a washroom stall where you
won't disturb others. Death makes people uncomfortable—and
distracts them from their work.

Death has never been a laugh-a-minute conversation starter.   7
But we've become less and less able to talk about it. We let others
prepare our loved ones' bodies for burial. We contract out the
wake. We insist on "happy" funerals, celebrations where wailing
is frowned upon and any sign that this is a grim affair is
discouraged. And if we dress entirely in black, it's only because
we live in Toronto, where dressing entirely in black is compulsory
year-round. We've turned grieving into an industry with
consultants and counselors and books to tell us how to do it
(quick: what stage am I in now?).

Part of that is because, these days, many of us have   8
surprisingly little personal experience with death. Thanks to
modern medicine and the luck of being born Canadian in the
latter half of the 20th century, we haven't lost siblings to smallpox
or flu or uncles and brothers and fathers to war or mothers and

aunts to childbirth. I'm amazed at how many people my age—35—have never even been to a funeral.

So, when a public figure dies or a tragedy like Littleton or 9 Taber turns someone like us into a public figure, we mourn. Why? If we've been lucky enough to be largely untouched by death in our own lives, we get to practise. It's virtual death: we're imagining what it would be like to be Caroline, a sister without a brother, or William and Harry, sons without a mother, or the minister and his wife in Taber, parents coping bravely with the loss of a son.

If we've got personal griefs of our own, we vent them 10 vicariously. We talk death to our friends, discuss the unfairness of a life cut short, share our fears about our own mortality—all of the things we wanted to talk about but couldn't when our own loved ones died. And we cry, we buy flowers, we even pen a bad poem or two.

I've shed lots of tears for celebrities in the past couple of 11 years. And with each one, I've thought of my friends Catherine and Keitha, my colleague Jim, my grandparents Kay, Edna and Tom, my childhood friends Suzie, Billy, Rhonda, and Michael. Yes, I've mourned those I never knew. But, more important, each time I've remembered those I did.

UNDERSTANDING DETAILS

1. What is Pittaway's position on the "celebrity death rituals" she refers to in paragraph 1? What purpose does Pittaway see these rituals performing?
2. According to Pittaway, what is our society's attitude toward mourning? What evidence does she give to support this point of view?
3. Pittaway claims "these days, many of us have surprisingly little experience with death" (paragraph 8). Why is this the case?

ANALYZING MEANING

1. What is Pittaway's purpose in writing this essay? Is she hoping to change people's behaviour or attitudes? Explain your answer.
2. Why do people have the need to mourn when someone dies? Why have "we become less and less able to talk" about death?
3. Explain the title of this essay. In what respect does it have a double meaning?

DISCOVERING RHETORICAL STRATEGIES

1. What tone does Pittaway establish in her essay? What is her reason for creating this particular tone? What is your reaction to it?
2. In paragraphs 1, 4, 9, and 11, Pittaway mentions specific people and places. Who are these people she mentions? What is the effect of the incorporation of these examples?
3. A *euphemism* is the substitution of a deceptively pleasant term for a straightforward, less pleasant one (e.g., "he has gone to a better place" rather than "he died"). Has Pittaway used euphemisms or straightforward terms in her essay? What effect does this choice have?

MAKING CONNECTIONS

1. In "Why We Crave Hot Stuff," Trina McQueen mentions some of the same celebrity examples that Pittaway cites in "Dead Wrong." Is McQueen's attitude to these examples consistent with Pittaway's, or is McQueen one of the people whose attitude Pittaway considers "dead wrong"?
2. Pittaway makes a case for acknowledging grief and not limiting our range of emotions to those that are considered acceptable by our society. How does this compare to Lynn Coady's ("Genius or Madness?") comments on socially unacceptable behaviour?
3. Stephen King ("Why We Crave Horror Movies") argues that horror movies are an outlet for our less socially acceptable emotions. How do you think King would respond to Pittaway's position on "celebrity death rituals"? Do you see the "flowery shrines and on-camera weeping by complete strangers" to be a comparable outlet for less socially acceptable emotion? Why or why not?

IDEAS FOR DISCUSSION/WRITING

Preparing to Write

Write freely about celebrities. What role do celebrities play in your life? What celebrities do you particularly admire? Why? How do you learn the details about the lives of celebrities? How do you respond to the life events that happen to celebrities? Have you ever visited a celebrity home? To what lengths would you go to meet a celebrity who you admired? What type of behaviour crosses the line between admiration and obsession?

Choosing a Topic

1. Celebrities often have profound effects on our lives, either through their behaviour or through things that happen to them. Write an essay in which you outline the effects on you of the actions or the fate of a particular celebrity.
2. The deaths resulting from the September 11, 2001, terrorist attacks on the United States caused an international outpouring of response. Write an essay in which you discuss how those attacks personally affected you or someone you know.
3. In an essay directed to your colleagues, explain the effect of a school or workplace policy that you believe doesn't respond adequately to the needs of the people it governs. Make it clear how consequent behaviour demonstrates the inadequacy of this policy.

Tony Leighton

THE NEW NATURE

Tony Leighton (1954–) is a freelance writer from Guelph, Ontario, whose work can be found in *Harrowsmith*, *Canadian Geographic*, *Explore* magazine, the *Globe and Mail*'s *Report on Business*, and *Equinox,* where "The New Nature" was first published late in 1994. Leighton was also the editor of the Bank of Montreal's customer newsletter, *Possibilities.*

Preparing to Read

"The New Nature" is an exploration of the growing industry of digital imaging, a process that is, in many ways, replacing traditional photography. Before reading Leighton's essay, think about photographs and the role that they play in our lives. What role do photographs play in newspapers and magazines, in conveying news stories, and in providing us with memories of specific events and people? It is often said that "a picture is worth a thousand words." Can you think of any other sayings about pictures? How reliable are pictures? Can you always believe your eyes?

340 Chapter 8 ■ Cause/Effect

O f all the media coverage that has whirled around O.J. 1
Simpson's indictment for murder, one image has had lingering impact. Shortly after Simpson's arrest on June 17, the Los
Angeles Police Department released a now infamous photograph
that appeared on the covers of both *Time* and *Newsweek*. It's not a
particularly striking image. Simpson is being arraigned at a court-
house. He is obviously tired and shaken. What's significant is what
Time did to it. The magazine's art department used a computer
to "process" the image digitally, darkening Simpson's features
and his day-old beard and making the background details appear
indistinct and shadowy. The result is unmistakably sinister. *Time*'s
Simpson looked more threatening than *Newsweek*'s.

Once discovered, *Time*'s use of computer manipulation was 2
hotly criticized as a cheat on an unsuspecting public. But it's
more than that. The Simpson episode reflects a broad trend in
contemporary media that's giving rise to a new ethical debate.
Thanks to the revolution of digital technology, the original source
materials of many cultural media, including photographs, films,
and recordings, can now be reshaped with amazing—and some
say alarming—felicity. Reality can be transfigured with a few
swift strokes of a keyboard. And it can be done with such skill
that the difference between an authentic image or sound and a
digitized fake is no longer recognizable.

For those who work in the fantasy business producing 3
movies, commercials, pop records, or fine art, digital
manipulation offers cost savings and enhanced creative power.
But when it is used to alter, say, news photography, it has much
darker implications. It can be argued that for every advancement
of technology, there is a price to pay. With the digitization of
photography, the price is veracity. We can no longer believe
what we see.

"It's that old thing about 'photography never lies,'" says 4
Doug Smith, a computer-support specialist at The Banff Centre
for the Arts in Alberta, where resident artists are taught digital
photography. "We know that photography lies, but we still rely
on newspapers, television, and magazines for truthful
information. I guess we have to trust somebody. If we know they
are manipulating images, it becomes just another of the many
things we have to mistrust."

Learning to mistrust may soon be a survival skill for the 5
customers of media, one that forces us to break some very old

habits of mind. "For a century and a half ... photographs appeared to be reliably manufactured commodities, readily distinguishable from other types of depictions," wrote William J. Mitchell, a professor of architecture and media arts at the Massachusetts Institute of Technology (MIT), in the February 1994 issue of *Scientific American*. "The emergence of digital imaging has irrevocably subverted these certainties, forcing us all to adopt a far more wary and vigilant interpretive stance ... We will have to take great care to sift the facts from the fictions and falsehoods."

Anyone who doubts the urgency of the issue need only 6 consider a handful of classic digital ploys. Last February, *New York Newsday* showed Olympians Tonya Harding and Nancy Kerrigan skating "together" shortly after the famous bashed-knee incident. The photo was a composite, with the skaters stitched in place electronically. In the musical realm, Frank Sinatra sang "duets" on a recent compact disc with artists he never met, their voices recorded digitally, some transmitted with flawless clarity over telephone lines. In Hollywood, John Candy's last movie, *Wagons East*, unfinished at the time of his death, was completed with digitally cloned images of the actor inserted into essential scenes.

Historically, of course, the media have always been able to 7 manipulate source materials one way or another. American Civil War battlefields were rigged with "dead" bodies by photographers drumming up sympathy for the Union's cause. Trying to rewrite history, Stalin had Trotsky expunged from a 1920 photograph that showed him at Lenin's side. What's the difference today? Those who altered photographs in the '20s used knives, light, silver-halide paper, and darkrooms, and only a handful of skilled specialists could work such magic. Today, with an hour of practice, you and I could do a much better job in a few minutes on a desktop computer.

Of all media, photography provides the most instructive look 8 at both the seductive power and the haunting price of the new digital technology. When the content of a conventional photograph is stored as digital code, it is transformed from a static reflection of reality frozen on film and paper to a fluid bit stream that is as alterable as a fantasy. In fact, most of what you see in newspapers, magazines, and books these days are no longer photographs at all. They are digital images.

Put most simply, digital code is a binary, or "on-off" 9
language, a kind of simplified alphabet with only two characters,
0 and 1. Any computer program is a huge script of these two
characters strung together into large, meaningful patterns that
ultimately command a word-processing program to place letters
on a screen, a spreadsheet to calculate, or a design program to
display an automobile part in three dimensions.

Photographs enter the digital realm by way of a tool called a 10
scanner. With a bar of intense light, it moves across a photograph,
reading colours and details, breaking down the original image
into thousands of tiny "picture elements," or "pixels," that are like
the dots that make up a television screen. Pack together enough
dots in sufficient density, and you have a picture. Once digitized,
an image can be redescribed at will. In other words, it can be
copied, transmitted, or altered with utter mathematical precision.

Working conventionally, a photographer must labour for 11
hours in a darkroom to alter what a camera and film captured
in the field. It is fussy, messy work to isolate certain elements in
a photograph and then "dodge" them (deny them light) to darken
them in the final print or "burn" them (expose them to more
light) to lighten them. Elaborate composites or montages used
to require multiple exposures and manual contrivances, to say
nothing of all the paper and caustic chemicals devoured in the
process. "Now," says Doug Smith, "you can do and undo
experimental changes ad infinitum without being in a darkroom,
without expending materials, and without standing on your feet
for hours and hours."

If you pay any attention to the popular media, you've 12
probably seen the products of digital imaging. Practised photo
manipulators have worked some cheeky digital deceptions:
Hillary Rodham Clinton's head on the barely dressed body of a
voluptuous young model (on the cover of *Spy* magazine). Arnold
Schwarzenegger and Queen Elizabeth as black people and black
director Spike Lee with white skin and green eyes (in *Colors*, a
magazine published by Italian clothier Benetton). And Marilyn
Monroe flirting arm-in-arm with Abraham Lincoln (on the cover
of *Scientific American*). These images are astonishing and stand as
the comic beginning of revolution in image control.

No organization has been quite as engaged in this tech- 13
nological leap as photographic giant Eastman Kodak Company
of Rochester, New York. Kodak recently hired chief executive

officer George Fisher, who aims to find a new way for the company synonymous with the old way of taking pictures, the analogue way. Fisher's strategy is to focus Kodak's energies on the highly competitive fray of consumer electronics (copiers, printers, Photo CD players) and, of course, to transform Kodak into the company synonymous with digital imaging. In the lobby of Kodak Canada's corporate offices in Toronto's west end, the writing is literally on the wall. The company's business lines are inscribed proudly on several mounted plaques: Printing and Publishing Imaging, Office Imaging, Professional Imaging, Consumer Imaging, Motion Picture and Television Imaging. Nowhere is the word "photography" used.

When asked whether photography is as good as dead, Neil   14
Buchanan, the national sales manager of Kodak Canada's Digital Imaging Group, says no, conventional silver-halide photography will coexist with digital imaging for many years to come. "Technologies don't get displaced," he says. "They just reinvent themselves."

But at the very moment Buchanan is explaining film's   15
importance, one of his colleagues in the same room is downloading an image that was captured moments ago on perhaps the single most subversive tool of the digital age: the filmless camera. Kodak's DCF 420 camera looks like a normal 35 mm model that a professional photographer might use. (And indeed, the main part of the body is a standard Nikon N90.) But inside it is the future of photography—a "charge-coupled device," or CCD array. A CCD is a chip composed of millions of microscopic light-sensing cells that generate millions of little electrical charges in proportion to the intensity of light that strikes them through the camera's lens. The charges are converted to numbers. The numbers describe pixels. In essence, the CCD snatches an image straight from the ether. The electronic image is then stored on a credit-card-sized cartridge that fits in an extension at the base of the camera. It can be downloaded directly to a computer or stored for later use.

The DCF 420 is not for you and me. It costs around $15,000.   16
The image it currently produces is not quite as sharp as a photograph, but it's not far off. And it's getting better with each new version of the camera.

The CCD is a key component in a whole digital desktop   17
system contained in Kodak's demonstration room that can, in

minutes, convert what we see around us into a finished colour print. No film. No chemicals. No monopolistic middlemen. No waiting. The system includes a Macintosh computer loaded with Adobe Photoshop software for altering digital images, a "continuous-tone digital-output device" for printing colour images straight from the computer, and if you want to store the images for later retrieval, Kodak's remarkable Photo CD technology that digitally encodes dozens of pictures on a compact disc.

Products such as Kodak's Photo CD and Adobe System's   18 Photoshop are technological watersheds. They have, within the past five years or so, vaulted the entire field of image capture and manipulation through a critical barrier. Granted, not many photographers are working extensively in the medium just yet, considering the cost factors and the leap of faith involved in leaving silver and celluloid behind. But those who have gone digital are proving its huge potential.

"This is about creative control," says Burton Robson,   19 Canadian director of Adobe Systems. "It's putting creative control in a photographer's hands or a designer's hands. Photographers can now provide concepts in advertising and promotions that couldn't be done before."

Toronto photographer Philip Rostron's advertising work is   20 a case in point. He estimates that about 70 percent of his photography is now altered with digital-imaging software, gaining him a creative and financial edge. His work on a Chrysler Canada ad for instance, featured a photograph of a car apparently roaring around a turn in an attractive rural landscape. But it is a landscape of deception. The grassy fields in the background, originally a limp grey-green, were warmed up in Photoshop with the roasted autumnal tones of a chaparral. The sky, in reality a thin blue, was dramatized with beguiling purple. The car, actually photographed when stationary but jacked up on one side to suggest motion, was touched up with a slight digital blur at its back end to create the illusion of speed. Its paint job was raised to the high lustre of polished lacquer. And to finish things off, an intrusive-looking lamp post was simply vaporized. "You could stay on location for two years and not see that landscape," says Rostron. "And it's very hard to justify $20,000 of location photography with no guarantee that God will cooperate."

Rostron says he still works hard to take the best possible   21 photographs. "The stronger the image that goes into the system," he says, "the better the final product that comes out." But he can rest a lot easier these days if a sky is pale or a model has a pimple. The computer will forgive the imperfections.

Digital technology has had a similar effect on Louis Fishauf, 22 a partner in Reactor Art & Design, one of Toronto's best-known graphic-design studios. Fishauf works exclusively on a Macintosh, frequently in Photoshop, and increasingly with Kodak's Photo CD. "The major change," says Fishauf, "has been that the whole process of design can now be telescoped into days, even hours, and be accomplished by one person."

Canada Post Corporation recently hired Reactor to create a 23 stamp and commemorative booklet to honour the 125th anniversary of The T. Eaton Company Limited. With access to a vast trove of Eaton's memorabilia from the Archives of Ontario, Fishauf and his associate, Stephanie Power, decided to do both the stamp and booklet in collage style, displaying as many old photos and illustrations as possible. They selected more than 300 items from the archives and had them photographed on 35 mm slides. All 300 images were then digitized onto Photo CDs.

"It was a great way of organizing so many images," says 24 Fishauf. "With an electronic collage, if you make a mistake or change your mind, you can reuse the same source elements, go back and make it bigger or smaller, change the colour balance, make it transparent, change the brightness or the contrast. You have all kinds of capabilities for manipulating imagery that don't exist in the real world."

The enthusiasm of users such as Rostron and Fishauf is not 25 universally shared. Some critics worry that the greater ease offered by digital technology will seduce us into modifying images without due reflection on a variety of ethical questions. This was a theme at a conference called Ethics, Copyright, and the Bottom Line: A Symposium on Digital Technologies and Professional Photography, held in 1992 at the Center for Creative Imaging in Camden, Maine. One of the speakers, Fred Ritchin, director of photography at *The New York Times Magazine*, summarized the double-edged nature of digital imagery. "As we applaud the technology—as we should," he said, "I think we have to simultaneously ask, 'Is this helping us to see, to understand the world?' You have this impulse to make it bigger, make it smaller, make it pink, because it is so easy. This is what some people have called the God Complex."

The God Complex may be harmless enough in the hands of   26
an artist retouching a mole on the cheek of a *Vogue* cover model,
but what about when it crosses over into photography that we are
conditioned to trust as documentary evidence? Ritchin gave the
example of a Swedish plane that crashed in Finland. No
photographer was present, so a newspaper interviewed three
eyewitnesses and created a composite image of a plane crash,
which it ran as a "news photo."

As Ritchin and others point out, historically we have relied   27
on the accuracy of photography (and film and video) to get the
truth—about Tiananmen Square, the Rodney King incident, Gary
Hart, and Marion Barry. Or for that matter, about the Civil War,
Auschwitz, Hiroshima, and the assassination of JFK. But when
truth can so easily be falsified and news travels so rapidly and
completely around the world through huge, centralized news
organizations or courtesy of the Pentagon, can we believe what
we see any more? Will photography ever be taken seriously as
evidence again? Will powerful people still need to be "afraid of
photographs," as Ritchin puts it?

All of this is good cause for soul-searching among   28
professional image makers. "I think there is a moral decision we
have to make," says Nancy Shanoff, another Toronto-based
commercial photographer. "We have to think about what engages
our minds. If I want to create a photographic illusion, that's one
thing, but manipulating a photograph in a news context, that
seems to me totally void of morality. Just because we have the
technological ability to do something, does that exonerate people
from moral obligation? I don't think so."

Olusegun Olaniyan, a Montreal graphic designer who teaches   29
digital imaging to photographers, gives a qualified endorsement
to photo manipulation. "I personally have no problem with it,
as long as I'm told. As humans, we have a need to know what
reality is. When our reality is being played around with, it puts
us in a shaky position. It's a state of mind."

If the ethics of current digital developments are difficult to   30
wrestle with, the future looks even more unsettling. As Ritchin
said in his conference talk: "We now have something called a
range-camera, which is a 360-degree scan that is being developed
at the MIT Media Lab. So you could basically encode George
Bush's data from any angle, and then you could reconstruct the
image from any angle you want any time you wanted, with any

stop, with any depth of field, any focus, any lighting, any people next to him that you want. Basically what you end up with is that you no longer need the photographer there."

There's also a persuasive argument to be made that computer 31 images have retarded creativity at least as much as they have advanced it. If ad agencies are now content with digital cut-and-pastes that avoid the high cost of putting a photographer in front of the Eiffel Tower or the Grand Canyon, will professionals become lastingly complacent? "Will we any longer be the originators of images?" asks Shanoff. "Or will we be reduced to image makers who supply pieces of images? This background, this person—like sampling music or actors?"

Shanoff is not an unschooled technophobe. Like Rostron, she 32 has spent hundreds of hours working with Photoshop. For clients who prefer their images in digital format, she now delivers her work on magnetic disk. Yet she is a reluctant participant. She doesn't alter her own images. She has hired an operator to use the computer in her studio. "I am a middle-aged woman, and I decided a long time ago I wasn't going to be left behind. [But conventional photography] is the craft I have spent my life training for, and there is an intrinsic human thing that doesn't want to let go of that."

In the long run, the impact of digital imaging on our culture 33 may be profound. The cognitive consequence of altering reality is dissonance, the uncomfortable befuddlement we feel when our anchor points are uprooted and there's nothing left to hang onto. News as entertainment does this to us. Television does it in general. Digitally altered photographs do it. As Marshall McLuhan said, "We become what we behold," and "We shape our tools, and afterwards, our tools shape us."

Lewis H. Lapham, the editor of *Harper's*, recounted these 34 words of McLuhan's in a recent editorial. Lapham believes that in the here-there-and-everywhere universe of modern media, "a world in which the stars of daytime soap opera receive 10,000 letters a week from fans who confess secrets of the heart that they dare not tell their husbands, their mothers, or their wives," our perceptions are being perilously reshuffled. As he argues it, we are moving intractably from the pre-electronic straight lines of intellectual cause and effect to nonlinear ways of thinking based on emotions, impressions, sensations—things that invite manipulation. When we allow our tools to shape us, he concludes, we "deconstruct the texts of a civilization" and "nothing necessarily follows from anything else."

The same can be said very specifically for rearranging our 35 photographic reality. If all things are digitally fluid, nothing necessarily follows from anything else. A photograph no longer tells the truth. It only suggests a possibility.

UNDERSTANDING DETAILS

1. What effect has the advent of digital imaging had on traditional photography? Give specific examples to support your answer.
2. How does the ability to manipulate photographs digitally differ from the manipulation of photographs practised earlier in this century?
3. Summarize the benefits that digital imaging can offer. What negative effects counter these positives?

ANALYZING MEANING

1. According to the various people cited in Leighton's article, what reaction to this new technology is now required from consumers? Why?
2. What has been the impact of digital imaging on the way that people view the world? Explain what ethical issues it raises.
3. Where is the line drawn between appropriate and inappropriate use of this form of new technology? Does everyone agree on what is acceptable? Whose view is closest to your own? Explain why.

DISCOVERING RHETORICAL STRATEGIES

1. Reread Leighton's introduction to this essay. What rhetorical technique has he used to introduce his topic and get his audience's attention? Is it effective? Why or why not?
2. Paragraph 20 has several good examples of words that have been carefully chosen for their connotations. List the words or phrases that emphasize the negative impression of the real and those that highlight the positive attitude toward the illusion.
3. Identify Leighton's intended audience in this essay. How has he tailored his discussion of digital imaging to suit this group of readers?

MAKING CONNECTIONS

1. Evan Solomon ("The Babar Factor") concludes his essay by choosing old technology over new. Do you think that Leighton views the new technology that he describes as positive or negative? Explain. What is your position on new technologies such as digital enhancement of photographs?

2. Trina McQueen ("Why We Crave Hot Stuff") alerts us to some of the dangers of journalistic storytelling. How would the information and examples in Tony Leighton's essay support McQueen's caution?

3. Several of the authors represented in *Reader's Choice* give vivid descriptions of places. Would the essays of Tomson Highway ("What a Certain Visionary Once Said"), Lesley Choyce ("Thin Edge of the Wedge"), Sharon Butala ("The Myth: The Prairies Are Flat"), Dave Bidini ("Kris King Looks Terrible"), and Will Ferguson ("The Sudbury Syndrome") be enhanced by photographs of their subjects? Why or why not? If photographs were to accompany their essays do you think that any of them would want to use digitally enhanced photographs? Explain your answer.

IDEAS FOR DISCUSSION/WRITING

Preparing to Write

Write freely about the reliable sources of information in your life. How do you obtain information on news items in your community? National events? International happenings? Historical events? How do you know that those sources are accurate? Who can you count on to tell you the truth? Have you ever found a reliable source to be inaccurate? Do newspaper or television reporters ever misrepresent a story? Do stories get different coverage by different reporters or by different media? Also consider information about personal matters. How have you learned about your family and your ancestors? What do you know about your friends? How do you know what they have told you is true?

Choosing a Topic

1. Many of the people cited in Leighton's essay discuss the situations where digital manipulation of photographs is and is not appropriate. What is your position on the use of digital imaging? What limits, if any, should restrict the use of this technology?

2. Find a picture of yourself that was taken at least five years ago, preferably at some memorable or significant event (e.g., a wedding, a party, a vacation, a holiday celebration). What does it convey about the reality of where and who you were at that time? If you could, is there anything about this picture that you would change? Explain why or why not.

3. In "The New Nature" Leighton quotes Marshall McLuhan as saying, "We shape our tools, and afterwards, our tools shape us." In a short essay, discuss the truth of this statement with reference to at least one specific example of a "tool" that you use in your life.

CHAPTER 9

ARGUMENT/PERSUASION

■ ■ ■

Inciting People to Thought or Action

Almost everything we do or say is an attempt to persuade. Whether we dress up to impress a potential employer or argue openly with a friend about an upcoming election, we are trying to convince various people to see the world our way. Some aspects of life are particularly dependent upon persuasion. Think, for example, of all the television, magazine, and billboard ads we see urging us to buy certain products, or of the many impassioned appeals we read and hear on such controversial issues as school prayer, abortion, gun control, and nuclear energy. Religious leaders devote their professional lives to convincing people to live a certain way and believe in certain religious truths, whereas scientists and mathematicians use rigorous logic and natural law to convince us of various hypotheses. Politicians make their living persuading voters to elect them and then support them throughout their terms of office. In fact, anyone who wants something from another person or agency, ranging from federal money for a research project to a new bicycle for Christmas, must use some form of persuasion to get what he or she desires. The success or failure of this type of communication is easily determined: If the people being addressed change their actions or attitudes in favour of the writer or speaker, the attempt at persuasion has been successful.

Defining Argument/Persuasion

The terms *argument* and *persuasion* are often used interchangeably, but one is actually a subdivision of the other. Persuasion names a purpose for writing. To persuade your readers is to convince them to think, act, or feel a certain way. Much of the writing you have been doing in this book has persuasion as one of its goals: A description of an African tribe has a "dominant impression" you want your readers to accept; in an essay comparing various ways of celebrating the New Year, you are trying to convince your readers to believe that these similarities and differences actually exist; and in writing an essay exam on the causes of the strife in the Middle East, you are trying to convince your instructor that your reasoning is clear and your conclusions sound. In a sense, some degree of persuasion propels all writing.

More specifically, however, the process of persuasion involves appealing to one or more of the following: to reason, to emotion, or to a sense of ethics. An *argument* is an appeal predominantly to your readers' reason and intellect. You are working in the realm of argument when you deal with complex issues that are debatable; opposing views (either explicit or implicit) are a basic requirement of argumentation. But argument and persuasion are taught together because good writers are constantly blending these three appeals and adjusting them to the purpose and audience of a particular writing task. Although reason and logic are the focus of this chapter, you need to learn to use all three methods of persuasion as skillfully as possible to write effective essays.

An appeal to reason relies upon logic and intellect and is usually most effective when you are expecting your readers to disagree with you in any way. This type of appeal can help you change your readers' opinions or influence their future actions through the sheer strength of logical validity. If you wanted to argue, for example, that pregnant women should refrain from smoking cigarettes, you could cite abundant statistical evidence that babies born to mothers who smoke have lower birth weights, more respiratory problems, and a higher incidence of sudden infant death syndrome than the children of nonsmoking mothers. Because smoking clearly endangers the health of the unborn child, reason dictates that mothers who wish to give birth to the healthiest possible babies should avoid smoking during pregnancy.

Emotional appeals, however, attempt to arouse your readers' feelings, instincts, senses, and biases. Used most profitably when your readers already agree with you, this type of essay generally validates, reinforces, and/or incites in an effort to get your readers to share your feelings or ideas. In order to urge our lawmakers to impose stricter jail sentences for alcohol abuse, you might describe a recent tragic accident involving a local twelve-year-old girl who was killed by a drunk driver as she rode her bicycle to school one morning. By focusing on such poignant visual details as the condition of her mangled bike, the bright blood stains on her white dress, and the anguish on the faces of parents and friends, you could build a powerfully persuasive essay that would be much more effective than a dull recitation of impersonal facts and nationwide statistics.

An appeal to ethics, the third technique writers often use to encourage readers to agree with them, involves cultivating a sincere, honest tone that will establish your reputation as a reliable, qualified, experienced, well-informed, and know-ledgeable person whose opinions on the topic under discussion are believable because they are ethically sound. Such an approach is often used in conjunction with logical or emotional appeals to foster a verbal environment that will result in minimal resistance from its readers. Ed McMahon, Johnny Carson's congenial announcer on the *Tonight Show* for many years and the host of *Star Search*, was an absolute master at creating this ethical, trustworthy persona as he coaxed his television viewers to purchase everything from dog food to beer. In fact, the old gag question "Would you buy a used car from this man?" is our instinctive response to all forms of attempted persuasion, whether the salesperson is trying to sell us Puppy Chow or gun control, hair spray or school prayer. The more believable we are as human beings, the better chance we will have of convincing our audience.

The following student paragraph is directed primarily toward the audience's logical reasoning ability. Notice that the writer states her assertion and then gives reasons to convince her readers to change their ways. The student writer also brings both emotion and ethics into the argument by choosing her words and examples with great precision.

> Have you ever watched a pair of chunky thighs, a jiggling pos-terior, and an extra-large sweatshirt straining to cover a beer belly and thought, "Thank God I don't look like that! I'm in pretty good shape ... for someone my age." Well, before you become too smug and self-righteous, consider what kind of shape you're really in. Just because you don't look like Shamu the Whale doesn't mean you're in good condition. What's missing, you ask? Exercise. You can diet all day, wear the latest slim-cut designer jeans, and still be in worse

shape than someone twice your age if you don't get a strong physical workout at least three times a week. Exercise is not only good for you, but it can also be fun—especially if you find a sport that makes you happy while you sweat. Your activity need not be expensive: Jogging, walking, basketball, tennis, and handball are not costly, unless you're seduced by the glossy sheen of the latest sporting fashions and accessories. Most of all, however, regular exercise is important for your health. You can just as easily drop dead from a sudden heart attack in the middle of a restaurant when you're slim and trim as when you're a slob. Your heart and lungs need regular workouts to stay healthy. So do yourself a favour and add some form of exercise to your schedule. You'll feel better and live longer, and your looks will improve, too!

Thinking Critically by Using Argument/Persuasion

Argument and persuasion require you to present your views on an issue through logic, emotion, and good character in such a way that you convince an audience of your point of view. This rhetorical mode comes at the end of this book because it is an extremely complex and sophisticated method of reasoning. The more proficient you become in this strategy of thinking and presenting your views, the more you will get what you want out of life (and out of school). Winning arguments means getting the pay raises you need, the refund you deserve, and the grades you've worked so hard for.

In a successful argument, your logic must be flawless. Your conclusions should be based on clear evidence, and your evidence must be organized in such a way that it builds to an effective, convincing conclusion. You should constantly have your purpose and audience in mind as you build your case; at the same time, issues of emotion and good character should support the flow of your logic.

Exercising your best logical skills is extremely important to all phases of your daily survival—in and out of the classroom. Following a logical argument in your reading and presenting a logical response to your course work are the hallmarks of a good student. Right now, put your best logic forward and work on your reasoning and persuasive abilities in the series of exercises below. Isolate argument and persuasion from the other rhetorical strategies so that you can practise it and strengthen your ability to argue before you combine it with other methods.

1. Bring to class two magazine ads—one ad that tries to sell a product and another that tries to convince the reader that a particular action or product is wrong or bad (unhealthy, misinterpreted, politically incorrect, etc.). How does each ad appeal to the reader's logic? How does the advertiser use emotion and character in his or her appeal?
2. Think of a recent book you have read. How could you persuade a friend either to read or not to read this book?
3. Fill in the following blanks: The best way to _____ is to _____ . (For example, "The best way to lose weight is to exercise.") Then, list ways you might persuade a reader to see your point of view in this statement.

Reading and Writing Persuasive Essays

Although persuasive writing can be approached essentially in three different ways—logically, emotionally, and/or ethically—our stress in this chapter is on logic and reason, because they are at the heart of most college writing. As a reader, you will see how various forms of reasoning and different methods of organization affect your reaction to an essay. Your stand on a particular issue will control the way you process information in argument and persuasion essays. As you read the essays in this chapter, you will also learn to recognize emotional and ethical appeals and the different effects they create. In your role as writer, you need to be fully aware of the options available to you as you compose. Although the basis of your writing will be logical argument, you will see that you can learn to control your readers' responses to your essays by choosing your evidence carefully, organizing it wisely, and seasoning it with the right amount of emotion and ethics—depending on your purpose and audience.

How to Read Persuasive Essays

Preparing to Read. As you prepare to read the essays in this chapter, spend a few minutes browsing through the preliminary material for each selection: What does Judy Rebick's title, "The Culture of Overwork," prepare you for? What can you learn from scanning Jennifer Cowan's essay, "TV Me Alone," and reading its synopsis in the Rhetorical Contents?

Also, you should bring to your reading as much information as you can from the authors' biographies: Why do you think Jennifer Cowan writes about keeping television out of public places in "TV Me Alone"? Does she have the appropriate qualifications to teach us about the proper time and place for TV? What is the source of David Suzuki's interest in "The Right Stuff"? For the essays in this chapter that present two sides of an argument, what biographical details prepare us for each writer's stand on the issue? Who were the original audiences for these pro and con arguments?

Last, before you read these essays, try to generate some ideas on each topic so that you can take the role of an active reader. In this text, the Preparing to Read questions will ready you for this task. Then, you should speculate further on the general subject of the essay: Do you believe that the collection of personal data is dangerous or desirable (Lawrence Solomon, "Too Much Privacy Can Be Hazardous to the Person")? What do you want to know from Rebick about workaholics?

Reading. Be sure to record your spontaneous reactions to the persuasive essays in this chapter as you read them for the first time: What are your opinions on each subject? Why do you hold these opinions? Be especially aware of your responses to the essays representing opposing viewpoints at the end of the chapter; know where you stand in relation to each side of the issues here.

Use the preliminary material before an essay to help you create a framework for your responses to it: Who was Jennifer Cowan's primary audience when her essay was first published? In what ways is the tone of her essay appropriate for that audience? What motivated Rebick to publish her arguments on the problem of workaholism? Why is Suzuki so interested in the high school science curriculum? Which argument do you find most convincing?

Your main job at this stage of reading is to determine each author's primary assertion or proposition (thesis statement) and to create an inquisitive environment for thinking critically about the essay's ideas. In addition, take a look at the questions after each selection to make sure you are picking up the major points of the essay.

Rereading. As you reread these persuasive essays, notice how the writers integrate their appeals to logic, to emotion, and to ethics. Also, pay attention to the emphasis the writers place on one or more appeals at certain strategic points in the essays: How does Cowan integrate these three appeals in "TV Me Alone"? Which of these appeals does she rely on to help bring her essay to a close? How persuasive is her final appeal? What combination of appeals does Rebick use in "The Culture of Overwork"? In what ways does the tone of her writing support what she is saying? How does she establish the tone?

Also, determine what other rhetorical strategies help these writers make their primary points. How do these strategies enable each writer to establish a unified essay with a beginning, a middle, and an end?

Then, answer the questions after each reading selection to make certain you understand the essay on the literal, interpretive, and analytical levels in preparation for the discussion/writing assignments that follow.

For a list of guidelines for the entire reading process, see the checklists on pages 15–16 of the Introduction.

How to Write Persuasive Essays

Preparing to Write. The first stage of writing an essay of this sort involves, as usual, exploring and then limiting your topic. As you prepare to write your persuasive paper, first try to generate as many ideas as possible—regardless of whether they appeal to logic, emotion, or ethics. To do this, review the prewriting techniques in the Introduction and answer the Preparing to Write questions. Then, choose a topic. Next, focus on a purpose and a specific audience before you begin to write.

Writing. Most persuasive essays should begin with an assertion or a proposition stating what you believe about a certain issue. This thesis should generally be phrased as a debatable statement, such as, "If the national government instituted a guaranteed income supplement for seasonal workers, it would provide security for workers in the natural resource sectors of the economy and minimize the draw on the Employment Insurance Fund." At this point in your essay, you should also justify the significance of the issue you will be discussing: "Such a program would help to support workers in industries vital to Canada's economy, would help to maintain the EI fund for people who become unexpectedly out of work, and would improve the image of seasonal workers among Canadians."

The essay should then support your thesis in a variety of ways. This support may take the form of facts, figures, examples, or opinions by recognized authorities, case histories, narratives/anecdotes, comparisons, contrasts, or cause/effect studies. This evidence is most effectively organized from least to most important when you are confronted with a hostile audience (so that you can lead your readers through the reasoning step by step) and from most to least important when you are facing a supportive audience (so that you can build on their loyalty and enthusiasm as you advance your thesis). In fact, you will be able to engineer your best support if you know your audience's opinions, feelings, and background before you write your essay, so that your intended "target" is as clear as possible. The body of your essay will undoubtedly consist of a combination of logical, emotional, and ethical appeals—all leading to some final summation or recommendation.

The concluding paragraph of a persuasive essay should restate your main assertion (in slightly different terms from those in your original statement) and should offer some constructive recommendations about the problem you have been discussing (if you haven't already done so). This section of your paper should clearly bring your argument to a close in one final attempt to move your audience to accept or act on the viewpoint you present. Let's look more closely now at each of the three types of appeals used in such essays: logical, emotional, and ethical.

To construct a *logical* argument, you have two principal patterns available to you: inductive reasoning or deductive reasoning. The first encourages an audience to make what is called an "inductive leap" from several particular examples to a single, useful generalization. In the case of a guaranteed income supplement, you might cite a number of examples, figures, facts, and case studies illustrating the effectiveness of a guaranteed income supplement plan, thereby leading to your firm belief that implementation of this program is essential to the survival of many of Canada's core industries. Used most often by detectives, scientists, and lawyers, the process of inductive reasoning addresses the audience's ability to think logically by moving it systematically from an assortment of selected evidence to a rational and ordered conclusion.

In contrast, deductive reasoning moves its audience from a broad, general statement to particular examples supporting that statement. In writing such an essay, you would present your thesis statement about a guaranteed income supplement first and then offer clear, orderly evidence to support that belief. Although the mental process we go through in creating a deductive argument is quite sophisticated, it is based on a three-step form of reasoning called the *syllogism*, which most logicians believe is the foundation of logical thinking. The traditional syllogism has:

a major premise: Seasonal workers are essential to the Canadian economy;

a minor premise: All workers must make enough money, through wages and/or supplements, to support themselves year round;

and a conclusion: Therefore, for the survival of the Canadian economy, seasonal workers need to receive enough money, through wages and/or supplements, to live adequately for the entire year.

As you might suspect, this type of reasoning is only as accurate as its original premises, so you need to be careful with the truth of the premises as well as with the logical validity of your argument.

In constructing a logical argument, you should take great care to avoid the two types of fallacies in reasoning found most frequently in college papers: giving too few examples to support an assertion and citing examples that do not represent the assertion fairly. If you build your argument on true statements and abundant, accurate evidence, your essay will be effective.

Persuading through *emotion* necessitates controlling your readers' instinctive reactions to what you are saying. You can accomplish this goal in two different ways: (1) by choosing your words with even greater care than usual and (2) by using figurative language whenever appropriate. In the first case, you must be especially conscious of using words that have the same general denotative (or dictionary) meaning but bear decidedly favourable or unfavourable connotative (or implicit) meanings. For example, notice the difference between *slender* and *scrawny*, *patriotic* and *chauvinistic*, or *compliment* and *flattery*. Your careful attention to the choice of such words can help readers form visual images with certain positive or negative associations that subtly encourage them to follow your argument and adopt your opinions. Second, the effective use of figurative language—especially similes and metaphors—makes your writing more vivid, thus triggering your readers' senses and encouraging them to accept your views. Both of these techniques will help you manipulate your readers into the position of agreeing with your ideas.

Ethical appeals, which establish you as a reliable, well-informed person, are accomplished through (1) the tone of your essay and (2) the number and type of examples you cite. Tone is created through deliberate word choice: Careful attention to the mood implied in the words you use can convince your readers that you are serious, friendly, authoritative, jovial, or methodical—depending on your intended purpose. In like manner, the examples you supply to support your assertions can encourage readers to see you as experienced, insightful, relaxed, or intense. In both of these cases, winning favour for yourself will usually also gain approval for your opinions.

Rewriting. To rework your persuasive essays, you should play the role of your readers and impartially evaluate the different appeals you have used to accomplish your purpose:

1. Is your thesis statement clear?
2. Is the main thrust of your essay argumentative (an appeal to reason)?
3. Will the balance of these appeals effectively accomplish your purpose with your intended audience?
4. Does your conclusion restate your argument, make a recommendation, and bring your essay to a close?

You should also look closely at the way your appeals work together in your essay:

1. When you use logic, is that section of your paper arranged through either inductive or deductive reasoning?
2. Is that the most effective order to achieve your purpose?
3. In appealing to the emotions, have you chosen your words with proper attention to their denotative and connotative effects?
4. Have you chosen examples carefully to support your thesis statement?
5. Are these examples suitable for your purpose and your audience?

Any additional guidance you may need as you write and revise your persuasive essays is furnished on pages 26–27 of the Introduction.

Student Essay: Argument/Persuasion at Work

The following student essay by an American uses all three appeals to make its point about the power of language in shaping our view of the world. First, the writer sets forth her character references (ethical appeal) in the first paragraph, after which she presents her thesis and its significance in paragraph 2. The support for her thesis is a combination of logical and emotional appeals, heavy on the logical, as the writer moves her paragraphs from general to particular in an effort to convince her readers to adopt her point of view and adjust their language use accordingly.

The Language of Equal Rights

Ethical appeal — Up front, I admit it. <u>I've been a card-carrying feminist since junior high school. I want to see an Equal Rights Amendment to the U.S. Constitution, equal pay for equal—and comparable—work, and I go dutch on dates. Furthermore, I am quite prickly on the subject of language. I'm one of those women who bristles at terms like</u> — Emotional appeal — *lady doctor* (you know they don't mean a gynecologist), *female policeman* (a paradox), and *mankind* instead of *humanity* (are they really talking about me?).

Many people ask "How important are mere words, anyway? You know what we really mean." A question like this ignores the symbolic and psychological importance of language. <u>What words</u> — Assertion or thesis statement — <u>"mean" can go beyond what a speaker or writer consciously intends, reflecting personal and cultural biases that run so deep that most of the time we aren't even aware they exist. "Mere words" are</u> Significance of assertion <u>incredibly important: They are our framework for seeing and understanding the world.</u>

Logical appeal — <u>*Man,* we are told, means woman as well as man, just as *mankind* supposedly stands for all of humanity.</u> In the introduction of a sociology textbook I recently read, the author was anxious to demonstrate his awareness of the controversy over sexist language and to — Examples organized deductively — assure his female readers that, despite his use of non-inclusive terms, he was not forgetting the existence or importance of women in society. He was making a conscious decision to continue to use *man* and *mankind* instead of *people, humanity,* etc., for ease of expression and aesthetic reasons. "Man" simply sounds better, he explained. I flipped through the table of contents and found "Man and Society," "Man and Nature," "Man and Technology," and, near the end, "Man and Woman." <u>At what point did *Man* quit</u> — Emotional appeal — <u>meaning people and start meaning men again?</u> The writer was obviously unaware of the answer to this question, because it is one he would never think to ask. Having consciously addressed the issue only to dismiss it, he reverted to form.

Logical appeal — <u>The very ambiguity of *man* as the generic word for our species ought to be enough to combat any arguments that we keep it because we all "know what it means" or because it is both</u>

traditional and sounds better. And does it really sound all that much better, or are we just more used to it, more comfortable? Our own national history proves that we can be comfortable with a host of words and attitudes that strike us as unjust and ugly today. A lot of white folks probably thought that Negroes were getting pretty stuffy and picky when they began to insist on being called blacks. After all, weren't there more important things to worry about, like civil rights? But black activists recognized the emotional and symbolic significance of having a name that was parallel to the name that the dominant race used for itself—a name equal in dignity, lacking that vaguely alien, anthropological sound. After all, whites were called *Caucasians* only in police reports, textbooks, and autopsies. *Negro* may have sounded better to people in the bad old days of blatant racial bigotry, but we adjusted to the word *black* and have now moved on to African American, and more and more people of each race are adjusting to the wider implications and demands of practical, as well as verbal labels.

[margin: Examples organized deductively]

[margin: Emotional appeal]

[margin: Logical appeal] In a world where *man* and *human* are offered as synonymous terms, I don't think it is a coincidence that women are still vastly underrepresented in positions of money, power, and respect. Children grow up learning a language that makes maleness the norm for anything that isn't explicitly designated as female, giving little girls a very limited corner of the universe to picture themselves in. Indeed, the language that nonfeminists today claim to be inclusive was never intended to cover women in the first place. "One man, one vote" and "All men are created equal" meant just that. Women had to fight for decades to be included even as an afterthought; it took constitutional amendments to convince the government and the courts that women are human, too.

[margin: Examples organized deductively]

[margin: Conclusion/ restatement] The message is clear. We have to start speaking about people, not men, if we are going to start thinking in terms of both women and men. A "female man" will never be the equal of her brother.

Some Final Thoughts on Argument/Persuasion

As you can tell from the selections that follow, the three different types of persuasive appeals usually complement each other in practice. Most good persuasive essays use a combination of these methods to achieve their purposes. Good persuasive essays also rely on various rhetorical modes we have already studied—such as example, process analysis, division/classification, comparison/

contrast, definition, and cause/effect—to advance their arguments. In the following essays, you will see a combination of appeals at work and a number of different rhetorical modes furthering the arguments.

Argument/Persuasion in Review

Reading Argument and Persuasion Essays

Preparing to Read

1. What assumptions can you make from the essay's title?
2. Can you guess what the general mood of the essay is?
3. What is the essay's purpose and audience?
4. What does the synopsis in the Rhetorical Table of Contents tell you about the essay?
5. What can you learn from the author's biography?
6. Can you guess what the author's point of view toward the subject is?
7. What are your responses to the Preparing to Read questions?

Reading

1. What is the author's main assertion or thesis?
2. What are the primary appeals at work in the essay?
3. Did you preview the questions that follow the essay?

Rereading

1. How does the writer integrate the appeals in the essay?
2. What is the tone of the essay? How does the author establish this tone?
3. What other rhetorical strategies does the author use to support the essay's purpose?
4. What are your responses to the questions after the essay?

Writing Argument and Persuasion Essays

Preparing to Write

1. What are your responses to the Preparing to Write questions?
2. Do you narrow and focus your material as much as possible?
3. What is your purpose?
4. Who is your audience?

Writing

1. Is your thesis a debatable question?
2. Do you justify the organization of your essay?
3. Is your essay organized effectively for what you are trying to accomplish?
4. Does the body of your essay directly support your thesis?
5. Do you understand your audience's opinions, convictions, and backgrounds so that you know what to emphasize?
6. Does your conclusion restate your main intention and offer some constructive recommendations?

Rewriting

1. Is your thesis statement clear?
2. Is the main thrust of your essay argumentative (an appeal to reason)?
3. Will the balance of these appeals effectively accomplish your purpose with your intended audience?
4. Does your conclusion restate your argument, make a recommendation, and bring your essay to a close?
5. When you use logic, is that section of your paper arranged through either inductive or deductive reasoning? Is that the most effective order to achieve your purpose?
6. In appealing to the emotions, have you chosen your words with proper attention to their denotative and connotative effects?
7. Have you chosen examples carefully to support your thesis statement?
8. Is this tone suitable for your purpose and your audience?

Jennifer Cowan

■ □ ■

TV ME ALONE

Jennifer Cowan (1965–) has spent more than a decade as a pop culture commentator, writer, director, and producer. Since graduating with a journalism degree from Carleton University in Ottawa, Cowan has become a regular contributor to *Wired*, CBC Stereo's *Realtime*, and *Shift*, from which this selection was taken. Also, in 1995 Cowan produced and directed the documentary *Douglas Coupland: Close Personal Friend*, which has been broadcast and screened at festivals across North America and Europe. Cowan's advice for writers: Have fun, be nice, and do good work.

Cowan's television experience has included work on *mediatelevision*, *Girltalk*, *ENG*, and *Wired for Sex* (a CBC *Witness* documentary). Cowan makes television, but in "TV Me Alone," she argues for keeping TV out of public places.

Preparing to Read

Jennifer Cowan's essay first appeared in *Shift* in the summer of 1995. Written on an overnight flight from Los Angeles to Toronto, "TV Me Alone" argues that television does not belong in public places. Before reading her argument, think about television and the role that it plays in your life. What do you watch on TV? What is your favourite program? What do you like least on TV? When do you watch television? Where do you watch it? What do you think of television in public places? Could you live without television?

■ _____ ■

I recently had the scrumptious opportunity to take the red-eye   1
from Los Angeles to Toronto. Buoyed by the three-hour stopover in Chicago, I swiped a mini-puft-pillow and set out to catch some sleep in the departure lounge. Sadly, the hum of 5 a.m. airport traffic was drowned out by the incessant loop of CNN airport television. Instead of some much needed zzzzs, I was repeatedly subjected to life-enhancing information on the nutritional value of stamps (two to eight calories per lick if you must know) and tips for the solo traveller (when in San Francisco rent a car and drive down the coast).

TV in public and quasi-public places has become as ubiquitous   2
as the word "ubiquitous." Flight attendants no longer demo

oxygen masks or point out exits with choreographed precision. Instead, pop-out screens serve up sanitized corporate videos with a unisexual Benetton cast. And while you have to pony up a few bucks to see an inflight movie, you can freely access the ABC and NBC news-feeds on short hauls.

Airports are not the only venue plagued by monitor   3 multiplication. Try banks. If being watched by their security cameras while picking underwear out of your bum wasn't enough media scrutiny, now financial institutions want to watch you as you watch them. So during the recent RSP blitz, they played video loops of sailing, sunset strolls on the beach and other dishy retirement options for the canny investor.

At the HMV music stores, the garish interiors and sadistic   4 display practices aren't the only consumer bonus. Toronto's Yonge Street mausoleum is fronted by a 20-foot video wall programmed with HMV's promotional choices of the moment.

Nary a retail space is free of TV. Used to be if you wanted to   5 watch TV in a department store, you had to go to the home entertainment section. Now a detour through the men's wear in Eaton's includes a how-to-open-an-umbrella TV demonstration courtesy of the Totes galoshes people. No doubt the women's accessories department plugs 50 ways to use a scarf clip. There are even TVs, according to *Entertainment Tonight*, tucked into gas pumps, so you can stay tuned while filling your car. The notion that TV is mindless and relaxing, I've discovered, has become as obsolete as manual channel-changing.

Even when there's nothing to see, televisions have taken on   6 an omniscient aura, staring like a Cyclops at the cultural psyche. On a recent visit to a bar, three overhead monitors screened the film *Blood Simple*, just in case my companion failed to provide enough visual enticement. Not to be outdone, a few blocks down, at the neighbouring Bovine Sex Club (where the interior design meshes chicken wire, doll parts and TVs), four big screens emanated everything from *Much Music* and anime to *Tommy* and *Night of the Living Dead*. Bloodshot eyes were glued. Even I found myself staring lemming-like, transfixed by the stream of cathode rays.

Don't get me wrong. I'm not trying to pull a Neil Postman. I   7 don't think TV will topple civilization and make us stop reading or talking or screwing. I love TV! Hell, I make TV. But I think TV has a time and a place—a personal time and a private place. No more.

When TV left our homes and went public, something curious 8 happened. It went from home appliance to tool of compliance. And TV continues to make inroads into the public domain because it reinforces our commonality. Or more specifically, our communality. This is good. I know I'm not alone in relishing mid-*Melrose Place* phone calls from friends dissing Amanda's roots, or Kimberly's lunacy. However, droning news packages, investment tips and how-to-dress techniques served up in buzzing public places don't inspire communal awe among strangers. The only thing I had in common with my fellow travellers at O'Hare during our airport television experience was peckishness and crankiness. United Airlines had united us in disdain, hardly the yummiest form of community.

Pundits keep spewing hoopla about the glowing blue future- 9 direct broadcast satellites, the 500-channel universe, video-on-demand—and we all blink in bewilderment. But if we open our eyes, we'll notice the 500-channel universe is already upon us, and someone else is holding the remote control! The TV nation is little more than a sea of TVs in every environment conceivable.

The fact is, TV should not be in airports or retail stores or 10 banks. TV should not be in doctors' waiting rooms (as the defunct Medical News Network discovered). And there's no need for it in supermarket checkouts. The power and wonder of TV is that it has an ability to create a community. It gives us things to laugh about, cry about and bitch about. But when it is forced upon us, all the things that give it power—intimacy, insularity, intensity— are deadened.

Moving through daily life should not be a battle to avoid the 11 relentless electronic assault. TV deserves so much more.

UNDERSTANDING DETAILS

1. List the range of public places Cowan mentions where TV can be found. Are there others you can add to this list?
2. What is Cowan's thesis or main point in this essay? Where in the essay can it be found?
3. What aspects of TV give it its power?

ANALYZING MEANING

1. How and why does television reinforce a sense of community? What other activities fill this role of creating and maintaining community?

2. Discuss the different reasons that various businesses and corporations have introduced TV into their public spaces.
3. Cowan says that the "notion that TV is mindless and relaxing ... has become as obsolete as manual channel-changing" (paragraph 5). Explain what view has replaced this antiquated notion.

DISCOVERING RHETORICAL STRATEGIES

1. Explain Cowan's perspective on the subject of this essay. What credentials does she have to write on this topic?
2. One strategy Cowan uses to strengthen her argument is specific, vivid examples. Identify four such examples and explain how they enhance her argument.
3. Cowan has made some careful deliberate word choices in "TV Me Alone." What is the effect of each of the following vocabulary choices: *mausoleum* (paragraph 4), *plagued* (paragraph 3), *lemming-like* (paragraph 6), and *zzzzs* (paragraph 1)?

MAKING CONNECTIONS

1. Cowan and Mark Kingwell ("Not Available in Stores") both write about the role of television in our society. On what points do they agree about the place of TV? On what points do they disagree?
2. Cowan's essay first appeared in *Shift* magazine as did "The Babar Factor" by Evan Solomon. From these two essays, what conclusions might you draw about the readers of *Shift*? What other essay in this book is also likely to appeal to this audience? Explain your answer.
3. Analyze the balance in Cowan's essay between logical, emotional, and ethical appeals. How is this balance different from that found in Judy Rebick's "The Culture of Overwork"? Which author uses more of an emotional appeal? Who uses more logic? Who relies most on ethical appeal? In what way does the mixture of appeals in each of these essays determine how convincing they are to you?

IDEAS FOR DISCUSSION/WRITING

Preparing to Write

Cowan says that one of the positive things TV has to offer is its ability to create a sense of community. Write freely about other shared aspects of life that create a sense of community. What filled this role before television was invented? What other things achieve this purpose today? How has TV contributed to the idea of the global community?

Choosing a Topic

1. Cowan loves TV, but she thinks TV has a time and a place. Write about a particular setting or time where you find television annoying. Explain clearly to your readers why television does not belong in that place or why it is not appropriate at that time.
2. In "TV Me Alone" Cowan says that TV's power is deadened when it is forced upon us. Choose another example of something that loses its power when it is forced on people, and write an essay in which you argue against its imposition.
3. TV is subject to a lot of criticism. Write an essay for *TV Guide* in which you present the benefits that TV has to offer its viewers.

Lawrence Solomon

TOO MUCH PRIVACY CAN BE HAZARDOUS TO THE PERSON

In addition to being the editor of (now defunct) *The Next City*, Lawrence Solomon (1948–) has contributed to many publications including the *Globe and Mail* and the *Wall Street Journal*. Solomon's areas of expertise include public utilities, public-private partnerships, and regulation. Solomon is also noted as a leading environmentalist, and in the late 1970s he was an advisor to President Carter's Task Force on the Global Environment. In addition, his work on energy deregulation, as presented in his books *Energy Shock* (1980), *Breaking Up Ontario Hydro's Monopoly* (1982), and *Power at What Cost?* (1984), has served as a model for privatization of the electricity industry in several countries, including the United Kingdom.

Preparing to Read

"Too Much Privacy Can Be Hazardous to the Person" first appeared in *The Next City,* described in its masthead as "a solutions-oriented magazine that tackles issues confronting our new urban society." In this essay, Lawrence Solomon responds to the concern shared by many that electronic data collection and storage are an undesirable invasion of our privacy. Before you begin reading, think about the idea of privacy. What things do you consider private? Do others share your opinion about what things are private? In what ways have you had your privacy invaded? Do you ever refuse to give people information that you consider to be private? What is the risk associated with having private information shared with others?

■ ─── ■

With vast computer network data bases storing detailed in-   1
formation about our private lives, many of us are becoming uneasy about invasions of privacy. Already, computers track our daily activities, time-stamping every credit and debit card transaction, monitoring who we call on the telephone or visit over the World Wide Web. Many businesses snoop on their employees, many municipalities film activities on city streets to cut down on red-light runners and other violators. Soon, every highway will be tolled, recording our comings and goings; and so will every neighbourhood road—satellite technology today tracks the movement of London cabbies, the better to dispatch them; tomorrow these satellites will economically track private automobiles, the better to bill their owners.

Some privacy concerns revolve around bothersome junk mail   2
and unwanted telemarketing calls: Air mile and other cards let marketers analyze your personal shopping habits, opening you up to an avalanche of targeted offers. Other concerns— particularly access to your genetic code, which contains intimate details about you and your likely future life—are anything but frivolous. A recent study by the Federal Bureau of Investigation and the Computer Security Institute found that "most organizations are woefully unprepared ... [making] it easier for perpetrators to steal, spy, or sabotage without being noticed and with little culpability if they are." After sampling 400 sites, the study found 42 per cent had experienced an intrusion or unauthorized use over the past year. Even sophisticated agencies are vulnerable. Pentagon computers suffered 250,000 attacks by

intruders in 1995, 65 per cent of whom gained entry to a computer network. That same year, the London *Sunday Times* reported that the contents of anyone's electronic health record could be purchased on the street for £150.

Because the dangers—ranging from financial exploitation to, in the worst case, a police state—can be profound, legislation of various types is being proposed. Some argue that all personal information should be our own private property, to prevent marketers from storing and exchanging information about us without our consent; others would severely restrict or even prohibit the collection of sensitive personal data. These approaches miss the mark. The collection of data—the accumulation of knowledge—is almost always desirable. The relevant question is, when does the information belong in the public sphere and when in the private? 3

The claim that we somehow have property rights to our personal information does not stand up to scrutiny. We all exchange information about others—"Did you see Andrea's new car?"; "I hear Jim got a promotion"—in our daily routines without requiring their consent, and a democratic society that respects free speech could not do otherwise. Even if we did enact laws to restrict or ban data banks from collecting information about us, it would generally backfire. Junk mail is unwanted precisely because it is indiscriminate and useless. If marketing succeeds in sending us useful, targeted information, many of us would have our goal of restricting unwanted mail. In one survey, 71 per cent of 18- to 20-year-olds wanted mail on products that interested them; in another, 52 per cent of consumers wanted to be profiled if that would lead to special offers. Those who don't want the mail or the offers will only need to make their views heard: Few companies would defy their customers by selling their names. 4

Valid restrictions governing free speech—such as slandering others or violating their copyright on personal works—are properly limited. But we should add one other restriction—control over the use of our genetic code, where privacy should take precedence over free speech. 5

The field of genetic information promises to be the greatest boon to science and medicine in human history. We suffer from at least 4,000 genetic diseases and conditions—everything from Huntington's disease to depression—that may one day be treated or cured as science unravels the mysteries of the human genome. 6

Even today, reading our genes can guide us in making decisions about our future, revealing whether we have predispositions for cancers or alcoholism, medical conditions that preventative measures could ameliorate. The information in your genetic code amounts to a probabilistic future diary that describes an important part of a unique and personal character—not just about your physical and mental health but also about your family, especially your parents, siblings, and children.

Yet this field also promises to lead to invasions of privacy 7
unprecedented in their nature and scale. Unlike your personal diary, in which you might reveal your innermost secrets, the information in your genetic code may become known to strangers but not to you. From our own experiences, we know that there are no shortages of people with motives to acquire such information. Insurers and employers would value this information for business purposes. Political operatives might want to discredit opponents, as might combatants in divorces or other domestic disputes. Even where stakes aren't high, people may have malicious curiosities about their friends, neighbors, co-workers, or romantic rivals.

Until the turn of the century, our privacy was recognized as 8
a property right and consequently given great legal weight. Our diaries and our secrets, particularly our medical secrets, were our own, in the United Kingdom as in North America. The genetic code, the epitome of that which is personal, is both a present document and a future diary. Giving each of us clear rights to our genetic code and requiring those who would use it to first obtain our consent would provide a necessary and indispensable ingredient to protecting our privacy.

Most day-to-day concerns that people have about privacy 9
will evaporate. Those who don't want consumer data collected on them can avoid air miles-type marketing. Those seeking anonymity in making a phone call or a toll road trip can purchase prepaid cards; other technologies will foil telemarketers and e-mail snoops. Those who value record keeping—primarily businesspeople who bill their time or track it for other purposes— will see this data collection as an added-value service. Most of us won't care much one way or the other.

In private spaces—banks, convenience stores, office 10
buildings—we have accepted cameras, taking little notice of them and worrying about their misuse even less. We understand the

proprietor's motives—to protect his property and the security of those who use it—and accept them as valid. Though we want similar protection in our public spaces, we are less trusting here, not because we value public property and security less but because we know the proprietor—the state—may have mixed motives. Too often government officials have used privileged information—whether medical data or income tax files—for self-serving ends. We do need safeguards governing surveillance in public spaces to allay legitimate public fears over the advent of the police state. Less privacy, ironically, would be one such safeguard.

Many criminal lawyers believe the police state arrived some 11 time ago, that law enforcement authorities effectively frame individuals whom they believe to be guilty. Guy Paul Morin is a case in point: Convinced of his guilt, police fudged the facts. When conflicting evidence frustrated their efforts—Morin left work too late to have travelled the 30 miles home in time to have murdered 9-year-old Christine Jessop—police ingenuity overcame this shortcoming.

Morin has plenty of company—Donald Marshall, David 12 Milgaard, and countless others have been convicted of murder and lesser offences because they could not establish where they were at some fateful time. Put another way, they were victims of their privacy. The vacuum of reliable information about their whereabouts created the opening for overzealous or overlazy police officers and prosecutors. Overzealous and overlazy authorities will always be with us, but vacuums of reliable information are increasingly becoming scarce. Had Jessop been murdered today, and had Morin travelled along an electronically tolled road such as Ontario's Highway 407, a record of when he got on and where he got off the highway would have established his whereabouts. The injustices perpetrated by the criminal justice system on this young man would never have occurred. Highway 407 was built too late to help Morin, but not for future travellers, whose record of their comings and goings—unbeknownst to them—adds a touch of security to their lives. So do new advances in DNA analysis, which eventually proved Morin innocent, as they are now doing for others around the world who were also falsely imprisoned.

A world in which we can verify our daily movements—the 13 very world that has been unfolding for decades—diminishes the number of miscarriages of justice that can occur. To fill a void with false information has always been easy; to rewrite data showing that someone drove 30 miles at a particular time along a particular electronic toll road involves reconstructing an alternate route and time, which involves alternate billing, which involves replacing the old invoice with a new one, and on and on. The effort required to spin a web of false information and then overlay it upon an existing factual network without getting tangled up would be so daunting as to virtually never occur. The very data base networks that some fear will usher in the police state, in the end, are really the best protection against it.

UNDERSTANDING DETAILS

1. Itemize the privacy concerns that Solomon identifies in his essay. How many are there in total?
2. What is Solomon's position on the collection and sharing of personal genetic information?
3. In what ways is our daily activity monitored and tracked according to Solomon? What has led to this type of collection of information?

ANALYZING MEANING

1. Explain how Guy Paul Morin, Donald Marshall, and David Milgaard were "victims of privacy."
2. Where does Solomon draw the line between the type of information that belongs in the public sphere and that which belongs in the private realm? Do you agree with him? Explain why or why not.
3. Explain why people are concerned about the collection of data. Are these concerns warranted? Why or why not?

DISCOVERING RHETORICAL STRATEGIES

1. In several places, Solomon uses statistics to help him advance his argument. Why does he incorporate survey and study results into his essay?
2. What is Solomon's thesis? Where in his essay does it appear? Why has he chosen to organize his argument in this way?
3. What type of appeal does Solomon primarily use in his essay? Is this an effective choice? Why or why not?

MAKING CONNECTIONS

1. Solomon discusses changes in our society that result from advances in technology. How are these changes similar to or different from the changes identified by Tony Leighton ("The New Nature")?
2. Electronic monitoring of our daily activities has the potential to affect our behaviour in many ways. How might electronic monitoring be used to combat racism (Cecil Foster, "Why Blacks Get Mad") or overwork (Judy Rebick, "The Culture of Overwork")?
3. Trina McQueen ("Why We Crave Hot Stuff") discusses the appeal of scandal, gossip, and stories about fascinating people. To what extent is information gathered through the types of electronic monitoring that Solomon describes fair game for media stories?

IDEAS FOR DISCUSSION/WRITING

Preparing to Write

Write freely about electronic monitoring of your daily activities. In what ways are your daily activities monitored? By whom? How do you feel about this monitoring? What are the consequences of the monitoring you have identified? Are these welcome outcomes or undesired consequences? Who should decide what activities are monitored?

Choosing a Topic

1. The electronic gathering of information about us enables marketers to send us unsolicited information or offers on various products and services. Write an essay in which you either promote the use of electronic gathering of data to support this activity or argue against the collection of this information to send "junk mail."
2. One person exercising the right to free speech may infringe on another's right to personal privacy. Write an essay in which you explain where the line should be drawn between free speech and personal privacy.
3. Solomon argues that the monitoring of our activities may protect us in many ways but he has reservations about the collection of genetic data. Write an essay in which you either support or argue against the collection of genetic data. Make sure you include specific examples to support your argument.

Judy Rebick

■ □ ■

THE CULTURE OF OVERWORK

A noted feminist and political commentator, Judy Rebick (1945–) can currently be seen on CBC Newsworld's *Straight from the Hip* and was previously the cohost of CBC's *Face Off*, a national debate show. In addition, Rebick has appeared on a variety of TV and radio shows, including *The Journal*, *Prime Time News*, *Canada AM*, *CBC Midday*, and CBC's *Morningside*. Rebick also writes regular columns for *Elm Street*, *The Ottawa Citizen*, *The London Free Press*, and *CBC Online* and is the author of two books, *Politically Speaking* and *Imagine Democracy*.

A graduate of McGill University with a degree in psychology, Rebick worked as the director of special projects for the Canadian Hearing Society. From 1990 to 1993, she served as the president of Canada's largest women's organization, the National Action Committee on the Status of Women. Most recently Rebick has taken on the role of publisher of rabble.ca, an online community of rabble-rousers.

Preparing to Read

In "The Culture of Overwork," which first appeared in *Elm Street* magazine in the spring of 2001, Judy Rebick discusses the growing problem of overwork and the effects that it has on individuals and society. Before you begin reading, think about overwork. How often do you respond "Busy" when people ask how you are? Do you feel overworked? Are the general expectations of your workplace realistic or excessive? How many hours do you think the ideal workweek should be? How would you spend your remaining time? Who should determine the appropriate number of hours in a standard workweek? What is a workaholic?

■—————————————————————————————————————■

The other day I sat down at the computer in my home office 1 and found that I just couldn't do any work. I was exhausted. At first I thought I was getting sick. Then I realized that I hadn't taken a day off in more than six weeks. I wound up sleeping and watching videos all weekend to recover. Still, I felt a little twinge of guilt that my work wasn't getting done even though years ago I had decided to break from the workaholic behaviour that was driving my life.

Overwork is becoming a cultural norm and it's bad for us. 2
Non-standard jobs, self-employment, cutbacks, weakened labour
standards, technology that permits us to work everywhere from
the car to the home, and the very male-defined norm that you
have to work endless hours to be a success are all contributing.

A Statistics Canada report from November 1999 says that 3
one-third of those aged 25 to 44 describe themselves as
workaholics. Studies show that long work hours are a major
contributor to stress, depression, burnout and a variety of other
illnesses. StatsCan data indicates that those who switched to a
workweek longer than 40 hours increased cigarette and alcohol
consumption and gained weight.

Irregular and long hours are stressful to families, too. A U.S. 4
study shows that family breakup is three to eight times more
likely in couples with children if one parent works nights or does
shift work. In Quebec, one parent works nights or weekends in
more than half of families.

But we don't just bring it on ourselves. In many of the fastest- 5
growing sectors, such as dot-coms, entertainment and business
services, small firms demand long hours and pay scant attention
to labour standards.

Two years ago, Tara Cleveland, now 25, got a job as a Web 6
page designer in a brand new dot-com business, so new that
they were working out of the owner's living room for a while. "I
worked 40 hours a week but they wanted more. They expected us
to stay late every night and on weekends, too. They were never
prepared to pay overtime." Cleveland, whose mother is a social
activist, refused the overtime and still kept the job. But "most
kids don't know what their rights are and they're just grateful
to have an interesting job," notes Cleveland.

If working long hours makes us unhappy and unhealthy, 7
why do we do it? Money is the obvious answer but, according to
StatsCan, most of the one-fifth of Canadians who worked
overtime during the first quarter of 1997 did so for free.

Chris Schenk, research director of the Ontario Federation of 8
Labour, says downsizing in the recession of the early 1990s meant
fewer people had to do more work. "It became an expectation
to work long hours and take work home, even in the broader
public sector," he explains. Just ask nurses or teachers how their
workload has increased.

Given these time stresses, you'd think that the length of a 9
workweek would be a major issue in Canada, but it wasn't even

mentioned in the recent federal election. Quebec—where the reality of women's lives seems to get more attention—has just reduced its legal workweek from 44 hours to 40 hours, joining four other provinces with a 40-hour week. But Ontario is going in the opposite direction with a proposal to extend the workweek to 60 hours if the employee and the employer agree.

In Europe, people want to live and work differently. France 10 adopted a legal 35-hour workweek last February. Norway just added a fifth week of paid vacation, Denmark a sixth. Last spring, the Netherlands passed a law permitting people who want to work a shorter week to request it from their employer, with the onus on the employer to explain why it couldn't be implemented. The same law permits part-time workers to request longer hours.

So what can we do about the situation at home? I'm going to 11 start booking time off in my agenda. We can challenge the culture of overwork by refusing overtime whenever possible and refusing to take work home. But individual action goes only so far. Women have to make overwork a major public policy issue. Let's look to Europe for the example and start demanding that the culture of work reflect the best interests of women and our families.

UNDERSTANDING DETAILS

1. What is "the culture of overwork"? According to Rebick, who and what is creating it?
2. What are the consequences of overwork?
3. How do the standards around working time in Europe compare with those in North America?

ANALYZING MEANING

1. How significant is the problem of overwork? Who does the culture of overwork affect to the greatest degree?
2. What is Rebick's thesis? What exactly is she advocating? Do you agree with this position? Why or why not?
3. Explain why people continue to work long hours despite the negative effects this behaviour has.

DISCOVERING RHETORICAL STRATEGIES

1. What is Rebick's purpose in writing this essay? Given the original source of this essay, who do you think is her intended audience?

2. In this essay, Rebick frequently uses statistics and quotations from authorities. Explain why she has incorporated these elements. How do they enhance her argument?

3. Is Rebick's essay an appeal primarily to logic, to emotion, or to ethics? Why do you think Rebick has made this choice?

MAKING CONNECTIONS

1. Amy Willard Cross writes about the demands on our time in "Life in the Stopwatch Lane." How do you think that Cross would respond to Rebick's position about the culture of overwork?

2. In "Dead Wrong," Kim Pittaway talks about the intolerance for public grieving and says, "Death makes people uncomfortable and distracts them from their work." How do you think Rebick would respond to this argument? In what way does Pittaway's essay support Rebick's argument?

3. Discuss the relative balance of the logical, emotional, and ethical appeals in the essays by Rebick and by David Suzuki ("The Right Stuff") and Lawrence Solomon ("Too Much Privacy Can Be Hazardous to the Person"). Which author uses logic most? Who relies most heavily on emotion? Whose ethical appeal is the strongest? What do the dominance of these appeals have to do with the subject matter of each essay?

IDEAS FOR DISCUSSION/WRITING

Preparing to Write

Write freely about changing societal expectations. How do you go about shifting attitudes about an issue such as overwork? What kind of action is appropriate to encourage a change in attitudes or public policy? What kind of action is effective? Can an individual make a difference? Why or why not?

Choosing a Topic

1. Write a letter to the premier of your province or the prime minister of Canada about the problem of overwork. Be clear about what actions you are responding to and what you expect from your reader.

2. Rebick argues that we need to reduce the average workweek, but she mentions a proposal in one province to extend the work-

week to 60 hours. In a coherent essay, persuade your colleagues that overwork is not a serious social problem and that the work-week should be lengthened.

3. Rebick concludes her essay with a call to action: "Let's look to Europe for the example and start demanding that the culture of work reflect the best interest of women and our families." Write an essay in which you either advance this argument or justify the culture of overwork that Rebick identifies.

David Suzuki

▪ □ ▪

THE RIGHT STUFF

From Vancouver, British Columbia, David Suzuki (1936–) is a geneticist, writer, broadcaster, educator, parent, and environmentalist. Suzuki received his university education from Amherst College, the University of Chicago, and the University of PEI. He began teaching zoology at the University of British Columbia in 1969 and has appeared on radio and television as the host of *Quirks and Quarks* and *The Nature of Things*. Suzuki's writings on science and the environment have appeared in columns in the *Globe and Mail* and the *Toronto Star* as well as many books, which include *Genethics* (1989), his *Looking at...* series for children, *It's a Matter of Survival* (1990), *Wisdom of the Elders* (1992), and *Inventing the Future* (1989), a collection of previously published essays from which "The Right Stuff" is taken.

Preparing to Read

As you prepare to read this essay, think about your associations with high school. What positive memories do you have of high school? What things would you rather not recall? What people do you remember from high school? Teachers? Friends? What was the building like? Did you attend a public school? A private school? A separate school? An alternative school? Are there any classes that stand out in your recollections? What was the most important thing that you learned in high school?

Years ago I read a marvellous book entitled *Is There Life After* 1
High School? In spite of the title, it was a serious comparison of
human relationships at different stages in life. The study revealed
that impressions formed in high school are more vivid and indelible than those formed at any other time in life. The author described how people in their seventies and eighties who had
difficulty remembering most of their associates in university and
at work would instantly recall most of their classmates by name
while leafing through their high school yearbooks. In the analysis
of the author, high school society is divided into two broad categories, the innies and the outies. The innies were football and basketball players and cheerleaders who set the whole social climate
of the school. The outies were all the rest, the majority of the student body, most of whom lusted to be innies. I sure hope it's different today because that description fits my recollection of high
school and it was awful. But I'm getting off the point.

Those high school memories are so intense because that is the 2
time when puberty occurs. The enormous physiological changes
that take place in response to the surge of new hormones through
the body completely transform both anatomy and mind. I always
feel kids lose about half their intelligence for a few years in response
to that blast of hormones. Relationships change radically. Suddenly
parents change from protective, loving gods to dictatorial wardens
incessantly imposing restrictions and criticizing everything. A
pubescent teenager perceives adults and members of their own
age group with totally new eyes. It's not surprising then that
attitudes to school, courses and studying also change dramatically.

In the early 1970s, I visited a small northern town to judge a 3
science fair. Back then, it was a tough town with a transient
population of men working in the oil fields and a high proportion
of Native people. The night I arrived, I dropped in to the bar of
the motel and a man came over and said, "I hear you're going
to talk to the students at the high school tomorrow." When I
affirmed it, he shocked me by adding, "They'll kill you. I'm the
science teacher there and I can tell you that all they think about
is sex, drugs and cars. They'll tear you apart."

Well, he really scared me. I immediately formed images of a 4
blackboard jungle, filled with switchblades and drug-crazed
hoods. The next day when I walked into that auditorium, it was
with great trepidation. There were 400 teenagers in the gym,

about a third of them Indians. They looked pretty normal, but I had been warned and knew they were just biding their time before turning into raving animals.

So I began by saying, "I'm a geneticist. I know that you're 5 basically walking gonads, so I'm going to talk about sex." That opener caught their attention. I started with the beginning of human life by describing eggs and sperm, talked about chromosomes and the X and Y basis for sex determination and went on from there. The kids were dead silent and attentive. I talked for about an hour and then opened it up for questions. I was astounded at the range of topics we covered. We discussed drugs and chromosomes, test-tube babies, amniocentesis and cloning. The principal finally had to step in to dismiss the group an hour and a half after that.

Science education in high school should be designed around 6 sex and human biology. It's a shock every time I hear that a school board has caved in to pressure and kept sex education out of schools. I am sure opponents of sex ed have no intention of providing that information to their own children. In a time of easy access to the most explicit films, videos, magazines and books, who can believe it's better to keep youngsters ignorant by denying them some accurate facts? They're going to get all kinds of anecdotal, apocryphal stuff about sex from their peer group, anyway.

By starting their instruction with human sexuality and 7 reproduction, teachers will be able to go on to practically every other subject in science. It just takes a hard look from a different perspective. After all, we are not trying to train future scientists (only a small percentage of high school graduates will go on in science), yet all of them will be able to use information that science can provide for the rest of their lives. And you can bet they will remember those lessons vividly in their life after high school.

UNDERSTANDING DETAILS

1. Why, according to Suzuki, are "impressions formed in high school more vivid and indelible than those formed at any other time in life"?
2. What is Suzuki's position on sex education in schools?
3. What changes in kids does Suzuki attribute to puberty?

ANALYZING MEANING

1. What arguments does Suzuki provide to support his position on high school science education? Are these arguments convincing? Why or why not?
2. What accounted for the reaction that Suzuki got from the students at the high school he visited? Was the science teacher right in saying, "all they think about is sex, drugs and cars" (paragraph 3)?
3. Why is sex education in schools such a controversial issue?

DISCOVERING RHETORICAL STRATEGIES

1. What do you think the writer's purpose is in "The Right Stuff"? Where does Suzuki state his thesis?
2. Characterize the tone that Suzuki adopts in this essay. What words and phrases does he use to create this tone?
3. What is the dominant type of appeal in this essay?

MAKING CONNECTIONS

1. Suzuki is presenting a somewhat controversial position in his essay as is Lawrence Solomon ("Too Much Privacy Can Be Hazardous to the Person"). Compare and contrast the strategies that these two writers have used to advance their positions and make their audiences more receptive to their views.
2. The incorporation of humour is one of the strategies that Suzuki uses in his essay. Compare and contrast his use of humour with that of Evan Solomon ("The Babar Factor") and Drew Hayden Taylor ("Pretty Like a White Boy").
3. Suzuki's essay presents a strategy for making scientific topics appealing and interesting to a lay audience. How do you think Maureen Littlejohn ("You Are a Contract Painkiller"), Michael Clugston ("Twice Struck"), or Stanley Coren ("Dogs and Monsters") would respond to Suzuki's strategy?

IDEAS FOR DISCUSSION/WRITING

Preparing to Write

Write freely about learning about sex. What was your primary source of information? How did you learn about sex? What role did your parents play? Your peers? The school? The church? What did you learn from films, videos, magazines, or books? Was there anything that you learned that you discovered later to be untrue? What was the source of that information? What is your primary source of information about sex now?

Choosing a Topic

1. Write a letter to your school board either advocating or arguing against Suzuki's suggestion for high school science curriculum design.
2. Write a proposal for a department head of your old high school proposing a way to make another subject area (other than science) relevant and interesting. Make sure you explain your idea clearly and provide adequate justification to make the changes.
3. The inclusion of many works of fiction in the high school curriculum has been challenged based on the sexual content. Find one book that has been subject to censorship challenge and write a letter to the editor of the paper expressing your views on whether or not such a book should be rejected from the classroom.

■▬▬▬▬▬▬▬▬▬▬▬▬▬□▬▬▬▬▬▬▬▬▬▬▬▬▬■

Naheed Mustafa

■□■

MY BODY IS MY OWN BUSINESS

Naheed Mustafa chose to voice her opinion about the traditional Muslim dress for women in an essay published in the "Facts and Arguments" column of the *Globe and Mail*. A graduate of the University of Toronto with a degree in political science and history, who went to study journalism at Ryerson University, Mustafa makes the point in her essay that she grew up in Canada, although she has moved to Pakistan since her article was originally published in 1993. Since its original publication, this essay has been reproduced in several anthologies and several websites.

Preparing to Read

In this essay, Naheed Mustafa discusses the ways in which appearance and clothing are related to the oppression of women. Before you read her essay, think about feminism and the oppression of women. What is feminism? Do you consider yourself a feminist? Why or why not? Traditionally, what aspects of society have oppressed women? Are there still barriers that women face today? How does the situation in Canada compare to that of other countries? What is the relationship between women's physical appearance and their oppression?

■───■

I often wonder whether people see me as a radical, fundamentalist 1
Muslim terrorist packing an AK-47 assault rifle inside my jean jacket. Or maybe they see me as the poster girl for oppressed womanhood everywhere. I'm not sure which it is.

I get the whole gamut of strange looks, stares and covert 2
glances. You see, I wear the *hijab*, a scarf that covers my head, neck and throat. I do this because I am a Muslim woman who believes her body is her own private concern.

Young Muslim women are reclaiming the *hijab*, reinterpreting 3
it in light of its original purpose—to give back to women ultimate control of their own bodies.

The Koran teaches us that men and women are equal, that 4
individuals should not be judged according to gender, beauty, wealth or privilege. The only thing that makes one person better than another is her or his character.

Nonetheless, people have a difficult time relating to me. After 5
all, I'm young, Canadian born and raised, university-educated—why would I do this to myself, they ask.

Strangers speak to me in loud, slow English and often appear 6
to be playing charades. They politely inquire how I like living
in Canada and whether or not the cold bothers me. If I'm in the
right mood, it can be very amusing.

But why would I, a woman with all the advantages of a 7
North American upbringing, suddenly, at 21, want to cover
myself so that with the *hijab* and the other clothes I choose to
wear, only my face and hands show?

Because it gives me freedom. 8

Women are taught from early childhood that their worth is 9
proportional to their attractiveness. We feel compelled to pursue
abstract notions of beauty, half realizing that such a pursuit is futile.

When women reject this form of oppression, they face ridicule 10
and contempt. Whether it's women who refuse to wear makeup
or to shave their legs or to expose their bodies, society, both men
and women, have trouble dealing with them.

In the Western world, the *hijab* has come to symbolize either 11
forced silence or radical, unconscionable militancy. Actually, it's
neither. It is simply a woman's assertion that judgment of her
physical person is to play no role whatsoever in social interaction.

Wearing the *hijab* has given me freedom from constant attention 12
to my physical self. Because my appearance is not subjected to
public scrutiny, my beauty, or perhaps lack of it, has been removed
from the realm of what can legitimately be discussed.

No one knows whether my hair looks as if I just stepped out 13
of a salon, whether or not I can pinch an inch, or even if I have
unsightly stretch marks. And because no one knows, no one cares.

Feeling that one has to meet the impossible male standards 14
of beauty is tiring and often humiliating. I should know, I spent
my entire teenage years trying to do it. I was a borderline bulimic
and spent a lot of money I didn't have on potions and lotions in
hopes of becoming the next Cindy Crawford.

The definition of beauty is ever-changing; waifish is good, 15
waifish is bad, athletic is good—sorry, athletic is bad. Narrow
hips? Great. Narrow hips? Too bad.

Women are not going to achieve equality with the right to 16
bare their breasts in public, as some people would like to have
you believe. That would only make us party to our own
objectification. True equality will be had only when women don't
need to display themselves to get attention and won't need to
defend their decision to keep their bodies to themselves.

UNDERSTANDING DETAILS

1. Why does Mustafa tell us that she has chosen to wear the hijab? What does the hijab represent to her?

ANALYZING MEANING

1. Mustafa claims that "because no one knows [details of her physical appearance], no one cares" (paragraph 13). How would someone with an opposing viewpoint respond to this argument?
2. What does wearing the hijab say about the respective roles of men and women, according to Mustafa's view?

DISCOVERING RHETORICAL STRATEGIES

1. How would you characterize Mustafa's audience?
2. Mustafa has personal characteristics that give her credibility in dealing with this subject. What aspects of Mustafa's life strengthen her argument?
3. Mustafa uses figurative language to help convey her point effectively. Find three examples of figurative language (e.g., metaphor, simile, alliteration) in each of these essays. What effect do these language choices have on each essay?

MAKING CONNECTIONS

1. Like Mustafa, Gloria Steinem ("The Politics of Muscle") and Laura Robinson ("Starving for the Gold") both write about aspects of the appearance of women. On what points do you think these writers would agree on this topic? On which points would they disagree? Explain your answer.

2. Drew Hayden Taylor ("Pretty Like a White Boy") and Cecil Foster ("Why Blacks Get Mad") frequently run into difficult situations as people make assumptions based on their appearance. How is their experience similar to that of Naheed Mustafa? How do their experiences differ?

3. Naheed Mustafa writes about some of the conflicts that arise as two cultures meet. How are the situations they describe similar to the one that Charlotte Gray presents in "The Temple of Hygiene" and that described by Wayson Choy in "I'm a Banana and Proud of It"?

IDEAS FOR DISCUSSION/WRITING

Preparing to Write

Write freely about clothing and the fashion industry. Why do we wear what we wear? What is the purpose of clothing? How do we choose the things that we wear? What does our clothing tell the world about us? Why do fashions change? Why is fashion such a major industry? What factors in our lives dictate the fashion choices we make?

Choosing a Topic

1. Write an essay in which you explain your threshold of tolerance when it comes to practices of various nationalities, religions, or ethnicities. What practices go beyond the realm of those you consider acceptable or tolerable?
2. The imposition of the values of one culture on another is always a difficult issue. In promoting multiculturalism, many immigrants to Canada are encouraged to maintain some traditional practices and lifestyles. Which practices should be maintained from an old culture and which Canadian values should be imposed upon newcomers? Write an essay for a group of newcomers to Canada in which you explain which values or practices are appropriate to maintain, and which Canadian values or practices should replace the ones with which they are familiar. Be sure that you present your argument in a clear, tactful, and diplomatic way.
3. The clothing we choose to wear tells the world a lot about who we are. Write an essay for a fashion magazine in which you explain how the fashion choices you make reflect your lifestyle and values.

CHAPTER 10

DOCUMENTED ESSAYS

■ ■ ■

Reading and Writing from Sources

We use sources every day in both informal and formal situations. We explain the source of a phone message, for example, or we refer to an instructor's comments in class. We use someone else's opinion in an essay, or we quote an expert to prove a point. We cite sources both in speaking and in writing through summary, paraphrase, and direct quotation. Most of your instructors will ask you to write papers using sources so they can see how well you understand the course material. The use of sources in academic papers requires you to understand what you have read and to integrate this reading material with your own opinions and observations—a process that requires a high level of skill in thinking, reading, and writing.

Defining Documented Essays

Documented essays provide you with the opportunity to perform sophisticated and exciting exercises in critical thinking; they draw on the thinking, reading, and writing abilities you have built up over the course of your academic career, and they often require you to put all the rhetorical modes to work at their most analytical level. Documented essays demonstrate the process of analytical thinking at its best in different disciplines.

In the academic world, documented essays are also called *research papers, library papers, and term papers*. Documented essays are generally written for one of three reasons: (1) to **report**, (2) to **interpret**, or (3) to **analyze**.

The most straightforward, uncomplicated type of documented essay **reports** information, as in a survey of problems that children have in preschool. The second type of documented essay both presents and **interprets** its findings. It examines a number of different views on a specific issue and weighs these views as it draws its own conclusions. A topic that falls into this category would be whether children who have attended preschool are more sociable than those who have not. After considering evidence on both sides, the writer would draw his or her own conclusions on this topic. A documented essay that **analyzes** a subject presents a hypothesis, tests the hypothesis, and analyzes or evaluates its conclusions. This type of essay calls for the most advanced form of critical thinking. It might look, for example, at the reasons preschool children are more or less socially flexible than non-preschool children. At its most proficient, this type of writing requires a sophisticated degree of evaluation that forces you to judge your reading, evaluate your sources, and ultimately scrutinize your own reasoning ability as the essay takes shape.

Each of these types of documented essays calls for a higher level of thinking, and each evolves from the previous category. In other words, interpreting requires some reporting, and analyzing draws on both reporting and interpreting.

In the following paragraph, a student reports, interprets, analyzes, and uses sources to document the problem of solid waste in the United States. Notice how the student writer draws her readers into the essay with a commonly used phrase about America and then questions the validity of its meaning. The student's opinions give shape to the paragraph, while her use of sources helps identify the problem and support her contentions.

> "America the Beautiful" is a phrase used to describe the many wonders of nature found throughout our country. America's natural beauty will fade, however, if solutions to our solid waste problems are not discovered soon. America is a rich nation socially, economically, and politically. But these very elements may be the cause of Americans' wastefulness. Americans now generate approximately 160 million tons of solid waste a year—3 1/2 pounds per person per day. We live in a consumer society where convenience, ready-to-use, and throwaway are words that spark the consumer's attention (Cook 60). However, many of the products associated with these words create a large part of our problem with

solid waste (Grossman 39). We are running out of space for our garbage. The people of America are beginning to produce responses to this problem. Are we too late? A joint effort between individuals, businesses, government industries, and local, state, and federal governments is necessary to establish policies and procedures to combat this waste war. The problem requires not one solution, but a combination of solutions involving technologies and people working together to provide a safe and healthy environment for themselves and future generations.

Reading and Writing Documented Essays

Reading and writing documented essays involves the skillful integration of two complex operations: research and writing. Reading documented essays critically means understanding the material and evaluating the sources as you proceed. Writing documented essays includes reading and understanding sources on the topic you have chosen and then combining this reading with your own conclusions. The two skills are, essentially, mirror images of one another.

How to Read Documented Essays

Preparing to Read. You should approach a documented essay in much the same way that you approach any essay. First, take a few minutes to look at the preliminary material for the selection: What can you learn from scanning Barbara Ehrenreich's essay ("The Ecstasy of War") or from reading the synopsis in the Rhetorical Table of Contents? What does Marilyn Dahl's title prepare you to read? And what questions do you have about "the ecstacy of war" before you read Ehrenreich's essay?

Also, you should learn as much as you can from the authors' biographies: What is Ehrenreich's interest in war? What biographical details prepare us for her approach to this topic? Who was the original audience for her essay? What is Dahl's background? Does she have the proper qualifications to write about the depiction of disabled people by the media?

Another important part of preparing to read a documented essay is surveying the sources cited. Turn to the end of the essay, and look at the sources. What publications does Ehrenreich draw from? Do you recognize any of the authorities that Dahl cites? Are these books and magazines well respected?

Last, before you read these essays, try to generate some ideas on the topics so you can participate as fully as possible in your reading. The Preparing to Read questions will get you ready for this task. Then, try to speculate further on the topic of the essay: What is the connection for Ehrenreich between war and ecstasy? What does this relationship tell us about human nature in general? What do you want to know from Dahl about disabilities and the media? Why do you think this topic has become such a major social issue?

Reading. As you react to the material in this chapter, you should respond to both the research and the writing. Record your responses as you read the essay for the first time: What are your reactions to the information you are reading? Are the sources appropriate? How well do they support the author's main points? Use the preliminary material before each essay to help you create a framework for your responses to it: Who was Dahl's primary audience when her essay was first published? In what ways is the tone of her essay appropriate for that audience? What motivated Ehrenreich to publish her argument on war? Do you find it convincing? Your main job at this stage is to determine the author's primary assertion (thesis statement), note the sources the author cites to support this thesis, and begin to ask yourself questions about the essay so you can respond critically to your reading. In addition, take a look at the questions after the selection to make certain you are comprehending the major ideas of the essay.

Rereading. As you reread this documented essay, take some time to become aware of the difference between fact and opinion, to weigh and evaluate the evidence brought to bear on the arguments, to consider the sources the writer uses, to judge the interpretation of the facts cited, to determine what the writer has omitted, and to confirm your own views on the issues at hand. All these skills demand the use of critical thinking strategies at their most sophisticated level.

You need to approach this type of argument with an inquiring mind, asking questions and looking for answers as you read the essay. Be especially conscious of the appeals (logical, emotional, and ethical) at work in the essay (see Chapter 9), and take note of other rhetorical strategies that support the author's main argument.

Also, be aware of your own thought processes as you sort facts from opinions. Know where you stand personally in relation to each side of the issues here.

For a list of guidelines for the entire reading process, see the checklists on pages 15–16 of the Introduction.

How to Write Documented Essays

Preparing to Write. Just as with any writing assignment, you should begin the task of writing a documented essay by exploring and limiting your topic. In this case, however, you draw on other sources to help you with this process. You should seek out both primary and secondary sources related to your topic. **Primary sources** are works of literature, historical documents, letters, diaries, speeches, eyewitness accounts, and your own experiments, observations, and conclusions; **secondary sources** explain and analyze information from other sources. Any librarian can help you search for both types of sources related to your topic.

After you have found a few sources on your general topic, you should scan and evaluate what you have discovered so you can limit your topic further. Depending on the required length of your essay, you want to find a topic broad enough to be researched, established enough so that you can find sources on it , and significant enough to demonstrate your abilities to grapple with ideas and draw conclusions. The Preparing to Write questions can help you generate and focus your ideas.

Once you have established these limitations, you might try writing a tentative thesis. At this point, asking a question and attempting to find an answer are productive. But you should keep in mind that your thesis is likely to be revised several times as the range of your knowledge changes and as your paper takes different turns while you research and write. Then, decide on a purpose and audience for your essay.

Once your tentative thesis is formed, you should read your sources for ideas and take detailed notes on your reading. These notes will probably fall into one of four categories: (1) *summary*— a condensed statement of someone else's thoughts or observations; (2) *paraphrase*—a restatement in your own words of someone else's ideas or observations; (3) *direct quotations from sources*; or (4) *a combination of these forms*. Be sure to make a distinction in your notes between actual quotations and paraphrases or summaries. Also, record the sources of all your notes—especially of quoted, summarized, and paraphrased material—that you may need to cite in your essay.

As you gather information, you should consider keeping a "research journal" where you can record your own opinions, interpretations, and analyses in response to your reading. This journal should be separate from your notes on sources. It is the place where you can make your own discoveries in relation to your topic by jotting down thoughts and relationships among ideas you are exposed to, by keeping a record of sources you read and others you want to pursue, by tracking and developing your own ideas and theories, and by clarifying your thinking on an issue.

Finally, before you write your first draft, you might want to write an informal working outline for your own information. Such an exercise can help you check the range of your coverage and the order and development of your ideas. With an outline, you can readily see where you need more information, less information, or more solid sources. Try to be flexible, however. This outline may change dramatically as your essay develops.

Writing. Writing the first draft of a documented essay is your chance to discover new insights and to find important connections between ideas that you may not be aware of yet. This draft is your opportunity to demonstrate that you understand the issue at hand and your sources on three increasingly difficult levels— literal, interpretive, and analytical; that you can organize your material effectively; that you can integrate your sources (in the form of summaries, paraphrases, or quotations) with your opinions; and that you can document (that is, cite) your sources.

To begin this process, look again at your thesis statement and your working outline, and adjust them to represent any new discoveries you have made as you read your sources and wrote in your research journal. Then, organize your research notes and information in some logical fashion.

When you begin to draft your paper, write the sections of the essay that you feel most comfortable about first. Throughout the essay, feature your own point of view and integrate summaries, paraphrases, and quotations from other sources into your analysis. Each point you make should be a section of your paper consisting of your own conclusion and your support for that conclusion (in the form of facts, examples, summaries, paraphrases, and quotations). Remember that the primary reason for doing such an assignment is to let you demonstrate your ability to synthesize material, draw your own conclusions, and analyze your sources and your own reasoning.

A documented paper usually blends three types of material:

1. *Common knowledge, such as the places and dates of events (even if you have to look them up).*

   Example: Neil Armstrong and Edwin Aldrin first walked on the moon on July 20, 1969.

2. *Your own thoughts and observations.*

   Example: Armstrong and Aldrin's brief walk on the moon's surface was the beginning of a new era in the U.S. space program.

3. *Someone else's thoughts and observations.*

   Example: President Richard Nixon reacted to the moonwalk in a telephone call to the astronauts: "For one priceless moment in the history of man all the people on this earth are truly one— one in their pride in what you have done and one in our prayers that you will return safely to earth."

Of these three types of information, you must document or cite your exact source only for the third type. Negligence in citing your sources, whether purposeful or accidental, is called *plagiarism*, which comes from a Latin word meaning "kidnapper." Among student writers, plagiarism usually takes one of three forms: (1) using words from another source without quotation marks; (2) using someone else's ideas in the form of a summary or paraphrase without citing your source; and (3) using someone else's paper as your own.

Avoiding plagiarism is quite simple: You just need to remember to acknowledge the sources of ideas or wording that you are using to support your own contentions. Acknowledging your sources also gives you credit for the reading you have done and for the ability you have developed to use sources to support your observations and conclusions.

Documentation styles vary from discipline to discipline. Ask your instructor about the particular documentation style he or she wants you to follow. The most common styles are the Modern Language Association (MLA) style, used in humanities courses, and the American Psychological Association (APA) style, used in behavioural sciences and science courses. (See any writing handbook for more details on documentation formats.)

The World Wide Web is a newer source of information for your research papers. Electronic sources include online journals and magazines, CD-ROMs, software programs, newsletters, discussion groups, bulletin boards, gopher sites, and e-mail. But, just as with sources in more traditional media, not all electronic sources are equally accurate and reliable. Based on your topic, you need to exercise your best judgment and get your instructor's help in assessing the most useful online sites for your purposes. If you use electronic sources in any of your papers, remember that you have two goals in any citation: (1) to acknowledge the author and (2) to help the reader locate the material. Then you should check the MLA or APA home pages for their current guidelines for online documentation: The URL for the Modern Language Association is **www.mla.org**, and for the American Psychological Association, **www.apa.org**.

Even though documentation styles vary somewhat from one discipline to another, the basic concept behind documentation is the same in all disciplines: You must give proper credit to other writers by acknowledging the sources of the summaries, paraphrases, and quotations that you use to support the topics in your documented paper. Once you grasp this basic concept and accept it, you will have no trouble avoiding plagiarism.

Rewriting. To rewrite your documented essay, you should play the role of your readers and impartially evaluate your argument and the sources you have used as evidence in that argument. To begin with, revise your thesis to represent all the discoveries you made as you wrote your first draft. Then, look for problems in logic throughout the essay; you might even develop an outline at this point to help evaluate your reasoning:

1. Are the essay's assertions clear? Are they adequately supported?
2. Are other points of view recognized and examined?
3. Does the organization of your paper further your assertions/argument?
4. Have you removed irrelevant material?

Next, check your documentation style:

1. Is your source material (either summarized, paraphrased, or quoted) presented fairly and accurately?
2. Have you rechecked the citations for all the sources in your paper?
3. Do you introduce the sources in your paper when appropriate?

4. Are your sources in the proper format according to your instructor's guidelines (MLA, APA, or another)?

Then, proofread carefully. Finally, prepare your paper to be submitted to your instructor:

1. Have you followed your instructor's guidelines for your title page, margins, page numbers, tables, and abstracts?
2. Have you prepared an alphabetical list of your sources for the end of your paper?

Any additional guidance you may need as you write and revise your documented essays is provided on pages 26–27 of the Introduction.

Student Essay: Documentation at Work

The following student essay uses documented sources to support its conclusions and observations about our eating habits today. First, the writer creates a profile of carnivorous species in contrast to human beings. She then goes on to discuss the harsh realities connected with eating meat. After recognizing and refuting some opposing views, this student writer ends her paper with her own evaluation of the situation and a list of some famous vegetarians. Throughout the essay, the student writer carefully supports her principal points with summaries, paraphrases, and quotations from other sources. Notice that she uses the MLA documentation style and closes the paper with an alphabetical list of "Works Cited."

Food for Thought

Background information — The next time you sit down to a nice steak dinner, pause for a moment to consider whether you are biologically programmed to eat meat. Unlike carnivores, such as lions and tigers, with claws and sharp front teeth allowing them to tear and eat raw flesh, humans are omnivores, with fingers that can pluck fruits and grains and flat teeth that can grind these vegetable foods. To digest their meals, Common knowledge — carnivores have an acidic saliva and a very strong hydrochloric acid digestive fluid. In contrast, we humans have an alkaline saliva, and our digestive fluids are only one-tenth as potent as those of carnivores. Common knowledge — Moreover, carnivores have an intestinal tract barely three times their body length, which allows for faster elimination of rotting flesh; humans have an intestinal tract eight to twelve times our

Paraphrase of secondary source body length, better enabling us to digest plant nutrients. These marked physiological distinctions clearly suggest that carnivorous animals and humans are adapted to very different kinds of foods (Diamond and Diamond, *Fit for Life II* 239). What happens, then, *Citation (MLA form)*

Thesis when we eat flesh? <u>The effects of a meat-based diet are far-reaching: massive suffering of the animals killed and eaten, a myriad of diseases in humans, and a devastating effect on world ecology.</u>

Student's first conclusion <u>The atrocities committed daily to provide meat should be enough to make a meat-based diet completely unconscionable.</u> According to Peter Singer, of People for the Ethical Treatment of *Summary of secondary source* Animals (PETA), every year several hundred million cattle, pigs, and sheep and 3 billion chickens are slaughtered to provide food for humans (*Animal Liberation* 92). That is equal to 6278 animals every minute of every day—and those are just the ones that make it to the slaughterhouse. Over 500 000 animals die in transit each *Support for conclusion #1* year (Singer, *Animal Liberation* 150).

Paraphrase of secondary source (fact) A slaughterhouse is not a pretty sight. Anywhere from 50 to 90 percent of the cattle are slaughtered in a "kosher" manner *Summary of secondary source* (Robbins 142). "Kosher" sounds innocent enough, but what it actually means is that the animal must be "healthy and moving" at the time of death. This requires the animals to be fully conscious as "a heavy chain is clamped around one of their rear legs; then they are jerked off their feet and hang upside down" for anywhere from two to five minutes, usually twisting in agony with a broken leg, while they are moved down the conveyer belt to be slaughtered (Robbins 140–41).

Student's opinion The pain doesn't start at the time of slaughter, however, for most of these animals, but rather at birth. An in-depth look at the animal most slaughtered by people, the chicken, reveals particularly horrendous treatment. Chickens are used in two ways: for their flesh and for their eggs. For egg manufacturers, the one-half *Examples to support opinion* million male chicks born every day are useless, so they are immediately thrown into garbage bags and left to suffocate. When *Paraphrase of secondary source (opinion)* you consider the life of their female counterparts, however, perhaps such brutal treatment is a blessing (Robbins 54).

Paraphrase of secondary source (facts) Chickens naturally belong to a flock with a specific pecking order. They seem to enjoy open spaces to stretch their wings as they scratch around, dust-bathe, and build nests for their eggs *Paraphrase of secondary source (facts)* (Singer, *Animal Liberation* 109). Today, however, chickens are housed in wire-mesh cages suspended over a trench to collect droppings. The typical cage is 30 by 45 cm, holding four or five hens for their entire productive life, which is at least a year or more (Mason in Singer, *Defense* 91). This overcrowding results in such high levels of stress that the hens resort to pecking each other's feathers out and to cannibalism (Singer, *Animal Liberation* 98). Rather than incur the expense of increasing space to alleviate these conditions, chicken farmers have routinely adopted the practice of debeaking the hens by slicing a hot knife through their highly sensitive beak tissue (Singer, *Animal Liberation* 99). Another result of this overcrowding is that the hens' toenails get tangled in the bottom wires of the cages; after some time the flesh grows onto the wire. The solution to this problem has become to cut off the chick's toes within a day or two of birth (Robbins 61). Conditions for other farm animals are equally despicable (Singer, *Defense*). *[margin: Analysis from secondary source] [margin: Paraphrase of secondary sources (facts)] [margin left: Paraphrase of secondary source (opinion)]*

While we would like to assume the animals we eat are healthy at the time of butchering, this is often not the case. Most veal calves, for example, are near death from anemia when sent to the butcher (Diamond and Diamond, *Fit for Life II* 238). Inspections have revealed leukosis (cancer) in 90 percent of the chickens (Robbins 67), pneumonia rates of 80 percent and stomach ulcers of 53 percent in pigs (Robbins 94). Salmonellosis is found in 90 percent of the chickens dressed and ready to be purchased (Robbins 303). *[margin: Student's opinion] [margin: Examples from secondary sources]*

How can the factory farming industry justify its behaviour? The answer boils down to money, for factory farming has become an incredibly huge business, and meat producers can't afford to be sentimental. As shown by USDA Economic Indicators for the Farm Sector, in 1988 the United States had cash receipts totalling over $150 billion from farm marketing (*State Financial Summary* 151) and nearly $80 billion from livestock and livestock products (153). As Fred Haley, head of a poultry farm with nearly 250 000 hens, has stated, "The object of producing eggs is to make money. When we forget this objective, we have forgotten what it is all about" (qtd. in Robbins 67). Cattle auctioneer Henry Pace has a similar comment about the treatment of cattle: "We believe we can be most efficient by not being emotional. We are a business, not a humane society, and our job is to sell merchandise at a profit. It's no different from selling paper clips or refrigerators" (qtd. in Robbins 104). *[margin: Student's opinion] [margin: Paraphrase of secondary sources] [margin: Quotation from secondary source] [margin: Quotation from secondary source]*

Even if we, like the industry leaders, could turn a cold heart to the plight of our fellow creatures, we would still find many reasons to warrant a vegetarian diet, beginning with our own health. Recapping just a few of the hundreds of studies that link diet to disease, we might consider the following: *[margin: Student's second conclusion]*

Paraphrase of secondary sources (facts) —A study of nearly 90 000 American women published in the *New England Journal of Medicine* reports that daily pork, lamb, or beef eaters have a 250 percent greater likelihood of developing colon cancer than people who consume these foods once a month or less ("Red Meat Alert"). *Support for second conclusion*

—The *Journal of the American Medical Association* stated that a vegetarian diet could prevent 97 percent of coronary occlusions (Robbins 247).

—Scientists now routinely screen cattle workers for BIV, a disease that "shares about 35 percent of its genetic makeup with HIV," the human AIDS retrovirus ("Cattle's Link with AIDS" 19).

Summary of secondary source Other equally shocking residual health problems associated with a meat diet are also being documented. For instance, people tend to think that vegetarians are at high risk for pesticide poisoning, but according to the EPA's *Pesticides Monitoring Journal*, most pesticides in the American diet come from foods originating from animals. Studies have shown that 95 to 99 percent of toxic chemicals in the North American diet come from meat, fish, and animal products (Robbins 315). These same pesticides are ending up in the milk of lactating mothers. A similar study in the *New England Journal of Medicine* showed that the breast milk of vegetarian mothers has contamination levels only 1 to 2 percent of the average (Robbins 345). Not only does vegetarian breast milk have strikingly lower levels of contamination, it also has higher levels of essential elements, such as selenium (Debski et al. 215). *Paraphrase of secondary sources (facts)*

Student's question But don't we need a lot of protein to be strong and healthy? The RDA for protein is 56 grams (just under 2 ounces) per day (Diamond and Diamond, *Fit for Life* 88). People seem to think that meat is the best (or the only) way to get protein, but think about this: Some of the world's strongest animals—elephants, horses, and gorillas—eat principally fruits, grain, or grass (Diamond, *Fit for Life* 89–90). Lest you believe that humans must eat meat to be strong and healthy, consider the following: Edwin Moses, undefeated in the 400-metre hurdles for eight years, is a vegetarian; Andreas Cahling, 1980 Mr. International Body Builder, is a vegetarian (Robbins 160–61); and Dave Scott, Ironman Triathlon winner four times (no one else has won it more than once), is a vegetarian (Robbins 158). In study after study, the consumption of protein is linked not with health but with such illnesses as heart disease, hypertension, various forms of cancer, arthritis, and osteoporosis (Diamond and Diamond, *Fit for Life* 87). *Paraphrase of secondary source (fact)*

Paraphrase of secondary source (fact)

Examples that answer protein question

Examples that answer protein question

The effects of meat diets go beyond causing human disease

Student's third conclusion and death. <u>Perhaps the most frightening legacy being left by America's dietary ritual is just now being realized, and that is the profound ecological impact factory farming is having on our planet.</u> Every 10 seconds, one hectare of forest is cleared in *Support for third conclusion* America, and one estimate is that 87 percent is cleared for either livestock grazing or growing livestock feed (Robbins 361). According to Christopher Uhl of the Pennsylvania State University *Paraphrase of secondary sources (facts)* Department of Biology and Geoffrey Parker of the Institute of Ecosystem Studies, 5m^2 of forest in Central America is lost for each hamburger eaten (642).

Student's opinion Forests are not all that we are sacrificing. Local governments are constantly calling for water conservation, yet over 50 percent of all water used in America goes into grain production for livestock (Robbins 367). According to one study, the water required to *Paraphrase of secondary sources (facts)* feed a meat eater for one day is 4,000 gallons, but it is only 1,200 gallons for a lacto-ovo (dairy and egg eating) vegetarian and 300 gallons for a vegan (one who consumes no animal-derived products) (Robbins 367). Not only is the vast amount of water wasted through a meat-based diet outrageous, but the added cost of controlling animal waste must also be taken into account. One cow produces sixteen times as much waste as one human (Robbins 372), and cattle waste produces ten times the water pollution that human waste does (Robbins 373).

Student's opinion A third loss is even more serious than the losses of forests and water. This year, 60 million people will die of starvation, yet in America, we feed 80 percent of our corn and 95 percent of our oats to farm animals. The feed given to cattle alone, excluding pigs and chickens, would feed double the population of humans worldwide (Robbins 352). Three and one-quarter acres of farm- *Paraphrase of secondary sources (facts)* land are needed to provide meat for one person per year. A lacto-ovo vegetarian can be fed from just one-half acre per year; a vegan needs only one-sixth of an acre. This means twenty vegans can eat a healthy diet for the same acreage needed to feed just one meat eater. Cutting our meat habit by only 10 percent would provide enough food for all of the 60 million people worldwide who will starve this year (Robbins 352–53).

Quotation from secondary source As John Robbins, who relinquished his inheritance of the largest ice cream company in America, Baskin-Robbins, said, "We live in a crazy time, when people who make food choices that are healthy and compassionate are often considered weird, while people are considered normal whose eating habits promote disease and are dependent on enormous suffering" (305).

Student's final remarks   With all the devastation the average North American diet is creating, we must begin to take responsibility for the consequences of our actions. Let us follow in the footsteps of such famous vegetarians as Charles Darwin, Leonardo da Vinci, Albert Einstein, Sir Isaac Newton, Plato, Pythagoras, Socrates, and Tolstoy (Parham 185). Every time we sit down to eat, we can choose either to contribute to or to help put an end to this suffering and destruction. Only one move matters, and that is the one we make with our forks.

Works Cited

"Cattle's Link with AIDS." *New Scientist* 8 Oct. 1987:19.

Debski, Bogdan, et al. "Selenium Content and Glutathione Peroxidase Activity of Milk from Vegetarian and Nonvegetarian Women." *Journal of Nutrition* 119 (1989):215–20.

Diamond, Harvey, and Marilyn Diamond. *Fit for Life*. New York: Warner, 1985.

———. *Fit for Life II, Living Health*. New York: Warner, 1987.

Parham, Barbara. *What's Wrong with Eating Meat?* Denver: Ananda Marga, 1981.

"Red Meat Alert." *New Scientist* 22/29 Dec. 1990.

Robbins, John. *Diet for a New America*. Walpole: Stillpoint, 1987.

Singer, Peter. *Animal Liberation: A New Ethics for Our Treatment of Animals*. New York: Hearst, 1975.

———, ed. *In Defense of Animals*. New York: Basil Blackwell, 1985.

State Financial Summary, 1988. Washington: Economic Indicators for the Farm Sector, 1988.

Uhl, Christopher, and Geoffrey Parker. "Our Steak in the Jungle." *Bio Science* 36 (1986):642.

Some Final Thoughts on Documented Essays

The essays that follow offer vigorous exercises in critical thinking. They use a combination of the three different types of persuasive appeals we studied in Chapter 9 (logical, emotional, and ethical) and draw on a wealth of rhetorical modes that we have studied throughout the book. In the first essay, Barbara Ehrenreich illustrates the Modern Language Association documentation style as she uses sources to support her thesis that people do not have a natural instinct to kill. The second essay, by Marilyn Dahl, examines the role the media play in our societal images of disability; its use of sources illustrates the American Psychological Association documentation style. As you read these essays, be aware of the combination of appeals at work, the various rhetorical modes the authors use to further their arguments, and the way each author uses sources to support the topics within the argument.

Documented Essays in Review

Reading Documented Essays

Preparing to Read

1. What assumptions can you make from the essay's title?
2. Can you guess what the general mood of the essay is?
3. What is the essay's purpose and audience?
4. What does the synopsis in the Rhetorical Table of Contents tell you about the essay?
5. What can you learn from the author's biography?
6. Can you guess what the author's point of view toward the subject is?
7. What are your responses to the Preparing to Read questions?

Reading

1. What are your initial reactions to the essay?
2. What is the author's main assertion or thesis?
3. What sources does the author cite to support the thesis?
4. What questions do you have about this topic?
5. Did you preview the questions that follow the essay?

Rereading

1. How does the author use facts and opinions in the essay?
2. Are the sources the writer cites valid and reliable?
3. Are the sources cited in the essay respected in the field?
4. Does the author interpret facts accurately?
5. Has the author omitted any necessary information?
6. What are your responses to the questions after the essay?

Writing Documented Essays

Preparing to Write

1. What are your responses to the Preparing to Write questions?
2. What is your purpose?
3. Who is your audience?

Writing

1. Do you have a thesis statement?
2. Do you use both primary and secondary sources in your essay?
3. Have you organized your material effectively?
4. Have you avoided plagiarism and cited your sources correctly?
5. Do you use the appropriate documentation style?

Rewriting

1. Are the essay's assertions clear? Are they adequately supported?
2. Are other points of view recognized and examined?
3. Does the organization of your paper further your assertions/argument?
4. Have you removed irrelevant material?
5. Is your source material (whether summarized, paraphrased, or quoted) presented fairly and accurately?
6. Have you rechecked the citations for all the sources in your paper?
7. Do you introduce the sources in your paper when appropriate?
8. Are your sources in the proper format according to your instructor's guidelines (MLA, APA, or another)?
9. Have you followed your instructor's guidelines for your title page, margins, page numbers, tables, and abstracts?
10. Have you prepared an alphabetical list of your sources for the end of your paper?

Barbara Ehrenreich

■ □ ■

THE ECSTASY OF WAR

Barbara Ehrenreich (1941–) is a respected author, lecturer, and social commentator with opinions on a wide range of topics. After earning a B.A. from Reed College in chemistry and physics and a Ph.D. from Rockefeller University in cell biology, she turned almost immediately to freelance writing, producing a succession of books and pamphlets on a dazzling array of subjects. Early publications examined student uprisings, health care in America, nurses and midwives, poverty, welfare, economic justice for women, and the sexual politics of disease. Her recent books include *The Worst Year of Our Lives: Irreverent Notes from a Decade of Greed* (1990)—an indictment of the 1980s that was described by the *New York Times* as "elegant, trenchant, savagely angry, morally outraged, and outrageously funny," *Blood Rites: Origins and History of the Passions of War,* and *Nickel and Dimed: On (Not) Getting by in America.* Ehrenreich is also well known as a frequent guest on television and radio programs, including *The Today Show, Good Morning America, NightLine, Canada AM,* and *Crossfire.* Her many articles and reviews have appeared in the *New York Times Magazine, Esquire,* the *Atlantic Monthly,* the *New Republic, Vogue, Harper's,* and the *Wall Street Journal.* She has been an essayist for *Time* since 1990. Ehrenreich, whose favourite hobby is "voracious reading," lives in Syosset, New York.

Preparing to Read

Taken from *Blood Rites: Origins and History of the Passions of War* (1997), the following essay analyzes the psychology of war. Its citations and bibliography illustrate proper MLA (Modern Language Association) documentation form. As you prepare to read this article, take a few minutes to think about aggression in society today: Do you think aggression plays a significant role in North American society? In other societies? What do you think is the origin of aggression? In your opinion, what role does aggression play in war? In everyday life? How do you react to aggressive behaviour? How do people you associate with react to aggressive behaviour?

■ ■

"So elemental is the human need to endow the shedding of blood with some great and even sublime significance that it renders the intellect almost entirely helpless" (Van Creveld 166).

Different wars have led to different theories of why men fight　2
them. The Napoleonic Wars, which bore along with them the
rationalist spirit of the French Revolution, inspired the Prussian
officer Carl von Clausewitz to propose that war itself is an entirely
rational undertaking, unsullied by human emotion. War, in his
famous aphorism, is merely a "continuation of policy ... by other
means," with policy itself supposedly resulting from the same
kind of clearheaded deliberation one might apply to a game of
chess. Nation-states were the leading actors on the stage of
history, and war was simply one of the many ways they
advanced their interests against those of other nation-states. If
you could accept the existence of this new superperson, the
nation, a battle was no more disturbing and irrational than, say,
a difficult trade negotiation—except perhaps to those who lay
dying on the battlefield.

World War I, coming a century after Napoleon's sweep　3
through Europe and northern Africa, led to an opposite assessment
of the human impulse of war. World War I was hard to construe
as in any way "rational," especially to that generation of European
intellectuals, including Sigmund Freud, who survived to ponder
the unprecedented harvest of dead bodies. History textbooks tell
us that the "Great War" grew out of the conflict between
"competing imperialist states," but this Clausewitzian
interpretation has little to do with the actual series of accidents,
blunders, and miscommunications that impelled the nations of
Europe to war in the summer of 1914.[1] At first swept up in the
excitement of the war, unable for weeks to work or think of
anything else, Freud was eventually led to conclude that there is
some dark flaw in the human psyche, a perverse desire to destroy,
countering Eros and the will to live (Stromberg 82).

So these are, in crude summary, the theories of war which　4
modern wars have left us with: That war is a means, however
risky, by which men seek to advance their collective interests
and improve their lives. Or, alternatively, that war stems from
subrational drives not unlike those that lead individuals to
commit violent crimes. In our own time, most people seem to
hold both views at once, avowing that war is a gainful enterprise,
intended to meet the material needs of the groups engaged in it,
and, at the same time, that it fulfills deep and "irrational"
psychological needs. There is no question about the first part of
this proposition—that wars are designed, at least ostensibly, to
secure necessaries like land or oil or "geopolitical advantage."

The mystery lies in the peculiar psychological grip war exerts on us.

In the 1960s and '70s, the debate on the psychology of war 5 centered on the notion of an "aggressive instinct," peculiar to all humans or only to human males. This is not the place to summarize that debate, with its endless examples of animal behavior and clashes over their applicability to human affairs. Here I would simply point out that, whether or not there is an aggressive instinct, there are reasons to reject it as the major wellspring of war.

Although it is true that aggressive impulses, up to and 6 including murderous rage, can easily take over in the heat of actual battle, even this statement must be qualified to take account of different weaponry and modes of fighting. Hand-to-hand combat may indeed call forth and even require the emotions of rage and aggression, if only to mobilize the body for bursts of muscular activity. In the case of action-at-a-distance weapons, however, like guns and bows and arrows, emotionality of any sort can be a distinct disadvantage. Coolness, and the ability to keep aiming and firing steadfastly in the face of enemy fire, prevails. Hence, according to the distinguished American military historian Robert L. O'Connell, the change in the ideal warrior personality wrought by the advent of guns in the fifteenth and sixteenth centuries, from "ferocious aggressiveness" to "passive disdain" (119). So there is no personality type—"hot-tempered," "macho," or whatever—consistently and universally associated with warfare.

Furthermore, fighting itself is only one component of the 7 enterprise we know as war. Wars are not barroom brawls writ large, or domestic violence that has been somehow extended to strangers. In war, fighting takes place within battles—along with much anxious waiting, of course—but wars do not begin with battles and are often not decided by them either. Most of war consists of *preparation* for battle—training, the organization of supplies, marching and other forms of transport—activities which are hard to account for by innate promptings of any kind. There is no plausible instinct, for example, that impels a man to leave his home, cut his hair short, and drill for hours in tight formation. As anthropologists Clifton B. Kroeber and Bernard L. Fontana point out, "It is a large step from what may be biologically innate leanings toward individual aggression to ritualized, socially sanctioned, institutionalized group warfare" (166).

War, in other words, is too complex and collective an activity   8
to be accounted for by a single warlike instinct lurking within
the individual psyche. Instinct may, or may not, inspire a man to
bayonet the first enemy he encounters in battle. But instinct does
not mobilize supply lines, manufacture rifles, issue uniforms, or
move an army of thousands from point A on the map to B. These
are "complicated, orchestrated, highly organized" activities, as
social theorist Robin Fox writes, undertaken not by individuals
but by entities on the scale of nations and dynasties (15). "The
hypothesis of a killer instinct," according to a commentator
summarizing a recent conference on the anthropology of war, is
"not so much wrong as irrelevant" (McCauley 2).

In fact, throughout history, individual men have gone to   9
near-suicidal lengths to avoid participating in wars—a fact that
proponents of a warlike instinct tend to slight. Men have fled
their homelands, served lengthy prison terms, hacked off limbs,
shot off feet or index fingers, feigned illness or insanity, or, if
they could afford to, paid surrogates to fight in their stead. "Some
draw their teeth, some blind themselves, and others maim
themselves, on their way to us" (Mitchell 42), the governor of
Egypt complained of his peasant recruits in the early nineteenth
century. So unreliable was the rank and file of the eighteenth-
century Prussian army that military manuals forbade camping
near a woods or forest: The troops would simply melt away into
the trees (Delbrück 303).

Proponents of a warlike instinct must also reckon with the   10
fact that even when men have been assembled, willingly or
unwillingly, for the purpose of war, fighting is not something
that seems to come "naturally" to them. In fact, surprisingly,
even in the thick of battle, few men can bring themselves to shoot
directly at individual enemies.[2] The difference between an
ordinary man or boy and a reliable killer, as any drill sergeant
could attest, is profound. A transformation is required: The man
or boy leaves his former self behind and becomes something
entirely different, perhaps even taking a new name. In small-
scale, traditional societies, the change was usually accomplished
through ritual drumming, dancing, fasting, and sexual
abstinence—all of which serve to lift a man out of his mundane
existence and into a new, warriorlike mode of being, denoted by
special body paint, masks, and headdresses.

As if to emphasize the discontinuity between the warrior   11
and the ordinary human being, many cultures require the would-

be fighting man to leave his human-ness behind and assume a new form as an animal.³ The young Scandinavian had to become a bear before he could become an elite warrior, going "berserk" (the word means, "dressed in a bear hide"), biting and chasing people. The Irish hero Cuchulain transformed himself into a monster in preparation for battle: "He became horrible, many-shaped, strange and unrecognizable," with one eye sucked into his skull and the other popping out of the side of the face (Davidson 84). Apparently this transformation was a familiar and meaningful one, because similarly distorted faces turn up frequently in Celtic art.

Often the transformation is helped along with drugs or social 12
pressure of various kinds. Tahitian warriors were browbeaten into fighting by functionaries called Rauti, or "exhorters," who ran around the battlefield urging their comrades to mimic "the devouring wild dog" (Keeley 146). The ancient Greek hoplites drank enough wine, apparently, to be quite tipsy when they went into battle (Hanson 126); Aztecs drank pulque; Chinese troops at the time of Sun Tzu got into the mood by drinking wine and watching "gyrating sword dancers" perform (Griffith in Sun Tzu 37). Almost any drug or intoxicant has served, in one setting or another, to facilitate the transformation of man into warrior. Yanomamo Indians of the Amazon ingest a hallucinogen before battle; the ancient Scythians smoked hemp, while a neighboring tribe drank something called "hauma," which is believed to have induced a frenzy of aggression (Rolle 94–95). So if there is a destructive instinct that impels man to war, it is a weak one, and often requires a great deal of help.

In seventeenth-century Europe, the transformation of man 13
into soldier took on a new form, more concerted and disciplined, and far less pleasant, than wine. New recruits and even seasoned veterans were endlessly drilled, hour after hour, until each man began to feel himself part of a single, giant fighting machine. The drill was only partially inspired by the technology of firearms. It's easy enough to teach a man to shoot a gun; the problem is to make him willing to get into situations where guns are being shot and to remain there long enough to do some shooting of his own. So modern military training aims at a transformation parallel to that achieved by "primitives" with war drums and paint: In the fanatical routines of boot camp, a man leaves behind his former identity and is reborn as a creature of the military—an automaton and also, ideally, a willing killer of other men.

This is not to suggest that killing is foreign to human nature 14
or, more narrowly, to the male personality. Men (and women)
have again and again proved themselves capable of killing
impulsively and with gusto. But there is a huge difference
between a war and an ordinary fight. War not only departs from
the normal; it inverts all that is moral and right: In war one *should*
kill, *should* steal, *should* burn cities and farms, should perhaps
even rape matrons and little girls. Whether or not such activities
are "natural" or at some level instinctual, most men undertake
them only by entering what appears to be an "altered state"—
induced by drugs or lengthy drilling, and denoted by face paint
or khakis.

The point of such transformative rituals is not only to put 15
men "in the mood." Returning warriors may go through equally
challenging rituals before they can celebrate victory or reenter
the community—covering their heads in apparent shame, for
example; vomiting repeatedly; abstaining from sex (Keeley 144).
Among the Maori, returning warriors could not participate in
the victory celebration until they had gone through a whaka-hoa
ritual, designed to make them "common" again: The hearts of
slain enemies were roasted, after which offerings were made to
the war god Tu, and the rest was eaten by priests, who shouted
spells to remove "the blood curse" and enable warriors to reenter
their ordinary lives (Sagan 18). Among the Taulipang Indians of
South America, victorious warriors "sat on ants, flogged one
another with whips, and passed a cord covered with poisonous
ants, through their mouth and nose" (Métraux 397). Such painful
and shocking postwar rites impress on the warrior that war is
much more than a "continuation of policy ... by other means."
In war men enter an alternative realm of human experience, as far
removed from daily life as those things which we call "sacred."

Notes

1. See, for example, Stoessinger, *Why Nations Go to War*, 14–20.

2. See Grossman, *On Killing.*

3. In the mythologies of the Indo-European tradition, Dumézil
   relates, thanks "either to a gift of metamorphosis, or to a monstrous heredity, the eminent warrior possesses a veritable animal nature" (140).

Works Cited

Davidson, Hilda Ellis. *Myths and Symbols in Pagan Europe: Early Scandinavian and Celtic Religions.* Syracuse, NY: Syracuse UP, 1988.

Delbrück, Hans. *History of the Art of War, vol. 4. The Dawn of Modern Warfare.* Lincoln: U of Nebraska P, 1985.

Dumézil, Georges. *Destiny of the Warrior.* Chicago: U of Chicago P, 1969.

Fox, Robin. "Fatal Attraction: War and Human Nature." *The National Interest* (Winter 1992/93): 11–20.

Grossman, Lt. Col. Dave. *On Killing: The Psychological Cost of Learning to Kill in War and Society.* Boston: Little, Brown, 1995.

Hanson, Victor Davis. *The Western Way of War: Infantry Battle in Classical Greece.* New York: Knopf, 1989.

Keeley, Lawrence H. *War Before Civilization: The Myth of the Peaceful Savage.* New York: Oxford UP, 1996.

Kroeber, Clifton B., and Bernard L. Fontana. *Massacre on the Gila: An Account of the Last Major Battle Between American Indians, with Reflections on the Origin of War.* Tucson: U of Arizona P, 1986.

McCauley, Clark. "Conference Overview." *The Anthropology of War.* Ed. Jonathan Haas. Cambridge: Cambridge UP, 1990, 1–25.

Métraux, Alfred. "Warfare, Cannibalism, and Human Trophies." *Handbook of South American Indians,* vol. 5. Ed. Julian H. Steward. New York: Cooper Square Publishers, 1963. 383–409.

Mitchell, Timothy. *Colonizing Egypt.* Berkeley: U of California P, 1991.

O'Connell, Robert L. *Of Arms and Men: A History of War, Weapons, and Aggression.* New York: Oxford UP, 1989.

Rolle, Renate. *The World of the Scythians.* Berkeley: U of California P, 1989.

Sagan, Eli. *Cannibalism: Human Aggression and Cultural Form.* New York: Harper and Row, 1974.

Stoessinger, John G. *Why Nations Go to War.* New York: St. Martin's Press, 1993.

Stromberg, Roland. *Redemption by War: The Intellectuals and 1914.* Lawrence: U of Kansas P, 1982.

Sun Tzu. *The Art of War.* Trans. Samuel B. Griffith. London: Oxford UP, 1971.

Van Creveld, Martin. *The Transformation of War.* New York: Free Press, 1991.

UNDERSTANDING DETAILS

1. What do you think Ehrenreich's main purpose is in this essay?
2. According to Ehrenreich, what is the difference between hand-to-hand combat and fighting at a distance?
3. What does Ehrenreich say are the various components of what we call "war"?
4. In what ways do some cultures ritualize the transformation from regular citizen to warrior? Give three examples.

ANALYZING MEANING

1. Do you believe war can ever be emotionless and rational, like "a difficult trade negotiation" (paragraph 2)?
2. What do Clifton B. Kroeber and Bernard L. Fontana mean when they say "It is a large step from what may be biologically innate leanings toward individual aggression to ritualized, socially sanctioned, institutionalized group warfare" (paragraph 7)?
3. Why is "the hypothesis of a killer instinct" "not so much wrong as irrelevant" to the "anthropology of war" (paragraph 8)?
4. Are you convinced by this essay that "In war men enter an alternative realm of human experience, as far removed from daily life as those things which we call 'sacred'" (paragraph 15)?

DISCOVERING RHETORICAL STRATEGIES

1. Who do you think is Ehrenreich's main audience? How did you come to this conclusion?
2. The author begins her discussion of war with different "theories of why men fight them [wars]" (paragraph 2). Is this an effective beginning for what Ehrenreich is trying to accomplish? Explain your answer.
3. What information in this essay is most persuasive to you? What is the least persuasive?
4. What tone does the author establish by citing frequent statistics and referring to other sources in her essay?

MAKING CONNECTIONS

1. Compare and contrast Ehrenreich's insights on the psychology of war with Stephen King's theories on "Why We Crave Horror Movies." How do their ideas support one another? How do they contradict each other?

2. Compare Ehrenreich's use of examples with those of Marilyn Dahl ("The Role of the Media in Promoting Images of Disability").
3. In a conversation between Ehrenreich and Steven Heighton ("Elegy in Stone") about the glorification of war in American society, on what points would they agree and disagree? Give examples.

IDEAS FOR DISCUSSION/WRITING

Preparing to Write

Write freely about aggression in general: Why do people fight? Why do countries go to war? What are some ways in which people take out their aggression? Have you ever noticed people fighting just for the sake of fighting? When is aggression acceptable? When is it unacceptable?

Choosing a Topic

1. Ehrenreich claims that "even when men have been assembled, willingly or unwillingly, for the purpose of war, fighting is not something that seems to come 'naturally' to them" (paragraph 10). Do you agree or disagree with this statement? Explain your reaction in a clearly reasoned argumentative essay. Cite Ehrenreich's selection whenever necessary.
2. In the last paragraph of her essay, Ehrenreich suggests that warriors often have to go through rituals to return to their civilizations. Use Ehrenreich's article as one of your sources; then read further on such transformations. Next, write a clear, well-documented argument expressing your opinion on a specific transformation. Organize your paper clearly, and present your suggestions logically, using proper documentation (citations and bibliography) to support your position.
3. Use additional sources to study the circumstances of a war you are familiar with. Then, referring to Ehrenreich's explanation of "the anthropology of war" (paragraph 8), write a well-documented argument explaining the causes and effects of the war by discussing or analyzing in depth the consequences you have discovered.

Before beginning your essay, you might want to consult the checklists on pages 407–408.

Marilyn Dahl

■ □ ■

THE ROLE OF THE MEDIA IN PROMOTING IMAGES OF DISABILITY— DISABILITY AS METAPHOR: THE EVIL CRIP

Marilyn Dahl (1931–) is a western Canadian nurse educator originally from Broderick, Saskatchewan, and now living in Port Coquitlam, B.C. After graduating as an R.N. in 1953 from the Victoria Hospital School of Nursing in Prince Albert, Dahl practised nursing in a variety of settings until 1977. During this time she was married, had three children, wrote a hospital teaching video, and also wrote and produced a weekly children's television program in Medicine Hat from 1967–69. Dahl then returned to school at the University of British Columbia to get her B.Sc.N. in 1979. In the 1980s Dahl worked as an instructor at the Douglas College Faculty of Nursing and became a disabled consumer advocate in 1980. In 1985 she assumed the position of president of the Canadian Hard of Hearing Association and three years later became the vice-president of the International Hard of Hearing Federation. Dahl completed her M.A. at Simon Fraser University in 1988 with a thesis looking at how disabled role identity is culturally produced in Canadian society. Her many publications include *Caring for the Patient Who Is Hard of Hearing* (1979). This essay appeared in the *Canadian Journal of Communication* in 1993.

Preparing to Read

Before reading this article think about how disabilities are portrayed by the media. Brainstorm a list of movies, television shows, and books that include characters with disabilities. What disabilities do these characters have? Is the disability the focus of the story or is it an incidental characteristic? How are these people with disabilities portrayed? What do you know about the characters apart from their disabilities?

■ _____ ■

It is a commonly held theory that one cannot legislate attitude   1
change. One can legislate behavioural change and hopefully changes in attitude will follow. Attitudes, beliefs, and misconceptions of society constitute a major barrier for people with disabilities.

Attitude change can follow on heightened awareness, increased contact, and increased meaningful communication between disabled and non-disabled people. Although personal interaction is the most effective medium for conveying the personal experience of disability, the mass media can be an effective vehicle for bringing about greater understanding, and a consequent gradual change in public perceptions, of people with disabilities.

Disability as a Metaphor

A review of our cultural forms of expression provides evidence 2 of the metaphoric role of disability which is deeply ingrained in our social values. It has been a convention of all literature and art that physical deformity, chronic illness, or any visible defect symbolizes an evil and malevolent nature and monstrous behaviour (Sontag, 1978). A summary look at literary distortions of handicapping conditions illustrates this point: Captain Hook (in *Peter Pan*) is intentionally an amputee with a prosthesis; Shakespeare links Richard III's hunchback to his evil lust. Somerset Maugham uses Philip's clubfoot (in *Of Human Bondage*) to symbolize his bitter and warped nature.

Occasionally a type of reaction formation is invoked and the 3 literary association to disability is instead quite sentimental. Hans Christian Andersen depicts The Little Lame Prince in maudlin tones, and some other childhood tales use the stereotype of the selfless dwarf, or the blind seer. Occasionally the protagonist copes nobly with a disability but even then it is depicted as a "curse" to bear. Cyrano de Bergerac with his grotesque nose and Quasimodo with his hunchback are remarked not for their deformity but because they are both deformed and good (as though one precludes the other). Rarely does there appear an average or ordinary person whose disability is incidental.

We are both repelled and intrigued by the cripple as 4 metaphor. Children's classics are particularly graphic and concrete in this regard. Villains are always ugly and deformed in some manner, heroes and heroines are possessed of beauty and grace. Fellini used freaks and disabilities to cue people to respond with revulsion and disgust to his film characters. Disney frequently promoted disability as metaphor. More recently, Hollywood has tended to sentimentalize the disabled with stock movies of two-dimensional characters who "learn to cope" and "live happily ever after." The deaf (*Voices*), the blind (*Ice Castles*), and quadriplegics (*The Other Side of the Mountain*) have all been treated within this formula. Film and television have also employed the metaphor of the disabled as helpless victim. Roughing up a cripple or a blind man is a device used to show a villain as a particularly evil person. At times television has tended to transform the metaphor by endowing the disabled person with superhuman characteristics, such as the Bionic Man; while in *Ironside*, the paraplegic was given a brilliant mind (Bird, Byrd, & Allen, 1977).

Research into the relationship between physical attractiveness   5 and crime in the various media found that physical ugliness and physical differences are often associated with media depictions of violence and crime (Needleman & Weiner, 1974). Horror movies make free use of this strategy. Gardner & Radel (1978), who analyzed American newspapers and television for references to disabled people, found that about one half of the items portrayed the disabled as dependent persons. A tenth of the items portrayed the disabled as being in some way deviant: "strange, antisocial or bizarre." Only about one quarter of the items portrayed the disabled as persons capable of independent living and of contributing to society. Cartoons and comic strip captions are also important carriers of prejudicial and discriminatory language and images of evil cripples. Words such as "stupid moron," "idiot," "crazy," are common jargon in strips such as *Beetle Bailey*, and the various "animal" comic strips. Everyday words which refer to specific conditions have become standardized as curse words, and stereotypes of conditions are reinforced (Weinberg & Santana, 1978).

In spite of these trends, there have been some changes in   6 American plays and films, which today present more sympathetic and romanticized views of the disabled. Gussow (1979) labelled the phenomenon "the time of the wounded hero." Some of the examples are *The Elephant Man* (congenital deformity), *Wings* (stroke), *Whose Life Is It Anyway?* (paralysis), and *Children of a Lesser God*. There have been more recent attempts to portray the disabled as "incidental" characters, neither hero nor victim. A policeman in a wheelchair on *Cagney and Lacey* portrayed an average role. The elderly, the ugly, the obese are seen more often as "normal." Marlee Matlin, as assistant district attorney in *Reasonable Doubts*, attempts to show a deaf person filling a professional role in much the same way as a hearing person. Made for television films in the 1980s have portrayed sensitive and realistic stories of schizophrenia and Alzheimer's victims.

L.A. Law portrays a mentally handicapped man in a sensitive way, and has a lawyer who wears a hearing aid.

Effects of Media Selectivity in Describing Disability

The media promote certain images of the disabled by selectively 7 covering certain events and ignoring others. Dr. Kenneth Jernigan, president of the National American Federation of the Blind, reported that reporters invited to a press conference on a highly political topic, ignored the political topic and wanted instead to photograph and report on the various walking aids, lead dogs, and other stereotypical symbols of blindness (Bogden & Biklen, 1977). In covering the Terry Fox story, the media focused on the "dying hero" and the medical model of illness, ignoring the counter-ideology issue of environmental pollution from nuclear fallout over the area where Fox was born in the 1950s, and its relationship to causes of cancer (Harrison, 1985).

The selective coverage of disability has led to the creation 8 of "heroes by hype." The power of the media in manipulating public response is seen in the media coverage of the disabled marathoners who in the 1980s were a uniquely Canadian phenomenon (Graham, 1987). While many marathoners crossed Canada for causes, it was only the young, attractive men with dramatic visual disabilities (Fox, Fonyo, and Hansen) who received orchestrated backing and media coverage. Promoters and handlers "packaged" the young man and directed the programs and publicity en route. A star was created. Increased coverage pressured corporations and politicians to be seen giving generously to the hero's cause. An exception was the "W5" program (CTV, 1987), which presented the misgivings held by disabled people themselves about what "disabled as superstar" portrays to the public.

The *Disability Network* (TVOntario) presents lifestyles of people 9 with disabilities, but most disabled people would prefer to be shown as part of the average population. The Bay's advertising flyer recently featured a model in a wheelchair, McDonald's ads have included people with different types of disabilities (King, 1992). These ads are the exception rather than the rule. Advertisers do not seem to think in terms of disabled people as customers— drinking beer, brushing their teeth, or buying a car. One particularly onerous depiction of disability remains a television regular: fund-raising telethons. The model for this is the Jerry Lewis Telethon which presents an alliance of business, high status public persons and service providers, plus a disabled child who is helpless and appealing. The images equate disability with childlike behaviour and an infantile condition, a minor role, while the healthy normal star has the spotlight, status, and prestige. Helping the disabled becomes entertainment (Dahl, 1987).

The mass media perpetuate stereotypes of disability through their portrayals of characters. But there is no evidence that the mass media have any major effect on manipulating the attitudes and opinions of its audience. Researchers state that it is difficult to discover what are the precise effects of the media on public opinion. It is possible that attitudes and opinions change dramatically as a result of what is seen or heard. There are indications of selective perception of what is viewed, namely that audiences tend to identify with that which reinforces their existing beliefs. On the whole it appears that "the potential of the mass media to create false impressions ... is tempered by the tendency of the public to neglect the mass media in favour of other sources of understanding social reality" (Howitt, 1982, p. 179). Some speculation is in order, however, on the effect of negative stereotyping on the disabled themselves, especially children with disabilities. "Self-identity is formed by what is communicated through the media as well as by interpersonal acts" (Gumpert & Cathcart, 1982, p. 13). To see oneself labelled and cast always in the role of the villain, helpless dependent, or victim is not an enviable fate.   10

Creating an "Average" Typification of the Disabled

Although there are no specific data showing attitude change in response to media communication, people tend to believe that the manner in which characters are portrayed is important. Characters presented on screen are sociocultural stereotypes designed to appeal to the majority of viewers, and reflect widely held values (albeit mostly American). It seems apparent that the repeated presentation of images in an acceptable and palatable manner will result in those images becoming a typification of everyday existence. The media are efficient in implanting new information and contributing new ideas and values, where they are not in conflict with strongly held views. The effect of mass communication on society is often more a contributory than a sole effect (Schramm, 1973). "Media images, however, can help to shape the meanings we find directly in the situation and what   11 we discover in the actual situation can influence the way we look at the media" (Kelly, 1981, p. 167).

The CRTC recognized the influence of broadcasting on viewers   12
in its 1986 policy statement: "Broadcasting is ... a powerful medium to reinforce [sex-role] stereotyping and can be equally powerful to correct it." Since 1979, the Treasury Board, the Advertising Management Group, the CRTC, and CBC have developed policies on the elimination of sexual stereotyping and cultural stereotyping. The CRTC called for self-regulation by the industry in regard to policy implementation. Guidelines are monitored by the CRTC, the industry, and consumer groups such as Mediawatch and Evaluation/Medias (in Quebec). The CRTC report (December, 1986) indicated that some sensitization to the issue of sex-role stereotyping had occurred, but significant reductions in such stereotyping had not been achieved. No separate set of guidelines exists with respect to persons with disabilities; such guidelines are included under regulations prohibiting discrimination. In 1990 the Department of Secretary of State, Canada, published two reports: *Worthless or Wonderful* includes recommendations on elimination of social stereotyping of disabled persons, modelled on the guidelines for sex-role and cultural stereotype elimination; *A Way With Words* (1990) provides guidelines and appropriate terminology for the portrayal of persons with disabilities.

We have moved somewhat away from the disabled as hero   13
or victim but we are still a long way from a normal depiction of disability. Disabled people could be depicted as living and working in a variety of situations, with a diverse range of responsibilities, and not necessarily overcoming great odds to achieve their status. The mass media affect public opinion and public perception of social reality by their ability to create typifications. Careful use of terminology and visual images of the disabled can gradually create a more acceptable and realistic typification of people with disabilities as "average" people.

References

Bird, E.K., Byrd, P.D., & Allen, C.M. (1977). Television programming and disability. *Applied Rehabilitation Counselling*, 8(1), 28–32.

Bogden, Robert, & Biklen, Douglas. (1977). *Handicapism*. Mimeographed paper, Social Policy Corporation, New York.

CRTC. (1986). *Sex role stereotyping in the broadcast media* (Report on Industry Self-Regulation). Ottawa: Supply and Services Canada.

CRTC. (1986). *Sex role stereotyping in the broadcast media* (Policy Statement). Ottawa: Supply and Services Canada.

Dahl, Marilyn. (1987). *The cultural production of the disabled role identity in contemporary Canadian society.* MA thesis, Simon Fraser University, Burnaby, BC.

Fiedler, Leslie. (1978). *Freaks, myths and images of the secret self.* New York: Simon & Shuster.

Gardner, J.M., & Radel, M. (1978). Portrait of the disabled in the media. *Journal of Community Psychology, 6,* 269–274.

Graham, R. (1987, January). On the road. *Saturday Night,* 102(1) 16ff.

Gumpert, Gary, & Cathcart, Robert. (1982). *Inter/media: Interpersonal communication in a media world.* New York: Oxford University Press.

Gussow, Mel. (1979, April 15). The time of the wounded hero. *The New York Times,* 11, 1–2.

Harrison, Deborah. (1985). The Terry Fox story and the media: A case study in ideology and illness. *Canadian Review of Sociology and Anthropology,* 22(4), 496–514.

Howitt, Dennis. (1982). *The mass media and social problems.* Oxford: Pergamon Press.

Kelly, John. (1981). *A philosophy of communication and culture.* London: Centre for Study of Communications and Culture.

King, Marsha. (1992, February 20). Companies doing the right thing. *The Province,* p. C9.

Needleman, B., & Weiner, N. (1974). *Faces of evil: The good, the bad and the ugly.* Mimeographed paper, Oswego State College Department of Sociology, New York.

Schramm, Wilbur. (1973). *Men, messages and media.* New York: Harper & Row.

Secretary of State. (1988). *Worthless or wonderful: The social stereotyping of persons with disabilities.* Ottawa: Minister of Supply and Services.

Secretary of State. (1988). *A way with words: Guidelines and appropriate terminology for the portrayal of persons with disabilities.* Ottawa: Minister of Supply and Services.

Sontag, Susan. (1978). *Illness as metaphor.* New York: Farrar, Strauss and Giroux.

Weinberg, Nancy, & Santana, Rosina. (1978, November–December). Comic books: Champions of the disabled stereotype. *Rehabilitation Literature,* pp. 11–12.

UNDERSTANDING DETAILS

1. According to Dahl, in what way does the mass media make life difficult for people with disabilities?
2. What does Dahl see as likely to cause attitude change regarding people with disabilities?
3. Why does Dahl not support fund-raising telethons for disabilities?

ANALYZING MEANING

1. Is Dahl optimistic or pessimistic about the current portrayal of people with disabilities by the mass media? Explain.
2. What is Dahl's attitude toward disabled marathoners such as Terry Fox, Steve Fonyo, or Rick Hansen?
3. Summarize the categories that Dahl establishes to organize portrayals of people with disabilities. Add one original example to each category.

DISCOVERING RHETORICAL STRATEGIES

1. From what you know about the source of this essay and the writer, describe Dahl's audience. Is this the same group that she usually addresses? How do you know this?
2. In this article is Dahl reporting, interpreting, or analyzing? How do Dahl's sources and statistics help advance her argument?
3. What main rhetorical modes does Dahl use to state her case? Give examples of each.

MAKING CONNECTIONS

1. Dahl contends that stereotyping can be diminished through changing the images that people see in the media and that legislation can promote the changes in these images. How would Cecil Foster ("Why Blacks Get Mad") react to Dahl's position on the importance of the images that people see in the media? What is your position on this issue?
2. Imagine that Dahl is having a conversation with Cecil Foster ("Why Blacks Get Mad"), Naheed Mustafa ("My Body Is My Own Business"), and Laura Robinson ("Starving for the Gold") about the effect of appearance. On what points would the three writers agree? On which would they disagree?

IDEAS FOR DISCUSSION/WRITING

Preparing to Write

Write freely about language and disability. What connotations are there to words like "maimed," "crippled," "handicapped," "physically challenged," "differently-abled," "disfigured," or "disabled"? What words are acceptable? Which ones are not? What associations do you have with the terms "retarded," "feeble-minded," and "moron"?

Choosing a Topic

1. In a letter to the organizers of one of the fundraising telethons for disabilities, explain the negative effects of their well-intentioned actions and encourage them to stop holding their telethon.
2. Dahl refers to the depiction of disabilities in fairy tales. In a well-documented essay, explore the portrayal of evil or bad characters in fairy tales. To what extent are disabilities used to reflect negative roles?
3. Using both primary and secondary sources, research the effects of including people with disabilities in advertisements. Write a well-documented essay in which you examine both the direct and indirect outcomes of this approach to advertising.

CHAPTER 11

THE STORIES

■ ■ ■

Storytelling is the mother of all literary arts, and
anyone who reads must occasionally speculate
on its enduring power.

—Robert Fulford

In his book *The Triumph of Narrative* (based on his Massey Lectures),
Robert Fulford examines the appeal of story in entertaining us
and helping us to make sense of the world around us: "Stories are
how we explain, how we teach, how we entertain ourselves, and
how we often do all three at once. They are the juncture where
facts and feelings meet. And for those reasons, they are central to
civilization...." We constantly use stories in both our personal and
our professional lives in order to communicate with each other
and to share the experiences and the essential truths of our lives.
The stories we tell may be factual, they may be imaginary, or they
may fall somewhere in between. What distinguishes a story from
a simple sequence of events is the truth about our lives that that
story conveys. Those stories become the primary vehicle through
which we explore our world, share our understanding of it, and
create connection and community with others.

The first ten chapters of this book focus on non-fiction. In
each of the preceding chapters, we have examined a single
rhetorical mode in order to focus attention on how writers use
that pattern to organize their thoughts. In this final chapter, we
move to a collection of short stories. These stories differ from the
earlier essays in their structure and their basis in fact, but, like
the essays, they are written to help us to better understand some
facet of our experience or some essential point about our world
and those who inhabit it. While stories may not be "true" in the
sense of being factually verifiable, they are our means of exploring
the greater truths about our world, ourselves, and humankind.

Our primary purpose in this text has been to show how thinking, reading, and writing work together like fine machinery to help all of us function as intelligent and productive human beings. Our introduction discusses the relationship of thinking, reading, and writing; the text itself illustrates the crucial interdependence of these skills; and this last chapter concludes the book by presenting short stories by some of Canada's best fiction writers.

In the stories you will find many of the same rhetorical strategies and techniques introduced earlier and employed by the essay writers. In addition, you will find that there are elements and strategies that are unique to fiction; David Arnason's "A Girl's Story" will give you a good overview of these. The questions that follow each of the selections will help you to focus on some of the writing strategies that make these stories effective, and will also offer further opportunities for you to practise your essay writing skills in your critical analysis of these pieces of fiction. The questions that accompany each selection are also intended to launch your exploration of the greater truths that each author is exploring.

> Stories touch all of us, reaching across cultures
> and generations, accompanying humanity down
> the centuries.
>
> — Robert Fulford

David Arnason

A GIRL'S STORY

The fact that the entire Spring 2001 issue of *Prairie Fire* is devoted to David Arnason is testament to his influence on the Canadian literary community and to the range of his talents. In the introduction to this issue of *Prairie Fire*, Douglas Reimer characterizes Arnason as "prodigious in his energy for the promotion of the arts and for life itself ..." as evidenced, in part, by his writing and publishing of plays, novels, short stories, poetry, drama, film scripts, essays, anthologies, songs, and works of criticism, by his service on various arts councils, and by his teaching at the University of Manitoba.

Arnason was born in Gimli, Manitoba in 1940, and now makes his home both in Gimli, where he does most of his writing, and in Winnipeg, where he teaches Canadian Literature and Creative Writing and is head of the English Department and of the Department of Icelandic Language and Literature. Arnason's most recent publication is a novel entitled *King Jerry* (2001); the story found here comes from *The Circus Performers' Bar*, a collection of short stories published in 1984.

■ _____ ■

You've wondered what it would be like to be a character in a   1
story, to sort of slip out of your ordinary self and into some other character. Well, I'm offering you the opportunity. I've been trying to think of a heroine for this story, and frankly, it hasn't been going too well. A writer's life isn't easy, especially if, like me, he's got a tendency sometimes to drink a little bit too much. Yesterday, I went for a beer with Dennis and Ken (they're real-life friends of mine) and we stayed a little longer than we should have. Then I came home and quickly mixed a drink and started drinking it so my wife would think the liquor on my breath came from the drink I was drinking and not from the drinks I had had earlier. I wasn't going to tell her about those drinks. Anyway, Wayne dropped over in the evening and I had some more drinks, and this morning my head isn't working very well.

To be absolutely frank about it, I always have trouble getting   2
characters, even when I'm stone cold sober. I can think of plots; plots are really easy. If you can't think of one, you just pick up a book, and sure enough, there's a plot. You just move a few things around and nobody knows you stole the idea. Characters are the problem. It doesn't matter how good the plot is if your characters are dull. You can steal characters too, and put them into different plots. I've done that. I stole Eustacia Vye from Hardy and gave her another name. The problem was that she turned out a lot sulkier than I remembered and the plot I put her in was a light comedy. Now nobody wants to publish the story. I'm still sending it out, though. If you send a story to enough publishers, no matter how bad it is, somebody will ultimately publish it.

For this story I need a beautiful girl. You probably don't   3
think you're beautiful enough, but I can fix that. I can do all
kinds of retouching once I've got the basic material, and if I miss
anything, Karl (he's my editor) will find it. So I'm going to make
you fairly tall, about five-foot eight and a quarter in your stocking
feet. I'm going to give you long blonde hair because long blonde
hair is sexy and virtuous. Black hair can be sexy too, but it doesn't
go with virtue. I've got to deal with a whole literary tradition
where black-haired women are basically evil. If I were feeling
better I might be able to do it in an ironic way, then black hair
would be okay, but I don't think I'm up to it this morning. If
you're going to use irony, then you've got to be really careful
about tone. I could make you a redhead, but redheads have a
way of turning out pixie-ish, and that would wreck my plot.

So you've got long blonde hair and you're this tall slender girl   4
with amazingly blue eyes. Your face is narrow and your nose is
straight and thin. I could have turned up the nose a little, but
that would have made you cute, and I really need a beautiful
girl. I'm going to put a tiny black mole on your cheek. It's
traditional. If you want your character to be really beautiful there
has to be some minor defect.

Now, I'm going to sit you on the bank of a river. I'm not   5
much for setting. I've read so many things where you get great
long descriptions of the setting, and mostly it's just boring. When
my last book came out, one of the reviewers suggested that the
reason I don't do settings is that I'm not very good at them. That's
just silly. I'm writing a different kind of story, not that old realist
stuff. If you think I can't do setting, just watch.

There's a curl in the river just below the old dam where the   6
water seems to make a broad sweep. That flatness is deceptive,
though. Under the innocent sheen of the mirroring surface, the
current is treacherous. The water swirls, stabs, takes sharp angles
and dangerous vectors. The trees that lean from the bank
shimmer with the multi-hued greenness of elm, oak, maple and
aspen. The leaves turn in the gentle breeze, showing their paler
green undersides. The undergrowth, too, is thick and green,
hiding the poison ivy, the poison sumac and the thorns. On a
patch of grass that slopes gently to the water, the only clear part
of the bank on that side of the river, a girl sits, a girl with long
blonde hair. She has slipped a ring from her finger and seems
to be holding it towards the light.

You see? I could do a lot more of that, but you wouldn't like 7
it. I slipped a lot of details in there and provided all those hints
about strange and dangerous things under the surface. That's
called foreshadowing. I put in the ring at the end there so that
you'd wonder what was going to happen. That's to create
suspense. You're supposed to ask yourself what the ring means.
Obviously it has something to do with love, rings always do,
and since she's taken it off, obviously something has gone wrong
in the love relationship. Now I just have to hold off answering
that question for as long as I can, and I've got my story. I've got
. a friend who's also a writer who says never tell the buggers
anything until they absolutely have to know.

I'm going to have trouble with the feminists about this story. 8
I can see that already. I've got that river that's calm on the surface
and boiling underneath, and I've got those trees that are gentle
and beautiful with poisonous and dangerous undergrowth.
Obviously, the girl is going to be like that, calm on the surface but
passionate underneath. The feminists are going to say that I'm
perpetuating stereotypes, that by giving the impression the girl
is full of hidden passion I'm encouraging rapists. That's crazy. I'm
just using a literary convention. Most of the world's great books
are about the conflict between reason and passion. If you take
that away, what's left to write about?

So I've got you sitting on the riverbank, twirling your ring. I 9
forgot the birds. The trees are full of singing birds. There are
meadowlarks and vireos and even Blackburnian warblers. I know
a lot about birds but I'm not going to put in too many. You've got
to be careful not to overdo things. In a minute I'm going to enter
your mind and reveal what you're thinking. I'm going to do this
in the third person. Using the first person is sometimes more
effective, but I'm always afraid to do a female character in the first
person. It seems wrong to me, like putting on a woman's dress.

Your name is Linda. I had to be careful not to give you a 10
biblical name like Judith or Rachel. I don't want any symbolism
in this story. Symbolism makes me sick, especially biblical
symbolism. You always end up with some crazy moral argument
that you don't believe and none of the readers believe. Then you
lose control of your characters, because they've got to be like the
biblical characters. You've got this terrific episode you'd like to
use, but you can't because Rachel or Judith or whoever wouldn't
do it. I think of stories with a lot of symbolism in them as sticky.

Here goes.   11

Linda held the ring up towards the light. The diamond flashed   12
rainbow colours. It was a small diamond, and Linda reflected
that it was probably a perfect symbol of her relationship with
Gregg. Everything Gregg did was on a small scale. He was careful
with his money and just as careful with his emotions. In one week
they would have a small wedding and then move into a small
apartment. She supposed that she ought to be happy. Gregg was
very handsome, and she did love him. Why did it seem that she
was walking into a trap?

That sounds kind of distant, but it's supposed to be distant.   13
I'm using indirect quotation because the reader has just met
Linda, and we don't want to get too intimate right away. Besides,
I've got to get a lot of explaining done quickly, and if you can
do it with the character's thoughts, then that's best.

Linda twirled the ring again, then with a suddenness that   14
surprised her, she stood up and threw it into the river. She was
immediately struck by a feeling of panic. For a moment she
almost decided to dive into the river to try to recover it. Then,
suddenly, she felt free. It was now impossible to marry Gregg. He
would not forgive her for throwing the ring away. Gregg would
say he'd had enough of her theatrics for one lifetime. He always
accused her of being a romantic. She'd never had the courage to
admit that he was correct, and that she intended to continue
being a romantic. She was sitting alone by the river in a long
blue dress because it was a romantic pose. Anyway, she thought
a little wryly, you're only likely to find romance if you look for
it in romantic places and dress for the occasion.

Suddenly, she heard a rustling in the bush, the sound of   15
someone coming down the narrow path from the road above.

I had to do that, you see. I'd used up all the potential in the   16
relationship with Gregg, and the plot would have started to flag
if I hadn't introduced a new character. The man who is coming
down the path is tall and athletic with wavy brown hair. He has
dark brown eyes that crinkle when he smiles, and he looks kind.
His skin is tanned, as if he spends a lot of time outdoors, and he
moves gracefully. He is smoking a pipe. I don't want to give too
many details. I'm not absolutely sure what features women find
attractive in men these days, but what I've described seems safe
enough. I got all of it from stories written by women, and I
assume they must know. I could give him a chiselled jaw, but
that's about as far as I'll go.

The man stepped into the clearing. He carried an old-fashioned   17
wicker fishing creel and a telescoped fishing rod. Linda remained
sitting on the grass, her blue dress spread out around her. The
man noticed her and apologized.

"I'm sorry, I always come here to fish on Saturday afternoons   18
and I've never encountered anyone here before." His voice was
low with something of an amused tone in it.

"Don't worry," Linda replied. "I'll only be here for a little   19
while. Go ahead and fish. I won't make any noise." In some way
she couldn't understand, the man looked familiar to her. She felt
she knew him. She thought she might have seen him on television
or in a movie, but of course she knew that movie and television
stars do not spend every Saturday afternoon fishing on the banks
of small, muddy rivers.

"You can make all the noise you want," he told her. "The   20
fish in this river are almost entirely deaf. Besides, I don't care if
I catch any. I only like the act of fishing. If I catch them, then I
have to take them home and clean them. Then I've got to cook
them and eat them. I don't even like fish that much, and the fish
you catch here all taste of mud."

"Why do you bother fishing then?" Linda asked him. "Why   21
don't you just come and sit on the riverbank?"

"It's not that easy," he told her. "A beautiful girl in a blue   22
dress may go and sit on a riverbank any time she wants. But a
man can only sit on a riverbank if he has a very good reason.
Because I fish, I am a man with a hobby. After a hard week of
work, I deserve some relaxation. But if I just came and sat on the
riverbank, I would be a romantic fool. People would make fun of
me. They would think I was irresponsible, and before long I
would be a failure." As he spoke, he attached a lure to his line,
untelescoped his fishing pole and cast his line into the water.

You may object that this would not have happened in real   23
life, that the conversation would have been awkward, that Linda
would have been a bit frightened by the man. Well, why don't
you just run out to the grocery store and buy a bottle of milk
and a loaf of bread? The grocer will give you your change without
even looking at you. That's what happens in real life, and if that's
what you're after, why are you reading a book?

I'm sorry. I shouldn't have got upset. But it's not easy you   24
know. Dialogue is about the hardest stuff to write. You've got
all those "he saids" and "she saids" and "he replieds." And
you've got to remember the quotation marks and whether the

comma is inside or outside the quotation marks. Sometimes you can leave out the "he saids" and the "she saids" but then the reader gets confused and can't figure out who's talking. Hemingway is bad for that. Sometimes you can read an entire chapter without figuring out who's on what side.

Anyway, something must have been in the air that afternoon. 25 Linda felt free and open.

Did I mention that it was warm and the sun was shining?   26

She chattered away, telling the stranger all about her life, 27 what she had done when she was a little girl, the time her dad had taken the whole family to Hawaii and she got such a bad sunburn that she was peeling in February, how she was a better water-skier than Gregg and how mad he got when she beat him at tennis. The man, whose name was Michael (you can use biblical names for men as long as you avoid Joshua or Isaac), told her he was a doctor, but had always wanted to be a cowboy. He told her about the time he skinned his knee when he fell off his bicycle and had to spend two weeks in the hospital because of infection. In short, they did what people who are falling in love always do. They unfolded their brightest and happiest memories and gave them to each other as gifts.

Then Michael took a bottle of wine and a Klik sandwich out 28 of his wicker creel and invited Linda to join him in a picnic. He had forgotten his corkscrew and he had to push the cork down into the bottle with his filletting knife. They drank wine and laughed and spat out little pieces of cork. Michael reeled in his line, and to his amazement discovered a diamond ring on his hook. Linda didn't dare tell him where the ring had come from. Then Michael took Linda's hand, and slipped the ring onto her finger. In a comic-solemn voice, he asked her to marry him. With the same kind of comic solemnity, she agreed. Then they kissed, a first gentle kiss with their lips barely brushing and without touching each other.

Now I've got to bring this to some kind of ending. You think 29 writers know how stories end before they write them, but that's not true. We're wracked with confusion and guilt about how things are going to end. And just as you're playing the role of Linda in this story, Michael is my alter ego. He even looks a little like me and he smokes the same kind of pipe. We all want this to end happily. If I were going to be realistic about this, I suppose I'd have to let them make love. Then, shaken with guilt and horror, Linda would go back and marry Gregg, and the doctor would go back to his practice. But I'm not going to do that. In the story from which I stole the plot, Michael turned out not to be a doctor at all, but a returned soldier who had always been in love with Linda. She recognized him as they kissed, because they had kissed as children, and even though they had grown up and changed, she recognized the flavour of wintergreen on his breath. That's no good. It brings in too many unexplained facts at the last minute.

I'm going to end it right here at the moment of the kiss. You 30 can do what you want with the rest of it, except you can't make him a returned soldier, and you can't have them make love then separate forever. I've eliminated those options. In fact, I think I'll eliminate all options. This is where the story ends, at the moment of the kiss. It goes on and on forever while cities burn, nations rise and fall, galaxies are born and die, and the universe snuffs out the stars one by one. It goes on, the story, the brush of a kiss.

UNDERSTANDING DETAILS

1. Itemize all the elements of a story that Arnason identifies in "A Girl's Story."
2. The narrator draws attention to his name choice for his central character. Why does he do this? Why has he chosen the name Linda?
3. According to the narrator, what is the theme of most great books? Is this the theme of "A Girl's Story"? Explain.

ANALYZING MEANING

1. What is the purpose of Arnason's "A Girl's Story"? Does the author have more than one purpose? How successfully does Arnason achieve his goal or goals with this story?
2. Explain the ending of the story. Why does it end at the moment of the kiss?
3. The narrator in this story claims to hate symbolism. Do you believe him? Why or why not? What symbols has he incorporated in the story?

DISCOVERING RHETORICAL STRATEGIES

1. Describe Arnason's tone in "A Girl's Story." What effect does the tone have on the reader? Why do you think Arnason has adopted this tone?
2. Discuss how Arnason uses point of view in "A Girl's Story." Where and why does he change the point of view? What effect does this have on the reader?
3. Arnason makes references to several other stories and writers within "A Girl's Story." Why does he do this? What role does literary tradition play in writing a story?

MAKING CONNECTIONS

1. Like Maureen Littlejohn in "You Are a Contract Painkiller," Arnason has chosen to address the reader directly in his story. Explain the effect of this use of second person point of view in these two pieces of writing.
2. The tone in Arnason's story is conversational and somewhat humorous. Compare his strategies for creating humour to those of Paul Quarrington ("Home Brew") and Drew Hayden Taylor ("Pretty Like a White Boy").

CHOOSING A TOPIC FOR DISCUSSION/WRITING

1. Write an essay using the second person point of view in which you take your reader on a tour of a place you know well. Be sure to incorporate specific details.
2. Write an essay in which you either support or counter Arnason's position that most great stories are about the conflict between reason and passion.
3. Write an essay in which you evaluate the effectiveness of Arnason's story in conveying a good understanding of the fundamental elements of a work of fiction.

Margaret Atwood

■ □ ■

DEATH BY LANDSCAPE

Arguably Canada's most widely recognized author internationally, Margaret Atwood has had a distinguished career as a writer of poems, short stories, novels, children's stories, essays, and critical works. Atwood was born in Ottawa in 1939, grew up primarily in Toronto, and was educated at the University of Toronto, Cambridge University, and Harvard University.

Atwood's published works include *The Edible Woman* (1969), *The Journals of Susanna Moodie* (1970), *Surfacing* (1972), *The Handmaid's Tale* (for which she won the Governor General's Award) (1985), *Cat's Eye* (1988), *The Robber Bride* (1993), *Alias Grace* (1996), *Morning in the Burned House* (1996), and, most recently, *The Blind Assassin* (2000), for which she won the Booker Prize. Atwood has won numerous awards for her writing, which has been translated into several languages, including French, German, Italian, Urdu, Estonian, Romanian, Serbo-Croatian, Catalan, Turkish, Russian, Finnish, Dutch, Danish, Norwegian, Swedish, Portuguese, Greek, Polish, Japanese, Icelandic, Spanish, and Hebrew. The story here comes from a collection of Atwood's short fiction entitled *Wilderness Tips* (1991).

■ ——————————————————————————— ■

Now that the boys are grown up and Rob is dead, Lois has 1
moved to a condominium apartment in one of the newer waterfront developments. She is relieved not to have to worry about the lawn, or about the ivy pushing its muscular little suckers into the brickwork, or the squirrels gnawing their way into the attic and eating the insulation off the wiring, or about strange noises. This building has a security system, and the only plant life is in pots in the solarium.

Lois is glad she's been able to find an apartment big enough 2
for her pictures. They are more crowded together than they were in the house, but this arrangement gives the walls a European look: blocks of pictures, above and beside one another, rather than one over the chesterfield, one over the fireplace, one in the

front hall, in the old acceptable manner of sprinkling art around so it does not get too intrusive. This way has more of an impact. You know it's not supposed to be furniture.

None of the pictures is very large, which doesn't mean they   3
aren't valuable. They are paintings, or sketches and drawings, by artists who were not nearly as well known when Lois began to buy them as they are now. Their work later turned up on stamps, or as silk-screen reproductions hung in the principals' offices of high schools, or as jigsaw puzzles, or on beautifully printed calendars sent out by corporations as Christmas gifts, to their less important clients. These artists painted mostly in the twenties and thirties and forties; they painted landscapes. Lois has two Tom Thomsons, three A. Y. Jacksons, a Lawren Harris. She has an Arthur Lismer, she has a J. E. H. MacDonald. She has a David Milne. They are pictures of convoluted tree trunks on an island of pink wave-smoothed stone, with more islands behind; of a lake with rough, bright, sparsely wooded cliffs; of a vivid river shore with a tangle of bush and two beached canoes, one red, one grey; of a yellow autumn woods with the ice-blue gleam of a pond half-seen through the interlaced branches.

It was Lois who'd chosen them. Rob had no interest in art,   4
although he could see the necessity of having something on the walls. He left all the decorating decisions to her, while providing the money, of course. Because of this collection of hers, Lois's friends—especially the men—have given her the reputation of having a good nose for art investments.

But this is not why she bought the pictures, way back then.   5
She bought them because she wanted them. She wanted something that was in them, although she could not have said at the time what it was. It was not peace: she does not find them peaceful in the least. Looking at them fills her with a wordless unease. Despite the fact that there are no people in them or even animals, it's as if there is something, or someone, looking back out.

When she was thirteen, Lois went on a canoe trip. She'd only   6
been on overnights before. This was to be a long one, into the trackless wilderness, as Cappie put it. It was Lois's first canoe trip, and her last.

Cappie was the head of the summer camp to which Lois had   7
been sent ever since she was nine. Camp Manitou, it was called;

it was one of the better ones, for girls, though not the best. Girls of her age whose parents could afford it were routinely packed off to such camps, which bore a generic resemblance to one another. They favoured Indian names and had hearty, energetic leaders, who were called Cappie or Skip or Scottie. At these camps you learned to swim well and sail, and paddle a canoe, and perhaps ride a horse or play tennis. When you weren't doing these things you could do Arts and Crafts and turn out dingy, lumpish clay ashtrays for your mother—mothers smoked more, then—or bracelets made of coloured braided string.

Cheerfulness was required at all times, even at breakfast. Loud 8
shouting and the banging of spoons on the tables were allowed, and even encouraged, at ritual intervals. Chocolate bars were rationed, to control tooth decay and pimples. At night, after supper, in the dining hall or outside around a mosquito-infested campfire ring for special treats, there were singsongs. Lois can still remember all the words to "My Darling Clementine," and to "My Bonnie Lies Over the Ocean," with acting-out gestures: a rippling of the hands for "the ocean," two hands together under the cheek for "lies." She will never be able to forget them, which is a sad thought.

Lois thinks she can recognize women who went to these 9
camps, and were good at it. They have a hardness to their handshakes, even now; a way of standing, legs planted firmly and farther apart than usual; a way of sizing you up, to see if you'd be any good in a canoe—the front, not the back. They themselves would be in the back. They would call it the stern.

She knows that such camps still exist, although Camp 10
Manitou does not. They are one of the few things that haven't changed much. They now offer copper enamelling, and functionless pieces of stained glass baked in electric ovens, though judging from the productions of her friends' grandchildren the artistic standards have not improved.

To Lois, encountering it in the first year after the war, Camp 11
Manitou seemed ancient. Its log-sided buildings with the white cement in between the half-logs, its flagpole ringed with whitewashed stones, its weathered grey dock jutting out into Lake Prospect, with its woven rope bumpers and its rusty rings for tying up, its prim round flowerbed of petunias near the office door, must surely have been there always. In truth it dated only

from the first decade of the century; it had been founded by
Cappie's parents, who'd thought of camping as bracing to the
character, like cold showers, and had been passed along to her as
an inheritance, and an obligation.

Lois realized, later, that it must have been a struggle for   12
Cappie to keep Camp Manitou going, during the Depression
and then the war, when money did not flow freely. If it had been
a camp for the very rich, instead of the merely well off, there
would have been fewer problems. But there must have been
enough Old Girls, ones with daughters, to keep the thing in
operation, though not entirely shipshape: furniture was battered,
painted trim was peeling, roofs leaked. There were dim
photographs of these Old Girls dotted around the dining hall,
wearing ample woollen bathing suits and showing their fat,
dimpled legs, or standing, arms twined, in odd tennis outfits
with baggy skirts.

In the dining hall, over the stone fireplace that was never   13
used, there was a huge moulting stuffed moose head, which
looked somehow carnivorous. It was a sort of mascot; its name
was Monty Manitou. The older campers spread the story that it
was haunted, and came to life in the dark, when the feeble and
undependable lights had been turned off or, due to yet another
generator failure, had gone out. Lois was afraid of it at first, but
not after she got used to it.

Cappie was the same: you had to get used to her. Possibly she   14
was forty, or thirty-five, or fifty. She had fawn-coloured hair that
looked as if it was cut with a bowl. Her head jutted forward,
jigging like a chicken's as she strode around the camp, clutching
notebooks and checking things off in them. She was like their
minister in church: both of them smiled a lot and were anxious
because they wanted things to go well; they both had the same
overwashed skins and stringy necks. But all this disappeared
when Cappie was leading a singsong, or otherwise leading. Then
she was happy, sure of herself, her plain face almost luminous.
She wanted to cause joy. At these times she was loved, at others
merely trusted.

There were many things Lois didn't like about Camp   15
Manitou, at first. She hated the noisy chaos and spoon-banging
of the dining hall, the rowdy singsongs at which you were
expected to yell in order to show that you were enjoying yourself.
Hers was not a household that encouraged yelling. She hated

the necessity of having to write dutiful letters to her parents claiming she was having fun. She could not complain, because camp cost so much money.

She didn't much like having to undress in a roomful of other 16 girls, even in the dim light, although nobody paid any attention, or sleeping in a cabin with seven other girls: some of whom snored because they had adenoids or colds, some of whom had nightmares, or wet their beds and cried about it. Bottom bunks made her feel closed in, and she was afraid of falling out of top ones; she was afraid of heights. She got homesick, and suspected her parents of having a better time when she wasn't there than when she was, although her mother wrote to her every week saying how much they missed her. All this was when she was nine. By the time she was thirteen she liked it. She was an old hand by then.

Lucy was her best friend at camp. Lois had other friends in 17 winter, when there was school and itchy woollen clothing and darkness in the afternoons, but Lucy was her summer friend.

She turned up the second year, when Lois was ten, and a 18 Bluejay. (Chickadees, Bluejays, Ravens, and Kingfishers—these were the names Camp Manitou assigned to the different age groups, a sort of totemic clan system. In those days, thinks Lois, it was birds for girls, animals for boys: wolves, and so forth. Though some animals and birds were suitable and some were not. Never vultures, for instance; never skunks, or rats.)

Lois helped Lucy to unpack her tin trunk and place the folded 19 clothes on the wooden shelves, and to make up her bed. She put her in the top bunk right above her, where she could keep an eye on her. Already she knew that Lucy was an exception, to a good many rules; already she felt proprietorial.

Lucy was from the United States, where the comic books 20 came from, and the movies. She wasn't from New York or Hollywood or Buffalo, the only American cities Lois knew the names of, but from Chicago. Her house was on the lakeshore and had gates to it, and grounds. They had a maid, all of the time. Lois's family only had a cleaning lady twice a week.

The only reason Lucy was being sent to *this* camp (she cast a 21 look of minor scorn around the cabin, diminishing it and also offending Lois, while at the same time daunting her) was that her mother had been a camper here. Her mother had been a

Canadian once, but had married her father, who had a patch
over one eye, like a pirate. She showed Lois the picture of him in
her wallet. He got the patch in the war. "Shrapnel," said Lucy.
Lois, who was unsure about shrapnel, was so impressed she
could only grunt. Her own two-eyed, unwounded father was
tame by comparison.

"My father plays golf," she ventured at last.   22

"*Everyone* plays golf," said Lucy. "My *mother* plays golf."   23

Lois's mother did not. Lois took Lucy to see the outhouses   24
and the swimming dock and the dining hall with Monty
Manitou's baleful head, knowing in advance they would not
measure up.

This was a bad beginning; but Lucy was good-natured, and   25
accepted Camp Manitou with the same casual shrug with which
she seemed to accept everything. She would make the best of it,
without letting Lois forget that this was what she was doing.

However, there were things Lois knew that Lucy did not.   26
Lucy scratched the tops off all her mosquito bites and had to be
taken to the infirmary to be daubed with Ozonol. She took her T-
shirt off while sailing, and although the counsellor spotted her
after a while and made her put it back on, she burnt spectacularly,
bright red, with the X of her bathing-suit straps standing out in
alarming white; she let Lois peel the sheets of whispery-thin
burned skin off her shoulders. When they sang "Alouette" around
the campfire, she did not know any of the French words. The
difference was that Lucy did not care about the things she didn't
know, whereas Lois did.

During the next winter, and subsequent winters, Lucy and   27
Lois wrote to each other. They were both only children, at a
time when this was thought to be a disadvantage, so in their
letters they pretended to be sisters, or even twins. Lois had to
strain a little over this, because Lucy was so blond, with
translucent skin and large blue eyes like a doll's, and Lois was
nothing out of the ordinary—just a tallish, thinnish, brownish
person with freckles. They signed their letters LL, with the L's
entwined together like the monograms on a towel. (Lois and
Lucy, thinks Lois. How our names date us. Lois Lane,
Superman's girlfriend, enterprising female reporter; "I Love
Lucy." Now we are obsolete and it's little Jennifers, little Emilys,
little Alexandras and Carolines and Tiffanys.)

They were more effusive in their letters than they ever were   28
in person. They bordered their pages with X's and O's, but when

they met again in the summers it was always a shock. They had changed so much, or Lucy had. It was like watching someone grow up in jolts. At first it would be hard to think up things to say.

But Lucy always had a surprise or two, something to show, 29 some marvel to reveal. The first year she had a picture of herself in a tutu, her hair in a ballerina's knot on the top of her head; she pirouetted around the swimming dock, to show Lois how it was done, and almost fell off. The next year she had given that up and was taking horseback riding. (Camp Manitou did not have horses.) The next year her mother and father had been divorced, and she had a new stepfather, one with both eyes, and a new house, although the maid was the same. The next year, when they had graduated from Bluejays and entered Ravens, she got her period, right in the first week of camp. The two of them snitched some matches from their counsellor, who smoked illegally, and made a small fire out behind the farthest outhouse, at dusk, using their flashlights. They could set all kinds of fires by now; they had learned how in Campcraft. On this fire they burned one of Lucy's used sanitary napkins. Lois is not sure why they did this, or whose idea it was. But she can remember the feeling of deep satisfaction it gave her as the white fluff singed and the blood sizzled, as if some wordless ritual had been fulfilled.

They did not get caught, but then they rarely got caught at 30 any of their camp transgressions. Lucy had such large eyes, and was such an accomplished liar.

This year Lucy is different again: slower, more languorous. She 31 is no longer interested in sneaking around after dark, purloining cigarettes from the counsellor, dealing in black-market candy bars. She is pensive, and hard to wake in the mornings. She doesn't like her stepfather, but she doesn't want to live with her real father either, who has a new wife. She thinks her mother may be having a love affair with a doctor; she doesn't know for sure, but she's seen them smooching in his car, out on the driveway, when her stepfather wasn't there. It serves him right. She hates her private school. She has a boyfriend, who is sixteen and works as a gardener's assistant. This is how she met him: in the garden. She describes to Lois what it is like when he kisses her—rubbery at first, but then your knees go limp. She has been forbidden to see him, and threatened with boarding school. She wants to run away from home.

Lois has little to offer in return. Her own life is placid and   32
satisfactory, but there is nothing much that can be said about
happiness. "You're so lucky," Lucy tells her, a little smugly. She
might as well say *boring* because this is how it makes Lois feel.

Lucy is apathetic about the canoe trip, so Lois has to disguise   33
her own excitement. The evening before they are to leave, she
slouches into the campfire ring as if coerced, and sits down with
a sigh of endurance, just as Lucy does.

Every canoe trip that went out of camp was given a special   34
send-off by Cappie and the section leader and counsellors, with
the whole section in attendance. Cappie painted three streaks of
red across each of her cheeks with a lipstick. They looked like
three-fingered claw marks. She put a blue circle on her forehead
with fountain-pen ink, and tied a twisted bandanna around her
head and stuck a row of frazzle-ended feathers around it, and
wrapped herself in a red-and-black Hudson's Bay blanket. The
counsellors, also in blankets but with only two streaks of red,
beat on tom-toms made of round wooden cheese boxes with
leather stretched over the top and nailed in place. Cappie was
Chief Cappeosota. They all had to say "How!" when she walked
into the circle and stood there with one hand raised.

Looking back on this, Lois finds it disquieting. She knows   35
too much about Indians: this is why. She knows, for instance,
that they should not even be called Indians, and that they have
enough worries without other people taking their names and
dressing up as them. It has all been a form of stealing.

But she remembers too, that she was once ignorant of this.   36
Once she loved the campfire, the flickering of light on the ring of
faces, the sound of the fake tom-toms, heavy and fast like a scared
heartbeat; she loved Cappie in a red blanket and feathers, solemn,
as a chief should be, raising her hand and saying, "Greetings,
my Ravens." It was not funny, it was not making fun. She wanted
to be an Indian. She wanted to be adventurous and pure, and
aboriginal.

"You go on big water," says Cappie. This is her idea—all their   37
ideas—of how Indians talk. "You go where no man has ever trod.
You go many moons." This is not true. They are only going for a
week, not many moons. The canoe route is clearly marked, they
have gone over it on a map, and there are prepared campsites

with names which are used year after year. But when Cappie says this—and despite the way Lucy rolls up her eyes—Lois can feel the water stretching out, with the shores twisting away on either side, immense and a little frightening.

"You bring back much wampum," says Cappie. "Do good 38 in war, my braves, and capture many scalps." This is another of her pretences: that they are boys, and bloodthirsty. But such a game cannot be played by substituting the word "squaw." It would not work at all.

Each of them has to stand up and step forward and have a 39 red line drawn across her cheeks by Cappie. She tells them they must follow in the paths of their ancestors (who most certainly, thinks Lois, looking out the window of her apartment and remembering the family stash of daguerreotypes and sepia-coloured portraits on her mother's dressing table, the stiff-shirted, black-coated, grim-faced men and the beflounced women with their severe hair and their corseted respectability, would never have considered heading off onto an open lake, in a canoe, just for fun).

At the end of the ceremony they all stood and held hands 40 around the circle, and sang taps. This did not sound very Indian, thinks Lois. It sounded like a bugle call at a military post, in a movie. But Cappie was never one to be much concerned with consistency, or with archaeology.

After breakfast the next morning they set out from the main 41 dock, in four canoes, three in each. The lipstick stripes have not come off completely, and still show faintly pink, like healing burns. They wear their white denim sailing hats, because of the sun, and thin-striped T-shirts, and pale baggy shorts with the cuffs rolled up. The middle one kneels, propping her rear end against the rolled sleeping bags. The counsellors going with them are Pat and Kip. Kip is no-nonsense; Pat is easier to wheedle, or fool.

There are puffy clouds and a small breeze. Glints come from 42 the little waves. Lois is in the bow of Kip's canoe. She still can't do a J-stroke very well, and she will have to be in the bow or the middle for the whole trip. Lucy is behind her; her own J-stroke is even worse. She splashes Lois with her paddle, quite a big splash.

"I'll get you back," says Lois. 43

"There was a stable fly on your shoulder," Lucy says. 44

Lois turns to look at her, to see if she's grinning. They're in   45
the habit of splashing each other. Back there, the camp has
vanished behind the first long point of rock and rough trees. Lois
feels as if an invisible rope has broken. They're floating free, on
their own, cut loose. Beneath the canoe the lake goes down,
deeper and colder than it was a minute before.

"No horsing around in the canoe," says Kip. She's rolled her   46
T-shirt sleeves up to the shoulder, her arms are brown and
sinewy, her jaw determined, her stroke perfect. She looks as if
she knows exactly what she is doing.

The four canoes keep close together. They sing, raucously   47
and with defiance; they sing "The Quartermaster's Store," and
"Clementine," and "Alouette." It is more like bellowing than
singing.

After that the wind grows stronger, blowing slantwise against   48
the bows, and they have to put all their energy into shoving
themselves through the water.

Was there anything important, anything that would provide   49
some sort of reason or clue to what happened next? Lois can
remember everything, every detail; but it does her no good.

They stopped at noon for a swim and lunch, and went on in   50
the afternoon. At last they reached Little Birch, which was the
first campsite for overnight. Lois and Lucy made the fire, while
the others pitched the heavy canvas tents. The fireplace was
already there, flat stones piled into a U. A burned tin can and a
beer bottle had been left in it. Their fire went out, and they had
to restart it. "Hustle your bustle," said Kip. "We're starving."

The sun went down, and in the pink sunset light they   51
brushed their teeth and spat the toothpaste froth into the lake. Kip
and Pat put all the food that wasn't in cans into a packsack and
slung it into a tree, in case of bears.

Lois and Lucy weren't sleeping in a tent. They'd begged to be   52
allowed to sleep out; that way they could talk without the others
hearing. If it rained, they told Kip, they promised not to crawl
dripping into the tent over everyone's legs: they would get under
the canoes. So they were out on the point.

Lois tried to get comfortable inside her sleeping bag, which   53
smelled of musty storage and of earlier campers, a stale salty
sweetness. She curled herself up, with her sweater rolled up
under her head for a pillow and her flashlight inside her sleeping

bag so it wouldn't roll away. The muscles of her sore arms were making small pings, like rubber bands breaking.

Beside her Lucy was rustling around. Lois could see the 54 glimmering oval of her white face.

"I've got a rock poking into my back," said Lucy. 55

"So do I," said Lois. "You want to go into the tent?" She 56 herself didn't, but it was right to ask.

"No," said Lucy. She subsided into her sleeping bag. After a 57 moment she said, "It would be nice not to go back."

"To camp?" said Lois. 58

"To Chicago," said Lucy. "I hate it there." 59

"What about your boyfriend?" said Lois. Lucy didn't answer. 60 She was either asleep or pretending to be.

There was a moon, and a movement of the trees. In the sky 61 there were stars, layers of stars that went down and down. Kip said that when the stars were bright like that instead of hazy it meant bad weather later on. Out on the lake there were two loons, calling to each other in their insane, mournful voices. At the time it did not sound like grief. It was just background.

The lake in the morning was flat calm. They skimmed along over 62 the glassy surface, leaving V-shaped trails behind them; it felt like flying. As the sun rose higher it got hot, almost too hot. There were stable flies in the canoes, landing on a bare arm or leg for a quick sting. Lois hoped for wind.

They stopped for lunch at the next of the named campsites, 63 Lookout Point. It was called this because, although the site itself was down near the water on a flat shelf of rock, there was a sheer cliff nearby and a trail that led up to the top. The top was the lookout, although what you were supposed to see from there was not clear. Kip said it was just a view.

Lois and Lucy decided to make the climb anyway. They didn't 64 want to hang around waiting for lunch. It wasn't their turn to cook, though they hadn't avoided much by not doing it, because cooking lunch was no big deal, it was just unwrapping the cheese and getting out the bread and peanut butter, but Pat and Kip always had to do their woodsy act and boil up a billy tin for their own tea.

They told Kip where they were going. You had to tell Kip 65 where you were going, even if it was only a little way into the woods to get dry twigs for kindling. You could never go anywhere without a buddy.

"Sure," said Kip, who was crouching over the fire, feeding 66
driftwood into it. "Fifteen minutes to lunch."

"Where are they off to?" said Pat. She was bringing their 67
billy tin of water from the lake.

"Lookout," said Kip.   68

"Be careful," said Pat. She said it as an afterthought, because 69
it was what she always said.

"They're old hands," Kip said.   70

Lois looks at her watch: it's ten to twelve. She is the watch- 71
minder; Lucy is careless of time. They walk up the path, which is
dry earth and rocks, big rounded pinky-grey boulders or split-
open ones with jagged edges. Spindly balsam and spruce trees
grow to either side, the lake is blue fragments to the left. The
sun is right overhead; there are no shadows anywhere. The heat
comes up at them as well as down. The forest is dry and crackly.

It isn't far, but it's a steep climb and they're sweating when 72
they reach the top. They wipe their faces with their bare arms, sit
gingerly down on a scorching-hot rock, five feet from the edge but
too close for Lois. It's a lookout all right, a sheer drop to the lake
and a long view over the water, back the way they've come. It's
amazing to Lois that they've travelled so far, over all that water,
with nothing to propel them but their own arms. It makes her
feel strong. There are all kinds of things she is capable of doing.

"It would be quite a dive off here," says Lucy.   73

"You'd have to be nuts," says Lois.   74

"Why?" says Lucy. "It's really deep. It goes straight down." 75
She stands up and takes a step nearer the edge. Lois gets a stab
in her midriff, the kind she gets when a car goes too fast over a
bump. "Don't," she says.

"Don't what?" says Lucy, glancing around at her 76
mischievously. She knows how Lois feels about heights. But she
turns back. "I really have to pee," she says.

"You have toilet paper?" says Lois, who is never without 77
it. She digs in her shorts pocket.

"Thanks," says Lucy.   78

They are both adept at peeing in the woods: doing it fast so 79
the mosquitoes don't get you, the underwear pulled up between
the knees, the squat with the feet apart so you don't wet your
legs, facing downhill. The exposed feeling of your bum, as if
someone is looking at you from behind. The etiquette when

you're with someone else is not to look. Lois stands up and starts
to walk back down the path, to be out of sight.

"Wait for me?" says Lucy.   80

Lois climbed down, over and around the boulders, until she   81
could not see Lucy; she waited. She could hear the voices of the
others, talking and laughing, down near the shore. One voice
was yelling, "Ants! Ants!" Someone must have sat on an ant hill.
Off to the side, in the woods, a raven was croaking, a hoarse
single note.

She looked at her watch: it was noon. This is when she heard   82
the shout.

She has gone over and over it in her mind since, so many   83
times that the first, real shout has been obliterated, like a footprint
trampled by other footprints. But she is sure (she is almost
positive, she is nearly certain) that it was not a shout of fear. Not
a scream. More like a cry of surprise, cut off too soon. Short, like
a dog's bark.

"Lucy?" Lois said. Then she called "Lucy!" By now she was   84
clambering back up, over the stones of the path. Lucy was not
up there. Or she was not in sight.

"Stop fooling around," Lois said. "It's lunchtime." But Lucy   85
did not rise from behind a rock or step out, smiling, from behind
a tree. The sunlight was all around: the rocks looked white. "This
isn't funny!" Lois said, and it wasn't, panic was rising in her, the
panic of a small child who does not know where the bigger ones
are hidden. She could hear her own heart. She looked quickly
around; she lay down on the ground and looked over the edge of
the cliff. It made her feel cold. There was nothing.

She went back down the path, stumbling; she was breathing   86
too quickly; she was too frightened to cry. She felt terrible—
guilty and dismayed, as if she had done something very bad, by
mistake. Something that could never be repaired. "Lucy's gone,"
she told Kip.

Kip looked up from her fire, annoyed. The water in the billy   87
can was boiling. "What do you mean, gone?" she said. "Where
did she go?"

"I don't know," said Lois. "She's just gone."   88

No one had heard the shout, but then no one had heard Lois   89
calling, either. They had been talking among themselves, by the
water.

Kip and Pat went up to the lookout and searched and called,   90
and blew their whistles. Nothing answered.

Then they came back down, and Lois had to tell exactly what   91
had happened. The other girls all sat in a circle and listened to
her. Nobody said anything. They all looked frightened, especially
Pat and Kip. They were the leaders. You did not just lose a
camper like this, for no reason at all.

"Why did you leave her alone?" said Kip.   92

"I was just down the path," said Lois. "I told you. She had to   93
go to the bathroom." She did not say *pee* in front of people older
than herself.

Kip looked disgusted.   94

"Maybe she just walked off into the woods and got turned   95
around," said one of the girls.

"Maybe she's doing it on purpose," said another.   96

Nobody believed either of these theories.   97

They took the canoes and searched around the base of the   98
cliff, and peered down into the water. But there had been no
sound of falling rock; there had been no splash. There was no
clue, nothing at all. Lucy had simply vanished.

That was the end of the canoe trip. It took them the same   99
two days to go back that it had taken coming in, even though
they were short a paddler. They did not sing.

After that, the police went in a motorboat, with dogs; they   100
were the Mounties and the dogs were German shepherds, trained
to follow trails in the woods. But it had rained since, and they
could find nothing.

Lois is sitting in Cappie's office. Her face is bloated with crying,   101
she's seen that in the mirror. By now she feels numbed; she feels
as if she has drowned. She can't stay here. It has been too much
of a shock. Tomorrow her parents are coming to take her away.
Several of the other girls who were on the canoe trip are also
being collected. The others will have to stay, because their parents
are in Europe, or cannot be reached.

Cappie is grim. They've tried to hush it up, but of course   102
everyone in camp knows. Soon the papers will know too. You
can't keep it quiet, but what can be said? What can be said that
makes any sense? "Girl vanishes in broad daylight, without a
trace." It can't be believed. Other things, worse things, will be
suspected. Negligence, at the very least. But they have always

taken such care. Bad luck will gather around Camp Manitou like a fog; parents will avoid it, in favour of other, luckier places. Lois can see Cappie thinking all this, even through her numbness. It's what anyone would think.

Lois sits on the hard wooden chair in Cappie's office, beside 103 the old wooden desk, over which hangs the thumbtacked bulletin board of normal camp routine, and gazes at Cappie through her puffy eyelids. Cappie is now smiling what is supposed to be a reassuring smile. Her manner is too casual: she's after something. Lois has seen this look on Cappie's face when she's been sniffing out contraband chocolate bars, hunting down those rumoured to have snuck out of their cabins at night.

"Tell me again, " says Cappie, "from the beginning." 104

Lois has told her story so many times by now, to Pat and 105 Kip, to Cappie, to the police, that she knows it word for word. She knows it, but she no longer believes it. It has become a story. "I told you," she said. "She wanted to go to the bathroom. I gave her my toilet paper. I went down the path, I waited for her. I heard this kind of shout ..."

"Yes," says Cappie, smiling confidingly, "but before that. 106 What did you say to one another?"

Lois thinks. Nobody has asked her this before. "She said you 107 could dive off there. She said it went straight down."

"And what did you say?" 108

"I said you'd have to be nuts." 109

"Were you mad at Lucy?" says Cappie, in an encouraging 110 voice.

"No," says Lois. "Why would I be mad at Lucy? I wasn't 111 ever mad at Lucy." She feels like crying again. The times when she has in fact been mad at Lucy have been erased already. Lucy was always perfect.

"Sometimes we're angry when we don't know we're angry," 112 says Cappie, as if to herself. "Sometimes we get really mad and we don't even know it. Sometimes we might do a thing without meaning to, or without knowing what will happen. We lose our tempers."

Lois is only thirteen, but it doesn't take her long to figure 113 out that Cappie is not including herself in any of this. By *we* she means Lois. She is accusing Lois of pushing Lucy off the cliff. The unfairness of this hits her like a slap. "I didn't!" she says.

"Didn't what?" says Cappie softly. "Didn't what, Lois?" 114

Lois does the worst thing, she begins to cry. Cappie gives 115
her a look like a pounce. She's got what she wanted.

Later, when she was grown up, Lois was able to understand 116
what this interview had been about. She could see Cappie's
desperation, her need for a story, a real story with a reason in
it; anything but the senseless vacancy Lucy had left for her to
deal with. Cappie wanted Lois to supply the reason, to be the
reason. It wasn't even for the newspapers or the parents, because
she could never make such an accusation without proof. It was
for herself: something to explain the loss of Camp Manitou and
of all she had worked for, the years of entertaining spoiled
children and buttering up parents and making a fool of herself
with feathers stuck in her hair. Camp Manitou was in fact lost. It
did not survive.

Lois worked all this out, twenty years later. But it was far 117
too late. It was too late even ten minutes afterwards, when she'd
left Cappie's office and was walking slowly back to her cabin to
pack. Lucy's clothes were still there, folded on the shelves, as if
waiting. She felt the other girls in the cabin watching her with
speculation in their eyes. *Could she have done it? She must have
done it.* For the rest of her life, she has caught people watching her
in this way.

Maybe they weren't thinking this. Maybe they were merely 118
sorry for her. But she felt she had been tried and sentenced, and
this is what has stayed with her: the knowledge that she had been
singled out, condemned for something that was not her fault.

Lois sits in the living room of her apartment, drinking a cup of 119
tea. Through the knee-to-ceiling window she has a wide view
of Lake Ontario, with its skin of wrinkled blue-grey light, and
of the willows of Centre Island shaken by a wind, which is silent
at this distance, and on this side of the glass. When there isn't
too much pollution she can see the far shore, the foreign shore;
though today it is obscured.

Possibly she could go out, go downstairs, do some shopping; 120
there isn't much in the refrigerator. The boys say she doesn't get
out enough. But she isn't hungry, and moving, stirring from this
space, is increasingly an effort.

She can hardly remember, now, having her two boys in the 121
hospital, nursing them as babies; she can hardly remember getting

married, or what Rob looked like. Even at the time she never felt she was paying full attention. She was tired a lot, as if she was living not one life but two: her own, and another, shadowy life that hovered around her and would not let itself be realized—the life of what would have happened if Lucy had not stepped sideways, and disappeared from time.

She would never go up north, to Rob's family cottage or to 122 any place with wild lakes and wild trees and the calls of loons. She would never go anywhere near. Still, it was as if she was always listening for another voice, the voice of a person who should have been there but was not. An echo.

While Rob was alive, while the boys were growing up, she 123 could pretend she didn't hear it, this empty space in sound. But now there is nothing much left to distract her.

She turns away from the window and looks at her pictures. 124 There is the pinkish island, in the lake, with the intertwisted trees. It's the same landscape they paddled through, that distant summer. She's seen travelogues of this country, aerial photographs; it looks different from above, bigger, more hopeless: lake after lake, random blue puddles in dark green bush, the trees like bristles.

How could you ever find anything there, once it was lost? 125 Maybe if they cut it all down, drained it all away, they might find Lucy's bones, some time, wherever they are hidden. A few bones, some buttons, the buckle from her shorts.

But a dead person is a body; a body occupies space, it exists 126 somewhere. You can see it; you put it in a box and bury it in the ground, and then it's in a box in the ground. But Lucy is not in a box, or in the ground. Because she is nowhere definite, she could be anywhere.

And these paintings are not landscape paintings. Because 127 there aren't any landscapes up there, not in the old, tidy European sense, with a gentle hill, a curving river, a cottage, a mountain in the background, a golden evening sky. Instead there's a tangle, a receding maze, in which you can become lost almost as soon as you step off the path. There are no backgrounds in any of these paintings, no vistas; only a great deal of foreground that goes back and back, endlessly, involving you in its twists and turns of tree and branch and rock. No matter how far back in you go, there will be more. And the trees themselves are hardly trees; they are currents of energy, charged with violent colour.

Who knows how many trees there were on the cliff just before   128
Lucy disappeared? Who counted? Maybe there was one more,
afterwards.

Lois sits in her chair and does not move. Her hand with the   129
cup is raised halfway to her mouth. She hears something, almost
hears it: a shout of recognition, or of joy.

She looks at the paintings, she looks into them. Every one   130
of them is a picture of Lucy. You can't see her exactly, but she's
there, in behind the pink stone island or the one behind that. In
the picture of the cliff she is hidden by the clutch of fallen rocks
towards the bottom, in the one of the river shore she is crouching
beneath the overturned canoe. In the yellow autumn woods she's
behind the tree that cannot be seen because of other trees, over
beside the blue sliver of pond; but if you walked into the picture
and found the tree, it would be the wrong one, because the right
one would be farther on.

Everyone has to be somewhere, and this is where Lucy is.   131
She is in Lois's apartment, in the holes that open inwards on the
wall, not like windows but like doors. She is here. She is entirely
alive.

UNDERSTANDING DETAILS

1. The setting in "Death by Landscape" is particularly important.
   When and where does this story take place? How do you know
   this?
2. Summarize the general experience of being a camper at Camp
   Manitou. Is it an appealing experience? Why or why not?
3. Describe the character of Lucy.

ANALYZING MEANING

1. What happens to Lucy when she disappears? Be sure to use
   specific details from the story to support your theory.
2. Explain the significance of the pictures on the walls of Lois's
   apartment in "Death by Landscape."
3. Explain how Atwood develops the character of Lois in "Death
   by Landscape" to make the reader empathize with her over the
   disappearance of her friend Lucy.

DISCOVERING RHETORICAL STRATEGIES

1. The disappearance of Lucy in "Death by Landscape" does not come as a complete surprise. How does Atwood foreshadow this event?
2. Atwood has used the technique of flashbacks to relate this story. Why has she made this choice? How would the story be different if it were told entirely from the perspective of the adult Lois?
3. Atwood has incorporated a significant amount of dialogue into "Death by Landscape." What is the effect of hearing the dialogue rather than a third person account of a conversation?

MAKING CONNECTIONS

1. Compare and contrast the attitude conveyed toward the Canadian wilderness in "Death by Landscape" with that portrayed by Tomson Highway in "What a Certain Visionary Once Said."
2. Both Lois and Beth (in Elizabeth Hay's "Cézanne in a Soft Hat") find significance in paintings. What role does visual art play in each of their lives?
3. Several of the stories in this collection deal with the effects of traumatic experience on individual characters. Compare and contrast the effects of Lucy's death on Lois ("Death by Landscape") with the effects of Clare's father's death on Clare (in Timothy Taylor's "Doves of Townsend").

CHOOSING A TOPIC FOR DISCUSSION/WRITING

1. Write a narrative essay telling the story of a person you encountered in childhood who has had a lasting impact on your life.
2. Read the poem by Margaret Atwood entitled "This Is a Photograph of Me" (available in many anthologies). Write a short essay in which you explain how this poem relates to "Death by Landscape."
3. The pictures on Lois's walls are particularly significant in this story. Write an essay in which you explain the role of some form of art (visual art, music, dance, etc.) in your life.

T. Coraghessan Boyle

■ ☐ ■

GREASY LAKE

Boyle's advice to young writers starting out (as found on his Web site), is as follows:

> Read. Find a writer who knocks you out and
> read and obsessively re-read his/her work.
> Writing is the expression of an assimilation of
> words, phrases, ideas, textures, structures. Read
> and absorb. And then see what comes out of the
> old fingertips. Read constantly.

Born in Peekskill, New York in 1948, Boyle was a history and English major at SUNY and began his career as a high school teacher. Boyle left his first teaching position to pursue graduate studies in writing and literature, then served as fiction editor for the *Iowa Review*. Since 1986, Boyle has been a Professor of English at the University of South California, Los Angeles, in addition to being a prolific writer. Boyle's novels, collections of short stories, and essays have earned him numerous awards; they include *Descent of Man* (1979), *World's End* (1987), *The Tortilla Curtain* (1995), and *Greasy Lake and Other Stories* (1985), which includes the selection found here.

It's about a mile down the dark side of Route 88.

—Bruce Springsteen

There was a time when courtesy and winning ways went out of   1
style, when it was good to be bad, when you cultivated decadence like a taste. We were all dangerous characters then. We wore torn-up leather jackets, slouched around with toothpicks in our mouths, sniffed glue and ether and what somebody claimed was cocaine. When we wheeled our parents' whining station wagons out into the street we left a patch of rubber half a block long.

We drank gin and grape juice, Tango, Thunderbird, and Bali Hai. We were nineteen. We were bad. We read André Gide and struck elaborate poses to show that we didn't give a shit about anything. At night, we went up to Greasy Lake.

Through the center of town, up the strip, past the housing 2 developments and shopping malls, street lights giving way to the thin streaming illumination of the headlights, trees crowding the asphalt in a black unbroken wall: that was the way out to Greasy Lake. The Indians had called it Wakan, a reference to the clarity of its waters. Now it was fetid and murky, the mud banks glittering with broken glass and strewn with beer cans and the charred remains of bonfires. There was a single ravaged island a hundred yards from shore, so stripped of vegetation it looked as if the air force had strafed it. We went up to the lake because everyone went there, because we wanted to snuff the rich scent of possibility on the breeze, watch a girl take off her clothes and plunge into the festering murk, drink beer, smoke pot, howl at the stars, savor the incongruous full-throated roar of rock and roll against the primeval susurrus of frogs and crickets. This was nature.

I was there one night, late, in the company of two dangerous 3 characters. Digby wore a gold star in his right ear and allowed his father to pay his tuition at Cornell; Jeff was thinking of quitting school to become a painter/musician/headshop proprietor. They were both expert in the social graces, quick with a sneer, able to manage a Ford with lousy shocks over a rutted and gutted blacktop road at eighty-five while rolling a joint as compact as a Tootsie Roll Pop stick. They could lounge against a bank of booming speakers and trade "man"s with the best of them or roll out across the dance floor as if their joints worked on bearings. They were slick and quick and they wore their mirror shades at breakfast and dinner, in the shower, in closets and caves. In short, they were bad.

I drove. Digby pounded the dashboard and shouted along 4 with Toots & the Maytals while Jeff hung his head out the window and streaked the side of my mother's Bel Air with vomit. It was early June, the air soft as a hand on your cheek, the third night of summer vacation. The first two nights we'd been out till dawn, looking for something we never found. On this, the third night, we'd cruised the strip sixty-seven times, been in and out of every bar and club we could think of in a twenty-mile radius, stopped twice for bucket chicken and forty-cent hamburgers, debated going to a party at the house of a girl Jeff's sister knew, and chucked two dozen raw eggs at mailboxes and hitchhikers. It was 2:00 A.M.; the bars were closing. There was nothing to do but take a bottle of lemon-flavored gin up to Greasy Lake.

The taillights of a single car winked at us as we swung into   5
the dirt lot with its tufts of weed and washboard corrugations; '57 Chevy, mint, metallic blue. On the far side of the lot, like the exoskeleton of some gaunt chrome insect, a chopper leaned against its kickstand. And that was it for excitement: some junkie half-wit biker and a car freak pumping his girlfriend. Whatever it was we were looking for, we weren't about to find it at Greasy Lake. Not that night.

But then all of a sudden Digby was fighting for the wheel.   6

"Hey, that's Tony Lovett's car! Hey!" he shouted, while I   7
stabbed at the brake pedal and the Bel Air nosed up to the gleaming bumper of the parked Chevy. Digby leaned on the horn, laughing, and instructed me to put my brights on. I flicked on the brights. This was hilarious. A joke. Tony would experience premature withdrawal and expect to be confronted by grim-looking state troopers with flashlights. We hit the horn, strobed the lights, and then jumped out of the car to press our witty faces to Tony's windows; for all we knew we might even catch a glimpse of some little fox's tit, and then we could slap backs with red-faced Tony, roughhouse a little, and go on to new heights of adventure and daring.

The first mistake, the one that opened the whole floodgate,   8
was losing my grip on the keys. In the excitement, leaping from the car with the gin in one hand and a roach clip in the other, I spilled them in the grass—in the dark, rank, mysterious nighttime grass of Greasy Lake. This was a tactical error, as damaging and irreversible in its way as Westmoreland's decision to dig in at Khe Sanh. I felt it like a jab of intuition, and I stopped there by the open door, peering vaguely into the night that puddled up round my feet.

The second mistake—and this was inextricably bound up   9
with the first—was identifying the car as Tony Lovett's. Even before the very bad character in greasy jeans and engineer boots ripped out of the driver's door, I began to realize that this chrome blue was much lighter than the robin's-egg of Tony's car, and that Tony's car didn't have rear-mounted speakers. Judging from their expressions, Digby and Jeff were privately groping toward the same inevitable and unsettling conclusion as I was.

In any case, there was no reasoning with this bad greasy 10
character—clearly he was a man of action. The first lusty
Rockette's kick of his steel-toed boot caught me under the chin,
chipped my favorite tooth, and left me sprawled in the dirt. Like
a fool, I'd gone down on one knee to comb the stiff hacked grass
for the keys, my mind making connections in the most dragged-
out, testudineous way, knowing that things had gone wrong,
that I was in a lot of trouble, and that the lost ignition key was my
grail and my salvation. The three or four succeeding blows were
mainly absorbed by my right buttock and the tough piece of
bone at the base of my spine.

Meanwhile, Digby vaulted the kissing bumpers and delivered 11
a savage kung-fu blow to the greasy character's collarbone. Digby
had just finished a course in martial arts for phys-ed credit and
had spent the better part of the past two nights telling us
apocryphal tales of Bruce Lee types and of the raw power invested
in lightning blows shot from coiled wrists, ankles and elbows.
The greasy character was unimpressed. He merely backed off a
step, his face like a Toltec mask, and laid Digby out with a single
whistling roundhouse blow ... but by now Jeff had got into the
act, and I was beginning to extricate myself from the dirt, a tinny
compound of shock, rage, and impotence wadded in my throat.

Jeff was on the guy's back, biting at his ear. Digby was on 12
the ground, cursing. I went for the tire iron I kept under the
driver's seat. I kept it there because bad characters always keep
tire irons under the driver's seat, for just such an occasion as
this. Never mind that I hadn't been involved in a fight since sixth
grade, when a kid with a sleepy eye and two streams of mucus
depending from his nostrils hit me in the knee with a Louisville
slugger; never mind that I'd touched the tire iron exactly twice
before, to change tires: it was there. And I went for it.

I was terrified. Blood was beating in my ears, my hands were 13
shaking, my heart turning over like a dirtbike in the wrong gear.
My antagonist was shirtless, and a single cord of muscle flashed
across his chest as he bent forward to peel Jeff from his back like
a wet overcoat. "Motherfucker," he spat, over and over, and I
was aware in that instant that all four of us—Digby, Jeff, and
myself included—were chanting "motherfucker, motherfucker,"
as if it were a battle cry. (What happened next? the detective
asks the murderer from beneath the turned-down brim of his
porkpie hat. I don't know, the murderer says, something came
over me. Exactly.)

Digby poked the flat of his hand in the bad character's face   14
and I came at him like a kamikaze, mindless, raging, stung with
humiliation—the whole thing, from the initial boot in the chin
to this murderous primal instant involving no more than sixty
hyperventilating, gland-flooding seconds—and I came at him
and brought the tire iron down across his ear. The effect was
instantaneous, astonishing. He was a stunt man and this was
Hollywood, he was a big grimacing toothy balloon and I was a
man with a straight pin. He collapsed. Wet his pants. Went loose
in his boots.

A single second, big as a zeppelin, floated by. We were   15
standing over him in a circle, gritting our teeth, jerking our necks,
our limbs and hands and feet twitching with glandular
discharges. No one said anything. We just stared down at the
guy, the car freak, the lover, the bad greasy character laid low.
Digby looked at me; so did Jeff. I was still holding the tire iron,
a tuft of hair clinging to the crook like dandelion fluff, like down.
Rattled, I dropped it in the dirt, already envisioning the headlines,
the pitted faces of the police inquisitors, the gleam of handcuffs,
clank of bars, the big black shadows rising from the back of the
cell … when suddenly a raw torn shriek cut through me like all
the juice in all the electric chairs in the country.

It was the fox. She was short, barefoot, dressed in panties   16
and a man's shirt. "Animals!" she screamed, running at us with
her fists clenched and wisps of blow-dried hair in her face. There
was a silver chain round her ankle, and her toenails flashed in the
glare of the headlights. I think it was the toenails that did it. Sure,
the gin and the cannabis and even the Kentucky Fried may have
had a hand in it, but it was the sight of those flaming toes that set
us off—the toad emerging from the loaf in *Virgin Spring*, lipstick
smeared on a child: she was already tainted. We were on her
like Bergman's deranged brothers—see no evil, hear none, speak
none—panting, wheezing, tearing at her clothes, grabbing for
flesh. We were bad characters, and we were scared and hot and
three steps over the line—anything could have happened.

It didn't.   17

Before we could pin her to the hood of the car, our eyes   18
masked with lust and greed and the purest primal badness, a
pair of headlights swung into the lot. There we were, dirty, bloody,
guilty, dissociated from humanity and civilization, the first of the
Ur-crimes behind us, the second in progress, shreds of nylon

panty and spandex brassiere dangling from our fingers, our flies open, lips licked—there we were, caught in the spotlight. Nailed.

We bolted. First for the car, and then, realizing we had no way   19 of starting it, for the woods. I thought nothing. I thought escape. The headlights came at me like accusing fingers. I was gone.

Ram-bam-bam, across the parking lot, past the chopper and   20 into the feculent undergrowth at the lake's edge, insects flying up in my face, weeds whipping, frogs and snakes and red-eyed turtles splashing off into the night: I was already ankle-deep in muck and tepid water and still going strong. Behind me, the girl's screams rose in intensity, disconsolate, incriminating, the screams of the Sabine women, the Christian martyrs, Anne Frank dragged from the garret. I kept going, pursued by those cries, imagining cops and bloodhounds. The water was up to my knees when I realized what I was doing: I was going to swim for it. Swim the breadth of Greasy Lake and hide myself in the thick clot of woods on the far side. They'd never find me there.

I was breathing in sobs, in gasps. The water lapped at my   21 waist as I looked out over the moon-burnished ripples, the mats of algae that clung to the surface like scabs. Digby and Jeff had vanished. I paused. Listened. The girl was quieter now, screams tapering to sobs, but there were male voices, angry, excited, and the high-pitched ticking of the second car's engine. I waded deeper, stealthy, hunted, the ooze sucking at my sneakers. As I was about to take the plunge—at the very instant I dropped my shoulder for the first slashing stroke—I blundered into something. Something unspeakable, obscene, something soft, wet, moss-grown. A patch of weed? A log? When I reached out to touch it, it gave like a rubber duck, it gave like flesh.

In one of those nasty little epiphanies for which we are   22 prepared by films and TV and childhood visits to the funeral home to ponder the shrunken painted forms of dead grandparents, I understood what it was that bobbed there so inadmissibly in the dark. Understood, and stumbled back in horror and revulsion, my mind yanked in six different directions (I was nineteen, a mere child, an infant, and here in the space of five minutes I'd struck down one greasy character and blundered into the waterlogged carcass of a second), thinking, The keys, the keys, why did I have to go and lose the keys? I stumbled back, but the muck took hold of my feet—a sneaker snagged, balance lost—and suddenly I was pitching face forward into the buoyant black mass, throwing out my hands in desperation while simultaneously conjuring the image of reeking frogs and muskrats revolving in slicks of their own deliquescing juices. AAAAArrrgh! I shot from the water like a torpedo, the dead man rotating to expose a mossy beard and eyes cold as the moon. I must have shouted out, thrashing around in the weeds, because the voices behind me suddenly became animated.

"What was that?"   23

"It's them, it's them: they tried, to tried to ... *rape* me!" Sobs.   24

A man's voice, flat, Midwestern accent. "You sons a bitches,   25
we'll kill you!"

Frogs, crickets.   26

Then another voice, harsh, r-less, Lower East Side: 27
"Motherfucker!" I recognized the verbal virtuosity of the bad greasy character in the engineer boots. Tooth chipped, sneakers gone, coated in mud and slime and worse, crouching breathless in the weeds waiting to have my ass thoroughly and definitively kicked and fresh from the hideous stinking embrace of a three-days-dead corpse, I suddenly felt a rush of joy and vindication: the son of a bitch was alive! Just as quickly, my bowels turned to ice. "Come on out of there, you pansy motherfuckers!" the bad greasy character was screaming. He shouted curses till he was out of breath.

The crickets started up again, then the frogs. I held my   28
breath. All at once there was a sound in the reeds, a swishing, a splash: thunk-a-thunk. They were throwing rocks. The frogs fell silent. I cradled my head. Swish, swish, thunk-a-thunk. A wedge of feldspar the size of a cue ball glanced off my knee. I bit my finger.

It was then that they turned to the car. I heard a door slam, a   29
curse, and then the sound of the headlights shattering—almost a good-natured sound, celebratory, like corks popping from the necks of bottles. This was succeeded by the dull booming of the fenders, metal on metal, and then the icy crash of the windshield. I inched forward, elbows and knees, my belly pressed to the muck, thinking of guerrillas and commandos and *The Naked and the Dead*, I parted the weeds and squinted the length of the parking lot.

The second car—it was a Trans-Am—was still running, its   30
high beams washing the scene in a lurid stagy light. Tire iron flailing, the greasy bad character was laying into the side of my mother's Bel Air like an avenging demon, his shadow riding up

the trunks of the trees. Whomp. Whomp. Whomp-whomp. The other two guys—blond types, in fraternity jackets—were helping out with tree branches and skull-sized boulders. One of them was gathering up bottles, rocks, muck, candy wrappers, used condoms, poptops, and other refuse and pitching it through the window on the driver's side. I could see the fox, a white bulb behind the windshield of the '57 Chevy. "Bobbie," she whined over the thumping, "come *on*." The greasy character paused a moment, took one good swipe at the left taillight, and then heaved the tire iron halfway across the lake. Then he fired up the '57 and was gone.

Blond head nodded at blond head. One said something to   31 the other, too low for me to catch. They were no doubt thinking that in helping to annihilate my mother's car they'd committed a fairly rash act, and thinking too that there were three bad characters connected with that very car watching them from the woods. Perhaps other possibilities occurred to them as well—police, jail cells, justices of the peace, reparations, lawyers, irate parents, fraternal censure. Whatever they were thinking, they suddenly dropped branches, bottles, and rocks and sprang for their car in unison, as if they'd choreographed it. Five seconds. That's all it took. The engine shrieked, the tires squealed, a cloud of dust rose from the rutted lot and then settled back on darkness.

I don't know how long I lay there, the bad breath of decay all   32 around me, my jacket heavy as a bear, the primordial ooze subtly reconstituting itself to accommodate my upper thighs and testicles. My jaws ached, my knee throbbed, my coccyx was on fire. I contemplated suicide, wondered if I'd need bridgework, scraped the recesses of my brain for some sort of excuse to give my parents—a tree had fallen on the car, I was blindsided by a bread truck, hit and run, vandals had got to it while we were playing chess at Digby's. Then I thought of the dead man. He was probably the only person on the planet worse off than I was: I thought about him, fog on the lake, insects chirring eerily, and felt the tug of fear, felt the darkness opening up inside me like a set of jaws. Who was he, I wondered, this victim of time and circumstance bobbing sorrowfully in the lake at my back. The owner of the chopper, no doubt, a bad older character come to this. Shot during a murky drug deal, drowned while drunkenly frolicking in the lake. Another headline. My car was wrecked; he was dead.

When the eastern half of the sky went from black to cobalt   33
and the trees began to separate themselves from the shadows, I
pushed myself up from the mud and stepped out into the open.
By now the birds had begun to take over for the crickets, and
dew lay slick on the leaves. There was a smell in the air, raw and
sweet at the same time, the smell of the sun firing buds and
opening blossoms. I contemplated the car. It lay there like a wreck
along the highway, like a steel sculpture left over from a vanished
civilization. Everything was still. This was nature.

I was circling the car, as dazed and bedraggled as the sole   34
survivor of an air blitz, when Digby and Jeff emerged from the
trees behind me. Digby's face was crosshatched with smears of
dirt; Jeff's jacket was gone and his shirt was torn across the
shoulder. They slouched across the lot, looking sheepish, and
silently came up beside me to gape at the ravaged automobile. No
one said a word. After a while Jeff swung open the driver's door
and began to scoop the broken glass and garbage off the seat. I
looked at Digby. He shrugged. "At least they didn't slash the
tires," he said.

It was true: the tires were intact. There was no windshield, the   35
headlights were staved in, and the body looked as if it had been
sledge-hammered for a quarter a shot at the county fair, but the
tires were inflated to regulation pressure. The car was drivable.
In silence, all three of us bent to scrape the mud and shattered
glass from the interior. I said nothing about the biker. When we
were finished, I reached in my pocket for the keys, experienced
a nasty stab of recollection, cursed myself, and turned to search
the grass. I spotted them almost immediately, no more than five
feet from the open door, glinting like jewels in the first tapering
shaft of sunlight. There was no reason to get philosophical about
it: I eased into the seat and turned the engine over.

It was at that precise moment that the silver Mustang with the   36
flame decals rumbled into the lot. All three of us froze; then
Digby and Jeff slid into the car and slammed the door. We
watched as the Mustang rocked and bobbed across the ruts and
finally jerked to a halt beside the forlorn chopper at the far end
of the lot. "Let's go," Digby said. I hesitated, the Bel Air wheezing
beneath me.

Two girls emerged from the Mustang. Tight jeans, stiletto   37
heels, hair like frozen fur. They bent over the motorcycle, paced
back and forth aimlessly, glanced once or twice at us, and then

ambled over to where the reeds sprang up in a green fence round the perimeter of the lake. One of them cupped her hands to her mouth. "Al," she called. "Hey, Al."

"Come on," Digby hissed. "Let's get out of here." 　　　　38

But it was too late. The second girl was picking her way across 39 the lot, unsteady on her heels, looking up at us and then away. She was older—twenty-five or -six—and as she came closer we could see there was something wrong with her: she was stoned or drunk, lurching now and waving her arms for balance. I gripped the steering wheel as if it were the ejection lever of a flaming jet, and Digby spat out my name, twice, terse and impatient.

"Hi," the girl said. 　　　　40

We looked at her like zombies, like war veterans, like deaf- 41 and-dumb pencil peddlers.

She smiled, her lips cracked and dry. "Listen," she said, 42 bending from the waist to look in the window, "you guys seen Al?" Her pupils were pinpoints, her eyes glass. She jerked her neck. "That's his bike over there—Al's. You seen him?"

Al. I didn't know what to say. I wanted to get out of the car 43 and retch, I wanted to go home to my parents' house and crawl into bed. Digby poked me in the ribs. "We haven't seen anybody," I said.

The girl seemed to consider this, reaching out a slim veiny 44 arm to brace herself against the car. "No matter," she said, slurring the *t*'s, "he'll turn up." And then, as if she'd just taken stock of the whole scene—the ravaged car and our battered faces, the desolation of the place—she said: "Hey, you guys look like some pretty bad characters—been fightin', huh?" We stared straight ahead, rigid as catatonics. She was fumbling in her pocket and muttering something. Finally she held out a handful of tablets in glassine wrappers: "Hey, you want to party, you want to do some of these with me and Sarah?"

I just looked at her. I thought I was going to cry. Digby broke 45 the silence. "No thanks," he said, leaning over me. "Some other time."

I put the car in gear and it inched forward with a groan, 46 shaking off pellets of glass like an old dog shedding water after a bath, heaving over the ruts on its worn springs, creeping toward the highway. There was a sheen of sun on the lake. I looked back. The girl was still standing there, watching us, her shoulders slumped, hand outstretched.

UNDERSTANDING DETAILS

1. In what sense is Greasy Lake the perfect setting for Boyle's story? How important to what happens in "Greasy Lake" is Greasy Lake itself?
2. How does the heroes' encounter with the two girls at the end of the story differ from their earlier encounter with the girl from the blue Chevy? How do you account for this difference?
3. Discuss the portrayal of the main character in "Greasy Lake." How does Boyle develop the narrator and convincingly convey the significant personality changes in this character?

ANALYZING MEANING

1. Boyle's stories focus on "bizarre action within seemingly normal settings." How is this true of "Greasy Lake"?
2. "Good short stories have the power to entertain and affect readers through time with their enduring themes." Discuss the relevance of "Greasy Lake" for a 21st-century audience.
3. In a review of *Greasy Lake and Other Stories* in the *Globe and Mail*, Nancy Wigston described Boyle's stories as "ribald, outrageous, sentimental, terrifying." How does this description apply to the title story?

DEVELOPING RHETORICAL STRATEGIES

1. Boyle has been noted for his technical skill in writing. With specific examples, explain how Boyle has effectively used devices of style, such as figurative language, in "Greasy Lake."
2. Explain how Boyle *shows* the true nature of the narrator and his friends rather than *telling* the audience what they are like.
3. Boyle is often called one of the great American humorists. What elements of humour are there in "Greasy Lake"?

MAKING CONNECTIONS

1. Imagine the reaction of Stephen King ("Why We Crave Horror Movies") to Boyle's story. How do you think King would account for the appeal of "Greasy Lake"? What do think Trina McQueen ("Why We Crave Hot Stuff") would have to say about the appeal of this story?

2. Compare and contrast the portrayal of nature in Margaret Atwood's "Death by Landscape" and "Greasy Lake."
3. Compare and contrast the depiction of the high school students in "Greasy Lake" and in David Suzuki's "The Right Stuff." How do you think the narrator and his friends in "Greasy Lake" would have responded to David Suzuki's lecture?

CHOOSING A TOPIC FOR DISCUSSION/WRITING

1. Write an essay about a situation where you felt in real danger from another person or group of people. How did you respond in this situation?
2. Write a process essay for an audience of teenagers in which you instruct them how to be the contemporary equivalent of "bad, dangerous characters."
3. Write an essay in which you classify the various groups of people at your school or workplace.

John Brooke

THE FINER POINTS OF APPLES

In 1998, John Brooke (1951–) was the winner of the Journey Prize for this story "The Finer Points of Apples," which originally appeared in the literary journal *Kairos*. His story is set in his home city of Montreal, where he has lived since the mid-1980s. After graduating from Trent University with a degree in English Literature and receiving a teaching certificate from the University of Toronto, Brooke worked in the Toronto film and television business and directed short films on modern dance. Since receiving recognition from the Journey Prize jury (and the $10,000 award) for this short story, Brooke has published *The Voice of Aliette Nouvelle* and *All Pure Souls*, both mysteries featuring Inspector Aliette Nouvelle. Brooke is currently making his living as a writer and translator.

"Mmm! You smell like apples." Bruce was nuzzling her hair, 1
pushing his knee against her thigh.

"Le vinaigre de cidre," said Geneviève, "the apple man sells it." 2

"Cider vinegar?" 3

"C'est bon pour le ... how do you say it? ... itching." 4

"Smells good." Then Bruce asked, "are we going to make 5
love tonight?"

"Pense pas." 6

"Ah ..." 7

"You would like that?" 8

"I could." 9

"Pas moi ... trop fatiguée." Geneviève rolled over. 10

"Maybe the apple guy has something for that too." 11

"Peut-être ... bonne nuit." 12

In fact, the apple guy did. 13

Gaston Le Gac had long fingers that knew how to reach deep 14
into her different openings to places Bruce had never been, or
scratch her breast at *le moment juste,* or slap her bottom with a
calculated measure of playful malice which could make her
insides flow. Or baking the apple: He would disengage
completely—maybe softly kiss—while pressing an apple against
her. She would ply herself upon its smoothness. It was birth in
reverse, the head of the child she had never made. No, she had no
regrets on that score. It's far too late for that. Rather, it was this
sense of being removed, of falling into a space between herself
and the life around her. Pure imagination. The erotic farside of
procreation ... The apple, after all, is forever. Gaston brought
Geneviève fresh sex and immortality.

And it was conversation—of the kind Bruce, eight years into 15
their liaison, had never quite caught onto. Oh, his French was
mostly fine at this point; but what could an English Canadian
ever really know of a French traveller's soul? Of her blood-borne
feelings?

They had determined that Gaston had arrived from Quimper 16
via Paris the very week she had walked off her flight from
Toulouse. That was twenty-three years ago. Now here at long
last was the inevitable meeting with a fellow countryman, the
kind she vaguely imagined as she'd set out, footloose, excited ...
then nibbled at from behind loneliness for the first two years at
wine and cheese things at l'Alliance or brunches at friends of
friends', then forgotten for a time when she'd met her first
stranger at a fern bar in Vancouver, and then encountered again

from a different kind of distance as the trail had wound in ever more diffuse circles, back here to Montréal.

Where there are lots of us.   17

Yes, but all re-attached, she thought. To them.   18

Twenty-three years, and it was this scruffy Breton, coming up 19 from Freleighsburg to sell his apples at le Marché Jean Talon.

His wife's apples, to be more exact. Well, her father's, really. 20 But almost hers and so Gaston's. Geneviève had heard that part too. It meant this could only be *une aventure*. A fling? An affair? Something on the side? Positioning it in English was something she would leave for the time being. Just *une aventure*, thought Geneviève, without a sense of any wrong. Because we have the passion and the practicality, and these are meant to be separate. The ability to keep each in its place is in our blood. It's what they know us by, our calling card ... Gaston's wife was a sturdy Québécoise. Micheline. She worked the stall the occasional day but there was no threat. And there were three children, and perhaps the eldest girl sensed something as she observed her papa chatting with this regular customer. This Française. But that girl was half French. His wife? Not a problem. She wouldn't know. Too far from her. Just like with Bruce. Never in a million years.

It was a question of breathing the same way. Or the finer 21 points of apples. They could talk for hours if they had to, right there in the middle of the market. The locals' eyes would glaze over and they'd get on with other things. It was a kind of natural protection, especially here in Montréal.

They were settling on Empire. The acidy element made the sweet 22 more precious, the pulp required real teeth, had character. But Gaston was still loath to dismiss the McIntosh.

"This is your basic apple," he said. "Sure, some will call it 23 bland, flaccid. Myself, I say it's soft, welcoming. This apple is fundamentally sweet. Sweetness is a quality where degrees begin in the ineffable and descend from there. A child will eat six of these McIntoshes before she realizes she is ill. None of them can match that. We are talking fruit, remember, something the Lord created and the Devil put to use."

"It is like our vin de pays," countered Geneviève; "solid, and 24 there for anyone. But low. No, there are no two ways about it— the McIntosh is low. If you want to know quality, you have to move up."

"True. Absolutely true."   25

"Now the Cortland," she ventured, "is almost a McIntosh. 26
That soft taste, as you characterize it ... and almost Empire as
well. Cortland's pulp is a force to be reckoned with. And it lacks
the sour bite. Yes, I would almost say Cortland is the best of both
worlds."

"But are we here to deal in almosts?" queried Gaston.   27

"No ... no," sighed Geneviève, smoothing her palm along 28
his hairy back, "we've come too far for that."

"If you want to challenge Empire you must side with 29
Spartan. You must go past the threshold of stringency. Spartan
compels the mouth to draw in upon itself. Not pleasant to my
taste—but vital!"

"But if we must explore those areas," and Geneviève was at 30
a point in her life where she did not like to speak of dryness,
"we must surely say Lobo is king."

"King of dryness, yes, no argument there ... But it is flat. 31
Lobo is soft but in all its negative connotations. Sweetness,
character ... there is nothing there! ... much like those waxy things
they send us from the west. *Delicious.* There's a marketing
triumph for you ... Lobo is entirely too easy. If McIntosh is for a
baby, Lobo's for a sauce and not much else." He rolled over,
sipped on her nipple. "It's my biggest seller though. I have to
love Lobo regardless of what I know is true."

"I know the feeling," said Geneviève, fingers in his stringy 32
hair—jet black and so familiar.

"Do you?"   33

"Oui," she mused, suddenly weighed down by subtlety, 34
"... some things are made to test us."

That morning she had tried to give Bruce a reason why *fini* 35
could not be used to express his feeling of exhaustion after a
fourth piece of toasted baguette, smothered, as usual, with peach
jam from her mother's village in the Midi, a half-hour north of
Sète:

"Yes, to say you are finished—as in *through eating*, which 36
anyone would be ..." Bruce never flinched at her jabs. "And yes,
if eating four pieces of toast like that will serve to break your
reputation into crumbs. Your social standing, or your business
credibility: these both could be fini ... Mais, tu ne peux pas dire
pour le moral. Jamais."

"I don't mean to use it for my morale," said Bruce. "I feel 37
fine. Wonderful! I'm just wiped out from eating four pieces of

toast and two bowls of your beautiful coffee. Je suis fini. As in *fatigué.*"

"You can't."	38
"You can in English ... whew! I'm finished!"	39
"Faux amis."	40
"Why?"	41
"C'est le moral."	42
"No ... c'est le physique."	43
"No, Bruce ... non."	44
"Think you're wrong this time, Gen."	45
So she'd got the dictionary and it took an hour.	46

She should have been used to it by that point, but no, it was 47 still surprising how much time they spent working with words. The mechanics. They were a shield against the gap and why deny it. Not a bridge; one cannot bridge a gap that will always, like sweetness, be ineffable. Just a shield. One more way to work around the gap so a bond could form. And it was not only with Bruce ... with the English. It happened with all the Québécois she knew as well. Gaston had said "and how!" (*tu parles!*) to that, referring to the three children he had engendered, but who lived *here*, in this slightly less-than state of culture.

Geneviève did not need to explain or argue language with 48 Gaston. Of like generation and both with a *Bacc A* ... philo or literature; not much real use like the *B* which was the economic sciences, and from a system that was now obsolete; but it meant they could speak the way one was meant to. So they did, and were free to delve straight into each other. Which is not to say that Geneviève and Gaston went gouging through the body to devour the soul. Not at all. A passion of sorts, yes, some days (self-respect demanded some); savagery, no. They were both too old for such behaviour. They both had things worth guarding.

She had Christmas in English now. Bruce's blue-rinsed 49 mother refused to consider chestnuts in the stuffing. His too-polite father really did believe in the English queen. But Geneviève had found the beginnings of a new family over in the western reaches of crumbling Montréal. Sure she fought it—the bond that could never be perfect. She was fighting it in this thing with Gaston. Or was wavering the better word? *Balancer.* Her instincts ... fears? Something had latched on to these people even while her mind continued to dissect their ways. Because Bruce had helped her shift up, at long last, into a more civilized way of living. He sent his daughter to college, and he kept his son supplied with music and those ridiculous clothes; yet he still contributed enough to allow Geneviève's one-woman translation operation to be enjoyable now. No more panic if the calls did not come. Since leaving his disaster in Westmount and moving in, Bruce's presence had allowed her to work with a view of the poplars in the lane and the Italian neighbours in their gardens, then, if she felt like it, leave it in the afternoon. Bruce and their home together: the practical side ... She would take her bicycle and pedal to the market, ten minutes away, for bread that was improving, sausage she had learned to like, real cheeses from France, good fish from the Greek, decent tomatoes in September. And apples.

Les Pommes Le Gac. You had to pass it. It was dead-centre,   50 where the two closed-in aisles met in winter, the nexus of the expanded open-air arrangement that came with summer. There were eight varieties of apple, six of which came from Le Gac's own orchards. They also offered apple butter, jelly, juice and cider, pies, a syrup ... a taffy in the winter, and the cider vinegar—with herbs, or straight. Geneviève had a healthy *mère* growing in a large jar of wine vinegar and replenished it with the dregs from each and every bottle opened in her home. So she had never tried this product. But she was a regular. She had been stopping at the stall for several years with no real thought for the proprietor with the Breton name. Bruce took an apple in his briefcase every day.

It was September when it started. It had been hot, Montréal   51 humidity lingering, but pleasant by then, and even cherished, with only three, maybe five more weeks till the seasons changed. She and Bruce had gone for their three weeks in Maman's house, then come home to pass August in the back yard. A cousin— Yves, on her father's side from Nantes—and his family had stopped over for a couple of days on their drive through Québec. Visitors always liked the market so she'd brought them along. Yves and Gaston traded pleasantries in their Breton dialect, everyone was delighted ... they came away with a complimentary bottle of the cider vinegar. Four weeks later Geneviève approached with a postcard from her cousin, to be forwarded to Monsieur Le Gac, and a bottle of the chewy southern wine she always brought back from Maman's village.

"You must drink it with me," said Gaston.   52

Yes, she thought, chatting on about Chirac and his atomic   53 bombs in Polynesia, perhaps I must.

It was not difficult. He kept a three-and-a-half opposite the 54
police station on St. Dominique, hardly a minute away.
Ramshackle. In need of a good fumigating. She watched officers
tucking in their shirts as they got out of their patrol cars and
slammed the doors.

"... handy," offered Geneviève. 55

"Practical," corrected Gaston, "otherwise I'd never sleep." 56

So it was September. But they did not rush into it. 57

They kissed on Referendum Day. A cold day, the bitterness 58
of Québec winter just arriving. It had been a joke actually, to
show their own small solidarity. Yet it was also, they both knew,
a recognition of its inevitability—the thing that was going to
happen. But they did not consummate it until January, with
Christmas and family well out of the picture, the day after
Mitterrand died.

Not difficult at all. There was the grotesque cold since New 59
Year's, historically unusual amounts of snow, a strike by the blue
collars which meant it stayed there, and, of course, the politics.
Apple buyers were sparse and sombre. Gaston wore two sweaters
and a Montréal Canadiens toque, making him look more of a
nul than Bruce's son. Not difficult ... But neither was it passion
that first carried them through.

Her Bruce was disappearing into the cold several nights a 60
week and on Sunday afternoons, leaving shows he loved
unwatched to drive through the cramped and broken streets,
out to the West Island, Westmount, and NDG, or down to McGill
for these meetings.

"*Seinfeld*, *The Health Show*, the hockey game, even his stupid 61
Super Bowl! ... And twice to the Townships, just near your place."

"They call it l'Estrie now," muttered Gaston, whose Micheline
had put everything aside while she prepared a speech she would
give at the town hall down in Burlington, Vermont, less than an
hour from the border which was five minutes from their farm, "to
tell them the real history of Québec ... and not to be afraid of it.
That's her message. They have a network. They're determined
to spread the good word from the Adirondacks over to Maine."

"Bruce's group is going over to the Outaouais next week ... 62
a weekend workshop, is what he's calling it."

"They don't have a chance." 63

"They don't care. They're expecting contingents from the 64
Gaspé, the Megantic, Pontiac County, even from up in Val D'Or."

"It's provocative."   65

"It's what they're thinking," shrugged Geneviève. "He says   66
they've got the Indians on their side."

"Not really. That's a whole other thing."   67

"Try telling him. He says his country had a near-death   68
experience and he's vowed never to let it happen again. It affected
him."

"Micheline says she has never felt more alive." He rolled his   69
bony jaw around in its sockets, shook his head and stared down
at the messy melange of police cars amid the drumlins of dirty
snow. "... alive in front of the computer for sixteen hours a day.
My children have it too. Not just from Maman. It's their teachers."

"So where do you stand, monsieur?"   70

"I don't care," said Gaston, glum. "I don't feel it."   71

"Mm," agreed Geneviève. "It all seems so unnecessary."   72

"Yes," reaching for her, "and so does all the snow."   73

"I've never been homesick," whispered Geneviève, "but I   74
feel quite left out by all this ... I feel cast aside."

He nodded. He knew.   75

And so, like that, they made love.   76

Then, sitting there in the apple farmer's pied-à-terre, they   77
watched a tribute to the wily Mitterrand. *Wily?* Some American's
word. But yes: a survivor—in the face of controversy and even,
for a while, mortal illness. They both identified with that.

They continued making love through the winter into the   78
spring. It was nice. It was necessary: a step back from the tense
bleakness colouring the cold. Endless Montréal winters made
life seem directionless in the best of times and these were
anything but. She was glad she'd done it ... In the rusty shower,
Gaston showed Geneviève the right mix of water and cider
vinegar. A simple rinse, to close the follicles after the shampoo.
With regular use, it worked; her itching all but disappeared. So
did Bruce's, once she'd started him on it. (It was, she felt, the
least that she could do.)

Yet, when it's up in the air like that—in three lime-coloured   79
rooms with water marks on the ceiling—you have to begin to
wonder where it could ever lead. Gaston seemed sustained by the
sex, a sharing of the odd perception, a laugh together at *Paris-
Match.* But Geneviève felt a need to push it; she found herself
saying things she had tried to stop thinking. "Every time I go back
I marvel at the cleanliness, the stream in the gutters every morning.
It's such a beautiful place because they keep it that way."

"They?"	80
"We ..."	81
"That's more like it."	82
"But if I went back, I'd be taxed through the nose the second	83
I put out my little shingle."
"To keep the water running in the gutter."	84
"They don't give you time to get going like they do here."	85
"But your money's stronger there. The *franc fort*—European	86
money ..."
"But would I make any? Who needs a French translation in	87
France? and especially in the south. I won't live in Paris ... never
again."
"They still take care of you if you fail."	88
"They're trying to get out of it ... they seem determined this	89
time." Juppé had sat tight and taken the strike right through
Christmas. "Can't afford it, just like anywhere. We're supposed
to care more about Europe than France now—for our own
supposed good."
"You know that's impossible," scoffed Gaston. "Besides,	90
there will always be a place for you. Monsieur Le Pen will see
to it."
True. Fifteen percent last time out and expected to rise.	91
"But do I want that," she asked.	92
"Do you want a job—or a clear conscience? The man speaks	93
from the heart ... our heart."
"Not mine ... not the one I left there."	94
"Nor mine," he sighed, eyes on the ceiling. Gaston could	95
make the dream of returning difficult.
But Gaston was all she had to share it with, and she persisted.	96
Some days it would be the fast train and the brilliant autoroutes,
signs at every *rond-point* that never left you guessing. And look
at Mitterrand's new monuments; only a true giant would have
dared! Pride was an ongoing sub-text; even, ironically, pride in
Algerian bombs along the railway track—as if to say, what do
Canadians know of trouble? Or the climbing rate of male suicide,
the highest rates of AIDS and psychiatrists, the neurotic line-ups
at pharmacies for sleeping pills and tranquillizers. (She and
Gaston both admitted to having brought this inclination with
them to Canada.) The declining state of French film was discussed
at Oscar time. And how the rampant cheating, from Juppé's rents
to Tapie's matches, was making the best and brightest look so

bad. And the growing malignant shadow behind the Church that was *l'Opus Dei* ...

Everything, good and bad, was set against the obsession 97 surrounding her. Her adopted home was trying to kill itself. The wish was building, morbidly—*les moutons de Panurge*; or as the English would say, *lemmings to the sea*. Either way, Geneviève did not need that. She was a citizen, but she did not know how she was meant to participate. She could not see herself as one of them. She should leave it.

Yet the more she prodded her lover and explored her 98 Frenchness ... and the France that existed now, the more she thought maybe she was too old and too far from the France she'd left to really think of going home. *Cosmo* magazine had even determined that 87% of married French women were faithful. Well, she was not married, but —

"Home?" asked Gaston, to challenge her ... to keep it going, 99 the talk that sculpted clarity. That very French thing.

"Home," she murmured, "like Bruce says: where does it 100 start? Where does it end?"

"And like Micheline," echoed Gaston, soothing her. "We'll 101 see what happens ... Look," slicing an apple into perfect halves, "each side shows a five-pointed star, the sign of immortality, the sign of the Goddess in her five stations from birth to death and back to birth again. It's a Celtic thing. You have that. Lots of it, according to your cousin Yves. Who you are lasts forever."

"I suppose it could." 102

And *une aventure* could become a holding pattern. 103

The Jean Talon Market is a cultural crossroads in the north end 104 of the city proper. The stalls in the centre are owned mainly by Québécois farmers selling fruit, flowers, vegetables, and eggs. But there is an Italian with his own kind of tomatoes, an Anglo egg man called Syd. Merchants in the surrounding shops are Greek, Italian, mid-eastern and north African ... with one Québécois butcher, baker, one more selling fruit. Everything is fresher and cheaper, and every sort of Montréaler goes there. Some Chinese can even be spotted, lured away from their own market downtown, and also some regulars from the cluster of Thai and Vietnamese grocery stores two blocks away at the corner of St. Denis. Any politician fighting for the hearts of the people will naturally find his way to the market, to glad-hand and smile, and be seen with all the various kinds of faces. *Look!* says the image, *our bustling community, happy together amid the bounty of our land.*

It was May and finally warm. Six months of soul-draining 105 winter lay between the comfort of that morning and the cold night of the former Premier's ugly words in the face of a narrow defeat. The idea of partitioning Québec still simmered, but without the fervour of those initial cries of war. It was a good time to start reaching out again. The new Premier showed up in corduroy and cashmere with his wife, two sons and the usual entourage of handlers and media representation.

Geneviève and Gaston had adjusted to Bruce on a Saturday. 106 They dealt with it without a blink. And they surpassed themselves when Micheline would decide to work the weekend, with the silent daughter behind her, keeping the $1 and $3 baskets full.

Bruce was deliberating between Cortland and McIntosh when 107 everything suddenly stopped. A crowd formed and pressed close. Lights went on over the eyes of the cameras. Gaston pushed the hair off his forehead and Micheline, looking good in tight denim (Geneviève always gave credit where it was due) beamed as the two boys sampled her apple juice. The Premier chose a basket of Lobos, and, being from Lac St. Jean, made a glib comment about blueberry season, still a good three months away.

"We close up for three weeks," joked Gaston, "they make 108 our apples lose their point."

That was untrue. Les Pommes Le Gac was never closed. But 109 it sounded good and everyone laughed.

Then Micheline presented his wife with a bottle of the cider 110 vinegar. It came with Gaston's small brochure explaining both the gastronomic and medicinal uses. The woman, an American, seemed impressed.

Yet no one paid for the apples. Geneviève wondered if 111 anyone else had noticed. Perhaps money was not a part of this sort of thing, and someone else took care of it later. Then the Premier, just another shopper with a sack of fruit, moved to shake some hands.

What are you supposed to do? It's Saturday, the market ... 112 Geneviève took his hand, looked into the baleful eyes and said, "Bonjour."

But Bruce, who was beside her, said, "Are you kidding? No 113 way!"

"Dommage monsieur." In that rumbly voice.   114
"Hell of a lot more than a pity, monsieur."   115

"I mean your manners. You are very rude."   116

"And you're dishonest."   117

"I am a democrat."   118

"Try dema*gogue* ..."   119

Geneviève watched it from that distance she had been   120
allowing herself to feel, the voice inside saying *oh these people* ...
and still from that removed vantage as Bruce was suddenly
yanked away from in front of the Premier's face—and smacked.
By Micheline.

"Va-t-en! We don't want the likes of you around our stall!"   121

"No ... I'm sure you don't," said Bruce when the blush had   122
faded. "Well to hell with you and your apples, madame. Your
children won't thank you when they wake up in the third world!"

A dour man in sunglasses made a move, but Bruce indicated   123
there was no need. The cameras panned away from the Premier,
following as Bruce pushed through the throng and walked away.

Geneviève hurried after him. Of course she did.   124

Her *aventure* was over before the next weekend. Gaston's   125
daughter had said something in the aftermath of the ugly
incident. Something about *la Française*, the Anglo's wife. Yes, he
knew she was not Bruce's wife. That was not the point. *He* was
someone's husband and that someone had caught on. Gaston
said that's it—*fini.*

Geneviève would have said the same thing, regardless of his   126
wife *la militante*. It was as good a time as any. She and Bruce
would be gone by mid-June, back to the village in the south—
for a month this time. She would be re-charged. Maybe they
would be renewed. Even Bruce wouldn't be able to think about
his politics with all those topless teenagers wandering around
on the beach.

But that was cynical and, happily, something that was burned   127
away by the Mediterranean sun.

Because she had watched the thing on television, in both   128
English and in French, and then again at eleven, with the sound
turned off. In fact she had taped it, and watched it again, alone,
brown and relaxed, the night they got back. Geneviève watched
herself: her reaction, the way she went straight-away after her
man—no hesitation. She realized she had a purpose, if not a
cause, right there in Montréal. A passion for something new had
brought her life to Canada and now she was involved in it. The
place and its people. She had been re-attached through love. Yes,
she thought—it had to be. It was there on Canadian television

... just look at my face: Jeanne Moreau. Arletty. Deneuve or Fanny Ardant. Very noble. Very knowing. Very right. Surely Gaston would have watched and seen as well.

Bruce never knew. For his sake, Geneviève bore the prick of feeling like an enemy whenever she passed Micheline Le Gac, there most days now, defiant in her stall. The apples were just as good at the other end of the market. Apples are apples. Unfortunately none of the other merchants was as ambitious or creative as Gaston when it came to developing spin-offs. No more cider vinegar. Although her scalp itched in the dryness of the next winter (Bruce's too), Geneviève forced herself to live with it. Besides, it was $10 a bottle—an outrageous amount to pay for vinegar. 129

There would be something in France to solve the itching. They would find something the next time they went, and bring it back. 130

UNDERSTANDING DETAILS

1. Describe le Marché Jean Talon. Where is it? Why does it appeal to politicians?
2. When and where does this story take place? How important is the setting to this story?
3. For Geneviève, what is the appeal of Gaston? What appeal does Bruce offer?

ANALYZING MEANING

1. Is "The Finer Points of Apples" a story primarily about love or about politics? Explain.
2. Why does the author have the characters spend time debating about the distinguishing characteristics of different types of apples?
3. What is the character of Geneviève like? What are the primary factors that govern her behaviour? How is her character revealed?

DISCOVERING RHETORICAL STRATEGIES

1. Brooke has incorporated many French words and expressions into this story. Why has he done this? Why is there so much attention paid to the differences between English and French expressions?
2. What is the tone of the story, and how is it established?
3. Explain how Brooke brings unity to his story through the introduction and conclusion.

MAKING CONNECTIONS

1. In "The Finer Points of Apples," Geneviève has the sense of being a foreigner whose true home is elsewhere. Compare her sense of home to that of Allen Abel ("A Home at the End of the Journey").
2. Brooke's story raises the issue of conflict between cultures. In what ways does this conflict in "The Finer Points of Apples" resemble the cultural conflict in "The Immaculate Conception Photography Gallery" (Govier)?
3. Food plays a significant role in Brooke's story. Explain the function of food in the stories by Hay ("Cézanne in a Soft Hat") and Brooke ("The Finer Points of Apples").

CHOOSING A TOPIC FOR DISCUSSION/WRITING

1. Brooke's story focuses on the personal side of a major political movement. Write an essay in which you explain the personal side of a political issue with which you are familiar.
2. Write a classification/division essay in which you choose a type of food (other than apples) and clearly distinguish various types that fall into that category. You might focus on types of oranges, grapes, breads, corn, rice, squash, or some other type of food.
3. "The Finer Points of Apples" takes place around the time of a Quebec referendum on separation. Imagine another such referendum is happening a month from now. Write a persuasive essay for all people in Quebec telling them how they should vote in this upcoming referendum.

Katherine Govier

THE IMMACULATE CONCEPTION PHOTOGRAPHY GALLERY

Sandro named the little photography shop on St. Clair Avenue   1
West, between Lord's Shoes and Bargain Jimmies, after the parish church in the village where he was born. He had hankered after wider horizons, the rippled brown prairies, the hard-edged mountains. But when he reached Toronto he met necessity in the form of a wife and babies, and, never having seen a western sunset, he settled down in Little Italy. He photographed the brides in their fat lacquered curls and imported lace, and their quick babies in christening gowns brought over from home. Blown up to near life size on cardboard cutouts, their pictures filled the windows of his little shop.

Sandro had been there ten years already when he first really   2
saw his sign, and the window. He stood still in front of it and
looked. A particularly buxom bride with a lace bodice and cap
sleeves cut in little scallops shimmered in a haze of concupiscence
under the sign reading Immaculate Conception Photography
Gallery. Sandro was not like his neighbours any more, he was
modern, a Canadian. He no longer went to church. As he stared,
one of the street drunks shuffled into place beside him. Sandro
knew them all, they came into the shop in winter. (No one ought
to have to stay outside in that cold, Sandro believed.) But he
especially knew Becker. Becker was a smart man; he used to be
a philosopher at a university.

"Immaculate conception," said Sandro to Becker. "What do   3
you think?"

Becker lifted his eyes to the window. He made a squeezing   4
gesture at the breasts. "I never could buy that story," he said.

Sandro laughed, but he didn't change the sign that year or the   5
next and he got to be forty-five and then fifty and it didn't seem
worth it. The Immaculate Conception Photography Gallery had
a reputation. Business came in from as far away as Rosedale and
North Toronto, because Sandro was a magician with a camera. He
also had skill with brushes and lights and paint, he reshot his
negatives, he lined them with silver, he had tricks even new
graduates of photography school couldn't (or wouldn't) copy.

Sandro was not proud of his tricks. They began in a gradual   6
way, fixing stray hairs and taking wrinkles out of dresses. He did
it once, then twice, then people came in asking for it. Perhaps
he'd have gone on this way, with small lies, but he met with a
situation that was larger than most; it would have started a feud
in the old country. During a very large and very expensive
wedding party Tony the bridegroom seduced Alicia the
bridesmaid in the basketball storage room under the floor of the
parish hall. Six months later Tony confessed, hoping perhaps to
be released from his vows. But the parents judged it was too late
to dissolve the union: Diora was used, she was no longer a virgin,
there was a child coming. Tony was reprimanded, Diora consoled,
the mothers became enemies, the newlyweds made up. Only
Alicia remained to be dealt with. The offence became hers.

In Italy, community ostracism would have been the   7
punishment of choice. But this was Canada, and if no one
acknowledged Alicia on the street, if no one visited her mother,
who was heavy on her feet and forced to sit on the sofa protesting

her daughter's innocence, if no one invited her father out behind to drink home-made wine, Alicia didn't care. She went off to her job behind the till in a drugstore with her chin thrust out much as before. The inlaws perceived that the young woman could not be subdued by the old methods. This being the case, it was better she not exist at all.

Which was why Diora's mother turned up at Sandro's counter 8 with the wedding photos. The pain Alicia had caused! she began. Diora's mother's very own miserable wages, saved these eighteen years, had paid for these photographs! She wept. The money was spent, but the joy was spoiled. When she and Diora's father looked at the row of faces flanking bride and groom there she was— Alicia, the whore! She wiped her tears and made her pitch.

"You can solve our problem, Sandro. I will get a new cake, we 9 will all come to the parish hall. You will take the photographs again. Of course," she added, "we can't pay you again."

Sandro smiled, it was so preposterous. "Even if I could afford 10 to do all that work for nothing, I hate to say it, but Diora's out to here."

"Don't argue with me." 11

"I wouldn't be so bold," said Sandro. "But I will not take the 12 photographs over."

The woman slapped the photographs where they lay on the 13 counter. "You will! I don't care how you do it!" And she left.

Sandro went to the back and put his negatives on the light 14 box. He brought out his magic solution and his razor blades and his brushes. He circled Alicia's head and shoulders in the first row and went to work. He felt a little badly, watching the bright circle of her face fade and swim, darken down to nothing. But how easily she vanished! He filled in the white spot with a bit of velvet curtain trimmed from the side.

"I'm like a plastic surgeon," he told his wife. "Take that patch 15 of skin from the inner thigh and put it over the scar on the face. Then sand the edges. Isn't that what they do? Only it isn't a face I'm fixing, it's a memory."

His wife stood on two flat feet beside the sink. She shook 16 the carrot she was peeling. "I don't care about Alicia," she said, "but Diora's mother is making a mistake. She is starting them off with a lie in their marriage. And why is she doing it? For her pride! I don't like this, Sandro."

"You're missing the point," said Sandro. 17

The next day he had another look at his work. Alicia's   18
shoulders and the bodice of her dress were still there, in front
of the chest of the uncle of the bride. He couldn't remove them;
it would leave a hole in Uncle. Sandro had nothing to fill the
hole, no spare male torsos in black tie. He considered putting a
head on top, but whose head? There was no such thing as a free
face. A stranger would be questioned, a friend would have an
alibi. Perhaps Diora's mother would not notice the black velvet
space, as where a tooth had been knocked out, between the
smiling faces.

Indeed she didn't but kissed his hand fervently and thanked   19
him with tears in her eyes. "Twenty-five thousand that wedding
cost me. Twenty-five thousand to get this photograph and you
have rescued it."

"Surely you got dinner and a dance too?" said Sandro.   20

"The wedding was one day. This is forever," said Diora's   21
mother.

"I won't do that again," said Sandro, putting the cloth over his 22
head and looking into his camera lens to do a passport photo.
In the community the doctored photograph had been examined
and re-examined. Alicia's detractors enjoyed the headless
shoulders as evidence of a violent punishment.

"No, I won't do that again at all," said Sandro to himself,   23
turning aside compliments with a shake of his head. But there
was another wedding. After the provolone e melone, the veal
piccata, the many-tiered cake topped with swans, the father of the
bride drew Sandro aside and asked for a set of prints with the
groom's parents removed.

"My God, why?" said Sandro.   24

"He's a bastard. A bad man."   25

"Shouldn't have let her marry his son, then," said Sandro,   26
pulling a cigarette out of the pack in his pocket. These
conversations made him nervous.

The father's weathered face was dark, his dinner-jacket did 27
not button around his chest. He moaned and ground his lower
teeth against his uppers. "You know how they are, these girls in
Canada. I am ashamed to say it, but I couldn't stop her."

Sandro said nothing.   28

"Look, I sat here all night long, said nothing, did nothing. I 29
don't wanna look at him for the next twenty years."

Sandro drew in a long tube of smoke.   30

"I paid a nice bundle for this night. I wanna remember it 31
nice-like."

The smoke made Sandro nauseous. He dropped his cigarette 32
and ground it into the floor with his toe, damning his own
weakness. "So what am I going to do with the table?"

The father put out a hand like a tool, narrowed his eyes, and 33
began to saw, where the other man sat.

"And leave it dangling, no legs?" 34

"So make new legs." 35

"I'm a photographer, not a carpenter," said Sandro. "I don't 36
make table legs."

"Where you get legs is your problem," said the father. "I'm 37
doing well here. I've got ten guys working for me. You look like
you could use some new equipment."

And what harm was it after all, it was only a photograph, 38
said Sandro to himself. Then too there was the technical challenge.
Waiting until they all got up to get their bonbonnière, he took a
shot of the head table empty. Working neatly with his scalpel,
he cut the table from this second negative, removed the inlaws
and their chairs from the first one, stuck the empty table-end
onto the table in the first picture, blended over the join neatly, and
printed it. Presto! Only one set of inlaws.

"I don't mind telling you, it gives me a sick feeling," said 39
Sandro to his wife. "I was there. I saw them. We had a conversation.
They smiled for me. Now ..." he shrugged. "An empty table. Lucky
I don't go to church any more. "

"Let the man who paid good money to have you do it 40
confess, not you," she said. "A photograph is a photograph."

"That's what I thought too," said Sandro. 41

The next morning Sandro went to the Donut House, got 42
himself a take-out coffee and stood on the street beside his
window.

"Why do people care about photographs so much?" he asked 43
Becker. Becker had newspaper stuffed in the soles of his shoes. He
had on a pair of stained brown pants tied up at the waist with a
paisley necktie. His bottle was clutched in a paper bag gathered
around the neck.

"You can put them on your mantel," said Becker. "They don't 44
talk back."

"Don't people prefer life?" said Sandro. 45

"People prefer things," said Becker. 46

"Don't they want their memories to be true?" 47

"No," said Becker.   48

"Another thing. Are we here just to get our photograph   49
taken? Do we have a higher purpose?"

Becker pulled one of the newspapers out of his shoe. There   50
were Brian and Mila Mulroney having a gloaty kiss. They were
smeared by muddy water and depressed by the joint in the ball
of Becker's foot.

"I mean real people," said Sandro. "Have we no loyalty to the   51
natural?"

"These are existential questions, Sandro," said Becker. "Too   52
many more of them and you'll be out here on the street with the
rest of us."

Sandro drained the coffee from his cup, pitched it in the bin   53
painted "Keep Toronto Clean" and went back into his gallery.
The existential questions nagged. But he did go out and get the
motor drive for the camera. In the next few months he eradicated
a pregnancy from a wedding photo, added a daughter-in-law
who complained of being left out of the Christmas shots, and
made a groom taller. Working in the dark-room, he was hit by
vertigo. He was on a slide, beginning a descent. He wanted to
know what the bottom felt like.

After a year of such operations a man from the Beaches came   54
in with a tiny black and white photo of a long-lost brother. He
wanted it coloured and fitted into a family shot around a picnic
table on Centre Island.

"Is this some kind of joke?" said Sandro. It was the only   55
discretion he practised now: he wanted to talk about it before
he did it.

"No. I'm going to send it to Mother. She thinks Christopher   56
wrote us all off."

"Did he?" said Sandro.   57

"Better she should not know."   58

Sandro neglected to ask if Christopher was fat or thin. He ended   59
up taking a medium-sized pair of shoulders from his own cousin
and propping them up behind a bush, with Christopher's head
on top. Afterward, Sandro lay sleepless in his bed. Suppose that
in the next few months Christopher should turn up dead, say
murdered. Then Mother would produce the photograph
stamped Immaculate Conception Photography Gallery, 1816 St.
Clair Avenue West. Sandro would be implicated. The police
might come.

"I believe adding people is worse than taking them away," he 60
said to his wife.

"You say yes to do it, then you do it. You think it's wrong, 61
you say no."

"Let me try this on you, Becker," said Sandro the next 62
morning. "To take a person out is only half a lie. It proves nothing
except that he was not in that shot. To add a person is a whole lie:
it proves that he was there, when he was not."

"You haven't proven a thing, you're just fooling around with 63
celluloid. Have you got a buck?" said Becker.

"It is better to be a murderer than a creator. I am playing 64
God, outplaying God at His own game." He was smarter than
Becker now. He knew it was the photographs that lasted, not
the people. In the end the proof was in the proof. Though he
hadn't prayed in thirty years, Sandro began to pray. It was like
riding a bicycle: he got the hang of it again instantly. "Make me
strong," he prayed, "strong enough to resist the new equipment
that I might buy, strong enough to resist the temptation to expand
the gallery, to buy a house in the suburbs. Make me say no to
people who want alterations."

But Sandro's prayers were not answered. When people 65
offered him money to dissolve an errant relative, he said yes. He
said yes out of curiosity. He said yes out of a desire to test his
skills. He said yes out of greed. He said yes out of compassion.
"What is the cost of a little happiness?" he said. "Perhaps God
doesn't count photographs. After all, they're not one of a kind."

Sandro began to be haunted, in slow moments behind the counter 66
in the Immaculate Conception, by the faces of those whose
presence he had tampered with. He kept a file—Alicia the lusty
bridesmaid, Antonia and Marco, the undesired inlaws. Their
heads, their shoes and their hands, removed from the scene with
surgical precision, he saved for the moment when, God willing,
a forgiving relative would ask him to replace them. But the day
did not come. Sandro was not happy.

"Becker," he said, for he had a habit now of buying Becker a 67
coffee first thing in the morning and standing out if it was warm,
or in if it was cold, for a chat. "Becker, let's say it's a good service
I'm doing. It makes people happy, even if it tells lies."

"Sandro," said Becker, who enjoyed his coffee, "these 68
photographs, doctored by request of the subjects, reflect back
the lives they wish to have. The unpleasant bits are removed,

the wishes are added. If you didn't do it, someone else would. Memory would. It's a service."

"It's also money," said Sandro. He found Becker too eager   69
to make excuses now. He liked him better before.

"You're like Tintoretto, painting in his patron, softening his   70
greedy profile, lifting the chin of his fat wife. It pays for the part
that's true art."

"Which part is that?" said Sandro, but Becker didn't answer.   71
He was still standing there when Diora came in. She'd matured,
she'd gained weight, and her twins, now six years old, were
handsome and strong. Sandro's heart flew up in his breast.
Perhaps she had made friends with Alicia, perhaps Diora had
come to have her bridesmaid reinstated.

"The long nightmare is over," said Diora. "I've left him."   72

The boys were running from shelf to shelf lifting up the   73
photographs with their glass frames and putting them down
again. Sandro watched them with one eye. He knew what she
was going to say.

"I want you to take him out of those pictures," she said.   74

"You'd look very foolish as a bride with no groom," he said   75
severely.

"No, no, not those," she said. "I mean the kids' birthday   76
shots."

They had been particularly fine, those shots, taken only two   77
weeks ago, Tony tall and dark, Diora and the children radiant
and blonde.

"Be reasonable, Diora," he said. "I never liked him myself.   78
But he balances the portrait. Besides, he was there."

"He was not there!" cried Diora. Her sons went on turning all   79
the pictures to face the walls. "He was never there. He was
running around, in his heart he was not with me. I was alone
with my children."

"I'll take another one," said Sandro. "Of you and the boys.   80
Whenever you like. This one stays like it is."

"We won't pay."   81

"But Diora," said Sandro, "everyone knows he's their father."   82

"They have no father," said Diora flatly.   83

"It's immaculate conception," said Becker gleefully.   84

But Diora did not hear. "It's our photograph, and we want   85
him out. You do your job. The rest of it's none of your business."
She put one hand on the back of the head of each of her twins
and marched them out the door.

Sandro leaned on his counter idly flipping the pages of a   86
wedding album. He had a vision of a great decorated room, with
a cake on the table. Everyone had had his way, the husband had
removed the wife, the wife the husband, the bridesmaid her
parents, and so forth. There was no one there.

"We make up our lives out of the people around us," he said   87
to Becker. "When they don't live up to standard, we can't just
wipe them out."

"Don't ask me," said Becker. "I just lit out for the streets.   88
Couldn't live up to a damn thing." Then he too went out the door.

"Lucky bugger," said Sandro.   89

Alone, he went to his darkroom. He opened his drawer of   90
bits and pieces. His disappeared ones, the inconvenient people.
His body parts, his halves of torsos, tips of shiny black shoes.
Each face, each item of clothing punctured him a little. He looked
at his negatives stored in drawers. They were scarred, pathetic
things. I haven't the stomach for it, not any more, thought Sandro.

As he walked home, St. Clair Avenue seemed very fine. The   91
best part was, he thought, there were no relationships. Neither
this leaning drunk nor that window-shopper was so connected to
any other as to endanger his, or her, existence. The tolerance of
indifference, said Sandro to himself, trying to remember it so
that he could tell Becker.

But Sandro felt ill at ease in his own home, by its very   92
definition a dangerous and unreliable setting. His wife was
stirring something, with her lips tight together. His children,
almost grown up now, bred secrets as they looked at television.
He himself only posed in the doorway, looking for hidden seams
and the faint hair-lines of an airbrush.

That night he stood exhausted by his bed. His wife lay on   93
her side with one round shoulder above the sheet. Behind her
on the wall was the photo he'd taken of their village before he left
Italy. He ought to reshoot it, take out that gas station and clean
up the square a little. His pillow had an indentation, as if a head
had been erased. He slept in a chair.

In the morning he went down to the shop. He got his best   94
camera and set up a tripod on the sidewalk directly across the
street. He took several shots in the solid bright morning light.
He locked the door and placed the CLOSED sign in the window.
In the darkroom he developed the film, floating the negatives in
the pungent fluid until the row of shop fronts came through
clearly, the flat brick faces, the curving concrete trim, the two

balls on the crowns. Deftly he dissolved each brick of his store, the window and the sign. Deftly he reattached each brick of the store on the west side to the bricks of the store to the east.

I have been many things in my life, thought Sandro, a presser   95
of shutters, a confessor, a false prophet. Now I am a bricklayer, and a good one. He taped the negatives together and developed them. He touched up the join and then photographed it again. He developed this second negative and it was perfect. Number 1812, Lord's Shoes, joined directly to 1820, Bargain Jimmies: the Immaculate Conception Photography Gallery at 1816 no longer existed. Working quickly, because he wanted to finish before the day was over, he blew it up to two feet by three feet. He cleared out his window display of brides and babies and stood up this new photograph—one of the finest he'd ever taken, he thought. Then he took a couple of cameras and a bag with the tripod and some lenses. He turned out the light, pulling the door shut behind him, and began to walk west.

UNDERSTANDING DETAILS

1. Why does Sandro start manipulating his photographs? Why does he continue to alter them? How does Sandro feel about the manipulation of his photographs? What does Becker think about the alteration of the pictures?
2. When and where does the story take place? What details reveal this information?
3. Govier draws particular attention to the name of Sandro's photography studio by using it as the title of her story. Explain the symbolic value of the name Immaculate Conception Photography Gallery.

ANALYZING MEANING

1. Explain the conclusion of "The Immaculate Conception Photography Gallery." Why does Sandro take the action he does? Where is he heading when he leaves the shop?
2. Discuss the portrayal of the main character in "The Immaculate Conception Photography Gallery." How does Govier develop the narrator and convincingly convey the significant personality changes in this character?
3. Explain the role of Becker in Govier's story.

DISCOVERING RHETORICAL STRATEGIES

1. Specific examples with specific details make Govier's story effective and memorable. Identify at least five examples that you found particularly effective and explain why.
2. Much of Govier's story is related through dialogue between the characters. Explain her choice to use the characters' own words.
3. Discuss the link between the introduction and the conclusion of "The Immaculate Conception Photography Gallery." How has Govier effectively framed her story?

MAKING CONNECTIONS

1. Tony Leighton's essay ("The New Nature") explores the world of digital manipulation of photographs. Imagine Leighton joining in one of the conversations between Sandro and Becker. What do you think Leighton's perspective would be on Sandro's alteration of the photographs?
2. "Cézanne in a Soft Hat" (Elizabeth Hay) explores the fluctuating terrain of friendship. How do you think the narrator of this story would respond to Sandro's comment that "We make up our lives out of the people around us ... When they don't live up to standard, we can't just wipe them out" (paragraph 87)?

CHOOSING A TOPIC FOR DISCUSSION/WRITING

1. Becker tells Sandro that people don't want their memories to be true (paragraph 48). Explain what Becker means by this. What role does memory play in people's lives?
2. In paragraph 38, Sandro justifies his actions by telling himself, "it was only a photograph." Write an essay for Sandro in which you try to convince him either that what he is doing is acceptable or that he should not be altering the photographs.
3. In a review of *The Immaculate Conception Photography Gallery*, Zaheera Jiwaji says,

> Katherine Govier's rule for writing short stories must be to have readers smiling within three or four paragraphs. This is not to say that her stories are riotously funny; rather, they amuse in a half-painful, half-pleasurable way. Govier's characters bare their human failings and foibles, leaving readers smiling at their own imperfection.

Discuss this view in relation to the title story of Govier's book.

Elizabeth Hay

■ □ ■

CÉZANNE IN A SOFT HAT

"Cézanne in a Soft Hat" comes from *Small Change* (1997), Elizabeth Hay's book of 20 linked stories about friendship told by a narrator named Beth. *Small Change* was Hay's fourth book (following a 1989 collection of short stories and two works of creative non-fiction published in the early 1990s) but the first to receive widespread attention. This book received many glowing reviews and was a finalist for the Governor General's Award for fiction, the Trillium Award, and the Rogers Communications Writers' Trust Fiction Prize. *A Student of Weather* (2000), Hay's first novel, received a similar reception; she is currently working on a second novel.

Hay, born in Owen Sound, Ontario in 1951, grew up in small Ontario towns before attending the University of Toronto and then living in Yellowknife, Winnipeg, and Toronto while working as a broadcaster for CBC Radio. In 1982, she moved to Mexico, where she worked as a documentary maker, and then lived in Manhattan. Hay now makes her home with her husband and children in Ottawa, Ontario.

Soon after we moved here, I picked up a small book about 1 Cézanne. This was in September. I opened the book to dry landscapes and cool still lifes, to late summer and early fall, to the pleasure and pain of seasonal change, the detachment of weather. This is the detachment we seek and usually fail to find in friendships—an unbegrudging, clear-eyed, undemanding, infinitely interesting and natural presence.

Here were pears on a table, apples in a bowl, a flowered 2 pitcher, a leafy piece of fabric. Everything gave the impression of being aware of every other thing but in a way that transcends the human.

I began to read the biographical notes and came upon the 3 description of Cézanne's friendship with Zola, a deep and long friendship that began in Aix in 1852 when Cézanne was thirteen, and ended in 1886 when Zola published a novel about a painter who hanged himself in front of the painting he couldn't complete. Everyone knew the painter was Cézanne.

I reread the paragraph about the end of their friendship. 4 "Although he spoke of it to no one, it could be seen that Cézanne's grief was bitter and irremediable. Perhaps it was partly because of the sincere compassion expressed in the novel that Cézanne's grief was so inconsolable."

I wondered how sincere Zola's compassion was. I wondered 5 how it was known that Cézanne's grief was inconsolable if he spoke of it to no one, and how it was known that he spoke of it to no one. I wondered about Zola's ulterior motives—his desire to hurt an old friend, his competitiveness, his honesty, his dishonesty. The book said that Zola had moved away from his Impressionist friends and no longer believed in them, having been their most valiant champion. But my main interest was Cézanne and the way he dealt with the discovery that his oldest and dearest friend considered him a failure and used him as subject matter in a book.

No more letters passed between them, apparently. There 6 were no more greetings, and they did not meet again.

In 1886 Cézanne was forty-seven. His friendship with Zola had 7 lasted more than thirty years. The first time Zola left for Paris and Cézanne remained in Aix, they were about twenty. Cézanne wrote to him: "Ever since you left I am tormented by grief. This is the truth. You would not recognize me. I feel heavy, stupid and slow."

The book has two self-portraits: an unfinished sketch in 1880 8 when he was forty-one, half bald, heavy forehead, dark beard, large face; then *Cézanne in a Soft Hat* ten years later, several years after the break with Zola and several years in the making. His nose and chin are more pointed than broad; his beard is white and grey; the colours of his coat, hat, and jacket are repeated in the colours of the wall; and he seems less massive—flimsier and more decorative. He is known for his persistence in the face of doubts and for how slowly he painted.

In early October we were beside a river with two friends. The 9 woman was telling us that old friends of theirs had just moved away. They had moved away one morning, and in the afternoon she had walked past the empty house and couldn't believe how relieved she felt. She laughed about it and went on talking, compelled to tell us, her new friends, about these old friends.

She said it was the woman in the couple who had pulled 10 away, and she had never understood why. Simply, the invitations stopped, the Christmas gifts ended, various courtesies vanished. With their disappearance arrived her confusion and sense of hurt, so that when she walked her dog past their house she was never sure whether the woman came down the steps because she wanted to say hello, or because she felt she had to.

She said, "I talked a lot about work with him, maybe she felt   11 left out. And then she went through a lot of changes herself and got her own friends."

But none of these reasons was sufficient to explain a change   12 so drastic, and she knew it.

She peeled a peach as she told the story. She avoided the   13 words *dropped* or *dumped* or *rejected*. She said only that she didn't understand, that once there had been steady contact and then there was none, that whenever they saw each other they all enjoyed themselves, but afterwards there was nothing.

The peach was from the market, carried in a knapsack, a little   14 bruised and one of eight. She peeled another, her fingers curving around the fruit, picking at the peel with her fingernail, then pulling it back. We sat on a blanket on the grass and ate tomatoes, bread, cheese, the peaches, a sausage. We ate with our hands and shared a napkin.

My friend dealt with being rejected by understanding and   15 not understanding, stating and understating, avoiding certain things but staying true to the general picture. Her husband was impatient. He couldn't be bothered, he said, worrying about such things.

This is the refreshing thing about men. They don't brood so   16 luxuriously about friendships gone wrong. They think about them very little, it seems, and talk about them less. Cézanne, for instance.

Ted said, "It's hard when one person wants the friendship   17 and another doesn't. People change."

But that only rubbed salt in the wound. Our friend wasn't   18 saying they didn't want her, she was saying they seemed to enjoy her company and this was the source of her confusion. She was unable to give up the hope that she was liked.

I was thinking about her again this morning when I peeled a   19 peach. I used the fingers of my left hand, picking the skin loose at the top as you pick one page free from the page below.

I was thinking about a conversation with Maureen. We were   20 in a park and it was warm, it might have been late spring or early fall. We were sitting on a stone wall and she was distributing food to the kids. (She was always much more prepared than I, never leaving the house without a variety of snacks and drinks.) She could not believe, she said, that certain friends with whom she had been incredibly close had faded away—she mentioned a roommate in university—yet she admitted it was so with tight lips, and I knew she foresaw our own end.

My sympathies are with Cézanne even though I am like Zola— 21 the realistic writer using the people he knows. What defence can Zola offer? When accused of using the life of a friend to further his artful ends, what can he say? That it was his life too? It was my life too.

UNDERSTANDING DETAILS

1. Who is Cézanne? Who is Zola? What was their relationship to each other? How did this relationship change over time?
2. Identify and describe the characters in this story.
3. Why does the narrator tell the story of the end of Cézanne and Zola's friendship? What links Cézanne and Zola's relationship with the narrator and her friends?

ANALYZING MEANING

1. Explain the title of the story. Why does the narrator focus on this particular self-portrait by Cézanne?
2. How do men and women differ in their attitudes toward and expectations of friendship? What essential truth about friendship is Hay communicating through this story?
3. There are several references to food in "Cézanne in a Soft Hat." What symbolic role does food carry?

DISCOVERING RHETORICAL STRATEGIES

1. Hay frequently constructs sentences with patterns of pairs (paragraphs 1, 15). Explain the effect this has in her writing.
2. Hay begins and ends her story with references to Cézanne and Zola. Explain the function of these references in this story.
3. "Cézanne in a Soft Hat" contains many visual elements. Identify details that appeal particularly to the sense of sight.

MAKING CONNECTIONS

1. Compare Hay's portrayal of friendship with that in Margaret Atwood's "Death by Landscape."
2. Hay's narrator points out the differences between the ways friendship is viewed by men and by women. How do these differing views fit with the respective roles of males and females as depicted in Alice Munro's "Boys and Girls"?

CHOOSING A TOPIC FOR DISCUSSION/WRITING

1. Write an essay in which you define friendship.
2. Write a process essay in which you relate the course of a friendship you have had that has undergone some significant change.
3. Hay's narrator sees a side of herself reflected in Zola. Write an essay in which you identify a less-than-flattering side of yourself that you have seen reflected in someone else.

Alistair MacLeod

AS BIRDS BRING FORTH THE SUN

After teaching literature and creative writing at the University of Windsor for 32 years, Alistair MacLeod has recently retired to a new level of international literary recognition since the publication of his first novel, *No Great Mischief*, in 1999, and the republication of a collection of his earlier short stories in *Island* (2000).

Born in Saskatchewan in 1936 and raised in Cape Breton, Nova Scotia, MacLeod's fiction focuses primarily on the often harsh lives of people living in the rural areas of Canada's East Coast who make a living through hard physical labour. Although he has worked as a miner, a logger, and a farmhand, MacLeod's primary careers have been as an academic and then as a writer.

"As Birds Bring Forth the Sun" was originally published as the title story in MacLeod's 1986 collection of stories and was also included in *Island* in 2000.

Once there was a family with a Highland name who lived be- 1 side the sea. And the man had a dog of which he was very fond. She was large and grey, a sort of staghound from another time. And if she jumped up to lick his face, which she loved to do, her paws would jolt against his shoulders with such force that she would come close to knocking him down and he would be forced to take two or three backward steps before he could regain his balance. And he himself was not a small man, being slightly over six feet and perhaps one hundred and eighty pounds.

She had been left, when a pup, at the family's gate in a small 2 handmade box and no one knew where she had come from or that she would eventually grow to such a size. Once, while still a small pup, she had been run over by the steel wheel of a horse-drawn cart which was hauling kelp from the shore to be used as fertilizer. It was in October and the rain had been falling for some weeks and the ground was soft. When the wheel of the cart passed over her, it sunk her body into the wet earth as well as crushing some of her ribs; and apparently the silhouette of her small crushed body was visible in the earth after the man lifted her to his chest while she yelped and screamed. He ran his fingers along her broken bones, ignoring the blood and urine which fell upon his shirt, trying to soothe her bulging eyes and her scrabbling front paws and her desperately licking tongue.

The more practical members of his family, who had seen 3 run-over dogs before, suggested that her neck be broken by his strong hands or that he grasp her by the hind legs and swing her head against a rock, thus putting an end to her misery. But he would not do it.

Instead, he fashioned a small box and lined it with woollen 4 remnants from a sheep's fleece and one of his old and frayed shirts. He placed her within the box and placed the box behind the stove and then he warmed some milk in a small saucepan and sweetened it with sugar. And he held open her small and trembling jaws with his left hand while spooning in the sweetened milk with his right, ignoring the needle-like sharpness of her small teeth. She lay in the box most of the remaining fall and into the early winter, watching everything with her large brown eyes.

Although some members of the family complained about 5 her presence and the odour from the box and the waste of time she involved, they gradually adjusted to her; and as the weeks passed by, it became evident that her ribs were knitting together in some form or other and that she was recovering with the resilience of the young. It also became evident that she would grow to a tremendous size, as she outgrew one box and then another and the grey hair began to feather from her huge front paws. In the spring she was outside almost all of the time and followed the man everywhere; and when she came inside during the following months, she had grown so large that she would no longer fit into her accustomed place behind the stove and was forced to lie beside it. She was never given a name but was referred to in Gaelic as *cù mòr glas*, the big grey dog.

By the time she came into her first heat, she had grown to a   6 tremendous height, and although her signs and her odour attracted many panting and highly aroused suitors, none was big enough to mount her, and the frenzy of their disappointment and the longing of her unfulfilment were more than the man could stand. He went, so the story goes, to a place where he knew there was a big dog. A dog not as big as she was, but still a big dog, and he brought him home with him. And at the proper time he took the *cù mòr glas* and the big dog down to the sea where he knew there was a hollow in the rock which appeared only at low tide. He took some sacking to provide footing for the male dog and he placed the *cù mòr glas* in the hollow of the rock and knelt beside her and steadied her with his left arm under her throat and helped position the male dog above her and guided his blood-engorged penis. He was a man used to working with the breeding of animals, with the guiding of rams and bulls and stallions and often with the funky smell of animal semen heavy on his large and gentle hands.

The winter that followed was a cold one and ice formed on   7 the sea and frequent squalls and blizzards obliterated the offshore islands and caused the people to stay near their fires much of the time, mending clothes and nets and harness and waiting for the change in season. The *cù mòr glas* grew heavier and even larger until there was hardly room for her around the stove or under the table. And then one morning, when it seemed that spring was about to break, she was gone.

The man and even his family, who had become more   8 involved than they cared to admit, waited for her but she did not come. And as the frenzy of spring wore on, they busied themselves with readying their land and their fishing gear and all of the things that so desperately required their attention. And then they were into summer and fall and winter and another spring which saw the birth of the man and his wife's twelfth child. And then it was summer again.

That summer the man and two of his teenaged sons were 9 pulling their herring nets about two miles offshore when the wind began to blow off the land and the water began to roughen. They became afraid that they could not make it safely back to shore, so they pulled in behind one of the offshore islands, knowing that they would be sheltered there and planning to outwait the storm. As the prow of their boat approached the gravelly shore, they heard a sound above them, and looking up they saw the *cù mòr glas* silhouetted on the brow of the hill which was the small island's highest point.

"*M'eudal cù mòr glas,*" shouted the man in his happiness— 10 *m'eudal* meaning something like dear or darling; and as he shouted, he jumped over the side of his boat into the waist-deep water, struggling for footing on the rolling gravel as he waded eagerly and awkwardly toward her and the shore. At the same time, the *cù mòr glas* came hurtling down toward him in a shower of small rocks dislodged by her feet; and just as he was emerging from the water, she met him as she used to, rearing up on her hind legs and placing her huge front paws on his shoulders while extending her eager tongue.

The weight and speed of her momentum met him as he tried 11 to hold his balance on the sloping angle with the water rolling gravel beneath his feet, and he staggered backwards and lost his footing and fell beneath her force. And in that instant again, as the story goes, there appeared over the brow of the hill six more huge grey dogs hurtling down toward the gravelled strand. They had never seen him before; and seeing him stretched prone beneath their mother, they misunderstood, like so many armies, the intention of their leader.

They fell upon him in a fury, slashing his face and tearing 12 aside his lower jaw and ripping out his throat, crazed with blood-lust or duty or perhaps starvation. The *cù mòr glas* turned on them in her own savagery, slashing and snarling and, it seemed, crazed by their mistake; driving them bloodied and yelping before her, back over the brow of the hill where they vanished from sight but could still be heard screaming in the distance. It all took perhaps little more than a minute.

The man's two sons, who were still in the boat and had 13 witnessed it all, ran sobbing through the salt water to where their mauled and mangled father lay; but there was little they could do other than hold his warm and bloodied hands for a few brief moments. Although his eyes "lived" for a small fraction of time, he could not speak to them because his face and throat had been torn away, and of course there was nothing they could do except to hold and be held tightly until that too slipped away and his eyes glazed over and they could no longer feel his hands holding theirs. The storm increased and they could not get home and so they were forced to spend the night huddled beside their father's body. They were afraid to try to carry the body to the rocking boat because he was so heavy and they were afraid that they might lose even what little of him remained and they were afraid also, huddled on the rocks, that the dogs might return. But they did not return at all and there was no sound from them, no sound at all, only the moaning of the wind and the washing of the water on the rocks.

In the morning they debated whether they should try to take 14 his body with them or whether they should leave it and return in the company of older and wiser men. But they were afraid to leave it unattended and felt that the time needed to cover it with protective rocks would be better spent in trying to get across to their home shore. For a while they debated as to whether one should go in the boat and the other remain on the island, but each was afraid to be alone and so in the end they managed to drag and carry and almost float him toward the bobbing boat. They laid him face-down and covered him with what clothes there were and set off across the still-rolling sea. Those who waited on the shore missed the large presence of the man within the boat and some of them waded into the water and others rowed out in skiffs, attempting to hear the tearful messages called out across the rolling waves.

The *cù mòr glas* and her six young dogs were never seen 15 again, or perhaps I should say they were never seen again in the same way. After some weeks, a group of men circled the island tentatively in their boats but they saw no sign. They went again and then again but found nothing. A year later, and grown much braver, they beached their boats and walked the island carefully, looking into the small sea caves and the hollows at the base of the wind-ripped trees, thinking perhaps that if they did not find the dogs, they might at least find their whitened bones; but again they discovered nothing.

The *cù mòr glas*, though, was supposed to be sighted here 16 and there for a number of years. Seen on a hill in one region or silhouetted on a ridge in another or loping across the valleys or glens in the early morning or the shadowy evening. Always in the area of the half perceived. For a while she became rather like the Loch Ness monster or the Sasquatch on a smaller scale. Seen but not recorded. Seen when there were no cameras. Seen but never taken.

The mystery of where she went became entangled with the 17 mystery of whence she came. There was increased speculation about the handmade box in which she had been found and much theorizing as to the individual or individuals who might have left it. People went to look for the box but could not find it. It was felt she might have been part of a *buidseachd* or evil spell cast on the man by some mysterious enemy. But no one could go much farther than that. All of his caring for her was recounted over and over again and nobody missed any of the ironies.

What seemed literally known was that she had crossed the 18 winter ice to have her pups and had been unable to get back. No one could remember ever seeing her swim; and in the early months at least, she could not have taken her young pups with her.

The large and gentle man with the smell of animal semen 19 often heavy on his hands was my great-great-great-grandfather, and it may be argued that he died because he was too good at breeding animals or that he cared too much about their fulfilment and well-being. He was no longer there for his own child of the spring who, in turn, became my great-great-grandfather, and he was perhaps too much there in the memory of his older sons who saw him fall beneath the ambiguous force of the *cù mòr glas*. The youngest boy in the boat was haunted and tormented by the awfulness of what he had seen. He would wake at night screaming that he had seen the *cù mòr glas a' bhàis*, the big grey dog of death, and his screams filled the house and the ears and minds of the listeners, bringing home again and again the consequences of their loss. One morning, after a night in which he saw the *cù mòr glas a' bhàis* so vividly that his sheets were drenched with sweat, he walked to the high cliff which faced the island and there he cut his throat with a fish knife and fell into the sea.

The other brother lived to be forty, but, again so the story 20 goes, he found himself in a Glasgow pub one night, perhaps looking for answers, deep and sodden with the whisky which had become his anaesthetic. In the half darkness he saw a large, grey-haired man sitting by himself against the wall and mumbled something to him. Some say he saw the *cù mòr glas a' bhàis* or uttered the name. And perhaps the man heard the phrase through ears equally affected by drink and felt he was being called a dog or a son of a bitch or something of that nature. They rose to meet one another and struggled outside into the cobblestoned passageway behind the pub where, most improbably, there were supposed to be six other large, grey-haired men who beat him to death on the cobblestones, smashing his bloodied head into the stone again and again before vanishing and leaving him to die with his face turned to the sky. The *cù mòr glas a' bhàis* had come again, said his family, as they tried to piece the tale together.

This is how the *cù mòr glas a' bhàis* came into our lives, and it   21 is obvious that all of this happened a long, long time ago. Yet with succeeding generations it seemed the spectre had somehow come to stay and that it had become *ours*—not in the manner of an unwanted skeleton in the closet from a family's ancient past but more in the manner of something close to a genetic possibility. In the deaths of each generation, the grey dog was seen by some—by women who were to die in childbirth; by soldiers who went forth to the many wars but did not return; by those who went forth to feuds or dangerous love affairs; by those who answered mysterious midnight messages; by those who swerved on the highway to avoid the real or imagined grey dog and ended in masses of crumpled steel. And by one professional athlete who, in addition to his ritualized athletic superstitions, carried another fear or belief as well. Many of the man's descendants moved like careful haemophiliacs, fearing that they carried unwanted possibilities deep within them. And others, while they laughed, were like members of families in which there is a recurrence over the generations of repeated cancer or the diabetes that comes to those beyond middle age. The feeling of those who may say little to others but who may say often and quietly to themselves, "It has not happened to me," while adding always the cautionary *"yet."*

I am thinking all of this now as the October rain falls on the   22 city of Toronto and the pleasant, white-clad nurses pad confidently in and out of my father's room. He lies quietly amidst the whiteness, his head and shoulders elevated so that he is in that hospital position of being neither quite prone nor yet sitting. His hair is white upon his pillow and he breathes softly and sometimes unevenly, although it is difficult ever to be sure.

My five grey-haired brothers and I take turns beside his   23 bedside, holding his heavy hands in ours and feeling their response, hoping ambiguously that he will speak to us, although we know that it may tire him. And trying to read his life and ours into his eyes when they are open. He has been with us for a long time, well into our middle age. Unlike those boys in that boat of so long ago, we did not see him taken from us in our youth. And unlike their youngest brother who, in turn, became our great-great-grandfather, we did not grow into a world in which there was no father's touch. We have been lucky to have this large and gentle man so deep into our lives.

No one in this hospital has mentioned the *cù mòr glas a' bhàis.* 24 Yet as my mother said ten years ago, before slipping into her own death as quietly as a grownup child who leaves or enters her parents' house in the early hours, "It is hard to *not* know what you do know."

Even those who are most sceptical, like my oldest brother 25 who has driven here from Montreal, betray themselves by their nervous actions. "I avoided the Greyhound bus stations in both Montreal and Toronto," he smiled upon his arrival, and then added, "Just in case."

He did not realize how ill our father was and has smiled little 26 since then. I watch him turning the diamond ring upon his finger, knowing that he hopes he will not hear the Gaelic phrase he knows too well. Not having the luxury, as he once said, of some who live in Montreal and are able to pretend they do not understand the "other" language. You cannot *not* know what you do know.

Sitting here, taking turns holding the hands of the man who 27 gave us life, we are afraid for him and for ourselves. We are afraid of what he may see and we are afraid to hear the phrase born of the vision. We are aware that it may become confused with what the doctors call "the will to live" and we are aware that some beliefs are what others would dismiss as "garbage." We are aware that there are men who believe the earth is flat and that the birds bring forth the sun.

Bound here in our own peculiar mortality, we do not wish to 28 see or see others see that which signifies life's demise. We do not want to hear the voice of our father, as did those other sons, calling down his own particular death upon him.

We would shut our eyes and plug our ears, even as we know 29 such actions to be of no avail. Open still and fearful to the grey hair rising on our necks if and when we hear the scrabble of the paws and the scratching at the door.

UNDERSTANDING DETAILS

1. What are the most significant characteristics of the man?
2. Characterize the relationship between the man and the big grey dog. What happens to the big grey dog when she becomes pregnant? How long is it until the man sees her again?
3. Describe the effect of the man's death on his family.

ANALYZING MEANING

1. None of the human characters in this story is named, and the dog is called only cù mòr glas. Why has MacLeod chosen to make his characters nameless?
2. Explain the irony of the man's death.
3. What is the meaning of the title of the story? How does the title link to the central theme of the story?

DISCOVERING RHETORICAL STRATEGIES

1. The language MacLeod uses is distinctively rhythmic. How does MacLeod achieve this effect? How is the rhythm of the language reflective of the setting of the story?
2. Who is the narrator of the story? How does the narrator know the events that he is relating?
3. Describe the tone of "As Birds Bring Forth the Sun." How has MacLeod created this tone?

MAKING CONNECTIONS

1. Compare the East Coast residents of MacLeod's story to those portrayed in Ray Guy's "When Jannies Visited."
2. MacLeod's story includes a descriptive depiction of the East Coast landscape. How does his description of the Nova Scotia coast compare to that of Lesley Choyce ("Thin Edge of the Wedge")?

CHOOSING A TOPIC FOR DISCUSSION/WRITING

1. "You cannot *not* know what you do know." Write an essay using a specific extended example that illustrates the truth of this statement.

2. The characters in MacLeod's story are haunted by the ghost of the *cù mòr glas a' bhàis*. Write an essay in which you examine the effect of a particular superstition or belief like the *cù mòr glas a' bhàis*.
3. Part of the power of MacLeod's story lies in the vivid sensory details. Write an essay in which you examine the way in which MacLeod incorporates these details into this story. You may also want to compare the use of detail in this story to another of MacLeod's stories.

Alice Munro

BOYS AND GIRLS

Hateship, Friendship, Courtship, Loveship, Marriage is the latest of Alice Munro's nine collections of short stories, and the critical acclaim this work is receiving reinforces the comments on the jacket of her earlier collection, *The Love of a Good Woman*: "Alice Munro continues to achieve the impossible, every story collection improving on the near-perfection of the last."

Munro was born in Wingham, Ontario in 1931, and grew up in southwestern Ontario. From 1949 to 1951, she attended the University of Western Ontario, majoring in English. In 1951, she married and moved to British Columbia, where she started a family. In 1963, she moved to Victoria, B.C., and, with her husband, started Munro's Books. Almost a decade later, her marriage ended and she returned to live in southwestern Ontario, where she remarried in 1976.

In addition to her collections of short stories, Munro has published a novel and has regularly had her stories published in periodicals, including *The New Yorker* and the *Atlantic Monthly*. In addition to being a three-time winner of the Governor General's Award for fiction (for *Dance of the Happy Shades* in 1968, *Who Do You Think You Are?* in 1978, and *The Progress of Love* in 1986), in 1997 Munro became the first Canadian to win the U.S. PEN/Malamud Award for Excellence in Short Fiction.

My father was a fox farmer. That is, he raised silver foxes, in 1
pens; and in the fall and early winter, when their fur was
prime, he killed them and skinned them and sold their pelts to
the Hudson's Bay Company or the Montreal Fur Traders. These
companies supplied us with heroic calendars to hang, one on each
side of the kitchen door. Against a background of cold blue sky and
black pine forests and treacherous northern rivers, plumed ad-
venturers planted the flags of England or of France; magnificent
savages bent their backs to the portage.

For several weeks before Christmas, my father worked after 2
supper in the cellar of our house. The cellar was whitewashed,
and lit by a hundred-watt bulb over the worktable. My brother
Laird and I sat on the top step and watched. My father removed
the pelt inside-out from the body of the fox, which looked
surprisingly small, mean and rat-like, deprived of its arrogant
weight of fur. The naked, slippery bodies were collected in a
sack and buried at the dump. One time the hired man, Henry
Bailey, had taken a swipe at me with this sack, saying, "Christmas
present!" My mother thought that was not funny. In fact she
disliked the whole pelting operation—that was what the killing,
skinning, and preparation of the furs was called—and wished it
did not have to take place in the house. There was the smell.
After the pelt had been stretched inside-out on a long board my
father scraped away delicately, removing the little clotted webs
of blood vessels, the bubbles of fat; the smell of blood and animal
fat, with the strong primitive odour of the fox itself, penetrated
all parts of the house. I found it reassuringly seasonal, like the
smell of oranges and pine needles.

Henry Bailey suffered from bronchial troubles. He would 3
cough and cough until his narrow face turned scarlet, and his
light blue, derisive eyes filled up with tears; then he took the lid
off the stove, and, standing well back, shot out a great clot of
phlegm—hsss—straight into the heart of the flames. We admired
him for this performance and for his ability to make his stomach
growl at will, and for his laughter, which was full of high
whistlings and gurglings and involved the whole faulty
machinery of his chest. It was sometimes hard to tell what he
was laughing at, and always possible that it might be us.

After we had been sent to bed we could still smell fox and 4
still hear Henry's laugh, but these things, reminders of the warm,
safe, brightly lit downstairs world, seemed lost and diminished,
floating on the stale cold air upstairs. We were afraid at night in

the winter. We were not afraid of *outside* though this was the time of year when snowdrifts curled around our house like sleeping whales and the wind harassed us all night, coming up from the buried fields, the frozen swamp, with its old bugbear chorus of threats and misery. We were afraid of *inside*, the room where we slept. At this time the upstairs of our house was not finished. A brick chimney went up one wall. In the middle of the floor was a square hole, with a wooden railing around it; that was where the stairs came up. On the other side of the stairwell were the things that nobody had any use for any more— a soldiery roll of linoleum, standing on end, a wicker baby carriage, a fern basket, china jugs and basins with cracks in them, a picture of the Battle of Balaclava, very sad to look at. I had told Laird, as soon as he was old enough to understand such things, that bats and skeletons lived over there; whenever a man escaped from the county jail, twenty miles away, I imagined that he had somehow let himself in the window and was hiding behind the linoleum. But we had rules to keep us safe. When the light was on, we were safe as long as we did not step off the square of worn carpet which defined our bedroom-space; when the light was off no place was safe but the beds themselves. I had to turn out the light kneeling on the end of my bed, and stretching as far as I could to reach the cord.

In the dark we lay on our beds, our narrow life rafts, and 5 fixed our eyes on the faint light coming up the stairwell, and sang songs. Laird sang "Jingle Bells," which he would sing any time, whether it was Christmas or not, and I sang "Danny Boy." I loved the sound of my own voice, frail and supplicating, rising in the dark. We could make out the tall frosted shapes of the windows now, gloomy and white. When I came to the part, *When I am dead, as dead I well may be*—a fit of shivering caused not by the cold sheets but by the pleasurable emotion almost silenced me. *You'll kneel and say, an Ave there above me*—What was an Ave? Every day I forgot to find out.

Laird went straight from singing to sleep. I could hear his 6 long, satisfied, bubbly breaths. Now for the time that remained to me, the most perfectly private and perhaps the best time of the whole day, I arranged myself tightly under the covers and went on with one of the stories I was telling myself from night to night. These stories were about myself, when I had grown a little older; they took place in a world that was recognizably mine, yet one that presented opportunities for courage, boldness and self-sacrifice, as mine never did. I rescued people from a bombed building (it discouraged me that the real war had gone on so far from Jubilee). I shot two rabid wolves who were menacing the schoolyard (the teachers cowered terrified at my back). I rode a fine horse spiritedly down the main street of Jubilee, acknowledging the townspeople's gratitude for some yet-to-be-worked-out piece of heroism (nobody ever rode a horse there, except King Billy in the Orangemen's Day parade). There was always riding and shooting in these stories, though I had only been on a horse twice— bareback because we did not own a saddle—and the second time I had slid right around and dropped under the horse's feet; it had stepped placidly over me. I really was learning to shoot, but I could not hit anything yet, not even tin cans on fence posts.

Alive, the foxes inhabited a world my father made for them. It   7 was surrounded by a high guard fence, like a medieval town, with a gate that was padlocked at night. Along the streets of this town were ranged large, sturdy pens. Each of them had a real door that a man could go through, a wooden ramp along the wire, for the foxes to run up and down on, and a kennel— something like a clothes chest with airholes—where they slept and stayed in winter and had their young. There were feeding and watering dishes attached to the wire in such a way that they could be emptied and cleaned from the outside. The dishes were made of old tin cans, and the ramps and kennels of odds and ends of old lumber. Everything was tidy and ingenious; my father was tirelessly inventive and his favourite book in the world was Robinson Crusoe. He had fitted a tin drum on a wheelbarrow, for bringing water down to the pens. This was my job in summer, when the foxes had to have water twice a day. Between nine and ten o'clock in the morning, and again after supper, I filled the drum at the pump and trundled it down through the barnyard to the pens, where I parked it, and filled my watering can and went along the streets. Laird came too, with his little cream and green gardening can, filled too full and knocking against his legs and slopping water on his canvas shoes. I had the real watering can, my father's, though I could only carry it three-quarters full.

The foxes all had names, which were printed on a tin plate   8 and hung beside their doors. They were not named when they were born, but when they survived the first year's pelting and were added to the breeding stock. Those my father had named were called names like Prince, Bob, Wally and Betty. Those I had

named were called Star or Turk, or Maureen or Diana. Laird named
one Maud after a hired girl we had when he was little, one Harold
after a boy at school, and one Mexico, he did not say why.

Naming them did not make pets out of them, or anything   9
like it. Nobody but my father ever went into the pens, and he
had twice had blood-poisoning from bites. When I was bringing
them their water they prowled up and down on the paths they
had made inside their pens, barking seldom—they saved that
for nighttime, when they might get up a chorus of community
frenzy—but always watching me, their eyes burning, clear gold,
in their pointed, malevolent faces. They were beautiful for their
delicate legs and heavy, aristocratic tails and the bright fur
sprinkled on dark down their backs—which gave them their
name—but especially for their faces, drawn exquisitely sharp in
pure hostility, and their golden eyes.

Besides carrying water I helped my father when he cut the   10
long grass, and the lamb's quarter and flowering money-musk,
that grew between the pens. He cut with the scythe and I raked
into piles. Then he took a pitchfork and threw fresh-cut grass all
over the top of the pens, to keep the foxes cooler and shade their
coats, which were browned by too much sun. My father did not
talk to me unless it was about the job we were doing. In this he
was quite different from my mother, who, if she was feeling
cheerful, would tell me all sorts of things—the name of a dog
she had had when she was a little girl, the names of boys she
had gone out with later on when she was grown up, and what
certain dresses of hers had looked like—she could not imagine
now what had become of them. Whatever thoughts and stories
my father had were private, and I was shy of him and would
never ask him questions. Nevertheless I worked willingly under
his eyes, and with a feeling of pride. One time a feed salesman
came down into the pens to talk to him and my father said, "Like
to have you meet my new hired man." I turned away and raked
furiously, red in the face with pleasure.

"Could of fooled me," said the salesman. "I thought it was   11
only a girl."

After the grass was cut, it seemed suddenly much later in the   12
year. I walked on stubble in the earlier evening, aware of the
reddening skies, the entering silences, of fall. When I wheeled
the tank out of the gate and put the padlock on, it was almost
dark. One night at this time I saw my mother and father standing
talking on the little rise of ground we called the gangway, in front

of the barn. My father had just come from the meathouse; he had his stiff bloody apron on, and a pail of cut-up meat in his hand.

It was an odd thing to see my mother down at the barn. She   13
did not often come out of the house unless it was to do something—hang out the wash or dig potatoes in the garden. She looked out of place, with her bare lumpy legs, not touched by the sun, her apron still on and damp across the stomach from the supper dishes. Her hair was tied up in a kerchief, wisps of it falling out. She would tie her hair up like this in the morning, saying she did not have time to do it properly, and it would stay tied up all day. It was true, too; she really did not have the time. These days our back porch was piled with baskets of peaches and grapes and pears, bought in town, and onions and tomatoes and cucumbers grown at home, all waiting to be made into jelly and jam and preserves, pickles and chili sauce. In the kitchen there was a fire in the stove all day, jars clinked in boiling water, sometimes a cheesecloth bag was strung on a pole between two chairs straining blue-black grape pulp for jelly. I was given jobs to do and I would sit at the table peeling peaches that had been soaked in the hot water, or cutting up onions, my eyes smarting and streaming. As soon as I was done I ran out of the house, trying to get out of earshot before my mother thought of what she wanted me to do next. I hated the hot dark kitchen in summer, the green blinds and the flypapers, the same old oilcloth table and wavy mirror and bumpy linoleum. My mother was too tired and preoccupied to talk to me, she had no heart to tell about the Normal School Graduation Dance; sweat trickled over her face and she was always counting under her breath, pointing at jars, dumping cups of sugar. It seemed to me that work in the house was endless, dreary and peculiarly depressing; work done out of doors, and in my father's service, was ritualistically important.

I wheeled the tank up to the barn, where it was kept, and I   14
heard my mother saying, "Wait till Laird gets a little bigger, then you'll have a real help."

What my father said I did not hear. I was pleased by the way   15
he stood listening, politely as he would to a salesman or a stranger, but with an air of wanting to get on with his real work. I felt my mother had no business down here and I wanted him to feel the same way. What did she mean about Laird? He was no help to anybody. Where was he now? Swinging himself sick on the swing, going around in circles, or trying to catch caterpillars. He never once stayed with me till I was finished.

"And then I can use her more in the house," I heard my 16
mother say. She had a dead-quiet, regretful way of talking about
me that always made me uneasy. "I just get my back turned and
she runs off. It's not like I had a girl in the family at all."

I went and sat on a feed bag in the corner of the barn, not 17
wanting to appear when this conversation was going on. My
mother, I felt, was not to be trusted. She was kinder than my
father and more easily fooled, but you could not depend on her,
and the real reasons for the things she said and did were not to
be known. She loved me, and she sat up late at night making a
dress of the difficult style I wanted, for me to wear when school
started, but she was also my enemy. She was always plotting.
She was plotting now to get me to stay in the house more,
although she knew I hated it (*because* she knew I hated it) and
keep me from working for my father. It seemed to me she would
do this simply out of perversity, and to try her power. It did not
occur to me that she could be lonely, or jealous. No grown-up
could be; they were too fortunate. I sat and kicked my heels
monotonously against a feedbag, raising dust, and did not come
out till she was gone.

At any rate, I did not expect my father to pay any attention 18
to what she said. Who could imagine Laird doing my work—
Laird remembering the padlock and cleaning out the watering-
dishes with a leaf on the end of a stick, or even wheeling the
tank without it tumbling over? It showed how little my mother
knew about the way things really were.

I have forgotten to say what the foxes were fed. My father's 19
bloody apron reminded me. They were fed horsemeat. At this
time most farmers still kept horses, and when a horse got too
old to work, or broke a leg or got down and would not get up, as
they sometimes did, the owner would call my father, and he and
Henry went out to the farm in the truck. Usually they shot and
butchered the horse there, paying the farmer from five to twelve
dollars. If they had already too much meat on hand, they would
bring the horse back alive, and keep it for a few days or weeks in
our stable, until the meat was needed. After the war the farmers
were buying tractors and gradually getting rid of horses
altogether, so it sometimes happened that we got a good healthy
horse, that there was just no use for any more. If this happened
in the winter we might keep the horse in our stable till spring, for
we had plenty of hay and if there was a lot of snow—and the

plow did not always get our road cleared—it was convenient to be able to go to town with a horse and cutter.

The winter I was eleven years old we had two horses in the   20
stable. We did not know what names they had had before, so we called them Mack and Flora. Mack was an old black workhorse, sooty and indifferent. Flora was a sorrel mare, a driver. We took them both out in the cutter. Mack was slow and easy to handle. Flora was given to fits of violent alarm, veering at cars and even at other horses, but we loved her speed and high-stepping, her general air of gallantry and abandon. On Saturdays we went down to the stable and as soon as we opened the door on its cosy, animal-smelling darkness Flora threw up her head, rolled her eyes, whinnied despairingly and pulled herself through a crisis of nerves on the spot. It was not safe to go into her stall; she would kick.

This winter also I began to hear a great deal more on the   21
theme my mother had sounded when she had been talking in front of the barn. I no longer felt safe. It seemed that in the minds of the people around me there was a steady undercurrent of thought, not to be deflected, on this one subject. The word *girl* had formerly seemed to me innocent and unburdened, like the word *child*; now it appeared that it was no such thing. A girl was not, as I had supposed, simply what I was; it was what I had to become. It was a definition, always touched with emphasis, with reproach and disappointment. Also it was a joke on me. Once Laird and I were fighting, and for the first time ever I had to use all my strength against him; even so, he caught and pinned my arm for a moment, really hurting me. Henry saw this, and laughed, saying, "Oh, that there Laird's gonna show you, one of these days!" Laird was getting a lot bigger. But I was getting bigger too.

My grandmother came to stay with us for a few weeks and   22
I heard other things. "Girls don't slam doors like that." "Girls keep their knees together when they sit down." And worse still, when I asked some questions, "That's none of girls' business." I continued to slam the doors and sit as awkwardly as possible, thinking that by such measures I kept myself free.

When spring came, the horses were led out in the barnyard.   23
Mack stood against the barn wall trying to scratch his neck and haunches, but Flora trotted up and down and reared at the fences, clattering her hooves against the rails. Snow drifts dwindled quickly, revealing the hard grey and brown earth, the familiar

rise and fall of the ground, plain and bare after the fantastic landscape of winter. There was a great feeling of opening-out, of release. We just wore rubbers now, over our shoes; our feet felt ridiculously light. One Saturday we went out to the stable and found all the doors open, letting in the unaccustomed sunlight and fresh air. Henry was there, just idling around looking at his collection of calendars which were tacked up behind the stalls in a part of the stable my mother had probably never seen.

"Come to say goodbye to your old friend Mack?" Henry 24 said. "Here, you give him a taste of oats." He poured some oats into Laird's cupped hands and Laird went to feed Mack. Mack's teeth were in bad shape. He ate very slowly, patiently shifting the oats around in his mouth, trying to find a stump of molar to grind it on. "Poor old Mack," said Henry mournfully. "When a horse's teeth's gone, he's gone. That's about the way."

"Are you going to shoot him today?" I said. Mack and Flora 25 had been in the stable so long I had almost forgotten they were going to be shot.

Henry didn't answer me. Instead he started to sing in a high, 26 trembly, mocking-sorrowful voice, *Oh, there's no more work, for poor Uncle Ned, he's gone where the good darkies go.* Mack's thick, blackish tongue worked diligently at Laird's hand. I went out before the song was ended and sat down on the gangway.

I had never seen them shoot a horse, but I knew where it 27 was done. Last summer Laird and I had come upon a horse's entrails before they were buried. We had thought it was a big black snake, coiled up in the sun. That was around in the field that ran up beside the barn. I thought that if we went inside the barn, and found a wide crack or a knothole to look through, we would be able to see them do it. It was not something I wanted to see; just the same, if a thing really happened, it was better to see it, and know.

My father came down from the house, carrying the gun. 28

"What are you doing here?" he said. 29

"Nothing." 30

"Go on up and play around the house." 31

He sent Laird out of the stable. I said to Laird, "Do you want 32 to see them shoot Mack?" and without waiting for an answer led him around to the front door of the barn, opened it carefully, and went in. "Be quiet or they'll hear us," I said. We could hear Henry and my father talking in the stable, then the heavy, shuffling steps of Mack being backed out of his stall.

In the loft it was cold and dark. Thin, crisscrossed beams of   33
sunlight fell through the cracks. The hay was low. It was a rolling
country, hills and hollows, slipping under our feet. About four
feet up was a beam going around the walls. We piled hay up in one
corner and I boosted Laird up and hoisted myself. The beam was
not very wide; we crept along it with our hands flat on the barn
walls. There were plenty of knotholes, and I found one that gave
me the view I wanted—a corner of the barnyard, the gate, part of
the field. Laird did not have a knothole and began to complain.

I showed him a widened crack between two boards. "Be   34
quiet and wait. If they hear you you'll get us in trouble."

My father came in sight carrying the gun. Henry was leading   35
Mack by the halter. He dropped it and took out his cigarette
papers and tobacco; he rolled cigarettes for my father and himself.
While this was going on Mack nosed around in the old, dead
grass along the fence. Then my father opened the gate and they
took Mack through. Henry led Mack way from the path to a
patch of ground and they talked together, not loud enough for us
to hear. Mack again began searching for a mouthful of fresh
grass, which was not to be found. My father walked away in a
straight line, and stopped short at a distance which seemed to
suit him. Henry was walking away from Mack too, but sideways,
still negligently holding on to the halter. My father raised the
gun and Mack looked up as if he had noticed something and my
father shot him.

Mack did not collapse at once but swayed, lurched sideways   36
and fell, first on his side; then he rolled over on his back and,
amazingly, kicked his legs for a few seconds in the air. At this
Henry laughed, as if Mack had done a trick for him. Laird, who
had drawn a long, groaning breath of surprise when the shot
was fired, said out loud, "He's not dead." And it seemed to me
it might be true. But his legs stopped, he rolled on his side again,
his muscles quivered and sank. The two men walked over and
looked at him in a businesslike way; they bent down and
examined his forehead where the bullet had gone in, and now I
saw his blood on the brown grass.

"Now they just skin him and cut him up," I said. "Let's go."   37
My legs were a little shaky and I jumped gratefully down into the
hay. "Now you've seen how they shoot a horse," I said in a
congratulatory way, as if I had seen it many times before. "Let's
see if any barn cat's had kittens in the hay." Laird jumped. He
seemed young and obedient again. Suddenly I remembered how,

when he was little, I had brought him into the barn and told him to climb the ladder to the top beam. That was in the spring, too, when the hay was low. I had done it out of a need for excitement, a desire for something to happen so that I could tell about it. He was wearing a little bulky brown and white checked coat, made down from one of mine. He went all the way up, just as I told him, and sat down on the top beam with the hay far below him on one side, and the barn floor and some old machinery on the other. Then I ran screaming to my father, "Laird's up on the top beam!" My father came, my mother came, my father went up the ladder talking very quietly and brought Laird down under his arm, at which my mother leaned against the ladder and began to cry. They said to me, "Why weren't you watching him?" but nobody ever knew the truth. Laird did not know enough to tell. But whenever I saw the brown and white checked coat hanging in the closet, or at the bottom of the rag bag, which was where it ended up, I felt a weight in my stomach, the sadness of unexorcised guilt.

I looked at Laird, who did not even remember this, and I 38 did not like the look on this thin, winter-pale face. His expression was not frightened or upset, but remote, concentrating. "Listen," I said, in an unusually bright and friendly voice, "you aren't going to tell, are you?"

"No," he said absently. 39

"Promise." 40

"Promise," he said. I grabbed the hand behind his back to 41 make sure he was not crossing his fingers. Even so, he might have a nightmare; it might come out that way. I decided I had better work hard to get all thoughts of what he had seen out of his mind—which, it seemed to me, could not hold very many things at a time. I got some money I had saved and that afternoon we went into Jubilee and saw a show, with Judy Canova, at which we both laughed a great deal. After that I thought it would be all right.

Two weeks later I knew they were going to shoot Flora. I 42 knew from the night before, when I heard my mother ask if the hay was holding out all right, and my father said, "Well, after tomorrow there'll just be the cow, and we should be able to put her out to grass in another week." So I knew it was Flora's turn in the morning.

This time I didn't think of watching it. That was something 43 to see just one time. I had not thought about it very often since, but sometimes when I was busy, working at school, or standing in front of the mirror combing my hair and wondering if I would be pretty when I grew up, the whole scene would flash into my mind: I would see the easy, practised way my father raised the gun, and hear Henry laughing when Mack kicked his legs in the air. I did not have any great feeling of horror and opposition, such as a city child might have had; I was too used to seeing the death of animals as a necessity by which we lived. Yet I felt a little ashamed, and there was a new wariness, a sense of holding-off, in my attitude to my father and his work,

It was a fine day, and we were going around the yard picking   44
up tree branches that had been torn off in winter storms. This was something we had been told to do, and also we wanted to use them to make a teepee. We heard Flora whinny, and then my father's voice and Henry's shouting, and we ran down to the barnyard to see what was going on.

The stable door was open. Henry had just brought Flora out,   45
and she had broken away from him. She was running free in the barnyard, from one end to the other. We climbed up on the fence. It was exciting to see her running, whinnying, going up on her hind legs, prancing and threatening like a horse in a Western movie, an unbroken ranch horse, though she was just an old driver, an old sorrel mare. My father and Henry ran after her and tried to grab the dangling halter. They tried to work her into a corner, and they had almost succeeded when she made a run between them, wild-eyed, and disappeared around the corner of the barn. We heard the rails clatter down as she got over the fence, and Henry yelled, "She's into the field now!"

That meant she was in the long L-shaped field that ran up   46
by the house. If she got around the center, heading towards the lane, the gate was open; the truck had been driven into the field this morning. My father shouted to me, because I was on the other side of the fence, nearest the lane, "Go shut the gate!"

I could run very fast. I ran across the garden, past the tree   47
where our swing was hung, and jumped across a ditch into the lane. There was the open gate. She had not got out, I could not see her up on the road; she must have run to the other end of the field. The gate was heavy. I lifted it out of the gravel and carried it across the roadway. I had it half-way across when she came in sight, galloping straight towards me. There was just time to get the chain on. Laird came scrambling through the ditch to help me.

Instead of shutting the gate, I opened it as wide as I could. I 48
did not make any decision to do this, it was just what I did. Flora
never slowed down; she galloped straight past me, and Laird
jumped up and down, yelling, "Shut it, shut it!" even after it was
too late. My father and Henry appeared in the field a moment
too late to see what I had done. They only saw Flora heading for
the township road. They would think I had not got there in time.

They did not waste any time asking about it. They went back 49
to the barn and got the gun and the knives they used, and put
these in the truck; then they turned the truck around and came
bouncing up the field towards us. Laird called to them, "Let me
go too, let me go too!" and Henry stopped the truck and they
took him in. I shut the gate after they were all gone.

I supposed Laird would tell. I wondered what would happen 50
to me. I had never disobeyed my father before, and I could not
understand why I had done it. Flora would not really get away.
They would catch up with her in the truck. Or if they did not
catch her this morning somebody would see her and telephone
us this afternoon or tomorrow. There was no wild country here
for her to run to, only farms. What was more, my father had paid
for her, we needed the meat to feed the foxes, we needed the
foxes to make our living. All I had done was make more work for
my father who worked hard enough already. And when my
father found out about it he was not going to trust me any more;
he would know that I was not entirely on his side. I was on
Flora's side, and that made me no use to anybody, not even to
her. Just the same, I did not regret it; when she came running at
me and I held the gate open, that was the only thing I could do.

I went back to the house, and my mother said, "What's all 51
the commotion?" I told her that Flora had kicked down the fence
and got away. "Your poor father," she said, "now he'll have to
go chasing over the countryside. Well, there isn't any use planning
dinner before one." She put up the ironing board. I wanted to tell
her, but thought better of it and went upstairs and sat on my bed.

Lately I had been trying to make my part of the room fancy, 52
spreading the bed with old lace curtains, and fixing myself a
dressing table with some leftovers of cretonne for a skirt. I
planned to put up some kind of barricade between my bed and
Laird's, to keep my section separate from his. In the sunlight,
the lace curtains were just dusty rags. We did not sing at night
any more. One night when I was singing Laird said, "You sound
silly," and I went right on but the next night I did not start. There

was not so much need to anyway, we were no longer afraid. We knew it was just old furniture over there, old jumble and confusion. We did not keep to the rules. I still stayed awake after Laird was asleep and told myself stories, but even in these stories something different was happening, mysterious alterations took place. A story might start off in the old way, with a spectacular danger, a fire or wild animals, and for a while I might rescue people; then things would change around, and instead, somebody would be rescuing me. It might be a boy from our class at school, or even Mr. Campbell, our teacher, who tickled girls under the arms. And at this point the story concerned itself at great length with what I looked like—how long my hair was, and what kind of dress I had on; by the time I had these details worked out the real excitement of the story was lost.

It was later than one o'clock when the truck came back. The 53
tarpaulin was over the back, which meant there was meat in it. My mother had to heat dinner up all over again. Henry and my father had changed from their bloody overalls into ordinary working overalls in the barn, and they washed their arms and necks and faces at the sink, and splashed water on their hair and combed it. Laird lifted his arm to show off a streak of blood. "We shot old Flora," he said, "and cut her up in fifty pieces."

"Well I don't want to hear about it," my mother said. "And 54
don't come to my table like that."

My father made him go and wash the blood off. 55

We sat down and my father said grace and Henry pasted his 56
chewing-gum on the end of his fork, the way he always did; when he took it off he would have us admire the pattern. We began to pass the bowls of steaming, overcooked vegetables. Laird looked across the table at me and said proudly, distinctly, "Anyway it was her fault Flora got away."

"What?" my father said. 57

"She could of shut the gate and she didn't. She just open' it 58
up and Flora run out."

"Is that right?" my father said. 59

Everybody at the table was looking at me. I nodded, 60
swallowing food with great difficulty. To my shame, tears flooded my eyes.

My father made a curt sound of disgust. "What did you do 61
that for?"

I did not answer. I put down my fork and waited to be sent 62
from the table, still not looking up.

But this did not happen. For some time nobody said 63
anything, then Laird said matter-of-factly, "She's crying."

"Never mind," my father said. He spoke with resignation, 64
even good humour, the words which absolved and dismissed
me for good. "She's only a girl," he said.

I didn't protest that, even in my heart. Maybe it was true. 65

UNDERSTANDING DETAILS

1. In "Boys and Girls" the relationship between the narrator and
   her brother changes quite dramatically. Outline this shift and explain why it happens.
2. What role was the girl expected to play? What lessons about
   being a girl does the girl seem to learn from her father? From her
   mother? From her grandmother?
3. Discuss the portrayal of the main character in "Boys and Girls."
   What is the main character like? How does Munro develop the
   narrator and convincingly convey the significant personality
   changes in this character?

ANALYZING MEANING

1. The narrator says she could not understand why she disobeyed
   her father and allowed the horse to escape (paragraph 50).
   Explain her action.
2. "Good short stories have the power to entertain and affect readers through time with their enduring themes." Discuss the relevance of "Boys and Girls" for a 21st-century audience.
3. In an interview with Graeme Gibson, Alice Munro said, "I'm
   very excited by what you might call the surface of life …" How
   does the surface presented in "Boys and Girls" reflect what is
   going on under the surface?

DEVELOPING RHETORICAL STRATEGIES

1. Munro is noted for her meticulous attention to detail. Identify
   at least five examples of Munro's use of very specific detail that
   makes the story strong.
2. Describe the tone of the language in this story. How does Munro
   achieve this tone?
3. Explain how Munro's choice of narrative voice helps to reinforce the theme of "Boys and Girls."

MAKING CONNECTIONS

1. Compare and contrast the roles of boys and girls in "Boys and Girls" and "Greasy Lake" (Boyle). What expectations are placed on each?
2. "Boys and Girls" (Munro) and "Death by Landscape" (Atwood) both relate experiences of young girls. In what ways have these authors chosen similar strategies in crafting these stories?

CHOOSING A TOPIC FOR DISCUSSION/WRITING

1. Write an essay in which you compare and contrast the movie *Boys and Girls* with the story of the same title by Alice Munro. Remember that the story is the original version, and focus your discussion on the differences and similarities that you see as being particularly significant rather than on trivial details.
2. Compare and contrast "Boys and Girls" to another story by Alice Munro. Consider the similarities and differences in elements such as character, setting, style, and theme.
3. Write an essay for your student newspaper about ways in which boys and girls (or men and women) have been treated differently in some situation in your experience. Were the differences justified?

Carol Shields

WINDOWS

A resident of Canada since she married at age 22, Carol Shields was born in Oak Park, Illinois, in 1935. Her novel *The Stone Diaries*, a winner of the Governor General's Award for fiction in Canada and the Pulitzer Prize in the United States, is probably the best known of her works, but Shields has also published several collections of short stories, including *Dressing Up for the Carnival: Short Stories* (from which this story, "Windows," was taken), books of poetry, plays, a book of criticism about Susanna Moodie, and a biography of Jane Austen.

In addition to her writing, Shields has been a professor at the University of Ottawa, the University of British Columbia, and the University of Manitoba and has served as the chancellor of the University of Winnipeg. Shields now lives with her husband in Victoria, B.C.

■ ──────────────────────────────────── ■

In the days when the Window Tax was first introduced M. J. used to say to me, "Stop complaining. Accept. Render unto Caesar. Et cetera." 1

I remember feeling at the time of the legislation that the two of us would continue to live moderately well as long as we had electricity to illuminate our days and nights, and failing that, kerosene or candles. But I knew that our work would suffer in the long run. 2

"Furthermore," M. J. continued, "the choice is ours. We can block off as many or as few windows as we choose." 3

This was true enough; the government, fearing rebellion, I suppose, has left the options open. Theoretically, citizens are free to choose their own level of taxation, shutting off, if they like, just one or two windows or perhaps half to two-thirds of their overall glazed area. In our own case, we immediately decided to brick up the large pane at the back of the house which overlooks the ravine. A picture window is how my parents would have described this wide, costly expanse of glass; M. J. prefers the trademark term "panorama vista," but at the same time squints ironically when it's mentioned. We loved the view, both of us, and felt our work was nourished by it, those immense swaying poplars and the sunlight breaking across the top of their twinkling leaves, but once we sat down and calculated the tax dollars per square inch of window, we decided we would have to make the sacrifice. 4

Next we closed off our bedroom windows. Who needs light in a bedroom, we reasoned, or the bathroom either, for that matter? We liked to think at the time that our choices represented a deliberate push towards optical derangement, and that this was something that might add a certain ... *je ne sais quoi* ... to a relationship that has never been easy. 5

Before the advent of the Window Tax, light had streamed into our modest-but-somehow-roomy house, and both M. J. and I rejoiced in the fact, particularly since we earn our living as artists— I work in oils; M. J.'s medium is also oils, but thinly, thinly applied 6 so that the look is closer to tempera. Light—natural light—was crucial to us. Just think what natural light allows one to see: the thousand varying shades of a late fall morning when the sky is brittle with a blue and gold hardness, or the folded, collapsed, watery tints of a February afternoon. Still, artificial light was better than no light at all. We did go to the trouble of applying to the government for a professional dispensation, a matter of filling out half a dozen forms, but naturally we were turned down.

We were, it could be argued, partly prepared for our 7 deprivation, since both of us had long since adjusted our work cycle to the seasonal rhythms, putting in longer hours in the summer and cutting back our painting time in the dark ends of winter days, quitting as early as three-thirty or four, brewing up a pot of green tea, and turning to other pursuits, occasionally pursuits of an amatory disposition; M. J.'s sensibility rises astonishingly in the midst of coziness and flickering shadow. Our most intimate moments, and our most intense, tend to fall into that crack of the day when the sun has been cut down to a bent sliver of itself and even that about to disappear on the horizon.

It is a fact that my work has always suffered at the approach 8 of winter. The gradual threatened diminishment of the afternoon sun encourages a false exuberance. Slap down the thick blades of colour while it is still possible. Hurry. Be bold (my brain shouts and prods), and out of boldness, while the clock drains away each thrifty second of possibility, will come that accident we call art.

It seldom does. What I imagine to be a useful recklessness 9 is only bad painting executed with insufficient light.

M. J.'s highly representational work prospers even less well 10 than mine during the late autumn days, not that the two of us have ever spoken of this. You will understand that two painters living together under one roof can be an invitation to discord, and its lesser cousin, irritation. Ideally artists would be better off selecting mates who are civil engineers or chiropractors or those who manufacture buttons or cutlery. It's relatively easy to respect disparate work, but how do we salute, purely, the creative successes of those we live with, those we stand beside while brushing our teeth? How to rule out envy, or worse, disdain, and to resist those little sideways words or faked encouragement, delivered with the kind of candour that is really presumption? And so when I say, rather disingenuously, that M. J.'s work prospers less well, is overly representational, employs too much purple and lavender, and so on, you will have to take my pronouncement with a certain skepticism. And then reflect on the problems of artistic achievement and its measurement, and the knowledge that systems of temperament are immensely complicated. The salt and wound of M. J.'s vulnerability, for instance, is stalked by an old tenderness, but also by the fear of being overtaken.

It seems that most artists are frightened by any notion of 11 subtraction, and, of course, the rationing of light falls into the category of serious deprivation. Without paint, artists can create images with their own blood or excrement if necessary, not that the two of us have ever been driven to such measures, but there is no real substitute for natural light. As the accustomed afternoon rays grow thinner, the work becomes more desperate, careless, and ineffectual. We often discussed this over our tea mugs during our mid-winter days when the year seemed at its weakest point, how scarcity can stifle production or else, as in my case, clear a taunting space to encourage it. It seemed to both of us monumentally unfair.

But then, with the new tax measures, the house was dark all 12 day. Like everyone else we had come to see the cutting back of natural light as a civic protest against a manipulative tax, *conscience de nos jours*, you might call it, and like all but the very rich we had filled in every one of our windows—with brick or stone or sheets of ugly plywood. *Obscura maxima* was the code phrase on our politicized tongues, and we spoke it proudly— and on our bumper stickers too—at least in the beginning. (Of course we left the window in our studio as long as we were able, and only boarded it up when we were made to feel we had failed in our civic responsibility.)

In another country, at a different latitude, we might have 13 packed up our easels and paints and sandwiches and worked *en plein air*, since no government, however avid for revenues, is able to control access to outdoor light. But "nature's studio," as the great Linnaeus called it, is seldom available in our northern climate. Our winters are long and bitter, and our summers filled with sultry air and plagues of mosquitoes. We are dependent, therefore, on a contrived indoor space, our *atelier*, as I sometimes like to call it, into which we coax as much light as possible—or at least we did before the enactment of the Window Tax.

The tax, when it was first introduced, had a beguiling logic, 14 and even the appearance of fairness. We know, every last one of us, how widespread the evils of tax evasion are, how even the

most morally attentive—and I would put M. J. and myself in
that category—inflate their travel receipts or conceal small
transactions which have brought them profit. More than once
I've exchanged little dashed-off paintings, still lifes mostly, for
such necessities as fuel oil and roof repairs, leaving behind not a
trace for my accountant's eye.

The genius of the new tax was its simplicity. Some forms of   15
wealth can be hidden in safe-deposit boxes or in dresser drawers,
but the dwellings we inhabit announce, loudly and publicly, our
financial standing—their size, their aesthetic proportions, the
materials with which they are fashioned. And what could be
more visible from the exterior than the number and size of one's
windows? What feature can be more easily calculated?

A formula was worked out: so many tax dollars per square   16
inch of window. A populist victory.

The results might have been foreseen. Overnight, with   17
windows an index to wealth, and thus a liability, the new form
of tax evasion became, as you can imagine, a retreat to mediaeval
darkness. One by one, and then hundreds by hundreds, our
wondrous apertures to the world were walled in with wood or
cardboard or solid masonry. As seen from the outside, the
hurriedly filled-in windows gave our houses the blank, stunned
look of abandonment. Inside was trapped the darkness of a
primitive world; we might just as well have been living in caves
or burrows.

The plotted austerities of our own domestic life, so appealing   18
at first, soon faded. A life in the dark is close to motionless; hour
by hour the outlines of our bodies are lost—there is no armature
of style, no gesture, no signifying softness of the mouth. What
follows is a curious amnesia of the self. I had thought that words
spoken in the dark might bring back the old force of language,
words becoming deeds, becoming defined moments, but I found
instead that the voice in the dark puts on a dignified yet hollow
sideshow, so that we ended up speaking to ourselves and not to
each other.

Of course there was always the alternative of artificial light,   19
which was in fact our only recourse. But a life performed under
the burnt yellow-whiteness of electric illumination condemns us
to perceptual distortion. There is that vicious snapping on and off
of current, and the unvarying intensity, always predictable, yet
always startling. The glare of a simple light bulb—think of it,
that unhandsome utilitarian contrivance of glass and wire—

insists on a sort of extracted/extruded truth, which those of us involved in long love affairs are wary of. Our postures and equivocations are harshly exposed, and the face we show the world subtly discoloured. Is there any love that doesn't in the end insist on naming itself, showing itself to other less fortunate people, oh look at me! at us!

When two people live and work under the same roof, the 20 solitary nature of consciousness is frayed with a million threads of incalculability, and one of those threads is a decision to avoid emotional dissonance and preserve for one's self certain areas of privacy. M. J. and I, in the months following the Window Tax, settled for an unspoken equipoise: I kept my self-doubts to myself and, in turn, was spared the usual strong doses of disrespect about my *attitude*.

No longer did we discuss our work or show our projects to 21 each other, though we occupied as always the same studio. We kept to our separate corners. I worked mainly during the day and M. J. at night, for with the loss of daylight it scarcely mattered to us anymore which was which. As for our *vie intime*, well, that had declined radically after just a few days spent under the parching electric lights. While M. J. slept, I worked steadily but with a constant ache of discouragement, attempting with my range of aromatic oils to re-create on canvas the warmth and shine of inflowing light, that which I'd known all my life but now could scarcely remember. This was a flat, dull width of time, though I have always recognized that long chapters of life go on without strong passion.

It occurred to me one day that my use of canvas might be at 22 fault. Stretched canvas, with its stiff industrial surface, possesses a withholding element and in the best of circumstances is reluctant at first to "open" its weave to what is offered. I knew that it had once been customary to paint on wood surfaces, hearty walnut planks or maple—this was an old and honourable tradition, and one that I thought worth trying.

At that moment my eyes fell on the slab of plywood we 23 had nailed over the studio window, and the thought came to me that I might overpaint its cheap fir grain with a diverting image: one of my tossed-off still lifes perhaps, a collection of lemons on a blue plate or a pitcher of pure water, something anyway that was more consoling than the life around me and less inviting of the late afternoon fits and starts brought on by the overhead lights.

The rectangularity of the wood seemed to demand a frame of   24
some kind, and this I carefully painted in, exchanging the rather
harsh orangeness of fir for a subtly grained and bevelled oak, a
generous four inches in width, working my way around the two
sides, the top and bottom, and then, finally, painting in a quartet
of fine mitred corners. An easy trick, you might think,
transforming one type of wood into another, but the task took
me the rest of the day—and half of the next.

When I paint I am composed, I am most truly myself, but I   25
wish I could tell you how much happiness this particular
craftsmanlike task gave me, exchanging wood for simple wood,
coaxing ripples from dead surfaces. My usual paintings are
compositionally complex and employ a rich colour field. I am
known for my use of the curved line. It's even been said that my
management of the curve has brought to contemporary painting
"an engagement for the eye and a seduction for the intellect."
And yet, the strict linearity of my new "oak" frame brought a
satisfaction my rondure illusions have never given.

At first I didn't know that what I was framing was, in fact, a   26
window; the knowledge came upon me slowly as I found my
brush dividing the framed space into a series of smaller
rectangles, bringing about a look that was oddly architectural.
Again I reached for a golden oakiness of colour; again I kept my
lines disciplined and sharp, but narrower now, more delicate
and refined.

Mullions. The word leapt into my head. A relic of an older   27
world from a wiser consciousness. These nonstructural bars
dividing the lights or panes of the window proved relatively
easy to master, being simple wood strips, slightly grooved on
their edges, glinting with their barely revealed woody highlights.
Each one of them pleased me, the verticals, the horizontals, and
most especially their shy intersections.

That phrase *most especially.* Did you notice? M. J. has no   28
patience with such locutions.

Harder to paint on the surface of ordinary plywood was the   29
image of glass, and so I was forced to experiment. Window glass,
as you will have observed, is a curious half-silvered substance, a
steaming liquid that has been frozen into a solid plane. Glass
possesses different colours at different hours of the day.
Sometimes it pretends it's a mirror. Other times it gathers checks
and streaks and bubbles of brilliance and elegant flexes of mood.
Its transparency winks back at you, yet it withholds, in certain

weathers, what is on the other side, revealing only a flash of wet garden grass, a shadow of a close-standing hedge, or perhaps a human figure moving across its width—the mail carrier or a neighbour or even M. J. out for a late afternoon stroll. Glass is green like water or blue like the sky or a rectangle of beaten gold when the setting sun strikes it or else a midnight black broken by starlight or the cold courteous reflection of the moon.

Glassiness evaded me. My brush halted; it swung in the air 30 like a metronome. What I produced were grey cloudy squares with a cardboardlike density, a kindergarten version of what a window might be.

It may have been that I was tired. Or that I was visited by 31 that old fear of failure or by the sense of lowered consequence that arrives out of nowhere, especially when I hear M. J. tiptoeing around in the kitchen, brewing yet another pot of tea. I decided to leave it until morning.

As always I rose early and went straight to the studio and 32 snapped on the electric lights. My "window" was waiting, but I saw immediately that it was altered. The shadows of my oak mouldings had acquired a startling trompe l'oeil vividness, their depth and shadow augmented and their woodiness enlivened by amber flecks and streaks. I had been pleased to arrive the day before at a primitive suggestiveness—window as architectural detail, window as gesturing towards windowness, just falling short of verisimilitude, but this was now a window so cunningly made that it could almost have been opened on its casement hinges. Hinges that had not existed yesterday. The glass panes too had been tampered with. I looked closely and recognized a slick oil shine superimposed on a lake of rainy mauve.

All day I worked on the glass. It went slowly, so slowly that 33 often an hour would pass with only one or two touches of my brush on the surface. My paint was mixed and layered, rubbed out, then reapplied. By evening I had managed to articulate, or so I thought, the spark and glance and surprise of glass without, of course, stretching towards the achievement of light or air.

I woke the next morning with a sense of excitement. Even 34 before entering the studio I could feel a soft-shoe dance in the region of my chest, and I reflected that it had been some years since my feelings had run so dangerously out of control. My "window" shone, its oak frame burning with an almost antique burnish, and the troublesome panes giving off their glassy gifts. How is it possible to make light dance on a flat surface, and how does anyone bring transparency to what is rigid and unyielding? I sighed, then readied myself for a day of work.

It was at least a week before the task was done. By coincidence 35 we were both there when it reached completion, standing side by side in one of our rare moments of tenderness, each of us with brush in hand. One of us reached forward to apply a final brush-stroke, though we weren't able to remember afterwards which it was. The moment was beautiful, but also blurred. We recall a sudden augmentation of brilliance, as though we witnessed the phenomenon with a single pair of eyes, our "window" bursting its substance, freed in such a way that light flowed directly through it.

Not real light, of course, but the idea of light—infinitely more 36 alluring than light itself. Illusion, accident, meticulous attention all played a part in the construction of a window that had become more than a window, better than a window, the window that would rest in the folds of the mind as all that was ideal and desirable in the opening, beckoning, sensuous world.

UNDERSTANDING DETAILS

1. Why is the Window Tax introduced? How do people react to it? What is the meaning of the "code phrase" *obscura maxima* (paragraph 12)?
2. What is the effect of the Window Tax on the narrator and M. J.?
3. Describe the relationship between the narrator and M. J.

ANALYZING MEANING

1. Explain how the characters of the narrator and M. J. are reflected in the contributions each makes to the painted window.
2. Describe the effect of the painted window on the narrator and M. J. and on their relationship.
3. What is the central theme or universal truth Shields is conveying in this story?

DISCOVERING RHETORICAL STRATEGIES

1. Who tells the story, and why has Shields chosen this form of narration?
2. The narrator draws attention in paragraph 28 to linguistic "locutions." Why does she do this? Where are other examples of this kind of language?

3. Shields' story is about a pair of visual artists. What descriptive details appeal particularly to the sense of sight?

MAKING CONNECTIONS

1. In "Windows," Shields is exploring ideas about the perception of reality. What connections do you see between this story and "The Immaculate Conception Photography Gallery" (Govier)?
2. Tony Leighton's essay ("The New Nature") explores how much truth there is to the expression "seeing is believing." How is this expression relevant to Shields' story?

CHOOSING A TOPIC FOR DISCUSSION/WRITING

1. Imagine that you are living in Shields' society, where the government has just imposed the window tax. Write a persuasive essay in which you apply for dispensation on professional or medical grounds .
2. The window tax is ostensibly a fair method of taxation that is easily tracked. Write an essay for your municipal, provincial, or federal government in which you propose some better alternative to the current methods of taxation.
3. Write a classification/division essay in which you discuss different types of light and the effect each has on people.

Timothy Taylor

DOVES OF TOWNSEND

After graduating with a degree in economics and an M.B.A., Timothy Taylor (1963–) moved from Alberta to Toronto and began his career as a banker. After a few years, however, he exchanged the hectic pace of Toronto for the more relaxed atmosphere of Vancouver (where he had lived for about a decade in his childhood), and in 1991 he made the shift from banking to freelance corporate writing and consulting. In this role,

Taylor has published non-fiction pieces on travel, arts, and business in magazines that include *Canadian Lawyer, Adbusters, Saturday Night*, and *The Georgia Straight* and has done extensive consulting work in the salmon fishing industry. This role also allowed Taylor more time for creative writing, and his stories have been published in a range of literary magazines, including *The Malahat Review*, where "Doves of Townsend" first appeared. "Doves of Townsend" subsequently won the 2000 Journey Prize (as well as a National Magazine Award), and Taylor's first novel, *Stanley Park* (2001), received a very positive critical reception, including making the shortlist for the Giller Prize. Taylor's first collection of short stories, *Silent Cruise*, is scheduled for publication in 2002 and Taylor is currently working on a novel entitled *El Primero*.

"Doves of Townsend, good morning."   1

This is me, answering the phone at the shop. After which I   2
frequently end up explaining the inherited family name. Sometimes (I admit) tired of telling the real story, I'll make something up. "There's a flock of doves found in Townsend, my dad's hometown," I'll start. Then I finish the story by saying the birds hunt as a pack and kill cats, or that they bring good luck if you catch one and pull out a tail feather. The mood of the story rides up and down on the sine wave of my menstrual cycle.

The truth is plain. My father came from Townsend and he   3
was a fanatical collector. Knives, as it happens, but it could have been anything. Magpie, hoarder, packrat, whatever you want to call him, I had long understood him to be obsessive-compulsive within certain categories. His suicide note read: *I fear I have covered the full length of this blade.* But at auctions, where he lived the happy parts of his life, he held up his wooden paddle and said his last name so the auctioneer would know who was bidding. "Dove," he'd say, eyes never leaving whatever dagger, cleaver, oiseau or machete had captivated him. And then—in case there was another Dove in the room—he'd say it again, louder: "Doves of Townsend."

So, here I am: "Doves of Townsend?"   4

It was two months ago, Alexander Galbraithe calling. He   5
wanted a set of chrome 1940s ashtrays, the ones with the DC-3 doing the flypast over the cigar butts. I've known Mr. Galbraithe since I was a child. When my father started Doves of Townsend as an extension of his own collecting (a very bad idea I came to think), Mr. Galbraithe was one of his first steady buyers. I assume

he stayed with me out of allegiance or sympathy, since after Dad's death I sold off the knife collection quickly and resolved never to replace it.

"Clare?" he said. "Are you familiar with the airplane ones?" 6

I knew he was talking about the famous deco ashtray since 7 none of the other things he collects—coach clocks, cigar cutters, Iranian block-print textiles, even knives as far as I know—come in an aeroplane model.

"Pedestal or tabletop?" I asked him. "Illuminated?" 8

We began to work out the specs. 9

"Real?" I asked, breathing a little into the phone. "Or fake?" 10

Mr. Galbraithe didn't laugh often, although he found many 11 things funny. What he did, instead, was roll his massive balding head back an inch or two, squint slightly and crinkle his cheeks. When he was done, he'd roll his head back to its normal position and resume where he left off.

This is what he did now. I could tell over the phone. And 12 when he returned he said, "Clare. My dear. Really."

It pays to be straight on this real-fake question. There's no point 13 looking for something real, something authentic and old and possibly rare, if the client has no preference. My sometimes-boyfriend Tiko used to send art directors my way from time to time, and all they cared about was that an object look good on camera. Some collectors, on the other hand, collect fakes. So go figure.

What's bad, clearly, is to get fake when you're after real. 14 Most dealers will learn this the hard way even if they resist being obsessive collectors themselves. Me, for example. I was just starting out. Dad had been gone a year, and I overcame all the good sense I had and bought a set of *les Frères* locking steak knives. I literally saw them in a shop window, stopped on the sidewalk—reconsidering everything I had resolved after my father slipped somewhere beyond reach, after he did what he did—then went in and bought them. Of course, I knew the famous French maker produced knives that were rare and beautiful, knives with a four-inch hand-forged blade folding into a black pear-wood handle with silver inlay and locking in place with a tiny gold clasp in the shape of a dove. I knew the *les Frères* dove had meant something special to my father, among all his knives. These were the first I had seen since his death and, for that instant, I was host to a perfectly synchronous collector's impulse.

What this lapse taught me was never to buy a thing merely   15
because it is rare and beautiful and you are able to construe some
tangled family significance. What I didn't know then was the
number of *les Frères* reproduction steak knives that had been
made over the years by Spanish, Korean and other manufacturers.
When I learned this, which was soon enough, I sold my
Taiwanese fakes for about one-twentieth what I paid for them. To
Mr. Galbraithe, in fact, who rescued me. Tried to pay much more
than they were worth, but I wouldn't let him.

"You see the clasp here, Clare?" he explained very kindly.   16
"The reproduction clasps are stamped flat from stainless steel,
then gold-plated. A real *les Frères* has a hammered dove figurine,
sculpted in three dimensions, in 18-karat gold."

"Fake," I said, shaking my head. "I should have known."   17

"But now you have seen it," he said, putting a large hand   18
weightlessly on my shoulder. "I am quite sure you won't miss it
again."

He was a huge presence, six-and-a-half feet tall; God knows   19
how many pounds. In his other hand, the knife looked like an
antique folding toothpick I'd once seen at auction. Mr. Galbraithe
always leaned a little forward when we spoke, canted just so, careful
to hear and understand everything that I said. He wore dark, heavy
double-breasted suits and two-tone black and white shoes. Tiko
met him once and referred to him thereafter as Sidney Greenstreet,
although he looked nothing like that. He brought to mind the force
of gravity, yes, but not the crushing pressure of it. Instead, he made
me think of the way some large things elegantly defy it. I've looked
at suspension bridges the way I looked at Mr. Galbraithe.

He folded the fake *les Frères* into his palm, first popping the   20
gold-plated clasp with his thumb, then clicking shut the blade
with his fingers. Then he wrote me a cheque using a large black
fountain pen. In the nineteenth century, I thought on occasion, I
could have ended up marrying the widowed Mr. Galbraithe
despite the thirty-year age difference.

"You have an eye for the fine line," Mr. Galbraithe said to   21
me another time, admiring a more successful purchase. I thought
the words left unsaid were something like: *but be careful, so did
your father.*

He wanted the ashtrays for his office, he explained.   22

"Of course," I said. He'd been a pilot at one time. During   23
the war, the Second I suppose. He kept a suite of offices out near

the airport, and when we talked on the phone I could hear the jets taking off and landing.

I began a fairly typical search: local, then national dealers. 24 Then American. Surprisingly, I turned up only a few singles, none in fine condition and none illuminated. I searched the Internet and found a few more, but I couldn't tell what condition they were in and I didn't know the dealer.

I phoned Mr. Galbraithe back. 25

"Where are they?" he asked. 26

I told him it was Los Angeles. It wouldn't have been the first 27 time he'd sent me off to inspect something. He flew me to Boston once to look over a case lot of clocks. He expressed deep trust in my judgement and reacted with gratitude, but not much surprise, when I produced exactly what he was looking for, time after time.

This didn't seem worth it, frankly. "Let's leave it for a while," 28 I said. "Something will turn up."

He asked about local dealers, and I told him I'd long 29 exhausted those options.

"Yes, yes. Of course you have...." A jet was coming in for a 30 landing just then. "What about the flea markets and what have you?"

It was an unusual suggestion from him. Everything in the 31 entire flea market might be worth as much as one of his coach clocks on a good Saturday. It was, in my view (which I kept to myself), a vast sea of junk.

I phoned Tiko on Saturday, got him in bed. He said: "Baby ... 32 what time is it?"

I told him, and then described my plans for the day. "Chances 33 of success are very slim, but it might be fun."

"What's Greenstreet want in a flea market?" he said, yawning 34 and stretching. I could hear the sheets sliding over him, slipping off his chest, down his stomach. But when I asked him again, he said only: "I can't, I'm going skiing."

Work is work. I went down without him. 35

The flea market was held every weekend in a massive 36 wooden warehouse in the industrial part of the city near the railway tracks. It's the kind of neighbourhood where the streets collude to form gigantic shallow ponds during the rainy season and an unlikely number of shopping carts spend their final days.

I paid my sixty-five-cent cover charge, took a big breath and 37 went into the main hall. I didn't go there often enough for its vastness and futility not to strike me again. Here there were hundreds of independent dealers set up at folding tables, which stretched in their rows far back into the gloom, the warehouse air smelling of boiled hot dogs and vinegar, body odour, cat litter. The aisles sluggish with people. The vendors pessimistic.

I let myself drift with the currents of this sea, eyes down as   38 I passed the tables, trolling through cheap, newish merchandise that would be of no interest to any collector now or in the foreseeable future. Acres of airport novels, CDs suspiciously unboxed, video games, socket wrench sets, Ren and Stimpy T-shirts and boxes of paper clips or batteries or ballpoint pens that presumably fell off the back of a truck somewhere. And scattered among these tables the personal collections, which for their madness and desperation held an increment more promise of delivering the unexpected. These were the tables heaped with costume jewellery, constellations of twinkling, unwearable rhinestone earrings, pendants, tiaras. Tables with shallow glass cases stuffed full of coins, or stamps, military medals, old wristwatches, brazenly ugly cufflinks and spent cigarette lighters. Tables stacked dangerously high, any item on top of any other, a collection of large-format Japanese glamour magazines balancing on a pyramid of teak salad bowls, fondue sets and a condiment tray in the shape of a dachshund. A glass fishing float, purple. A collection of faded teacups, none Royal Doulton, most chipped, worth no more or less than the fifty cents marked on masking tape and stuck to each handle.

I imagined Mr. Galbraithe here, however unlikely. He would   39 hover at each table just briefly, I thought. He would ask questions with respect, his eye scanning, sorting and cataloguing in an instant the incomprehensible rubble pulled together by these other collectors.

I was getting on towards the back of the warehouse by this   40 point, having seen nothing of real interest. Here the black creosote-soaked timbers rose to a distant roof, netted under with sheets of small mesh to keep the pigeons from roosting there. It had only worked to keep them in, judging from the six or seven mummified birds lying suspended in the net. But it made me think of one of the Doves of Townsend stories I used to tell, the one about the doves living in the rafters of the Townsend railway station. And that thought brought me back to where I was, what I was supposed to be doing. I closed my mouth and looked down.

I was standing near a group of tables, a personal collection 41
although no person was apparent. The mounds of junk on some
of the tables had been covered over in orange tarps. A sign read
The Shickey Shack, scrawled in crayon on a piece of two-by-
four nailed to an upright. There were stacks of magazines—
years' worth of something called *American Rifleman*—which I
leafed through, not curious about the content but about the
person who would buy such a collection. Who might collect it in
the first place.

There were other books, adhering to a military theme. Many 42
dozen drinking glasses, no two the same. A large quartz polar
bear with zirconium eyes, and a stack of room-service silverware
from the Hotel Vancouver. I picked some of these up, wondering
if the dull clang of the worn plate cover against the warped plate
would call forward someone from behind one of these piles.

Under the plate cover, in the middle of the service platter, 43
there was a butterfly.

It startled me enough that I took a step back from the table 44
before I realized that it was dead, entombed in a clear plastic
silver-dollar-sized coin case. I put the plate cover aside and picked
up the butterfly, forced to smile.

It was fixed neatly to a square of Styrofoam cut to fit the box. 45
The front wings were burnt orange darkening to coffee-brown
at the tips. The back wings were white, covered with a lacy grey
pattern, impossibly complex. The two brittle antennae curled
away to tiny clublike tips. It was an exquisite thing, quivering
on its pin as I rolled the box in my fingers.

Looking around the table with renewed interest, I saw there 46
were several more. A few were strewn among the hotel
silverware, others dropped carelessly through the boxes of
magazines and among the books. I pulled together a small pile of
cases, a dozen or fifteen specimens, each one different. And before
I even looked at them closely I began to sift through the junk on
the rest of the table. In a beer mug marked "Oktoberfest 1988" I
found another six. There was an old naval officer's cap sitting
upside down at the very back of the table. I leaned as far as I
could, got it by the rim and felt immediately that it was heavy
with many more.

Large and small. Of more colours than I knew. None of the 47
boxes labelled, although the names wouldn't have meant much
to me. A tiny one with rounded dark khaki wings. One with
notched brown wings and a pronounced nose. Another lacy

pattern, this one brown and orange, fading to light brown on white like a melting snowbank. A large, regal yellow one with black trailing pieces like counterweights on each wing. And a dull grey, mothlike creature, which up close was not grey at all but a shimmering, luminescent blue. I stacked and restacked the boxes in small piles as I browsed, at first by size but then by wing shape and colour, arranging the boxes in a spectrum from the blacks and dark browns to the palest gold and shining white.

There was still nobody around, nobody to answer the 48 questions that were forming. Where from? Significance of? Even, how much? It didn't occur to me then that I had no buyer in mind for these. That I had no personal need for what appeared to be dozens of dead butterflies that were probably worth nothing in the first place. Still, I had become curious and interested, imagining that if I didn't buy them somebody else might only for the delicate, colourful improbability of them being there.

"Very strange," I said aloud, shaking my head and picking up 49 a case that held a black butterfly with blood-red stains in the centre of each forward wing.

At which point a small, rusty voice from nowhere said: "The 50 purpose of butterflies will not be found...."

I was startled a second time. In fact I think I yelped. 51

The voice started again: "The purpose of butterflies will not 52 be found ... in the few flowers they may inadvertently pollinate." And then the man got up from where he had been sitting on a milk crate, and stepped out from behind one of the tables tented in orange tarp.

"I'm sorry?" I said, hand on my throat. 53

He stood looking down at his own merchandise without 54 curiosity. "From a book," he said. "A butterfly book. William Howe."

"Oh yes?" I said. 55

"Nor in the numbers of parasitic wasps they may support," 56 he carried on, his voice building up to an insistent scrape. "And to peer beneath a microscope at their dissected fragments will in no way elucidate the reason for their being."

He stopped and thought. 57

"Where are they from?" I asked, but he didn't hear me. He 58 had grizzled sideburns that tapered to points and wore a chocolate-milk-coloured thigh-length leather jacket, green gabardine flood pants with two-inch cuffs. His blue wool socks collapsed casually to the top of the arch of his chisel-toed black loafers. If it weren't for the missing front teeth and his age, I thought he could have stepped from a Prada ad. Past hip though, not knowingly funky. Just poor.

He was reciting the last line again, to himself. "... *their dissected* 59 *fragments will in no way elucidate the reason for their being....*" Then his voice rose to full volume again as he remembered the remaining lines: "Their purpose is their beauty and the beauty they bring into the lives of those of us who have paused long enough from the cares of the world to listen to their fascinating story."

He nodded once, satisfied with his recitation, then returned 60 behind the table and produced a heavy, crumbling encyclopaedia of a book. "*On Butterflies and Moths.* William H. Howe."

It crossed my mind that the book was probably worth 61 something. It was full of colour plates that could be removed and sold individually. I took the book in my hands, ignoring the fact that I didn't deal prints, that I didn't know them or their buyers particularly well.

"Twenty dollars," the man said, looking away, across the 62 warehouse. Adhering to flea market convention by communicating a dry certainty that I would not buy.

"It's beautiful," I said, my hand drifting across the brocade 63 pattern on the binding. And then I heard myself ask: "And the collection?"

"This is a Tiger Swallowtail," he said, not answering, but 64 picking up the large yellow butterfly with black tails on its wings. I took it from him and admired it. "And this," he said, tapping another box on the table. "Ringlet. Here's a Pearly Eye. Pine White here. This guy's a Little Wood Satyr."

"A what?" I asked, incredulous. He repeated himself, 65 handing me a case holding a tiny butterfly, less than an inch across, with dark green-brown wings, spots like eyes, each rimmed in ghostly white.

"You like them?" he asked. "There's a collector's log here 66 too...." And reaching again into a box behind the table, he took out a spiral-bound notebook, the precise journal kept by the original collector. On its pages, in achingly tidy rows and columns, had been recorded the capture data for each butterfly: date, place (latitude, longitude and altitude), time, prevailing weather, vegetation and topography of the habitat, full species name. And so I read that the butterfly known as the Postman was to lepidopterists the *Heliconius melpomene* of the family *Nymphalidae*. And that the Postman in this collection had been found in a tangle of brush at the edge of a tropical forest not far from the Orinoco River, some day's drive south of San Tomé in Venezuela. When netted, the notes went on, this particular Postman had been feeding near passion vines.

I had never thought about butterflies before. Not the species, 67 nor the thing that might be collected. Although for a few seconds I imagined them wall-mounted, a dozen in a frame. And the loose ones, this Postman included, scattered in their little clear boxes across my desk for me to pick up and handle, to admire from time to time while working.

"Buck apiece," the man said, jarring me from my thoughts. 68 "There's sixty-two of them. Seventy bucks and I'll throw in the book, the collector's log and this too."

He brought out the killing jar and held it up for me to admire. 69 But I was already coming out of it. The price had startled me awake, having the reverse effect of the hydrocyanic acid gas that the man was explaining to me emanated from the plaster of paris at the bottom of the killing jar and put a butterfly painlessly, permanently to sleep. In an instant, by being so affordable, so not-exorbitant, the seventy-dollar price tag reminded me that this was exactly the kind of thing you can spend an unhappy lifetime picking up at auctions and flea markets, dollar by dollar, day by day without purpose or analysis until you need a bigger warehouse, a bigger line of credit. Until you wake up one morning—like this butterfly collector undoubtedly did—riding alone across the vast and lonely landscape to which you have been driven, the only place wide enough, unpeopled enough that it will accommodate the obsession you have allowed to spread tangled within you.

"They're very pretty," I said, clearing my throat. 70

"Not what you're looking for though," he said, shaking his 71 head, just short of disgust.

"No," I said, although it wasn't clear even to me whether I 72 was disagreeing or agreeing with him.

"Didn't think so," he said. "A gift maybe?" And he hoisted 73 the quartz polar bear, with effort. It appeared to weigh twenty or thirty pounds.

I remembered then what I had come looking for, and blurted 74 it out in one ragged breath, as if eager to convince him that I did have a purpose. When I was finished, he laughed out loud.

"Airplane ashtrays?" he said, the immensity of the world's 75 foolishness revealed to him in full. "Those shiny things like from the movies?"

"I suppose," I said.   76

"Little whirly bits and lights?"   77

"Yes," I said, weakly.   78

1940s chrome-and-slag-glass DC-3 pedestal ashtrays. He 79
pulled back the orange tarp on one of the covered tables and
there they were. Filthy, but they cleaned up well. Back at the
shop, a week later after I had the wiring fixed, the propellers
turned and all the little windows on the airplanes lit up. One in
this condition would have been rare. A matching set of four from
something called the Long Island Flying Club was without
question a very good find.

I delivered them to Alexander Galbraithe's office myself. I 80
didn't remember the last time I had been as excited about finding
something exactly right. But there I was, heart beating lightly,
quickly. I had the ashtrays on a flatbed mover's dolly, covered in
a white sheet. He would know immediately what they were; he
would react with his usual low-key appreciation, but he would
know they were perfect.

His secretary let me into his office with an expectant smile. 81
He came out from behind his broad mahogany desk, glided
across the room-sized Tabriz to take my hand, gently, raised it to
his lips like he had so many times before, always somewhere
between chivalry and self-deprecation.

"Clare. My dear."   82

I was grinning like an idiot. "Check this out," I said, as I 83
sometimes do, becoming a teenager around him. I was pointing
at the dolly, the sheet tented across the four objects underneath.
His eyes went round. His eyebrows lifted high. When he pulled
back the sheet, he actually drew in a breath, theatrically, and
stared at them for several seconds, touching one lightly with his
fingertips in disbelief. "Incredible," he said, finally. "Did you...."
And here he spun very slowly on one foot to face me. "Did you
go to Los Angeles?"

He knew I hadn't; it had been his suggestion I go to the flea 84
market in the first place. And with this thought I registered Mr.
Galbraithe's unusual surprise at my having performed just as I
always did.

"No," I said. "I didn't."   85

"Well where then, my dear girl?" he asked. Which was about 86
when I decided he was faking it.

"Um ..." I said, stumbling on the answer, because now, not 87
only was I transfixed by the thought that he had set the whole

thing up, my mind was also sweeping across the history of his patronage. After my father's suicide he had never pressed, only been nearby. I knew where to find him, and I confess I looked from time to time. Not just to find for him his various objects of desire, I talked boys to him once. I told him a sad story, early-Tiko no doubt, before I had come to accept the limits of what that relationship was all about. Mr. Galbraithe had taken me out for a drink at the Wedgewood. I was talking between sips of a crantini. He was holding a gimlet judiciously between his index finger and his thumb, sitting forward in the wingback lounge chair that was too small for his full frame, listening, listening always. I think he said: "Well. Clare. It may be no reassurance ... but let me say this. There are certain types of unkindness that will bleed out of a young man as he matures."

"The flea market," I said, finally answering his question. "I 88 found them at the flea market, just as you suggested."

Sure enough, his face flattened with recognition. And his 89 eyes did squint, and his cheeks did crinkle, and his bald head did roll back in silent recognition. But I wasn't seeing the humour in any of this.

I didn't say anything else. It felt impossible. I worried a range 90 of things at once. Mutually assured embarrassment. That it was too late to unwind anything that had been done. That unwanted favours can't be graciously accepted or easily rejected. That I didn't know what I thought of the favour anyway. He defied gravity, Mr. Galbraithe did. He hovered without effort, a teacup in his hand now. He listened as I mechanically told of the flea market. He laughed silently at my description of the place, its strange topography and population, the very terrain over which he had walked himself to plant something in my path.

I charged him what I'd paid The Shickey Shack, claiming 91 that I paid much less. He objected and used the opportunity to counsel me on profit margins until his secretary removed my teacup from my hand. I had my coat on again and was actually in the elevator, the doors sliding shut.

Tiko took me to dinner, a surprise. He was back from a shoot in 92 Whistler that had taken much longer than expected and he took me to the Alibi Room. New, hip, sexy, full of film types.

I told him about the flea market, at least most of the story. I 93 left out the butterflies, not sure why. But I told him about finding the ashtrays. I told him about the strange feeling I had that Mr. Galbraithe must have known they were there. Must have put them there for me to find.

Tiko didn't understand. I told the story three ways before 94 he finally said: "You mean he goes to the flea market, gives the guy these ashtrays, then sends you there to find them?"

From a nearby table a woman's indignant words wafted 95 over: *If he thinks I'm coming back from New York for a ten-minute short ... well....*

"It's an incredible coincidence," I said. "These things are 96 hard to find. Impossible to find at a flea market."

"Why though?" Tiko said, frowning. 97
"Because they're rare," I said. 98
"Not that." He was angry. "Why do it? Is it, like, a test?" 99
I hadn't really thought of that. 100
"Is he making fun of you? Having some kind of sport?" 101
I hadn't thought of that either. 102
"They're all total nut cases," Tiko said then, his nose 103 wrinkling with distaste for my clientele. "Greenstreet's no different, just fatter."

Our peach consommé arrived just then, and Tiko ordered 104 decaf espressos from a waiter who was almost embarrassingly eager to please. From the corner of my eye, I could see the woman with the indignant voice looking in our direction.

Tiko looked somewhere beyond beautiful, as always. There 105 were times I thought the only descriptor of his good looks was the word *ridiculous*. His eyes were brilliant green, his hair dark, thick, perfectly unkempt. His jawline descended like an executive order from his cheekbones.

He had work in Montreal, he told me. A perfume ad. 106
"Will you miss acting?" I asked him, when the espressos 107 arrived.
"It's still acting," he said. "I wouldn't actually wear Yves St 108 Laurent."
We kissed in the elevator going up to my place. I liked to 109 touch his face, to trace it with my fingers. In the apartment, the blinds were up and the mercury glow from the street lights was awash over everything. He undressed me in the living room, led me by the hand to the bedroom, pushed me down onto the bed before taking his own clothes off. He stood over me, stripped off his jacket, then his shirt, unbuckled his belt very slowly. It was

borderline Chippendale, but still sexy. I would have liked him to sleep there, wake up with me. But the fact that he had to leave, had to catch a flight in the morning, the fact of his rough kiss, the wool of his overcoat brushing my breasts and his scarf falling to the pillow beside my head ... all this stayed somehow romantic.

He said, just before he left: "Lying there ... you are so   110 beautiful."

Weeks passed. Mr. Galbraithe left a message, which he had never   111 done before. He said: "Clare. I am very fond of them. Thank you again."

"Doves of Townsend?"   112

The caller identified himself as an art director.   113

"Tiko says...." The art director spoke like he was waiting to   114 hear an echo. "... that no *matter* ... how obscure the item ... and no *matter* ... how much craziness you have to wade through in its pursuit ... you, Clare, always find The Object of Desire."

"When did you talk to Tiko?" I asked him.   115

"He told me about your airplane things," the art director   116 said.

"Oh yes," I said, but I have to admit I was distracted thinking   117 about where Tiko was at the moment. Montreal? Or back in Whistler?

"You know, women...." The art director seemed to be holding   118 the phone away from his head. "Women are *made* ... to find *things*. I believe."

"What?" I said.   119

"Well certainly you are." And here I imagined that the art   120 director leaned back in his ergonomic chair and kicked his feet up on a glass desk mounted on the backs of two giant black ceramic elephants. Cracked the micro-blinds with the tips of his fingers to peer into the parking lot. "You see, in old times ... very old times ... Jurassic Park-type old times ... women found the thing ... and then men killed the thing. There was this ... division of labour."

I agreed to go down and see him anyway. He had a film on   121 the go, an unhappy director. They had a character, he explained. "He needs a little *je ne sais quoi*."

And no, he didn't know where Tiko was.   122

The art director's office turned out to be brightly lit,   123 swatches and tile samples lying around. I was right about the blinds and the chair, but the resting place for the art director's pink-bunny-slipper-clad feet was actually a massive ball-and-claw partner's desk.

"Come in," he called across the room. The art director had 124 flowing black hair, a large, thin nose and wore contacts the colour of a Bombay Sapphire gin bottle. He brought to mind a bust of one of the bad Caesars. "Coffee?"

"Sure, thanks." I took in his room, then his slippers as they 125 disappeared off the desk and reappeared on the parquet hardwood, padding across to the espresso machine in the kitchenette.

"Cappuccino, espresso, flavouring?" 126

"Black," I said. 127

"Americano is it?" the art director answered, delighted with 128 whatever this revealed, humming now as he burped out the espresso into old Wedgwood cups. A discontinued pattern. Kimono, I thought.

"So?" he said, handing me the cup. It was Kimono. 129

"So," I answered. "Tell me about this character." 130

He nodded, then lifted the coffee cup to his lips, pinky 131 quivering erect. "All business," he observed, as if he found women a bit useless to work with normally. "Male. Thirties. A loser I'm afraid. Tight for money."

They needed something for his apartment, it seemed. 132 Something that would make a subconscious comment on the character's head, his heart and history. "We tried boxing posters, to emphasize his physicality," the art director said. "But in the rushes it came out too Sean Penn."

"So who is this guy?" I asked. Part of me always became 133 impatient with these types of clients, although they paid well. "What does this man do in the film?"

I should have known better. Scripts are state secrets and all the 134 art director gave me was: "Travis Bickle in Kafka's *Metamorphosis*."

I wanted to laugh, but didn't. 135

No family, no interest in girls. 136

"Metamorphosis?" I asked. 137

"Yes," the art director explained. "Because he is one thing, 138 then changes into another thing. A very dramatic, colourful change."

I was thinking of the stages, which I tried to remember while 139 sipping my coffee. Egg, larva, pupa, adult. The last stage brief, a moment of beauty. The struggle to emerge followed by that instant of first flight.

"Say ..." I said, as the idea fluttered into my head, bursting   140
into the fullness of what it could be.

Perhaps the most appealing aspect of the idea was the way   141
that something I had been tricked into finding could be used to
lead me on towards my own discovery. That by resisting the
collector's impulse, I had yet been rewarded.

I went to the flea market the following Saturday, first thing   142
in the morning. I took an enthusiastic breath of the fragrant air
inside the turnstile and jogged the length of the warehouse to
The Shickey Shack. He didn't let on that he recognized me. But
they were still there, the butterflies scattered once again without
order across his tables. The naval officer's cap had been refilled.
The black butterfly with the blood-red stains sat at the very edge
of the table, and I picked this up first, failing to suppress a small
smile of recognition.

"The Postman," he said wearily.   143

"This is the Postman?" I said, remembering the name.   144

He cracked a look up at me. "There's sixty-two in total," he   145
said.

I asked him how much, casually.   146

"Some people think they're worthless," the man said,   147
scratching his head. "Buncha dead bugs, know what I mean?
But to the right person, these are priceless."

We talked back and forth a bit, and I admit faking much   148
greater knowledge of the collection than I had. I said it was on
the small side, with a common assortment of specimens,
although in pretty good shape. He saw right through me,
apparently, and upped his quote to a hundred and fifty dollars
for everything, the specimens, the William Howe book, the
collector's log and the killing jar, which he pulled out and
proceeded to explain all over again.

I held onto them for a week before phoning the art director.   149
I left them scattered on my desk. I used the book and the log to
figure out their names. Part of me also knew that this drove up the
drama value of the delivery. I even wrapped them for maximum
impact on opening. I kept the books and the killing jar—the art
director wouldn't be interested in those—but loaded all the
butterflies carefully into a small wooden crate, wrapped the box
in heavy brown waxed paper, then tied it up with butcher's twine.
It might have been shipped in from the Amazon Basin.

"Good God," the art director said, staring at the elaborate   150
package. And when it was open, there was an instant when the

small clear boxes spilled onto the table, and it seemed that the butterflies had escaped, that they had been released and would now fly away, each to its own home.

"Remarkable," the art director said. Shifting his pale blue, 151 faintly distrusting gaze onto me. "Quite remarkable."

When he asked how much, I suggested he make me an offer. 152 I hadn't thought this strategy over and I had never used it before. But without thinking, it came out: "These are worthless or priceless, depending on how you look at it. What are they worth to you?"

Spending somebody else's money, this did not strike him as 153 disingenuous.

"How about a thousand?" he said finally. 154

I hadn't heard from Tiko in almost three weeks, not the longest 155 stretch by any degree, just a disappearance, of striking similarity to many others. The kiss. The final words. "So beautiful." The sound of the door closing behind him.

I phoned his agent and learned only that he was "out East." 156 I wasn't at a good place on the sine wave. "A lot of things are out East," I snapped, and hung up.

It made me think dismally of my father, I confess. There 157 came a day following his death—day 111, day 147, I don't remember—but there was one day different from every other day that he had been gone. It was the day I woke up not envisioning his absence as a separation, a distance that might be somehow closed through my efforts. Instead, that day, I woke up knowing the space between my father and me to be measureless, just as the time that stretched ahead of me into the unwritten future.

I thought of this, and then of phoning Alexander Galbraithe. 158 Something that hadn't occurred to me in several weeks and an impulse I quickly suppressed.

I went to the flea market that weekend, no reason, no objective. 159 No Object of Desire for me to find or miss. I just rolled with the uneasy crowds. I bought the purple glass fishing float. Fifteen dollars bargained down to ten. Why negotiate? I couldn't say.

I walked by The Shickey Shack but didn't stop. The American 160 Riflemen were still there, ditto the quartz polar bears. My man was nowhere to be seen, but I knew he was on his milk crate, head in his hands, socks collapsed around his tired ankles.

Past The Shickey Shack were the darkest corners of the 161 warehouse, such undesirable real estate apparently that not all the tables were in use. Here is where the new worthless junk and the madly compiled personal junk gave way to the utterly unsellable junk. Headless golf clubs, TVs with cracked screens, torn couches, bent bicycles. These were the people selling anything they could lift and carry here, their own things. These were the people burning furniture to stay warm, selling organs, consuming themselves.

At a table against the very back wall I stood and inspected a   162
computer with foreign characters on the keys, no English. A skinny man in a faded grey suit offered to demonstrate. He turned it on, typed in the password—the name of his father, I wondered, a favourite drink or food from home—then flashed up the various programs, all written over with the same language. He finished the demo with a winning smile. I made a sympathetic face. We both shrugged.

I turned away from the table and left the flea market. Out   163
past the pessimistic vendors, cutting through the sluggish crowds, under the dead hanging pigeons, through the turnstile and into a light afternoon rain. Driving unnecessarily fast across town, it occurred to me that the skinny man had only one potential flea market buyer for his computer: himself. And he already owned one. There was a painful irony in his linkage to that thing from his home, his past, a painful emblematic power in his attempt to sever the connection.

I found myself stopped in front of a well-known antique   164
dealer on Granville Street. Not a place I used often anymore. The woman at the counter recognized me, but could not place my name. When I gave her my card, she nodded immediately and said: "Yes of course, Doves of Townsend. I knew your father."

She had more knives to choose from than I could bear to consider. And in all of these, she had one set of *les Frères*.

They were in a square black wooden box, with a very worn   165
blue satin lining. The knives themselves were immaculate, like something gifted with eternal youth, forever fresh as the mundane world aged around them. A set of two *les Frères* steak knives, the black pear-wood inlaid handle at once familiar. I picked one up, turning it over in my hands. Letting my fingers ride over the sculpted, golden dove figurine. Three dimensional, very real. It released smoothly under my thumb, the blade unsheathing, extending, locking rigidly in place. Still very sharp, I noticed.

Sharp enough to cut flesh.   166

And then I was crying at the glass counter of an expensive 167
antique store on Granville Street. Weeping. Inconsolable, although
the woman did not try. She only stood at a distance, respectful of
my grief. I suppose she didn't have to share it to sense that it
came from memory. From lives already lived.

It was my idea to go to dinner. It's just possible, thinking about 168
it now, he might never have called me again. Let it go finally,
released to the future.

So I phoned him. A jet roared in the background. 169

There is a French bistro downtown, dark but comfortable, 170
the food hearty in the Parisian style. Walls covered with
photographs of famous people, some who had visited the
restaurant. Others who could not have, but who one might
imagine spending an evening here. Jack Johnson. Carl Sandburg.

I knew this to be one of his guilty pleasures. A quiet table 171
at this bistro, a companion. *Steak Frites* and a bottle of Burgundy.

I arrived first and took a seat in the corner I had reserved, 172
at a small table covered with a thick white cloth. I sat with my
back to the wall, under a photograph of Sigmund Freud, enjoying
a clear view of the restaurant and the door.

When he came in, the maitre d' bowed just slightly at the 173
waist, and they exchanged a few words. Then he turned into the
room, spotted me, and began his weightless navigation through
the tables. The *Queen Mary* approaching the jetty, all double-
breasted grace and size.

"Clare. My dear." His lips floated down to my hand. Then to 174
my cheek. He smelled just faintly of soap. Of wool and oak.

I kept my surprise until the main course arrived, the filet a 175
delicate island in a pool of dark demi-glaze. The pile of potato-
straw *frites* a cloud at one corner of the plate. Seven pomegranate
seeds and a spray of snow-pea pods providing balance.

The waiter produced steak knives, and when he had gone, 176
Alex held up his glass and said: "Santé."

We touched glasses, sipped. 177

"Now wait," I said. And I pulled out the black box from the 178
seat beside me and slid it across the table to him.

This time, his surprise was genuine and warranted. He untied 179
the red ribbon I had tied around it, and when it was open he
looked down at the knives for some time without touching them.
"Oh my, oh my," he said. And when he did finally take one of the
knives in his hand, he only held it, unopened, touching the clasp.

"Real," I said.   180

"Oh quite, yes," he said. And he looked at me with a small   181
smile.

We walked afterwards. I held his arm, which meant reaching   182
up just slightly. It was cold but clear now, and we walked from
the restaurant all the way down to the water, then along the sea
wall as far as English Bay. A boat churned past, heading to berth
in False Creek. There was phosphorescence in the water. We
talked only a little. Alex held the box of knives tightly under his
other arm, as if they made him very proud.

At the beach houses we turned out onto the sand, and found   183
a log to sit on. It was enormous. He helped me up onto it, then sat
himself, his black-and-white shoes comfortably reaching the sand.

Neither of us said anything for some time.   184

"They're very beautiful, Clare. Thank you."   185

"You've been good to me," I said, not looking at him. "And   186
I appreciate it."

"I am devoted to the Doves of Townsend," he answered.   187
"For a long time, yes?"

"Doves," I said, holding up an imaginary bidding paddle   188
and speaking with what had been my father's imperial cadence.
"Doves of Townsend."

Alex smiled at the memory. "A name for which you once   189
gave me a very colourful, if not entirely truthful explanation."

"Did I?" I asked, not remembering immediately.   190

"Oh yes," he said. "You told me that in Townsend there were   191
doves that lived their entire lives in the rafters of the train station.
When they died, you told me, they would fall onto the trains
and be carted off throughout the countryside. The opposite of
homing pigeons, I think you said."

"Gosh," I said. "Did I tell you that really?"   192

"I think perhaps you were in a black mood that day," he   193
said.

"Quite possible," I answered. "Although it could have been   194
worse." And then I told him how I had remembered this story in
the flea market, looking up at the pigeons that had been caught
and suspended after death.

He cocked his head at me. "Where you found my *les Frères*,   195
perhaps?"

I let the corner of my mouth twitch into a small smirk. "I'm   196
not that lucky," I said. "Not twice." But I told him where I had
bought them, and how I got there after an unusual trip to the

flea market. "Just wandering around without objective," I said. "Very unlike me."

His soft eyes were resting on my face, my hair. "That can't 197 always be bad," he said. "Wandering without objective, that is."

It wasn't, and I admitted it. 198

"You know?" he said, exhaling a tiny breath of resolve. "I 199 left you a gift there once."

"A gift?" I feigned surprise. 200

"Yes," he said, looking out at the sea. "I left you something 201 there that I wanted you to find. Something I wanted you to find by accident."

I didn't say anything. 202

"Aren't you going to ask me what it was?" For all his 203 immense weightlessness, I could feel him next to me now. I could feel his gaze on me, on my skin.

I turned on the log, shifting to face him. "What it was?" I 204 said.

"I thought you might wonder." 205

I put a hand gently on his arm. "I didn't know when I first 206 found them that they were a gift," I said. "But I figured it out once I got to your office."

He looked back at me curiously, processing this. 207

"The ashtrays," I said, squeezing his arm. 208

I wondered if I had embarrassed him by knowing about it, if 209 I had spoiled the kindness he had shown. But he didn't say anything right away. He slipped his fingers into his jacket pocket for what I expected to be one of his cigars, and brought his hand out closed around something small.

"Ashtrays." He said the word like he had just learned what 210 it meant.

"I don't mind, Alex," I said. "Maybe I was a little angry at the 211 time, but I'm not now."

"The airplane ashtrays," he said again. "I'm fond of them." 212 I nodded.

"They look very handsome in my office," he went on. "I 213 receive compliments daily."

"I'm glad," I said. 214

"But I wouldn't give them as a gift," he said. And he shook his 215 head slowly, thinking of how improbable this would be. "Not to you. Besides, would they really be a gift if you didn't keep them?"

I was still nodding for some reason but I wasn't certain. 216

Alexander Galbraithe opened his large hand. My eyes were   217
drawn immediately to the middle of his palm.

It was a small clear plastic box. In it, I recognized the fragile   218
stamp of colour. The blood-red spots on black wings, the tendril
antennae with their clublike tips.

I took the single butterfly from him, staring down at the case,   219
hearing the sound of their wings as they exploded from the box,
released back to their grasslands, their forests, their mignonette,
mustard or passion vine, each to their own corner of the world.

"Oh no," I said.   220

He had no doubt I would find them. That once there I would   221
search the place thoroughly, ask questions. "I was confident they
would haunt even you." But he smiled as he said this.

One of the sixty-three, he kept. There had been two Postmen   222
in the collection. And with that one, pressed from his large
palm down into my own, he considered the gift given. And I
accepted it.

And yes, sometime later I did track down my art director   223
and I did ask if I might buy the others back, but he couldn't find
them. "What do you mean, can't find them?" I didn't get angry.
I kept my cool.

They hadn't been sold he was certain. They hadn't been   224
thrown out that he recalled. He thought that the prop master
might have returned them to the antique store where they had
rented the furniture.

Did he remember the name of this store? Well … he could   225
find out and get back to me.

"Surely you can find some more?" he said. "How's Tiko?"   226

"Probably not," I answered. "And I have no idea,   227
respectively."

Alex laughed silently when I told him. He said: "I don't mind   228
that someone else will have discovered them, found them
beautiful."

"They are beautiful," I said, still wishing, wishing. "I could   229
have kept them so easily, they made me want them."

"Clare. Dearest," he said, his warm hand on the side of my   230
face. "Of course they did. Their purpose is their beauty. It's what
they're for."

I still have the books and the killing jar. The Postman I keep   231
on my desk as I imagined the others would have been kept. From

time to time I imagine them out there, want them to return, and then I may spend a week or two looking in shops, asking around. No one has ever seen them, and I know that the more time passes the further away from me they will have flown.

I went into a shop once, idle, directionless on a Saturday. I   232
asked about my butterflies. Described them: a collection maybe, in small plastic cases? The proprietor considered this very carefully, then produced a stuffed toad and asked me if I wanted that instead.

It doesn't matter. The Postman, where I am now, is very real.   233
It sits there on the corner of my desk, and every day it tells me a fascinating story.

UNDERSTANDING DETAILS

1. What happened to the narrator's father? How is this related to Clare's weeping in the Granville Street antique store (paragraph 167)?
2. What does Clare find at the Shickey Shack that attracts her attention? How did that item come to be at the Shickey Shack?
3. Why does Clare initially go to the flea market? Is it entirely good luck that she finds exactly what she is looking for? Explain why or why not.

ANALYZING MEANING

1. Why did Galbraithe plant the gift of butterflies at the flea market rather than giving them directly to Clare? Characterize the relationship between Clare and Alex Galbraithe.
2. Explain the symbolic value of the butterflies.
3. Why does Clare buy the *les Frères* steak knives for Alexander Galbraithe? What is the significance of these knives?

DISCOVERING RHETORICAL STRATEGIES

1. Identify the instances of foreshadowing that Taylor incorporates into his story. What clues can you find that point to Alex Galbraithe's actions?
2. Describe the character of Alexander Galbraithe. How does Taylor develop the character of Galbraithe?
3. From what perspective is this story told? What is the effect of Taylor's choice of narrative voice?

MAKING CONNECTIONS

1. "Doves of Townsend" and "The Finer Points of Apples" (Brooke) are both Journey Prize winners. What general conclusions might you draw about the Journey Prize based on these two stories? Consider both the criteria for the prize as well as the effect of being selected for recognition by this jury.
2. What do people's collections say about them? Discuss the role of paintings in the life of Lois in "Death by Landscape" (Atwood) and ashtrays, coach clocks, and cigar cutters in the life of Alex Galbraithe in "Doves of Townsend."

CHOOSING A TOPIC FOR DISCUSSION/WRITING

1. "Doves of Townsend" concerns people who are collectors of various items. Why do people collect things? Write a cause and effect essay in which you consider both the reasons that people have collections and the effect that collecting has on their lives.
2. Visit a local flea market and then write a descriptive essay in which you give your reader a clear sense of the market, including the people you find there.
3. Write a classification essay in which you divide the world into those who collect and those who discard. What characteristics readily identify each? What motivates the individuals who fall into each of these categories?

CREDITS

Allen Abel, "A Home at the End of the Journey," originally published in *Maclean's*, January 9, 1995. Reprinted with permission of the author. • David Arnason, "A Girl's Story," from *The Circus Performer's Bar*, by David Arnason ©1984 Talonbooks, Vancouver. Reprinted by permission. • Margaret Atwood, "Death by Landscape," from *Wilderness Tips* by Margaret Atwood. Used by permission, McClelland & Stewart Ltd. *The Canadian Publishers.* • Dave Bidini, "Kris King Looks Terrible," from *Tropic of Hockey* by Dave Bidini. Used by permission, McClelland & Stewart Ltd. *The Canadian Publishers.* • Neil Bissoondath, "Campfire, Idealism, and Pieces of Sky," from *Pieces of Sky* by Neil Bissoondath, from *If You Love This Country: Fifteen Voices for a Unified Canada.* Copyright © 1995 Penguin Books Canada Ltd. • T. Coraghessan Boyle, "Greasy Lake," from *Greasy Lake and Other Stories*, by T. Coraghessan Boyle, copyright © 1979, 1981, 1982, 1983, 1984, 1985 by T. Coraghessan Boyle. Used by permission of Viking Penguin, a division of Penguin Putnam Inc. • John Brooke, "The Finer Points of Apples," from *Kairos* by John Brooke. Used by permission, McClelland & Stewart Ltd. *The Canadian Publishers.* • Sharon Butala, "The Myth: The Prairies Are Flat," originally appeared in *enRoute.* (Spafax Canada, September 2001) © 2001 by Sharon Butala. With permission of *enRoute.* • Wayson Choy, "I'm a Banana and Proud of It," originally appeared in *The Globe and Mail* "Facts and Arguments" column; © Wayston Choy, All Rights Reserved by the author. • Lesley Choyce, "Thin Edge of the Wedge," published in *Canadian Geographic* (March/April 1997). Reprinted with permission of the author. • Michael Clugston, "Twice Struck," originally published in *Equinox* (July/Aug 1991). Copyright © by Michael Clugston. Reprinted by permission. • Lynn Coady, "Genius or Madness?" reprinted with permission of the author. • Stanley Coren, "Dogs and Monsters," originally published in *Saturday Night* (May 2000). Reprinted by permission of the author. • Jennifer Cowan, "TV Me Alone," originally published in *Shift* (July/Aug 1995). Copyright © by Jennifer Cowan. Reprinted by permission. • Amy Willard Cross, "Life in the Stopwatch Lane," originally appeared in *The Globe and Mail* (July 5, 1990, p. A18). Reprinted by permission of the author. • Marylin Dahl, "The Role of the Media in Promoting Images of Disability," from the *Canadian Journal of Communication.* Reprinted by permission of the Canadian Journal of Communication Inc. • Gwynne Dyer, "Flagging Attention," originally appeared in *enRoute.* Reprinted by permission of the author. • Barbara Ehrenreich, "The Ecstasy of War," from *Blood Rights: Origins and History of the Passions of War* by Barbara Ehrenreich. Copyright © 1997 by Barbara Ehrenreich. Reprinted by permission of Henry Holt and Company, Inc. • Will Ferguson, "The Sudbury Syndrome," from *Why I Hate Canadians* by Will Ferguson. Copyright © 1997, reprinted with permission from Groundwood Books, Douglas & McIntyre Publishing Group. • Joe Fiorito, "Breakfast in Bed," from *Comfort Me with Apples*, published by Nuage Editions. Reprinted by permission. • David Foot, "Boomers Dance to a New Beat," originally appeared in *The Globe and Mail* (Jan. 9, 1998). Reprinted by permission of David Foot, Professor of Economics, University of Toronto, and co-author of *Boom, Bust & Echo 2000: Profiting from the Demographic Shift in the New Millennium.* • Cecil Foster, "Why Blacks Get Mad," originally appeared in *Chatelaine*, November 1992. Reprinted by permission of the author. • Malcolm Gladwell, "Is The Belgian Coca-Cola

Hysteria the Real Thing?" originally appeared in *The New Yorker* (July 1999). Reprinted by permission of the author. • Katherine Govier, "The Immaculate Conception Photography Gallery" from the *Immaculate Conception Photography Gallery*, by Katherine Govier. Copyright © 1994 by Katherine Govier. Reprinted by permission of Random House Canada, a division of Random House of Canada Limited. • Charlotte Gray, "The Temple of Hygiene," originally appeared in *Saturday Night* (Sept. 1989). Reprinted by permission of the author • Ray Guy, "When Jannies Visited," published in *Canadian Geographic* (Nov/Dec 1993). Reprinted by permission of the author. • Elizabeth Hay, "Cézanne in a Soft Hat," from *Small Change* by Elizabeth Hay. Used by permission, McClelland & Stewart Ltd. *The Canadian Publishers*. • Steve Heighton, "Elegy in Stone," from *Admen Move on Lhasa* by Steve Heighton. ©1997 Stoddart Publishing Co. Limited. Reprinted by permission. • Tomson Highway, "What a Certain Visionary Once Said," Copyright © 1992 by Tomson Highway. Reprinted by permission of the author and the Susan Schulman Literary Agency, 454 West 44th Street, New York, NY 10036. • Stephen King, "Why We Crave Horror Movies," originally appeared in *Playboy* Magazine, 1982. Reprinted with permission of the author's agent, Arthur B. Greene, New York. • Mark Kingwell, "Not Available in Stores," originally appeared in *Saturday Night* (July/August 1996). Reprinted with permission of Mark Kingwell, University of Toronto. • Evelyn Lau, "I Sing the Song of My Condo," originally published in *The Globe and Mail* (June 17, 1994). With permission of the author. • Tony Leighton, "The New Nature," originally appeared in *Equinox* (Dec. 1994). Copyright © Tony Leighton. Reprinted by permission. • Michele Lemon, "Understanding Does Not Always Lead to Tolerance," originally appeared in *The Globe and Mail* (Jan. 31, 1995). • Brian Lewis, "Teeth," originally appeared in *Up Here/Life in Canada's North*. Reprinted by permission of *Up Here/Life*. • Maureen Littlejohn, "You Are a Contract Painkiller," originally published in *Equinox* (April/May 1997). Reprinted with permission of Maureen Littlejohn, feature writer, editor, and journalist. • Alistair MacLeod, "As Birds Bring Forth the Sun," from *Island: the Collected Stories of Alistair MacLeod* by Alistair MacLeod. Used by permission, McClelland & Stewart Ltd. *The Canadian Publishers*. • Michael McKinley, "Opera Night in Canada," originally appeared in *Saturday Night* (Dec. 2000). Reprinted with permission of the author. • "Why We Crave Hot Stuff" by Trina McQueen, president of Discovery Channel Canada. Originally published in *The Globe and Mail* (Sept. 26, 1998). Reprinted by permission. • Alice Munro, "Boys and Girls," from *Dance of the Happy Shades* by Alice Munro. Copyright ©1968 reproduced with permission of McGraw Hill Ryerson Ltd. • Naheed Mustafa, "My Body Is My Own Business," originally appeared in *The Globe and Mail* (June 29 1993). Copyright © by Naheed Mustafa. Reprinted by permission. • Kim Pittaway, "Dead Wrong," originally appeared in *Chatelaine*. Reprinted with permission of the author. • Paul Quarrington, "Home Brew," originally published in *Harrowsmith* 17(1) (May/June 1992). Reprinted by permission of the author. • Judy Rebick, "The Culture of Overwork," originally appeared in *Elm Street* (Feb/Mar 2001). Reprinted with permission of the author. • Laura Robinson, "Starving For the Gold," originally appeared in *The Globe and Mail* (April 11, 1992). Copyright © by Laura Robinson. Reprinted by permission • Carol Shields, "Windows," from *Dressing Up for the Carnival* by Carol Shields. Copyright © 2000, by Carol Shields. Reprinted by permission of Random House Canada, a division of Random House of Canada Limited. • Evan Solomon, "The Babar

INDEX OF AUTHORS AND TITLES